College Accounting

FOURTH EDITION 16–29

Douglas J. McQuaig
Wenatchee Valley College

HOUGHTON MIFFLIN COMPANY   Boston

Dallas   Geneva, Illinois   Palo Alto   Princeton, New Jersey

This text and its related materials
are dedicated to the students who
will use them. My dream is to give
them a tool that is both practical
and understandable.

Printed in the U.S.A.

Library of Congress Catalog Card No.: 88-81345

ISBN: 0-395-48707-2

ABCDEFGHIJ-VH-9543210/89

Contents

Preface   vii

Review: Chapters 1–15   xix

16 Accounting for Notes Payable   509

Promissory Notes / Calculating Interest / Determining Due Dates / Transactions Involving Notes Payable / End-of-Fiscal-Period Adjustments

C● Computerized Practice Set: Colony Collectibles

17 Accounting for Notes Receivable   541

Transactions for Notes Receivable / Dishonored Notes Receivable / Discounting Notes Receivable / End-of-Fiscal-Period Adjustments: Accrued Interest on Notes Receivable

18 Accounting for Valuation of Receivables   571

The Credit Department / Matching Bad Debt Losses with Sales / The Allowance Method of Accounting for Bad Debts / Aging Accounts Receivable / Writing Off Uncollectible Accounts / Collection of Accounts Previously Written Off / Specific Charge-off of Bad Debts / Requirements of the Tax Reform Act of 1986 / Computers at Work: Computerized Collection

19 Accounting for Valuation of Inventories   605

The Importance of Inventory Valuation / The Need for Inventories / Methods of Assigning Costs to Ending Inventory / Lower-of-Cost-or-Market Rule / Perpetual Inventories / Computers at Work: Managing with the Computer

Appendix D: Estimating the Value of Inventories   632

20 Accounting for Valuation of Plant and Equipment   645

Initial Costs of Plant and Equipment / Differentiating Costs of Land, Land Improvements, and Buildings / The Nature and Recording of Depreciation / Calculating Depreciation / Depreciation for Periods of Less Than a Year / Capital

and Revenue Expenditures / Extraordinary-Repairs
Expenditures / Disposition of Plant and Equipment / Plant
and Equipment Records / Depreciation for Federal Income
Tax / Computers at Work: Computers to the Rescue—
Depreciation

Review of T Account Placement and Representative Transactions: Chapters 16 Through 20   681

Appendix E: Modified Accelerated Cost Recovery System of Depreciation   686

21   The Voucher System of Accounting   697

Objective of the Voucher System / Vouchers / The
Vouchers Payable Account / The Voucher Register / The
Check Register / Handling of Unpaid Vouchers / Filing
Paid Vouchers / Situations Requiring Special Treatment /
The Voucher System as a Management Tool / Recording
Purchases at the Net Amount / Computers at Work:
Embezzling with a Computer

22   Accounting for Partnerships   733

Characteristics of a Partnership / Advantages of a
Partnership / Disadvantages of a Partnership / Partnership
Agreements / Accounting Entries for Partnerships /
Division of Net Income or Net Loss / Financial Statements
for a Partnership / Dissolution of a Partnership

Practice Set: Phoenix Mountain Bikes

23   Corporations: Organization and Capital Stock   769

Definition of a Corporation / Advantages of the
Corporation / Disadvantages of the Corporate Form /
Forming a Corporation / Structure of a Corporation /
Capital Stock / Issuing Stock / Illustration of a Corporate
Balance Sheet / New Accounts and the Fundamental
Accounting Equation

24   Corporations: Work Sheet, Taxes, and Dividends   805

Procedure for Recording and Paying Income Taxes /
Work Sheet for a Corporation / Reasons for
Appropriating Retained Earnings / Declaration and
Payment of Dividends / Stock Split / Statement of
Retained Earnings and a Balance Sheet for a Corporation /
Fundamental Guidelines for Accounting Reports

25 Corporations: Long-Term Obligations   843

Classification of Bonds / Why a Corporation Issues
Bonds / Accounting for the Issuance of Bonds / Bond
Sinking Fund / Redemption of Bonds / Balance Sheet

Review of T Account Placement and Representative Transactions: Chapters 21 Through 25   870

26 Departmental Accounting   877

Gross Profit by Departments / Income from Operations
by Departments / Departmental Margin / Branch
Accounting / Computers at Work: Management
Information Systems

27 Analyzing and Interpreting Financial Statements   915

Types of Comparison / Comparative Statements / Trend
Percentages / Industry Comparisons / Analysis by
Creditors and Management / Analysis by Owners and
Management / Computers at Work: Spreadsheets and
Models

28 Statement of Cash Flows   949

A Broad Look at the Statement of Cash Flows /
Classifications of Cash Flows / Form of the Statement of
Cash Flows / Developing the Statement of Cash Flows /
Interpreting the Statement of Cash Flows / Schedule of
Noncash Investing and Financing Transactions

29 Manufacturing Accounting   993

Comparison of Income Statements for Merchandising and
Manufacturing Enterprises / Statement of Cost of Goods
Manufactured / Elements of Manufacturing Costs / Balance
Sheet for a Manufacturing Firm / Work Sheet for a Manu-
facturing Firm / Accounting Cycle for a Manufacturing
Firm / Determining the Value of Ending Inventories /
Computers at Work: The Factory of the Future

Glossary of Terms: Chapters 1 Through 15   G-1

Index   I-1

Preface

The goals for the fourth edition of *College Accounting* are the same as they have been for the previous editions: To provide students with a sound basic knowledge of accounting terms, concepts, and procedures, always taking into consideration students' widely varying objectives:

- Preparation for students entering the job market in accounting
- A practical background in accounting for students embarking on other careers, such as clerical, secretarial, technical, sales, and management positions
- Preparation and background for students planning more advanced studies in accounting

Based on more than 30 years teaching experience, the author has developed a method of presentation that reflects the need for an understandable and teachable basic accounting text that is logically organized, liberally illustrated, and paced in such a manner that it is easy for students to read and understand. This same approach has made previous editions successful with many teachers and students. At the same time, however, based on extensive reviews, campus visits, and conversations with many accounting teachers, the author has updated, revised, and improved both the text and the ancillary materials.

The accounting principles described are those endorsed by the Financial Accounting Standards Board and its predecessor, the Accounting Principles Board. Pertinent areas of the Tax Reform Act are included in the appropriate chapters.

CHARACTERISTICS OF COLLEGE ACCOUNTING

Accent on the Fundamentals

College Accounting, Fourth Edition presents the fundamentals of accounting in a practical, easy-to-understand manner that students can understand. Appropriate repetition enables students to develop confidence in themselves and to make progress in easy stages. This repetition is accomplished through extensive use of examples and illustrations.

Since an understanding of accounting fundamentals is based on understanding accounting transactions, great stress is devoted to analysis of transactions. Each newly introduced transaction is fully illustrated and supported with T account examples. Comprehensive reviews of T accounts, organized in relation to the fundamental accounting equation, appear after Chapters 20 and 25 to assist students as they review material during their course of study.

Reading Comprehension

College Accounting, Fourth Edition is a very readable text. Capitalizing on a direct approach, the author writes in short sentences that are supported by many illustrations that help students to understand the discussion. Each chapter is limited to the presentation of one major concept, which is well illustrated with business documents and report forms. As terms are introduced, they are defined thoroughly and are used in subsequent examples. Comprehension is also enhanced through the use of unique "Remembers." These short, marginal notes present a learning hint or a capsule summary of a major point made in preceding paragraphs. New end-of-chapter summaries also enhance comprehension.

Terminology

The author firmly believes that accounting is the language of business and that learning new terminology is an important part of a first course. Each key term is printed in red and is explained when it is first introduced. The end-of-chapter glossary repeats the definitions of the terms presented in the chapter.

Questions, Exercises, and Problems

College Accounting, Fourth Edition provides a wealth of exercise and problem material that is fully supported by the Working Papers, offering instructors a wide choice for classroom illustrations and assignments. Each chapter ends with comprehensive review and study material consisting of a chapter summary, a glossary, eight discussion questions, eight exercises, and two sets of comparable A and B problems. Exercises and problems have been rewritten for this edition.

- **Questions** Eight questions, based on the main points in the text, are included at the end of each chapter.
- **Classroom Exercises** For practice in applying concepts, eight exercises are provided with each chapter.
- **Problems** Each chapter contains four A problems and four B problems. The A and B problems are parallel in content and level of difficulty. They are arranged in order of difficulty, with Problems 1A and 1B in each chapter being the simplest and the last problem in each series being the most comprehensive.

NEW FOUR-COLOR PEDAGOGY

The author, in conjunction with Houghton Mifflin Company, has developed a color-coded pedagogy that is designed to help students recognize and remember key points, understand the flow of accounting data, rec-

The Use of Color in McQuaig

Red	Green	Blue
Inputs $\longrightarrow$	Process $\longrightarrow$	Outputs

Source Documents
Bank Statements and
  Reconciliations
Tax Forms
	Trial Balances
	Journals
	Ledgers
	Work Sheets
	Schedules
	Registers
	Inventory, Plant,
	  and Equipment
	  Records
		**Financial
		Statements**
		  Income Statements
		  Statements of
		    Owner's Equity
		  Balance Sheets
		  Statements of
		    Retained Earnings
		  Statements of Cash
		    Flows

Also
  Learning Objectives
  Tables
  Key Terms
  Emphasis
		Also
		  Chapter Heads
		  Remembers
		  Computers at Work

ognize different types of documents and reports used in accounting, identify the learning objectives for each chapter, see how each exercise and problem relates to the learning objectives for the chapter, and review material efficiently and effectively.

- **Learning objectives** are set in red throughout the text. They are listed at the beginning of each chapter and restated alongside the related text discussion. They are referenced by learning objective number in the chapter summary and in the exercises and problems.
- **Key terms** are highlighted in red. They are defined in the text and repeated in a glossary at the end of the chapter.
- **Remembers,** which are printed in blue, are learning hints or summaries placed in the margin of the text. These marginal notes often alert students to common pitfalls and help them complete their work successfully.
- **Tables** are highlighted with a red screen, helping students quickly identify material that must be examined as a unit and is not part of running text.

The fourth edition's innovative use of color extends to the treatment of accounting forms, financial statements, and documents in the text and end-of-chapter assignments.

- **Working papers, journals, ledgers, trial balances, and other forms and schedules** used as part of the internal accounting process are shown in green.

- **Financial statements,** including balance sheets, income statements, statements of owner's equity, and statements of cash flows, are shown in blue.
- **Source documents,** such as invoices, bank statements, facsimiles, and other material that originates with outside sources, are shown in red.

This distinctive treatment differentiates these elements and helps students to see where each element belongs in the accounting cycle. Seeing these relationships helps students understand how accountants transform data into useful information.

CHAPTER COVERAGE

College Accounting 16–29 is designed for use by students who have completed *College Accounting 1–15*. The text may be divided into modules: Chapters 16–20 cover notes payable and receivable as well as the valuation of receivables, inventories, and plant assets. Chapters 21–25 cover vouchers, partnerships, and corporations. Chapters 26–29 cover analysis of financial statements and the statement of cash flows, as well as departmental and manufacturing accounting.

Two appendixes expand content coverage and increase the instructor's options for structuring the course.

- **Appendix D: Estimating the Value of Inventories** (after Chapter 19)   Describes the retail and gross profit methods.
- **Appendix E: Modified Accelerated Cost Recovery System of Depreciation** (after Chapter 20)   Presents definitions and depreciation schedules of recovery property.

COMPUTERS AT WORK

Microcomputers have brought major changes to the work environment in which today's graduates will be expected to function. The new *Computers at Work* boxes, highlighted in blue, offer instructors a springboard for explaining the impact of these changes to students. Topics have been selected for their relevance to accounting and include:
- Computerized Collection
- Managing with the Computer
- Depreciation
- Embezzling
- M.I.S.
- Spreadsheets
- The Factory of the Future

CONTENT CHANGES IN THE FOURTH EDITION

The author has carefully revised and updated the entire text and the end-of-chapter materials. Changes include an increased emphasis on explaining transactions and a step-by-step approach to transaction analysis and error correction. The learning objectives have been analyzed and improved by adding new learning objectives and breaking down complex learning objectives to increase student comprehension and understanding. A new chapter on the statement of cash flows replaces the chapter on the statement of changes in financial position.

Much care has been taken to make sure that *College Accounting*, Fourth Edition is as current as possible. The text discussion and examples have been revised in light of the Tax Reform Act of 1986. Appendixes have been replaced or updated. Practice sets have been completely revised to reflect business situations with inherent appeal to today's students.

QUALITY CONTROL

Successful use of an accounting text depends on more than the interesting and memorable presentation of material by the instructor and the text. The overall quality of the examples, illustrations, end-of-chapter questions, exercises and problems, and ancillary materials are critical to learning and retention of the facts and concepts covered in the course. Instructors and students must be assured that these materials are complete, consistent, and accurate.

The author and the publisher of *College Accounting*, Fourth Edition have taken a multistep approach to ensure quality materials for classroom use. The quality control system begins with in-depth reviews of the original manuscript and concludes with accuracy reviews of page proof provided by academics teaching the course and by the international accounting firm of Arthur Young & Company.

SUPPLEMENTARY LEARNING AIDS FOR STUDENTS

For the fourth edition we have assembled the most comprehensive package of student and instructor aids to complement a wide variety of teaching styles and course emphases.

Working Papers

The Working Papers now include the learning objectives for each chapter, chapter summaries, lists of key terms, study questions, an extended demonstration problem and solution for each chapter (which is reproduced in the Instructor's Manual), forms for A and B problems and for problems in appendixes, and answers to the study questions, a list of check figures, and additional blank working paper forms.

Practice Sets

After Chapter 16   *Colony Collectibles* (new), a computer-assisted accounting cycle practice set, focuses on receivables, payables, depreciation, and inventory for a merchandising company.

After Chapter 22   *Phoenix Mountain Bikes* (new) is a one-month manual practice set utilizing a voucher system for a partnership merchandising business

Computer Applications for College Accounting: A General Ledger Package

This easy-to-use general ledger package offers complete coverage of accounting concepts and procedures, including graduated problems, exercises, and tutorials. Selected problems from *College Accounting*, Fourth Edition can be completed with this package. The icon in the margin identifies these problems in the text. A template disk is available to adopters.

Computerized Demonstration Problems: A Tutorial Approach

This exciting new program enables students to test their knowledge of accounting procedures by examining the demonstration problems from the Working Papers that accompany the McQuaig text. Unlike practice sets that require students to enter problem data and then print out the results, this tutorial prompts students to answer true-false or multiple-choice questions on a series of accounting procedures. As students respond to these questions, the program dynamically demonstrates—through moving displays of ledgers and journals—how transaction data flow through an accounting system and impact accounts. Available for Chapters 1–15.

Lotus Problems for Accounting: A Working Papers Approach

This innovative accounting software allows students to solve end-of-chapter problems using the Lotus 1-2-3 spreadsheet software. Students can select from 20 prepared templates and use them to solve most end-of-chapter problems. A template guide is included in the Instructor's Manual.

SOFTWARE SOLUTIONS SERIES

The Software Solutions Series offers a choice from seven popular application software packages. These inexpensive tutorial manuals and educational versions of popular software provide hands-on experience for your students. The seven manuals include:

Using PageMaker®
Using Lotus 1-2-3® Version 2.0
Using dBASE III Plus™
Using SuperCalc® 4

Using WordStar® 4.0
Using WordPerfect™ 4.2
Using Microsoft® Works

SUPPLEMENTARY TEACHING AIDS FOR INSTRUCTORS

Instructor's Manual with Solutions

This instructor's manual includes teaching suggestions for each chapter as well as complete solutions to all questions and exercises. Solutions to all A and B problems are shown on the same forms used in the Working Papers.

New to this edition are lecture outlines, key terms, learning objectives, chapter summaries, and a duplicate of the demonstration problems that appear in the Working Papers, as well as a cross-reference for each problem to the corresponding page of the Working Papers. Also new is a template guide for *Lotus Problems for Accounting: A Working Papers Approach.*

Teaching and Solutions Transparencies

Mylar transparencies are available to adopters. The improved two-color, typeset solutions cover every exercise and problem. Approximately 25 teaching and supplemental blank transparencies are also provided in this improved format.

Test Bank

For this edition, the number of questions has increased, and they are presented on a chapter-by-chapter basis. True-false, multiple-choice, and matching questions, as well as short problems are offered for each chapter. Final examinations with answers are presented in two versions.

The test problems and final examinations are presented in a format suitable for copying and distributing to classes. Also included are achievement test facsimiles. A microcomputer-based version of the main test bank and a call-in testing service are available. Final examinations covering Chapters 16–29 are provided in ready-to-reproduce format.

Achievement Tests

Preprinted tests are ready for class use. Each test covers two to three chapters in the text. Series A, which covers Chapters 1–15 and Chapters 16–29, provides 32 copies of each test. Series B is an alternative set of tests covering the same material.

The Video Workshop

New to this edition, a professionally prepared VHS video tape is available. Video Workshop presents key accounting topics and survival skills for students. A Video Guide with teaching tips is included.

Grade Performance Analyzer

Provided free to instructors, this computerized gradebook program for IBM PC and Apple II microcomputers facilitates orderly recordkeeping, calculation, and posting of student grades.

ACKNOWLEDGMENTS

Again, I would sincerely like to thank the editorial staff of Houghton Mifflin for their continuous support. I am still deeply appreciative of the assistance given to me during the preparation of the first edition of this text by Professors Hobart Adams, University of Akron, and Joseph Goodman, Chicago State University. The cooperation of my colleagues, Professors Audrey Chan-Nui, Geneva Knutson, and John Wisen, has been most helpful. Also, I want to thank my many students at Wenatchee Valley College for their observations and evaluations. Especially, I want to thank Donna L. Randall Lacey, Bunker Hill Community College, and Suzanne M. Williamson, C.P.A., for their diligent and comprehensive reviews. Patricia A. Bille, Highline Community College, provided invaluable help in her role as consulting editor. Her work in developing the Computers at Work boxed inserts is particularly appreciated.

During the writing of the fourth edition, I visited many users of the text throughout the country. Their constructive suggestions are reflected in the changes that have been made. Unfortunately, space does not permit mention of all those who have contributed to this volume. Some of those, however, who have been supportive and have influenced my efforts are:

Joseph F. Adamo, Cazenovia College
Stanley Augustine, Santa Rosa Junior College
Catherine Berg, Nassau Community College
Linda J. Block, Embry-Riddle Aeronautical University
Kenneth W. Brown, College of Technology, University of Houston—
   University Park
Anita Brownstein, Drake Business School
Howard Bryan, Santa Rosa Junior College
Theresa Capretta, North Harris County College
Clairmont P. Carter, University of Lowell
Michael S. Chaks, Riverside Community College
John Chestnutt, Allan Hancock College
Trudy Chiaravalli, Lansing Community College
Judith Chowen, Cerritos College
Dana Crismond, Mt. Empire Community College
Martha J. Curry, Huston-Tillotson College
Leonard Delury, Portland Community College—Sylvania Campus
Irving Denton, Northern Virginia Community College
Allan Doyle, Pima Community College
Jerry Sue Dyess, San Jacinta College—Central Campus
William Evans, Cerritos College
Thaddeus Flood, Royal Business School
Mary Foster, Illinois Central College
Walter A. Franklin, Palm Beach Junior College
Alan Fraser, Rio Hondo College

William French, Albuquerque Technical-Vocational Institute
Stuart M. Fukushige, Leeward Community College
Helen Gerrard, Miami University—Hamilton and Middletown Regional
  Campuses
Steven R. Graham, Vincennes University
Charles Grant, Skyline College
Marie Gressel, Santa Barbara City College
Robert E. Hartzell, Colorado Mountain College—Timberline Campus
C. Robert Hellmer, Milwaukee Area Technical College
Joyce Henzel, Rogers State College
Carol Holcomb, Spokane Falls Community College
Donald L. Holloway, Long Beach City College
Andrea Holmes, Renton Vocational-Technical Institute
Janis Hutchins, Lamar University—Port Arthur
George Ihorn, El Paso Community College
Thomas Jackson, Cerritos College
Eugene Janner, Blinn College
Edward H. Julius, California Lutheran University
Andre E. Kelton, American Business Institute, New York
Jimmy King, McLennan Community College
Lydia C. K. Kinoshita, Cannon's Business College
Bobbie Krapels, Branell College
Frances Kubicek, Kalamazoo Valley Community College
Ronald Kulhanek, Great Lakes Junior College
Nathan R. Larsen, Ricks College
Kenneth J. Levi, CBM Education Center
Elliott S. Levy, Bentley College
Loren Long, Elgin Community College
Joyce Loudder, Houston Community College
Donald MacGilvra, Shoreline Community College
Elizabeth Barnard Miller, Columbus State Community College
Paul C. Maziarz, Bryant & Stratton Business Institute, Buffalo
Robert Mills, Texarkana Community College
V. Eva Molnar, Riverside Community College District
Donald Morehead, Henry Ford Community College
Robert Nash, Henry Ford Community College
M. Salah Negm, Prince George's College
Dolores Osborn, Central Washington University
Vincent Pelletier, College of DuPage
Mary E. Retterer, San Bernardino Valley College
Paul T. Ryan, Jackson State Community College
John T. Saleh, Tyler Junior College
H. Lee Schlorff, Bentley College
Steven Schmidt, Butte Community College
Linda Scott, Aims Community College
Nelda Shelton, Tarrant County Junior College

Eliot H. Sherman, Northeastern University
Elaine Simpson, St. Louis Community College at Florissant Valley
Sharon Smith, Texas Southmost College
Gary Stanton, Erie Community College—City
Harold Steinhauser, Rock Valley Community College
Rahmat Tavallali, Wooster Business College
Alan Tucker, Everett Community College
Catherine P. Varca, Bryant & Stratton Business Institute, Buffalo
William G. Vendemia, Youngstown State University
Russell Vermillion, Prince George's Community College
Florence G. Waldman, Kilgore College
Emma Watts, Westark Community College
Robert Weaver, Malcolm X College
Penny Westerfeld, North Harris County College
Maxine Wilson, Los Angeles City College

A special note of thanks to the individuals who contributed greatly by reviewing and checking the end-of-chapter questions, exercises, and problems.

Carmela C. Caputo, Empire State College
Janet Cassagio, Nassau Community College
Carl Dauber, Southern Ohio College
Vicky C. Dominguez, Clark County Community College
Marlin Gerber, Kalamazoo Valley Community College
Ann King, Branell College, Riverdale Campus
Jan Mardon, Green River Community College
Bernard Piwkiewicz, Laney College
Joseph Stoffel, Waubonsee Community College
Ron Summers, Oklahoma City Community College
Stan Weikert, College of the Canyons

As always, I would like to thank my family for their understanding and cooperation. Without their support, this text would never have been written. My heartfelt appreciation is extended to my wife, Beverlie, for her detailed proofreading and for her willingness to put up with me. Pertinent suggestions for updating the material were given by my daughter, Judith Britton, C.P.A., of Bunday, Britton, and Horikawa; my son, John McQuaig, C.P.A., of McQuaig and Welk; and my son-in-law, Christopher Britton, C.P.A., of Touche Ross.

Douglas J. McQuaig

Review: Chapters 1–15

This prechapter briefly reviews the material covered in *College Accounting 1–15*. The glossary at the end of this book lists all the key terms from Chapters 1–15 with their definitions. Glossaries for the key terms in Chapters 16 through 29 are found at the end of each chapter.

DEFINITION OF ACCOUNTING

Accounting is the process of analyzing, classifying, recording, summarizing, and interpreting business transactions. A business **transaction** is an event that has a direct effect on the operation of an **economic unit** (a business or a nonprofit organization such as a church, club, or government) and can be expressed in terms of money. Buying and selling goods, paying rent and wages, and buying insurance are all examples of transactions.

ACCOUNTING FOR THE SOLE PROPRIETORSHIP SERVICE BUSINESS

Assets, Liabilities, and Owner's Equity

Assets are properties or things of value, such as cash, equipment, and land, owned by an economic unit or business entity. A business entity is considered to be separate from the persons who supply its assets. The owner's right or claim is expressed in the term **equity** (other terms include *capital, investment,* and *net worth*). **Liabilities** include the amount that the business owes or is liable to its creditors. The relationship between these three elements is expressed by the **fundamental accounting equation:**

Assets	=	Liabilities	+	Owner's Equity
(things owned)		(amount owed to creditors)		(investment or net worth)

Recording Business Transactions

The accountant's job is to record each business transaction, making changes in the appropriate accounts. The **accounts** are categories under the main headings of the fundamental accounting equation. Before recording any transaction, the accountant sets up a **chart of accounts,** which lists each account the business uses and assigns it to one of the parts of the fundamental accounting equation. As transactions are recorded, the total of one side of the fundamental accounting equation should always equal the total of the other side. From this we get **double-entry accounting,** for each transaction must be recorded in at least two accounts, and the equation must be kept in balance.

The Balance Sheet

The **balance sheet** is a financial statement that summarizes the balances of the assets, liabilities, and owner's equity accounts on a given date; it is sometimes referred to as a *statement of financial position.* There are two formats commonly used for the balance sheet: the **account form,** in which the elements of the accounting equation appear side by side; and the **report form,** in which they are presented one on top of the other.

Revenue and Expense Accounts

The remaining two classifications in the fundamental accounting equation are revenues and expenses. **Revenues** are the amounts earned by a business; examples are money earned from the sale of merchandise, fees for services, and rental income collected for use of property. **Expenses** are the costs that relate to the earning of revenue, or the costs of doing business. Wages, utility, and advertising costs are all examples of expenses. Revenue and expense are placed in the fundamental accounting equation under the "umbrella" of owner's equity. Revenue increases owner's equity, while expenses decrease it. When total revenue is greater than total expenses, there is a **net income;** when expenses are greater than revenue, there is a **net loss.**

$$\text{Assets} = \text{Liabilities} \quad + \quad \text{Owner's Equity}$$
$$\text{Revenues} - \text{Expenses}$$

Accounts Receivable

A business uses its **Accounts Receivable** account to record amounts owed by charge customers. These amounts are usually due in thirty days. At the time the service is performed or the merchandise is sold, an increase is recorded in the Accounts Receivable account and in the appropriate revenue account. When the customer pays the bill in cash, it is recorded as an increase in Cash and a decrease in Accounts Receivable. No new entry needs to be made to the revenue account.

Drawing Account

The **Drawing** account is used to record personal withdrawals by the owner (usually in the form of cash). The Drawing account is a deduction from the owner's Capital account. At the end of the fiscal period, the Drawing account is closed into the Capital account.

Financial Statements

The **income statement** shows total revenue minus total expenses for a fiscal period, thus yielding the net income or net loss for that period. The income statement, unlike the balance sheet, covers a period of time (usually one month or year); it portrays the results of business transactions over time.

The **statement of owner's equity** shows how—and why—the owner's equity, or Capital, account has changed between the beginning and the end of the time period. The statement of owner's equity shows the balance of the Capital account at the beginning of the time period plus the net income (or minus the net loss) minus withdrawals.

In all financial statements, the heading requires three lines:

1. Name of company (or owner, if there is no company name)
2. Title of financial statement
3. Period of time covered by financial statement, or its date

The T Account Form

Before introducing the T account form, let's review what steps to take in analyzing any transaction:

1. Determine what accounts are involved.
2. Determine the classification of each account involved (where it fits into the fundamental accounting equation).
3. Decide whether the transaction results in an increase or decrease in each of these accounts.

In addition, always remember that after each transaction has been recorded, the total of one side of the accounting equation must equal the total of the other side.

The **T account form** is an informal method used by accountants to record business transactions. One side of the T account is used to record increases, and the other side is used to record decreases. The total of each side of a T account is called a **footing,** and the balance of the account is determined by subtracting the smaller from the larger footing, which (with a few exceptions) will be on the plus side. The plus side is called the **normal balance** of the account. In T accounts, the left side is always the **debit** side, and the right is always the **credit** side, regardless of which side is plus and which is minus. It is important to remember that the amount recorded on the left side of one T account or accounts must equal the amount recorded on the right side of another T account or accounts. Here are the T accounts for the five categories of the fundamental accounting equation:

Assets	=	Liabilities	+	Owner's Equity	+	Revenue	–	Expenses
+ –		– +		– +		– +		+ –
Left Right		Left Right		Left Right		Left Right		Left Right
Debit Credit		Debit Credit		Debit Credit		Debit Credit		Debit Credit

The Trial Balance

The **trial balance** is a tool used by the accountant to prove that the debit balances of the accounts equal the credit balances—to prove, in effect, the equality of both sides of the fundamental accounting equation. In preparing the trial balance, the accountant records the balances of the accounts in the order in which they appear in the **ledger** (a book, binder, or file containing all the accounts of an enterprise). This order follows the accounting equation so that all assets are listed first, then liabilities, owner's equity, revenue, and expenses.

The General Journal

The **general journal** is a book for recording business transactions as they occur. The general journal is like a diary for the business, in which the accountant records all financial events daily. The journal is also called the **book of original entry,** because transactions are always recorded first in the journal and later transferred to the ledger accounts. Information concerning transactions is taken from business papers like checks, invoices, and credit memorandums—which are called **source documents,** and which should be identified in the journal entry. The general journal contains two money columns. The column on the left is used to record debit amounts; the column on the right is used to record credit amounts.

The General Ledger

The **general ledger** is a book that contains all the accounts, arranged according to the chart of accounts. Each account is given an **account number,** which indicates its classification. Most businesses follow the fundamental accounting equation when assigning account numbers, so all accounts under Assets have numbers starting with 1, Liabilities with 2, and so on. The ledger is generally arranged in the four-column account form with balance columns. This arrangement, called the running balance format, helps the accountant to keep track of the balance at all times. Transferring amounts from the journal to the general ledger accounts is called **posting.**

The Posting Process

1. Write the date of the transaction in the account's Date column.
2. Write the amount of the transaction in the Debit or Credit column,

and enter the new balance in the Balance columns under Debit or Credit.

3. Write the page number of the journal in the Posting Reference column of the ledger account (this is a **cross-reference**).
4. Record the ledger account number in the Posting Reference column in the journal (this is also a cross-reference).

Initial Steps in the Accounting Process

1. Record the transaction in a journal—remember to include an explanation based on source documents.
2. Post to the accounts in the ledger.
3. Prepare a trial balance.

Correction of Errors

When errors are made in recording journal entries or posting to the ledger accounts, it is important that the accountant not erase them. There are two approved methods for correcting errors: the **ruling method,** in which a line is drawn through the incorrect number or label and the accountant initials it; and the **correcting entry method,** in which an additional general journal entry is recorded to cancel or correct an incorrect entry.

The Work Sheet

The **work sheet** is a tool used by accountants to prepare the financial statements. **Adjustments** are considered internal transactions and are used to bring certain account balances up to date at the end of the time period covered. The following accounts require adjustments:

Supplies   Each purchase of supplies has been recorded as an increase in the Supplies account. But by the end of the fiscal period, some of these supplies have been used. An inventory is taken to determine the amount of supplies remaining. The **adjusting entry** is computed by subtracting the amount of supplies remaining from the balance of the Supplies account. This amount represents the supplies used; it is taken out of the Supplies account and transferred to the Supplies Expense account (debit Supplies Expense and credit Supplies).

Prepaid Insurance   Suppose a premium has been paid in advance for a two-year insurance policy. If the fiscal period is one month, the accountant divides the total premium by 24 to determine the amount of the premium that has been "used" or is expired. The adjusting entry is to deduct the used portion of the premium from the Prepaid Insurance account and transfer it to the Insurance Expense account (debit Insurance Expense and credit Prepaid Insurance).

Depreciation of Equipment   Items recorded as Equipment are expected to last longer than 1 year. Nevertheless, all of these assets will eventually either wear out or become obsolete. Therefore, we should systematically spread out their costs over the period of their useful lives. We write off the cost of the assets as an expense over the estimated useful life of the equipment and call it **depreciation.** In an asset account such as Equipment, we must keep the original cost recorded in the account; so the amount of depreciation has to be recorded in another account. This account is called Accumulated Depreciation and is referred to as a **contra account** because it is contrary to, or a deduction from, the respective asset (in this case, Equipment). The adjusting entry for depreciation is a debit to Depreciation Expense and a credit to Accumulated Depreciation. On the balance sheet, the balance of Accumulated Depreciation is subtracted from the balance of the asset account. This figure is called the **book value** of the asset.

Accrued Wages   When the fiscal period ends in the middle of an employees' payroll period, the wages that have been earned and not recorded are called **accrued wages.** The accounting term *accrue* means to recognize an expense or revenue that has been incurred or earned but has not yet been recorded. In the case of wages, we're dealing with an expense, and the adjusting entry is to debit the Wages Expense account and credit Wages Payable.

Journalizing Adjusting Entries

Adjustments are first recorded in the work sheet. Since the work sheet does not constitute a journal, the accountant must journalize the adjustments to bring the ledger accounts up to date. The accountant takes the information for these entries directly from the Adjustments columns of the work sheet, debiting and crediting exactly the same accounts and amounts in the journal entries.

Here is the work sheet, showing the placement of the account classifications in the various columns.

Account Classification	Trial Balance		Adjustments		Adjusted Trial Balance		Income Statement		Balance Sheet	
	Debit	Credit	Debit	Credit	Debit	Credit	Debit	Credit	Debit	Credit
Assets	X				X				X	
Liabilities		X				X				X
Capital		X				X				X
Drawing	X				X				X	
Revenue		X				X		X		
Expenses	X				X		X			

Closing Entries

The income statement covers a definite period of time. So, when a fiscal period ends, we want to start from scratch for the next period, closing off the revenue, expense, and Drawing accounts. These accounts are called temporary-equity or nominal accounts. The **closing entry** serves to close off these accounts. (Accountants refer to this procedure as "clearing the accounts.") The asset, liability, and owner's equity accounts are called real or permanent accounts and remain open.

Procedure for Closing   The four steps in the closing procedure are as follows:

1. Close the revenue account(s) into the Income Summary account.
2. Close the expense accounts into the Income Summary account.
3. Close the Income Summary account into the Capital account.
4. Close the Drawing account into the Capital account.

The procedure for closing is simply to balance off each account, to make the balance equal zero. For example, if an account has a debit balance of $300, we credit the account for $300.

Post-Closing Trial Balance

After posting the closing entries and before going on to the next fiscal period, the accountant verifies the equality of the debit and credit balances of the accounts that remain open. To do this, the accountant makes up a **post-closing trial balance,** which lists the final balance figures from the ledger accounts (assets, liabilities, and the Capital account).

Steps in the Accounting Cycle

1. Record business transactions in a journal.
2. Post journal entries to the accounts in the ledger.
3. Prepare a trial balance.
4. Gather adjustment data and record the adjusting entries in a work sheet.
5. Complete the work sheet.
6. Based on the work sheet, complete the financial statements.
7. Based on the work sheet, journalize and post the adjusting entries.
8. Journalize and post the closing entries.
9. Prepare a post-closing trial balance.

The Three Approved Bases of Accounting

Accrual Basis   In the **accrual basis** of accounting revenue is recorded when it is earned and expenses when they are incurred.

Cash-Receipts-and-Disbursements Basis Under the **Cash-Receipts-and-Disbursements basis,** revenue is counted only when it is received in cash, and expenses are recorded only when they are paid in cash. This basis is used most often for preparing personal income tax returns.

Modified Cash Basis Professional enterprises (in law, medicine, dentistry, or architecture, for example), as well as many small businesses (particularly service-type firms) use the **modified cash basis** of accounting. Revenue is not recorded until it is received in cash, and most expenses are recorded only when they are paid in cash. Exceptions are made for expenditures on items having a useful life of more than one year and on some prepaid items. Examples include supplies, prepaid insurance, and depreciation, which result in adjustments for supplies used, insurance expired, and depreciation expense.

The Combined Journal

The combined journal is especially useful for small businesses whose transactions are not extensive. The **combined journal** replaces the general journal and has the advantage of speed and accuracy. Most transactions can be recorded on one line. Special column totals may be posted to the most frequently used account. No explanations are given in the combined journal. After the equality of the debits and credits has been tested, the special column totals are posted at the end of the month rather than as individual amounts. The combined journal has Sundry Debit and Credit columns to handle infrequently used accounts that cannot be recorded in the special columns. Amounts in the Sundry columns are usually posted daily.

Bank Accounts and Bank Reconciliations

A bank maintains an independent record of a company's cash as long as the business deposits all incoming cash in the bank and issues checks for all payments. A **bank reconciliation** is made to uncover the reason for the difference between the balance listed on the bank statement and the balance in the company's books (the Cash account). Possible reasons for the difference include outstanding checks, deposits in transit, service charges, and NSF checks among others.

The Petty Cash Fund

The petty cash fund is a separate kitty of cash for things like postage, delivery charges, and other small items. The entry to establish the petty cash fund is a debit to Petty Cash Fund (an asset account that is listed below Cash) and a credit to Cash. Once the fund has been created, it is not debited again. The entry to reimburse the petty cash fund is a debit to the accounts for which money was expended and a credit to Cash. The money is accounted for by means of **petty cash vouchers** and/or a **petty cash payments record.**

The Change Fund

The change fund is created to deal with the need to make change for a company's cash transactions. The change fund consists of a variety of denominations of bills and coins. The entry to establish a change fund is a debit to Change Fund (an asset account that is listed below Cash) and a credit to Cash. At the end of each day the change fund is reimbursed by withholding a portion of the cash on hand.

Cash Short and Over

The **Cash Short and Over** account is established to correct for errors in making change. A shortage is recorded by a debit to Cash Short and Over; an overage is recorded as a credit to Cash Short and Over. At the end of the fiscal period a net shortage (debit balance in Cash Short and Over) is recorded as a Miscellaneous Expense on the income statement. A net overage (credit balance in Cash Short and Over) is recorded as Miscellaneous Income.

Payroll Accounting

Payroll accounting is concerned both with collecting accurate data to compute the compensation due each employee in each payroll period and with completing various government reports that are required of all employers. There are several laws and regulations that affect employees' pay and employers' responsibilities. Among them are federal and state income tax withholding requirements, the Fair Labor Standards Act, the Federal Insurance Contributions Act, Federal and State Unemployment Tax Acts, and workers' compensation laws.

The Payroll Register

The **payroll register** is used to list employees' earnings and deductions for a payroll period. It contains the following columns: Earnings (regular and overtime), Cumulative Earnings, Taxable Earnings (Unemployment and FICA), and Deductions (Federal and State Income Taxes, FICA, Medical Insurance, and Other). To comply with government regulations, a firm has to keep correct data on each employee's accumulated earnings, deductions, and net pay. The information is transferred from the payroll register to the **employee's individual earnings record** each payday.

The Payroll Entry

The **payroll entry** is based on totals in the payroll register. The entry is a debit to Salary or Wages Expense and credits to Employees' Federal Income Tax Payable, Employees' State Income Tax Payable, FICA Taxes Payable, Employees' Medical Insurance Payable, and other deduction accounts and to Salaries Payable, or Cash (for the amount of the employees' net pay—gross pay minus deductions). Assuming the use of a separate payroll bank account (from which the actual paychecks are issued), the second entry is a debit to Salaries Payable and a credit to Cash.

W-4 Form

Each employee must fill out an **Employee's Withholding Allowance Certificate,** or **W-4 form,** as authorization for the employer to withhold money for the employee's federal income tax. On the W-4 form, the employee lists the number of exemptions he or she claims. An **exemption** is the amount of an individual's earnings that is nontaxable. One exemption per dependent can be claimed (this is in addition to the one personal exemption each individual is allowed).

Employer's Payroll Taxes

An employer's payroll taxes are based on the gross wage paid by an employer to its employees. Unemployment taxes are levied on the employer only, but FICA tax is imposed on both employer and employee. The accountant deducts the employee's share of the FICA tax from gross wages and records it in the payroll entry under FICA Tax Payable (an account used for the employer's share also). Next, the accountant determines the employer's share by multiplying the FICA tax rate times the total FICA-taxable earnings (this information comes from the payroll register). The entry for FICA and unemployment taxes is a debit to Payroll Tax Expense (an account that is closed at the end of the year along with other expense accounts) and a credit to FICA Tax Payable, State Unemployment Tax Payable, or Federal Unemployment Tax Payable.

Journal Entries for Recording Payroll   The payroll entry (from the payroll register) is recorded first, followed by the entry to record the employer's payroll tax. Finally, an entry is made to record the issuance of one check payable to a payroll bank account—separate payroll checks to each employee will be issued from this account.

Payments of FICA Taxes and Employee's Income Tax Withheld   The employer is required to make federal tax deposits for (1) employees' federal income tax withheld, (2) employees' FICA taxes withheld, and (3) the employer's share of FICA taxes. The timing of these payments depends on the amount of undeposited taxes.

Payments of Unemployment Insurance   The FUTA (Federal Unemployment Tax Act) tax is payable quarterly. If the accumulated tax liability is greater than $100, the tax is deposited in a commercial bank or a Federal Reserve bank, accompanied by a preprinted federal tax deposit card, like the form used to deposit employees' federal income tax withholding and FICA taxes. State unemployment taxes vary; different states have different rules with regard to both the rate and taxable base of unemployment insurance. The Employer's Annual Federal Unemployment Tax Return (Form 940) is prepared using information from the state unemployment tax return, which is prepared quarterly. Payment of unemployment insurance is a debit to Federal or State Unemployment Tax Payable and a credit to Cash.

Employer's Quarterly Federal Tax Return (FORM 941)   This return, which applies to federal income taxes withheld and FICA taxes, must be filed by the end of the month following the end of the quarter. The due dates for a calendar-year taxpayer are first quarter, April 30; second quarter, July 31; third quarter, October 31; and fourth quarter, January 31.

Employer's Annual Federal Income Tax Reports   The employer sends copy A of each employee's W-2 (withholding) form to the District Director of Internal Revenue on or before February 28 (the employer keeps copy D; other copies go to the employee for individual tax returns). The accountant attaches the W-2 forms to Form W-3, the Transmittal of Income and Tax Statements. Along with these, the employer sends the Quarterly Federal Tax Return for the fourth quarter.

Worker's Compensation Insurance   Most states require employers to provide workers' compensation insurance to pay medical bills if an employee is hurt on the job. Because some jobs are more dangerous than others (and therefore have a higher insurance rate assigned them), it is important to properly identify and classify each employee with regard to the insurance premium categories. Generally, the employer pays a premium in advance based on the estimated payrolls for the year. After the year ends the exact premium is calculated, and the employer either pays an additional premium or is entitled to a credit for overpayment.

ACCOUNTING FOR MERCHANDISING

A merchandising business depends for its revenue on the sale of goods, or merchandise. **Merchandise** consists of a stock of goods that the firm buys and intends to resell at a profit. Because a merchandising firm has to record transactions involving purchases and sales, it uses accounts and procedures we have not yet discussed. Here is the fundamental accounting equation showing the new T accounts to be introduced:

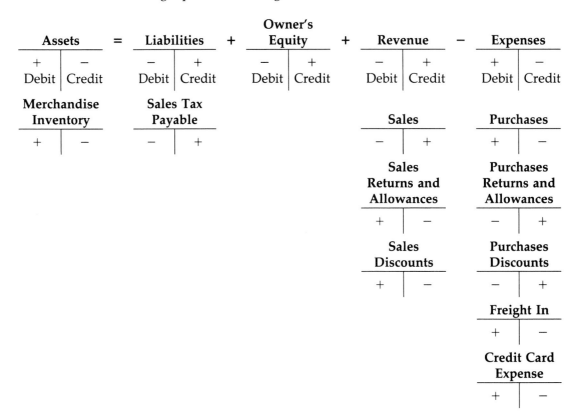

The Sales Account is a revenue account used for recording sales of merchandise.

The Purchases Account is used to record the cost of merchandise acquired for resale. Purchases is placed under the heading of Expenses only because the accountant closes it at the end of the fiscal period.

Sales Returns and Allowances is an account used to record physical returns of merchandise or a reduction in a bill due to defect or damage. It is treated as a deduction from Sales.

Purchases Returns and Allowances is used to record a return or reduction in price of merchandise purchased by the firm for resale. It is treated as a deduction from Purchases.

The accountant makes entries involving Merchandise Inventory only when the firm takes an actual physical count of the goods in stock; otherwise this account is left strictly alone.

The Sales Journal

The **sales journal** records sales of merchandise on account only. The entry involves a debit to Accounts Receivable and a credit to Sales. One type of sales journal has one column only, headed Accounts Receivable

Debit, Sales Credit. Listing the invoice number makes it easier to check the details of a particular sale at a later date. Another type of sales journal has three columns, with separate headings for Accounts Receivable Debit and Sales Credit, as well as a Sales Tax Payable column to provide for sales tax. Using the sales journal saves time and space in posting to the ledger accounts, as the accountant can make a **summarizing entry** (a single posting to these accounts for the amount of the total as of the last day of the month).

Posting Directly from Sales Invoices

Companies with a large volume of sales sometimes use copies of their sales invoices in place of a sales journal. The accountant posts to the charge accounts in the accounts receivable ledger directly from the invoices. At the end of the month, the accountant totals the sales invoices and makes a summarizing entry in the general journal debiting Accounts Receivable and crediting Sales.

The Accounts Receivable Ledger

Because it is impossible to tell from the general ledger how much each charge customer owes, most businesses keep a separate account for each charge customer in a subsidiary ledger called the **accounts receivable ledger.** At the end of each month the total balances of the charge customer accounts must equal the balance of the Accounts Receivable account in the general ledger. The account in the general ledger is called a **controlling account** because it summarizes the balances of a subsidiary ledger.

Sales Returns and Allowances

The source documents for entries in the Sales Returns and Allowances account are **credit memorandums.** The journal entry is a debit to Sales Returns and Allowances and a credit to Accounts Receivable. This entry is posted both in the general ledger account and in the charge customer accounts in the accounts receivable ledger. Sales Returns and Allowances is deducted from Sales in the income statement.

Purchases Returns and Allowances

The **Purchases Returns and Allowances** account is a deduction from Purchases (bear in mind that the Purchases account is used exclusively for the buying of merchandise intended for resale—in other words, not equipment, supplies, or other assets or liabilities). When a credit memo is received for the return of merchandise or as an allowance for damaged merchandise that was purchased on a credit basis, the buyer debits Accounts Payable and credits Purchases Returns and Allowances.

Freight Charges on Incoming Merchandise

Freight In is an expense account used to record transportation costs of merchandise intended for resale that has been purchased **FOB** (free on board) **shipping point.** Merchandise may be purchased FOB shipping point or FOB destination. With FOB shipping point, the buyer is responsible for paying the freight charges. With FOB destination, the seller is responsible for paying the freight charges. Unless the title to the goods is expressly reserved, whoever is responsible for paying the freight charges has title to the goods while they are in transit.

The Accounts Payable Ledger

We saw how the Accounts Receivable account in the general ledger was a controlling account and how the accountant created a subsidiary ledger to increase speed and convenience. The accountant does the same thing with the Accounts Payable account, keeping track in a subsidiary ledger of the individual accounts of creditors.

Purchases Journal (Three-Column)

The purchases journal is used to record the purchase of merchandise on account only. In this special journal, totals are posted to the general ledger each month. The columns are Purchases Debit, Freight In Debit, and Accounts Payable Credit. Entries are posted daily to the accounts payable ledger.

Multicolumn Purchases Journal (Invoice Register)

The **multicolumn purchases journal,** or **invoice register,** handles not only freight charges and purchases, but anything bought on account (including supplies and equipment). This special journal has columns for Accounts Payable Credit, three special columns for the most commonly used accounts, and a Sundry column for miscellaneous purchases. Accounts Payable Credit amounts are posted daily to the accounts payable ledger. Amounts in the Sundry column are usually posted daily to the general ledger. Amounts in the special columns are posted as totals at the end of the month.

Posting Directly from Purchase Invoices

As a further shortcut, a firm may post to the accounts of the individual creditors in the accounts payable ledger directly from invoices of items bought on credit. At the end of the month the accountant makes a summarizing entry in the general journal, debiting Purchases, Freight In, and any assets that were acquired and crediting Accounts Payable for the total of the invoices.

New Accounts

Credit Card Expense—used to record the discount taken by a bank for credit card sales.

Sales Discounts—used to record the amount a firm allows its customers as a deduction for prompt payment in cash (this account is considered a deduction from Sales).

Purchases Discount—used to record the amount a firm benefits by paying its bills promptly (this amount is considered a deduction from Purchases).

Cash Receipts Journal

When a company uses a **cash receipts journal,** all transactions resulting in a debit to Cash must be recorded in it. The journal includes special columns in which to record debits and credits to frequently used accounts (like the ones listed above and Accounts Receivable). Entries are recorded in the Sundry column when there is no appropriate special column. Amounts in the Accounts Receivable Credit column are posted daily to individual charge customers' accounts in the accounts receivable ledger. Amounts in the Sundry column are usually posted daily. The special columns are posted as totals at the end of the month.

Cash Payments Journal

A **cash payments journal** is just like a cash receipts journal, only it handles all transactions resulting in a credit to Cash. Special columns are included to take care of debits and credits to accounts used frequently, as well as Accounts Payable and Sundry columns. The posting procedure is similar to that used with the cash receipts journal. The cash payments journal for a merchandise firm is slightly different than that for a service business. This difference has to do with the cash discounts available to a merchandise business (see below). The buyer considers the cash discount to be a Purchases Discount, and it is treated as a deduction from Purchases in the buyer's income statement.

Credit Terms and Discounts

The seller always sets the credit terms, determining how much time the customer has to pay the full amount (this is called the **credit period**). Wholesalers and manufacturers often specify a **cash discount** in their credit terms, that is, a cash discount is given to the customer who can pay the full amount within a set amount of time (shorter than the regular credit period). Credit terms of 2/10, n/30 indicate a 2 percent discount for full payment within 10 days, and a regular due date of 30 days.

In transactions involving trade discounts, the purchase price is calculated by subtracting the trade discount(s) from the list price. Both buyers and sellers record the transaction at the purchase price.

Adjustment for Merchandise Inventory

When we introduced the merchandise inventory account, we mentioned that it is only changed after an actual physical count of the stock of goods has taken place. This is consistent with a system of **periodic inventories.** (Under this system a physical inventory must be taken at least once a year.) Adjusting entries need to be made to take off the beginning inventory and add on the ending inventory. The first entry is made to eliminate or close the Merchandise Inventory account into Income Summary by debiting Income Summary and crediting Merchandise Inventory for the amount of the beginning inventory (the amount of goods in stock at the beginning of the fiscal period covered). The second entry is made to enter, or add on, the ending inventory by debiting Merchandise Inventory and crediting Income Summary for the amount of the ending inventory. On the Merchandise Inventory line of the work sheet, the amount of the ending inventory is carried over to the Balance Sheet Debit column. On the Income Summary line of the work sheet, the debit and credit amounts in the Adjustment columns are carried over directly to the Income Statement Debit and Credit columns.

Adjustment for Unearned Revenue

The adjustment for unearned revenue could pertain to a service as well as a merchandising business. The **Unearned Revenue** account includes all money received in advance for services or goods not to be received by the customer or client until the next fiscal period. For the present fiscal period, these amounts are considered Unearned Revenue. This account is classified as a liability, because the firm is liable for the amount received in advance until it is earned. Assuming that the amount received was originally recorded as a debit to Cash and a credit to Unearned Revenue, the adjusting entry to record the amount of revenue actually earned is a debit to the Unearned Revenue account (such as Unearned Course Fees—for a college, say) and a credit to the Revenue account (such as Course Fees Income). On the Unearned Revenue line of the work sheet, Unearned Revenue is carried over to the Balance Sheet Credit column.

The Income Statement

The outline for the income statement follows a logical pattern and is much the same for any type of merchandising business.

Revenue from Sales   Sales, minus Sales Returns and Allowances, minus Sales Discounts: this equals Net Sales. Notice that we record these items in the same order in which they appear in the ledger.

Cost of Merchandise Sold   This is the most complicated part of the income statement. We start with the beginning Merchandise Inventory, then add Net Purchases (which is Purchases minus Purchases Returns and Allowances and Purchases Discounts plus Freight In) to arrive at Merchandise Available for Sale; then subtract the amount of the ending Merchandise Inventory to determine Cost of Merchandise Sold.

Net Sales − Cost of Merchandise Sold = Gross Profit

Operating Expenses   These are the regular expenses of doing business. We list the accounts and their balances in the order that they appear in the ledger. Many firms use subclassifications of operating expenses, such as selling expenses, general expenses, and the like.

Gross Profit − Operating Expenses = Income from Operations

Other Income   This category includes income from anything other than sales: Rent Income, Interest Income, Miscellaneous Income, Gain on Disposal of Plant and Equipment, etc.

Other Expenses   Nonoperating expenses include Interest Expense, Loss on Disposal of Plant and Equipment, etc.

Income from Operations + Other Income − Other Expenses = Net Income

The Balance Sheet

Balance sheet classifications are generally uniform for all types of business enterprises.

Current Assets   These consist of cash and any other assets or resources that are expected to be realized in cash or to be sold or consumed during the operating cycle of the business (usually one year). These accounts are listed in the order of their **liquidity** (convertibility to cash).

Plant and Equipment   These long-lived assets are sometimes referred to as **fixed assets.** These accounts are listed in the order of length of life; the asset with the longest life is placed first. Each separate asset is followed by its Accumulated Depreciation account.

Current Liabilities   These are debts that will become due within the normal operating cycle of the business; these accounts are listed in the order of their expected payment.

Long-Term Liabilities   These are debts payable over a comparably long period; Mortgage Payable is often the only account in this category for a sole-proprietorship business.

Working Capital and Current Ratio

Working capital is current assets minus current liabilities. The **current ratio** is determined by dividing a firm's current assets by its current liabilities. Both figures are useful in determining a business's ability to operate successfully and to pay its bills. When banks are considering granting loans to merchandising firms, a minimum current ratio of 2 : 1 is generally required.

Reversing Entries

The closing and adjusting procedures for a merchandising firm are the same as for a service or professional enterprise. The **reversing entry** is an entry made on the first day of the new fiscal period to reverse an adjusting entry. To determine which adjusting entries need to be reversed, follow this rule: if an adjusting entry increases an asset account or liability account that does not have a previous balance, reverse the adjusting entry. After the first year Merchandise Inventory and contra accounts such as Accumulated Depreciation always have previous balances; therefore, they are exceptions and should never be reversed.

16 Accounting for Notes Payable

LEARNING OBJECTIVES

After you have completed this chapter, you will be able to do the following:

1. Recognize a promissory note.
2. Calculate the interest on promissory notes.
3. Determine the due dates of promissory notes.
4. Make journal entries for (a) notes given to secure an extension of time on an open account, (b) payment of an interest-bearing note at maturity, (c) notes given in exchange for merchandise or other property purchased, (d) notes given to secure a cash loan, when the borrower receives full face value of the note, (e) notes given to secure a cash loan, when the bank discounts the note, (f) renewal of a note at maturity, (g) adjustment for accrued interest on notes payable, (h) adjustment for prepaid interest on notes payable.

Credit plays an extremely important role in the operation of most business enterprises. We have seen that credit may be extended on a charge-account basis, with payment generally due in thirty days. This type of credit involves the Accounts Payable and Accounts Receivable accounts. Credit may also be granted on the basis of giving or receiving notes for specific transactions. This sort of credit involves the Notes Payable and Notes Receivable accounts. The notes, which represent formal instruments of credit, are known as *promissory notes.* They are customarily used as evidence of credit transactions for periods longer than thirty days. For example, promissory notes may be used in sales of equipment on the installment plan and for transactions involving large amounts of money.

Promissory notes are also used to grant extensions of credit beyond the regular credit terms. For example, suppose that the Smith Company buys merchandise from Parker Brothers on the basis of 2/10, n/30. The Smith Company finds that it can't pay its bill within the thirty-day period. To preserve its credit standing, the Smith Company offers a note. The advantages to Parker Brothers are as follows: (1) they now have specific evidence of the transaction, (2) the note may carry interest, and (3) they can borrow from the bank by pledging the note as security for a loan. Business concerns may also borrow from banks by issuing their own promissory notes.

In general, then, most companies at one time or another become involved with notes, either by issuing notes to creditors, receiving notes from customers, or issuing notes to banks in order to borrow money. Consequently, an accountant must be acquainted with the procedures for handling promissory notes. In this chapter we shall discuss transactions involving notes payable. Chapter 17 will describe transactions involving notes receivable.

PROMISSORY NOTES

Objective 1

Recognize a promissory note.

A **promissory note**—usually referred to simply as a *note*—is a written promise to pay a certain sum at a fixed or determinable future time. Like a check, it must be payable to the order of a particular person or firm, known as the **payee.** It must also be signed by the person or firm making the promise, known as the **maker.** In Figure 16-1 Adkins Manufacturing Company is the payee, and City-Wide Electric Supply is the maker.

FIGURE 16-1

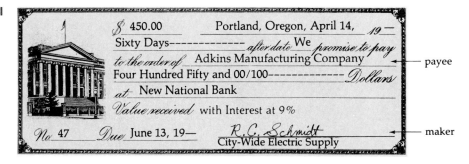

CALCULATING INTEREST

Interest is a charge made for the use of money. To the maker of the note, interest is an expense. The amount of interest a maker pays is expressed as a certain percentage of the principal of the note for a period of one year (or less). The following formula is used to calculate interest:

Objective 2

Calculate the interest on promissory notes.

| **Interest** (in dollars) | = | **Principal** of note (in dollars) | × | **Rate** of interest (as a percentage of the principal) | × | **Time** of note (expressed as a year or fraction of a year) |

The **principal** is the face amount of the note. The *rate of interest* is a percentage of the principal, such as 8 percent or 9 percent. Since 1 percent equals $1/100$ or .01, then 8 percent equals $8/100$ or .08.

Time, or the length of life of the note, is expressed in terms of days or months. It is the period between the date of issue of the note (starting date) and the **maturity date** of the note (the due date or interest payment date). It is stated in terms of a year or fraction of a year. Examples are

$$1 \text{ year} = 1 \qquad 6 \text{ months} = \frac{6}{12} \qquad 3 \text{ months} = \frac{3}{12}$$

$$90 \text{ days} = \frac{90}{360} \qquad 24 \text{ days} = \frac{24}{360}$$

The usual commercial practice is to use a 360-day year, thus making the denominator of the fraction 360. However, agencies of the federal government use the actual number of days in the year.

Example 1 $2,000, 8 percent, 1 year.

Interest = Principal × Rate × Time
Interest = $2,000 × .08 × 1 = $160

Example 2 $4,000, 9 percent, 3 months.

Interest = Principal × Rate × Time

$$\textbf{Interest} = \$4,000 \times .09 \times \frac{3}{12}$$

$$= \$4,000 \times .09 \times 3 \div 12 = \underline{\underline{\$90}}$$

Example 3 $6,000, 11 percent, 60 days.

Interest = Principal × Rate × Time

$$\textbf{Interest} = \$6,000 \times .11 \times \frac{60}{360}$$

$$= \$6,000 \times .11 \times 60 \div 360 = \underline{\underline{\$110}}$$

Example 4 $3,640, 12 percent, 45 days.

Interest = Principal × Rate × Time

$$\textbf{Interest} = \$3,640 \times .12 \times \frac{45}{360}$$

$$= \$3,640 \times .12 \times 45 \div 360 = \underline{\underline{\$54.60}}$$

Example 5 $5,684, 8 percent, 23 days.

$$\text{Interest} = \text{Principal} \times \text{Rate} \times \text{Time}$$

$$\text{Interest} = \$5,684 \times .08 \times \frac{23}{360}$$

$$= \$5,684 \times .08 \times 23 \div 360 = \underline{\$29.05}$$

DETERMINING DUE DATES

Objective 3

Determine the due dates of promissory notes.

As we have said, the period of time a note has to run may be expressed in either days or months. If the time of the note is expressed in months, the maturity date is the corresponding day in the month after the specified number of months have elapsed. For example, a note dated March 12 with a time period of three months has a due date of June 12. In those cases in which there is no date in the month of maturity that corresponds to the issuance date, the due date becomes the last day of the month. For example, a three-month note dated January 31 would be due on April 30.

But suppose that the period of time a note has to run is expressed in days. When counting the number of days, begin with the day after the date the note was issued, since the note states "after date." The last day, however, is counted. Let us say that the due date of a promissory note is specified as 60 days after April 14. The calendar below shows that the due date is June 13.

April						
S	M	T	W	T	F	S
		1	2	3	4	5
6	7	8	9	10	11	12
13	14	15	16	17	18	19
20	21	22	23	24	25	26
27	28	29	30			

16 days
15th through the 30th
30 − 14 = 16 days left

May						
S	M	T	W	T	F	S
				1	2	3
4	5	6	7	8	9	10
11	12	13	14	15	16	17
18	19	20	21	22	23	24
25	26	27	28	29	30	31

+ 31 days

June						
S	M	T	W	T	F	S
1	2	3	4	5	6	7
8	9	10	11	12	13	14
15	16	17	18	19	20	21
22	23	24	25	26	27	28
29	30					

= 47 days have passed
60 − 47 = 13 days remaining after May 31
June 13 due date

In summary, the due date is determined by the following steps:

1. Determine the number of days remaining in the month of issue by subtracting the date of the note from the number of days in the month in which it is dated.

2. Add as many full months as possible without exceeding the number of days in the note, counting the full number of days in these months.
3. Determine the number of days remaining in the month in which the note matures by subtracting the total days counted so far from the number of days in the note, as shown here.

April (30 − 14)   = 16 days left in April
May   = 31 days
_____
Total days so far = 47 days
June (60 − 47)   = 13th day of June (due date)

Let's look at another example. Suppose you have a 120-day note dated May 27:

May (31 − 27)   = 4 days left in May
June   = 30 days
July   = 31 days
August   = 31 days
_____
Total days so far   = 96 days
September (120 − 96) = 24th day of September (due date)

TRANSACTIONS INVOLVING NOTES PAYABLE

The following types of transactions involve the issuance and payment of notes payable:

1. Note given to a supplier in return for an extension of time for payment of an open account (charge account)
2. Note given in exchange for merchandise or other property purchased
3. Note given as evidence of a loan
4. Note renewed at maturity

In our examples, we assume all the notes are due within one year, and so they are classified on a balance sheet as Current Liabilities. However, if notes are due in a period longer than one year, they are classified as Long-Term Liabilities. Interest Expense is classified on an income statement as Other Expense.

Objective 4a

Make journal entries for notes given to secure an extension of time on an open account.

Note Given to Secure an Extension of Time on an Open Account

When a firm wishes to obtain an extension of time for the payment of an account, the firm may ask a supplier to accept a note for all or part of the amount due. For example, let's say that City-Wide Electric Supply prefers to not pay its open account with Adkins Manufacturing Company when it becomes due. Adkins agrees to accept a 60-day, 9 percent, $450 note from City-Wide Electric in settlement of the charge account. The entry that caused the account to be put on Adkins's books in the first place came about when City-Wide Electric bought merchandise on account on March 15, with terms 2/10, n/30. In general journal form the entry looks like this:

GENERAL JOURNAL   PAGE_____

	DATE	DESCRIPTION	POST. REF.	DEBIT	CREDIT	
1	19–					1
2	Mar. 15	Purchases		450 00		2
3		Accounts Payable, Adkins				3
4		Manufacturing Co.			450 00	4
5		Terms 2/10, n/30.				5
6						6

On April 14 City-Wide Electric records the issuance of the note in its general journal.

GENERAL JOURNAL   PAGE_____

	DATE	DESCRIPTION	POST. REF.	DEBIT	CREDIT	
1	19–					1
2	Apr. 14	Accounts Payable, Adkins				2
3		Manufacturing Co.		450 00		3
4		Notes Payable			450 00	4
5		Gave a 60-day, 9 percent note				5
6		in settlement of our open				6
7		account.				7

By T accounts, the transactions look like this:

Purchases		Accounts Payable		Notes Payable	
+	−	−	+	−	+
Mar. 15 450		Apr. 14 450	Mar. 15 450		Apr. 14 450

Observe that the above entry cancels out the Accounts Payable, Adkins Manufacturing Company account and substitutes Notes Payable. The note does not *pay* the debt, it merely changes the liability status from an account payable to a note payable. Adkins prefers the note to the open account because, in the case of default and a subsequent lawsuit to collect, the possession of the note improves Adkins's legal position. The note is written evidence of the debt and the amount owed. In addition, Adkins is, in this case, entitled to 9 percent interest.

Payment of an Interest-bearing Note at Maturity

Objective 4b

Make journal entries for payment of an interest-bearing note at maturity.

When a note payable falls due, payment may be made directly to the holder, or it may be made to a bank in which the note was left for collection. The maker of course knows the identity of the original payee, but he or she may not know who the holder of the note is at maturity. The payee may have transferred the note by endorsement to another party or may have left it with a bank for collection. When a note is left with a bank for collection, the bank usually mails the maker a **notice of maturity** specifying the terms and due date of the note. For example, Adkins Manufacturing Company turned the note over to its bank, the New National Bank, for collection. Accordingly, the bank sent City-Wide Electric a notice of maturity of the note.

City-Wide Electric Supply pays the note on June 13. In general journal form, the entry is as follows:

	DATE	DESCRIPTION	POST. REF.	DEBIT	CREDIT	
1	*19–*					1
2	*June 13*	*Notes Payable*		4 5 0 00		2
3		*Interest Expense*		6 75		3
4		*Cash*			4 5 6 75	4
5		*Paid note to Adkins*				5
6		*Manufacturing Co.*				6
7						7

GENERAL JOURNAL   PAGE_____

Because Interest = Principal × Rate × Time, we perform these calculations:

Interest = $450 × .09 × 60 ÷ 360 = $6.75

The organization for the entry is shown by T accounts:

Cash		Notes Payable		Interest Expense	
+	–	–	+	+	–
	456.75	450.00		6.75	

In practice, transactions such as this one are recorded directly in the cash payments journal rather than in the general journal. However, to simplify the discussion of the entries, all transactions will be presented here in general journal form. As stated earlier, Notes Payable is listed in the Current Liabilities section of a balance sheet. Interest Expense is listed in the Other Expense section of an income statement.

Note Given in Exchange for Assets Purchased

Objective 4c

Make journal entries for notes given in exchange for merchandise or other property purchased.

Occasionally, when the price of an item is high or the credit period is long, a buyer gives a note instead of buying the item on account. For example, City-Wide Electric Supply issues a 60-day, 8 percent interest-bearing note for $2,400 to the Sutton Equipment Company in exchange for equipment purchased May 3 and records the transaction in the general journal as follows:

	DATE		DESCRIPTION	POST. REF.	DEBIT	CREDIT	
1	19–						1
2	May	3	Store Equipment		2 4 0 0 00		2
3			Notes Payable			2 4 0 0 00	3
4			Acquired shelves and counters				4
5			from Sutton Equipment				5
6			Company, 60 days, 8 percent.				6

By T accounts, it looks like this:

Store Equipment		Notes Payable	
+	–	–	+
2,400			2,400

When City-Wide Electric pays the note at maturity, the entry in its books is the same as the entry it makes for the payment of any interest-bearing note. In general journal form, the entry looks like this:

	DATE		DESCRIPTION	POST. REF.	DEBIT	CREDIT	
1	19–						1
2	July	2	Notes Payable		2 4 0 0 00		2
3			Interest Expense		3 2 00		3
4			Cash			2 4 3 2 00	4
5			Paid note to Sutton Equipment				5
6			Company.				6

May (31 − 3)   = 28 days left in May
June   = 30 days

Total days so far = 58 days
July (60 − 58)   = 2nd day of July (due date)

And since Interest = Principal × Rate × Time,

Interest = $2,400 × .08 × 60 ÷ 360 = $32

Note Given to Secure a Cash Loan

Businesses frequently need to stock up on merchandise in large amounts in order to meet seasonal demands. Sometimes their usual receipts from customers are not enough to cover the sudden volume of purchases. During such periods, business firms customarily borrow money from banks, through the medium of short-term notes, to finance their operations.

Borrowing from a Bank When Borrower Receives Full Face Value of Note

Objective 4d

Make journal entries for notes given to secure a cash loan, when the borrower receives full face value of the note.

In one type of bank loan, a business firm signs an interest-bearing note and receives the full face value of the note. The borrower repays the principal plus interest. For example, on May 11 City-Wide Electric Supply borrows $1,200 from Flagel National Bank for 120 days with interest of 7 percent payable at maturity. The entry to record the transaction is as follows:

	DATE		DESCRIPTION	POST. REF.	DEBIT	CREDIT	
1	*19–*						1
2	*May*	*11*	*Cash*		1 2 0 0 00		2
3			*Notes Payable*			1 2 0 0 00	3
4			*Gave Flagel National Bank a*				4
5			*120-day, 7 percent note.*				5
6							6

May (31 − 11)   = 20 days left in May
June   = 30 days
July   = 31 days
August   = 31 days

Total days so far   = 112 days
September (120 − 112) = 8th day of September (due date)

Note Paid to the Bank at Maturity

After City-Wide Electric has paid the note and interest, its accountant makes the following entry on the books:

	DATE	DESCRIPTION	POST. REF.	DEBIT	CREDIT	
1	19–					1
2	Sept. 8	Notes Payable		1 2 0 0 00		2
3		Interest Expense		2 8 00		3
4		Cash			1 2 2 8 00	4
5		Paid note to Flagel National				5
6		Bank.				6
7						7

Interest = Principal × Rate × Time

Interest = $1,200 × .07 × 120 ÷ 360 = $28

Borrowing from a Bank When Bank Discounts Note (Deducts Interest in Advance)

In another type of bank loan, the bank deducts the interest in advance, which is called **discounting a note payable**. For example, on May 19 City-Wide Electric Supply borrows $6,000 for 60 days from Northwest National Bank; the bank requires City-Wide Electric to sign a note. From the face value of the note, the bank deducts 9 percent interest for 60 days, so City-Wide Electric actually gets only $5,910. This interest deducted in advance by a bank is called the **discount**. The principal of the loan left after the discount has been subtracted is called the **proceeds,** which is the amount the borrower has available to use. The calculations are as follows:

Interest = Principal × Rate × Time

Interest = $6,000 × .09 × 60 ÷ 360 = $90

As we said, the bank deducts the discount from the face amount of the note, before making the money available to the borrower.

Principal	$6,000
− Discount	90
Proceeds	$5,910

Entry When Note Discounted at Bank Matures Before End of Fiscal Period

Objective 4e

Make journal entries for notes given to secure a cash loan, when the bank discounts the note.

As long as a note begins and matures during the same fiscal period, the borrower may debit all the interest (or discount) to Interest Expense. The 60-day note that City-Wide Electric Supply submits to the bank is dated May 19 and therefore matures July 18. Since City-Wide Electric's fiscal period is from January 1 to December 31, City-Wide Electric can include the entire amount of interest in Interest Expense. Accordingly, City-Wide Electric records the transaction as follows:

	DATE		DESCRIPTION	POST. REF.	DEBIT	CREDIT	
1	19–						1
2	May	19	Cash		5 9 1 0 00		2
3			Interest Expense		9 0 00		3
4			Notes Payable			6 0 0 0 00	4
5			Discounted our 60-day				5
6			non-interest-bearing note at				6
7			the Northwest National Bank,				7
8			discount rate 9 percent.				8
9							9

Note Paid to the Bank at Maturity

When the note becomes due, City-Wide Electric Supply pays the bank just the *face value of the note*, and records the transaction as follows:

	DATE		DESCRIPTION	POST. REF.	DEBIT	CREDIT	
1	19–						1
2	July	18	Notes Payable		6 0 0 0 00		2
3			Cash			6 0 0 0 00	3
4			Paid Northwest National Bank				4
5			on our note payable discounted.				5
6							6

May (31 − 19)   = 12 days left in May
June   = 30 days

Total days so far = 42 days
July (60 − 42)   = 18th day of July (due date)

Entry When Note Discounted at Bank Matures After End of Fiscal Period

Now suppose that the time period of the note extends into the next fiscal period. City-Wide Electric Supply must then record the discount as a debit to Discount on Notes Payable. **Discount on Notes Payable is a contra liability account;** in other words, it is a deduction from Notes Payable. Recall that we defined the Accumulated Depreciation account as a contra asset—for example, a deduction from Equipment with the plus and minus signs switched around. Similarly, Discount on Notes Payable is another contra account—a deduction from Notes Payable with the plus and minus signs switched around. In T account form, using hypothetical (made-up) amounts, these accounts look like this:

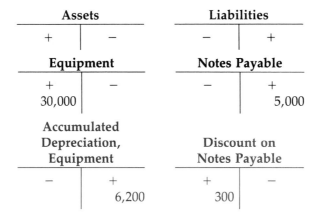

Also, on a balance sheet, the contra account is deducted as shown below:

Balance Sheet

Assets			
Plant and Equipment:			
Equipment	$ 30 0 0 0 00		
Less Accumulated Depreciation	6 2 0 0 00	$ 23 8 0 0 00	
Liabilities			
Current Liabilities:			
Notes Payable	$ 5 0 0 0 00		
Less Discount on Notes Payable	3 0 0 00	$ 4 7 0 0 00	

At the end of the fiscal period, an adjusting entry must be made to record the amount of interest expense for the time between the date the note is issued until the end of the fiscal period. We will describe the adjusting entry on page 525.

Let's say that on December 1 City-Wide Electric Supply borrows $1,800 from the First State Bank for 120 days. The bank deducts 8 percent interest (in advance) for 120 days, $48, and gives City-Wide Electric $1,752. City-Wide Electric's fiscal period is from January 1 through December 31, so its accountant's entry in the general journal is like this:

	DATE		DESCRIPTION	POST. REF.	DEBIT	CREDIT	
1	*19–*						1
2	*Dec.*	*1*	*Cash*		1 7 5 2 00		2
3			*Discount on Notes Payable*		4 8 00		3
4			*Notes Payable*			1 8 0 0 00	4
5			*Discounted our 120-day*				5
6			*non-interest-bearing note at*				6
7			*the First State Bank; discount*				7
8			*rate 8 percent.*				8
9							9

Remember

If a note payable discounted at a bank comes due before the end of the fiscal period, debit Interest Expense for the amount of the discount. If the note comes due after the end of the fiscal period, debit Discount on Notes Payable for the amount of the discount.

In a discounted-note transaction, since all the interest is deducted at the time the loan is made, the note must state that only the face amount is to be paid at maturity. Payment of this note is discussed on page 528 as part of End-of-Fiscal-Period Adjustments.

Renewal of Note at Maturity

Objective 4f

Make journal entries for renewal of a note at maturity.

What if the maker (or borrower) is unable to pay a note in full at maturity? Then he or she may arrange to renew all or part of the note. At this time, he or she usually pays the interest on the old note. For example, assume that on May 27 City-Wide Electric Supply issues a 60-day note to Draper, Inc., for $1,500, with interest at 8 percent. The original entry in general journal form is as follows:

	DATE		DESCRIPTION	POST. REF.	DEBIT	CREDIT	
1	*19–*						1
2	*May*	*27*	*Accounts Payable, Draper, Inc.*		1 5 0 0 00		2
3			*Notes Payable*			1 5 0 0 00	3
4			*Issued a 60-day, 8 percent*				4
5			*note.*				5
6							6

Renewal of Note with Payment of Interest

When a firm renews an interest-bearing note, the accountant first makes an entry to pay the interest on the existing note, up to the present date. This entry occurs on July 26, the maturity date of the note.

	DATE		DESCRIPTION	POST. REF.	DEBIT	CREDIT	
1	*19–*						1
2	*July*	*26*	*Interest Expense*		*2 0 00*		2
3			*Cash*			*2 0 00*	3
4			*Interest payment on note to*				4
5			*Draper, Inc.*				5

May (31 − 27)   = 4 days left in May
June   = 30 days

Total days so far = 34 days
July (60 − 34)   = 26th day of July (due date)

Interest = Principal × Rate × Time

Interest = $1,500 × .08 × 60 ÷ 360 = $\underline{\underline{\$20}}$

    The accountant then makes a separate entry for the issuance of the new note, to run for 30 days at 9 percent (the interest rate has been increased) as follows:

	DATE		DESCRIPTION	POST. REF.	DEBIT	CREDIT	
11	*19–*						11
12	*July*	*26*	*Notes Payable*		*1 5 0 0 00*		12
13			*Notes Payable*			*1 5 0 0 00*	13
14			*Canceled note to Draper, Inc.,*				14
15			*by issuing 30-day, 9 percent note.*				15

Renewal of Note with Payment of Interest and Part Payment of Principal

Now, what if the maker decides to pay only *part* of a note at maturity? Let us assume that, instead of taking the course of action we have just described, City-Wide Electric pays $500 on the principal of the note that is due (the old note), and also pays the entire interest on it. In other

Remember

For a renewal of a note payable, debit the old note to take it off the books, and credit the new note to put it on the books.

words, the maker pays the interest up to the present date for the old note, plus $500 to reduce the principal from $1,500 to $1,000, and issues a *new* note for $1,000.

	DATE	DESCRIPTION	POST. REF.	DEBIT	CREDIT	
11	**19–**					11
12	**July 26**	**Notes Payable**		5 0 0 00		12
13		**Interest Expense**		2 0 00		13
14		**Cash**			5 2 0 00	14
15		*Interest payment on note to*				15
16		*Draper, Inc., and part payment*				16
17		*on the principal.*				17
18						18
19	**26**	**Notes Payable**		1 0 0 0 00		19
20		**Notes Payable**			1 0 0 0 00	20
21		*Canceled note to Draper, Inc.,*				21
22		*by issuing 30-day, 9 percent*				22
23		*note.*				23

Ordinarily, small business firms issue notes to relatively few creditors. These firms can record the details of the notes on stubs similar to check stubs, or they can just keep duplicate copies of the notes. However, if a firm issues many notes, it may be more convenient to keep a **notes payable register.** In an abbreviated form, here's an illustration of a notes payable register for City-Wide Electric Supply through July 26.

NOTES PAYABLE REGISTER

DATE	PAYEE	AMOUNT	TIME	RATE	INTEREST	DUE DATE	DATE PAID	REMARKS
19–								
Apr. 14	*Adkins Manufac-*							
	turing Co.	4 5 0 00	*60 days*	*9%*	6 75	*6/13*	*6/13*	*Open account.*
May 3	*Sutton Equipment*							
	Co.	2 4 0 0 00	*60 days*	*8%*	3 2 00	*7/2*	*7/2*	*Bought equipment.*
11	*Flagel National*							*Loan, received full*
	Bank	1 2 0 0 00	*120 days*	*7%*	2 8 00	*9/2*	*9/2*	*principal.*
19	*Northwest National*							
	Bank	6 0 0 0 00	*60 days*	*9%*	9 0 00	*7/18*	*7/18*	*Loan, discount $90.*
27	*Draper, Inc.*	1 5 0 0 00	*60 days*	*8%*	2 0 00	*7/26*	*Renewed*	*Open account.*
July 26	*Draper, Inc.*	1 5 0 0 00	*30 days*	*9%*	1 1 25	*8/25*		*Renewed May 27 note.*

More elaborate notes payable registers may include columns listing note numbers, addresses of payees, places of payment, and similar information.

At the end of the fiscal period, the firm may prepare a schedule of notes payable by listing the unpaid notes that appear in the notes payable register. This schedule is similar to a schedule of accounts payable. The total of the schedule is compared with the balance of the controlling account (Notes Payable).

END-OF-FISCAL-PERIOD ADJUSTMENTS

In the case of notes that start in one fiscal period and mature in the next, adjusting entries must be made both for accrued interest and for discounts on notes payable. Otherwise, neither the expenses incurred by the business firm during a fiscal period nor its liabilities at the end of the fiscal period would be correctly stated.

Accrued Interest on Notes Payable

On all interest-bearing notes, interest expense *accrues*, or *accumulates*, daily. Consequently, if any notes payable are outstanding at the end of a fiscal period, the **accrued interest on notes payable** (that is, the interest due but not yet paid) should be calculated and recorded. For example, assume that a firm has two notes payable outstanding as of December 31, the end of the current fiscal period:

$2,000, 90 days, 9%, dated December 5
$3,600, 60 days, 7%, dated December 16

We can diagram the period of each note like this:

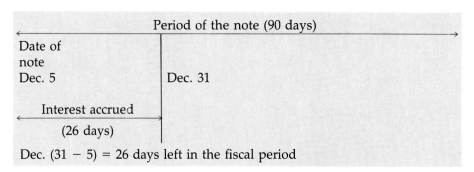

Interest = Principal × Rate × Time
Interest = $2,000 × .09 × 26 ÷ 360 = $13

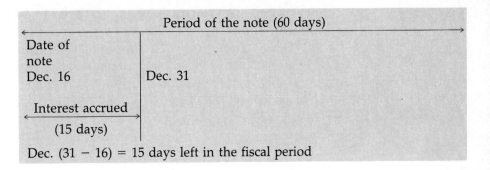

Interest = Principal × Rate × Time

Interest = \$3,600 × .07 × 15 ÷ 360 = $\underline{\$10.50}$

Obviously both notes extend into the next fiscal period; if they didn't, there would be no need for an adjustment. When one is paying interest on notes—except for notes discounted at a bank—one usually pays the principal and interest together, on the day the note matures, or falls due. But since *these* notes have not matured, naturally the interest expense has been neither paid nor recorded. Therefore the firm has to make an adjustment, since the accountant tries to portray the firm's expenses and liabilities for the current fiscal period as accurately as possible. In general journal form, the adjusting entry for the interest expense accrued on the two notes is as follows:

Objective 4g

Make journal entries for adjustment for accrued interest on notes payable.

	DATE	DESCRIPTION	POST. REF.	DEBIT	CREDIT	
1	19–					1
2		*Adjusting Entry*				2
3	Dec. 31	*Interest Expense*		2 3 50		3
4		*Interest Payable ($13 + $10.50)*			2 3 50	4
5						5
6						6
7						7

Like all other adjustments, this one is first recorded in the Adjustments columns of the work sheet. By T accounts, it looks like this, assuming a balance of \$724 before adjustment of Interest Expense:

Interest Expense			**Interest Payable**	
+		−	−	+
Dec. 31 Bal. 724.00				Dec. 31 Adj. 23.50
Dec. 31 Adj. 23.50				

On the balance sheet, Interest Payable is classified as a current liability.

This situation parallels that of the adjustment for accrued salaries, in which the objective is to record the extra amount of salaries owed at the end of the year. In each adjusting entry, debit an expense account and credit a payable account.

Salary Expense		Salaries Payable	
+	−	−	+
Dec. 31 Adj. xxx			Dec. 31 Adj. xxx

There is another similarity between the adjustment for accrued interest and the adjustment for accrued salaries: Both require reversing entries (recall Chapter 15). **The rule for reversing entries is: If an adjusting entry increases an asset or liability account that does not have a previous balance, then reverse the adjusting entry.** Entries involving contra accounts are never reversed. The credits to Interest Payable and Salaries Payable both represent increases to liability accounts. The reversing entry enables one to make the routine entry for the payment of an interest-bearing note at maturity as a debit to Notes Payable, a debit to Interest Expense, and a credit to Cash.

Discount on Notes Payable

Recall that when a note payable is discounted at a bank, the bank deducts the interest (based on the principal of the note) in advance. If the note begins and ends during one fiscal period, the interest is recorded as Interest Expense and no adjustment is needed. But if the note extends into the next fiscal period, the interest is recorded as Discount on Notes Payable. An adjusting entry will be needed to record the interest from the day the note started until the last day of the fiscal period.

Now let us recall our original entry (stated on page 521) made on December 1, in which the firm discounted its note at the bank.

	DATE		DESCRIPTION	POST. REF.	DEBIT	CREDIT	
1	19–						1
2	Dec.	1	Cash		1 7 5 2 00		2
3			Discount on Notes Payable		4 8 00		3
4			Notes Payable			1 8 0 0 00	4
5			Discounted our 120-day				5
6			non-interest-bearing note at				6
7			the First State Bank; discount				7
8			rate 8 percent.				8
9							9

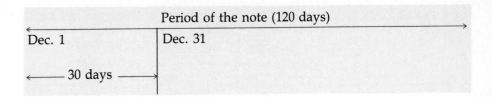

Interest = Principal × Rate × Time

Interest = $1,800 × .08 × 30 ÷ 360 = $12

Objective 4h

Make journal entries for adjustment for prepaid interest on notes payable.

Since 30 days elapse between December 1 and December 31, City-Wide Electric's accountant has to make an adjusting entry to record the Interest Expense:

	DATE	DESCRIPTION	POST. REF.	DEBIT	CREDIT	
1	19–					1
2		*Adjusting Entry*				2
3	Dec. 31	Interest Expense		1 2 00		3
4		*Discount on Notes Payable*			1 2 00	4
5						5
6						6
7						7
8						8
9						9
10						10
11						11
12						12
13						13
14						14

In T accounts, it looks this way:

Interest Expense		Discount on Notes Payable	
+	–	+	–
Dec. 31 Adj. 12		Dec. 1 48	Dec. 31 Adj. 12

In addition to recording Interest Expense, the adjusting entry also serves to reduce the balance of Discount on Notes Payable to its correct amount. This adjustment as well as the adjusting entry for accrued interest payable is shown in Figure 16-2 at the top of the next two pages.

At the end of the year, the Interest Expense account is closed along with all the other expense accounts.

FIGURE 16-2

	ACCOUNT NAME
Discount on Notes Payable	
Interest Expense	
Interest Payable	

Now let us proceed one step further and make the entries for the final payment of the discounted note to the bank. These may be separated into two entries; the first is like the payment of any discounted note.

	DATE		DESCRIPTION	POST. REF.	DEBIT	CREDIT	
1	19–						1
2	Mar.	31	Notes Payable		1 8 0 0 00		2
3			Cash			1 8 0 0 00	3
4			Paid the bank the 120-day				4
5			non-interest-bearing note, dated				5
6			December 1, and discounted				6
7			at 8 percent				7
8							8

The Discount on Notes Payable that was on the books has now become entirely an expense, so it is converted into Interest Expense.

			DESCRIPTION		DEBIT	CREDIT	
9		31	Interest Expense		3 6 00		9
10			Discount on Notes Payable			3 6 00	10
11			To expense the discount for the				11
12			current year for the 120-day				12
13			note, dated December 1, and				13
14			discounted at 8 percent.				14

TRIAL BALANCE		ADJUSTMENTS				INCOME STATEMENT		BALANCE SHEET	
DEBIT	CREDIT	DEBIT		CREDIT		DEBIT	CREDIT	DEBIT	CREDIT
4 8 00				(b)	1 2 00			3 6 00	
7 2 4 00		(a)	2 3 50			7 5 9 50			
		(b)	1 2 00						
				(a)	2 3 50				2 3 50

In T accounts, it looks like this:

Interest Expense				Discount on Notes Payable			
+		−		+		−	
Dec. 31 Adj.	12	Dec. 31 Clos.	12	Dec. 1	48	Dec. 31 Adj.	12
Mar. 31	36					Mar. 31	36

SUMMARY

L.O. 1   A business can obtain credit by means of an open account or charge account, or by writing a promissory note providing for payment of the principal either in one sum or in installments.

L.O. 2   The formula for calculating interest is: Interest = Principal × Rate × Time. The principal is the face amount of the note. The rate is a percentage of the principal. The time is a year or fraction of a year. Normally, in deter-

L.O. 3   mining the maturity date of a note expressed in days, one uses the exact number of days in each month.

We have concentrated on analyzing the debits and credits for each transaction. The entries were shown in general journal form to portray the debits and credits in a clear manner. However, if a firm is using a cash receipts journal and a cash payments journal, any entries involving cash should be recorded in one of these journals. They should not be recorded in a general journal.

To illustrate the use of the cash journals, we will show the related entries again. To conserve space in showing the general journal, we omit explanations.

L.O. 4a   Apr.   14 Issued a 60-day, 9 percent note for $450, payable to Adkins Manufacturing Company, in place of the open-book account.

GENERAL JOURNAL   PAGE _____

	DATE	DESCRIPTION	POST. REF.	DEBIT	CREDIT	
1	19–					1
2	Apr. 14	Accounts Payable, Adkins				2
3		Manufacturing Co.		4 5 0 00		3
4		Notes Payable			4 5 0 00	4

L.O. 4b   June   13 Paid at maturity the note given to Adkins Manufacturing Company.

CASH PAYMENTS JOURNAL   PAGE _____

	DATE	CK. NO.	ACCOUNT NAME	POST. REF.	SUNDRY ACCOUNTS DEBIT	ACCOUNTS PAYABLE DEBIT	PURCHASES DISCOUNT CREDIT	CASH CREDIT	
1	19–								1
2	June 13		Notes Payable		4 5 0 00				2
3			Interest Expense		6 75			4 5 6 75	3
4									4

L.O. 4c   May   3 Issued a 60-day, 8 percent note for $2,400, payable to the Sutton Equipment Company, for equipment.

GENERAL JOURNAL   PAGE _____

	DATE	DESCRIPTION	POST. REF.	DEBIT	CREDIT	
1	19–					1
2	May 3	Store Equipment		2 4 0 0 00		2
3		Notes Payable			2 4 0 0 00	3
4						4

July   2 Paid at maturity the note given to Sutton Equipment Company.

CASH PAYMENTS JOURNAL   PAGE _____

	DATE	CK. NO.	ACCOUNT NAME	POST. REF.	SUNDRY ACCOUNTS DEBIT	ACCOUNTS PAYABLE DEBIT	PURCHASES DISCOUNT CREDIT	CASH CREDIT	
1	19–								1
2	July 2		Notes Payable		2 4 0 0 00				2
3			Interest Expense		3 2 00			2 4 3 2 00	3
4									4

L.O. 4d   May   11 Borrowed $1,200 from the Flagel National Bank, giving in exchange a 120-day, 7 percent note (received full face amount).

CASH RECEIPTS JOURNAL   PAGE

	DATE	ACCOUNT NAME	POST. REF.	SUNDRY ACCOUNTS CREDIT	ACCOUNTS RECEIVABLE CREDIT	SALES CREDIT	CASH DEBIT	
1	19–							1
2	May 11	Notes Payable		1 2 0 0 00			1 2 0 0 00	2
3								3

Sept.   8 Paid loan in full, at maturity, to the Flagel National Bank.

CASH PAYMENTS JOURNAL   PAGE

	DATE	CK. NO.	ACCOUNT NAME	POST. REF.	SUNDRY ACCOUNTS CREDIT	ACCOUNTS RECEIVABLE CREDIT	PURCHASES DISCOUNT CREDIT	CASH CREDIT	
1	19–								1
2	Sept. 8		Notes Payable		1 2 0 0 00				2
3			Interest Expense		2 8 00			1 2 2 8 00	3
4									4

L.O. 4e   May   19 Borrowed $6,000 from Northwest National Bank for 60 days; discount rate is 9 percent; issued a note for $6,000.

CASH RECEIPTS JOURNAL   PAGE

	DATE	ACCOUNT NAME	POST. REF.	SUNDRY ACCOUNTS DEBIT	SUNDRY ACCOUNTS CREDIT	SALES CREDIT	CASH DEBIT	
1	19–							1
2	May 19	Interest Expense		9 0 00				2
3		Notes Payable			6 0 0 0 00		5 9 1 0 00	3
4								4

July   18 Paid bank when loan matured.

CASH PAYMENTS JOURNAL   PAGE

	DATE	CK. NO.	ACCOUNT NAME	POST. REF.	SUNDRY ACCOUNTS DEBIT	ACCOUNTS PAYABLE DEBIT	PURCHASES DISCOUNT CREDIT	CASH CREDIT	
1	19–								1
2	July 18		Notes Payable		6 0 0 0 00			6 0 0 0 00	2
3									3

Dec.   1 Borrowed $1,800 from First State Bank for 120 days; discount rate is 8 percent; issued a discounted note for $1,800.

CASH RECEIPTS JOURNAL   PAGE _____

	DATE		ACCOUNT NAME	POST. REF.	SUNDRY ACCOUNTS		SALES CREDIT	CASH DEBIT	
					DEBIT	CREDIT			
1	19–								1
2	Dec.	1	Discount on Notes Payable		4 8 00				2
3			Notes Payable			1 8 0 0 00		1 7 5 2 00	3
4									4

L.O. 4f   May   27 Issued a 60-day note payable to Draper, Inc., for $1,500, with interest at 8 percent, in place of open-book account.

GENERAL JOURNAL   PAGE _____

	DATE		DESCRIPTION	POST. REF.	DEBIT	CREDIT	
1	19–						1
2	May	27	Accounts Payable, Draper, Inc.		1 5 0 0 00		2
3			Notes Payable			1 5 0 0 00	3

L.O. 4f,g   July   26 Paid interest up to the present date on note given to Draper, Inc., and issued a new 30-day note for $1,500 with interest at 9 percent.

CASH PAYMENTS JOURNAL   PAGE _____

	DATE	CK. NO.	ACCOUNT NAME	POST. REF.	SUNDRY ACCOUNTS DEBIT	ACCOUNTS PAYABLE DEBIT	PURCHASES DISCOUNT CREDIT	CASH CREDIT	
1	19–								1
2	July 26		Interest Expense		2 0 00			2 0 00	2
3									3

Also we would have:

GENERAL JOURNAL   PAGE _____

	DATE		DESCRIPTION	POST. REF.	DEBIT	CREDIT	
1	19–						1
2	July	26	Notes Payable		1 5 0 0 00		2
3			Notes Payable			1 5 0 0 00	3
4							4

GLOSSARY

Accrued interest on notes payable For notes payable beginning in one fiscal period and maturing in the following fiscal period, accrued interest is the unpaid interest expense from the date of issue of the note until the last day of the fiscal period.

Discount Interest deducted in advance by a bank that makes a loan.

Discounting a note payable The procedure by which a bank deducts interest in advance when it loans money.

Interest A charge made for the use of money.

Maker An individual or firm that signs a promissory note.

Maturity date The due date of a promissory note.

Notes payable register An auxiliary record used for listing the details of notes issued.

Notice of maturity A notice specifying the terms and due date of a promissory note that has been left with a bank for collection; mailed by the bank to the maker.

Payee The party receiving payment.

Principal The face amount of a note.

Proceeds The principal of a loan less the discount.

Promissory note A written promise to pay a certain sum at a fixed or determinable future time.

QUESTIONS, EXERCISES, AND PROBLEMS
Discussion Questions

1. How do you determine the maturity date of a note?
2. Name three characteristics of a note.
3. Identify the two parties to a promissory note.
4. What is the basic formula for the calculation of interest?
5. What are two advantages of keeping up a notes payable register.
6. What is the difference between a regular note and a discounted note?
7. Explain why it is necessary to make an adjusting entry for accrued interest on an interest-bearing note payable. Should the entry be reversed?
8. Explain the Discount on Notes Payable account. What is its classification?

Exercises

L.O. 2 **Exercise 16-1** Determine the interest on the following notes:

	Principal	Number of Days	Interest Rate
(a)	$ 1,400	60	9%
(b)	1,500	60	8%
(c)	12,000	90	10%
(d)	8,400	63	12%
(e)	960	45	$7\frac{1}{2}\%$

L.O. 3   **Exercise 16-2** Determine the maturity dates on the following notes:

	Date of Issue	**Time Period**
(a)	April 16	60 days
(b)	October 12	90 days
(c)	December 21	3 months
(d)	June 20	30 days
(e)	July 2	120 days

L.O. 2,3,4b   **Exercise 16-3** On March 14, C. E. Alkire gives a 90-day, 9 percent note to Michel and Company, a creditor, in the amount of $8,400.

  a. What is the due date of the note?
  b. How much interest is to be paid on the note at maturity?
  c. On Alkire's books, show entries in general journal form to record both issuance of the note by the maker, and payment of the note at maturity.

L.O. 4b,e   **Exercise 16-4** As a result of a loan from the Lopez State Bank, the Blake Company signed a 90-day note for $16,000 that the bank discounted at 11 percent. Present the entries for the maker in general journal form to record the following, assuming that the note is paid in the same fiscal period:

  a. Issuance of the note.
  b. Payment of the note at maturity.

L.O. 2,4e   **Exercise 16-5** In arranging for a 60-day loan from a bank, Walton Company has the option of either (1) giving a $54,000, 9 percent interest-bearing note that will be accepted at face value, or (2) giving a $54,000 note that will be discounted at 9 percent.

  a. What is the amount of interest in each case?
  b. What is the amount Walton Company actually receives in each case?
  c. Which of the two alternatives is more favorable to Walton Company?

L.O. 4b,c   **Exercise 16-6** On March 1, Whitney Lumber bought the land and building that it was formerly renting. The terms of sale are: land, $10,000; building, $38,000; cash downpayment, $12,000; with the balance in the form of a 10 percent note, secured by a ten-year mortgage on the property. The terms of the note provide for 120 monthly payments of $300 each on the principal plus interest on the unpaid balance. Give entries in general journal form to record the following:

  a. The transaction on March 1.
  b. The payment of the first installment on April 1.
  c. The payment of the second installment on May 1.

L.O. 4b,g   **Exercise 16-7** On October 5, S. L. Whittier issued a 90-day, 12 percent note to Yeager Construction, a creditor, for $7,800. Present the entries in general journal form to record the following:

a. Issuance of the note on October 5.
b. Adjusting entry for accrued interest on December 31, the end of the fiscal year.
c. Reversing entry on January 1.
d. Payment of the note plus interest on January 3.

L.O. 4e,h **Exercise 16-8** On December 2, F. C. Young borrowed $8,400 from Malaga State Bank for 60 days, with a discount rate of 10 percent. Accordingly, F. C. Young signed a note for $8,400. The end of the fiscal year is December 31. Give entries in general journal form to record the following:

a. Issuance of the note on December 2.
b. Adjusting entry on December 31.
c. Payment of the note at maturity (two entries) on January 31.

Problem Set A

L.O. 2,4a,b,d **Problem 16-1A** The following were among the transactions of the Jordan Company:

Jan. 11 Bought merchandise on account from the Nakata Company, $3,350; terms, 2/10, n/30.
20 Paid the Nakata Company for the invoice of January 11.
Feb. 15 Bought merchandise on account from Godfrey and Company, $4,200; terms net 30 days.
Mar. 17 Gave a 30-day, 10 percent note for $4,200 to Godfrey and Company to apply on account.
Apr. 16 Paid Godfrey and Company the amount owed on the note of March 17.
May 27 Borrowed $9,600 from Keller State Bank, giving a 60-day, 11 percent note for that amount (received full face value).
July 26 Paid Keller State Bank the amount due on the note of May 27.

Instructions

Record these transactions in general journal form.

L.O. 4a,b,e,f **Problem 16-2A** The following were among the transactions of Novasky and Company during this year (January 1 through December 31):

Jan. 24 Bought merchandise on account from Noyd and Dietz, $3,240; terms, net 30 days.
Feb. 25 Gave a 30-day, 9 percent note for $3,240 to Noyd and Dietz to apply on account.
Mar. 27 Paid Noyd and Dietz the amount owed on the note of February 25.
Apr. 1 Bought merchandise on account from Bush and Company, $7,200; terms, 2/10, n/30.
May 2 Gave a 30-day, 10 percent note for $7,200 to Bush and Company to apply on account.

June 1 Paid Bush and Company the interest due on the note of May 2, and renewed the obligation by issuing a new 60-day, 11 percent note for $7,200.

July 31 Paid Bush and Company the amount owed on the note of June 1.

Aug. 17 Borrowed $14,400 from Cannon National Bank for 90 days; discount rate is 10 percent. Accordingly, signed a discounted note for $14,400.

Nov. 15 Paid Cannon National Bank at maturity of loan.

Instructions

Record these instructions in general journal form.

L.O. 4a,b,e,f,g **Problem 16-3A** The following were among the transactions of Darwin Camera during this year. Darwin Camera's fiscal year ends on December 31.

Jan. 27 Bought merchandise on account from Rowe Company, $4,200; terms, 2/10, n/30.

Feb. 26 Gave a 30-day, 9 percent note to Rowe Company, dated February 26, to apply on account, covering purchase of January 27.

Mar. 28 Paid $1,000 as part payment on principal as well as the full interest on the note given to Rowe Company; issued a new note for $3,200, 60 days, 10 percent, dated March 28.

May 27 Paid amount owed on the note dated March 28.

July 20 Borrowed $7,240 from Southern Trust Bank for 90 days, discount rate is 10 percent. Accordingly, signed a discounted note for $7,240.

Oct. 18 Paid the amount owed on the note given to Southern Trust Bank, dated July 20.

Nov. 16 Bought display tables and shelves for $2,426 from Boyd's Woodworking Shop. Issued a 90-day, 8 percent note, dated Nov. 16.

Dec. 31 Recorded the adjusting entry for accrued interest on the note given to Boyd's Woodworking Shop.

Instructions

Using the cash receipts journal, the cash payments journal, and the general journal, record these transactions in the appropriate journal.

L.O. 4b–h **Problem 16-4A** The following were among the transactions of Younce and Company during the year ended December 31:

June 4 Gave a 60-day, 10 percent note, dated June 4, to Lee Brothers, Inc., $52,000, for an addition to the building.

25 Borrowed $28,200 from Meier Mutual Bank signing a 3-month, 8 percent note for that amount, dated June 25 (received full face value).

July 14 Gave a note to Seco and Cohn for the purchase of office equipment, $12,400, at 9 percent for 90 days, dated July 14. The invoice was not previously recorded.

Aug.   3 Paid the amount owed on the note given to Lee Brothers, Inc.

Sept. 25 Paid interest on the note given to Meier Mutual Bank; renewed loan by issuing note for 60 days at 8 percent, dated September 25.

Oct.   12 Paid amount owed on the 90-day note given to Seco and Cohn.

       27 Gave two notes to Maki Manufacturing Company in settlement of their October 27 invoice for merchandise, as follows: $10,800, 30 days, 8 percent, dated October 27; $10,800, 60 days, 8 percent, dated October 27. The invoice was not previously recorded.

Nov. 24 Paid the note given to Meier Mutual Bank.

       26 Paid the amount owed on the 30-day note given to Maki Manufacturing Company.

Dec.   11 Issued a 60-day, 10 percent note, dated December 11, payable to Grantelli Company, in settlement of November 11 bill for merchandise, $20,700. The invoice was previously recorded.

       16 Borrowed $28,800 from Aiken National Bank for 60 days; discount rate is 9 percent; issued a discounted note for $28,800 (debit Discount on Notes Payable since the note extends into the next fiscal period).

       26 Paid amount owed on the 60-day note given to Maki Manufacturing Company.

Instructions

1. Record these transactions in a general journal.
2. Make the adjusting entries, dated December 31, to record the interest expense on notes issued to Grantelli Company and Aiken National Bank.

Problem Set B

L.O. 2,4a,b,d   **Problem 16-1B**   The following were among the transactions of Jack's Boats and Motors during the year:

Jan.   11 Bought merchandise on account from Eastern Marine, $6,420; terms, 2/10, n/30.

       19 Paid Eastern Marine for the invoice of January 11.

Feb. 22 Bought merchandise on account from Benton and Company, $4,200; terms, net 30 days.

Mar. 24 Gave a 60-day, 10 percent note for $4,200 to Benton and Company to apply on account.

May   23 Paid Benton and Company the amount owed on the note of March 24.

June   5 Borrowed $9,400 from Nelson State Bank, giving a 90-day, 11 percent note for that amount (received full face value).

Sept. 3 Paid Nelson State Bank the amount due on the note of June 5.

Instructions

Record these transactions in general journal form.

L.O. 4a,b,e,f   **Problem 16-2B**   The following were among the transactions of Novak Fine Fabrics during this year (January 1 through December 31):

Feb.	16	Bought merchandise on account from Kafer Mills, $3,260; terms, net 30 days.
Mar.	17	Gave a 30-day, 9 percent note for $3,260 to Kafer Mills to apply on account.
Apr.	16	Paid Kafer Mills amount owed on the note of March 17.
May	6	Bought merchandise on account from Wheeler Company, $7,400; terms, net 30 days.
June	5	Gave a 30-day, 10 percent note for $7,400 to Wheeler Company to apply on account.
July	5	Paid Wheeler Company the interest due on the note of June 5 and renewed the obligation by issuing a new 60-day, 11 percent note for $7,400.
Sept.	3	Paid Wheeler Company the amount owed on the note of July 5.
	29	Borrowed $12,000 from Peninsula National Bank for 90 days; discount rate is 12 percent. Accordingly, signed a discounted note for $12,000.
Dec.	28	Paid Peninsula National Bank at maturity of loan.

Instructions

Record these transactions in general journal form.

L.O. 4a,b,e,f,g   **Problem 16-3B**   The following were among the transactions of Sylvan Appliances during this year. The firm's fiscal year ends on December 31.

Jan.	14	Bought merchandise on account from Slavich Company, $4,628; terms, net 30 days.
Feb.	13	Gave a 30-day, 8 percent note to Slavich Company, dated February 13, to apply on account, covering purchase of January 14.
Mar.	15	Paid $1,400 as part payment of principal as well as the full interest on the note given to Slavich Company; issued new note for $3,228, 60 days, 8 percent, dated March 15.
May	12	Borrowed $9,600 from Texas National Bank for 90 days, discount rate is 10 percent. Accordingly, signed a discounted note for $9,600.
	14	Paid the amount owed on the note issued to Slavich Company, dated March 15.
Aug.	10	Paid the amount owed on the note issued to Texas National Bank, dated May 12.
Nov.	22	Bought a cash register for $3,640 from Kelly Business Machines. Issued a 60-day, 10 percent note, dated November 22.
Dec.	31	Recorded the adjusting entry for accrued interest on the note given to Kelly Business Machines.

Instructions

Using the cash receipts journal, the cash payments journal, and the general journal, record these transactions in the appropriate journal.

L.O. 4b–h   **Problem 16-4B**   The following were among the transactions of Tate Distributing Company during the year ended December 31:

May   26 Gave a 60-day, 8 percent note for $50,400, dated May 26, to Phipps and Howard, for addition to the warehouse.

June   23 Borrowed $16,800 from Big Apple Savings Bank, signing a 3-month, 8 percent note for that amount, dated June 23 (received full face value).

July   17 Gave a note to Blake Cabinet Shop for display cases, $28,920, at 9 percent for 90 days, dated July 17. The invoice was not previously recorded.

       25 Paid the amount due on the note given to Phipps and Howard.

Sept.   23 Paid interest on the note issued to Big Apple Savings Bank; renewed loan by issuing new 60-day, 8 percent note, dated September 23.

Oct.   15 Paid amount owed on the note given to Blake Cabinet Shop.

       29 Gave two notes to Wentz and Company in settlement of their October 29 invoice for merchandise, as follows: $16,200 note for 30 days at 8 percent, dated October 29; $16,200 note for 60 days at 8 percent, dated October 29. The invoice was not previously recorded.

Nov.   22 Paid the note given to Big Apple Savings Bank.

       28 Paid the amount owed on the 30-day note given to Wentz and Company.

Dec.   11 Issued a 60-day, 9 percent note, dated December 11, to Olson and Son in settlement of November 12 invoice for merchandise, $13,800. The invoice was previously recorded.

       21 Borrowed $22,500 from Slater National Bank for 60 days; discount rate is 10 percent; signed a discounted note for $22,500 (debit Discount on Notes Payable, since note extends into next fiscal period).

       28 Paid amount owed on the 60-day note given to Wentz and Company.

Instructions

1. Record these transactions in general journal form.
2. Make the adjusting entries, dated December 31, to record interest expense on notes issued to Olson and Son and Slater National Bank.

17 Accounting for Notes Receivable

LEARNING OBJECTIVES

After you have completed this chapter, you will be able to write journal entries to record these transactions:

1. Receipt of a note from a charge customer.
2. Receipt of payment of an interest-bearing note at maturity.
3. Receipt of a note as a result of granting a personal loan.
4. Receipt of a note in exchange for merchandise or other property.
5. Renewal of a note at maturity.
6. Dishonored notes receivable.
7. Collection on a note receivable formerly dishonored.
8. Discounting an interest-bearing note.
9. Dishonoring of a discounted note receivable.
10. Adjustment for accrued interest on notes receivable.

Business firms receive promissory notes for a variety of reasons, either regularly or occasionally. Sometimes a business firm accepts a promissory note from a customer at the time of sale. Companies frequently accept promissory notes from charge account customers who request an extension of time to settle past-due accounts. In effect, they substitute notes receivable for open accounts. The net result is that the charge customer gets an extension of time for the payment of a debt.

Obviously, getting a note receivable is not as good as having cash in hand. However, it offers several advantages to the company: (1) the note represents proof of the original transaction, (2) the note may bear interest, and (3) the note may be pledged as security for a loan from a bank. Banks, in fact, loan a higher proportion of the face value on notes (Notes Receivable) than on open accounts (Accounts Receivable). For example, banks may grant loans for 100 percent of the face value of notes but only 60 percent of the face value of open accounts.

Notes receivable also come into being when a company grants loans to employees or preferred customers or suppliers. In some business fields, the credit period is often longer than thirty days; here, the transactions are frequently evidenced by notes rather than by open accounts. Examples are sales of farm machinery, construction equipment, and trucks.

Let us now see how one journalizes transactions involving notes receivable. The accounts particularly involved are Notes Receivable (classified as a current asset on the balance sheet in our examples, although they could be classified as a long-term asset if the repayment period is longer than a year) and Interest Income (classified as other income on the income statement).

TRANSACTIONS FOR NOTES RECEIVABLE

First, let's say that all notes received are recorded in a single current asset account, Notes Receivable. Second, throughout this chapter we are going to use City-Wide Electric Supply to illustrate such transactions. Now let's begin with a simple example.

Notes from Charge Customers to Extend Time on Their Accounts

Objective 1

Receipt of a note from a charge customer.

On March 7, City-Wide Electric Supply sold $480 worth of merchandise to Harrells Electric, with the customary terms of 2/10, n/30, and made the original entry in its sales journal. On April 6, Harrells Electric sent City-Wide Electric a note for $480, payable within 30 days, at 8 percent interest. The note, dated April 6, was in settlement of the transaction of March 7. City-Wide Electric Supply recorded this new development in its general journal as follows:

GENERAL JOURNAL   PAGE_____

	DATE		DESCRIPTION	POST. REF.	DEBIT	CREDIT	
1	*19–*						1
2	*Apr.*	*6*	*Notes Receivable*		*4 8 0 00*		2
3			*Accounts Receivable, Harrells*				3
4			*Electric*			*4 8 0 00*	4
5			*Received a 30-day, 8 percent*				5
6			*note, dated April 6, in*				6
7			*settlement of open account.*				7
8							8

T accounts for the transactions look like this:

Accounts Receivable		Sales		Notes Receivable	
+	−	−	+	+	−
Mar. 7 480	Apr. 6 480		Mar. 7 480	Apr. 6 480	

<table>
<tr><td></td><td colspan="2">Objective 2</td></tr>
</table>

Objective 2

Receipt of payment of an interest-bearing note at maturity.

Receipt of Payment of an Interest-Bearing Note at Maturity

On May 6, Harrells paid City-Wide Electric in full: principal plus interest. City-Wide Electric recorded the transaction in the general journal as follows:

	DATE		DESCRIPTION	POST. REF.	DEBIT	CREDIT	
1	19–						1
2	May	6	Cash		4 8 3 20		2
3			Notes Receivable			4 8 0 00	3
4			Interest Income			3 20	4
5			Received full payment of				5
6			Harrells' note.				6
7							7

Let's look at the T accounts for this entry:

Cash		Notes Receivable	
+	−	+	−
May 6 483.20		Apr. 6 480.00	May 6 480.00

Interest Income	
−	+
	May 6 3.20

In practice, this transaction would be recorded directly in the cash receipts journal rather than in the general journal. But, for the sake of simplicity and clarity, we will use the general journal format to illustrate entries throughout this chapter.

Objective 3

Receipt of a note as a result of granting a personal loan.

Notes Received as a Result of Granting Personal Loans

Sometimes employees, preferred customers, or suppliers may want to borrow cash from the business. When that is the case, the business often accepts a note receivable. Let's say that Bryan Hanson, an employee of City-Wide Electric Supply, borrows $336 from his employer, for 3 months at 6 percent. His note is dated April 8. In general journal form, the entry is as shown below:

	DATE		DESCRIPTION	POST. REF.	DEBIT	CREDIT	
1	19–						1
2	Apr.	8	Notes Receivable		3 3 6 00		2
3			Cash			3 3 6 00	3
4			Granted a loan to Bryan				4
5			Hanson, 3 months, 6 percent,				5
6			dated April 8.				6
7							7

When the loan reaches maturity, Hanson pays the principal plus interest.

	DATE		DESCRIPTION	POST. REF.	DEBIT	CREDIT	
1	19–						1
2	July	8	Cash		3 4 1 04		2
3			Notes Receivable			3 3 6 00	3
4			Interest Income			5 04	4
5			Received full payment of				5
6			Bryan Hanson's note, dated				6
7			April 8.				7
8							8
9							9
10							10

Note Received in Exchange for Merchandise or Other Property

Business firms that sell high-priced durable goods in which the credit period is longer than the normal thirty days may accept notes from their customers fairly regularly.

On April 9, City-Wide Electric Supply sold merchandise to Johnson Heating and Air Conditioning for $900. Johnson gave City-Wide Electric a promissory note, promising to pay the full amount within 60 days; the note specified 7 percent interest. When this type of transaction occurs occasionally, the transaction is recorded in the general journal as follows:

Objective 4

Receipt of a note in exchange for merchandise or other property.

	DATE		DESCRIPTION	POST. REF.	DEBIT	CREDIT	
1	*19–*						1
2	*Apr.*	*9*	*Notes Receivable*		*9 0 0 00*		2
3			*Sales*			*9 0 0 00*	3
4			*Johnson Heating and Air*				4
5			*Conditioning, 60-day, 7 percent*				5
6			*note, dated April 9.*				6
7							7
8							8

However, if this type of transaction were to occur frequently, City-Wide Electric would use a Notes Receivable Debit column in the sales journal to record such transactions.

Renewal of Note at Maturity and Payment of Interest

Objective 5

Renewal of a note at maturity.

If the maker of a note is unable to pay the entire principal at maturity, he or she may be allowed to renew all or a part of the note.

Now suppose that Johnson Heating and Air Conditioning is not able to pay the note at maturity and offers to pay the interest on the current note and to issue a new note, for 30 days at 8 percent. City-Wide Electric makes the entries in the general journal as shown below. Note that two entries are required. One entry is to record the interest on the old note. The second entry is to cancel the old note and record the new note.

	DATE		DESCRIPTION	POST. REF.	DEBIT	CREDIT	
1	*19–*						1
2	*June*	*8*	*Cash*		*1 0 50*		2
3			*Interest Income*			*1 0 50*	3
4			*Received payment of interest*				4
5			*on Johnson Heating and Air*				5
6			*Conditioning note, dated*				6
7			*April 9.*				7
8							8
9		*8*	*Notes Receivable*		*9 0 0 00*		9
10			*Notes Receivable*			*9 0 0 00*	10
11			*Johnson Heating and Air*				11
12			*Conditioning renewal of note,*				12
13			*dated April 9; new note is*				13
14			*dated June 8, 30 days, 8*				14
15			*percent.*				15
16							16

Remember

For a renewal of a note receivable, credit the old note to take it off the books, and debit the new note to put it on the books.

Actually, there is only one Notes Receivable ledger account. However, when a note is renewed, it is customary for the debtor or maker to pay up the interest on the old note and then issue a new note.

Renewal of Note with Payment of Interest and Partial Payment of Principal

Sometimes the maker of a note cancels the original note by paying the interest, plus part of the principal, and issuing a new note. Suppose that as a substitute for the $900 note described above, Johnson gives City-Wide Electric $300 toward the principal and a new note for $600, in addition to the interest on the old note.

City-Wide Electric records the transactions in the general journal as follows:

	DATE		DESCRIPTION	POST. REF.	DEBIT	CREDIT	
1	19–						1
2	June	8	Cash		3 1 0 50		2
3			Notes Receivable			3 0 0 00	3
4			Interest Income			1 0 50	4
5			Johnson Heating and Air				5
6			Conditioning note, dated				6
7			April 9, partial payment of the				7
8			principal and interest payment.				8
9							9
10		8	Notes Receivable		6 0 0 00		10
11			Notes Receivable			6 0 0 00	11
12			Johnson Heating and Air				12
13			Conditioning renewal of note				13
14			dated April 9; the new note is				14
15			dated June 8, 30 days,				15
16			8 percent.				16
17							17
18							18

DISHONORED NOTES RECEIVABLE

When the maker of a note fails to pay the principal amount or to renew the note at maturity, the note is said to be a **dishonored note receivable.** The maker of the note is still obligated to pay the principal plus interest, and the creditor should take legal steps to collect the debt. However, the balance of the Notes Receivable account shows only the principal of notes that have not yet matured. A note that is past due, or dishonored, should be removed from the Notes Receivable account and returned to the Accounts Receivable account; the amount listed should be the principal plus interest. In other words, once a note receivable comes due and is not collected, it's "dead." But the maker still owes us, so we put the amount owed (principal plus interest) back into Accounts Receivable.

Objective 6

Dishonored notes receivable.

For example, City-Wide Electric Supply holds a 60-day, 7 percent note for $800, dated April 20, from Baker Building Supplies, which fails to pay by the due date. Thus the note is dishonored at maturity. Accordingly, City-Wide Electric makes the following entry in its general journal to remove the dishonored note from the Notes Receivable account:

	DATE		DESCRIPTION	POST. REF.	DEBIT	CREDIT	
1	19–						1
2	June	19	Accounts Receivable, Baker				2
3			Building Supplies		8 0 9 33		3
4			Notes Receivable			8 0 0 00	4
5			Interest Income			9 33	5
6			Baker Building Supplies dis-				6
7			honored their 60-day, 7 percent				7
8			note for $800, dated April 20.				8
9							9
10							10
11							11
12							12

Remember

For a dishonored interest-bearing note receivable, interest income is recorded, and the note is removed from the Notes Receivable account.

Baker Building Supplies owes both the principal and the interest, and the account should reflect the full amount owed. Note particularly that City-Wide Electric credits the Interest Income account, even though Baker did not pay the interest. This is consistent with the accrual basis of accounting: Revenue is recorded when it is *earned*, rather than when it is received. If Baker Building Supplies should ever ask City-Wide Electric to act as a credit reference, or if Baker ever asks for credit in the future, subsidiary records will show all past dealings, including the dishonored note.

Collection of a Dishonored Note

Objective 7

Collection on a note receivable formerly dishonored.

Now suppose that 30 days after its note has been dishonored, Baker Building Supplies pays up the balance of its account, plus an additional 30 days' interest at 7 percent on the amount owed. The entry in City-Wide Electric's general journal is shown on page 548.

GENERAL JOURNAL   PAGE _____

	DATE		DESCRIPTION	POST. REF.	DEBIT	CREDIT	
1	*19–*						1
2	*July*	*19*	*Cash*		8 1 4 05		2
3			*Accounts Receivable, Baker*				3
4			*Building Supplies*			8 0 9 33	4
5			*Interest Income*			4 72	5
6			*Baker Building Supplies paid*				6
7			*the dishonored note, plus*				7
8			*interest for 30 days at*				8
9			*7 percent.*				9
10							10
11							11
12							12
13							13

City-Wide Electric gets its money in the long run anyway, and it can now consider the matter closed.

DISCOUNTING NOTES RECEIVABLE

Instead of keeping notes receivable until they come due, a firm can raise cash by selling its notes receivable to a bank or finance company. This type of financing is usually called **discounting notes receivable** because the bank deducts the interest from the maturity value of the note to determine the proceeds (that is, the amount of money received by the firm). The **maturity value** is the principal (face value) of the note plus interest from the date of the note until due date.

In the process of discounting a note receivable, the firm endorses the note (as in a check) and delivers it to the financial institution. The financial institution gives out cash now in exchange for the privilege of collecting the principal and interest when the note comes due. The discount rate is the annual rate (percentage of maturity value) charged by the financial institution for buying the note.

A Discounted Note: Example 1   City-Wide Electric Supply granted an extension on an open account by accepting a 60-day, 8 percent note for $540, dated April 20, from Chavez Hardware. To raise cash to buy additional merchandise, City-Wide Electric sold the note to Flagel National Bank on May 5. The bank charged a discount rate of 7 percent. A diagram of the situation looks like this:

Period of the note (60 days)	
Date of note Apr. 20	Date discounted May 5
City-Wide Electric holds note (15 days)	Bank holds note (discount period) (60 − 15 = 45 days)

The discount period of the note consists of the interval between the date the note is given to the bank and the maturity date of the note. This is referred to as the **discount period**. (In other words, the discount period is the time the note has left to run.) Now we ask: How many days are there in the discount period? For emphasis, let's repeat the diagram.

Period of the note (60 days)	
Date of note Apr. 20	Date discounted May 5
City-Wide Electric holds note	Bank holds note (discount period)

Next we determine the value of the note at maturity and deduct the amount of the bank's discount from it, using the following listing or formula.

Principal ($540)
+ Interest to maturity date (8%, 60 days)
  Value at maturity
− Discount (7%, 45 days)
  Proceeds

After we set up the problem, we can complete the calculation:

Principal	$540.00	Interest = Principal × Rate × Time
+ Interest (8%, 60 days)	7.20	$\rightarrow$ Interest = $540 \times .08 \times \dfrac{60}{360} = \underline{\$7.20}$
Value at maturity	$547.20	
− Discount (7%, 45 days)	4.79	
Proceeds	$542.41	$\rightarrow$ Interest = $547.20 \times .07 \times \dfrac{45}{360} = \underline{\$4.788}$

Objective 8

Discounting an interest-bearing note.

Note that in our calculations we figure the discount on the value of the note at maturity ($547.20, 7 percent, 45 days). The proceeds are the amount that City-Wide Electric Supply receives from the bank; this amount is therefore debited to Cash. *If the amount of the proceeds is greater* *than the amount of the principal, the difference represents Interest Income* since City-Wide Electric Supply made money on the deal. *If the amount of the proceeds is less than the principal, on the other hand, the deficiency represents Interest Expense.* Look at the entry in City-Wide Electric's general journal.

	DATE		DESCRIPTION	POST. REF.	DEBIT	CREDIT	
1	*19–*						1
2	*May*	*5*	*Cash*		*5 4 2 41*		2
3			*Notes Receivable*			*5 4 0 00*	3
4			*Interest Income*			*2 41*	4
5			*Discounted at the bank Chavez*				5
6			*Hardware's note, dated*				6
7			*April 20. The bank discount*				7
8			*rate is 7 percent.*				8
9							9
10							10
11							11
12							12
13							13

Contingent Liability

At the time City-Wide Electric Supply discounted Chavez's note at the bank, City-Wide Electric had to endorse the note. By this endorsement, City-Wide Electric agreed to pay the note when it became due if the maker did not pay it. Therefore the endorser has a **contingent liability** for payment of the note. If the maker dishonors the note, the endorser is liable. In other words, the liability of the endorser is contingent on the possible dishonoring of the note by the maker. It follows that if the credit rating of the endorser of the note is good, a bank is usually willing to accept and discount a note. The endorser, by virtue of his or her endorsement or guarantee, agrees to pay the note at maturity *if it is not paid by the maker.* The fact that the note receivable is pledged as security, along with the amount of the contingent liability, should be shown as a footnote to the endorser's balance sheet.

Payment of a Discounted Note by the Maker

The bank collects the principal plus the interest on a discounted note directly from the maker. When the maker pays the bank, the endorser no longer has any contingent liability; the footnote to the endorser's balance sheet can be eliminated when the note is paid. A journal entry is not required.

A Discounted Note: Example 2   On April 25, City-Wide Electric Supply received a 90-day, 6 percent $600 note, dated April 24, from Davison Service Company. On May 4 City-Wide Electric discounted the note at the bank. The discount rate charged by the bank is 7 percent. In handling discounted notes receivable, you should by all means follow a definite step-by-step procedure.

1. Diagram the situation.

Period of the note (90 days)	
Date of note Apr. 24	Date discounted May 4
(10 days)	Discount period (90 − 10 = 80 days)

2. Determine the discount period. Endorser (City-Wide Electric) holds the note, April 24 through May 4.

April (30 − 24) = 6 days left in April
May   = 4 days
Days held   = 10 days

Discount period (bank holds note)
90 days − 10 days = 80 days

3. Record the formula.

      Principal ($600)
   + Interest (6%, 90 days)
      Value at maturity
   − Discount (7%, 80 days)
      Proceeds

4. Complete the formula.

Principal	$600.00	
+ Interest (6%, 90 days)	9.00	Interest = $600 × .06 × $\frac{90}{360}$ = $\underline{\underline{\$9.00}}$
Value at maturity	$609.00	
− Discount (7%, 80 days)	9.47	
Proceeds	$599.53	Interest = $609 × .07 × $\frac{80}{360}$ = $\underline{\underline{\$9.473}}$

5. Make the entry, recognizing that the amount of the proceeds is a debit to Cash. If the amount of the proceeds is less than the principal, debit Interest Expense for the difference.

	DATE		DESCRIPTION	POST. REF.	DEBIT	CREDIT	
1	19–						1
2	May	4	Cash		5 9 9 53		2
3			Interest Expense		47		3
4			Notes Receivable			6 0 0 00	4
5			Discounted at the bank				5
6			Davison Service Company's				6
7			note, dated April 24.				7
8			The bank discount rate is				8
9			7 percent.				9
10							10
11							11
12							12
13							13
14							14

Dishonor of a Discounted Note by the Maker

Suppose that the bank cannot get the maker of the note to pay the principal plus the interest on a pledged note. The bank immediately notifies the firm that endorsed and discounted the note. To take legal advantage of the contingent-liability relationship of the endorser, the bank must formally protest the note. It does so by preparing and mailing to each endorser a Notice of Dishonor and Protest. This statement, signed by a notary public, identifies the note and states that the note was duly presented to the maker for payment and that payment was refused. The fee levied by the bank, known as a **protest fee,** is charged first to the endorser, who passes this fee along to the maker. In essence, any amount that the endorser must pay on behalf of the maker is charged to the maker.

Objective 9

Dishonoring of a discounted note receivable.

For example, let's say that Davison Service Company dishonors its note that was discounted at the bank by City-Wide Electric Supply. The bank issues a formal Notice of Dishonor and Protest and charges a protest fee of $8. As a consequence, the bank deducts $617 from the account of City-Wide Electric Supply ($600 principal + $9 interest + $8 protest fee). City-Wide Electric Supply makes the entry in its general journal as follows:

	DATE		DESCRIPTION	POST. REF.	DEBIT	CREDIT	
1	*19–*						1
2	*July*	*23*	*Accounts Receivable, Davison*				2
3			*Service Company*		6 1 7 00		3
4			*Cash*			6 1 7 00	4
5			*Dishonor of Davison Service*				5
6			*Company's note, dated April 24,*				6
7			*90 days, 6 percent, principal*				7
8			*$600, interest $9, and protest*				8
9			*fee $8.*				9
10							10
11							11
12							12

It's only fair that the protest fee be charged against the maker, and as a result the maker's account at City-Wide Electric is increased by this amount. **There is no account called "Protest Fee."**

Maker Pays Dishonored Note Plus Additional Interest

Now assume that Davison Service Company finally comes through. On July 31 it pays the note, dated April 24 and dishonored on July 23, plus 7 percent interest from July 23 until July 31. In City-Wide Electric's general journal, the entry looks like this:

	DATE		DESCRIPTION	POST. REF.	DEBIT	CREDIT	
1	*19–*						1
2	*July*	*31*	*Cash*		6 1 7 96		2
3			*Accounts Receivable, Davison*				3
4			*Service Company*			6 1 7 00	4
5			*Interest Income*			96	5
6			*Received payment on the*				6
7			*Davison Service Company note,*				7
8			*dated April 24, discounted at*				8
9			*the bank on May 4, dishonored*				9
10			*on July 23; received additional*				10
11			*interest at 7 percent for period*				11
12			*July 23 through 31.*				12
13							13
14							14
15							15

A Discounted Note: Example 3 On May 10 Cromwell and Son gave City-Wide Electric Supply a 60-day, 8 percent note for $2,640, dated May 9. On June 2 City-Wide Electric Supply discounted the note at the bank. The bank charges a discount rate of 7½ percent.

1. Diagram the situation.

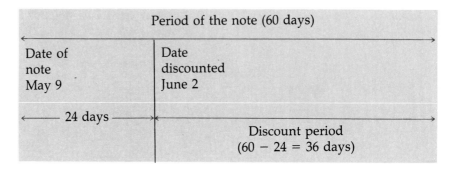

Period of the note (60 days)

Date of note May 9	Date discounted June 2

24 days ← → Discount period (60 − 24 = 36 days)

2. Determine the discount period. Endorser (City-Wide Electric) holds note through June 2.

May (31 − 9) = 22 days left in May
June   = 2 days
Days held   = 24 days

Discount period (bank holds note)
60 days − 24 days = 36 days

3. Record the formula.

Principal ($2,640)
+ Interest (8%, 60 days)
  Value at maturity
− Discount (7½%, 36 days)
  Proceeds

4. Complete the formula.

Principal	$2,640.00	Interest = Principal × Rate × Time
+ Interest (8%, 60 days)	35.20	→ Interest = $2,640 × .08 × $\frac{60}{360}$ = $35.20
Value at maturity	$2,675.20	
− Discount (7½%, 36 days)	20.06	
Proceeds	$2,655.14	→ Interest = $2,675.20 × .075 × $\frac{36}{360}$ = $20.064

5. Record the entry as shown. If the amount of the proceeds is greater than the principal, credit Interest Income for the difference.

	DATE		DESCRIPTION	POST. REF.	DEBIT	CREDIT	
1	*19–*						1
2	*June*	*2*	*Cash*		2 6 5 5 14		2
3			*Notes Receivable*			2 6 4 0 00	3
4			*Interest Income*			1 5 14	4
5			*Discounted at bank the note*				5
6			*received from Cromwell and*				6
7			*Son dated May 9; discount*				7
8			*rate, 7½ percent.*				8
9							9
10							10
11							11
12							12
13							13

Notes Receivable Register

Companies that have a significant number of notes receivable may find it worthwhile to set up a separate list to keep track of them. This list is called a **notes receivable register.** It is similar to the notes payable register presented in Chapter 16. Information is taken from the face of each note. Columns are included to record the specifics of each note, such as: amount, date issued, time period, due date, interest rate, date discounted, where payable, date paid. At the end of the fiscal period, the accountant makes a schedule of notes receivable by listing the unpaid notes that appear in the notes receivable register. Also, the total of the schedule is compared with the balance of the controlling account (Notes Receivable).

END-OF-FISCAL-PERIOD ADJUSTMENTS: ACCRUED INTEREST ON NOTES RECEIVABLE

Accrued interest income on notes receivable runs parallel to accrued interest expense on notes payable (Chapter 16). Whenever a firm receives *or* issues an interest-bearing note, the interest accrues or accumulates daily. As a result, any interest-bearing notes that overlap two or more fiscal periods require adjusting entries in order for the financial statements to present a true picture of the firm's net income and financial condition.

For example, let's say that a firm has two notes receivable on December 31, the end of the fiscal period:

$4,000, 90 days, 8%, dated November 28
$5,200, 60 days, 7%, dated December 20

We can diagram the situation as follows:

Period of the note (90 days)	
Date of note Nov. 28	Dec. 31
Interest accrued	
(33 days)	

Nov. (30 − 28) = 2 days left in November
Dec.   = 31 days
Total   33 days left in the fiscal period

Interest = Principal × Rate × Time

$$\text{Interest} = \$4{,}000 \times .08 \times \frac{33}{360} = \underline{\$29.33}$$

Period of the note (60 days)	
Date of note Dec. 20	Dec. 31
Interest accrued (11 days)	

FIGURE 17-1

ACCOUNT NAME	TRIAL BALANCE	
	DEBIT	CREDIT
Notes Receivable	9 2 0 0 00	
Interest Income		6 1 9 70
Interest Receivable		

L.O. 2   May   6 Received a payment at maturity of principal plus interest on the Harrells Electric Company's note.

CASH RECEIPTS JOURNAL   PAGE _____

	DATE	ACCOUNT CREDITED	POST. REF.	SUNDRY ACCOUNTS CREDIT	ACCOUNTS RECEIVABLE CREDIT	SALES CREDIT	CASH DEBIT	
1	19–							1
2	May 6	Notes Receivable		480 00				2
3		Interest Income		3 20			483 20	3
4								4

L.O. 3   April   8 Granted a loan to Bryan Hanson, an employee, for $336, for three months, 6 percent, dated April 8.

CASH PAYMENTS JOURNAL   PAGE _____

	DATE	CK. NO.	ACCOUNT DEBITED	POST. REF.	SUNDRY ACCOUNTS DEBIT	ACCOUNTS PAYABLE DEBIT	PURCHASES DISCOUNT CREDIT	CASH CREDIT	
1	19–								1
2	Apr. 8		Notes Receivable		336 00			336 00	2
3									3

July   8 Received payment from Bryan Hanson of principal plus interest on the three-month, 6 percent loan granted him on April 8.

CASH RECEIPTS JOURNAL   PAGE _____

	DATE	ACCOUNT CREDITED	POST. REF.	SUNDRY ACCOUNTS CREDIT	ACCOUNTS RECEIVABLE CREDIT	SALES CREDIT	CASH DEBIT	
1	19–							1
2	July 8	Notes Receivable		336 00				2
3		Interest Income		5 04			341 04	3

L.O. 4   April   9 Received a note for $900 from Johnson Heating and Air Conditioning for merchandise, 60 days, 7 percent, dated April 9.

	DATE	DESCRIPTION	POST. REF.	DEBIT	CREDIT	
1	19–					1
2	Apr. 9	Notes Receivable		900 00		2
3		Sales			900 00	3
4						4

June   8 Received interest from Johnson Heating and Air Conditioning on its note of April 9.

CASH RECEIPTS JOURNAL   PAGE _____

	DATE	ACCOUNT CREDITED	POST. REF.	SUNDRY ACCOUNTS CREDIT	ACCOUNTS RECEIVABLE CREDIT	SALES CREDIT	CASH DEBIT	
1	*19–*							1
2	*June 8*	*Interest Income*		1 0 50			1 0 50	2

L.O. 5   Then it agreed to renewal of the note by issuance of a new note, 30 days, 8 percent, dated June 8.

	DATE	DESCRIPTION	POST. REF.	DEBIT	CREDIT	
1	*19–*					1
2	*June 8*	*Notes Receivable*		9 0 0 00		2
3		*Notes Receivable*			9 0 0 00	3

L.O. 6   June   19 Baker Building Supplies dishonored its note of April 20 for $800, at 7 percent, for 60 days.

	DATE	DESCRIPTION	POST. REF.	DEBIT	CREDIT	
1	*19–*					1
2	*June 19*	*Accounts Receivable, Baker*				2
3		*Building Supplies*		8 0 9 33		3
4		*Notes Receivable*			8 0 0 00	4
5		*Interest Income*			9 33	5
6						6
7						7

L.O. 7   July   19 Baker Building Supplies paid its dishonored note, plus additional interest for 30 days at 7 percent.

CASH RECEIPTS JOURNAL   PAGE _____

	DATE	ACCOUNT CREDITED	POST. REF.	SUNDRY ACCOUNTS CREDIT	ACCOUNTS RECEIVABLE CREDIT	SALES CREDIT	CASH DEBIT	
1	*19–*							1
2	*July 19*	*Baker Building Supplies*			8 0 9 33			2
3		*Interest Income*		4 72			8 1 4 05	3

L.O. 8   May   5 Discounted at Flagel National Bank the note received from Chavez Hardware, dated April 20, $540, 8 percent, 60 days. The discount rate is 7 percent.

CASH RECEIPTS JOURNAL   PAGE _____

	DATE		ACCOUNT CREDITED	POST. REF.	SUNDRY ACCOUNTS CREDIT	ACCOUNTS RECEIVABLE CREDIT	SALES CREDIT	CASH DEBIT	
1	19–								1
2	May	5	Notes Receivable		5 4 0 00				2
3			Interest Income		2 41			5 4 2 41	3
4									4
5									5
6									6

May   4 Discounted at Flagel National Bank the note received from Davison Service Company, dated April 24, $600, 6 percent, 90 days. The discount rate is 7 percent.

CASH RECEIPTS JOURNAL   PAGE _____

	DATE		ACCOUNT NAME	POST. REF.	SUNDRY ACCOUNTS DEBIT	SUNDRY ACCOUNTS CREDIT	SALES CREDIT	CASH DEBIT	
1	19–								1
2	May	4	Notes Receivable			6 0 0 00			2
3			Interest Expense		47			5 9 9 53	3
4									4
5									5
6									6

L.O. 9   July   23 Notified by Flagel National Bank that Davison Service Company dishonored its note previously discounted on May 4. Paid bank the principal, $600, plus interest, $9, plus protest fee, $8.

CASH PAYMENTS JOURNAL   PAGE _____

	DATE		CK. NO.	ACCOUNT DEBITED	POST. REF.	SUNDRY ACCOUNTS DEBIT	ACCOUNTS PAYABLE DEBIT	PURCHASES DISCOUNT CREDIT	CASH CREDIT	
1	19–									1
2	July	23		Accounts Receivable,						2
3				Davison Service Company		6 1 7 00			6 1 7 00	3
4										4
5										5
6										6

July   31 Davison Service Company paid the note dated April 24, previously discounted at the bank and dishonored, plus $.96 interest from July 23 through 31. The same entry in a cash receipts journal looks like this:

CASH RECEIPTS JOURNAL   PAGE _____

	DATE	ACCOUNT CREDITED	POST. REF.	SUNDRY ACCOUNTS CREDIT	ACCOUNTS RECEIVABLE CREDIT	SALES CREDIT	CASH DEBIT	
1	19–							1
2	July 31	Davison Service Company			6 1 7 00			2
3		Interest Income		96			6 1 7 96	3
4								4

June   2 Discounted at Flagel National Bank the note received from Cromwell and Son, dated May 9, $2,640, 8 percent, 60 days. The discount rate is 7 ½ percent.

CASH RECEIPTS JOURNAL   PAGE _____

	DATE	ACCOUNT CREDITED	POST. REF.	SUNDRY ACCOUNTS CREDIT	ACCOUNTS RECEIVABLE CREDIT	SALES CREDIT	CASH DEBIT	
1	19–							1
2	June 2	Notes Receivable		2 6 4 0 00				2
3		Interest Income		1 5 14			2 6 5 5 14	3

GLOSSARY

Accrued interest income on notes receivable   When a note receivable begins in one fiscal period and matures in the following one, accrued interest represents interest income earned but not yet received—for example, from the date of the note until the last day of the fiscal period.

Contingent liability   A liability that may develop—for example, if a note receivable is discounted at a bank and then the maker does not pay.

Discounting a note receivable   The process by which a firm may raise cash by selling a note receivable to a bank or finance company. The bank deducts the interest from the maturity value of the note to determine the proceeds (amount of money) that the firm receives.

Discount period   The time between the date a note receivable is discounted and the date it matures.

Dishonored note receivable   When the maker of a note fails to pay the principal and interest at the maturity date, the maker is said to be dishonoring the note.

Maturity value   The principal (face value) of a note plus interest from the date of the note until due date.

Notes receivable register   A supplementary record in which a firm lists details of notes received.

Protest fee   If the maker of a note receivable that has been discounted by a bank dishonors the note (fails to pay the bank by the due date), the bank charges a protest fee for compiling and mailing a Notice of Dishonor and Protest.

QUESTIONS, EXERCISES, AND PROBLEMS

Discussion Questions

1. What do accountants mean when they talk about the maturity value of a note?
2. Describe possible situations in which notes receivable may come into existence.
3. Why is a note receivable considered superior to an account receivable?
4. What is meant by dishonoring a note receivable? What journal entry would you make to handle a dishonored interest-bearing note receivable?
5. Explain what *contingent liability* means in relation to the endorser of a note.
6. Where are Notes Receivable due within a year and Interest Income placed in classified financial statements?
7. Why is it necessary to make an adjusting entry for accrued interest on an interest-bearing note receivable? Should the adjusting entry be reversed?
8. Describe a discounted note receivable. How do you compute the proceeds?

Exercises

L.O. 1   **Exercise 17-1**   On March 9 the J. M. Stark Company received a 90-day, 12 percent note for $1,800, dated March 9 from C. P. Bell, a charge customer.

a. What is the due date of the note?
b. How much interest is due at maturity?

L.O. 1,2   **Exercise 17-2**   Given the data in Exercise 17-1, write entries in general journal form on the books of the J. M. Stark Company to record the following:

a. Receipt of the note from Bell.
b. Receipt of the principal and interest at maturity.

Given the data in Exercise 17-1, write entries in general journal form on C. P. Bell's books to record the following:

c. Issuance of the note by Bell.
d. Payment of the note at maturity.

L.O. 1,2,10   **Exercise 17-3**   Write entries in general journal form to record the following transactions for the Macon Company, whose fiscal year ends on December 31:

Dec.   3 The Macon Company receives from B and N Leasing a $6,000, 120-day, 10 percent note, dated December 3, as an extension of a charge account.
       31 The adjusting entry for accrued interest.
       31 The closing entry, assuming no other interest income is involved.
Jan.   1 The reversing entry.
Apr.   2 Receipt of the principal and interest at maturity.

L.O. 4,8   **Exercise 17-4**   On May 8, the Marcia Stein Company received a 90-day, 10 percent note for $8,000, dated May 8, for merchandise sold to the Purcell Company. Stein endorsed the note in favor of its bank on May 28. The bank discounted the note at 9 percent, paying the proceeds to Stein. Determine the following facts:

a. Number of days the Marcia Stein Company held the note
b. Number of days in the discount period
c. Face value
d. Maturity value
e. Proceeds
f. Interest income or expense recorded by the payee (the Marcia Stein Company)

L.O. 1,8   **Exercise 17-5**   Prepare entries in general journal form to record the following:

June   12 Sold merchandise on account to D. C. Slade; terms, 2/10, n/30; $1,440.
July   12 Received $240 in cash from D. C. Slade and a 60-day, 10 percent note for $1,200, dated July 12.
Aug.   17 Discounted the note at the bank at 9 percent.

L.O. 9   **Exercise 17-6**   A discounted note receivable is dishonored by the maker, C. M. Lange. The endorser pays the bank the face value of the note, $900; the interest, $12.60; plus a protest fee, $9. In general journal form, journalize the entry on September 16 to record the payment by the endorser.

L.O. 1,2,8,9   **Exercise 17-7**   The T accounts below show a series of six transactions concerning a sale of merchandise on account and subsequent payment of the amount owed. Describe the nature of each transaction.

Cash				Accounts Receivable				Sales			Interest Income	
(d)	894	(e)	909	(a)	930	(b)	30		(a)	930	(f)	4
(f)	913			(e)	909	(c)	900					
						(f)	909					

Sales Returns and Allowances				Notes Receivable				Interest Expense		
(b)	30			(c)	900	(d)	900	(d)	6	

L.O. 1,8,9 **Exercise 17-8** Write entries in general journal form to record the following transactions for the Cons Company:

Mar. 5 The Cons Company received from Newsom Stores a $12,000, 90-day, 10 percent note, dated March 4, as an extension of a charge account.

17 Discounted the note at the bank at 12 percent.

June 3 Newsom Stores dishonored the note; Cons paid the bank the amount due on the note plus a protest fee of $4.

July 3 Cons received from Newsom Stores the amount due on the dishonored note, plus interest for 30 days at 12 percent on the total amount owed.

Problem Set A

L.O. 1,2 **Problem 17-1A** Following are selected transactions carried out by Neeley and Company this year:

Jan. 12 Sold merchandise on account to O. C. Wentz Company; 2/10, n/30; $2,420.

22 Received check from O. C. Wentz Company for the sale of January 12.

Feb. 17 Sold merchandise on account to Marson, Inc.; 2/10, n/30; $3,240.

Mar. 18 Received a 30-day, 9 percent note, dated this day, for $3,240 from Marson, Inc., on account.

Apr. 17 Received a check from Marson, Inc., for the amount owed on the note of March 18.

June 1 Sold merchandise to Bracken and Riley, $3,850, receiving a 90-day, 10 percent note, dated this day. (This sale was not previously recorded.)

Aug. 30 Received payment from Bracken and Riley for the amount owed on the note of June 1.

Instructions

Record the above transactions in a general journal.

L.O. 1,2,5,8 **Problem 17-2A** Here are some of the transactions carried out by Thomas Trading Company this year:

Jan. 6 Sold merchandise on account to Pier Forty-One Imports; 2/10, n/30; $3,220.

Feb. 5 Received a 30-day, 9 percent note, dated this day, for $3,220 from Pier Forty-One Imports on account.

Mar. 7 Pier Forty-One Imports paid the amount due on its note of February 5.

Apr. 25 Sold merchandise on account to Taft Gift Shop; 2/10, n/30; $2,640.

May 25 Received a 45-day, 11 percent note, dated this day, for $2,640 from Taft Gift Shop on account.

July 9 Taft Gift Shop paid the interest on its note of May 25 and renewed the obligation by issuing a new 60-day, 12 percent note for $2,640, dated July 9.

Sept.   7 Received check from Taft Gift Shop for the amount owed on its note of July 9.

14 Sold merchandise on account to Len Scott, Inc., $4,200, receiving its 30-day, 10 percent note. (The sale was not previously recorded.)

24 Discounted the note received from Len Scott, Inc., at the Bates National Bank; discount rate, 9 percent.

Instructions

Record these transactions in a general journal.

L.O. 1,2,4,5,6,8,9   **Problem 17-3A**   Selected transactions of the Sports Center carried out this year are as follows:

Jan.   10 Sold merchandise on account to Millard Stores; 2/10, n/30; $4,668.

Feb.   9 Received a 30-day, 9 percent note from Millard Stores, $4,668, dated February 9.

Mar.   11 Received $2,703.01 from Millard Stores as part payment on its note dated February 9: $2,668 as part payment on the principal and $35.01 as interest on $4,668 for 30 days at 9 percent. Received a new 30-day, 10 percent note, dated March 11, in the amount of $2,000.

Apr.   4 Sold merchandise to The Enberg, $2,790, receiving their 90-day, 9 percent note, dated April 4 (not previously recorded).

10 Received a check from Millard Stores for the amount owed on its note of March 11.

12 Discounted the note received from The Enberg at the Ludlum State Bank; discount rate, 8 percent.

May   8 Sold merchandise on account to Newton, Inc.; 2/10, n/30; $2,244.

June   7 Received a 45-day, 9 percent note for $2,244 from Newton, Inc., dated June 7.

July   22 Newton, Inc., dishonored its note dated June 7.

Instructions

Using a sales journal, a cash receipts journal, and a general journal, record the above transactions in the appropriate journal.

L.O. 1,2,4,5,6,8,9,10   **Problem 17-4A**   Here are some selected transactions of Brasso Produce carried out during the year ended December 31:

June   9 Received a 60-day, 9 percent note, dated June 9, for $3,720 from Associated Foods for merchandise. (The sale was not previously recorded.)

21 Received a 30-day, 10 percent note, dated June 21, for $4,200 from Bracken Restaurants, a charge customer, for a sale recorded previously.

July   1 Received a 90-day, 10 percent note, dated July 1, for $2,140 from Aikens and Coe, a charge customer, for a sale recorded previously.

July 21 Received a check from Bracken Restaurants in payment of principal and interest on its note.

Aug. 8 Received payment of interest from Associated Foods for its note of June 9 and a new 30-day, 9 percent note, for $3,720, dated August 8.

20 Received a 60-day, 8 percent note, dated August 20, from C. C. Phillips, a charge customer, for $2,400, for a sale recorded previously.

Sept. 7 Associated Foods paid its note dated August 8, principal plus interest.

9 Discounted the note received from C. C. Phillips, dated August 20, at the Molson State Bank; discount rate, 10 percent.

29 Aikens and Coe dishonored its note dated July 1.

Dec. 6 Received a 60-day, 9 percent note, dated December 6 from T. C. Smith, a charge customer, for $2,390, for a sale recorded previously.

Instructions

1. Record the transactions in general journal form.
2. Make the adjusting entry.

Problem Set B

L.O. 1,2   **Problem 17-1B**   The Connell Lighting Company carried out the following transactions this year:

Jan. 16 Sold merchandise on account to Monroe Company; 2/10, n/30; $2,120.

26 Received check from Monroe Company for the sale of January 16.

Feb. 23 Sold merchandise on account to Shaw and Rowe; 2/10, n/30; $1,970.

Mar. 24 Received a 60-day, 9 percent note, dated this day, for $1,970 from Shaw and Rowe for the amount owed on account.

May 23 Received a check from Shaw and Rowe for the amount owed on the note of March 24.

June 8 Sold merchandise on account to Tidwell Interiors for $2,610, receiving its 90-day, 10 percent note, dated June 8 (not previously recorded).

Sept. 6 Received payment from Tidwell Interiors for the amount owed on its note of June 8.

Instructions

Record the above transactions in general journal form.

L.O. 1,2,5,8   **Problem 17-2B**   Nelson and Company carried out the following transactions this year:

Jan. 11 Sold merchandise on account to L. B. Shafer; 1/10, n/30; $2,140.

Feb. 10 Received a 30-day, 9 percent note, dated this day, for $2,140 from L. B. Shafer on account.

Mar.   12   L. B. Shafer paid the amount due on its note of February 10.

Apr.   28   Sold merchandise on account to Epsom Gallery; 1/10, n/30; $2,700.

May   28   Received a 60-day, 10 percent note, dated this day, for $2,700 from Epsom Gallery on account.

July   27   Epsom Gallery paid the interest on its note of May 28 and renewed the obligation by issuing a new 60-day, 11 percent note for $2,700, dated July 27.

Sept.   25   Received check from Epsom Gallery for the amount owed on its note of July 27.

Oct.   1   Sold merchandise to Dennis, Inc., for $4,200, receiving a 30-day, 7 percent note dated this day (not previously recorded).

     21   Discounted the note received from Dennis, Inc., at the Macon State Bank; discount rate, 8 percent.

Instructions

Record the above transactions in general journal form.

L.O. 1,2,4,5,6,8,9   **Problem 17-3B**   Here are some selected transactions carried out by the Van Dyke Nursery this year:

Jan.   6   Sold merchandise on account to Ulrich Gardens; 2/10, n/30; $2,790.

Feb.   5   Received a 30-day, 11 percent note from Ulrich Gardens for $2,790, dated February 5.

Mar.   7   Received $1,215.58 from Ulrich Gardens as payment on its note dated February 5; $1,190 as part payment on the principal, $25.58 as interest on $2,790 for 30 days at 11 percent. Received a new 30-day, 10 percent note for $1,600, dated March 7.

Apr.   6   Received a check from Ulrich Gardens for the amount owed on its note, dated March 7.

     13   Sold merchandise to C. T. Jarvis, receiving her 60-day, 10 percent note, dated April 13, in the amount of $3,940 (not previously recorded).

     21   Discounted the note received from C. T. Jarvis at the Lincoln First Bank; discount rate, 10 percent.

May   23   Sold merchandise on account to Ames and Company; 2/10, n/30; $3,644.

June   22   Received a $3,644 note from Ames and Company for 90 days at 11 percent, dated June 22.

Sept.   20   Ames and Company dishonored its note dated June 22.

Instructions

Use a sales journal, a cash receipts journal, and a general journal to record the above transactions. Record each transaction in the appropriate journal.

L.O. 1,2,4,5,6,8,9,10   **Problem 17-4B**   Exacto Printing Company completed the following transactions during the year ended December 31:

June   14 Received a 60-day, 9 percent note, dated June 14, for $2,640 from Nolte Office Supply for the sale of services. (The sale was not previously recorded.)

           26 Received a 30-day, 10 percent note, dated June 25, for $3,222 from Byrd and Meeker, a charge customer, for a sale recorded previously.

July   7 Received a 90-day, 10 percent note, dated July 7, for $4,200 from City Office Supply, a charge customer, for a sale recorded previously.

           25 Received a check from Byrd and Meeker in payment of principal and interest on its note.

Aug.   13 Received payment of interest from Nolte Office Supply for its note of June 14 and also a new 30-day, 10 percent note, dated August 13, for $2,640.

           22 Received a 60-day, 8 percent note, dated August 22, for $2,900 from Wilson and Company, a charge customer, for a sale recorded previously.

Sept.   12 Nolte Office Supply paid its note dated August 13, principal plus interest.

           14 Discounted the note received from Wilson and Company, dated August 22, at the Turner State Bank; discount rate, 10 percent.

Oct.   5 City Office Supply dishonored its note dated July 7.

Dec.   16 Received a 60-day, 8 percent note, dated December 15, for $5,200 from Hoyt and Lee, a charge customer, for a sale recorded previously.

Instructions

1. Record the above transactions in a general journal.
2. Make the adjusting entry.

18 Accounting for Valuation of Receivables

LEARNING OBJECTIVES

After you have completed this chapter, you will be able to do the following:

1. Make the adjusting entry to record estimated bad debt losses by using the allowance method of handling bad debts.
2. Determine the amount of the adjusting entry by aging Accounts Receivable.
3. Determine the amount of the adjusting entry by using a percentage of Accounts Receivable.
4. Calculate the amount of the adjusting entry by using a percentage of Sales or net sales.
5. Journalize the entries to write off Accounts Receivable as being uncollectible using the allowance method of accounting for bad debt losses.
6. Journalize entries to reinstate Accounts Receivable previously written off using the allowance method.
7. Journalize the entries to write off Accounts Receivable as being uncollectible using the specific charge-off method of accounting for bad debt losses.
8. Journalize entries to reinstate Accounts Receivable previously written off using the specific charge-off method.

The use of credit for both buying and selling goods and services has become standard practice for business firms of all types and levels: retailers, wholesalers, and manufacturers. By now, you have learned to record sales of merchandise on account as a debit to Accounts Receivable and a credit to Sales. You have also learned to debit Cash and credit Accounts Receivable when the account is collected.

Business firms selling goods or services on credit inevitably find that not all the Accounts Receivable are collected in full. Consequently, the unpaid accounts must eventually be written off as uncollectible, or as a bad debt. In other words, a firm that grants credit "can't win 'em all," so the firm is obliged to provide for the anticipated losses. In this chapter we'll discuss ways to provide for losses as well as to write off customer accounts that are no longer collectible.

We shall examine two methods of accounting for uncollectible accounts: the allowance method, and the specific charge-off method. The allowance method is consistent with the matching principle, in that it enables firms to match up sales of one year with bad debt losses of the same year, and is consistent with the accrual method of accounting required by generally accepted principles of accounting. The specific charge-off method traditionally has been used by small businesses. Now, in accordance with the Tax Reform Act of 1986, the specific charge-off method is the only method approved for federal income tax purposes. Many companies, especially larger firms, use the allowance method for their own accounting system of internal reporting, that is, for their own financial statements. They use the specific charge-off method for federal income tax reporting, that is, for their tax returns. The adjustments required on their tax returns are not entered in the companies' books. Incidentally, by the terms *write-off* and *charge-off*, we mean the same thing.

THE CREDIT DEPARTMENT

Because it governs the extension of credit to charge customers, the Credit Department has to keep a watchful eye on present customers, evaluate the debt-paying ability of prospective customers, and determine the maximum amount of credit to be extended to each customer. Retail stores selling to individuals rely on reports from local retail credit bureaus. When wholesalers and manufacturers grant credit to customers, they utilize reports of national credit-rating institutions such as Dun and Bradstreet, wholesale credit bureaus, and the financial statements of prospective customers. Business firms that make many sales on credit find it worthwhile to subscribe to credit bureaus or credit-rating agencies. These credit-reporting organizations maintain files of current financial information on charge customers, establish credit ratings for each charge customer, and conduct special investigations on request.

It's always bad, of course, if a business firm has high credit losses, since any firm needs to be paid for its sales on account. Surprisingly, it may be bad if a firm has no credit losses. Such a record indicates that the firm must be turning down applications for credit, even though most applicants would indeed pay their bills. In this last situation, the firm not only loses many immediate sales but reaps considerable ill will as well because it turns down so many prospective customers. A sound credit policy should provide for a limited amount of credit losses. It is the responsibility of the Credit Department to keep losses within acceptable limits.

MATCHING BAD DEBT LOSSES WITH SALES

A basic principle of the accrual basis of accounting is that revenue for a fiscal period must be matched by the expenses incurred during that same period to earn that revenue. This matching principle is consistent with our earlier presentation of adjusting entries. As you recall, depreciation represents the loss in usefulness of, say, equipment for a particular year. In making the adjustment, we allocate this expense to one year of operations. For example, we debit Depreciation Expense, Equipment and credit Accumulated Depreciation, Equipment. By the same token, when a firm sells merchandise on account to a customer who may eventually default on the obligation, the firm has a bad debt loss potential. The firm must try to match the loss with the revenue earned for the year in which the sale is made.

At the time of making the sale, the company does not *know* that it has incurred a loss because it anticipates that the customer will pay the obligation. Otherwise the company would not have extended credit to that particular customer. In other words, the firm making the credit sale has increased its revenue account, but it does not know at the time of the sale whether or not the revenue will be collected. As a matter of fact, the firm will not be certain of the loss until it has repeatedly failed in attempts to collect the bill, so the final recognition of the loss will probably occur many months after the sale. *In order to match up the bad debt losses of the year with the sales of the same year, the firm must make an estimate of the losses as a means of providing for them in advance.* The **allowance method of accounting for bad debt losses** provides the means for matching bad debt losses with the applicable sales in the company's financial statements. For tax purposes, however, the rules are different after 1986.

Think of the situation from the standpoint of a company paying its income tax. The company makes sales on account during the year. Sales are counted as revenue, so the company pays income tax on these sales. But some of these sales will not be collected. In other words, the company paid too much income tax. In a later fiscal period, the company writes off the uncollectible accounts as bad debts and deducts the amount of the write-offs as an expense on its income tax. Now the company is able to get even on its previous overpayment of income tax. The difference between tax return "bad debts" and financial statement "bad debts" results in an adjustment to deferred or prepaid taxes (a subject that is covered in later accounting courses).

THE ALLOWANCE METHOD OF ACCOUNTING FOR BAD DEBTS

Most big business firms use the allowance method of accounting for bad debt losses for financial reporting, which is consistent with the accrual method of accounting required by generally accepted accounting principles (GAAP). An adjusting entry is recorded first in the Adjustment columns of the work sheet—much like the adjustment for depreciation, which was described in Chapter 5. In general journal and T account form, the adjusting entry for the estimated bad debt losses is shown in the following examples:

	DATE	DESCRIPTION	POST. REF.	DEBIT	CREDIT	
1	19–	*Adjusting Entry*				1
2	Dec. 31	Bad Debts Expense		7 0 0 00		2
3		Allowance for Doubtful Accounts			7 0 0 00	3
4						4

Bad Debts Expense		Allowance for Doubtful Accounts	
+	–	–	+
Adj. 700			Bal. 1,100
			Adj. 700

Objective 1

Make the adjusting entry to record estimated bad debt losses by using the allowance method of handling bad debts.

The purpose of the adjusting entry is to increase Bad Debts Expense by the amount of the estimated loss, and also to show a realistic figure for the book value of Accounts Receivable. *Allowance for Doubtful Accounts is classified as a deduction from Accounts Receivable. As such, it is a contra account, similar to Accumulated Depreciation.* Just as the book value of Equipment equals the cost of Equipment minus Accumulated Depreciation, Equipment, the book value of Accounts Receivable equals Accounts Receivable minus Allowance for Doubtful Accounts. Accountants also refer to the book value of Accounts Receivable as the **expected realizable value.**

Because a firm cannot know with certainty which accounts won't be fully collected, it's not possible to credit Accounts Receivable directly. Think of a life insurance company that insures 1,000 newborn infants. The insurance company doesn't know *who* will be alive at age 21, but on

FIGURE 18-1

	ACCOUNT NAME
	Accounts Receivable
	Allowance for Doubtful Accounts
	Equipment
	Accumulated Depreciation, Equipment
	Bad Debts Expense
	Depreciation Expense, Equipment

the basis of experience, it can estimate *how many* will be alive at age 21. Similarly, on the basis of its experience, a business firm is able to estimate what this year's bad debt losses will be. The firm bases its estimate on a year's sales, but it can't designate with certainty *which* credit sales will not be paid.

Prior to the adjustments, the **Bad Debts Expense account has no previous balance, as the account is not used during the fiscal period.** The firm's accountant makes an adjusting entry to increase Bad Debts Expense and immediately closes the account along with all other expense accounts. Allowance for Doubtful Accounts, on the other hand, has a balance that is carried over from previous years and is not closed. Notice where these accounts appear in the partial worksheet shown in Figure 18-1.

Note that Accounts Receivable is recorded in the debit column, and Allowance for Doubtful Accounts is recorded in the credit column. The $700 adjustment is added to the previous credit balance of $1,100, resulting in $1,800 being recorded in the Balance Sheet Credit column. As you can see, Allowance for Doubtful Accounts is handled much like Accumulated Depreciation. Both are recorded as credits in the Adjustments and Balance Sheet columns of the work sheet; also, the adjustments are never reversed because both accounts have previous balances after the first year of operations.

Bad Debts Expense and Allowance for Doubtful Accounts on Financial Statements

The Bad Debts Expense account appears on the income statement as an operating expense. Some firms subdivide operating expenses into selling expenses and general expenses, in which case they list Bad Debts Expense in the category of general expenses. (*Reason:* The decision to grant credit is usually a function of the administrative rather than the sales staff.)

TRIAL BALANCE		ADJUSTMENTS		INCOME STATEMENT		BALANCE SHEET	
DEBIT	CREDIT	DEBIT	CREDIT	DEBIT	CREDIT	DEBIT	CREDIT
60 0 0 0 00						60 0 0 0 00	
	1 1 0 0 00		(e) 7 0 0 00				1 8 0 0 00
74 0 0 0 00						74 0 0 0 00	
	22 0 0 0 00		(h) 6 0 0 0 00				28 0 0 0 00
		(e) 7 0 0 00		7 0 0 00			
		(h) 6 0 0 0 00		6 0 0 0 00			

Allowance for Doubtful Accounts is listed immediately below Accounts Receivable in the Current Assets section of the balance sheet, as in Figure 18-2.

Jacoby and Company
Balance Sheet
December 31, 19–

Assets				
Current Assets:				
Cash			$ 12 0 0 0 00	
Notes Receivable			8 0 0 0 00	
Accounts Receivable	$60 0 0 0 00			
Less Allowance for Doubtful Accounts	1 8 0 0 00		58 2 0 0 00	
Merchandise Inventory			96 0 0 0 00	
Supplies			4 0 0 00	
Total Current Assets				$ 174 6 0 0 00
Plant and Equipment:				
Equipment	$74 0 0 0 00			
Less Accumulated Depreciation	28 0 0 0 00	$ 46 0 0 0 00		

FIGURE 18-2

The $58,200 represents the anticipated net realizable value of Accounts Receivable; this is also known as the **book value of Accounts Receivable.** Again, one classifies Allowance for Doubtful Accounts as a *valuation* or *contra account* since it is a deduction from an asset. Sometimes accountants use other names for this account, such as Allowance for Bad Debts, Allowance for Uncollectible Accounts, and Estimated Uncollectible Accounts.

Estimating the Amount of Bad Debts Expense

Management—on the basis of its judgment and past experience—has to make a reasonable estimate of the amount of its uncollectible accounts. Of course, it stands to reason that any such estimate is modified by business trends. In a period of prosperity and high employment, one can expect fewer losses from uncollectible accounts than in a period of recession.

The next question is, "How does management estimate the dollar amount of bad debts expense?" The estimate can be made in several ways; we will present three methods here:

1. Aging Accounts Receivable
2. Using a percentage of Accounts Receivable
3. Using a percentage of Sales or net sales

AGING ACCOUNTS RECEIVABLE

The most common technique for estimating the total uncollectible amount of Accounts Receivable is to **age** each charge customer's account by (1) determining the number of days old each account is and (2) determining the number of days the account is past due. On a working paper, the accounts in a company's accounts receivable ledger are listed by name and amount. Columns are set up for various age groups. As an example, we will use the Accounts Receivable of Norma Sanders Company. Here is the partial aging schedule:

ANALYSIS OF ACCOUNTS RECEIVABLE BY AGE

CUSTOMER'S NAME	BALANCE	NOT YET DUE	DAYS PAST DUE 1-30	31-60	61-90	91-180	181-365	OVER 365
A. B. Allen	722.00	722.00						
B. N. Baker	464.00				464.00			
C. L. Chase	136.90			136.90				
D. R. Dalton	914.00	914.00						
E. V. Early	593.10			593.10				
Total	90,000.00	78,200.00	4,030.00	3,280.00	1,975.00	1,260.00	834.00	421.00

Based on its past experience, a company can estimate that a given percentage of each age group of accounts will be uncollectible. Next, the accountant multiplies the total amount for each age group by the percentage for that group. This results in the amount estimated to be uncollectible for that group. We now continue with the Accounts Receivable of Norma Sanders Company. Naturally, the older the account, the greater the possibility that it is uncollectible.

Age Interval	Amount	Estimated Percentage Uncollectible	Allowance for Doubtful Accounts
Not yet due	$78,200	2	$78,200 × .02 = $1,564.00
1 to 30 days past due	4,030	4	$4,030 × .04 = 161.20
31 to 60 days past due	3,280	10	$3,280 × .10 = 328.00
61 to 90 days past due	1,975	20	$1,975 × .20 = 395.00
91 to 180 days past due	1,260	30	$1,260 × .30 = 378.00
181 to 365 days past due	834	50	$834 × .50 = 417.00
More than 365 days past due	421	80	$421 × .80 = 336.80
	$90,000		$3,580.00

Objective 2

Determine the amount of an adjusting entry by aging Accounts Receivable.

In the ledger of Norma Sanders Company, the new balance in Allowance for Doubtful Accounts should be $3,580 (amount estimated by aging to be uncollectible). **The accountant now makes an adjusting entry large enough to make the balance of Allowance for Doubtful Accounts the same as the estimated uncollectible amount.** Norma Sanders Company had a credit balance of $410 in Allowance for Doubtful Accounts. We now make an adjusting entry to bring the balance of the account up to $3,580. The amount of the adjusting entry is $3,170 ($3,580 − $410). This situation is illustrated by T accounts as follows:

Bad Debts Expense		Allowance for Doubtful Accounts	
+	−	−	+
Adj. 3,170			Bal. 410
			Adj. 3,170
			3,580

To sum up: The firm estimates that $3,580 of Accounts Receivable is uncollectible. *It now has to bring the balance of Allowance for Doubtful Accounts up to the desired figure of $3,580.* Allowance for Doubtful Accounts has a present credit balance of $410, so the firm adjusts for the difference, $3,170. After the accountant posts the adjusting entry, the footing of Allowance for Doubtful Accounts indicates the desired balance, as determined by the aging analysis. The adjusting data and their effect on the accounts are illustrated in Figure 18-3.

Bad Debts Expense ($3,170) will appear on the income statement in the general-expense portion of Operating Expenses. Like all expenses, it will

FIGURE 18-3

ACCOUNT NAME
Accounts Receivable
Allowance for Doubtful Accounts
Bad Debts Expense

be closed at the end of the fiscal period into Income Summary. For emphasis, let's repeat the placement of the accounts in the balance sheet.

Norma Sanders Company
Balance Sheet
December 31, 19–

Assets		
Current Assets:		
Cash		$9 2 0 0 00
Notes Receivable		4 0 0 0 00
Accounts Receivable	$90 0 0 0 00	
Less Allowance for Doubtful Accounts	3 5 8 0 00	86 4 2 0 00

Incidentally, aging Accounts Receivable is easily accomplished by existing computer accounting programs.

Estimating Bad Debts as a Percentage of Accounts Receivable

Some business firms feel that the aging procedure is too time-consuming; they prefer a quicker but less exact method for estimating the amount of uncollectible Accounts Receivable. These firms take an average of the actual bad debt losses of previous years as a percentage of Accounts

Norma Sanders Company
Work Sheet
For Year Ended December 31, 19–

TRIAL BALANCE		ADJUSTMENTS		INCOME STATEMENT		BALANCE SHEET	
DEBIT	CREDIT	DEBIT	CREDIT	DEBIT	CREDIT	DEBIT	CREDIT
90 0 0 0 00						90 0 0 0 00	
	4 1 0 00		(a)3 1 7 0 00				3 5 8 0 00
		(a)3 1 7 0 00		3 1 7 0 00			

Receivable. For example, the Robert Frank Company calculated the amount of the adjustment for uncollectible accounts as follows:

End of Year	Balance of Accounts Receivable	Total Actual Losses from Accounts Receivable (Accounts Receivable Written Off)
19x1	$22,000	$ 770
19x2	28,000	764
19x3	24,000	686
	$74,000	$2,220

The firm's average loss over three consecutive years was 3 percent.

$$\frac{2,220}{74,000} = .03 = \underline{\underline{3\%}}$$

Objective 3

Determine the amount of the adjusting entry by using a percentage of Accounts Receivable.

Assume that, at the end of 19x4, the balance of Accounts Receivable is $29,200 and the credit balance of Allowance for Doubtful Accounts is $172. The amount of Accounts Receivable the company estimated to be uncollectible is $876 ($29,200 × .03 = $876). Since $876 is the desired figure, the amount of the adjustment is $704 ($876 − $172 = $704). As in the case of aging Accounts Receivable, when you figure the adjustment for bad debts as a percentage of Accounts Receivable, *you make an adjust-*

FIGURE 18-4

ACCOUNT NAME

Cash
Notes Receivable
Accounts Receivable
Allowance for Doubtful Accounts

Bad Debts Expense

ing entry to bring the balance of Allowance for Doubtful Accounts up to the desired figure. Notice how the adjusting entry looks in the following T accounts:

Bad Debts Expense		Allowance for Doubtful Accounts	
+	−	−	+
Adj. 704			Bal. 172
			Adj. 704
			876

You would then record the adjustment in the work sheet (Figure 18-4).

Let's examine a portion of the balance sheet derived from the work sheet.

Robert Frank Company
Balance Sheet
December 31, 19x4

Assets			
Current Assets:			
Cash			$16 8 9 1 00
Notes Receivable			1 6 0 0 00
Accounts Receivable	$29 2 0 0 00		
Less Allowance for Doubtful Accounts	8 7 6 00	28 3 2 4 00	

In this statement, the book value of Accounts Receivable is shown as $28,324.

Robert Frank Company
Work Sheet
For Year Ended December 31, 19x4

TRIAL BALANCE		ADJUSTMENTS		INCOME STATEMENT		BALANCE SHEET	
DEBIT	CREDIT	DEBIT	CREDIT	DEBIT	CREDIT	DEBIT	CREDIT
16 8 9 1 00						16 8 9 1 00	
1 6 0 0 00						1 6 0 0 00	
29 2 0 0 00						29 2 0 0 00	
	1 7 2 00		(e) 7 0 4 00				8 7 6 00
		(e) 7 0 4 00		7 0 4 00			

Estimating Bad Debts as a Percentage of Sales

Calculate the amount
of the adjusting entry
by using a percentage
of Sales or net sales.

Some business firms prefer a simplified method for determining the amount of the adjustment for Bad Debts Expense. They multiply the current year's sales by a set percentage rate and then record the adjusting entry for the exact amount.

For example, the actual losses from sales on account for the A. D. Yancey Company have averaged approximately 1 percent of net sales (Sales less Sales Returns and Allowances and less Sales Discount). The firm makes virtually all sales on credit. On the basis of this information, the company computes the amount of the adjustment as 1 percent of net sales.

Here is the figure for net sales, as shown in the income statement:

A. D. Yancey Company
Income Statement
For Year Ended June 30, 19x5

Revenue from Sales:			
Sales		$640 0 0 0 00	
Less: Sales Returns and Allowances	$26 0 0 0 00		
Sales Discount	1 2 0 0 00	27 2 0 0 00	
Net Sales			$612 8 0 0 00

Now 1 percent of net sales is $6,128 ($612,800 × .01), **so the firm uses this amount directly for the adjusting entry,** adding it to both accounts, as shown in the T accounts on the next page.

FIGURE 18-5

ACCOUNT NAME
Accounts Receivable
Allowance for Doubtful Accounts
Sales
Sales Returns and Allowances
Sales Discount
Bad Debts Expense

Bad Debts Expense			Allowance for Doubtful Accounts	
+	–		–	+
Adj. 6,128				Bal. 216
				Adj. 6,128
				6,344

Figure 18-5 shows how to record the adjustment in the work sheet. A portion of the balance sheet is shown below.

A. D. Yancey Company
Balance Sheet
June 30, 19x5

Assets			
Current Assets:			
Accounts Receivable	$48 0 0 0 00		
Less Allowance for Doubtful Accounts	6 3 4 4 00	41 6 5 6 00	

Many companies that sell on both a cash and a credit basis compute the amount of their adjustment for bad debts on net credit sales. As an example, we will use another company, the Ziegler Company. Charge sales, recorded in a sales journal, total $490,000. Sales Returns and Allowances and Sales Discounts relating to credit sales are $18,000 and $2,900, respectively. The Ziegler Company records the adjustment for

A. D. Yancey Company
Work Sheet
For Year Ended June 30, 19x5

TRIAL BALANCE		ADJUSTMENTS		INCOME STATEMENT		BALANCE SHEET	
DEBIT	CREDIT	DEBIT	CREDIT	DEBIT	CREDIT	DEBIT	CREDIT
48 0 0 0 00						48 0 0 0 00	
	2 1 6 00		(e)6 1 2 8 00				6 3 4 4 00
	640 0 0 0 00				640 0 0 0 00		
26 0 0 0 00				26 0 0 0 00			
1 2 0 0 00				1 2 0 0 00			
		(e)6 1 2 8 00		6 1 2 8 00			

bad debts at ¾ percent of net credit sales. Look at the adjustment and the calculation that follow:

Credit (charge) sales		$490,000
Less: Sales Returns and Allowances	$18,000	
Sales Discounts	2,900	20,900
Net credit sales		$469,100

$ 469,100
× .0075
$3,518.25

By T accounts, the adjustment looks like this:

Bad Debts Expense			Allowance for Doubtful Accounts		
+		−		−	+
Adj. 3,518.25				Bal. 220.32	
				Adj. 3,518.25	
					3,738.57

Note that a firm using this simplified method multiplies net sales or net credit sales by the given percentage in order to determine the amount of the adjustment. **The present balance of Allowance for Doubtful Accounts is not involved in determining the amount of the adjustment.** If the given percentage does not adequately provide for the firm's losses (that is, if it yields either too little or too much), the firm merely changes the percentage.

WRITING OFF UNCOLLECTIBLE ACCOUNTS

Up to now, we have seen that the firm's accountant first records the adjusting entry for bad debts in the appropriate columns of the work sheet. For the sake of additional clarification, the relevant accounts are illustrated in T accounts.

Bad Debts Expense			Allowance for Doubtful Accounts		
+		−		−	+
Adj. 3,518.25				Bal. 220.32	
				Adj. 3,518.25	
					3,738.57

Next the firm's accountant closes Bad Debts Expense, along with all expenses, into the Income Summary account. **The Bad Debts Expense account is not used during the year, so the only entries in it are the ad-**

justing entry and the closing entry. This represents the beginning and the end of Bad Debts Expense for the fiscal period. In other words, the only entry in Bad Debts Expense is the adjusting entry, and, as we said, this account is immediately closed out. After the adjusting entry and closing entry have been posted, the accounts look like this:

Bad Debts Expense		Allowance for Doubtful Accounts	
+	−	−	+
Adj. 3,518.25	Clos. 3,518.25		Bal. 220.32
			Adj. 3,518.25

Allowance for Doubtful Accounts

It is apparent that Allowance for Doubtful Accounts remains open. Rather than have the balance continually increase because of the successive adjustments on the credit side of the account, the accountant uses the debit side of the account to write off charge accounts that are considered definitely uncollectible.

We can consider Allowance for Doubtful Accounts as a reservoir: We fill it up at the end of the year through the medium of the adjusting entry by crediting the account. During the following year, we drain off the reservoir through the medium of write-offs by debiting the account. To avoid the possibility of the reservoir's "running dry," *the accountant should make the adjusting entry large enough to provide for all possible write-offs.*

Objective 5

Journalize the entries to write off Accounts Receivable as being uncollectible using the allowance method of accounting for bad debt losses.

Entry to Write Off a Charge Account in Full

Suppose that a firm decides, after all attempts to collect a customer's debt have failed, that the account is definitely uncollectible. In such a case, the firm should write off the amount due. Assume that on July 1, the A. D. Yancey Company decides that the account of a customer, Ronald D. Jones, is uncollectible. The accountant records the write-off by making the following entry:

	DATE		DESCRIPTION	POST. REF.	DEBIT	CREDIT	
			GENERAL JOURNAL			PAGE _116_	
1	*19x5*						1
2	*July*	*1*	*Allowance for Doubtful Accounts*		7 1 40		2
3			*Accounts Receivable, Ronald D.*				3
4			*Jones*			7 1 40	4
5			*Wrote off the account as*				5
6			*uncollectible.*				6
7							7

By T accounts, the entry looks like this:

Accounts Receivable				Allowance for Doubtful Accounts		
+		**–**		**–**		**+**
Bal.	48,000.00	July 1	71.40	July 1 71.40	Bal.	6,344.00
				(Jones's write-off)		

The accountant also posts the entry to the account of Ronald D. Jones in the accounts receivable subsidiary ledger.

NAME   *Ronald D. Jones*

ADDRESS   *217 Barclay Road*

Boston, MA 02101

DATE		ITEM	POST. REF.	DEBIT	CREDIT	BALANCE
19x2						
May	1	Balance	√			71 40
19x5						
July	1		J116		71 40	——

Note that the above entry does not change the net realizable value or book value of the Accounts Receivable.

Account Name	Balances Before Write-offs	Balances After Write-offs
Accounts Receivable	$48,000.00	$47,928.60
Less Allowance for Doubtful Accounts	6,344.00	6,272.60
Book value (net realizable value)	$41,656.00	$41,656.00

Also note that **the entry to write off an account does not involve an expense account.** The adjusting entry, which was made long before this time, provides for the expense. The estimated expense was recorded *during the year in which the sale was made,* even though this account is written off in a later year.

Compound Entry to Write Off a Number of Accounts as Uncollectible

Rather than writing off each uncollectible account separately during the year, a firm may write off a number of accounts at the end of the year by using a compound entry. For example, assume that on December 31 the Linton Company writes off the following accounts of charge customers as being uncollectible: C. D. Davis, $72.00; M. R. Gardner, $29.00; O. C. Hammil, $18.00; and M. A. Tilden, $93.00. The accountant records the write-offs by making the following entry:

	DATE		DESCRIPTION	POST. REF.	DEBIT	CREDIT	
1	*19x5*						1
2	*Dec.*	*31*	*Allowance for Doubtful Accounts*		2 1 2 00		2
3			*Accounts Receivable, C. D. Davis*			7 2 00	3
4			*Accounts Receivable, M. R.*				4
5			*Gardner*			2 9 00	5
6			*Accounts Receivable, O. C.*				6
7			*Hammil*			1 8 00	7
8			*Accounts Receivable, M. A.*				8
9			*Tilden*			9 3 00	9
10			*Wrote off the accounts as*				10
11			*uncollectible.*				11
12							12
13							13
14							14
15							15
16							16
17							17

Entry to Write Off a Charge Account Paid in Part

Sometimes a part payment is involved in a write-off of an account. When this happens, it may be due to a bankruptcy settlement. The federal laws governing **bankruptcy** legally excuse a debtor from paying off certain obligations. For example, on April 21 the A. D. Yancey Company received 10 cents on the dollar in settlement of a $364 account owed by its customer, M. A. Farris, a bankrupt. In general journal form, the entry is as follows:

	DATE		DESCRIPTION	POST. REF.	DEBIT	CREDIT	
1	*19x5*						1
2	*Apr.*	*21*	*Cash*		3 6 40		2
3			*Allowance for Doubtful Accounts*		3 2 7 60		3
4			*Accounts Receivable, M. A.*				4
5			*Farris*			3 6 4 00	5
6			*Settlement in bankruptcy,*				6
7			*wrote off account balance*				7
8			*as uncollectible.*				8

Write-offs Seldom Agree with Previous Estimates

The total amount of Accounts Receivable written off during a given year does not ordinarily agree with the estimates of uncollectible accounts previously debited to Bad Debts Expense and credited to Allowance for Doubtful Accounts. In the usual situation, the amounts written off as uncollectible turn out to be less than the estimated amount. At the end of a given year there is normally a credit balance in Allowance for Doubtful Accounts. However, if (as sometimes happens) the amounts written off are greater than the estimated amounts, Allowance for Doubtful Accounts temporarily has a debit balance. The debit balance will be eliminated by the adjusting entry at the end of the year, which results in a credit to, or increase in, Allowance for Doubtful Accounts.

COLLECTION OF ACCOUNTS PREVIOUSLY WRITTEN OFF

Objective 6

Journalize entries to reinstate Accounts Receivable previously written off using the allowance method.

Every now and then the sun shines when you least expect it, and an account previously written off as uncollectible may later be recovered, either in part or in full. In such cases, the firm's accountant restores the account to the books, or reinstates it, by an entry that is the exact opposite of the write-off entry.

As an example, the A. D. Yancey Company sells merchandise on account to B. L. Little for $405, on May 5, 19x6. Here is the entry in general journal form:

	DATE		DESCRIPTION	POST. REF.	DEBIT	CREDIT	
1	*19x6*						1
2	*May*	*5*	*Accounts Receivable, B. L. Little*		4 0 5 00		2
3			*Sales*			4 0 5 00	3
4			*Sold merchandise on account,*				4
5			*2/10, n/30.*				5
6							6
7							7
8							8

The A. D. Yancey Company makes many futile attempts to collect, and the **statute of limitations** finally expires. Since the statute of limitations is set at three years in many states, let's say that the A. D. Yancey Company has not been able to collect any money at all from Little during a three-year period and that Little has remained within the jurisdiction of the court. This means that the debt is outlawed by the statute of limitations. In other words, the firm cannot use the courts to force the debtor to pay up. Accordingly, three years later in 19x9, the accountant for A. D. Yancey Company writes off the account of B. L. Little as uncollectible.

	DATE		DESCRIPTION	POST. REF.	DEBIT	CREDIT	
1	*19x9*						1
2	*June*	*10*	*Allowance for Doubtful Accounts*		4 0 5 00		2
3			*Accounts Receivable, B. L. Little*			4 0 5 00	3
4			*Wrote off the account as*				4
5			*uncollectible.*				5
6							6
7							7

But on September 15, 19x9, B. L. Little suddenly pays his account in full! The entry to reinstate the account is the reverse of the entry used to write off the account.

	DATE		DESCRIPTION	POST. REF.	DEBIT	CREDIT	
1	*19x9*						1
2	*Sept.*	*15*	*Accounts Receivable, B. L. Little*		4 0 5 00		2
3			*Allowance for Doubtful Accounts*			4 0 5 00	3
4			*Reinstated the account.*				4
5							5

The way is now clear to record the collection of the account.

	DATE		DESCRIPTION	POST. REF.	DEBIT			CREDIT			
1	19x9										1
2	Sept.	15	Cash		4 0 5	00					2
3			Accounts Receivable, B. L. Little					4 0 5	00		3
4			Collection in full of account.								4

Now suppose that B. L. Little had gone into bankruptcy and settled his account with the A. D. Yancey Company by paying it 5 cents on the dollar. The A. D. Yancey Company would realize that there was no hope of collecting any more, so the accountant would reinstate the account only for the amount collected, like this:

	DATE		DESCRIPTION	POST. REF.	DEBIT			CREDIT			
1	Sept.	15	Accounts Receivable, B. L. Little		2 0	25					1
2			Allowance for Doubtful Accounts					2 0	25		2
3			Settlement in bankruptcy,								3
4			5 percent of $405; reinstated								4
5			the account to the extent of								5
6			the settlement.								6

The subsequent entry to record the cash payment would be as follows:

	DATE		DESCRIPTION	POST. REF.	DEBIT			CREDIT			
1	Sept.	15	Cash		2 0	25					1
2			Accounts Receivable, B. L. Little					2 0	25		2
3			Settlement in bankruptcy,								3
4			5 percent of $405.								4
5											5

SPECIFIC CHARGE-OFF OF BAD DEBTS

The **specific charge-off method of accounting for bad debt losses** is a simpler system for writing off charge accounts determined to be uncollectible. No adjusting entry is made, since there is no attempt to provide

Objective 7

Journalize the entries to write off Accounts Receivable as being uncollectible using the specific charge-off method.

for bad debt losses in advance or to match revenue with related expenses. Instead, when a firm decides that a specific customer account is never going to be paid, the accountant makes an entry in the general journal debiting Bad Debts Expense and crediting Accounts Receivable. Thus Allowance for Doubtful Accounts does not exist in the firm's charts of accounts. Traditionally, this method has been used primarily by small companies and professional enterprises. As we stated previously, the specific charge-off method is required for federal income tax reporting. We will get back to the requirements of the Tax Reform Act of 1986, but first let's show an illustration.

For example, on April 16, 1987 the Coe Company sold merchandise on account to C. T. Owens for $44.20, making the following entry in the general journal.

	DATE		DESCRIPTION	POST. REF.	DEBIT	CREDIT	
1	*1987*						1
2	*Apr.*	*16*	*Accounts Receivable, C. T. Owens*		*44 20*		2
3			*Sales*			*44 20*	3
4			*Sale of merchandise on*				4
5			*account, n/30.*				5
6							6

Owens never pays his bill. Finally, three years later, on September 1, the account is written off as follows.

	DATE		DESCRIPTION	POST. REF.	DEBIT	CREDIT	
1	*1990*						1
2	*Sept.*	*1*	*Bad Debts Expense*		*44 20*		2
3			*Accounts Receivable, C. T. Owens*			*44 20*	3
4			*To write off an uncollectible*				4
5			*account.*				5
6							6
7							7

By T accounts, the entries look like this.

Accounts Receivable			Sales			Bad Debts Expense	
+	−		−	+		+	−
1987	1990		1987	1987		1990	
Apr. 16 44.20	Sept. 1 44.20		Dec. 31 Closed	Apr. 16 44.20		Sept. 1 44.20	

You can see that revenue does not match expenses for a particular year. The Coe Company counted the original sale of $44.20 in 1987, thereby overstating true revenue for that year. It counted Bad Debts Expenses three years later in 1990 thereby overstating expenses for that year. Note that the Coe Company did not use the account titled Allowance for Doubtful Accounts. In other words, if you wait until you consider an account to be a bad debt and then write it off, with no provision for realistically estimating the losses in advance, you are operating in a rather precarious situation. On the balance sheet, Accounts Receivable is stated at the gross amount only; there is no book value or net realizable value.

Objective 8

Journalize entries to reinstate Accounts Receivable previously written off using the specific charge-off method.

As an illustration of reinstating an account previously written or charged off, let's go on and say that on May 2, 1991, C. T. Owens returns and pays his $44.20 bill. We will show the entries in general journal form.

GENERAL JOURNAL PAGE_____

	DATE		DESCRIPTION	POST. REF.	DEBIT	CREDIT	
1	1991						1
2	May	2	Accounts Receivable, C. T. Owens		44 20		2
3			Bad Debts Recovered			44 20	3
4			Reinstated the account.				4
5							5
6		2	Cash		44 20		6
7			Accounts Receivable, C. T. Owens			44 20	7
8			Collection in full of				8
9			account.				9
10							10
11							11
12							12
13							13

By T accounts, the entries look like this:

Accounts Receivable				Bad Debts Recovered			Cash	
+		−		−	+		+	−
1991		1991			1991		1991	
May 2	44.20	May 2	44.20		May 2	44.20	May 2	44.20

For a small company that uses the specific charge-off method alone, the account entitled Bad Debts Recovered is classified as a revenue account and would be listed in the Other Income section of an income statement. The Accounts Receivable account was placed back on the books, so that the firm would have a record of C. T. Owens's account. Note that this method of accounting is not consistent with the accrual method.

REQUIREMENTS OF THE TAX REFORM ACT OF 1986

All taxpayers, except for financial institutions, are required to use the specific charge-off method for reporting on their federal income tax returns. Before 1987, both the specific charge-off method and the allowance method were approved for federal income tax reporting. Consequently, a company formerly using the allowance method (also called the reserve method) had a balance in its Allowance for Doubtful Accounts account. The balance of Allowance for Doubtful Accounts, as of January 1, 1987, must be transferred to, or included in, income in equal amounts over a four-year period starting with the 1987 tax year. For example, assume that Beesley Company had a credit balance of $80,000 in Allowance for Doubtful Accounts. For each of the four years, Beesley's accountant makes an entry debiting Allowance for Doubtful Accounts for $20,000 and crediting a revenue account such as Write-off of Allowance for Doubtful Accounts for $20,000. Write-off of Allowance for Doubtful Accounts would be classified as an Other Income account on an income statement.

For companies reporting bad debt losses, a separate record should be maintained. For each account charged off, the records must contain the following:

1. A description of the debt, including the amount, and the date it became due.
2. The name of the debtor.
3. The efforts that have been made to collect the debt.
4. Why it is decided that the debt is worthless.

SUMMARY

For accounting purposes, companies may account for bad debts by two different methods; the allowance method and the specific charge-off method. A great advantage of the allowance method is that it enables a firm to match the bad debt losses with the revenue of the same period and is consistent with generally accepted accounting principles (GAAP). The allowance method requires an adjusting entry at the end of the fiscal period debiting Bad Debts Expense and crediting Allowance for Doubtful Accounts for the estimated amount of bad debt losses for the period.

L.O. 1   Regarding the allowance method, three techniques were described for determining the amount of the adjusting entry: (1) aging the Accounts Receiv-

L.O. 2,3 able, (2) using a given percentage of Accounts Receivable, and (3) using a percentage of Sales or net sales. In the first two methods, the accountant makes the adjusting entry, then he or she brings the balance of Allowance for Doubtful Accounts up to the desired figure. The present balance of Allowance for Doubtful Accounts must be used in the calculation. When the

L.O. 4 method is based on a percentage of Sales or net sales, the accountant simply finds the percentage amount and uses that figure directly in the adjusting entry.

Also, under the allowance method, a company does not use the Bad Debts Expense account during the fiscal period, but only at the end of the period, to make an adjusting entry. The accountant then closes Bad Debts Expense immediately, along with the expense accounts. Bad Debts Expense appears in the income statement under the General Expense section of Operating Expenses. Allowance for Doubtful Accounts is a contra account, since it is a deduction from Accounts Receivable. It appears immediately below Accounts Receivable in the Current Assets section of the balance sheet.

L.O. 5   To write off a customer's account as being uncollectible, the accountant debits Allowance for Doubtful Accounts and credits Accounts Receivable. To re-

L.O. 6   instate an account previously written off, the accountant makes an entry which is the opposite of this entry.

L.O. 7   The specific charge-off method of accounting for bad debts is required for reporting on federal income tax returns. With this method, the accountant does not make any adjusting entry, and so does not use the Allowance for Doubtful Accounts account. When a company considers an account to be uncollectible, an entry is made debiting Bad Debts Expense and crediting

L.O. 8   Accounts Receivable. For any account written off previously and collected at a later time, the entry to reinstate the account is a debit to Accounts Receivable and a credit to Bad Debts Recovered (an Other Income account). A second entry is made debiting Cash and crediting Accounts Receivable.

GLOSSARY

Age (Accounts Receivable)   To analyze the composition of Accounts Receivable by classifying the outstanding balance of each charge customer's account according to the amount of time it has been outstanding. One can then multiply the totals for each time period by a percentage deemed to be uncollectible.

Allowance method of accounting for bad debt losses   An adjusting entry is required to debit Bad Debts Expense and to credit Allowance for Doubtful Accounts. Write-offs of uncollectible accounts are debited to Allowance for Doubtful Accounts and credited to Accounts Receivable.

Bankruptcy   A federal law excusing a debtor from certain obligations incurred.

Book value of Accounts Receivable   The balance of Accounts Receivable after one has deducted the balance of Allowance for Doubtful Accounts; also called the *net realizable value* of Accounts Receivable.

Specific charge-off method of accounting for bad debt losses   This method, used by small business firms, requires no adjusting entry. The accountant debits write-offs of uncollectible accounts to Bad Debts Expense and credits them to Accounts Receivable. This method is required for federal income tax reporting.

Statute of limitations   Laws that limit the period of time during which the courts may force a debtor to pay a debt; usually three years for charge accounts.

OMPUTERS AT WORK

Computerized Collection

Many companies have recently begun to pay more attention to collecting on overdue accounts receivable. More people are using more credit, in part as a result of the rise in home equity loans and the current ease with which many people can get credit cards. Companies are realizing that collecting on their receivables can do more for their cash flow than anything else. Credit departments of many large companies find themselves swamped in the paperwork that collection has traditionally required. For these and other reasons, many businesses are turning to computer systems to help them determine a customer's credit rating and collect on receivables.

Typically, a collection agent will have a terminal tied into the company's mainframe computer. From the company's data base, the agent can get information about the customer's payment history. Branch offices of the company may also supply such information, often computer-to-computer over phone lines. Outside services offer the agent information about the customer's credit history with other companies. The agent can also gather data about a customer's industry or peer group.

Armed with such information, the agent can start making calls. Working at a fully automated workstation, the agent can dial a number that's listed on the computer screen simply by pushing one key on the computer terminal. While talking to the delinquent customer, the agent can hit a single key to display "promise to pay" on the screen, allowing the agent to record any promises quickly and store them in the customer's file. Some collection agents use automatic dialers and taped messages that require only occasional human intervention.

The payoffs of moving to such a computerized system are large and often immediate. Individual collectors can handle from 30 to 75 percent more work. The company can reduce its collection personnel and still cut bad debt losses by up to 40 percent. A bank with a computerized accounts receivable system can make information about delinquent accounts available to all bank personnel, ensuring that a customer who's a bad credit risk won't be given another loan or allowed to cash a check. Computerized systems provide collectors with up-to-date information. They reduce the number of unnecessary calls, allow collectors to contact customers as soon as an account becomes overdue, and give collectors more thorough knowledge of delinquent customers' patterns. Faced with recent challenges to prove that they have been fair in denying a customer credit, companies can count on their computers to remember the truth, the whole truth.

Sources: Daniel A. Hosage, "Automated Workstations Raise Productivity," *Business Credit*, January 1988, 24–27; John S. Sargent, "Downloading for Credit Decision Support," *Business Credit*, January 1988, 33–36; Beth Stetenfeld, "Collection Connection," *Credit Union Management*, January 1988, 23–24.

QUESTIONS, EXERCISES, AND PROBLEMS

Discussion Questions

1. For each item stated below, indicate whether it would appear on an income statement or a balance sheet and under what heading it should be shown:

   a. Interest Receivable
   b. Bad Debts Expense
   c. Notes Payable
      (due in ten months)
   d. Allowance for Doubtful Accounts
   e. Discount on Notes Payable
   f. Interest Payable

2. What do accountants mean when they talk about the matching principle?
3. Explain the nature of Allowance for Doubtful Accounts, how it comes into existence, and what happens to it.
4. Describe the process of aging Accounts Receivable.
5. In what situation would Allowance for Doubtful Accounts have a debit balance?
6. How is the book value of Accounts Receivable figured?
7. Why is the allowance method of handling bad debts considered more effective than the specific charge-off method? Is the specific charge-off method ever acceptable?
8. When an account is written off under the allowance method of accounting for bad debts, why doesn't the book value of Accounts Receivable decrease?

Exercises

L.O. 2   **Exercise 18-1**   The Russo Company analyzed its Accounts Receivable balances on December 31 and determined the following aged balances:

Age Interval	Balance	Estimated Percentage Uncollectible
Not yet due	$100,000	1
30 to 60 days past due	20,000	2
61 to 120 days past due	8,000	5
121 to 365 days past due	2,000	30
More than 1 year past due	4,600	60
	$134,600	

The credit balance of Allowance for Doubtful Accounts is $2,050. What is the adjusting entry for estimated credit losses on December 31?

L.O. 1,3   **Exercise 18-2**   The Vinyard Company uses the allowance method of handling losses from bad debts. Vinyard Company considers estimated losses to be 3 percent of Accounts Receivable. On December 31 the Accounts Receivable balance was $82,000, and Allowance for Doubtful Accounts had a credit balance of $214. Journalize the adjusting entry to record the estimated bad debt losses.

L.O. 1,4   **Exercise 18-3**   The Roman Company uses the allowance method of handling losses due to bad debts. On December 31, before any adjustments have been recorded, the ledger contains the following balances:

Sales	$160,000
Sales Returns and Allowances	19,000

The company estimates that bad debt losses will be ½ percent of net sales. Journalize the adjusting entry to record the estimated bad debt losses. The Allowance for Doubtful Accounts account has a credit balance of $210.

L.O. 1,4   **Exercise 18-4**   At the end of the year, the Tenney Company's Accounts Receivable account has a balance of $92,000. Net sales for the year total $996,000. Present the adjusting entry to record the estimated bad debt losses under each of the following conditions. Assume that Allowance for Doubtful Accounts has a credit balance of $627.

a. Analysis of the charge accounts in the accounts receivable ledger indicates doubtful accounts of $5,240.
b. Bad debt losses are estimated at ½ percent of net sales.

L.O. 1,4   **Exercise 18-5**   With reference to Exercise 18-4, determine the amount of the Tenney Company's entry to record the estimated bad debt losses and make the entry under each of the following conditions.

a. Analysis of the charge accounts in the accounts receivable ledger indicates doubtful accounts of $4,862.
b. Bad debt losses are estimated at ¾ percent of net sales.

L.O. 1,4,5,6   **Exercise 18-6**   Hobby-Time Plaster Crafts had the following transactions this year. Assuming that Hobby-Time Plaster Crafts uses the allowance method of accounting for bad debt losses, record the three transactions in general journal form. The present balance of Allowance for Doubtful Accounts is a credit balance of $346.

a. Wrote off the account of C. Sutter as uncollectible, $164.
b. Reinstated the account of L. Bradey that had been written off during the preceding year, $54; received $54 cash in full payment.
c. Estimated bad debt losses to be 1 percent of sales of $76,200.

L.O. 7   **Exercise 18-7**   With reference to Exercise 18-6 assume that Hobby-Time Plaster Crafts uses the specific charge-off method of accounting for bad debt losses. Record transactions **a** and **b** in general journal form.

L.O. 5   **Exercise 18-8**   Record the following transactions in general journal form for the Sykes Company; these transactions occurred during this fiscal year:

Jan.   10 Sold merchandise to C. R. Sutcliff on account, $5,260; terms, 2/10, n/30.
         18 Received a check from C. R. Sutcliff in settlement of her account.

Mar.   19 Sold merchandise on account to M. O. James, $4,200; terms, 2/10, n/30.

Apr.   19 Received a 90-day, 10 percent note, dated this day, from M. O. James in settlement of his account, $4,200.

May   19 Discounted James's note at the bank; the bank levied a discount rate of 8 percent.

July   18 James dishonored his note previously discounted. The Sykes Company paid the bank the principal, plus interest, plus a protest fee of $4.

Dec.   27 Wrote off the account of M. O. James as worthless. Assume Sykes Company uses the allowance method of providing for bad debt losses.

Problem Set A

L.O. 1

Problem 18-1A   The balance sheet prepared by D. H. Allen, Inc., for December 31 of last year includes $206,400 in Accounts Receivable and $12,192 (credit) in Allowance for Doubtful Accounts. The following transactions occurred during January of this year:

a. Sales of merchandise on account, $193,400.

b. Sales returns and allowances related to sales of merchandise on account, $5,027.

c. Cash payments by charge customers (no cash discounts), $181,946.

d. Accounts Receivable from Sims and Towne written off as uncollectible, $1,216.

e. By the process of aging Accounts Receivable, on January 31 it was decided that Allowance for Doubtful Accounts should be adjusted to a balance of $19,412.

f. Closed Bad Debts Expense account.

Instructions

1. Record the entries in general journal form. Record the letter in the Date column.

2. Record the balance in Allowance for Doubtful Acounts.

3. Post the appropriate journal entries to the accounts for Allowance for Doubtful Accounts and Bad Debts Expense.

L.O. 1,2,5

Problem 18-2A   Johnson Company uses the aging method of estimating bad debts as of December 31, the end of the fiscal year. Terms of sales are net 30 days. While in the process of completing the aging schedule, the accountant became very ill and was unable to finish the job. The accountant's report, as far as she had done it, appears as follows:

Customer Name	Balance	Not Yet Due	Days Past Due			
			1–30	31–60	61–90	More than 90
Balance Forward	$389,900	$249,200	$76,280	$38,848	$15,032	$10,540

The accountant had the following accounts left to analyze:

Account	Amount	Due Date
B. Finch	$3,840	November 28
L. Flanagan	920	January 16 (next year)
C. Giller	6,480	November 6
L. Hernandez	9,420	January 27 (next year)
P. Lamb	3,700	September 20
C. Newman	1,160	October 16

From past experience, the company has found that the following rates of estimated uncollectible accounts produce an adequate balance for Allowance for Doubtful Accounts:

Time Past Due	Estimated Percentage Uncollectible
Not yet due	2
1–30 days	4
31–60 days	20
61–90 days	30
Over 90 days	50

Prior to aging Accounts Receivable, Allowance for Doubtful Accounts has a credit balance of $4,346.

Instructions

1. Enter the forward balances and complete the aging schedule.
2. Complete the table for estimating an allowance for doubtful accounts.
3. Record the adjusting entry in general journal form.

L.O. 1,4,5,6   **Problem 18-3A**   On January 1 of this year, Noss Company's Allowance for Doubtful Accounts account had a $1,926 credit balance. During the year Noss Company completed the following transactions:

Feb.   10 Wrote off the $654 account of Newton Company; the company had gone out of business, leaving no assets.

May   5 Wrote off the account of C. Tidwell as uncollectible, $348.32.

18 Received $182 unexpectedly from C. Weiss. The account had been written off two years earlier. Reinstated the account for $182 and recorded the collection of $182.

Aug.   3 Collected 10 percent of the $252 owed by C. C. Mack, a bankrupt. Wrote off the remainder as worthless.

Sept.   21 Received $180 from C. Tidwell as part payment of the account written off on May 5. He wrote a letter stating that he expects to pay the balance in the near future. Accordingly, reinstated the account for the amount of the original obligation, $348.32.

Dec.   29 Journalized a compound entry to write off the following accounts: N. C. Allen, $352.40; R. L. Barnes, $248.72; C. Ellis, $228.

         31 Recorded the adjusting entry for estimated bad debt losses at $1/2$
percent of charge sales of $303,426.

         31 Closed the Bad Debts Expense account.

Instructions

1. Record the opening balance in the ledger account of Allowance for
Doubtful Accounts.
2. Record the entries in general journal form.
3. Post the entries to ledger accounts for Allowance for Doubtful Accounts
and Bad Debts Expense.

L.O. 1,2,5,6   **Problem 18-4A**   The following are among the transactions completed by
Wheeler Building Supplies this year:

Jan.   7 Sold merchandise on account to B. O. Webster, $1,480.

Feb.   6 Wrote off the account of Malo, Inc., $1,211.17. The company
went out of business, leaving no assets to attach.

        6 Received a note from B. O. Webster, $1,480, 9 percent, 60 days,
in settlement of the sale of January 7. The note is dated February
6.

Mar.   12 Reinstated the account of L. Ward that had been written off in
the preceding year; received $217.16 in full payment.

Apr.   7 B. O. Webster dishonored his note today. Charged principal plus
interest to Accounts Receivable.

Aug.   17 Received $144 unexpectedly from C. P. Beech. The account had
been written off last year in the amount of $144. Reinstated the
account and recorded the collection of $144.

Sept.   27 Received 10 percent of the $1,502.20 balance owed by B. O. Web-
ster from the referee in bankruptcy and wrote off the remainder
as worthless.

Oct.   15 Reinstated the account of Dahl and Son that had been written off
two years earlier and received $749.30 in full payment.

Dec.   29 Journalized a compound entry to write off the following accounts
as uncollectible: D. C. Lang, $328; R. R. Mann, $752.28; N.
Shearer, $1,274.41; D. Terry, $1,562.15.

       31 On the basis of an analysis of Accounts Receivable, which
amounted to $87,811.14, estimated that $4,991 will be uncollectible. Recorded the adjusting entry.

       31 Recorded the entry to close the appropriate account to Income
Summary.

Instructions

1. Open the following accounts, recording the credit balance as of January 1
of this fiscal year:

114 Allowance for Doubtful Accounts $5,272.36
313 Income Summary   _____
542 Bad Debts Expense   _____

2. Journalize in general journal form the transactions as well as the adjusting and closing entries described above. After each entry, post to the three selected ledger accounts.

3. Prepare the Current Assets section of the balance sheet. Other pertinent accounts are: Cash, $12,621.42; Merchandise Inventory, $144,567; Supplies, $1,940.50; Prepaid Insurance, $756.

Problem Set B

L.O. 1 CO **Problem 18-1B** On December 31 of last year, the accountant for Bristol, Inc., prepared a balance sheet that included $197,900 in Accounts Receivable and $12,618 (credit) in Allowance for Doubtful Accounts. Selected transactions occurred during January of this year, as follows:

a. Sales of merchandise on account, $181,900.

b. Sales returns and allowances related to sales of merchandise on account, $4,922.

c. Cash payments by charge customers (no cash discounts), $168,461.24.

d. Accounts Receivable from Cooke Company written off as uncollectible, $1,217.27.

e. By the process of aging Accounts Receivable, on January 31 it was decided that Allowance for Doubtful Accounts should be adjusted to a balance of $20,011.14.

f. Closed Bad Debts Expense account.

Instructions

1. Record the entries in general journal form.

2. Record the balance in Allowance for Doubtful Accounts.

3. Post the appropriate entries to the accounts for Allowance for Doubtful Accounts and Bad Debts Expense.

L.O. 1,2,5 **Problem 18-2B** Malcolm Company uses the aging method of estimating bad debts as of December 31, the end of the fiscal year. Terms of sales are net 30 days. While preparing the aging schedule, the accountant became very ill and was unable to finish the job. The accountant's report, as complete as he left it, appears as follows:

Customer Name	Balance	Not Yet Due	Days Past Due			
			1–30	31–60	61–90	More than 90
Balance Forward	$352,292	$192,800	$94,400	$37,452	$14,960	$12,680

The accountant still had to analyze the accounts shown at the top of page 602.

Account	Amount	Due Date
P. Noss	$3,480	January 12 (next year)
R. Novak	2,360	December 22
L. Pomeroy	7,820	November 2
C. Quinn	8,280	August 18
T. Renn	1,520	December 3
P. Roma	1,160	January 22 (next year)

From past experience, the company has found that the following rates of estimated uncollectible accounts produce an adequate balance for Allowance for Doubtful Accounts:

Time Past Due	Estimated Percentage Uncollectible
Not yet due	2
1–30 days	4
31–60 days	20
61–90 days	30
Over 90 days	50

Prior to aging the accounts receivable, Allowance for Doubtful Accounts has a credit balance of $7,248.

Instructions

1. Enter the forward balances and complete the aging schedule.
2. Complete the table for estimating an allowance for doubtful accounts.
3. Write the adjusting entry in general journal form.

L.O. 1,4,5,6   **Problem 18-3B**   On January 1 of this year, Ronald's Wholesale Meats had a credit balance of $4,234 in Allowance for Doubtful Accounts. During the year, the company completed the following selected transactions:

Feb.   8 Wrote off as uncollectible a $432 account of Seaforth Market, which had gone out of business, leaving no assets.

May   3 Wrote off the account of Marci's Catering as uncollectible, $250.80.

     17 Collected 5 percent of the $1,444 owed by Lee Company, a bankrupt. Wrote off the remainder as worthless.

Aug.   2 Received $228.40 unexpectedly from Day Company, whose account had been written off two years earlier. Reinstated the account for $228.40 and recorded the collection.

Sept.   11 Received $162 from Marci's Catering as part of the account written off on May 3. She wrote a letter saying that she expects to pay the balance soon. Accordingly, reinstated the account for the amount of the original obligation, $250.80.

Dec.   30 Journalized a compound entry to write off the following accounts as uncollectible: C. D. Finch, $384.32; Southway Inn, $272.82; Hall's Drive-In, $566.30.

        31 Recorded the adjusting entry for estimated bad debt losses at ½ percent of charge sales of $584,260.

        31 Closed the Bad Debts Expense account.

Instructions

1. Record the balance in the ledger accounts of Allowance for Doubtful Accounts.
2. Record entries in general journal form.
3. Post entries to the ledger accounts for Allowance for Doubtful Accounts and Bad Debts Expense.

L.O. 1,2,5,6   **Problem 18-4B**   The following transactions were among those completed by Caldwell Wholesale Jewelers this year:

Jan.   6 Sold merchandise on account to Castle Jewelers, $1,216.

Feb.   15 Wrote off as uncollectible the account of Malin, Inc., $1,412.50. This company had gone out of business, leaving no assets to attach.

        17 Received a note dated February 17 from Castle Jewelers for $1,216, 8 percent, 60 days, in settlement of the sale of January 6.

Mar.   14 Reinstated the account of Golding, Inc., which had been written off in the preceding year; received $372.12 in full of account.

Apr.   18 Castle Jewelers dishonored their note due today. Charged principal plus interest to Accounts Receivable.

July   27 Received $214.26 unexpectedly from Craig and Son, whose account had been written off last year in the amount of $214.26. Reinstated the account and recorded the collection of $214.26.

Sept.   4 Received 10 percent of the $1,232.21 balance owed by Castle Jewelers from the referee in bankruptcy and wrote off the remainder as worthless.

Oct.   14 Reinstated the account of C. P. Stewart that had been written off two years earlier and received $614 in full payment.

Dec.   28 Journalized a compound entry to write off as uncollectible the following accounts: L. Browning, $315; C. Godfrey, $332.16; Engle and Burns, $716.42; Gable Jewelry, $2,739.60.

        31 On the basis of an analysis of Accounts Receivable of $184,164.22, estimated that $5,514 will be uncollectible. Recorded the adjusting entry.

        31 Recorded the entry to close the appropriate account to Income Summary.

Instructions

1. Open the following accounts, recording the credit balance as of January 1 of this fiscal year:

114 Allowance for Doubtful Accounts $5,112.16

313 Income Summary   _____

542 Bad Debts Expense   _____

2. Record in general journal form the transactions as well as the adjusting and closing entries described above. After each entry, post to the three selected ledger accounts.

3. Prepare the Current Assets section of the balance sheet. Other pertinent accounts are: Cash, $14,782.41; Notes Receivable, $2,720; Merchandise Inventory, $321,417; Supplies, $1,796.41; Prepaid Insurance, $720.

19 Accounting for Valuation of Inventories

LEARNING OBJECTIVES
After you have completed this chapter, you will be able to do the following:

1. Determine the understatement or overstatement of cost of merchandise sold, gross profit, and net income resulting from a change in the ending merchandise inventory amount.

2. Determine unit cost, the value of the ending inventory, and the cost of merchandise sold by the following methods: (a) specific identification, (b) weighted-average cost, (c) first-in, first-out, and (d) last-in, first-out.

3. Journalize transactions relating to perpetual inventories.

4. Complete a perpetual inventory record card.

One of the most important aspects of the operation of any merchandising business is the accounting for, and valuation of, the merchandise in stock. Let us look back briefly at what we have said so far. We defined *merchandise inventory* as goods purchased by the company and held for resale to customers in the ordinary course of business. We pictured Merchandise Inventory and related T accounts as follows:

Assets		Revenue		Expenses	
+	−	−	+	+	−

Merchandise Inventory		Sales		Purchases	
+	−	−	+	+	−
Record only as an adjusting entry at end of fiscal period			Record the sale of merchandise at its selling price	Record the purchase at its cost	

	Sales Returns and Allowances		Purchases Returns and Allowances
+ Record the return of or allowance on merchandise previously sold at its selling price	−	−	+ Record the return of or allowance on merchandise previously purchased at its cost

	Sales Discount		Purchases Discount
+ Record cash discounts taken by customers	−	−	+ Record cash discounts taken on buying merchandise

	Freight In
+ Record freight charges on incoming merchandise shipments at cost	−

We have assumed that firms take a physical inventory at the end of their fiscal periods. At this time, the most up-to-date figure is included in the Adjustments columns of the work sheet. As we discussed in Chapter 15, Merchandise Inventory involves two adjusting entries:

a. The first one closes off or "reverses out" the value of the beginning merchandise inventory.
b. The second adds in the value of the ending merchandise inventory.

Assume that a firm has a beginning merchandise inventory amounting to $84,000. The cost of the ending merchandise inventory is $92,000. The adjustment was first described by T accounts as follows:

Merchandise Inventory				Income Summary			
+		−		(a)	84,000	(b)	92,000
Bal.	84,000	(a)	84,000				
(b)	92,000						

The same adjustments appear in the work sheet.

In this example, the ending inventory figure of $92,000 is given. However, in a practical business situation, the cost of the ending inventory must be determined. Counting the goods on hand is a relatively easy but time-consuming procedure compared with the more difficult task of assigning a dollar amount to them in a time of changing prices. We will talk mainly about the Merchandise Inventory account because of its relative importance. However, the same principle applies to other assets, such as supplies for a service business or raw materials for a manufacturer.

We are going to tackle the valuation of inventories in two ways: First, some merchandising firms take a physical inventory of merchandise on hand and then attach a value to it. This is known as a **periodic inventory system,** as shown in the example above involving the two adjusting entries for Merchandise Inventory. Second, other merchandising firms keep running records of inventories by recording all transactions, so that at any given time they know what they have on hand and the current cost of each item. This is known as a **perpetual inventory system**.

THE IMPORTANCE OF INVENTORY VALUATION

Objective 1

Determine the understatement or overstatement of cost of merchandise sold, gross profit, and net income resulting from a change in the ending merchandise inventory amount.

Merchandise Inventory is the only account that can appear on both major financial statements. On the balance sheet, it appears under Current Assets. On the income statement, it is listed under Cost of Merchandise Sold. Why is the valuation of merchandise inventory so important? In many business firms, merchandise inventory is the asset with the largest dollar amount. Likewise, as a part of Cost of Merchandise Sold, it vitally affects the net income because the Cost of Merchandise Sold is the largest deduction from Sales. As a result, inventory determination plays an important role in matching costs with revenue for a given period.

Differing costs of ending merchandise inventory have a dramatic effect on net income. We can see this in the partial income statements that follow (Figures 19-1 through 19-4).

FIGURE 19-1

YEAR 1

Sales (net)		$ 203 0 0 0 00
Cost of Merchandise Sold:		
Merchandise Inventory (beginning)	$ 84 0 0 0 00	
Purchases (net)	160 0 0 0 00	
Merchandise Available for Sale	$ 244 0 0 0 00	
Less Merchandise Inventory (ending)	92 0 0 0 00	
Cost of Merchandise Sold		152 0 0 0 00
Gross Profit		$ 51 0 0 0 00
Expenses		30 0 0 0 00
Net Income		$ 21 0 0 0 00

Now assume that instead of setting $92,000 as the value for ending merchandise inventory, one could quite legally set its value at $82,000. The result would be a net income of only $11,000 (Figure 19-2), instead of $21,000. Of course, this would result in lower income taxes as well.

FIGURE 19-2

YEAR I

Sales (net)			$ 203 0 0 0 00
Cost of Merchandise Sold:			
Merchandise Inventory (beginning)	$ 84 0 0 0 00		
Purchases (net)	160 0 0 0 00		
Merchandise Available for Sale	$ 244 0 0 0 00		
Less Merchandise Inventory (ending)	82 0 0 0 00		
Cost of Merchandise Sold		162 0 0 0 00	
Gross Profit		$ 41 0 0 0 00	
Expenses		30 0 0 0 00	
Net Income		$ 11 0 0 0 00	

From Figures 19-1 and 19-2 we can see that if the ending merchandise inventory is overstated (too high) by $10,000, the net income will be overstated (too high) by $10,000, because the two are directly proportional to each other. Similarly, **if the ending merchandise inventory is understated (too low), net income will be understated (too low).**

But there is something else you have to take into account. Since the *ending* inventory of one year becomes the *beginning* inventory of the following year, the net income of the following year is also affected, but in an opposite manner. Let's continue with our example into year 2. The $92,000 *ending* inventory of year 1 becomes the *beginning* inventory of year 2 (Figure 19-3).

FIGURE 19-3

YEAR 2

Sales (net)			$ 236 0 0 0 00
Cost of Merchandise Sold:			
Merchandise Inventory (beginning)	$ 92 0 0 0 00		
Purchases (net)	184 0 0 0 00		
Merchandise Available for Sale	$ 276 0 0 0 00		
Less Merchandise Inventory (ending)	100 0 0 0 00		
Cost of Merchandise Sold		176 0 0 0 00	
Gross Profit		$ 60 0 0 0 00	
Expenses		35 0 0 0 00	
Net Income		$ 25 0 0 0 00	

Look at Figure 19-4 to see what happens when the $82,000 ending inventory of year 1 becomes the beginning inventory of year 2.

FIGURE 19-4

YEAR 2

Sales (net)		$ 236 0 0 0 00
Cost of Merchandise Sold:		
Merchandise Inventory (beginning)	$ 82 0 0 0 00	
Purchases (net)	184 0 0 0 00	
Merchandise Available for Sale	$ 266 0 0 0 00	
Less Merchandise Inventory (ending)	100 0 0 0 00	
Cost of Merchandise Sold		166 0 0 0 00
Gross Profit		$ 70 0 0 0 00
Expenses		35 0 0 0 00
Net Income		$ 35 0 0 0 00

We can see that if the beginning merchandise inventory is overstated by $10,000, the net income will be understated by $10,000 because the two are inversely proportional to each other. Similarly, **if the beginning merchandise inventory is understated, net income will be overstated.**

In other words, over a two-year period, the net income will be correct, since the overstatement of one year cancels out the understatement of the following year, and vice versa. We can summarize all this as shown in the following table:

Year	Ending Inventory of $92,000	Ending Inventory of $82,000
	Net Income	Net Income
1	$21,000	$11,000
2	25,000	35,000
Total	$46,000	$46,000

If *ending* inventory is *overstated*, net income for the period will be *overstated*.

If *ending* inventory is *understated*, net income for the period will be *understated*.

If *beginning* inventory is *overstated*, net income for the period will be *understated*.

If *beginning* inventory is *understated*, net income for the period will be *overstated*.

THE NEED FOR INVENTORIES

Firms that want to satisfy their customers have to maintain large and varied inventories because naturally all of us would rather shop in stores that offer a wide selection. This assumes, of course, that the firm does not run out of goods at the end of the year. The successful firm has to buy enough merchandise in advance to satisfy the demands of its customers. Efficient purchasing also dictates that the firm take advantage of quantity discounts as well as special buys of seasonal or distressed goods. So, well-run business firms keep fairly large stocks of merchandise on hand at all times.

Taking a Physical Inventory

Many merchandising firms, at a given moment in time, possess no record that shows the exact quantity and cost of merchandise on hand. They do make spot checks from time to time as part of inventory control, but they can determine *exact* amounts only by physically counting the goods on hand. Even stores that use computers or other means to maintain a perpetual inventory system need to take a physical inventory from time to time. Stores that carry a particularly wide array of merchandise in large amounts wait until their stock is reasonably low before they attempt to count it. Many department stores, for example, take a physical inventory of their stock toward the end of January, after the holiday rush and the postholiday special sales.

When they do take inventory, firms use various procedures and internal checks to be certain that they do not miss any items or include any items more than once. Usually employees work in pairs, with one person counting the items and the other recording the information on inventory schedules. Companies frequently use a system of tagging or marking bins or shelves. An inventory tag lists the type of item, size, and number of units in the inventory count. Some firms use an electronic recorder. As part of internal control, people from the management level may make spot checks on the inventory counts. Most firms take inventory after regular business hours and record data on inventory sheets, such as the one shown in Figure 19-5 for City-Wide Electric Supply.

When people take inventory, they must be careful to count only goods belonging to the firm. They must exclude goods that have been sold and are awaiting shipment, as well as goods held on a consignment basis. Merchandise sold on the basis of FOB destination should be included in the ending inventory of the seller while it is being transported, since the seller is paying the freight charges and thus still has title. Sometimes a firm must also count goods that it does not have on hand. This situation occurs when the supplier has turned the goods over to a transportation company and the goods are shipped FOB shipping point. Remember, this means that the buyer is paying the freight charges and as a result normally has title to the goods.

INVENTORY

DATE *January 2, 19–*   SHEET NO. *326*

CALLED BY *Jack Lyon*   COSTED BY *H. H. C*

ENTERED BY *Tom Peterson*   METHOD OF COSTING *LIFO*

DEPARTMENT *Fittings*   EXTENDED BY *J. C.*

LOCATION *Store & Warehouse*   EXAMINED BY *M. R.*

DESCRIPTION	QUANTITY	UNIT	UNIT COST	EXTENSIONS	TOTAL COST
Reducing washers ¾" to ½"	273	ea.	67 @ .19 206 @ .23	$ 12.73 47.38	$ 60.11
1 ½" to 1 ¼"	319	ea.	146 @ .32 173 @ .38	46.72 65.74	112.46
Locknuts ¾"	976	ea.	200 @ .14 400 @ .16 376 @ .17	28.00 64.00 63.92	155.92
1 ¼"	818	ea.	600 @ .31 218 @ .32	186.00 69.76	255.76
1 ½"	149	ea.	149 @ .59	87.91	87.91
P81 covers	733	ea.	140 @ .33 593 @ .37	46.20 219.41	265.61
					$937.77

FIGURE 19-5

METHODS OF ASSIGNING COSTS TO ENDING INVENTORY

Objective 2

Determine unit cost, the value of the ending inventory, and the cost of merchandise sold by the following methods: (a) specific identification, (b) weighted-average cost, (c) first-in, first-out, and (d) last-in, first-out.

After the items are described and counted, the unit costs are inserted in the inventory sheet and the total costs are extended. How does one determine unit cost? You might think that this would be rather elementary. Indeed, it would be—*if* all the purchases of a given article had been made at the same price per unit. To determine the total unit cost, you would only need to look up one invoice, check the unit price, then multiply it by the number of items present. Simple! But nothing is ever that simple, unfortunately. Usually a firm buys a number of batches of a given item during the year, and—especially these days—the unit cost varies. A can of shoe polish that cost 80 cents in January may cost 90 cents in October. So which unit cost should one assign to the goods on hand?

There are four main methods of assigning costs to goods in the ending inventory: (1) specific identification, (2) weighted-average cost, (3) first-in, first-out, and (4) last-in, first-out.

Inventory Evaluation: Example I   City-Wide Electric Supply keeps an inventory of electric safety switches (3 phase, 240 volt, 60 amp) purchased from Adkins Manufacturing Company. This year City-Wide Electric sells eighty of these switches and has twenty-six remaining in stock. The company started out the year with twenty-two in stock, and bought more as the year went by, as follows:

Jan. 1	Beginning inventory	22 units @ $57 each = $1,254
Mar. 16	Purchase	30 units @ 62 each = 1,860
July 29	Purchase	36 units @ 65 each = 2,340
Nov. 18	Purchase	18 units @ 68 each = 1,224
	Total available	106 units $6,678

Now let's compute the cost of merchandise sold (eighty safety switches) and the value of the ending inventory (twenty-six safety switches). We will use the four different methods.

Specific Identification

When a firm sells big-ticket items (cars, appliances, furniture, jewelry, and so forth), it can keep track of the purchase price of each individual article and determine the exact cost of the merchandise sold. Such a firm uses the **specific-identification method** of inventory control. Because the safety switches have imprinted manufacture date codes, City-Wide Electric can identify each switch with a separate purchase invoice listing the unit cost. When City-Wide Electric takes inventory at the end of the year, it finds that there are twenty-six safety switches left in stock; four of these were bought in March, ten were bought in July, and twelve were bought in November. Costs are assigned to the ending inventory as follows:

Mar. 16	Purchase	4 units @ $62 each = $ 248
July 29	Purchase	10 units @ 65 each = 650
Nov. 18	Purchase	12 units @ 68 each = 816
	Total	26 units $1,714

City-Wide Electric Supply determines the cost of merchandise sold by subtracting the value of the ending inventory from the total available for sale:

Total safety switches available (106 units)	$6,678
Less ending inventory (26 units)	1,714
Cost of merchandise sold (80 units)	$4,964

Weighted-Average Cost

An alternative to keeping track of the cost of each item purchased is to find the **weighted-average cost** per unit of all like articles available for sale during the period. First, City-Wide Electric finds the total cost of the safety switches it had on hand during the year by multiplying the number of units by their respective purchase costs.

Jan. 1	Beginning inventory	22 units @ $57 each = $1,254
Mar. 16	Purchase	30 units @ 62 each = 1,860
July 29	Purchase	36 units @ 65 each = 2,340
Nov. 18	Purchase	18 units @ 68 each = 1,224
	Total available	106 units $6,678

Next City-Wide Electric finds the average cost per switch.

$6,678 ÷ 106 units = $63 average cost per unit

Value of ending inventory = 26 units × $63 each = $1,638

Cost of merchandise sold = 80 units × $63 each = $5,040

According to this method, the beginning inventory is *weighted* (that is, multiplied by the number of units it comprises). Each purchase thereafter is weighted by the number of units involved in that purchase. In other words, the more you buy at a time, the more that purchase influences the average cost.

First-In, First-Out (FIFO) Method

Remember

First-in, first-out refers to the way goods are sold. The ending inventory consists of those items purchased most recently.

The **first-in, first-out (FIFO) method** is based on the flow-of-cost assumption that merchandise sold should be charged against revenue in the order in which the costs were incurred. To determine the cost of merchandise sold, the accountant records the first (oldest) cost first, then the next-oldest cost, and so on. First-in, first-out is a logical way for a firm to rotate its stock of merchandise. Think of a grocery store selling milk. Because milk will sour, the oldest milk is moved up to the front of the shelf. As a result, the ending inventory consists of the freshest milk.

Again, let us return to City-Wide Electric's safety switches. To repeat, 106 safety switches were available for sale during the year:

Jan. 1	Beginning inventory	22 units @ $57 each = $1,254
Mar. 16	Purchase	30 units @ 62 each = 1,860
July 29	Purchase	36 units @ 65 each = 2,340
Nov. 18	Purchase	18 units @ 68 each = 1,224
	Total available	106 units $6,678

City-Wide Electric sold eighty units. The accountant calculates the total cost of the switches on a first-in, first-out (FIFO) basis, like this:

Jan. 1	Beginning inventory	22 units @ $57 each = $1,254
Mar. 16	Purchase	30 units @ 62 each = 1,860
July 29	Purchase	28 units @ 65 each = 1,820
	Total	80 units $4,934

City-Wide Electric has the twenty-six newest or most recently purchased units on hand in the ending inventory. The accountant records the ending inventory at the most recent costs, like this:

Nov. 18	Purchase	18 units @ $68 each = $1,224
July 29	Purchase	8 units @ 65 each = 520
	Total	26 units $1,744

The accountant now verifies the total cost of the eighty units sold:

Total available − Ending inventory = Cost of merchandise sold
$6,678 − $1,744 = \underline{$4,934}

Last-in, First-Out (LIFO) Method

The **last-in, first-out (LIFO) method** is based on the flow-of-cost assumption that the most recently purchased articles are sold first and the articles remaining in the ending inventory are the oldest items. As an example, think of a coal yard selling coal. When the coal yard buys coal from its supplier, the new coal is added to the top of the pile. When the coal yard sells coal to its customer, coal is taken off the top of the pile. Consequently, the ending inventory consists of those first few tons at the bottom of the pile. And unless the pile is exhausted, they will never be sold.

Meanwhile, back at City-Wide Electric, the firm sold eighty units. The accountant calculates the cost of the switches on a last-in, first-out (LIFO) basis:

Remember

Last-in, first-out refers to the way goods are sold. The ending inventory consists of the items purchased earliest.

Nov. 18	Purchase	18 units @ $68 each = $1,224
July 29	Purchase	36 units @ 65 each = 2,340
Mar. 16	Purchase	26 units @ 62 each = 1,612
	Total	80 units $5,176

City-Wide Electric has the twenty-six oldest units (or the units at the bottom of the pile) on hand in the ending inventory. The accountant records the ending inventory at the earliest costs, like this:

Jan. 1	Beginning inventory	22 units @ $57 each = $1,254
Mar. 16	Purchase	4 units @ 62 each = 248
	Total	26 units $1,502

The accountant now verifies the total cost of the eighty units sold:

Total available − Ending inventory = Cost of merchandise sold
$6,678 − $1,502 = $5,176

Comparison of Methods

If prices don't change very much, all inventory methods give just about the same results. However, in a dynamic market where prices are constantly rising and falling, each method may yield different amounts. Here is a comparison of the results of the sale of the safety switches using the four methods we described:

Method	Cost of Merchandise Sold (80 Units)	Ending Inventory (26 Units)
Specific identification	$4,964	$1,714
Weighted-average cost	5,040	1,638
First-in, first-out	4,934	1,744
Last-in, first-out	5,176	1,502

Assume that City-Wide Electric sells the eighty safety switches for $90 apiece. The four methods yield the following gross profits:

	Specific Identification	Weighted-Average Cost	First-In, First-Out	Last-In, First-Out
Sales	$7,200	$7,200	$7,200	$7,200
Cost of merchandise sold	4,964	5,040	4,934	5,176
Gross profit	$2,236	$2,160	$2,266	$2,024

We can see from all this that the effects of the methods are as follows:

1. Specific identification matches costs exactly with revenues.
2. Weighted-average cost is a compromise between LIFO and FIFO, both for the amount of the ending inventory and for the cost of merchandise sold.
3. FIFO portrays the most realistic figure for ending merchandise inventory in the Current Assets section of the balance sheet. The ending inventory is valued at the most recent costs.
4. LIFO portrays the most realistic figure for the Cost of Merchandise Sold section of the income statement because the items that have been sold will have to be replaced at the most recent costs.

Concerning the specific identification method, for City-Wide Electric Supply we chose safety switches as a realistic example. Besides safety switches, it should be mentioned that the firm carries a variety of products. Consequently, keeping track of the cost of each item of product may prove difficult and costly. However, as we mentioned previously, for companies selling a few high-priced products, the specific identification method may be ideal. Additional examples are heavy construction equipment and boats.

Tax Effect of LIFO

In a period of rising prices, LIFO yields the lowest gross profit and hence the lowest income tax, because the most recent costs are assigned to the cost of merchandise sold. For the past forty years, prices have just kept going up in most industries, providing a built-in tax advantage for users of LIFO. In effect, the business is postponing paying taxes. Since the money is not paid to the government, the business has the use of this money. Consequently, the money saved can be used for financing more inventories or paying off interest-bearing debts. When prices fall, companies using LIFO are at a disadvantage from the standpoint of taxes.

Bear in mind that the cost figure determined by the different methods may have nothing to do with the physical flow of the goods. By physical flow, we mean the way that specific items are taken out of inventory and sold.

The **consistency principle** is a fundamental principle of accounting. We have seen that a firm can increase or decrease its gross profit, and likewise its net income and income tax, by changing the flow-of-cost assumption from one method to another—from FIFO to LIFO, for example. Although a firm may change its method of assigning inventory costs, it may not change back and forth repeatedly. Consistency in the method of determining cost of merchandise sold and the related cost of the ending inventory is necessary. For one thing, the government has said that a firm cannot switch back and forth in order to evade some of its income tax. In addition, the firm must stick to a single method of reporting in financial statements to its owners and creditors.

LOWER-OF-COST-OR-MARKET RULE

All the above methods for determining the cost of the ending inventory are based on the cost per unit. In our examples prices were generally rising. However, sometimes the replacement cost of items in stock is *less* than the original market cost. The word *market* refers to the current price charged in the market. It is the price at which, *at the time of taking the inventory*, the items could be bought through the usual channels and in the usual quantities. The current prices may be quoted in catalogs or reflect contract quotations.

The **lower-of-cost-or-market rule** says that under certain conditions when the replacement or market cost is lower than the original cost, the inventory should be valued at the lowest cost. For example, the inventory of a store consists of 20 ski parkas purchased originally for $22 each (total, $440). At the time the inventory is being taken, the same type of ski parkas may be purchased (replaced) for $18 each (total, $360). Under the lower-of-cost-or-market rule, the inventory is valued at $360. In this example, the original cost of $22 may have been determined by the specific-identification method, the weighted-average-cost method, or the FIFO method. Under the tax law, the cost may *not* be determined by the LIFO method, since this method already offers tax advantages.

PERPETUAL INVENTORIES

Objective 3

Journalize transactions relating to perpetual inventories.

Business firms such as equipment or appliance dealers that sell a limited variety of products of relatively high value maintain book records of their inventories on hand. They *record additions to or deductions from their inventories directly in Merchandise Inventory accounts*. This is known as the perpetual inventory system because the firms perpetually (or continually) *know* the *amount* of goods on hand. With computers, many firms have adopted the perpetual inventory system. This system involves the following accounts, as illustrated by T accounts:

Merchandise Inventory		Cost of Merchandise Sold		Sales	
+	−	+	−	−	+
Record the purchase of merchandise at cost	Record the sale of merchandise at cost	Record the sale of merchandise at cost			Record the sale of merchandise at selling price

The adjusting entries at the end of the year are the only entries firms using the periodic system make in Merchandise Inventory. But firms

using the perpetual inventory system make entries directly in the Merchandise Inventory account throughout the year. The perpetual inventory system enables the firm to do away with the Purchases and Purchases Returns and Allowances accounts.

To illustrate the perpetual inventory system, let's look at a series of entries in general journal form, with transactions recorded at the gross amount.

Feb.   14 Bought merchandise on account, from Dever, Inc.; 2/10, n/30; $800.

	DATE	DESCRIPTION	POST. REF.	DEBIT	CREDIT	
1	19–					1
2	Feb. 14	Merchandise Inventory		8 0 0 00		2
3		Accounts Payable, Dever, Inc.			8 0 0 00	3
4		Terms: 2/10, n/30.				4
5						5

Merchandise Inventory		Accounts Payable	
+	–	–	+
800			800

Feb.   24 Paid the invoice within the discount period.

	DATE	DESCRIPTION	POST. REF.	DEBIT	CREDIT	
1	19–					1
2	Feb. 24	Accounts Payable, Dever, Inc.		8 0 0 00		2
3		Cash			7 8 4 00	3
4		Purchases Discount			1 6 00	4
5		Paid invoice within discount				5
6		period.				6
7						7

Accounts Payable		Cash		Purchases Discount	
–	+	+	–	–	+
800			784		16

Mar.   5 Sold the merchandise on account to S. T. Dunn for $950. (The cost of the merchandise is $800. Two entries are required to record a sale under a perpetual inventory system.)

	DATE		DESCRIPTION	POST. REF.	DEBIT	CREDIT	
1	*19–*						1
2	*Mar.*	*5*	*Accounts Receivable, S. T. Dunn*		*9 5 0 00*		2
3			*Sales*			*9 5 0 00*	3
4			*Sold merchandise on account.*				4
5							5
6		*5*	*Cost of Merchandise Sold*		*8 0 0 00*		6
7			*Merchandise Inventory*			*8 0 0 00*	7
8			*Relating to $950 sale to*				8
9			*S. T. Dunn.*				9

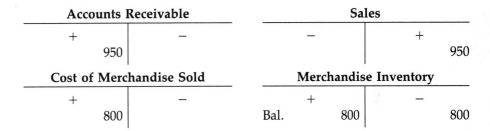

Accounts Receivable			Sales	
+	–		–	+
950				950

Cost of Merchandise Sold			Merchandise Inventory	
+	–		+	–
800		Bal.	800	800

For a firm using a perpetual inventory system, one can compare the Cost of Merchandise Sold account to an expense account: both are increased by debits, and both are closed at the end of the year.

Firms may take physical inventories both during and at the end of the year to verify the book value of the perpetual inventory. If there is a difference between the book value and the physical count, an adjustment is made to the Merchandise Inventory account. In this adjustment, Cost of Merchandise Sold is used as the off-setting account. Suppose the book value figure for Merchandise Inventory is $16,250 and the physical count shows $16,140 of merchandise on hand. The adjusting entry looks like this:

	DATE		DESCRIPTION	POST. REF.	DEBIT	CREDIT	
1	*19–*		*Adjusting Entry*				1
2	*June*	*30*	*Cost of Merchandise Sold*		*1 1 0 00*		2
3			*Merchandise Inventory*			*1 1 0 00*	3
4							4

When a firm uses the perpetual inventory system, Merchandise Inventory is a controlling account. The firm maintains an individual record in the subsidiary ledger for each kind of product, recording the number of units received as "units received" and the number of units sold as "units

Objective 4

Complete a perpetual
inventory record card.

sold." The firm records the remaining balance after each receipt or sale. Companies may keep perpetual inventories by any of the four methods we talked about. For example, assume City-Wide Electric Supply maintains a perpetual inventory on heaters, on a LIFO basis, as shown in Figure 19-6.

INVENTORY RECORD CARD

ITEM _Wall-mounted recessed heaters_   LOCATION _Warehouse Heater Section_

MAXIMUM _40_   MINIMUM _8_   METHOD _LIFO_

DATE	PURCHASED AT COST			COST OF MERCHANDISE SOLD			INVENTORY AT COST		
	UNITS	COST	TOTAL	UNITS	COST	TOTAL	UNITS	COST	TOTAL
1/2	Bal.						14	$72	$1,008
2/6				4	$72	$288	10	72	720
2/22	30	$75	$2,250				{ 10	72	720
							{ 30	75	2,250
3/14				6	75	450	{ 10	72	720
							{ 24	75	1,800
3/29				8	75	600	{ 10	72	720
							{ 16	75	1,200
Total	30	—	$2,250	18	—	$1,338	—	—	

FIGURE 19-6

The ending balance of twenty-six units amounts to $1,920 ($720 + $1,200). Assuming that the eighteen heaters were sold at $120 each for total sales of $2,160, gross profit is $822.

Sales (from sales journal)	$2,160
Less Cost of Merchandise Sold	1,338
Gross Profit	$ 822

The weighted-average-cost flow can be used with a perpetual inventory system. Rather than computing the average price for each inventory item at the end of a period, a new average is calculated each time a purchase is made. This average method is called a **moving average.** When goods are sold, their cost is determined by multiplying the number of units sold by the moving-average cost existing at that time. Further discussion of moving averages is reserved for more advanced accounting texts.

Perpetual-Inventory Records in Electronic Data Processing Accounting Systems

Several years ago, perpetual inventory systems were most appropriate for firms selling a limited variety of products of relatively high value. This was true because they had to depend on hand-operated techniques.

However, electronic computers—which have large data storage capacities and can retrieve an item of stored information in fractions of a second—have enabled business firms to maintain perpetual inventories involving a wide variety of products and a large volume of transactions. Let's take as an example an automobile parts distribution center. Think of the benefits a computer terminal would have for an auto parts store.

Each item of stock in the inventory is assigned a code number. Whenever the amounts of the items change, information concerning the changes is fed into the computer by means of an on-line data entry terminal. The computer performs the arithmetic operations and determines the new balance in accordance with the inventory method in use: LIFO, FIFO, or moving average. Thus the firm can determine the current status of any given item instantaneously. Whenever desired, the computer can list the balances of all the items in the inventory, in terms of both units and dollars. Some firms get such a listing or printout daily.

As another illustration, in many large department stores the cash registers (terminals) are linked directly to a computer center. When a sale is made, the salesclerk can punch in the item number, the quantity, and the price of the item being sold. In other stores clerks use a wand or gun to scan bar codes on individual tickets. And in supermarkets across the country, cashiers pass purchased items over scanners at the checkout register. With the information about the sale stored in the computer, management may obtain inventory quantities, costs, and total sales at any time.

Our discussion of perpetual inventories has been geared to merchandising firms. However, manufacturing concerns use perpetual inventories almost exclusively. A lumber mill, for example, uses the balances of daily inventories as a basis for deciding which sizes of lumber to cut: $2'' \times 4'' \times 8'$, $1'' \times 3'' \times 6'$, and so on.

SUMMARY

L.O. 1   The value of the merchandise inventory appears in the Cost of Merchandise Sold section of the income statement.

If the ending inventory is	Net income will be
Overstated	Overstated
Understated	Understated

If the beginning inventory is	Net income will be
Overstated	Understated
Understated	Overstated

The value of the ending merchandise inventory also appears in the Current Assets section of the balance sheet.

L.O. 2   There are four methods of determining the cost of the ending inventory:

1. Specific identification: Used for high-value items when a firm can identify each item on hand with its respective price.
2. Weighted-average cost: Number of units of each purchase × Unit price = Cost of each purchase. Cost of beginning inventory + Costs of each purchase = Total cost. Total cost ÷ Total units = Weighted-average cost per unit.
3. First-in, first-out (FIFO): Costs are charged against revenue in the order in which they were incurred. This method portrays the most realistic figure for the Current Assets section of the balance sheet.
4. Last-in, first-out (LIFO): Costs that are charged against revenue are the most recent costs. Emphasis is placed on the income statement. This method portrays the most realistic figure for the Cost of Merchandise Sold section of the income statement.

In an era of rising prices, the LIFO method yields the lowest net income. Firms must be consistent in their use of inventory methods.

L.O. 3   Perpetual inventories are book records of what a firm has in stock. The Merchandise Inventory account is a controlling account. Merchandise Inventory is debited when goods are bought and credited when goods are sold. Cost of Merchandise sold is a specific account, handled much like an expense account.

L.O. 4   Firms that use a perpetual inventory system keep track of each item bought or sold on a perpetual inventory card, if they are using a manual system, or in a computer file, if they are using a computerized system.

GLOSSARY

Consistency principle An accounting principle that requires that a particular accounting procedure, once adopted, will not be changed from one fiscal period to another fiscal period.

First-in, first-out (FIFO) method Process of assigning costs to merchandise sold, based on the flow-of-cost assumption that units are sold in the order in which they were acquired. Unsold units on hand at date of inventory are assumed to be valued at the most recent costs.

Last-in, first-out (LIFO) method Process of assigning costs to merchandise sold, based on the flow-of-cost assumption that units sold are recorded at the costs of the most recently acquired units. Unsold units on hand at date of inventory are assume to be valued at the earliest costs.

Lower-of-cost-or-market rule When there is a difference between the cost price and the market price of goods, the lower price is used for determining the value of the ending inventory. The term *market price* means current replacement price.

Moving average A modification of the weighted-average-cost method, used for computing the average cost of a perpetual inventory. The firm determines the moving-average unit price each time it buys more units.

Periodic inventory system Determining the amount of goods on hand by periodically taking a physical count and then attaching a value to it.

C●MPUTERS AT WORK

Managing with the Computer

At the beginning of the computer revolution, software programs tended to serve only one function, and often only specially trained users or programmers could work with them. Recently, however, software has been changing. Programs written for huge mainframe computers are being rewritten for microcomputers and their owners. They're becoming less specialized and more versatile, often linking different parts of a company's operations. Among the software providing links useful to an accountant are inventory control and data base management programs.

Besides the new technology that connects the cash register to the factory floor, there are many programs that allow a company to manufacture most efficiently. Modern "just-in-time" manufacturing techniques require suppliers to arrive at just the right moment with just the right amount of material. Such techniques virtually eliminate costly inventory, but they also require both manufacturers and suppliers to meet a high standard of reliability and efficiency. Inventory software allows management to track the records of its suppliers, noting which ones are most often on time with the highest quality of goods. It also monitors shop floor production and the use of supplies and finished goods both in the factory and in any of the company's remote locations, enabling management to continue perfecting the "just-in-time" process.

Such inventory tracking programs are just one of many types of data base management systems (DBMS). Originally, a DBMS was modeled on the principle of a manual filing system, allowing the user to enter data into various files and retrieve it in a variety of ways. As these systems have become more sophisticated, they have enabled users to retrieve information in more different ways, for more purposes. "We can slice the data from any conceivable angle," says the head of one software company.[1]

Besides increasing the software's ability to combine and format data in a variety of ways, software companies are also writing programs that anyone can understand and that don't require the user to know programming languages. They're competing to make new programs compatible with the leading spreadsheet and DBMS programs. With the integration of different kinds of software and hardware within a company, many businesses are approaching the day when anyone who needs information will be able to tap into one central data base and retrieve the information in the most useful form.

[1] Sopko, "Database Management Software," p. 80.

Sources: Robert Francis, "The Age of Friendly DBMSs Draws Closer for Micro Users," *Datamation,* January 15, 1988, 24–26; Larry Roches, "Keeping on Top of the Basics," *Systems 3X/World,* 54; Sandra Sopko, "Database Management Software: Tailor It," *The Office,* February 1988, 78–80.

Perpetual inventory system   A book record of the ending inventory showing the unit costs of the items received and the items sold. This gives the
firm a running balance of the inventory on hand and the current cost of
each item.

Specific-identification method   Counting the actual cost of each individual
item in the ending inventory.

Weighted-average cost   A method of determining the cost of the ending inventory by multiplying the weighted-average cost per unit by the number
of remaining units.

QUESTIONS, EXERCISES, AND PROBLEMS
Discussion Questions

1. List an advantage and a disadvantage of LIFO.
2. Explain how to calculate the weighted-average cost.
3. Due to an error, merchandise costing $2,600 was omitted from the ending
   inventory. What effect does the omission have on the company's gross
   profit?
4. What is the difference between the periodic (physical) system and the
   perpetual system of accounting for inventories?
5. When a perpetual inventory system is in use, what are the necessary
   journal entries for buying merchandise on account and selling merchandise on account?
6. In a perpetual inventory system, what happens to the Cost of Merchandise Sold account at the end of the fiscal period?
7. If the physical inventory count is less than the balance in the perpetual
   inventory record, what should be done about it?
8. What is meant by the specific identification method of pricing inventory?
   Give an example of a situation where this method would be suitable.

Exercises

L.O. 1   **Exercise 19-1**   Condensed income statements for Morrison Company for
two years are presented below:

			1991			1992
Sales (net)			$88 0 0 0 00			$80 0 0 0 00
Cost of Merchandise Sold:						
Beginning Merchandise Inventory	$14 0 0 0 00			$12 0 0 0 00		
Purchases (net)	48 0 0 0 00			46 0 0 0 00		
Merchandise Available for Sale	$62 0 0 0 00			$58 0 0 0 00		
Less Ending Merchandise Inventory	12 0 0 0 00			13 0 0 0 00		
Cost of Merchandise Sold			50 0 0 0 00			45 0 0 0 00
Gross Profit			$38 0 0 0 00			$35 0 0 0 00
Operating Expenses			18 0 0 0 00			17 0 0 0 00
Net Income			$20 0 0 0 00			$18 0 0 0 00

After the end of 1992, it was discovered that an error had been made in 1991. Ending inventory in 1991 should have been $10,000 instead of $12,000. Determine the corrected net income for 1991 and 1992. What is the amount of the total net income for the two-year period both without the correction and with the correction?

L.O. 2b,c,d **Exercise 19-2** Beggs Garden Center maintains an inventory of lawn mowers. The beginning inventory of mowers and the purchases of them during the year were as follows. (Round all computations to two decimal places.)

Jan.   1 Inventory of 22 units @ $84 each
Mar.   6 Purchased 32 units @ $84 each
May   12 Purchased 18 units @ $87 each
       30 Purchased 12 units @ $89 each

The ending inventory, by physical count, is 26 units. Determine the value of the ending inventory and the cost of merchandise sold by the following methods: weighted-average cost; first-in, first-out; last-in, first-out.

L.O. 1 **Exercise 19-3** Referring to Exercise 19-2, if the lawn mowers during the year were sold for $109 each, determine the cost of merchandise sold and the gross profit using weighted-average cost; first-in, first-out; last-in, first-out methods.

L.O. 3 **Exercise 19-4** The S. R. Phillips Company's fiscal year is from January 1 through December 31. The following figures are available:

Inventory, January 1 $183,000 (by physical count)
Inventory, December 31   197,000 (by physical count)

a. Record the adjusting entries, assuming that the company uses the periodic inventory system.
b. Record the adjusting entry, assuming that the company uses the perpetual inventory system and that the book balance of the ending inventory is $197,250.

L.O. 4 **Exercise 19-5** Seeley Lumber keeps perpetual inventories on storm doors, using the first-in, first-out method. Determine the cost of merchandise sold in each sale and the inventory balance after each sale for the following purchases and sales of storm doors:

Jan.   1 Inventory of 30 units @ $47 each
       22 Sold 16 units
Feb.   3 Purchased 20 units @ $50 each
       14 Sold 17 units
Mar.   1 Sold 10 units
       17 Purchased 16 units @ $52

L.O. 2b,c,d **Exercise 19-6** Baxter School Supply's beginning inventory of staplers for June consisted of 3,200 units at $3 each. Purchase and sales during June are shown on the next page.

June   4 Sold 1,100 units
          10 Purchased 1,600 units @ $3.10 each
          12 Sold 2,000 units
          24 Purchased 1,800 units @ $3.20 each
          30 Sold 600 units

Calculate the cost of the ending inventory under each of the following pricing methods: weighted-average cost; first-in, first-out; last-in, first-out. (Round all computations to two decimal places.)

L.O. 1   **Exercise 19-7**   An abbreviated income statement for Sherbrooke and Company for this fiscal year is shown below:

Sales (net)		$160 0 0 0 00
Cost of Merchandise Sold		
Merchandise Inventory, January 1	$ 37 0 0 0 00	
Purchases (net)	128 0 0 0 00	
Merchandise Available for Sale	$165 0 0 0 00	
Merchandise Inventory, December 31	42 0 0 0 00	
Cost of Merchandise Sold		123 0 0 0 00
Gross Profit		$ 37 0 0 0 00
Expenses		20 0 0 0 00
Net Income		$ 17 0 0 0 00

An accountant discovers that the ending inventory is overstated by $5,000. What effect does this have on cost of merchandise sold, gross profit, and net income in this fiscal year?

L.O. 2   **Exercise 19-8**   The records of Compu Store show the following data as of January 31, the end of the fiscal year. Determine the value of the ending merchandise inventory.

a. Cost of merchandise on hand, based on a physical count, $194,600.
b. Cost of defective merchandise (to be thrown away) included in **a**, $160.
c. Cost of merchandise shipped out FOB destination on January 29, with an expected delivery date of approximately four days, $940; not included in **a**.
d. Merchandise purchased January 30, FOB shipping point, delivered to the transportation company on January 31, $720.
e. Cost of merchandise sold to a customer on January 30, which is paid for in full and is awaiting shipping instructions, $370; not included in **a** above.

Problem Set A

L.O. 2,b,c,d   **Problem 19-1A**   Baisch and Company, on January 1 of one year, had an inventory of XN244 of 12,000 gallons, costing $.41 per gallon. In addition to this beginning inventory, purchases during the next six months were as follows:

Date	Quantity (Gallons)	Cost per Gallon	Total Cost
Jan. 1 Inventory	12,000	$.41	$4,920
14	9,000	.42	3,780
Feb. 21	8,000	.43	3,440
Mar. 7	6,000	.43½	2,610
Apr. 19	11,000	.43	4,730
May 5	8,000	.44	3,520
June 2	9,000	.45	4,050
29	7,000	.45	3,150

The inventory on June 30 was 16,000 gallons. During this six-month period, Baisch and Company sold XN244 for $.57 per gallon. Assume that no liquid was lost through evaporation or leakage.

Instructions

1. Find the cost of the ending inventory by the following methods:

   a. Weighted-average cost (Round to two decimal places.)
   b. First-in, first-out
   c. Last-in, first-out

2. Determine the cost of merchandise sold according to the three methods of costing inventory.
3. Determine the amount of the gross profit according to the three methods of costing inventory.

L.O. 2b,c,d   **Problem 19-2A**   Bingham Jewelers uses the periodic inventory system. Data pertaining to the inventory on January 1, the beginning of the fiscal year, as well as purchases during the year and the inventory count on December 31, are as follows:

	Model		
	JP314	CL247	9L21
Inventory, Jan. 1	11 @ $432	3 @ $786	21 @ $318
First purchase	17 @ 444	7 @ 782	28 @ 322
Second purchase	22 @ 452	9 @ 788	30 @ 322
Third purchase	16 @ 452	6 @ 796	32 @ 330
Fourth purchase	12 @ 458		26 @ 332
Inventory, Dec. 31	15	7	31

Instructions

1. Determine the cost of the inventory on December 31 by the weighted-average-cost method. (Round to two decimal places.)

2. Determine the cost of the inventory on December 31 by the first-in, first-out method.

3. Determine the cost of the inventory on December 31 by the last-in, first-out method.

L.O. 3   **Problem 19-3A**   The Matthews Company made the following transactions during the year:

Jan.	2	Bought merchandise on account from Upton Products; terms 2/10, n/30; FOB destination; $7,640.
	4	Received credit memo no. 1421 from Upton Products for the return of merchandise bought on January 2, $426.
	11	Issued check no. 2912 to Upton Products, in payment of the invoice dated January 2.
	14	Sold merchandise on account to C. N. Lewis, $3,510; the cost of the merchandise was $2,492.
	30	Sold merchandise on account to S. T. Clark, $4,672; the cost of the merchandise was $3,317.
Dec.	31	Made adjusting entries: The ending merchandise inventory determined by physical count is $140,316. The beginning inventory was $137,294. The balance in the inventory account under the perpetual inventory system is $140,892. Accrued interest on notes payable is $221. Accrued interest on notes receivable is $118. Allowance for Doubtful Accounts is to be increased by $1,310.

Instructions

1. Record the above transactions in general journal form, assuming that Matthews Company uses the perpetual inventory system and records purchases at the gross amount.

2. Record the above transactions in general journal form, assuming that Matthews Company uses the periodic inventory system and records purchases at the gross amount.

L.O. 4   **Problem 19-4A**   The Brady Company's beginning inventory of C215 is 160 units at a cost of $44 each. Dates of purchases and sales for a three-month period are shown at the top of the next page.

Brady Company maintains a perpetual inventory record using the first-in, first-out method. Data for the month of January are recorded in the Working Papers.

Instructions

1. Record the data for purchases and sales of item C215 and for cost of merchandise sold in a perpetual inventory record using the first-in, first-out method for the months of February and March.

2. Determine the total cost of merchandise sold during the three-month period.

3. Determine the total sales for the three-month period.

4. Determine the gross profit from sales of item C215 for the period.

Date	Purchases		Sales	
	Units	Cost per Unit	Units	Price per Unit
Jan. 16	220	$44.20		
18			70	$52.00
29			140	52.00
Feb. 5	240	45.60		
14			130	53.00
22			190	53.00
26	220	46.20		
Mar. 4			70	54.00
11	150	48.00		
17			80	54.00
30			145	56.00

Problem Set B

L.O. 2b,c,d **Problem 19-1B** Howell Chemical's inventory of NC221 on January 1 of one year was 7,000 gallons, which cost them $.52 per gallon. In addition to the beginning inventory, the firm bought more NC221 during the next six months, as follows:

Date	Quantity (Gallons)	Cost per Gallon	Total Cost
Jan. 1 Inventory	7,000	$.52	$3,640
26	10,000	.52½	5,250
Feb. 4	12,000	.53	6,360
21	9,000	.53	4,770
Mar. 7	11,000	.53½	5,885
24	8,000	.55	4,400
Apr. 19	9,000	.55	4,950
May 31	6,000	.55	3,300
June 15	4,000	.56	2,240

Howell Chemical's inventory on June 30 was 11,000 gallons. During this six-month period, the firm sold all its NC221 at $.69 per gallon. Assume that no liquid was lost through evaporation or leakage. (Round all computations to four decimal places.)

Instructions

1. Find the cost of the ending inventory by the following methods:

   a. Weighted-average cost (Round to two decimal places.)
   b. First-in, first-out
   c. Last-in, first-out

2. Determine the cost of merchandise sold according to the three methods of costing inventory.
3. Determine the amount of the gross profit according to the three methods of costing inventory.

L.O. 2b,c,d   **Problem 19-2B**   Hoffman Stereo uses the periodic inventory system. Data for their inventories on January 1, the beginning of their fiscal year, as well as purchases during the year and the inventory count at December 31, are shown below:

	Model		
	JP314	CL247	9L21
Inventory, Jan. 1	6 @ $436	4 @ $692	17 @ $336
First purchase	9 @ 450	7 @ 722	21 @ 344
Second purchase	11 @ 460	8 @ 722	33 @ 344
Third purchase	8 @ 460	6 @ 736	14 @ 348
Fourth purchase	7 @ 466		
Inventory, Dec. 31	8	7	23

Instructions

1. Determine the cost of the inventory on December 31 by the weighted-average-cost method. (Round to two decimal places.)
2. Determine the cost of the inventory on December 31 by the first-in, first-out method.
3. Determine the cost of the inventory on December 31 by the last-in, first-out method.

L.O. 3   **Problem 19-3B**   The McNeil Company carried out the following transac-
C●   tions during the year:

Jan.   3 Bought merchandise on account from Sadler, Inc.; terms 2/10, n/30; FOB destination; $12,200.

        5 Received credit memo no. 1642 from Sadler, Inc., for the return of merchandise bought on January 3, $720.

    12 Issued check no. 2141, payable to Sadler, Inc., in payment of the invoice dated January 3.

    20 Sold merchandise on account to Schick and Son, $6,420; the cost of the merchandise was $5,292.

    30 Sold merchandise on account to O'Donnell and Company, $5,212; the cost of the merchandise was $3,744.

Dec.   31 Made the following adjusting entries: The ending inventory determined by physical count is $225,814. The balance in the inventory account under the perpetual inventory system is $225,975. The beginning inventory was $198,524. Accrued interest on notes payable is $79. Accrued interest on notes receivable is $112. Allowance for Doubtful accounts is to be increased by $1,540.

Instructions

1. Assuming that McNeil Company uses the perpetual inventory system, record the transactions in general journal form, with purchases recorded at the gross amount.
2. Assuming that McNeil Company uses the periodic inventory system, record the transactions in general journal form, with purchases recorded at the gross amount.

L.O. 4 **Problem 19-4B**   The Brown Company's beginning inventory of C430 is 160 units at a cost of $88 each. Dates of purchases and sales for a three-month period are as follows:

	Purchases		Sales	
Date	Units	Cost per Unit	Units	Price per Unit
Jan. 16	220	$88.40		
18			70	$104.00
29			140	104.00
Feb. 2	180	92.00		
11			120	106.00
17	200	96.00		
27			170	112.00
Mar. 9			90	112.00
14	120	97.20		
22			75	112.00
29			70	112.80

Brown Company maintains a perpetual inventory record using the first-in, first-out method. Data for the month of January are recorded in the Working Papers.

Instructions

1. Record the data for purchases and sales of item C430 and for cost of merchandise sold in a perpetual inventory record using the first-in, first-out method for the months of February and March.
2. Determine the total cost of merchandise sold during the three-month period.
3. Determine the total sales for the three-month period.
4. Determine the gross profit from sales of item C430 for this period.

APPENDIX D
Estimating the Value of Inventories

In Chapter 1, we described accounting as the eyes and ears of management. Management sees and hears through the medium of financial reports that summarize the results of business operations. Management, to function efficiently, must have interim income statements and balance sheets prepared monthly. Management needs a physical inventory at the end of the year because inventory balance figures are an integral element of financial statements. However, because it is both time-consuming and expensive to take a physical inventory, management finds it more expedient to estimate the value of the ending inventories each month and to use these estimates on the monthly financial statements. Let's take a look at the two most frequently used methods of estimating the value of inventories: the retail method and the gross-profit method.

RETAIL METHOD OF ESTIMATING THE VALUE OF INVENTORIES

As the name implies, this method is widely used by retail concerns, particularly department stores. The retailer buys merchandise at cost, then adds the normal markup, and prices the goods at the retail level. The normal markup—which is the normal amount, or percentage, that you add to the cost of an item to arrive at its selling price—covers operating expenses and profit. When a firm uses the retail method of estimating inventories, it must record the Purchases-related accounts at both cost and retail values. The firm's accountant records retail values in supplementary records; he or she also records the physical inventory taken at the end of the previous year at both cost and retail values.

Example 1 Nicholson Company takes a physical inventory at the end of each year and estimates the value of the ending inventory at the end of each month for its monthly financial statements.

The accountant for Nicholson Company needs to determine the following information to estimate the value of the ending merchandise inventory at cost:

• Cost value and retail value of merchandise on hand at the beginning of the month. (The inventory at the beginning of a given month is the same as the inventory at the end of the preceding month.)

		AT COST	AT RETAIL
Merchandise Inventory (beginning)		41 2 0 0 00	68 6 0 0 00

- Net purchases of merchandise during the month, both cost value and retail value. The retail figures include the cost plus the company's standard markup, as shown.

		AT COST			AT RETAIL
Purchases plus Freight In			87 1 0 0 00		145 1 6 7 00
Less: Purchases Returns and Allowances	3 2 0 0 00				
Purchases Discounts	1 0 0 0 00	4 2 0 0 00			7 0 0 0 00
Net Purchases			82 9 0 0 00		138 1 6 7 00

- Net sales for the month. All sales are recorded at retail price levels, as listed on sales slips and cash register tapes.

			AT RETAIL
Sales			151 6 5 0 00
Less: Sales Returns and Allowances	7 0 0 0 00		
Sales Discounts	2 6 5 0 00		9 6 5 0 00
Net Sales			142 0 0 0 00

The accountant can determine this information by following these four steps:

1. Determine the dollar value of merchandise available for sale, at cost and at retail. The cost figures are the same as the Merchandise Available for Sale, which is part of the Cost of Merchandise Sold section of the income statement.

	At Cost	At Retail
Beginning inventory	$ 41,200	$ 68,600
Plus net purchases	82,900	138,167
Merchandise available for sale	$124,100	$206,767

2. Find the ratio of the cost value of merchandise available for sale to the retail value of merchandise available for sale.

$$\frac{\text{Cost value of merchandise available for sale}}{\text{Retail value of merchandise available for sale}} = \frac{\$124,100}{\$206,767} = \underline{\underline{60\%}}$$

3. Determine the retail value of ending inventory.

Retail value of merchandise available	$206,767
Less net sales	142,000
Retail value of ending inventory	$ 64,767

Think of the retail value of the ending inventory this way: If the firm had $206,767 of merchandise available for sale, and $142,000 was actually sold, then the amount left over should be $64,767.

4. Convert the retail value of the ending inventory into the cost value of the ending inventory by using this formula:

$$\$64,767 \times 60\% = \$64,767 \times .6 = \underline{\$38,860}$$

Therefore, on its income statement for the month, Nicholson Company records the value of the ending inventory as $38,860. If the retail value is $64,767 and 40 percent of this figure represents markup, the remaining 60 percent must be the cost.

Example 2   Mattson Company had the following account balances, as shown by T accounts:

Merchandise Inventory				Purchases				Sales	
+		−		+		−		−	+
Bal. 210,160				720,327					985,000

Purchases Returns and Allowances			Sales Returns and Allowances	
−	+		+	−
	32,716		25,000	

Purchases Discount	
−	+
	14,082

Freight In	
+	−
37,911	

Retail value of beginning inventory, $296,000 (the accountant picks up this figure from a report dated the end of the preceding month).

Net Purchases = Purchases + Freight In
$\qquad$ − Purchases Returns and Allowances − Purchases Discount
$\qquad$ = $720,327 + $37,911 − $32,716 − $14,082
$\qquad$ = $711,440

Retail value of net purchases, $984,000 (the normal markup is added to the cost figure).

Net Sales = Sales − Sales Returns and Allowances
$\qquad$ = $985,000 − $25,000
$\qquad$ = $960,000

Again, the information is obtained by following the four steps:

1. Determine the dollar value of merchandise available for sale, at cost and at retail.

	At Cost	At Retail
Beginning inventory	$210,160	$ 296,000
Plus net purchases	711,440	984,000
Merchandise available for sale	$921,600	$1,280,000

2. Find the ratio of the cost value of merchandise available for sale to the retail value of merchandise available for sale.

$$\frac{\text{Cost value of merchandise available for sale}}{\text{Retail value of merchandise available for sale}} = \frac{\$921,600}{\$1,280,000} = 72\%$$

3. Find the retail value of ending inventory, as follows:

Retail value of merchandise available	$1,280,000
Less net sales	960,000
Retail value of ending inventory	$ 320,000

4. Convert retail value of ending inventory into cost value of ending inventory by using this formula:

$320,000 × 72% = $320,000 × .72 = $230,400

In the above examples, there is a built-in assumption that the retailer will maintain the normal markup. In other words, we are assuming that the composition or mix of the items in the ending inventory, in terms of the ratio of cost price to retail price, will remain the same for the entire stock of merchandise available for sale.

Markups and Markdowns

In our examples, the retailers used normal markups, but some stores use additional markups and markdowns. Retailers impose additional markups on top of normal markups when the merchandise involved is in great demand. Because of the highly desirable nature of the goods (for example, up-to-the minute fashion in clothes), a store may feel that it can get higher-than-normal prices for the goods. Conversely, a store uses markdowns to sell slow-moving merchandise during a clearance sale.

When a store using the retail inventory method imposes additional markups and markdowns, it must keep track of them, so that it can calculate the ratio of the cost value of merchandise available to the retail value of merchandise available. Look at the following example of how a store keeps track of markups and markdowns.

Step 1   Merchandise available for sale, at cost and at retail.

	At Cost	At Retail
Beginning inventory	$ 60,000	$ 90,000
Plus net purchases	110,000	165,000
Plus additional markups		4,000
Merchandise available for sale	$170,000	$259,000

Step 2   Ratio of cost value of merchandise available for sale to retail value of merchandise available for sale is as follows:

$$\frac{\text{Cost value of merchandise available for sale}}{\text{Retail value of merchandise available for sale}} = \frac{\$170,000}{\$259,000} = 66\%$$

Step 3   Retail value of ending inventory.

Retail value of merchandise available for sale	$259,000
Less net sales	200,000
Less markdowns	3,000
Retail value of ending inventory	$ 56,000

Step 4   Convert retail value of ending inventory into cost value of ending inventory:

$56,000 \times .66 = \$36,960$

The accountant adds any additional markups in the retail column of his or her working paper because such markups result in an increase in the retail value of the merchandise available for sale. For example, let's say that the price of a popular item is $40, so a store seizes the opportunity and marks it up to $49; this is a $9 increase in the retail value of the merchandise available for sale. On the other hand, when a store marks down the price of an item, the accountant deducts the amount of the markdown from the retail value of the merchandise available for sale (step 3) to obtain the retail value of the merchandise inventory at the end of a given month. For example, say that the price tag of an item is $389, but nobody is buying, so the store marks it down to $359. This means that there has been a $30 decrease in the retail value of this merchandise available for sale.

END-OF-YEAR PROCEDURE

As we have said, it is very important to take a physical inventory at the end of the year. Physical inventories may also be taken periodically during the year to spot-check the estimated inventories. Most retail stores record items in stock on the inventory sheets at retail prices (in other words, they take the total of all the price tags). It is then necessary to convert the total of the retail values into the total of the cost values, as in step 4. For example, suppose that the total retail value of the merchandise on all the inventory sheets is $96,000, and the ratio of cost value to retail value is

$$\frac{\text{Cost value of merchandise available}}{\text{Retail value of merchandise available}} = \underline{\underline{70\%}}$$

The cost value of the merchandise is $96,000 \times .7 = $67,200$. The only difference between the steps taken to prepare the end-of-the-year statement and the steps taken to prepare the interim or monthly statements is that, at the end of the year, there is a physical count of the merchandise, and consequently one begins with step 4.

However, to find out the magnitude of shoplifting, or to verify the accuracy of the evaluation of the physical inventory, some firms go through the full procedure of estimating the value of the inventory at the end of the year. Then they take a physical count of the goods on hand and compare this value with the value of the estimated inventory.

GROSS-PROFIT METHOD OF ESTIMATING THE VALUE OF INVENTORIES

Sometimes a firm may find that the total of the retail prices of the beginning inventory and purchases is not readily available; in such cases, the firm naturally cannot use the retail method of estimating the value of the ending inventory. The gross-profit method is an alternative procedure that achieves the same objective. As the name implies, the key element in this method of estimating the value of inventories is the percentage of gross profit the firm makes over a given period of time.

The term *gross profit*, as used on income statements, represents net sales less cost of merchandise sold.

Net sales	$60,000
Less cost of merchandise sold	45,000
Gross profit	$15,000

You arrive at the figure for the percentage of gross profit by dividing the gross profit by the net sales, like this:

$$\text{Percentage of gross profit} = \frac{\text{Gross profit}}{\text{Net sales}} = \frac{\$15,000}{\$60,000} = 25\%$$

A 25 percent gross-profit rate means that there is 25¢ of gross profit for every $1 of net sales. *Gross profit* is the profit earned on the sale of merchandise *before* expenses are deducted. You can compute the gross-profit rate or percentage by using figures from a recent income statement. Alternatively, you may compute the percentage of gross profit from income statements from past years, using averages of figures. The variation from year to year is usually relatively minor, unless marked changes have taken place in the buying and selling policies of the firm.

You need the following information for the current year:

- Sales (balance of account to date)
- Sales Returns and Allowances (balance of account to date)
- Sales Discounts (balance of account to date, if any)
- Beginning Merchandise Inventory (ending inventory of the previous period)
- Purchases (balance of account to date)
- Purchases Returns and Allowances (balance of account to date)
- Purchases Discount (balance of account to date)
- Freight In (balance of account to date)

Example I   On the night of April 29, the Holloway Variety Store was destroyed by fire. However, a heroic salesclerk ran into the building and rescued the company's books and records of transactions. For insurance purposes, the owner must estimate the value of the inventory by the gross-profit method. The owner knows that the average gross-profit percentage for the past five years is 32 percent. By journalizing and posting the transactions of the current month, the company's accounts can be brought up to date from these sources:

- Sales (from sales journal, cash receipts journal, and invoices for April 29)
- Sales Returns and Allowances (from cash receipts and general journal)
- Merchandise Inventory, December 31 (ending inventory of last fiscal period)
- Purchases (from purchases journal and invoices for April 29)

Holloway Variety Store
Income Statement
For Period January 1 through April 29, 19–

Revenue from Sales:				
Sales				$217 0 0 0 00
Less Sales Returns and Allowances				17 0 0 0 00
Net Sales				$200 0 0 0 00
Cost of Merchandise Sold:				
Merchandise Inventory, January 1, 19–			$ 72 0 0 0 00	
Purchases		$136 0 0 0 00		
Less: Purchases Returns and Allowances	$ 14 0 0 0 00			
Purchases Discount	2 4 0 0 00	16 4 0 0 00		
		$119 6 0 0 00		
Add Freight In		7 4 0 0 00		
Net Purchases			127 0 0 0 00	
Merchandise Available for Sale			$199 0 0 0 00	
Less Merchandise Inventory, April 29, 19–			⬭	
Cost of Merchandise Sold				⬭
Gross Profit				$ ⬭

FIGURE D-I

- Purchases Returns and Allowances (from general journal)
- Purchases Discount (from cash payments journal)
- Freight In (from purchases journal, cash payments journal, and invoices for April 29)

The owner of Holloway Variety arranges these figures in the customary income statement format, extending from Sales to Gross Profit (see Figure D-1).

$$\text{Percentage of gross profit} = \frac{\text{Gross profit}}{\text{Net sales}} = \frac{\text{Gross profit}}{\$200,000} = \underline{\underline{32\%}}$$

Gross profit $= .32 \times \$200,000 = \underline{\$64,000}$

Now we fill in the Gross Profit blank in the income statement (see Figure D-2).

To find the value of the merchandise at the end (April 29), we should work backward. The cost of merchandise sold is the difference between net sales and gross profit, or $136,000 ($200,000 − $64,000). The equation is as shown here:

Cost of merchandise sold $=$ Net sales $-$ Gross profit
$= \$200,000 - \$64,000$
$= \underline{\underline{\$136,000}}$

Holloway Variety Store
Income Statement
For Period January 1 through April 29, 19–

Revenue from Sales:						
Sales					$217 0 0 0 00	
Less Sales Returns and Allowances					17 0 0 0 00	
Net Sales					$200 0 0 0 00	
Cost of Merchandise Sold:						
Merchandise Inventory, January 1, 19–				$ 72 0 0 0 00		
Purchases			$136 0 0 0 00			
Less: Purchases Returns and Allowances	$ 14 0 0 0 00					
Purchases Discount	2 4 0 0 00		16 4 0 0 00			
			$119 6 0 0 00			
Add Freight In			7 4 0 0 00			
Net Purchases				127 0 0 0 00		
Merchandise Available for Sale				$199 0 0 0 00		
Less Merchandise Inventory, April 29, 19–						
Cost of Merchandise Sold						
Gross Profit					$ 64 0 0 0 00	

FIGURE D-2

Now that we have filled in the figures for Gross Profit and Cost of
Merchandise Sold, the partial income statement (from Merchandise
Available for Sale through Gross Profit) looks like this:

Merchandise Available for Sale	$199,000.00
Less Merchandise Inventory, Apr. 29, 19–	
Cost of Merchandise Sold	136,000.00
Gross Profit	$ 64,000.00

The value of the merchandise inventory on April 29 is the difference
between the value of the merchandise available for sale and the cost of
merchandise sold, or $63,000 ($199,000 − $136,000). The equation is as
follows:

Value of ending inventory = Value of merchandise available for sale
− Cost of merchandise sold
= $199,000 − $136,000
= $63,000

Merchandise Available for Sale	$199,000.00
Less Merchandise Inventory, Apr. 29, 19–	63,000.00
Cost of Merchandise Sold	136,000.00
Gross Profit	$ 64,000.00

The income statement is a very useful device in the box of tools that
you have been accumulating. That is why we suggested earlier that you

memorize the form initially to implant it firmly in your mind; then it will always be at your fingertips when you need it to do a specific job.

Example 2   Hoffman Beauty Supply has an average gross-profit rate of 34 percent. Its account balances on May 31 of this year are shown by the T accounts and by the partial income statement in Figure D-3.

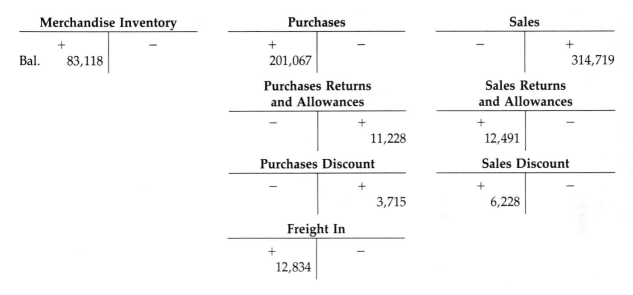

Merchandise Inventory		Purchases		Sales	
+	−	+	−	−	+
Bal. 83,118		201,067			314,719

Purchases Returns and Allowances		Sales Returns and Allowances	
−	+	+	−
	11,228	12,491	

Purchases Discount		Sales Discount	
−	+	+	−
	3,715	6,228	

Freight In	
+	−
12,834	

FIGURE D-3

Hoffman Beauty Supply
Income Statement
For Period January 1 through May 31, 19–

Revenue from Sales:				
Sales				$314 7 1 9 00
Less: Sales Returns and Allowances		$ 12 4 9 1 00		
Sales Discount		6 2 2 8 00	18 7 1 9 00	
Net Sales			$296 0 0 0 00	
Cost of Merchandise Sold:				
Merchandise Inventory, January 1, 19–		$ 83 1 1 8 00		
Purchases	$201 0 6 7 00			
Less: Purchases Returns and Allowances	$ 11 2 2 8 00			
Purchases Discount	3 7 1 5 00	14 9 4 3 00		
		$186 1 2 4 00		
Add Freight In		12 8 3 4 00		
Net Purchases		198 9 5 8 00		
Merchandise Available for Sale		$282 0 7 6 00		
Less Merchandise Inventory, May 31, 19–		(86 7 1 6 00)		
Cost of Merchandise Sold			195 3 6 0 00	
Gross Profit			($100 6 4 0 00)	

$$\text{Percentage of gross profit} = \frac{\text{Gross profit}}{\text{Net sales}} = \frac{\text{Gross profit}}{\$296,000} = 34\%$$

$$\text{Gross profit} = \text{Net sales} \times .34 = \$296,000 \times .34$$
$$= \underline{\underline{\$100,640}}$$

The cost of merchandise sold is equal to net sales minus gross profit, or $195,360 ($296,000 − $100,640). The ending merchandise inventory is the value of the merchandise available for sale minus the cost of merchandise sold, or $86,716 ($282,076 − $195,360).

Problems

Problem D-1 You are given the following information for D and R Audio at the end of its fiscal year, October 31:

	At Cost	At Retail
Sales		$264,789
Sales Returns and Allowances		10,659
Purchases plus Freight In	$160,848	268,134
Purchases Returns and Allowances	7,026	11,712
Merchandise Inventory, Beginning	59,172	98,640

Instructions

1. Determine the cost value of the ending merchandise inventory as of October 31, presenting details of your computations.
2. At the end of the year, D and R Audio takes a physical inventory at marked selling prices and finds that the retail stock totals $98,889. There is a possibility that the difference between the estimated ending inventory and the actual physical inventory is due to shoplifting. Convert the value of the physical inventory at retail into its value at cost and determine the amount of the loss.

Problem D-2 On May 10 of this year, a fire in the night destroyed the entire stock of merchandise of Del's Athletic Attic. Most of the accounting records were destroyed also. However, from assorted statements and documents, the firm's accountant was able to piece together the balances of several accounts. Over the past three years, the percentage of gross profit averaged 40 percent.

Merchandise Inventory, January 1	
(beginning of fiscal year)	$125,187
Account balances, as of May 10	
Purchases	163,970
Purchases Returns and Allowances	984
Freight In	7,906
Sales	213,420
Sales Returns and Allowances	660

Instructions

Determine the cost value of the ending merchandise inventory as of May 10, giving details of your computations.

Problem D-3   On the morning of July 27, the owner of Fran's Needle Nook opened her store and discovered that a robbery had taken place over the weekend. A large part of the stock had been stolen. However, the following information for the period January 1 through July 27 was available. Each year during the past four years, the store had earned an average 34 percent gross profit on sales.

Merchandise Inventory, January 1 (beginning of fiscal year)	$190,257
Account balances, as of July 27	
Purchases	408,692
Purchases Returns and Allowances	10,986
Purchases Discount	8,244
Freight In	24,703
Sales	596,238
Sales Returns and Allowances	6,438

Instructions

1. Determine the cost value of the ending merchandise inventory as of July 27, giving details of your computations.
2. By physical count, the cost value of the remaining inventory on hand is $80,940. What is the amount of the loss to be claimed for insurance purposes?

20 Accounting for Valuation of Plant and Equipment

After you have completed this chapter, you will be able to do the following:

1. Allocate costs to Land, Land Improvements, and Buildings accounts.
2. Calculate depreciation by the straight-line method, units-of-production method, double-declining-balance method, and sum-of-the-years'-digits method.
3. Differentiate between capital expenditures and revenue expenditures.
4. Differentiate between expenditures for ordinary and for extraordinary repairs.
5. Prepare journal entries for discarding of assets fully depreciated, discarding of assets not fully depreciated, sale of assets involving a loss, sale of assets involving a gain, exchange of assets involving a loss on the trade, and exchange of assets involving a gain on the trade.
6. Maintain a plant and equipment subsidiary ledger.

We described plant and equipment as an account classification in Chapter 15, in connection with the classified balance sheet. Assets in this category have a useful life longer than one year and so are often referred to as long-lived or fixed assets. Such assets are originally purchased for use in the business, as opposed to merchandise, which is bought for the purpose of resale. Items most frequently classified as plant and equipment are equipment, furniture, machinery, tools, buildings, land improvements, and land.

INITIAL COSTS OF PLANT AND EQUIPMENT

The original cost of plant and equipment includes all normal expenditures necessary to acquire and install the plant and equipment. For example, the cost of a cash register includes not only its invoice price (less any discount for paying cash) but sales tax, freight charges, insurance costs while it is being transported, and costs of unpacking and assembling. Assuming that the buyer of the cash register pays these additional charges in cash, the accountant for the buyer debits Store Equipment and credits Cash. Suppose the firm bought a second-hand cash register and had to have it repaired before it could be used. The cost of the repairs would be debited to the relevant asset account, in this case Store Equipment.

The accountant should debit only normal and necessary costs to the asset accounts, which rules out expenditures that result from carelessness, vandalism, or other abnormal causes. For example, suppose that an employee dropped the cash register while unpacking it. The cost of the repair is not part of the cost of the cash register; that cost is charged to an expense account, such as Repair Expense or Miscellaneous Expense. The cost is charged as an expense and not as an asset because the repair does not *add* to the usefulness of the cash register—it simply restores its usefulness.

DIFFERENTIATING COSTS OF LAND, LAND IMPROVEMENTS, AND BUILDINGS

Objective 1

Allocate costs to Land, Land Improvements, and Buildings accounts.

There is no legal recognition for the depreciation of land. Yet a buyer usually buys a package including the land, land improvements, and the building. In other words, the buyer pays one price for one package. So the question is: How should the price be allocated among the three elements?

When there is no qualified appraisal available, then one accepts the ratio established by the county or municipal assessor. For example, suppose that someone buys some real property, including land and a building, for $500,000. The assessor valued this property for tax purposes at $300,000: $60,000 for the land and $240,000 for the building. The percentage the assessor allocated to the land is $60,000/$300,000 = 20 percent. The percentage allocated to the building is $240,000/$300,000 = 80 percent. Therefore, the value that the buyer should allocate to the land is $500,000 × .2 = $100,000; to the building, $500,000 × .8 = $400,000. For bookkeeping purposes, one separates land improvements from buildings because of the different lengths of life involved.

LAND

Suppose that someone buys a piece of land—just land, no building. The cost of the land includes the amount paid for the land plus incidental charges connected with the sale: real estate agents' commissions, escrow and legal fees, delinquent taxes paid by the buyer, plus any costs of surveying, clearing, draining, or grading the land. In addition, the municipality or county—either at the time of purchase or later—may assess the buyer for such improvements as the installation of paved streets, curbs, sidewalks, and sewers. The buyer debits these items to the Land account, since the items are considered to be as permanent as the land. If a business entity buys land for a building site and the land happens to have old buildings standing on it, the firm debits the cost of the structures as well as the costs of demolishing them to the Land account.

Land Improvements

An accountant uses the asset account **Land Improvements** to record expenditures for improvements that are (1) not as permanent as the land, or (2) not directly associated with a building. Examples are driveways, parking lots, trees and shrubs, fences, and outdoor lighting systems.

Buildings

The cost of a building includes not only money spent for labor and materials but architectural and engineering fees, money spent for insurance premiums during construction, interest on construction loans during the period of construction, and all other necessary and normal expenditures applicable to the project.

THE NATURE AND RECORDING OF DEPRECIATION

When accountants use the term *depreciation*, they mean loss in usefulness of long-lived assets (assets that will last longer than one year). Examples of long-lived assets are buildings, office furniture, store fixtures, machines, computers, trucks, and automobiles. Assets lose their usefulness to companies for two reasons: (1) **physical depreciation**—simply wearing out or being used up, such as an automobile becoming beyond repair; (2) **functional depreciation**—becoming obsolete or inadequate, such as a machine being outdated because more efficient machines have been developed. As we said in Chapter 5, depreciation represents a systematic procedure for spreading out the cost of plant and equipment to the fiscal periods in which the company receives services from the assets.

An item of supplies is bought and used up in one fiscal period; its cost is charged to the same fiscal period. In contrast, equipment is used over several fiscal periods. So the cost of the equipment must be spread out over the several periods, and this is consistent with the matching principle.

The firm treats depreciation as a debit to Depreciation Expense and a credit to Accumulated Depreciation. It treats Accumulated Depreciation as a deduction from the related asset account. Accumulated Depreciation is thus a contra account. We referred to this entry earlier as an *internal transaction,* because no outside business or person is involved. One can record depreciation as an adjusting entry at the end of each month or postpone recording it until the end of the fiscal year, except when there is a change in the assets, such as a sale or a trade-in. In that case, one first records depreciation of the asset from the beginning of the fiscal year until the date of the change *before* making any other accounting entries.

Determining the Amount of Depreciation

To determine the depreciation of a long-lived asset, one must take into account three elements:

1. The **depreciation base,** which is the full depreciation of an asset. Full depreciation is the total cost of an asset less the trade-in or salvage value.
2. The length of the useful life of the asset.
3. The method of depreciation chosen to allocate the depreciation base over the useful life of the asset.

Depreciation Base

When a business entity first puts an asset into service, it is hard to predict the amount of the trade-in or salvage value, especially when such a trade-in will not take place for many years. Many firms make estimates based on their own experience or on data supplied by trade associations or government agencies. If the firm expects the salvage value to be insignificant in comparison with the cost of the asset, the accountant often assumes the salvage value to be zero.

Useful Life

As we said, the length of an asset's useful life is affected not only by the amount of physical wear and tear it is subjected to but also by technological change and innovation. For accounting purposes, the useful life of an asset is based on the expected use of the asset, in keeping with the company's replacement policy. An average car, for example, may have a useful life of five years. However, for reasons of competition, a car rental company may replace its cars every year in order to offer customers the latest models. And a company operating a fleet of cars for its sales force may replace the cars every three years.

CALCULATING DEPRECIATION

Objective 2

Calculate depreciation by the straight-line method, units-of-production method, double-declining-balance method, and sum-of-the-years'-digits method.

The objective of recording depreciation is to spread out systematically the cost of a long-lived asset over the length of the asset's useful life. However, a firm need not use the same method of depreciation for all its assets.

The four most common methods of computing depreciation are the (1) straight-line method, (2) units-of-production method, (3) double-declining-balance method, and (4) sum-of-the-years'-digits method. Methods 3 and 4 represent **accelerated depreciation**. In accelerated depreciation, depreciation is speeded up, in that larger amounts of depreciation are taken during an asset's early life, and smaller amounts are taken during an asset's later life.

Straight-line Method

A firm that uses the straight-line method of calculating depreciation charges an equal amount of depreciation for each year of service anticipated. The accountant computes the annual depreciation by dividing the depreciation base (cost minus trade-in value, if any) by the number of years of useful life predicted for the asset. This is the type of depreciation we illustrated in Chapter 5. The percentage rate of depreciation per year is determined by dividing the number of years of useful life into 1. For instance, take an asset with a life of eight years:

$$\frac{1}{8 \text{ years}} = .125 \qquad .125 \times 100 = \underline{\underline{12.5\%}}$$

One always applies the depreciation rate against the depreciation base (cost less trade-in value):

$$\text{Depreciation per year} = \frac{\text{Cost} - \text{Trade-in value}}{\text{Useful life (in years)}}$$

Now let's look at two examples.

Example 1 A truck costs \$18,000 and has a useful life of six years. The estimated trade-in value at the end of six years is \$2,400.

$$\text{Depreciation per year} = \frac{\$18,000 - \$2,400}{6} = \frac{\$15,600}{6} = \underline{\underline{\$2,600}}$$

$$\text{Depreciation rate per year} = \frac{1}{6 \text{ years}} = .1667 \qquad .1667 \times 100 = \underline{\underline{16.67\%}}$$

Example 2 A neon sign costs \$2,400 and has a useful life of eight years. The estimated trade-in value at the end of eight years is zero.

$$\text{Depreciation per year} = \frac{\$2,400 - 0}{8} = \frac{\$2,400}{8} = \underline{\underline{\$300}}$$

$$\text{Depreciation rate per year} = \frac{1}{8 \text{ years}} = .125 \qquad .125 \times 100 = \underline{\underline{12.5\%}}$$

Units-of-Production Method

The units-of-production method enables one to allow for an asset that is used a great deal more in one year than in another. You can obtain the depreciation charge per unit of production by dividing the depreciation base by the total estimated units of production.

$$\text{Depreciation per unit of production} = \frac{\text{Cost} - \text{Trade-in value}}{\text{Estimated units of production}}$$

Example 1   A salesperson's car costs \$10,800 and has a useful life of 60,000 miles. The estimated trade-in value at the end of 60,000 miles is \$2,400. The car is driven 18,000 miles this year.

$$\text{Depreciation per mile} = \frac{\$10,800 - \$2,400}{60,000 \text{ miles}} = \frac{\$8,400}{60,000 \text{ miles}}$$

$$= \underline{\underline{\$.14}} \text{ per mile } (14¢)$$

$$\text{Depreciation for 18,000 miles} = 18,000 \text{ miles} \times \$.14 \text{ per mile}$$

$$= \underline{\underline{\$2,520}}$$

Example 2   A bulldozer costs \$70,000 and has a useful life of 4,000 hours. The estimated salvage value after 4,000 hours is \$6,000. The firm uses the bulldozer for 380 hours this year.

$$\text{Depreciation per hour} = \frac{\$70,000 - \$6,000}{4,000 \text{ hours}} = \frac{\$64,000}{4,000 \text{ hours}} = \underline{\underline{\$16}} \text{ per hour}$$

Depreciation for 380 hours = 380 hours × \$16 per hour = $\underline{\underline{\$6,080}}$

Double-Declining-Balance Method

The double-declining-balance method is popular because it allows larger amounts of depreciation to be taken in the early years of an asset's life. Some accountants reason that the amount charged to depreciation of an asset should be higher during the asset's early years so as to offset the higher repair and maintenance expenses of the asset's later years. The total annual expense would then tend to be equalized over the entire life of the asset.

For an asset that has a life of three years or more, this method allows a firm to calculate depreciation by *multiplying the book value (cost less accumulated depreciation) at the beginning of the year by* twice *the straight-line rate.*

Trade-in or salvage value is not counted in determining depreciation by the double-declining-balance method until the end of the depreciation schedule. As with other methods, an asset may not be depreciated below its salvage value.

To compute depreciation by the double-declining-balance method, follow these steps:

1. Calculate the straight-line depreciation rate.
2. Multiply the straight-line rate by 2.
3. Multiply the book value of the asset at the beginning of the year by double the straight-line rate.

During the first year, the book value of an asset will be the same as its cost, since no depreciation has been taken. So for the first year only, multiply the cost by twice the straight-line rate.

Example 1 A firm's word processing equipment costs $20,000 and has a useful life of five years. The estimated trade-in value at the end of five years is zero.

1. Compute the straight-line depreciation rate:

$$\text{Straight-line depreciation rate} = \frac{1}{5 \text{ years}} = .2 \qquad .2 \times 100 = \underline{\underline{20\%}}$$

2. Twice the straight-line rate = $.2 \times 2 = .4$ \qquad $.4 \times 100 = \underline{\underline{40\%}}$
3. Depreciation per year = Book value at beginning of year $\times$ .4.

Year	Book Value at Beginning of Year	Depreciation Expense	Book Value at End of Year
1	$20,000.00	$20,000 × .4 = $ 8,000.00	$20,000 − $8,000.00 = $12,000.00
2	$12,000.00	$12,000 × .4 = 4,800.00	$12,000 − $4,800.00 = $ 7,200.00
3	$ 7,200.00	$ 7,200 × .4 = 2,880.00	$ 7,200 − $2,880.00 = $ 4,320.00
4	$ 4,320.00	$ 4,320 × .4 = 1,728.00	$ 4,320 − $1,728.00 = $ 2,592.00
5	$ 2,592.00	$ 2,592 × .4 = 1,036.80	$ 2,592 − $1,036.80 = $ 1,555.20
Total		$18,444.80	

(Under the double-declining-balance method, book value never reaches zero. Therefore, a company typically switches over to the straight-line basis at the point where straight-line depreciation exceeds double-declining-balance.)

Example 2 A delivery van costs $12,000 and has a useful life of six years. The estimated trade-in value at the end of six years is $2,000.

1. Compute the straight-line depreciation rate:

$$\text{Straight-line depreciation rate} = \frac{1}{6 \text{ years}} = .1667$$

$$.1667 \times 100 = 16.67\% = \underline{\underline{\tfrac{1}{6}}}$$

Since the decimal equivalent of $\tfrac{1}{6}$ has a remainder (.1667), it is more accurate to use the fraction.

2. Twice the straight-line rate $= \tfrac{1}{6} \times 2 = \tfrac{2}{6} = \underline{\underline{\tfrac{1}{3}}}$.

3. Depreciation per year $=$ Book value at beginning of year $\times$ $\tfrac{1}{3}$.

Year	Book Value at Beginning of Year	Depreciation Expense	Book Value at End of Year
1	$12,000.00	$12,000.00 × $\tfrac{1}{3}$ = $ 4,000.00	$12,000.00 − $4,000.00 = $8,000.00
2	$ 8,000.00	$ 8,000.00 × $\tfrac{1}{3}$ = 2,666.67	$ 8,000.00 − $2,666.67 = $5,333.33
3	$ 5,333.33	$ 5,333.33 × $\tfrac{1}{3}$ = 1,777.78	$ 5,333.33 − $1,777.78 = $3,555.55
4	$ 3,555.55	$ 3,555.55 × $\tfrac{1}{3}$ = 1,185.18	$ 3,555.55 − $1,185.18 = $2,370.37
5	$ 2,370.37	$ 2,370.37 − $2,000 = 370.37	$ 2,370.37 − $370.37 = $2,000.00
6	$ 2,000.00	0	$ 2,000.00 − $0 = $2,000.00
Total		$10,000.00	

Remember

The double-declining-balance method is the only method in which one figures in the trade-in value at the end of the depreciation schedule.

Observe carefully that the trade-in or salvage value is not counted until the last year. When one uses the double-declining-balance method and there is a trade-in value involved, the book value gradually declines until it reaches the amount of the trade-in value. *An asset must not be depreciated beyond its trade-in value.* For example, take the delivery van. During the fifth year, the normal depreciation would be one-third of the book value at the beginning of the year. One would determine depreciation for the year and the ending book value as follows:

Depreciation expense $= \$2,370.37 \times \tfrac{1}{3} = \underline{\$790.12}$

Book value at end of year $= \$2,370.37 - 790.12 = \underline{\$1,580.25}$

Obviously, if one calculates depreciation in this manner the book value of the van ($1,580.25) dips below its established trade-in value ($2,000). Consequently, one must make an adjustment during this year so that the van's ending book value will be the same as its trade-in value. Even though its useful life was set at six years, the van is actually depreciated to the limit in five years.

Sum-of-the-Years'-Digits Method

The sum-of-the-years'-digits method yields a large proportion of depreciation during the early years of an asset's life. It does this on a reducing-fraction basis. To compute depreciation by this method, follow these steps:

1. Decide how many years the asset is likely to last. Then find the sum of the years' digits. For example, suppose the asset has an expected life of three years. Then add to find the sum of year 1, year 2, and year 3:

$$1 + 2 + 3 = 6$$

One can also determine the sum of the years by the following formula:

$$\frac{\text{Life}^2 + \text{Life}}{2}$$

For example, a life of three years would be

$$\frac{3^2 + 3}{2} = \frac{9 + 3}{2} = \frac{12}{2} = \underline{\underline{6}}$$

Some accountants use the letter N to represent the number of years of an asset's life. Thus the formula is

$$\frac{N^2 + N}{2}$$

2. Record the years in reverse (or descending) order in the numerator (top) of the fraction and the sum of the years' digits in the denominator (bottom) of the fraction:

$$\frac{3}{6} + \frac{2}{6} + \frac{1}{6} = \frac{6}{6}$$

3. Multiply the decreasing fractions by the depreciation base (cost less trade-in value).

Example 1 A stamping machine costs $11,200 and has a useful life of five years. The estimated salvage value at the end of five years is $400. The depreciation base is $10,800 ($11,200 − $400).

Step 1	Step 2	Step 3	
		Year	Depreciation Expense
1	$\frac{5}{15}$	1	$\frac{5}{15}$ × $10,800 = $ 3,600
2	$\frac{4}{15}$	2	$\frac{4}{15}$ × $10,800 = 2,880
3	$\frac{3}{15}$	3	$\frac{3}{15}$ × $10,800 = 2,160
4	$\frac{2}{15}$	4	$\frac{2}{15}$ × $10,800 = 1,440
5	$\frac{1}{15}$	5	$\frac{1}{15}$ × $10,800 = 720
$\underline{15}$	$\frac{15}{15}$		$10,800

Example 2 A fork-lift truck costs $9,000 and has a useful life of six years. The estimated salvage value at the end of six years is $600.

Step 1	Step 2	Year	Depreciation Expense
1	$\frac{6}{21}$	1	$\frac{6}{21} \times \$8,400 = \$2,400$
2	$\frac{5}{21}$	2	$\frac{5}{21} \times \$8,400 = 2,000$
3	$\frac{4}{21}$	3	$\frac{4}{21} \times \$8,400 = 1,600$
4	$\frac{3}{21}$	4	$\frac{3}{21} \times \$8,400 = 1,200$
5	$\frac{2}{21}$	5	$\frac{2}{21} \times \$8,400 = 800$
6	$\frac{1}{21}$	6	$\frac{1}{21} \times \$8,400 = 400$
21	$\frac{21}{21}$		$\$8,400$

Comparison of Three Methods

You can see in the following charts that the double-declining-balance method and the sum-of-the-years'-digits method yield relatively large amounts of depreciation during the early years of use of an asset. For this reason they are examples of *accelerated depreciation*. In the example shown, assume that a hoist costs $6,000 and has a useful life of four years. Estimated salvage value at the end of four years is $400.

	Straight-line Method		
Year	Depreciation Expense	Accumulated Depreciation	Book Value at End of Year
1	$\dfrac{\$6,000 - \$400}{4 \text{ years}} = \quad \$1,400$	$1,400	$6,000 − $1,400 = $4,600
2	1,400	$1,400 + $1,400 = $2,800	$6,000 − $2,800 = $3,200
3	1,400	$2,800 + $1,400 = $4,200	$6,000 − $4,200 = $1,800
4	1,400	$4,200 + $1,400 = $5,600	$6,000 − $5,600 = $400
Total	$5,600		

		Double-declining-balance Method (Based on Twice the Straight-line Rate)		
Year	Beginning Book Value	Depreciation Expense	Accumulated Depreciation	Book Value at End of Year
1	$6,000	$6,000 × .5 = $3,000	$3,000	$6,000 − $3,000 = $3,000
2	$3,000	$3,000 × .5 = $1,500	$3,000 + $1,500 = $4,500	$6,000 − $4,500 = $1,500
3	$1,500	$1,500 × .5 = 750	$4,500 + $750 = $5,250	$6,000 − $5,250 = $750
4	$750	$750 − $400 = 350	$5,250 + $350 = $5,600	$6,000 − $5,600 = $400
Total		$5,600		

Sum-of-the-years'-digits Method		
Year	Depreciation Expense	Accumulated Depreciation	Book Value at End of Year
1	$\frac{4}{10} \times \$5,600 = \$2,240$	$\$2,240$	$\$6,000 - \$2,240 = \$3,760$
2	$\frac{3}{10} \times \$5,600 = 1,680$	$\$2,240 + \$1,680 = \$3,920$	$\$6,000 - \$3,920 = \$2,080$
3	$\frac{2}{10} \times \$5,600 = 1,120$	$\$3,920 + \$1,120 = \$5,040$	$\$6,000 - \$5,040 = \ \ \$960$
4	$\frac{1}{10} \times \$5,600 = \ \ \ \ 560$	$\$5,040 + \ \ \ \$560 = \$5,600$	$\$6,000 - \$5,600 = \ \ \$400$
10	$\frac{10}{10} \qquad \qquad \$5,600$		

A firm may calculate its regular depreciation by any of these methods: straight-line, double-declining-balance, or sum-of-the-years'-digits. Or it may use other available methods. For each separate asset, a company should use the same method of depreciation for each year, to follow the principle of **consistency**. Since depreciation is an expense, its amount will be subtracted from total revenue to arrive at net income. If the depreciation method is changed from year to year, it becomes impossible to compare the firm's performance for one year with its performance for another year.

DEPRECIATION FOR PERIODS OF LESS THAN A YEAR

Businesses do not acquire (or get rid of) all their depreciable assets on the first and last days of their fiscal period. They buy and sell assets throughout the year. How, then, do they calculate depreciation? As you look at the examples in the table below, remember that when a business entity acquires a depreciable asset during the year, the accountant usually figures depreciation to the nearest whole month. If the firm held the as-

Date Acquired	Cost	Trade-in Value	Method	Useful Life	Depreciation for First Year
April 12	$9,000	$1,000	Straight-line	5 years	$\dfrac{\$9,000 - \$1,000}{5 \text{ years}} = \$1,600$ per year $\$1,600 \times \frac{9}{12} = \$1,200$ for 9 months
October 19	6,000	200	Double-declining-balance	8 years	$\$6,000 \times \frac{1}{4} = \$1,500$ for first year $\$1,500 \times \frac{2}{12} = \$250$ for 2 months
August 8	6,800	500	Sum-of-the-years'-digits	6 years	$\$6,300 \times \frac{6}{21} = \$1,800$ for first year $\$1,800 \times \frac{5}{12} = \$750$ for 5 months

set for *less* than half a given month, the accountant doesn't count that month. But if the firm has held it for half of a given month or more, the accountant counts it as a whole month. All of the examples in the table on page 655 assume that the firm's fiscal year ends on December 31.

Suppose a firm buys an asset on June 11. Depreciation is computed from June 1, counting the entire month. But if the firm bought that asset any time after June 15, no depreciation would be computed for the month of June.

It should be mentioned that computer programs are readily available for calculating and keeping track of depreciation by the various methods.

CAPITAL AND REVENUE EXPENDITURES

Objective 3

Differentiate between capital expenditures and revenue expenditures.

The term *expenditure* refers to spending, either by paying cash now or by promising to pay in the future for services received or assets purchased. After paying the initial price for an asset, one often has to pay out more, either to maintain the asset's operating efficiency or to increase its capacity. So there are two classifications of expenditures: capital and revenue.

Capital expenditures include the initial costs of plant and equipment; they also include any costs of increasing the capacity or prolonging the life of assets. You reap the benefits of capital expenditures during more than one accounting period. Examples are expenditures for buying a building, enlarging it, putting in air conditioning, and replacing a stairway with an elevator. All these expenditures result in debits to an asset account.

Revenue expenditures include the costs of maintaining the operation of an asset, such as the expense of making normal repairs. Examples are expenditures for painting, plumbing repairs, fuel, property taxes, and so on. These expenditures provide benefit only during the current accounting period and are recorded as debits to expense accounts.

EXTRAORDINARY-REPAIRS EXPENDITURES

Objective 4

Differentiate between expenditures for ordinary and for extraordinary repairs.

In accounting, **extraordinary-repairs expenditures** refer to a major overhaul or reconditioning that either extends the useful life of an asset beyond its original estimated life or increases its estimated salvage value. An accountant usually records expenditures for extraordinary repairs as debits to Accumulated Depreciation and credits to Cash or Accounts Payable.

For example, on January 3, 1988, a firm bought a used car for $6,000; the car's estimated useful life is four years, and its trade-in value is $1,600; straight-line annual depreciation expense is $1,100. On January 6,

1991, the firm puts in a new engine and has other major repairs done, for which it spends $1,400 in cash. The entry in general journal form is as follows:

	DATE		DESCRIPTION	POST. REF.	DEBIT	CREDIT	
1	*1991*						1
2	*Jan.*	*6*	*Accumulated Depreciation,*				2
3			*Automobile*		*1 4 0 0 00*		3
4			*Cash*			*1 4 0 0 00*	4
5			*New engine installed in*				5
6			*company car.*				6

This extraordinary repair extends the life of the car from the present one additional year to three additional years. Here are relevant balances, together with the $1,400 payment as shown by T accounts:

Automobile				Accumulated Depreciation, Automobile			
+		−		−		+	
Jan. 3, 1988	6,000			Jan. 6, 1991 1,400		Dec. 31, 1988	1,100
						Dec. 31, 1989	1,100
						Dec. 31, 1990	1,100

The car's book value before the extraordinary repair was $2,700 ($6,000 − $3,300). The accountant debits the Accumulated Depreciation account (rather than the asset account) to preserve the original cost figure in the asset account. In this example, the car that the firm bought cost $6,000, not $7,400. We can see this in the balance sheet as follows:

Plant and Equipment:			
Automobile	*$6 0 0 0 00*		
Less Accumulated Depreciation	*1 9 0 0 00*	*$4 1 0 0 00*	

When it comes to recording the remaining depreciation on this asset, the accountant now has a new cost base, which he or she uses to determine the new depreciation base. Assume that the trade-in value is still $1,600.

New book value ($6,000 − $1,900)	$4,100
Less trade-in value	1,600
New depreciation base	$2,500

$2,500 ÷ 3 years = $833.33

The adjusting entry for depreciation of the car at the end of 1991 is:

	DATE		DESCRIPTION	POST. REF.	DEBIT	CREDIT	
1	*1991*		*Adjusting Entry*				1
2	*Dec.*	*31*	*Depreciation Expense, Automobile*		8 3 3 33		2
3			*Accumulated Depreciation,*				3
4			*Automobile*			8 3 3 33	4
5							5

Remember

For an extraordinary
repair cost, debit
Accumulated
Depreciation instead of
Repair Expense, and
credit Cash or
Accounts Payable.

Assuming that no additional expenditures are made for extraordinary repairs, the adjusting entries for the remaining two years (1992 and 1993) will be $833.33 for 1992 and $833.34 for 1993.

DISPOSITION OF PLANT AND EQUIPMENT

Objective 5

Prepare journal entries
for discarding of assets
fully depreciated,
discarding of assets not
fully depreciated, sale
of assets involving a
loss, sale of assets
involving a gain,
exchange of assets
involving a loss on the
trade, and exchange of
assets involving a gain
on the trade.

Sooner or later a business entity disposes of its long-lived assets by (1) discarding or retiring them, (2) selling them, or (3) trading them in for other assets. **If the assets are not fully depreciated, the accountant must first make an entry to bring the depreciation up to date.** Let's look at some examples. (Ordinarily entries involving Cash would be recorded in the cash journals; however, for simplification and clarity, we shall present all the following entries in general journal form.)

Discarding or Retiring Plant and Equipment

When long-lived assets are no longer useful to the business and have no market value, a firm discards them.

Discarding of Fully Depreciated Assets   A display case that cost $1,400 and has been fully depreciated is given away as junk. The present status of the accounts is as follows:

Store Equipment		Accumulated Depreciation, Store Equipment	
+	–	–	+
Bal. 1,400			Bal. 1,400

The journal entry to record the disposal of the asset looks like this:

DATE	DESCRIPTION	POST. REF.	DEBIT	CREDIT	
1	*Accumulated Depreciation, Store*				1
2	*Equipment*		1 4 0 0 00		2
3	*Store Equipment*			1 4 0 0 00	3
4	*Discarded a fully depreciated*				4
5	*display case.*				5
6					6

Although fully depreciated assets are retained on the books as long as they remain in use, the firm may not take any additional depreciation on them. Once an asset is fully depreciated, the asset's book value will remain at its estimated salvage value unless an extraordinary repair is made or the company disposes of the asset.

Discarding an Asset Not Fully Depreciated   A firm discards a time clock that cost $1,600. No salvage value is realized. Accumulated Depreciation up to the end of the previous year is $1,450; depreciation for the current year is $90. The present balances of the accounts are as follows:

Office Equipment		Accumulated Depreciation, Office Equipment	
+	−	−	+
Bal. 1,600			Bal. 1,450

Record the entry to depreciate the asset up to date:

DATE	DESCRIPTION	POST. REF.	DEBIT	CREDIT	
1	*Depreciation Expense, Office*				1
2	*Equipment*		9 0 00		2
3	*Accumulated Depreciation, Office*				3
4	*Equipment*			9 0 00	4
5	*Depreciation on time clock for*				5
6	*the partial year.*				6

The T accounts look like this:

Depreciation Expense, Office Equipment		Accumulated Depreciation, Office Equipment	
+	−	−	+
90			Bal. 1,450
			90

The journal entry to record the disposal of the asset is as follows:

	DATE	DESCRIPTION	POST. REF.	DEBIT	CREDIT	
1		*Accumulated Depreciation, Office*				1
2		*Equipment*		1 5 4 0 00		2
3		*Loss on Disposal of Plant and*				3
4		*Equipment*		6 0 00		4
5		*Office Equipment*			1 6 0 0 00	5
6		*Discarded a time clock.*				6
7						7
8						8
9						9

The T accounts look like this:

Accumulated Depreciation, Office Equipment		Loss on Disposal of Plant and Equipment		Office Equipment	
−	+	+	−	+	−
1,540	Bal. 1,450	60		Bal. 1,600	1,600

The book value of the asset is $60 ($1,600 − $1,540). Because the firm realized nothing from the disposal of the asset, the loss is for the same amount as the book value.

Loss on Disposal of Plant and Equipment is an expense account that appears under Other Expense in the income statement.

Selling of Plant and Equipment

Naturally it is very hard to estimate the exact trade-in or salvage value of a long-lived asset. It is quite likely that when a firm sells or trades in such an asset, the amount realized will differ from the estimated amount.

Sale of an Asset at a Loss   Suppose that a firm sells a drill press for $135. This drill press originally cost $1,900; accumulated depreciation up to the end of the previous year was $1,560. Yearly depreciation is $180. The drill press is sold on August 21.

The present balances of the accounts are as follows:

Factory Equipment			Accumulated Depreciation, Factory Equipment		
+		−	−	+	
Bal.	1,900			Bal.	1,560

We record the depreciation of the asset to the present date:

	DATE		DESCRIPTION	POST. REF.	DEBIT		CREDIT		
1	*19–*								1
2	*Aug.*	*21*	*Depreciation Expense, Factory*						2
3			*Equipment*		*1 2 0 00*				3
4			*Accumulated Depreciation,*						4
5			*Factory Equipment*				*1 2 0 00*		5
6			*Depreciation on drill press for*						6
7			*8 months ($180 × 8/12 = $120).*						7
8									8
9									9
10									10
11									11

By T accounts, the situation looks like this:

Depreciation Expense, Factory Equipment		Accumulated Depreciation, Factory Equipment	
+	−	−	+
120			Bal. 1,560
			120

The entry, in general journal form, to record the sale of the drill press is as follows:

	DATE		DESCRIPTION	POST. REF.	DEBIT		CREDIT		
1	*Aug.*	*21*	*Cash*		*1 3 5 00*				1
2			*Accumulated Depreciation, Factory*						2
3			*Equipment*		*1 6 8 0 00*				3
4			*Loss on Disposal of Plant and*						4
5			*Equipment*		*8 5 00*				5
6			*Factory Equipment*				*1 9 0 0 00*		6
7			*Sold a drill press for $135,*						7
8			*having an original cost of $1,900*						8
9			*and accumulated depreciation*						9
10			*of $1,680.*						10
11									11
12									12
13									13
14									14

For purposes of illustration, let us record the above entry in the T accounts as follows:

	Cash	
+		−
	135	

Accumulated Depreciation, Factory Equipment		
−	+	
1,680	Bal.	1,560
		120

Loss on Disposal of Plant and Equipment		
+		−
85		

	Factory Equipment	
+		−
Bal.	1,900	1,900

Note that the book value of the drill press is $220 ($1,900 − $1,680). When the firm sells it for $135, the loss is $85, since the amount received for the item is $85 less than its book value.

Sale of an Asset at a Gain   Suppose that a firm sells an electronic analyzer for $310. The firm had originally paid $4,200; accumulated depreciation up to the end of the previous year was $3,960. Yearly depreciation is $120. The electronic analyzer is sold on October 18. The present balances of the accounts are as follows:

	Shop Equipment	
+		−
Bal.	4,200	

Accumulated Depreciation, Shop Equipment		
−	+	
	Bal.	3,960

We record the depreciation of the asset to the present date:

	DATE		DESCRIPTION	POST. REF.	DEBIT	CREDIT	
1	19–						1
2	Oct.	18	Depreciation Expense, Shop				2
3			Equipment		1 0 0 00		3
4			Accumulated Depreciation, Shop				4
5			Equipment			1 0 0 00	5
6			Recorded depreciation through				6
7			October 18. Depreciation for				7
8			10 months is $100				8
9			($120 × 10/12 = $100).				9
10							10
11							11

By T accounts, the situation looks like this:

Depreciation Expense, Shop Equipment		Accumulated Depreciation, Shop Equipment	
+	−	−	+
100			Bal. 3,960
			100

The general journal entry to record the sale of the electronic analyzer is as follows:

	DATE		DESCRIPTION	POST. REF.	DEBIT	CREDIT	
1	19—						1
2	Oct.	18	Cash		3 1 0 00		2
3			Accumulated Depreciation, Shop				3
4			Equipment		4 0 6 0 00		4
5			Shop Equipment			4 2 0 0 00	5
6			Gain on Disposal of Plant and				6
7			Equipment			1 7 0 00	7
8			Sold an electronic analyzer for				8
9			$310, having an original cost				9
10			of $4,200 and accumulated				10
11			depreciation of $4,060.				11

The T accounts look like this:

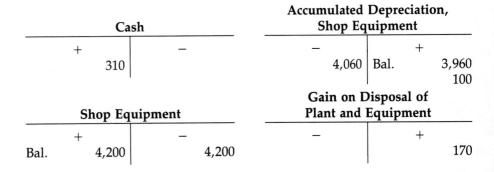

The revenue account **Gain on Disposal of Plant and Equipment** appears under Other Income in the income statement.

The book value of the electronic analyzer is $140 ($4,200 − $4,060). When the firm sells the electronic analyzer for $310, the firm's gain is $170, since the amount received for the item is $170 more than its book value.

Exchange of Long-lived Assets for Other Assets without Recognition of Gain or Loss

Often a business trades in one asset for another, using the old item as part payment for the new one. The trade-in allowance may differ from the book value of the asset. If the trade-in allowance is greater than the book value, the firm has a gain; if less than the book value, it has a loss. However, federal income tax laws state that when assets held for productive use are exchanged for similar assets, *no gain or loss is recognized*. In effect, the gain or loss is absorbed into the recorded cost of the new asset.

Exchange When Trade-in Value Is Less Than Book Value

Suppose that a firm bought a delivery truck for $14,700. Four years later, the truck has an accumulated depreciation of $12,600. The firm buys a new truck, with a list price of $16,800, trading in the old one, for which they are allowed only $1,200, and paying the difference in cash. Assume that the depreciation for the year is already up to date. The present status of the accounts is as follows:

Delivery Equipment		Accumulated Depreciation, Delivery Equipment	
+	−	−	+
Bal. 14,700		Bal. 12,600	

The firm's accountant records the transaction by the following steps:

1. Credit cash, $15,600 (quoted price of new truck, $16,800 minus $1,200, which is the trade-in allowance on old truck).
2. Close or clear the account of the old asset: credit Delivery Equipment, $14,700.
3. Close or clear the Accumulated Depreciation account of the old asset: debit Accumulated Depreciation, $12,600.
4. Debit the account of the new asset for the difference between total debits and total credits, $17,700 ($15,600 + $14,700 − $12,600 = $17,700), which is the book value of the old asset plus the amount of cash or notes given.

The entries in general journal form with the steps labeled are shown at the top of the next page.

You can see from this that when you use the income tax method of accounting, the loss is absorbed in the cost of the new equipment. In this case the accountant added the loss of $900 to the price of the new equipment, as follows:

	DATE	DESCRIPTION	POST. REF.	DEBIT	CREDIT	
1		(4) Delivery Equipment		17 7 0 0 00		1
2		(3) Accumulated Depreciation, Delivery				2
3		Equipment		12 6 0 0 00		3
4		(1) Cash			15 6 0 0 00	4
5		(2) Delivery Equipment			14 7 0 0 00	5
6		Bought a new delivery truck				6
7		having a list price of $16,800.				7
8		Received a trade-in allowance				8
9		of $1,200 on old delivery truck,				9
10		having an original cost of				10
11		$14,700 and accumulated				11
12		depreciation of $12,600.				12
13						13

Cost of old equipment	$14,700
Less accumulated depreciation	12,600
Book value	$ 2,100
Less trade-in allowance	1,200
Loss	$ 900
Quoted price of new equipment	$16,800
Plus loss absorbed in record cost of new equipment	900
Recorded cost of new equipment	$17,700

You can also use this technique to verify the cost recorded for the new equipment. For income tax purposes, the firm cannot count the $900 loss at this time; however, the firm does have an additional $900 that it can take in depreciation in the future.

Exchange When Trade-in Value Is Greater Than Book Value

A business bought an automated file for $2,600. After some years the business decides to trade it in on a new model. The old file has an accumulated depreciation of $2,480 *on the date of the trade-in,* leaving a book value of $120. The new file has a list price of $3,350; however, the salesperson gives the firm a generous trade-in allowance of $310 on the old equipment, and the firm pays the difference in cash. The present status of the accounts is shown in the following T accounts:

Office Equipment		Accumulated Depreciation, Office Equipment	
+	−	−	+
Bal. 2,600			Bal. 2,480

The firm's accountant records the transaction by the following steps:

1. Credit Cash, $3,040 (quoted price of new file, $3,350, minus the $310 trade-in allowance on old model).
2. Close or clear the account of the old asset: credit Office Equipment, $2,600.
3. Close or clear the Accumulated Depreciation account on the old asset: debit Accumulated Depreciation, $2,480.
4. Debit the account of the new asset for the difference between the total debits and credits, $3,160 ($3,040 + $2,600 − $2,480 = $3,160), which is the book value of the old asset plus the amount of cash or notes given.

Here is how one records the entries in general journal form with the steps labeled:

	DATE	DESCRIPTION	POST. REF.	DEBIT	CREDIT	
1		(4) Office Equipment		3 1 6 0 00		1
2		(3) Accumulated Depreciation, Office				2
3		Equipment		2 4 8 0 00		3
4		(1) Cash			3 0 4 0 00	4
5		(2) Office Equipment			2 6 0 0 00	5
6		Bought a new automated file				6
7		having a list price of $3,350.				7
8		Received a trade-in allowance				8
9		of $310 on old file, which had				9
10		an original cost of $2,600 and				10
11		accumulated depreciation of				11
12		$2,480.				12
13						13
14						14

The accountant records the cost of the new equipment at less than the list price, which indicates that a gain is involved. This gain has been absorbed in the price of the new equipment.

Cost of old equipment	$2,600
Less accumulated depreciation	2,480
Book value	$ 120
Less trade-in allowance of $310	
Gain	$310 − $120 = $190
Quoted price of new equipment	$3,350
Less gain absorbed in recorded cost of new equipment	190
Recorded cost of new equipment	$3,160

For income tax purposes, the firm does not count the gain at this time. However, the amount that the firm can take in depreciation in the future has been reduced by $190.

PLANT AND EQUIPMENT RECORDS

Objective 6

Maintain a plant and equipment subsidiary ledger.

Depreciation, which is regarded as an expense, vitally affects the net income of any business. Because net income is affected, the amount of income taxes owed is likewise affected. And not only Depreciation Expense, but also Loss (or Gain) on Disposal can affect net income. For income tax purposes, the business must be able to justify the amount of depreciation taken, as well as the gain or loss on disposal of assets.

We have discussed Plant and Equipment as a category on a classified balance sheet. Accountants use the term *plant* to include land, land improvements, and buildings.

Each asset represents a functional group. Following is an illustration of the Plant and Equipment section of a balance sheet:

Plant and Equipment:			
Land		$ 6 0 0 0 00	
Land Improvements	$ 3 0 0 0 00		
Less Accumulated Depreciation	2 3 0 0 00	7 0 0 00	
Building	$40 0 0 0 00		
Less Accumulated Depreciation	28 0 0 0 00	12 0 0 0 00	
Office Equipment	$ 6 0 0 0 00		
Less Accumulated Depreciation	4 5 0 0 00	1 5 0 0 00	
Store Equipment	$18 0 0 0 00		
Less Accumulated Depreciation	14 0 0 0 00	4 0 0 0 00	
Delivery Equipment	$20 0 0 0 00		
Less Accumulated Depreciation	12 0 0 0 00	8 0 0 0 00	
Total Plant and Equipment			32 2 0 0 00

The Store Equipment account represents a functional group; it includes all types of equipment used in the operation of a store. Examples of store equipment are display cases, cash registers, counters, and storage shelves. To account for the depreciation of each item of store equipment, accountants maintain a separate record card for each item in the plant and equipment ledger. **Store Equipment is a controlling account; the plant and equipment ledger is a subsidiary ledger.** This relationship is like that of Accounts Receivable, which is a controlling account, and the accounts receivable ledger, which is a subsidiary ledger with an account for each individual charge customer. Figure 20-1 shows a record

PLANT AND EQUIPMENT RECORD

ITEM   *Cash Register*   ACCOUNT NO.   *128-1*

SERIAL NO.   *ND37-4163*   MAKER   *Security, Inc.*

FROM WHOM PURCHASED   *Rogers Equipment Company*

ESTIMATED LIFE   *5*   ESTIMATED SALVAGE VALUE   *$50*

DEPRECIATION METHOD   *Straight line*   DEPRECIATION PER YEAR   *$150.00*   DEPRECIATION PER MONTH   *$12.50*   RATE OF DEPRECIATION   *20%*

		ASSET			ACCUMULATED DEPRECIATION			BOOK VALUE
DATE	EXPLANATION	DEBIT	CREDIT	BALANCE	DEBIT	CREDIT	BALANCE	
7/3/87		800		800				800
12/31/88						75	75	725
12/31/89						150	225	575
12/31/90						150	375	425

FIGURE 20-1

card in a firm's plant and equipment ledger. Posting to the subsidiary ledger will also be marked by a check mark in the journal's Post. Ref. column when the asset accounts and the related accumulated depreciation accounts are debited or credited.

Account 128 is the number of the general ledger account for Store Equipment. Account 128-1 is the first piece of equipment listed under Store Equipment in the plant and equipment ledger.

The plant and equipment record enables the accountant to calculate the total amount of the adjusting entry to be recorded on the company's work sheet. The total of the adjusting entry is found by adding the fiscal period's depreciation for each separate asset contained in the plant and equipment ledger. The amount of depreciation for each asset is determined by the schedule of depreciation for that asset. Also, plant and equipment records are invaluable when a business has to submit insurance claims in the event of insured losses.

DEPRECIATION FOR FEDERAL INCOME TAX

Businesses are entitled to deduct depreciation expenses when calculating the amounts of income taxes owed to the federal government. However, the amount of depreciation recorded on a company's income statement may differ from the amount used for income tax purposes. Before 1981, firms frequently used the double-declining-balance or sum-of-the-years'-digits methods for determining their income tax deductions, and they used the straight-line method for their income statements. In other

COMPUTERS AT WORK

Computers to the Rescue— Depreciation

Depreciation is a simple concept that has complex, ever-changing applications. Back in the days when all accounting was done with pencil and paper, all an accountant did to calculate depreciation was divide the cost of an asset by its useful life, using what we now call the straight-line method. The resulting figure was then entered as an expense, and that was that. Since that time, virtually every federal tax bill has changed some aspect of depreciation, creating a tangle of rules and choices. Anyone who has switched to computerized depreciation after trying to keep up with the changes using paper and pencil knows why many accountants feel that computers were invented just for them.

Keeping track of the depreciation of fixed assets requires a bewildering amount of record keeping, in part because so many depreciation options are available. The various methods of computing accelerated depreciation allow a company to deduct more of the cost of a fixed asset early in that asset's life and therefore save on taxes. But a company that uses accelerated depreciation for tax purposes may want to use the straight-line method for financial reporting, requiring more record keeping. To further complicate matters, when Congress made one change in the depreciation method, the Accelerated Cost Recovery System, it decided that the system could be used only for tax reporting, not for financial reporting.

The useful life periods assigned to various assets have also changed, as have the ability of a business to receive an investment tax credit and the records that a company needs to keep in order to claim depreciation. Therefore, companies have to record not just when an asset was purchased and how much it cost, but how long it was expected to last, what depreciation method was used for financial and tax purposes, and what the difference was between the Accelerated Cost Recovery System and regular depreciation.

Computer programs written especially for keeping such records have made the accountant's job immeasurably easier. The programs keep track of all the necessary information and then provide it in the most useful form for auditors verifying asset values, tax return preparers, and company controllers preparing financial statements and stockholder information. Depreciation software has also made it much easier for a company to compare various ways of handling fixed assets, deciding whether to lease or buy and which depreciation methods to use.

Hundreds of software companies now produce depreciation programs for both mainframe and personal computers. The companies tailor the programs for the needs of individual clients and update them with each change in tax law and accounting procedures. As a result, thousands of accountants each year can be heard mumbling to their computer screens, "What would I do without you?"

words, companies use one depreciation method for accounting purposes and another depreciation method for income tax purposes. Since the first two methods yield the greatest amount of depreciation during the earlier years of an asset's life, businesses were able to reduce their income taxes during this period. By using accelerated methods, they were able to delay paying their taxes and were able to put the money to productive use. However, in most situations, the straight-line method of depreciation is more closely related to the way assets wear out and consequently need to be replaced.

In 1981, Congress passed the Economic Recovery Act, which introduced the Accelerated Cost Recovery System (ACRS). ACRS provided for depreciation deductions that approximated the 150 percent declining-balance method. However, the assigned lives of assets (called recovery periods) were much shorter than their actual useful lives. The base for calculating depreciation was the asset's cost, since trade-in or scrap value was not counted. Assets were divided into classes according to length of life (three, five, ten, fifteen, or eighteen years). For example, automobiles were given a three-year life or recovery period, machinery five years, most buildings eighteen years. Percentages for annual depreciation of each class of asset were published in a series of tables developed by the federal government.

In 1986, Congress passed the Tax Reform Act, which revised allowable depreciation under ACRS. The new schedule of allowable depreciation is called the Modified Accelerated Cost Recovery System (MACRS). Assets put into use after 1986 are divided into eight classes according to length of life. Depreciation for most property except real estate is approximated by the 200 percent (double) declining-balance method. However, the allowable lives of most assets have been extended. As examples, automobiles, light trucks, and light tools were classified as three-year property under ACRS. Under the new law, light tools continue to be three-year property, but automobiles and light trucks are classified as five-year property. Following is a comparison of the allowable percentages and depreciation under ACRS versus the Tax Reform Act for an automobile or light truck costing $10,000:

ACRS—3-year Property			MACRS Tax Reform Act—5-year Property		
Year	Percentage	Depreciation	Year	Percentage	Depreciation
1	25	$2,500 ($10,000 × .25)	1	20	$2,000 ($10,000 × .2)
2	38	3,800 ($10,000 × .38)	2	32	3,200 ($10,000 × .32)
3	37	3,700 ($10,000 × .37)	3	19.2	1,920 ($10,000 × .192)
	100	$10,000	4	11.52	1,152 ($10,000 × .1152)
			5	11.52	1,152 ($10,000 × .1152)
			6	5.76	576 ($10,000 × .0576)
				100.00	$10,000

This presentation of allowable deductions for depreciation for federal income tax purposes is intended purely as an introduction. Because of the frequent revisions and the complexity of tax issues, consult the Internal Revenue Code for a more detailed discussion.

SUMMARY

L.O. 1   The figures listed for original costs of plant and equipment comprise all necessary and normal expenditures, including transportation and installation costs of an asset. An accountant may use the tax assessor's ratio to separate the value of land from the value of buildings when the two have been purchased as one package. Land improvements are depreciable; these improvements include the costs of driveways, parking lots, trees and shrubs, and outdoor lighting systems.

L.O. 2   Depreciation represents the decline in usefulness of an asset resulting from such causes as physical wear and tear, inadequacy, and obsolescence.

Depreciation is recorded as a debit to the Depreciation Expense of the asset and a credit to the Accumulated Depreciation of the asset. The depreciation base is the cost of the asset less the trade-in or salvage value. We introduced four methods of determining depreciation:

$$\text{Straight-line method} = \frac{\text{Cost} - \text{Trade-in value}}{\text{Useful life (in years)}}$$

$$\text{Units-of-production method} = \frac{\text{Cost} - \text{Trade-in value}}{\text{Estimated units of production}}$$

$$\text{Double-declining-balance method} = \text{Book value at beginning of year} \times \text{Twice straight-line rate}$$

$$\text{Sum-of-the-years'-digits method} = \text{Reducing fraction} \times (\text{Cost} - \text{Trade-in value})$$

For the sum-of-the-years'-digits method, the numerator of the fraction is the years of the asset's life placed in reverse order. The denominator of the fraction is the sum of the years of the asset's life. (The trade-in value is counted at the end of the schedule of depreciation.)

L.O. 3,4   Capital expenditures, which are debited to the asset accounts, are costs incurred to buy or increase the capacity of assets. Extraordinary-repairs expenditures either significantly prolong the life of an asset or increase its estimated salvage value. These expenditures are recorded as debits to the Accumulated Depreciation account of the asset.

L.O. 5   When a firm changes its Plant and Equipment accounts, as a result of selling, exchanging, or discarding its assets, the accountant must close or clear the asset accounts along with their respective Accumulated Depreciation accounts. When a firm discards, sells, or trades in an asset that has not yet been fully depreciated, the accountant must first depreciate the asset up to the present date. When the amount received for the old asset is less than the asset's book value, the accountant debits Loss on Disposal of Plant and Equipment. When a firm receives more for an asset than its book value, on the other hand, Gain on Disposal of Plant and Equipment is credited.

When a firm trades in one asset for a similar asset, the accountant's entry must include the four steps shown on pages 664 and 666.

L.O. 6   Plant and equipment records should consist of a controlling account and a subsidiary ledger. The subsidiary ledger should contain a card for each piece of equipment, listing the date acquired, cost, and depreciation taken to date. For income tax purposes, a subsidiary ledger is a must.

GLOSSARY

Accelerated depreciation Relatively large amounts of depreciation recorded during the early years of an asset's use; decreasing in later years.

Capital expenditures Costs incurred for the purchase of plant and equipment, as well as the cost of increasing the capacity of assets; the firm receives services or benefits from this plant and equipment for more than one accounting period.

Consistency The accounting concept that requires that a particular accounting procedure, once adopted, will not be changed from one fiscal period to another period.

Depreciation base Total cost of an asset less the trade-in or salvage value.

Extraordinary-repairs expenditures Costs incurred for major overhauls or reconditioning of assets; repairs that either significantly prolong the life of the asset or increase its estimated salvage value.

Gain on Disposal of Plant and Equipment When a firm sells or trades in an asset and receives an amount in excess of the book value for that asset, the gain is recorded in this account, which appears under Other Income in the income statement.

Land Improvements An asset account covering the cost of expenditures for improvements that are (1) not as permanent as the land, or (2) not directly associated with a building. These include driveways, parking lots, trees and shrubs, fences, and outdoor lighting systems.

Loss on Disposal of Plant and Equipment When a firm sells or trades in an asset and receives an amount less than the book value for that asset, the loss is recorded in this expense account.

Revenue expenditures Costs incurred to maintain the operation of assets, such as normal repair expenses and fuel expenses.

QUESTIONS, EXERCISES, AND PROBLEMS
Discussion Questions

1. How do income tax laws treat the exchange of similar items of plant and equipment?
2. Distinguish between expenditures for ordinary repairs and expenditures for extraordinary repairs.
3. Describe the use and operation of a plant and equipment ledger. What items are listed on each card in the ledger?
4. Which of the following would be listed under Plant and Equipment?
   a. Parking lot for company employees

    b. Car held for sale by a car dealer

    c. Microcomputer used by an office employee

    d. Pollution-control equipment that does not reduce the cost or improve the efficiency of the factory

    e. Stamping machine used in the manufacturing operations but now fully depreciated

5. How does the accountant's meaning of the term *depreciation* differ from the nonaccountant's meaning of the term?

6. Name four things that an accountant must know about an asset, classified as plant and equipment, to calculate its depreciation expense.

7. Which methods of depreciation are classified as accelerated depreciation?

8. Distinguish between capital expenditures and revenue expenditures.

Exercises

L.O. 1,3   **Exercise 20-1**   Brinks Manufacturing Company purchased land adjacent to its factory for the installation of a parking lot. Expenditures by the company were as follows: purchase price, $120,000; broker's fees, $6,500; title search and other fees, $550; demolition of a shack on the property, $2,400; grading, $2,800; paving $16,400; lighting, $10,300; signs, $950. Determine the amount that should be debited to the Land account.

L.O. 2   **Exercise 20-2**   T accounts for Truck and its related depreciation are presented below:

Truck		Accumulated Depreciation, Truck	
1/1/x1 8,000		12/31/x1 1,600	
		12/31/x2 1,600	
		12/31/x3 1,600	

    a. What is the book value of the truck as of 12/31/x3?

    b. If the trade-in value of the truck is $1,600, what is the estimated life of the truck?

    c. If the truck were sold for $3,950 on 12/31/x3, what would be the amount of the gain or loss?

L.O. 3   **Exercise 20-3**   Poe Woolen Mills bought a loom for $29,000; terms 2/10, n/30, FOB factory. Poe paid the invoice within the discount period, along with $520 for freight charges. Poe also paid installation costs of $1,210 and power connection costs of $620. How much should Poe debit to its Plant and Equipment account?

L.O. 2   **Exercise 20-4**   At the beginning of the fiscal year, Cox Furniture bought a delivery truck for $10,500, with an estimated trade-in value of $1,500 and an estimated useful life of five years. Determine the amount of the depreciation for the first and second years by the following methods:

    a. Straight-line

    b. Double-declining-balance method at twice the straight-line rate

    c. Sum-of-the-years'-digits

L.O. 5   **Exercise 20-5**   On August 24, Seibert and Company discarded a carpet (Office Equipment) with no salvage value. The following details are taken from the subsidiary ledger: cost, $720; accumulated depreciation as of the previous December 31, $549; monthly depreciation, $9. Journalize entries to record the depreciation of the carpet up to date and to record the disposal of the carpet.

L.O. 5   **Exercise 20-6**   On May 28, Sero Cab Company sold a taxicab for cash, $300. The following details are taken from the subsidiary ledger: cost, $7,450; accumulated depreciation as of the previous December 31, $6,380; monthly depreciation, $110. Make entries in general ledger form to record the depreciation up to date and the sale of the asset.

L.O. 5   **Exercise 20-7**   On October 19, Higgins Florists traded in its old delivery truck on a new one, which cost $9,880. Higgins got a trade-in allowance of $840 on the old truck and paid the difference in cash. The subsidiary account shows the following: cost (of old truck), $7,580; accumulated depreciation as of last December 31, $6,436; monthly depreciation, $96. Without recognizing gain or loss, make entries in general journal form to record the depreciation of the old truck up to date and to record the exchange of assets.

L.O. 5   **Exercise 20-8**   On May 22, Durco Cannery trades in a machine on a new one priced at $7,692, receiving a trade-in allowance of $820 on the old machine. Durco makes a downpayment of $1,000 in cash, and issues a 60-day, 8 percent note for the remainder. The subsidiary account shows the following: cost, $5,564; accumulated depreciation as of last December 31, $4,552; monthly depreciation, $68. Without recognizing gain or loss, make entries in general journal form to record the depreciation of the old machine up to date and to record the exchange of assets.

Problem Set A

L.O. 2   **Problem 20-1A**   The Simpson Company, at the beginning of a fiscal year, buys a machine for $40,000. The machine has an estimated life of five years and an estimated trade-in value of $4,000.

Instructions

Using the following three methods, determine the annual depreciation of the machine for each of the expected five years of its life, the accumulated depreciation at the end of each year, and the book value of the machine at the end of each year. Use the columns provided in the Working Papers.

a. Straight-line method
b. Double-declining-balance method
c. Sum-of-the-years'-digits method

L.O. 2,5   **Problem 20-2A**   During a three-year period, Megan Motel completed the following transactions pertaining to its pick-up truck:

Year 1

Jan. 11 Bought a used pick-up truck for cash, $6,700.

Nov. 16 Paid garage for maintenance repairs to pick-up truck, $138.

Dec. 31 Made the adjusting entry to record depreciation for the fiscal year, using the straight-line method of depreciation. The estimated life of the pick-up truck is four years, and it has an estimated trade-in value of $1,200.

      31 Closed the expense accounts to the Income Summary account.

Year 2

Mar.   4 Paid garage for tune-up and minor repairs, $56.

May   27 Bought a tire, $69.

Dec. 31 Recorded the adjusting entry for depreciation.

      31 Closed the expense accounts to the Income Summary account.

Year 3

Feb. 13 Paid garage for maintenance repairs to pick-up truck, $326.

June 22 Traded in the pick-up truck for another pick-up truck priced at $9,460, receiving a trade-in allowance of $1,040; paid the difference in cash. Recorded the entry to depreciate the old truck up to date. Made the entry to record the exchange, assuming gain or loss is not recognized.

Dec. 31 Recorded adjusting entry for depreciation of the new pick-up truck for the fiscal year using the straight-line method of depreciation. The estimated life of the new truck is six years, and it has an estimated trade-in value of $1,500.

      31 Closed the expense accounts to the Income Summary account.

Instructions

1. Record all these transactions in general journal form.
2. After journalizing each entry, post to the following ledger accounts: Truck; Accumulated Depreciation, Truck; Truck Repair Expense; Depreciation Expense, Truck.

L.O. 2,5 **Problem 20-3A** During a three-year period, the Bingham Construction Company completed the following transactions connected with its bulldozer:

Year 1

June 30 Bought a bulldozer, $120,400, paying $40,400 in cash, and issuing a series of four notes for $20,000 each, to come due at six-month intervals. Payments are to include principal plus 9 percent interest to maturity of each note.

July   2 Paid transportation charges for the bulldozer, $3,600.

Dec. 31 Paid the principal, $20,000, plus interest of $900 on the first note.

      31 Made the adjusting entry to record depreciation on the bulldozer for the fiscal year, using the double-declining-balance method at twice the straight-line rate ($24,800; verify this figure). The estimated life of the bulldozer is five years, and it has an estimated salvage value of $11,600.

      31 Closed the expense accounts to the Income Summary account.

Year 2

Apr.   24 Paid for maintenance repairs to the bulldozer, $5,836.

June   30 Paid the principal, $20,000, plus interest of $1,800 on the second note.

Dec.   31 Paid the principal, $20,000, plus interest of $2,700 on the third note.

       31 Made the adjusting entry to record depreciation for the fiscal year ($99,200 × 2/5 = $39,680; verify this figure).

       31 Closed the expense accounts to the Income Summary account.

Year 3

May   19 Paid for maintenance repairs to the bulldozer, $2,094.

June   30 Paid the principal, $20,000, plus interest of $3,600 on the fourth note.

Sept. 29 Bingham Construction decides to get rid of its bulldozer and use the services of an equipment rental firm in the future. Sold the bulldozer for $24,000, receiving cash. Made the entry to depreciate the bulldozer up to date ($17,856; verify this figure). Made the entry accounting for the sale of the machine.

Dec.   31 Closed the expense accounts to the Income Summary account.

Instructions

1. Record the transactions in general journal form.
2. After making each journal entry, post to the following ledger accounts: Equipment; Accumulated Depreciation, Equipment; Depreciation Expense, Equipment; Equipment Maintenance Expense; Interest Expense; Loss on Disposal of Plant and Equipment.

L.O. 2,5,6   **Problem 20-4A**   The general ledger of the Dillow Insurance Agency includes controlling accounts for Office Equipment and for Accumulated Depreciation, Office Equipment. Dillow's accountant also records the details of each item of office equipment in a subsidiary ledger. The following transactions affecting office equipment occurred during a three-year period:

Year 1

Jan.   4 Bought the following items from Graham Office Supplies for cash:

Executive desk, $810, account no. 123-1, estimated life ten years, trade-in value zero.

Executive chair, $285, account no. 123-2, estimated life ten years, trade-in value zero.

Filing cabinet, metal, $180, account no. 123-3, estimated life fifteen years, trade-in value zero.

(The above assets will be depreciated using the straight-line method.)

       9 Paid Sears Cabinet Shop $1,080 for a custom-made counter, account no. 123-4, estimated life ten years, trade-in value zero; depreciation by straight-line method.

       12 Purchased for cash a Van Dusen electric typewriter from Regal Office Machines, $570, serial no. VPL2155, account no. 123-5, estimated life five years, estimated trade-in value, $75; depreciation by sum-of-the-years'-digits method.

Dec.   31 Made the adjusting entry to record depreciation of Office Equipment for the fiscal year (total depreciation, $394.50; verify this figure).

31 Closed the Depreciation Expense, Office Equipment account into the Income Summary account.

Year 2

June   27 Bought a rug from Franklin Furniture on account, $720, account no. 123-6; estimated life eight years, trade-in value zero; depreciation by double-declining-balance method at twice the straight-line rate.

Dec.   31 Recorded the adjusting entry for depreciation of office equipment for the fiscal year (depreciation for six months on the rug; total depreciation, $451.50; verify this figure).

31 Closed the Depreciation Expense, Office Equipment account into the Income Summary account.

Year 3

June   23 Traded in the executive desk for a new one, which cost $1,020, from Sellwood, Inc., account no. 123-7, receiving a trade-in allowance of $480 on the old desk and paying the balance in cash. Expected life of the new desk is eight years, with a zero trade-in value. Use straight-line method of depreciation. Made the entry to depreciate the old desk up to date. Made the entry to record the exchange of assets, without recognizing gain or loss.

Dec.   31 Made the adjusting entry to record depreciation of office equipment for the fiscal year (depreciation for six months on the desk; total depreciation, $476.72; verify this figure).

31 Closed the Depreciation Expense, Office Equipment account into the Income Summary account.

Instructions

1. Record the transactions in general journal form.
2. With the purchase of each new asset, open an account in the subsidiary ledger.
3. After each entry, post to the two controlling accounts and to the subsidiary ledger.
4. Make a list of balances at the end of year 3 in the subsidiary ledger accounts and compare the totals with the balances of the two controlling accounts.

Problem Set B

L.O. 2   **Problem 20-1B**   At the beginning of a fiscal year, the Franco Potato Chip Company buys a truck for $18,000. The truck's estimated life is five years, and its estimated trade-in value is $3,000.

Instructions

Using the following three methods, determine the annual depreciation for each of the estimated five years of life, the accumulated depreciation at the end of each year, and the book value of the truck at the end of each year. Use the columns provided in the Working Papers.

a. Straight-line method
b. Double-declining-balance method
c. Sum-of-the-years'-digits method

L.O. 2,5 **Problem 20-2B** During a three-year period, Braden Electric completed the following transactions related to its service truck:

Year 1

Jan.   4 Bought a used service truck for cash, $12,600.
Nov.   21 Paid garage for maintenance repairs to the truck, $146.
Dec.   31 Recorded the adjusting entry for depreciation for the fiscal year. The estimated life of the truck is four years, and it has an estimated trade-in value of $2,800. Braden uses the straight-line method of depreciation.
       31 Closed the expense accounts to the Income Summary account.

Year 2

Apr.   2 Paid garage for tune-up of truck, $76.
May   24 Paid $345 for tires for the truck.
Dec.   31 Recorded the adjusting entry for depreciation for the fiscal year.
       31 Closed the expense accounts to the Income Summary account.

Year 3

June   6 Paid garage for maintenance repairs to truck, $342.
       27 Traded in the used truck for a new truck, which cost $21,600, receiving a trade-in allowance of $8,400 and paying the difference in cash. Made the entry to record the depreciation on the truck up to the present date. Made the entry to record the exchange, assuming gain or loss is not recognized.
Dec.   31 Recorded the adjusting entry for depreciation of the new truck for the fiscal year. The estimated life of the truck is six years, and it has an estimated trade-in value of $2,600. Braden Electric uses the straight-line method of depreciation.
       31 Closed the expense accounts to the Income Summary account.

Instructions

1. Record the transactions in general journal form.
2. After journalizing each entry, post to the following ledger accounts: Truck; Accumulated Depreciation, Truck; Truck Repair Expense; Depreciation Expense, Truck.

L.O. 2,5 **Problem 20-3B** During a three-year period, Fowler Excavation completed the following transactions pertaining to its printing press:

Year 1

June   30 Bought a front-end loader, $42,640, paying $10,640 in cash, and issuing a series of four notes for $8,000 each, to come due at six-month intervals. Payments are to include principal plus interest of 9 percent to maturity of each note.
July   1 Paid transportation charges for the loader, $560.
Dec.   31 Paid the principal, $8,000, plus interest of $360 on the first note.

Dec. 31 Made the adjusting entry to record depreciation for the fiscal year. The estimated life of the loader is four years; it has a salvage value of $4,000. Fowler's accountant uses the double-declining-balance method, at twice the straight-line rate ($10,800; verify this figure).

31 Closed the expense accounts to the Income Summary account.

Year 2

Mar. 14 Paid for normal mechanical repairs, $516.

June 30 Paid the principal, $8,000, plus interest of $720 on the second note.

Dec. 31 Paid the principal, $8,000, plus interest of $1,080 on the third note.

31 Recorded the adjusting entry for the fiscal year ($16,200; verify this figure).

31 Closed the expense accounts to the Income Summary account.

Year 3

Apr. 21 Paid for normal mechanical repairs, $823.

June 30 Paid the principal, $8,000, plus interest of $1,440 on the fourth note.

Sept. 27 Fowler Excavation decides to get rid of its loader and use the services of an equipment rental firm in the future. Sold the loader for $8,400 cash. Made the entry to depreciate the loader up to date ($6,075). Made the entry to account for the sale of the press.

Dec. 31 Closed the expense accounts to the Income Summary account.

Instructions

1. Record the transactions in general journal form.
2. After making each journal entry, post to the following ledger accounts: Equipment; Accumulated Depreciation, Equipment; Depreciation Expense, Equipment; Equipment Maintenance Expense; Interest Expense; Loss on Disposal of Plant and Equipment.

L.O. 2,5,6 **Problem 20-4B** The general ledger of the Coski Personnel Service includes controlling accounts for Office Equipment and Accumulated Depreciation, Office Equipment. Coski's accountant also records the details of each item of office equipment in a subsidiary ledger. During a three-year period, the following transactions affecting office equipment took place:

Year 1

Jan. 5 Bought the following from Abingdon, Inc., for cash:
Filing cabinet, $240, account no. 123-1, expected life fifteen years, trade-in value zero.
Executive desk, $960, account no. 123-2, expected life twelve years, trade-in value zero.
Executive chair, $360, account no. 123-3, expected life twelve years, trade-in value zero.
(The above assets will be depreciated using the straight-line method.)

7 Paid Butler and Robbins $1,280 for a custom-made counter, account no. 123-4, expected life ten years, trade-in value zero; straight-line rate method.

Jan. 10 Bought for cash a Sinclair typewriter, serial no. N-1522A, account no. 123-5, from Garland Office Supplies for $720; estimated life five years, estimated trade-in value $120; sum-of-the-years'-digits method.

Dec. 31 Made the adjusting entry to record depreciation of office equipment for the fiscal year (total depreciation, $454; verify this figure).

31 Closed the Depreciation Expense, Office Equipment account into the Income Summary account.

Year 2

June 29 Bought a carpet from Beel Floor Coverings on account, account no. 123-6, price $1,280, estimated life eight years, trade-in value zero; double-declining-balance method at twice the straight-line rate.

Dec. 31 Made the adjusting entry to record depreciation of office equipment for the fiscal year (depreciation for six months on the carpet; total depreciation, $574; verify this figure).

31 Closed the Depreciation Expense, Office Equipment account into the Income Summary account.

Year 3

June 30 Traded in the executive chair for a new one from Garcia and Wentz, account no. 123-7. The new chair cost $520, has an estimated life of eight years, and a zero trade-in value. Coski Personnel Service received a trade-in allowance of $230 on the old chair and paid the balance in cash. Recorded the entry to depreciate the old chair up to date using the straight-line method of depreciation. Made the entry to record the exchange of assets, without recognizing gain or loss.

Dec. 31 Made the adjusting entry to record depreciation of office equipment for the fiscal year (depreciation for six months on the chair; total depreciation, $659.94; verify this figure).

31 Closed the Depreciation Expense, Office Equipment account into the Income Summary account.

Instructions

1. Record the transactions in general journal form.
2. Each time Coski buys a new asset, open an account in the subsidiary ledger.
3. After each entry, post to the two controlling accounts and to the subsidiary ledger.
4. Make a list of the balances at the end of year 3 in the subsidiary ledger accounts and compare the totals with the balances of the two controlling accounts.

REVIEW OF T ACCOUNT PLACEMENT AND REPRESENTATIVE TRANSACTIONS: CHAPTERS 16 THROUGH 20

Review of T Account Placement

The following sums up the placement of T accounts covered in Chapters 16 through 20 in relation to the fundamental accounting equation. Color indicates that an account is treated as a deduction from the account above it.

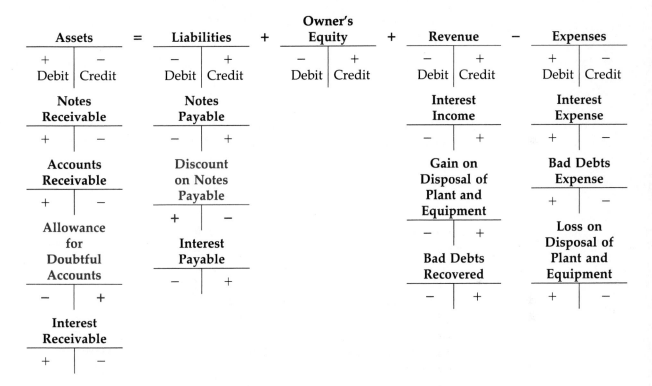

Review of Representative Transactions

The table on the following pages summarizes the recording of transactions covered in Chapters 16 through 20, along with the classification of the accounts involved. Note that, in this table, OE stands for Other Expenses.

Transaction	Accounts Involved	Class.	Increase or Decrease	Therefore Debit or Credit	Financial Statement
Gave a note to secure an extension of time on an open account.	Accounts Payable Notes Payable	CL CL	D I	Debit Credit	Balance Sheet Balance Sheet
Paid an interest-bearing note at maturity.	Notes Payable Interest Expense Cash	CL OE CA	D I D	Debit Debit Credit	Balance Sheet Income State. Balance Sheet
Borrowed from a bank; bank deducted interest in advance. Time period of note does not extend into next fiscal period.	Cash Interest Expense Notes Payable	CA OE CL	I I I	Debit Debit Credit	Balance Sheet Income State. Balance Sheet
Paid the bank at maturity of loan, previously discounted.	Notes Payable Cash	CL CA	D D	Debit Credit	Balance Sheet Balance Sheet
Borrowed from a bank; bank deducted interest in advance. Time period of note expires next fiscal period.	Cash Discount on Notes Payable Notes Payable	CA CL CL	I I I	Debit Debit Credit	Balance Sheet Balance Sheet Balance Sheet
Adjusting entry for interest expired.	Interest Expense Discount on Notes Payable	OE CL	I D	Debit Credit	Income State. Balance Sheet
Renewed a note and paid interest up to date.	Notes Payable Interest Expense Notes Payable Cash	CL OE CL CA	D I I D	Debit Debit Credit Credit	Balance Sheet Income State. Balance Sheet Balance Sheet
Adjusting entry for accrued interest on notes payable.	Interest Expense Interest Payable	OE CL	I I	Debit Credit	Income State. Balance Sheet
Reversing entry for accrued interest on notes payable.	Interest Payable Interest Expense	CL OE	D D	Debit Credit	Balance Sheet Income State.

Transaction	Accounts Involved	Class.	Increase or Decrease	Therefore Debit or Credit	Financial Statement
Received a note from a charge customer to gain an extension of time.	Notes Receivable Accounts Receivable	CA CA	I D	Debit Credit	Balance Sheet Balance Sheet

Received amount due on an interest-bearing note.	Cash
	   Notes Receivable
	   Interest Income
		CA
		CA
		OI
			I
			D
			I
				Debit
				Credit
				Credit
					Balance Sheet
					Balance Sheet
					Income State.

Maker dishonored an interest-bearing note at maturity.	Accounts Receivable
	   Notes Receivable
	   Interest Income
		CA
		CA
		OI
			I
			D
			I
				Debit
				Credit
				Credit
					Balance Sheet
					Balance Sheet
					Income State.

Discounted an interest-bearing note receivable; proceeds are less than the principal.	Cash Interest Expense Notes Receivable	CA OE CA	I I D	Debit Debit Credit	Balance Sheet Income State. Balance Sheet
Maker dishonored a note receivable previously discounted, involving a protest fee.	Accounts Receivable Cash	CA CA	I D	Debit Credit	Balance Sheet Balance Sheet
Adjusting entry for accrued interest on notes receivable.	Interest Receivable Interest Income	CA OI	I I	Debit Credit	Balance Sheet Income State.
Reversing entry for accrued interest on notes receivable.	Interest Income Interest Receivable	OI CA	D D	Debit Credit	Income State. Balance Sheet

Adjusting entry for estimated bad-debt losses.	Bad Debts Expense
	  Allowance for
	  Doubtful Accounts
		GE
		
		CA
			I
			
			I
				Debit
				
				Credit
					Income State.
					
					Balance Sheet

Wrote off an account as uncollectible using the allowance method.	Allowance for Doubtful Accounts Accounts Receivable	CA CA	D D	Debit Credit	Balance Sheet Balance Sheet

Transaction	Accounts Involved	Class.	Increase or Decrease	Therefore Debit or Credit	Financial Statement
Received part payment in bankruptcy settlement of amount owed by charge customer using the allowance method.	Cash Allowance for Doubtful Accounts Accounts Receivable	CA CA CA	I D D	Debit Debit Credit	Balance Sheet Balance Sheet Balance Sheet
Reinstated an account previously written off using the allowance method.	Accounts Receivable Allowance for Doubtful Accounts	CA CA	I I	Debit Credit	Balance Sheet Balance Sheet
Wrote off an account as uncollectible using the specific charge-off method	Bad Debts Expense Accounts Receivable	GE CA	I D	Debit Credit	Income State. Balance Sheet
Reinstated an account previously written off using the specific charge-off method.	Accounts Receivable Bad Debts Recovered	CA OI	I I	Debit Credit	Balance Sheet Income State.
Using the perpetual-inventory method, bought merchandise on account.	Merchandise Inventory Accounts Payable	CA CL	I I	Debit Credit	Balance Sheet Balance Sheet
Adjusting entry for merchandise inventory under a perpetual-inventory system; physical count is less than book value.	Cost of Merchandise Sold Merchandise Inventory	CMS CA	I D	Debit Credit	Income State. Balance Sheet
Adjusting entry for depreciation of building housing general office.	Depreciation Expense, Building Accumulated Depreciation, Building	GE P & E	I I	Debit Credit	Income State. Balance Sheet

Transaction	Accounts Involved	Class.	Increase or Decrease	Therefore Debit or Credit	Financial Statement
Discarded equipment that was fully depreciated and had a zero salvage value.	Accumulated Depreciation, Equipment Equipment	P & E P & E	D D	Debit Credit	Balance Sheet Balance Sheet
Sold for cash, equipment having a book value that is less than the amount received.	Cash Accumulated Depreciation, Equipment Equipment Gain on Disposal of Plant and Equipment	CA P & E P & E OI	I D D I	Debit Debit Credit Credit	Balance Sheet Balance Sheet Balance Sheet Income State.
Sold for cash, equipment having a book value that is greater than the amount received.	Cash Accumulated Depreciation, Equipment Loss on Disposal of Plant and Equipment Equipment	CA P & E OE P & E	I D I D	Debit Debit Debit Credit	Balance Sheet Balance Sheet Income State. Balance Sheet
Traded in old equipment, receiving a trade-in allowance that is more or less than the book value.	Equipment (new) Accumulated Depreciation, Equipment Cash Equipment (old)	P & E P & E CA P & E	I D D D	Debit Debit Credit Credit	Balance Sheet Balance Sheet Balance Sheet Balance Sheet
Paid for extraordinary repairs to equipment, prolonging life of equipment three years.	Accumulated Depreciation, Equipment Cash	P & E CA	D D	Debit Credit	Balance Sheet Balance Sheet

APPENDIX E
Modified Accelerated Cost Recovery System of Depreciation

The Tax Reform Act of 1986 introduced the Modified Accelerated Cost Recovery System (hereafter referred to as MACRS). MACRS calls for a change in the classification of assets and length of lives as stated in the Accelerated Cost Recovery System, which was passed by Congress and took effect as of January 1, 1981.

Recovery property is tangible property, such as equipment and buildings, that is subject to depreciation. The term *recovery* refers to the right of a business to recover its cost of plant and equipment by deducting the cost of each asset on its federal income tax return. Each asset's cost is deducted in the form of depreciation. **MACRS pertains to property placed in service on or after January 1, 1987.**

Property is depreciable if it meets the following requirements:

1. It must be used in business or held for the production of income.
2. It must have a determinable life, and that life must be longer than one year.
3. It must be something that wears out, decays, gets used up, becomes obsolete, or loses value from natural causes.

In general, if property does not meet all three of these conditions, it is not depreciable.

CLASSES OF PROPERTY

Under MACRS, property falls into one of eight classes. Each of the classes has an officially recognized length of life. The table at the top of the next page shows the property classes and the types of assets for each class.

Depreciation or cost recovery is based on the full cost of each asset. This means that *the cost of an asset is not reduced by the asset's trade-in value or salvage value.* Companies can use either a straight-line method of depreciation, as defined by the Internal Revenue Service (IRS), or a declining-balance method involving schedules approved by the IRS. Generally, companies choose the method that gives them the greatest amount of tax-deductible depreciation in the early years.

Property Class	Description
3-year property	Certain horses and tractor units for use over the road
5-year property	Autos, trucks, computers, typewriters, and copiers
7-year property	Office furniture and fixtures and any property that does not have a class life and that is not, by law, in any other class
10-year property	Vessels, barges, tugs, and similar water transportation equipment
15-year property	Wharves, roads, fences, and any municipal wastewater treatment plant
20-year property	Certain farm buildings and municipal sewers
27.5-year residential rental property	Rental houses and apartments
31.5-year real property	Office buildings and warehouses

SCHEDULES OF DEPRECIATION: THREE-, FIVE-, AND SEVEN-YEAR PROPERTY

Depreciation for all three-, five-, and seven-year property is based on the 200 percent (double)-declining-balance method. During the first year, assets in these classifications may be depreciated for only half the year. Regardless of when the asset was acquired, whether on January 5 or August 12, only one-half year's depreciation may be taken on that asset. Taking only half a year's depreciation during the first year is called the **half-year convention.** The remaining half year is taken in the year following the end of the recovery period unless the property is sold or otherwise disposed of before it has been fully depreciated. In that case, one-half of a year's depreciation may be taken during the year it was sold, regardless of when it was sold in that year.

Following are the approved schedules of percentage of cost allocated (written off or depreciated) each year for three-year, five-year, and seven-year property:

Year	Three-Year	Five-Year	Seven-Year
1	33.33	20.00	14.29
2	44.45	32.00	24.49
3	14.81	19.20	17.49
4	7.41	11.52	12.49
5	100.00	11.52	8.93
6		5.76	8.92
7		100.00	8.93
8			4.46
			100.00

To determine the depreciation for the year, multiply the cost of the asset by the percentage figure. The following examples compare allowable depreciation for five- and seven-year property according to the approved schedules with straight-line depreciation for five- and seven-year property as defined by the IRS.

Example for Five-Year Property

On April 2 a business purchased a pick-up truck (five-year property) that cost $10,000.

MACRS Depreciation

Year	Depreciation Expense	Accumulated Depreciation	Book Value at End of Year
1	$10,000 × .2 = $ 2,000	$2,000	$10,000 − $2,000 = $8,000
2	$10,000 × .32 = 3,200	$2,000 + $3,200 = $5,200	$10,000 − $5,200 = $4,800
3	$10,000 × .192 = 1,920	$5,200 + $1,920 = $7,120	$10,000 − $7,120 = $2,880
4	$10,000 × .1152 = 1,152	$7,120 + $1,152 = $8,272	$10,000 − $8,272 = $1,728
5	$10,000 × .1152 = 1,152	$8,272 + $1,152 = $9,424	$10,000 − $9,424 = $576
6	$10,000 × .576 = 576	$9,424 + $576 = $10,000	$10,000 − $10,000 = -0-
	$10,000		

Using the 200 percent declining-balance method with the truck's cost of $10,000, the percentages of MACRS depreciation were calculated by the following steps:

1. Calculate the straight-line rate:

$$\frac{1}{5 \text{ years}} = 1/5 = \underline{\underline{.2}}$$

2. Multiply the straight-line rate by 2: .2 × 2 = $\underline{\underline{.4}}$
3. Multiply the book value at the beginning of the year by double the straight-line rate

   Percentage amounts: *First year:* $10,000 × .4 = $4,000

   One-half year $4,000 × .5 = 2,000

$$\text{Percentage of cost} = \frac{\$2,000}{\$10,000} = .2 = \underline{\underline{20\%}}$$

Second year: $\$8,000 \times .4 = \$3,200$

$$\text{Percentage of cost} = \frac{\$3,200}{\$10,000} = .32 = \underline{\underline{32\%}}$$

Third year: $\$4,800 \times .4 = \$1,920$

$$\text{Percentage of cost} = \frac{\$1,920}{\$10,000} = .192 = \underline{\underline{19.2\%}}$$

Straight-Line Depreciation   (IRS Method)

$$\text{Straight-line depreciation rate} = \frac{1}{5 \text{ years}} = .2 \text{ per year}$$

Year	Depreciation Expense	Accumulated Depreciation	Book Value at End of Year
1	$\$10,000 \times .2 \times .5 = \$1,000^*$	$\$1,000$	$\$10,000 - \$1,000 = \$9,000$
2	$\$10,000 \times .2 \quad = 2,000$	$\$1,000 + \$2,000 = \$3,000$	$\$10,000 - \$3,000 = \$7,000$
3	$\$10,000 \times .2 \quad = 2,000$	$\$3,000 + \$2,000 = \$5,000$	$\$10,000 - \$5,000 = \$5,000$
4	$\$10,000 \times .2 \quad = 2,000$	$\$5,000 + \$2,000 = \$7,000$	$\$10,000 - \$7,000 = \$3,000$
5	$\$10,000 \times .2 \quad = 2,000$	$\$7,000 + \$2,000 = \$9,000$	$\$10,000 - \$9,000 = \$1,000$
6	$\$10,000 \times .2 \times .5 = \underline{1,000^*}$	$\$9,000 + \$1,000 = \$10,000$	$\$10,000 - \$10,000 = \quad \text{-0-}$
	$\underline{\$10,000}$		

*The half-year convention is applied to the first year and to the year following the end of the recovery period.

Example for Seven-Year Property

On August 4 a company purchased office equipment (seven-year property) that cost $4,200.

MACRS Depreciation

Year	Depreciation Expense	Accumulated Depreciation	Book Value at End of Year
1	$4,200 × .1429 = $ 600.18	$600.18	$4,200 − $600.18 = $3,599.82
2	$4,200 × .2449 = 1,028.58	$600.18 + $1,028.58 = $1,628.76	$4,200 − $1,628.76 = $2,571.24
3	$4,200 × .1749 = 734.58	$1,628.76 + $734.58 = $2,363.34	$4,200 − $2,363.34 = $1,836.66
4	$4,200 × .1249 = 524.58	$2,363.34 + $524.58 = $2,887.92	$4,200 − $2,887.92 = $1,312.08
5	$4,200 × .0893 = 375.06	$2,887.92 + $375.06 = $3,262.98	$4,200 − $3,262.98 = $937.02
6	$4,200 × .0892 = 374.64	$3,262.98 + $374.64 = $3,637.62	$4,200 − $3,637.62 = $562.38
7	$4,200 × .0893 = 375.06	$3,637.62 + $375.06 = $4,012.68	$4,200 − $4,012.68 = $187.32
8	$4,200 × .0446 = 187.32	$4,012.68 + $187.32 = $4,200.00	$4,200 − $4,200.00 = -0-
	$4,200.00		

Straight-Line Depreciation   (IRS Method)

$$\text{Straight-line depreciation rate} = \frac{1}{7 \text{ years}} = \frac{1}{7} = .1429 \text{ per year}$$

For convenience we will use the one-seventh fraction in our calculations.

Year	Depreciation Expense	Accumulated Depreciation	Book Value at End of Year
1	$4,200 × $\frac{1}{7}$ × $\frac{1}{2}$ = $300*	$300	$4,200 − $300 = $3,900
2	$4,200 × $\frac{1}{7}$ = 600	$300 + $600 = $900	$4,200 − $900 = $3,300
3	$4,200 × $\frac{1}{7}$ = 600	$900 + $600 = $1,500	$4,200 − $1,500 = $2,700
4	$4,200 × $\frac{1}{7}$ = 600	$1,500 + $600 = $2,100	$4,200 − $2,100 = $2,100
5	$4,200 × $\frac{1}{7}$ = 600	$2,100 + $600 = $2,700	$4,200 − $2,700 = $1,500
6	$4,200 × $\frac{1}{7}$ = 600	$2,700 + $600 = $3,300	$4,200 − $3,300 = $900
7	$4,200 × $\frac{1}{7}$ = 600	$3,300 + $600 = $3,900	$4,200 − $3,900 = $300
8	$4,200 × $\frac{1}{7}$ × $\frac{1}{2}$ = 300*	$3,900 + $300 = $4,200	$4,200 − $4,200 = -0-
	$4,200		

*The half-year convention is applied to the first year and to the year following the end of the recovery period.

Automobiles

Although passenger cars are classified as five-year property, the amount of depreciation allowed is limited for those placed in service beginning in 1987. Here are the maximum deductions by years: first year, $2,560; second year, $4,100; third year, $2,450; succeeding years, $1,475 each.

FIFTEEN- AND TWENTY-YEAR PROPERTY

For all fifteen- and twenty-year property, the 150 percent declining-balance method is used with the *half-year convention*.

For example, depreciation of a farm building (twenty-year property) for the first year, having a cost of $36,000, is figured like this:

Straight-line rate: $\dfrac{1}{20 \text{ years}} = \dfrac{1}{20} = \underline{\underline{.05}}$

Straight-line rate $\times$ 1.5: $.05 \times 1.5 = \underline{.075}$

$36,000 \times .075 = \underline{\underline{\$2,700}}$

One-half year $= \dfrac{\$2,700}{2} = \underline{\underline{\$1,350}}$

TWENTY-SEVEN AND ONE-HALF- AND THIRTY-ONE AND ONE-HALF-YEAR PROPERTY

For all residential and nonresidential rental property, the straight-line depreciation must be used with *a midmonth convention*. In other words, half a month is taken during the first month of the first year of operation, regardless of the day of the month the property was purchased. Also, during the first year, all the full months are counted. For example, on November 3, a store building is purchased for $120,000 ($100,000 for building and $20,000 for land). Depreciation for the first year is calculated like this:

One year's depreciation $= \dfrac{\$100,000}{31.5 \text{ years}} = \$3,174.60$

One month's depreciation $= \dfrac{\$3,174.60}{12 \text{ months}} = \$264.55$

One-half month's depreciation $= \dfrac{\$264.55}{2} = \$132.28$

For the first year:

November (one-half month)	$132.28
December (one full month)	264.55
Total	$396.83

EXCEPTION TO THE HALF-YEAR CONVENTION FOR THREE-, FIVE-, SEVEN-, AND TEN-YEAR PROPERTY

During any tax year, if the total property placed in service during the last three months (last quarter) of the year is greater than 40 percent of all property placed in service during that year, a midquarter convention is used instead of a half-year convention. (Incidentally, residential and nonresidential property is not counted.) The intent is to discourage companies from buying a lot of property during the last month of the tax year and then taking half a year's depreciation on that property.

Under the midquarter convention, all property placed in service during any quarter (three-month period) of a tax year is treated as being placed in service at the midpoint of that quarter. Since each quarter equals 25 percent, one-half quarter is 25 percent divided by 2, or 12.5 percent. This amount is then subtracted from the total percentage allowed for the number of quarters remaining in the year. The first quarter, which is 100 percent minus 12.5 percent, equals 87.5 percent. Here is a schedule of percentages to be applied to the full year's depreciation according to the quarter in which the assets are placed in service: first quarter, 87.5 percent; second quarter, 62.5 percent; third quarter, 37.5 percent, fourth quarter, 12.5 percent.

For example, Bowlen Company's fiscal year extends from January 1 through December 31. Bowlen bought a typewriter for $520 on February 5 and a computer for $5,400 on December 20. During the last three months, more than 40 percent of the property was purchased. (As a matter of fact, 91 percent was purchased during the last three months: $5,400 ÷ $5,920 = .91 = 91 percent.) Bowlen Company must use the midquarter convention. The depreciation for each item is calculated like this:

Typewriter (purchased during first quarter)   Five-year property using 200 percent declining balance:

Straight-line rate: $\frac{1}{5} = \underline{\underline{.2}}$

Double straight-line rate: $.2 \times 2 = \underline{\underline{.4}}$

First year's depreciation: $520 \times .4 = \underline{\underline{\$208}}$

Depreciation allowed using the midquarter convention: $208 \times .875 = \underline{\underline{\$182}}$

Computer (purchased during fourth quarter)   Five-year property using 200 percent declining balance:

Straight-line rate: $\frac{1}{5} = \underline{\underline{.2}}$

Double straight-line rate $= .2 \times 2 = \underline{\underline{.4}}$

First year's depreciation $= \$5,400 \times .4 = \underline{\underline{\$2,160}}$

Depreciation allowed using the midquarter convention:
$2,160 \times .125 = \underline{\underline{\$270}}$

SALE OF AN ASSET

The gain or loss on the sale of an asset must be computed using the MACRS schedules of cost recovery or depreciation. Referring back to our illustration of the pick-up truck on page 688, let's say that the company sells the truck for $1,500 on May 7 during the fourth year of use. First, record depreciation for the fourth year. One-half year is allowed according to the half-year convention. Next, record the sale. These entries are shown in general journal form below. We'll label the entries (1) and (2).

	DATE		DESCRIPTION	POST. REF.	DEBIT	CREDIT	
1	19–						1
2	May	7	Depreciation Expense Truck		576 00		2
3			Accumulated Depreciation, Truck			576 00	3
4			Recorded depreciation for				4
5	(1)		one-half year during the				5
6			fourth year of use.				6
7			$10,000 \times .1152 = $576				7
8			2				8
9		7	Cash		1500 00		9
10			Accumulated Depreciation, Truck		7696 00		10
11	(2)		Loss on Disposal of Plant and				11
12			Equipment		804 00		12
13			Truck			10000 00	13
14			Sold light truck.				14
15							15
16							16
17							17
18							18

GENERAL JOURNAL   PAGE _____

The T accounts look like this:

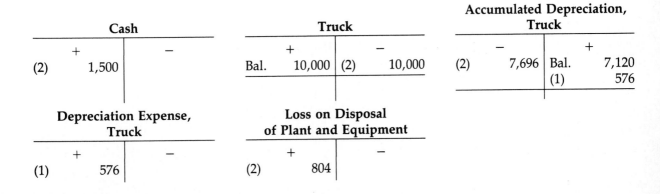

Cash	
+	−
(2) 1,500	

Truck	
+	−
Bal. 10,000	(2) 10,000

Accumulated Depreciation, Truck	
−	+
(2) 7,696	Bal. 7,120
	(1) 576

Depreciation Expense, Truck	
+	−
(1) 576	

Loss on Disposal of Plant and Equipment	
+	−
(2) 804	

MACRS VERSUS DEPRECIATION METHODS USED FOR THE COMPANY'S BOOKS

Remember

Since lives of property under MACRS may differ from the actual useful lives of assets, a company may use MACRS for its federal income tax return and other methods of depreciation for financial reporting purposes.

The actual lives of many assets differ significantly from the lives assigned to them by the IRS. For that reason, many firms use MACRS depreciation for federal taxes and straight-line depreciation, accounting method, for computing net income on their own financial statements. Assuming that the dollar amount of property acquisitions is about the same from year to year, using these two methods would show the highest net income to the owner(s) and the lowest net income to the IRS. Firms that follow this procedure maintain a double set of accounts for Depreciation Expense and Accumulated Depreciation.

Problems

Problem E-1   On April 9, 1988, Bowman Company bought a computer for $5,200. No other plant and equipment was purchased during the year. Therefore, the midquarter convention does not apply.

Instructions

Determine the annual depreciation, the accumulated depreciation at the end of each year, and the book value at the end of each year using the MACRS schedule of depreciation.

Problem E-2   During a three-year period, Papez Company completed the following transactions pertaining to its office furniture. No other assets were acquired earlier in the year. Therefore, the midquarter convention does not apply.

Year 1

Aug.   16 Bought office furniture for cash, $5,400.

Dec.   31 Recorded the adjusting entry for depreciation for the fiscal year using the MACRS method.

         31 Closed the appropriate account to the Income Summary account.

Year 2

Dec.   31 Made the adjusting entry to record depreciation for the fiscal year using the MACRS method.

         31 Closed the appropriate account to the Income Summary account.

Year 3

Dec.   31 Made the adjusting entry to record depreciation for the fiscal year using the MACRS method.

         31 Closed the appropriate account to the Income Summary account.

Instructions

Record the transactions in general journal form.

Problem E-3 During a four-year period, Walters Company completed the following transactions related to its pick-up truck. No other assets were purchased during the year. Therefore, the midquarter convention does not apply.

Year 1
Sept.   12 Bought a pickup truck for $10,600 from Travis Motors, paying $3,000 in cash, with the remainder due in 30 days.
Oct.   11 Paid the balance due on the purchase of the pickup truck.
Dec.   31 Made the adjusting entry to record depreciation of the truck for the fiscal year using the MACRS method.
       31 Closed the appropriate account to the Income Summary account.

Year 2
Dec.   31 Made the adjusting entry to record depreciation for the fiscal year using the MACRS method.
       31 Closed the appropriate account to the Income Summary account.

Year 3
Dec.   31 Made the adjusting entry to record depreciation for the fiscal year using the MACRS method.
       31 Closed the appropriate account to the Income Summary account.

Year 4
May   19 Sold the truck for cash, $4,150.
Dec.   31 Closed the appropriate accounts to the Income Summary account.

Instructions

1. Record the transactions in general journal form.
2. Post to the following ledger accounts after journalizing each entry: Truck; Accumulated Depreciation, Truck; Gain on Disposal of Plant and Equipment; Depreciation Expense, Truck.

21

The Voucher System of Accounting

LEARNING OBJECTIVES

After you have completed this chapter, you will be able to do the following:

1. Prepare vouchers.
2. Record vouchers in a voucher register.
3. Record payment of vouchers in a check register.
4. Record transactions involving canceling or altering an original voucher.
5. Record the receipt and payment of invoices by the net-amount method.

We have often used the term *internal control* in connection with cash receipts and payments. The objectives of internal control are (1) to prevent errors, (2) to prevent the stealing of cash or other assets by employees and customers, and (3) to provide for the efficient management of the owner's investment. To meet these objectives, business transactions should be recorded in such a way that one person acts as a check or verification on another person. In other words, no one person is alone and "out on a limb." As the size of the economic unit increases, the owner becomes less directly involved in the transactions and internal control becomes more important. The voucher system has been devised as a means of achieving internal control and enabling the owner or manager to maintain contact with day-by-day transactions.

OBJECTIVE OF THE VOUCHER SYSTEM

The objective of the **voucher system** is to *control the incurring of all liabilities and the making of all expenditures*—in other words, to control the purchase of (1) merchandise or materials, (2) other assets, and (3) services. An owner or chief executive who uses the voucher system can delegate authority while maintaining control over these transactions through the medium of signatures. An executive who signs a voucher has presumably read it and signifies that he or she approves the incurring of an obligation or the making of a payment. That is how the voucher system provides for the efficient management of the owner's investment. This feature is of vital importance, especially when large sums of money are involved.

The following four steps all involve the efficient management of resources. The steps are not, of course, exclusive to the voucher system. However, when a firm is using the voucher system, these four steps are implied.

1. All expenditures must be backed up by purchase orders or other authorizations.
2. Goods and services received must be inspected and approved.
3. Invoices from suppliers must be checked against their respective purchase orders and verified as to accuracy of the computations of the amounts listed, shipping costs, and credit terms. Computation of amounts listed on the invoices, such as unit prices multiplied by the number of units purchased, are called **price extensions.**
4. All payments must be made by check, except for payments made from petty cash.

The voucher system focuses on the four steps listed and includes the following components, each of which we shall describe in detail:

- Vouchers
- Voucher register
- Check register
- Unpaid Voucher file
- Paid Voucher file
- General journal

At the outset, bear in mind that the voucher system is appropriate only for medium- to large-sized businesses. The volume of transactions must be big enough to make the extra paperwork economically feasible, and the firm must customarily pay its bills when they are due rather than making part payments or installment payments. Also bear in mind that the voucher system has fixed channels in which to record routine types of transactions. Nonroutine transactions do not fit into these channels and therefore require special entries in the general journal.

VOUCHERS

The dictionary defines a **voucher** as a piece of paper that serves as proof of a transaction. Recall that we used the word in Chapter 8 in connection with petty cash. The petty cash voucher not only describes the transaction but also provides for signatures of the employee in charge of the fund and of the person receiving payment.

When a business is using the voucher system, a voucher must be filled out for *every* invoice or bill received, *whether it is to be paid immediately or in the future*. The voucher describes the terms of the transaction, and the invoice or bill is attached (usually stapled) to the voucher. If a business is buying merchandise, the voucher lists the name and address of the supplier, the date of the invoice, the amount, and the credit terms. There are always blanks for the necessary signatures, signifying approval of amounts, terms, and so forth.

Characteristics of Vouchers

Just as the form of *invoices* varies from one company to another, so too the form of *vouchers* varies from one company to another. In some enterprises, the voucher is in the form of a jacket and has a pocket or envelope so that the invoice can be included with the voucher.

Although vouchers for different business firms or government units do vary a bit from one to another, the following characteristics are usually present:

- Vouchers must be prepared for every incoming bill, and vouchers are numbered consecutively.
- Name and address of the payee or creditor appear on vouchers.
- Amount and credit terms of the invoice appear on vouchers.
- Vouchers state due dates so that firms can take advantage of possible cash discounts.
- For internal control, vouchers require signatures (1) approving payment and (2) showing that payment has been recorded in the account books.
- Vouchers record payment: date paid and check number.

A completed voucher, with the invoice or bill stapled to it, describes an entire transaction as well as the procedure for processing the voucher.

Preparation and Approval of Vouchers

Objective 1

Prepare vouchers.

Each voucher bears an identification number, which appears both inside and outside the voucher. To cite a familiar example, let's assume that City-Wide Electric Supply has now achieved such a volume of business that it is using a voucher system. Let's also assume that City-Wide has received from its supplier, Draper, Inc., the invoice shown in Figure 21-1.

FIGURE 21-1

DRAPER, INC.
1616 Madera Ave.
Los Angeles, CA 90026

INVOICE

SOLD TO	*City-Wide Electric Supply* *1968 N.E. Allen St.* *Portland, OR 97201*	DATE:	*October 1, 19–*
		INVOICE NO.:	*3394*
		ORDER NO.:	*9764*
		SHIPPED BY:	*Western Freight Line*
		TERMS:	*2/10, n/30*

QUANTITY	DESCRIPTION	UNIT PRICE	TOTAL
26	*Butler Electronic Thermostats* *Freight*	26 70	694 20 20 80 715 00

City-Wide Electric's accountant, using the invoice as the source of information, fills out the voucher shown in Figure 21-2. The inside or face of the voucher lists the particulars of the transaction.

The accountant staples the invoice to the voucher and circulates the two items for the required approval signatures. When the voucher and the attached invoice get back to the accounting department, the accountant fills in the following required information on the outside of the voucher: the accounts to be debited and credited, the due date, the name and address of the payee, and the payment information (see Figure 21-3 on page 702).

The Account Distribution section is used to record the account titles and amounts to be debited, the total amount to be credited to Vouchers Payable, and the initials of the person authorized to determine the distribution. The accounts to be debited depend, of course, on the types of goods and services purchased.

The *due date* represents the last day on which one can take advantage of the cash discount, taking into consideration the time required for mail delivery. For example, the invoice of Draper, Inc., was dated October 1, with terms of 2/10, n/30. The discount period ends on October 11. However, if three days are necessary for mail delivery, the due date is moved back from October 11 to October 8 so that the cash will be in the hands of the creditor by October 11.

FIGURE 21-2

CITY-WIDE ELECTRIC SUPPLY   No. 118
1968 N.E. Allen Street
Portland, OR 97201

VOUCHER

PAY
TO: *Draper, Inc.*
       1616 Madera Ave.
       Los Angeles, CA 90026   DATE ___10/1___

DATE OF INVOICE	TERMS	DESCRIPTION	AMOUNT	
10/1	*2/10, n/30*	*Invoice No. 3394*	*694*	*20*
		Less discount	*13*	*88*
		Freight	*20*	*80*
		Net amount payable	*701*	*12*

APPROVAL	DATES	APPROVED BY
Extensions and footings verified	*10/2*	MCL
Prices in agreement with purchase order	*10/2*	J.T.
Credit terms in agreement with purchase order	*10/2*	J.T.
Quantities in agreement with receiving report	*10/2*	JDS
Approved for payment	*10/7*	RLR

THE VOUCHERS PAYABLE ACCOUNT

When you use a voucher system, you substitute the Vouchers Payable account for Accounts Payable. For example, when a firm buys merchandise on account, the accountant enters it as a debit to Purchases and a credit to Vouchers Payable. Similarly, when a firm buys store equipment on account, the accountant records it as a debit to Store Equipment and a credit to Vouchers Payable. The voucher now represents the amount of the invoice or bill. When the obligation is paid, the payment is recorded as a debit to Vouchers Payable and a credit to Cash.

The Voucher System and Expenses

We have stressed the fact that when you are using a voucher system, you have to write out a voucher *every time you incur a liability,* and this in-

FIGURE 21-3

ACCOUNT DISTRIBUTION		VOUCHER NO. _118_
ACCOUNT DEBITED	**AMOUNT**	**Due Date** *10/8*
Purchases	694.20	**Pay To** *Draper, Inc.*
Freight In	20.80	*161 Madera Ave.*
Supplies		*Los Angeles, CA 90026*
Wages Expense		
Miscellaneous Expense		

SUMMARY OF CHARGES

Amount of invoice	*$715.00*
Less cash discount	*13.88*
Net amount	*$701.22*

RECORD OF PAYMENT

Paid by check no.	*390*
Date of check	*10/8*
Amount of check	*701.12*

Total Vouchers Payable Cr.   715.00

ACCOUNT DISTRIBUTION by _RRH_   ENTERED IN VOUCHER REG. by _M.C.L._

cludes liabilities incurred for expenses as well as those incurred for acquiring assets. For example, suppose that when the telephone bill comes
in, you notice some long-distance toll charges. First verify that these
were business calls, then make out a voucher and attach the telephone
bill to the inside of it. In the column headed Account Distribution, record
the bill as a debit to Telephone Expense and a credit to Vouchers
Payable. When a check is issued in payment of the voucher, record the
entry in the check register as a debit to Vouchers Payable and a credit to
Cash. Again let us emphasize that *all* liabilities are recorded in the
Vouchers Payable account.

THE VOUCHER REGISTER

Objective 2

Record vouchers in a
voucher register.

The **voucher register** has the status of a journal; it is a book of original
entry. All vouchers must be recorded in it, in numerical order. Think of it
as a multicolumn purchases journal. The voucher register has only one

credit column, Vouchers Payable Credit, but a number of debit columns. Headings for the debit columns are selected on the basis of their frequency of use. A merchandising business, for example, would always have a Purchases Debit column, because a merchant naturally buys a great volume of merchandise on account. The voucher register may vary widely, of course, depending on the size of the business and the number of accounts. In addition to the money columns, the voucher register also has space for recording the voucher number, name of creditor, date of payment, and check number. The voucher register for City-Wide Electric Supply is shown in Figure 21-4 on the next two pages.

When you first record the voucher, leave the Payment Date and Check Number columns blank. After you have recorded the payment in the check register, go back to the voucher register and enter the date of payment and the number of the check. In Figure 21-4, vouchers no. 123 and no. 149 have not been paid yet; voucher no 126 was "paid" by issuing a note (this transaction will be discussed later in this chapter); voucher no. 122 was issued payable to a payroll account. (It is assumed that this payroll entry was previously recorded in the general journal, crediting Wages Payable.)

Posting from the Voucher Register

The entries in the Sundry Accounts columns are posted *daily* to the general ledger, just as the Sundry Accounts columns of the other special journals are posted daily. The check mark ($\sqrt{}$) under the column total means "do not post." At the end of the month, total all the columns, and prove the equality of the debit and credit entries by comparing the combined total of the debit columns with the total of the Vouchers Payable Credit column. After you have proved the voucher register to be in balance, post the special-column totals to the general ledger. To show that each total has been posted, write the account number in parentheses immediately below the column total. In the ledger accounts write the letters VR and the page number to show that the posting came from the voucher register.

Remember

A voucher is prepared for every invoice or bill the company receives.

THE CHECK REGISTER

Objective 3

Record payment of vouchers in a check register.

Any economic unit using a voucher system uses the check register, like the one shown in Chapter 13, as a book of original entry, in conjunction with the voucher register. The procedure works this way: Since checks are issued only in payment of approved and recorded vouchers, the entry in the check register is always a debit to Vouchers Payable and a credit to Cash. A Vouchers Payable Debit column in the check register offsets the Vouchers Payable Credit column in the voucher register. Recall that after you record the entry in the check register, you enter the no-

FIGURE 21-4

	DATE	VOU. NO.	CREDITOR	PAYMENT		VOUCHERS PAYABLE CREDIT	PURCHASES DEBIT
				DATE	CK. NO.		
1	19–						
2	Oct.	1 117	Reliable Express Co.	10	1 383	4 2 00	
3		2 118	Draper, Inc.	10	8 390	7 1 5 00	6 9 4 20
4		3 119	Davenport Of. Sup.	10	3 384	4 8 72	
5		5 120	Rockland Insurance				
6			Company	10	5 387	7 4 00	
7		9 121	Reilly and Peters Co.	10	18 404	3 2 8 00	3 0 6 00
8		10 122	Payroll Bank Acc.	10	10 393	1 6 9 0 00	
9		12 123	Northwest Journal			7 6 00	
10		12 124	Dundee Equip. Co.	10	12 395	1 1 6 00	
11		15 125	R. C. Schmidt	10	15 399	5 0 0 00	
12		15 126	T. R. Wetzel, Inc.	10	18 *By note*	4 2 1 00	4 2 1 00
18		29 149	Adkins Mfg. Co.			7 1 4 00	7 1 4 00
19		30 150	Safety National Bank	10	30 412	1 5 0 7 50	
20							
21	31					10 6 9 8 68	4 3 6 1 90
22						(2 1 2)	(5 1 1)
23							
24							

Remember

The check mark (√) under the total of the Sundry Accounts Debit column means "do not post," since the individual amounts are posted separately.

Remember

Since the check register replaces the cash payments journal and the voucher register replaces the purchases journal, the special column totals from the voucher register must be posted before those from the check register.

tation of the payment on the appropriate line in the voucher register and on the outside of the voucher in the Record of Payment section. First prove the column totals of the check register to see that the debits equal the credits, then post the amounts as totals, as shown in Figure 21-5.

HANDLING OF UNPAID VOUCHERS

Business firms usually prepare vouchers in duplicate. In the system used by City-Wide Electric Supply, invoices are attached to the original copy of the voucher. Then the voucher is circulated within the company for the necessary signatures. After a voucher is recorded in the voucher register, it is filed under the name of the creditor. (Other companies prepare only one voucher and file it only under the date on which it is supposed to be paid.) At City-Wide Electric, the Unpaid Voucher file also contains any other outstanding vouchers or credit memos. This file, listed by names of creditors, now comprises a subsidiary ledger. In fact, at City-Wide Electric this file substitutes for the accounts payable ledger.

VOUCHER REGISTER   PAGE 3

FREIGHT IN DEBIT	WAGES PAYABLE DEBIT	SUPPLIES DEBIT	MISCELLANEOUS EXPENSE DEBIT	SUNDRY ACCOUNTS DEBIT			
				ACCOUNT	POST. REF.	AMOUNT	
							1
4 2 00							2
2 0 80							3
		4 8 72					4
							5
				Prepaid Insurance	116	7 4 00	6
2 2 00							7
	1 6 9 0 00						8
				Advertising Expense	518	7 6 00	9
				Sales Returns and Allowances	412	1 1 6 00	10
				R. C. Schmidt, Drawing	312	5 0 0 00	11
							12
							18
				Notes Payable	211	1 5 0 0 00	19
				Interest Expense	534	7 50	20
1 9 1 30	3 3 1 4 00	1 2 1 79	8 3 69			2 6 2 6 00	21
(5 1 4)	(2 1 3)	(1 1 5)	(5 1 9)			(√)	22
							23
							24

CHECK REGISTER   PAGE 11

	DATE	CK. NO.	PAYEE	VOU. NO.	VOUCHERS PAYABLE DEBIT	PURCHASES DISCOUNT CREDIT	CASH CREDIT	
1	19–							1
2	Oct. 1	383	Reliable Express Company	117	4 2 00		4 2 00	2
3	3	384	Davenport Office Supplies	119	4 8 72		4 8 72	3
4	3	385	Sullivan Manufacturing Company	114	2 0 6 00	2 06	2 0 3 94	4
5	4	386	Adkins Manufacturing Company	115	5 4 0 00	1 0 80	5 2 9 20	5
6	5	387	Rockland Insurance Company	120	7 4 00		7 4 00	6
7	6	388	Void					7
8	6	389	Reilly and Peters Company	116	4 6 4 00	9 28	4 5 4 72	8
9	8	390	Draper, Inc.	118	7 1 5 00	1 3 88	7 0 1 12	9
10								10
11	30	412	Safety National Bank	150	1 5 0 7 50		1 5 0 7 50	11
12	31				6 4 0 4 98	7 5 42	6 3 2 9 56	12
13					(2 1 2)	(5 1 3)	(1 1 1)	13
14								14

FIGURE 21-5

The *second* copy of the voucher goes to the treasurer, who files it chronologically by due date. This Unpaid Voucher file helps the treasurer to forecast the amount of cash that will be needed to pay outstanding bills and to take advantage of cash discounts.

At the end of the month, the accountant lists all the vouchers payable, taking the information directly from the Unpaid Voucher file. She or he writes the amount owed, as well as the name of each creditor. This same procedure was used to prepare the schedule of accounts payable, as you recall.

City-Wide Electric Supply
Schedule of Vouchers Payable
October 31, 19–

VOU. NO.	NAME OF CREDITOR	AMOUNT
123	*Northwest Journal*	$ 76 00
149	*Adkins Manufacturing Company*	714 00
	Total Vouchers Payable	$ 790 00

FILING PAID VOUCHERS

Now let's assume that the firm has paid its bill. The vouchers with their attached invoices are first removed from the Unpaid Voucher files, and the payment is recorded in the check register and in the Payment column of the voucher register. Then the two vouchers are combined, marked paid, and filed in numerical order in a Paid Vouchers file. Many firms staple a copy of the check to the paid voucher, which means that the Paid Vouchers file contains complete documents for every cash payment.

SITUATIONS REQUIRING SPECIAL TREATMENT

Objective 4

Record transactions involving canceling or altering an original voucher.

When a firm is using the voucher system, it inevitably runs into an occasional nonroutine type of transaction that does not fit into the fixed channels of the voucher system and therefore requires an entry in the general journal. One can consider such treatment as an adjustment to the voucher system. Let us now look at six such types of transactions, two occurring before the original voucher has been recorded and four occurring after the original voucher has been recorded.

Return of a Purchase Before Original Voucher Has Been Recorded

Normally, if a firm with an efficient purchasing department is going to return any merchandise, it returns the merchandise before the vouchers are recorded in the voucher register. The accountant records the deduction right on the invoice and records the invoice in the voucher register for the net amount. For example, City-Wide Electric Supply buys $1,200 worth of merchandise FOB destination on account. Before its accountant records the voucher, City-Wide Electric returns $100 worth of the merchandise to the supplier and receives a credit memorandum. The accountant staples the credit memorandum to the invoice, deducts $100 from the face amount, and records the invoice in the voucher register as a debit to Purchases for $1,100 and a credit to Vouchers Payable for $1,100.

Return of a Purchase After Original Voucher Has Been Recorded

Now what happens when a firm returns an item after the accountant has recorded the voucher listing its purchase in the voucher register?

On September 29, City-Wide Electric Supply bought $566 worth of merchandise FOB shipping point (freight to be billed separately by carrier) from Adkins Manufacturing Company. City-Wide Electric's accountant recorded the transaction in the voucher register as a debit to Purchases for $566 and a credit to Vouchers Payable for $566, as shown:

				PAYMENT		VOUCHERS PAYABLE CREDIT	PURCHASES DEBIT
	DATE	VOU. NO.	CREDITOR	DATE	CK. NO.		
1	Sept. 29	115	Adkins Mfg. Co.			5 6 6 00	5 6 6 00
2							

VOUCHER REGISTER PAGE 2

A few days later, City-Wide Electric returned $26 worth of defective merchandise to Adkins and got a credit memorandum from Adkins. City-Wide Electric's accountant recorded this transaction in the general journal shown in Figure 21-6 on the next page.

You will recognize that this entry is like a normal entry for the return of merchandise, except that here one uses Vouchers Payable instead of Accounts Payable and does not have to post anything to the accounts payable ledger. City-Wide Electric's accountant deducts the amount of the return ($26) on voucher no. 115 and staples Adkins's credit memorandum to it; then the accountant makes a notation in the Payment column of the voucher register, on the upper half of the line used to

FIGURE 21-6

GENERAL JOURNAL   PAGE _37_

	DATE		DESCRIPTION	POST. REF.	DEBIT	CREDIT	
1	19–						1
2	Oct.	3	Vouchers Payable		2 6 00		2
3			Purchases Returns and				3
4			Allowances			2 6 00	4
5			Returned defective merchandise				5
6			to Adkins Manufacturing				6
7			Company, receiving their credit				7
8			memo no. 4611, voucher				8
9			no. 115.				9

record the original voucher. City-Wide Electric pays the invoice on October 4 and the accountant records the issuance of check no. 386 in the check register as a debit to Vouchers Payable for $540.00, a credit to Purchases Discount for $10.80, and a credit to Cash for $529.20. The notations in the Payment column of the voucher register look like this:

VOUCHER REGISTER   PAGE _2_

	DATE	VOU. NO.	CREDITOR	PAYMENT DATE	PAYMENT CK. NO.	VOUCHERS PAYABLE CREDIT	PURCHASES DEBIT	
1	19–							
2	Sept. 29	115	Adkins Mfg. Co.	10 3 / 10 4	Ret. / 386	5 6 6 00	5 6 6 00	
3								

By T accounts, the entries look like this:

Purchases			
+		–	
Sept. 29 VR2	566		

Vouchers Payable			
–		+	
Oct. 3 J37	26	Sept. 29 VR2	566
Oct. 4 CkR11	540		

Purchases Returns and Allowances			
–		+	
		Oct. 3 J37	26

Cash in Bank			
+		–	
		Oct. 4 CkR11	529.20

Purchases Discount			
–		+	
		Oct. 4 CkR11	10.80

Issuing a "Note Payable" After Original Voucher Has Been Recorded

Suppose that someone in the firm issues a note canceling a voucher; then an entry is made in the general journal debiting Vouchers Payable and crediting Notes Payable. For example, let's say that on October 15 City-Wide Electric Supply bought $421 worth of merchandise from T. R. Wetzel, Inc., FOB destination and issued voucher no. 126, which was recorded in the voucher register (see Figure 21-4). On October 18, City-Wide Electric issued a 30-day, 8 percent note for $421, canceling the original voucher. City-Wide Electric's general journal entry is as follows:

GENERAL JOURNAL   PAGE _37_

	DATE		DESCRIPTION	POST. REF.	DEBIT	CREDIT	
1	19–						1
2	Oct.	18	Vouchers Payable		4 2 1 00		2
3			Notes Payable			4 2 1 00	3
4			Canceled voucher no. 126,				4
5			payable to T. R. Wetzel, Inc.,				5
6			and issued a 30-day,				6
7			8 percent note, dated				7
8			October 18.				8

In the Payment columns of the voucher register, on the line on which voucher no. 126 is recorded, the accountant writes "10/18" in the Date column and "By note" in the Check Number column.

VOUCHER REGISTER   PAGE _3_

	DATE		VOU. NO.	CREDITOR	PAYMENT DATE		CK. NO.	VOUCHERS PAYABLE CREDIT	PURCHASES DEBIT	FREIGHT IN DEBIT	
1	Oct.	15	126	T. R. Wetzel, Inc.	10	18	By note	4 2 1 00	4 2 1 00		
2											
3											

The accountant makes a notation on the voucher as well, indicating that it has been canceled by the issuance of a note, then transfers the voucher from the Unpaid Voucher file to the Paid Voucher file.

On November 17, when the note comes due, City-Wide Electric prepares a new voucher and records it in the voucher register as a debit to Notes Payable for $421 in the Sundry Accounts Debit column, a debit to Interest Expense for $2.81 in the Sundry Accounts Debit column ($421,

8 percent, 30 days), and a credit to Vouchers Payable for $423.81 in the Vouchers Payable Credit column. Next, the voucher is paid; City-Wide Electric's accountant records the payment in the check register in the usual manner as a debit to Vouchers Payable for $423.81 and a credit to Cash for $423.81. By T accounts, the entries appear as follows:

Purchases	
+	−
Oct. 15 VR3 421.00	

Interest Expense	
+	−
Nov. 17 VR4 2.81	

Cash	
+	−
	Nov. 17 CkR12 423.81

Vouchers Payable	
−	+
Oct. 18 J37 421.00	Oct. 15 VR3 421.00
Nov. 17 CkR12 423.81	Nov. 17 VR4 423.81

Notes Payable	
−	+
Nov. 17 VR4 421.00	Oct. 18 J37 421.00

Installment Payments Planned at Time of Original Purchase

In a voucher system, invoices generally are paid in full. Sometimes, however, management prefers to pay for an item in installments. When this happens, the company's accountant prepares a separate voucher and records it in the voucher register for each installment. As an illustration, assume that on November 2, City-Wide Electric bought an office safe for $750 from Newell Office Equipment Company, with a downpayment of $250, and two installments of $250 each, payable on November 17 and December 2. City-Wide Electric's accountant prepares three vouchers and records each of them in the voucher register:

VOUCHER REGISTER   PAGE 4

	DATE	VOU. NO.	CREDITOR	PAYMENT DATE	CK. NO.	VOUCHERS PAYABLE CREDIT	ACCOUNT	POST. REF.	AMOUNT	
1										1
2										2
3	Nov. 2	154	Newell Office							3
4			Equipment Co.			250 00				4
5		2 155	Newell Office							5
6			Equipment Co.			250 00				6
7		2 156	Newell Office							7
8			Equipment Co.			250 00	Office Equipment		750 00	8
9										9
10										10

Each voucher's due date corresponds to the date that installment is to be paid. Voucher no. 154 is paid immediately; voucher no. 155 is filed according to its due date, November 17; voucher no. 156 is filed according to its due date, December 2.

Installment Payments After Original Voucher Has Been Recorded

However, suppose that the buyer records the entire amount of the invoice on one voucher and *later* decides to pay the invoice in installments. The accountant must now cancel the original voucher by means of a general journal entry and issue new vouchers for each installment.

Suppose that City-Wide Electric buys merchandise from Donaldson and Farr FOB destination and records the transaction in the voucher register as follows except that the information in the Payment columns, which appears in color, is not included at this time:

VOUCHER REGISTER   PAGE ___2___

| | DATE | VOU. NO. | CREDITOR | PAYMENT | | VOUCHERS PAYABLE CREDIT | PURCHASES DEBIT | FREIGHT IN DEBIT |
				DATE	CK. NO.			
1								
2								
3	Sept. 21	103	Donaldson and Farr	10	16	V127, 128, 9	9 0 0 00	9 0 0 00
4								

Remember, when City-Wide Electric's accountant originally records the transaction, he or she leaves the Payment column blank. On October 16, City-Wide Electric arranges to pay the $900 debt in three installments of $300 each, with due dates of October 21, November 5, and November 21. Accordingly, the accountant makes an entry in the general journal as follows:

	DATE	DESCRIPTION	POST. REF.	DEBIT	CREDIT	
1	Oct. 16	Vouchers Payable		9 0 0 00		1
2		Purchases			9 0 0 00	2
3		Canceled voucher no. 103				3
4		payable to Donaldson and				4
5		Farr, the amount to be paid				5
6		in three equal installments,				6
7		due October 21, November 5,				7
8		and November 21.				8
9						9

The accountant then notes "10/16" and the voucher number for the installments in the Payment column of the voucher register and makes entries in the voucher register for three new vouchers, as shown:

VOUCHER REGISTER   PAGE ___3___

	DATE	VOU. NO.	CREDITOR	PAYMENT DATE	CK. NO.	VOUCHERS PAYABLE CREDIT	PURCHASES DEBIT	FREIGHT IN DEBIT
1								
2								
3	Oct. 16	127	Donaldson and Farr			3 0 0 00	3 0 0 00	
4	16	128	Donaldson and Farr			3 0 0 00	3 0 0 00	
5	16	129	Donaldson and Farr			3 0 0 00	2 5 7 00	4 3 00
6								

City-Wide Electric then puts voucher no. 103—the original voucher that was canceled—in the Paid Voucher file, and puts vouchers no. 127, no. 128, and no. 129 in the Unpaid Voucher file, in the usual manner.

Correcting an Amount After Original Voucher Has Been Recorded

The required approvals and verifications of records demanded by the voucher system will not entirely eliminate errors. However, these procedures should reduce errors to a minimum. If an error is discovered *after* a voucher has been recorded in the voucher register, the accountant can correct it by means of a general journal entry. The purpose of the entry is to cancel the original voucher by reversing the original entry. Since this has the effect of clearing the accounts, it paves the way for the issuance of a new voucher for the correct amount. For example, City-Wide Electric Supply bought merchandise, FOB destination, from Adkins Manufacturing Company for $546 and issued voucher no. 102, as follows:

VOUCHER REGISTER   PAGE ___2___

	DATE	VOU. NO.	CREDITOR	PAYMENT DATE	CK. NO.	VOUCHERS PAYABLE CREDIT	PURCHASES DEBIT	FREIGHT IN DEBIT
1								
2								
3	Sept. 20	102	Adkins Mfg. Co.	10 19	V130	5 4 6 00	5 4 6 00	
4								

When City-Wide Electric's accountant recorded the voucher, he or she left the Payment columns of the voucher register blank. On October 19, someone discovered an error in the price extensions; the correct amount of the invoice should have been $518. The entry necessary to correct the situation is as follows: first, cancel out the original voucher; next, record a new voucher for the correct amount.

	DATE	DESCRIPTION	POST. REF.	DEBIT	CREDIT	
1	Oct. 19	Vouchers Payable		5 4 6 00		1
2		Purchases			5 4 6 00	2
3		Canceled voucher no. 102 pay-				3
4		able to Adkins Manufacturing				4
5		Company because of error in				5
6		amount of invoice.				6

GENERAL JOURNAL PAGE ____

VOUCHER REGISTER PAGE 3

	DATE	VOU. NO.	CREDITOR	PAYMENT DATE	CK. NO.	VOUCHERS PAYABLE CREDIT	PURCHASES DEBIT	FREIGHT IN DEBIT
1								
2								
3	Oct. 19	130	Adkins Mfg. Co.			5 1 8 00	5 1 8 00	
4								
5								

The accountant makes a notation in the Payment columns of the voucher register that voucher no. 102 has been canceled by writing "10/19" and the new voucher number, "130." He or she makes a similar notation on voucher no. 102 itself, then places it in the Paid Voucher file. If the accountant discovers the error during the same month that the voucher was issued, he or she can handle the correction in this way or make the correction directly on the original voucher and in the voucher register by drawing a line through the incorrect amount and inserting the correct one. The accountant can do this because the transaction has not yet been posted.

THE VOUCHER SYSTEM AS A MANAGEMENT TOOL

The voucher system illustrates how well the accounting procedure aids internal control and how the voucher system helps organizations manage financial resources efficiently. In this respect, it has the following advantages. (Computers can also serve these functions.)

1. Vouchers supply up-to-date information on due dates and amounts owed. The financial manager is more interested in knowing *when* payment is due than in knowing to whom the amount is payable; she or he needs to plan for cash requirements. This information is provided in the **tickler file** (unpaid vouchers filed by due dates).
2. Vouchers systematize the taking of cash discounts. A firm that takes cash discounts saves a lot of money. The tickler file helps to ensure that a business will save this money by informing the firm about the last day to take advantage of cash discounts.
3. Payments cover specific invoices. Each check issued covers a specific invoice, which eliminates confusion about amounts owed to creditors.
4. Authority may be delegated and responsibility fixed. This advantage stems from the system of required approval signatures. Because the approval is given when the goods arrive or the service is received, if something is not satisfactory, it is given immediate attention.

RECORDING PURCHASES AT THE NET AMOUNT

Objective 5

Record the receipt and payment of invoices by the net-amount method.

Until now, even when we were discussing the voucher system, we always assumed that the firm's accountant recorded the cost of purchases at the gross amount. For example, Figure 21-1 showed an invoice from Draper, Inc., for $715; terms 2/10, n/30. City-Wide Electric's accountant recorded the invoice as a debit of $694.20 to Purchases, a debit of $20.80 to Freight In, and a credit of $715 to Vouchers Payable. (If City-Wide Electric had not been using the voucher system, Accounts Payable would have been credited.) As an alternative, firms that try to take advantage of all cash discounts use the **net-amount method.** They record all purchases at the net amount, which would be $701.12 ($694.20 less the 2 percent cash discount plus $20.80 for freight).

Recording purchases at the net amount means recording the amount of a purchase after the cash discount has been deducted.

A company that records purchases at the net amount does not necessarily have to use a voucher system. However, since firms that use voucher systems are usually medium- to large-sized business operations that take advantage of cash discounts whenever possible, many of these concerns do record purchases at the net amount. This method can be used with either a periodic or perpetual inventory system.

To compare the gross-amount procedure with the net-amount procedure, let's look at some sample transactions in general journal form, using both methods side by side. We will use a different company as an illustration.

Transaction (a) Bought merchandise on account from Barker and Fox, terms 2/10, n/30; FOB destination; $6,000. Issued voucher no. 2811.

Transaction (b) Issued check no. 3748 in payment of voucher no. 2811, less the cash discount.

Gross-Amount Procedure			Net-Amount Procedure		
(a) *In voucher register:*			**(a)** *In voucher register:*		
Purchases	6,000		Purchases	5,880	
Vouchers Payable		6,000	Vouchers Payable		5,880
(b) *In check register:*			**(b)** *In check register:*		
Vouchers Payable	6,000		Vouchers Payable	5,880	
Purchases Discount		120	Cash		5,880
Cash		5,880			

Using the net-amount method to record purchases eliminates the Purchases Discount account. But both methods yield the same Net Purchases that appears in the Cost of Merchandise Sold section of the income statement, because Purchases Discount must be deducted from Gross Purchases to arrive at Net Purchases.

Enterprises using the net-amount system naturally take advantage of all cash discounts available to them. However, sometimes, because of carelessness or oversight, one may miss out on the cash discount. In this case, one uses the account Discounts Lost, as illustrated here:

Transaction (c) Bought merchandise on account from C. R. Milton Company; terms 2/10, n/30; FOB destination; $3,200. Issued voucher no. 3092, May 17.

Transaction (d) Issued check no. 4167 in payment of voucher no. 3092, $3,200, June 17.

Gross-Amount Procedure			Net-Amount Procedure		
(c) *In voucher register:*			**(c)** *In voucher register:*		
Purchases	3,200		Purchases	3,136	
Vouchers Payable		3,200	Vouchers Payable		3,136
(d) *In check register:*			**(d)** *In check register:*		
Vouchers Payable	3,200		Vouchers Payable	3,136	
Cash		3,200	Discounts Lost	64	
			Cash		3,200

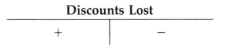

DATE		PAYMENT	CHECK NO.
June	17	Discount Lost	

When the net-amount method is used in conjunction with a voucher system, a notation in the Payment column of the voucher register indicates any discounts lost, as shown at left.

Under such a system, the check register contains a Discounts Lost Debit column. **Discounts Lost** is classified as an expense account:

Discounts Lost	
+	−

This account is closed into Income Summary along with all other expense accounts in the one large compound entry. On the income statement, Discounts Lost appears under Other Expenses. Additional accounts in this classification are Interest Expense and Loss on Disposal of Plant and Equipment (recall Chapter 15). For internal control, the prime advantage of using the net-amount method is that if a firm fails to take a discount, this fact is apparent to management, since it stands out as an exception. If this loss is due to someone's carelessness, management can take steps to see that the oversight does not recur. As an alternative, some accountants put the balance of Discounts Lost in the Cost of Merchandise Sold section of the income statement.

SUMMARY

L.O. 1 The voucher system is a procedure for recording and paying all liabilities incurred by a firm. The firm prepares a voucher in duplicate for each invoice (or bill) received, whether the obligation is to be paid immediately or in the future. The documents, consisting of the purchase invoice, or bill, and the purchase order are attached to the first copy of the voucher, which is circulated to the appropriate people so that they can add their official approval

L.O. 2 signatures. Next, the accountant records the voucher in the voucher register and files both copies of the vouchers in separate Unpaid Voucher files. The accountant files the original voucher, with documents attached, in the Unpaid Voucher file that is arranged alphabetically by names of creditors, and the second copy in the Unpaid Voucher file that is arranged chronologically by due dates (the tickler file). The accountant uses the alphabetical file to prepare the schedule of vouchers payable. When a firm is using the voucher system, it substitutes the Vouchers Payable account for Accounts Payable.

L.O. 3 Firms that use a voucher system use a check register. The Vouchers Payable debit column in the check register offsets the Vouchers Payable credit column in the voucher register. Both the check register and voucher register are books of original entry.

L.O. 4 The voucher system promotes internal control and the efficient management of financial resources. However, it is rigid, in that it establishes fixed

COMPUTERS AT WORK

Embezzling with a Computer

Businesses have always faced the threat of being "held up" by their own employees, robbed by people working from the inside. These crimes are generally more complex than a clerk simply walking off with the day's cash receipts. Some crafty criminals have used the company's own technology against it. Shift supervisors turned the time clocks against one company: they "punched in" phantom employees with their own time clock and then handed out paychecks to the phantoms. The scheme was uncovered only when the mother of a summer employee called the company to find out why it had over-reported her son's income to the government, making him ineligible for loans. The son's name, it turns out, had been on the payroll all year, although he stopped work in August.

Such embezzlement is not new to American companies, but it has recently taken on a new face, as computer and modems have become the embezzler's favorite tools. While teenage computer hackers make headlines by breaking into data banks to change grades or order airline tickets, trusted adult employees with access to computers are embezzling millions, perhaps billions, of dollars from American companies. No one really knows how much is stolen, in part because so few computer criminals are caught or prosecuted. The FBI estimates that only one in 20,000 computer criminals goes to jail. As computers become more widespread in the workplace, more people have access to them. And more are tempted by the tremendous potential computers offer for seemingly easy thefts, crimes that can be pulled off without leaving fingerprints.

Some computer crimes are fairly simple. An Indiana court convicted a county employee of using less than $10 worth of computer time without authorization. At Arizona's Veteran's Memorial Coliseum, a clerk sold full-price tickets, recorded them on the computer at half-price, and pocketed the difference.

More costly and complicated computer crimes are committed by sophisticated, trusted, high-level employees who have access to the accounts of a bank or other large institution. By creating phony accounts or phony transactions, or by siphoning off a few cents on thousands of real transactions, such people can cost their employers millions and sometimes lead their companies to bankruptcy. Only recently have companies started investing in security systems that prevent unauthorized use of computer systems and keep multiple copies of accounting records. It seems certain that the future of computerized accounting will involve new layers of checks and balances to make sure that no one is turning all those bytes and bits to dollars and cents of personal gain.

Sources: J. J. Buck BloomBecker, "New Federal Law Bolsters Computer Security Efforts," *Computerworld*, October 27, 1986, 53–66; Philip Elmer-DeWitt, "Surveying the Data Diddlers," *Time*, February 17, 1986, 95; Sanford L. Jacobs, "Owners Who Ignore Security Make Worker Dishonesty Easy," *The Wall Street Journal*, March 11, 1985, 31; Mike Lewis, "Computer Crime: Theft in Bits and Bytes," *Nation's Business*, February 1985, 57–58.

channels for handling routine transactions. Nonroutine transactions that do not fit into fixed channels require special treatment in the form of special entries in the general journal. Nonroutine transactions may involve the following: (1) returning part (or all) of the merchandise, (2) issuing a notes payable, (3) making part payments in the form of installments, or (4) making a correction on a bill or invoice *after the original voucher has been recorded.*

L.O. 5   When a firm uses the net-amount method, it records purchase invoices at the net figure (gross amount less cash discount). Normally, when the invoice is paid, the transaction is listed as a debit to Vouchers Payable and a credit to Cash. If the invoice is not paid within the discount period, at the time of payment the firm has to record the transaction as a debit to Vouchers Payable, a debit to Discounts Lost, and a credit to Cash. Or, if the firm is not using the voucher system, it substitutes Accounts Payable for Vouchers Payable. Under both systems, the Discounts Lost account is generally classified as an Other Expense account.

GLOSSARY

Discounts Lost   An account for recording the amount of cash discounts not taken, when the net-amount method of recording purchases of merchandise is used.

Net-amount method   A procedure by which incoming invoices are recorded at the net amount (gross amount less cash discount).

Price extensions   Computations of amounts listed on an invoice; unit prices multiplied by the number of units purchased, for example.

Tickler file   A file of unpaid vouchers arranged chronologically by due dates.

Voucher   A paper or document summarizing the terms of a transaction. It includes signatures or initials that vouch for its correctness, authorize its entry in the books, and approve its payment at the appropriate time.

Voucher register   A book of original entry in which all vouchers are recorded as credits to Vouchers Payable and debits to other accounts.

Voucher system   A procedure for the recording and payment of all liabilities incurred through the issuance of vouchers. It involves a voucher register and check register, Unpaid Voucher files, and Paid Voucher files.

QUESTIONS, EXERCISES, AND PROBLEMS
Discussion Questions

1. Why is the voucher system more appropriate for large- or medium-sized business firms than for small business firms?
2. When a business is using a voucher system, what types of transactions require that a voucher be filled out?
3. Describe each of the two Unpaid Voucher files.

4. Regarding the purchase of merchandise, describe what must be done when a credit memorandum is received after the original voucher has been recorded.
5. When a voucher system is in use, is it necessary to have an accounts payable ledger?
6. Explain briefly how the voucher system serves as a management tool.
7. Regarding the purchase of merchandise, what happens when installment payments are decided on after the original voucher has been recorded?
8. Describe the net-amount method for recording purchases.

Exercises

L.O. 2,3 **Exercise 21-1** Using the gross-amount method, record in general journal form the following related transactions. Assume the use of a voucher register, check register, and general journal. Identify the book of original entry in which each transaction would be recorded.

June   7 Bought merchandise on account from Weikert Company; terms 2/10, n/30; FOB destination; $9,200. Issued voucher no. 416.

10 Received credit memo no. D23 from Weikert Company for return of defective merchandise purchased June 7, $322.

15 Issued check no. 2029 in payment of voucher no. 416 less the return and less the discount.

L.O. 2,3 **Exercise 21-2** Enter the following in general journal form. Assume the use of a voucher register, check register, and general journal. Identify the book of original entry in which each transaction would be recorded.

a. Issued voucher no. 722 to establish a Petty Cash Fund, $85.
b. Prepared check no. 932 in payment of voucher no. 722, $85.
c. The present balance in the Petty Cash Fund is $9.06. Petty cash receipts indicate the following expenditures:

Store supplies	$11.44
Office supplies	16.20
Miscellaneous expense	48.30

Issued voucher no. 832 to reimburse the Petty Cash Fund, $75.94.

L.O. 2,3 **Exercise 21-3** Using the gross-amount method, record the following transactions in general journal form. Assume the use of a voucher register, check register, and general journal. Identify the book of original entry in which each transaction would be recorded.

Feb.   1 Prepared voucher no. 627 for $840, in favor of Freid Realty for rent for the month.

3 Prepared voucher no. 628, in favor of Hogan Company, for merchandise purchased; terms 2/10, n/30; FOB shipping point; $2,784; freight prepaid and added to the invoice, $116 (total $2,900).

5 Issued check no. 741 in payment of voucher no. 627.

Feb. 12 Issued check no. 742 in payment of voucher no. 628 less the amount of the cash discount.

17 Prepared voucher no. 629 in favor of Pioneer Paper Products for bags and cardboard cartons purchased, $241.62.

19 Issued check no. 743 in payment of voucher no. 629.

L.O. 2,3 **Exercise 21-4** Record in general journal form the following transactions. Assume the use of a voucher register, check register, and general journal. Identify the book of original entry in which each transaction would be recorded.

a. Issued voucher no. 7 to establish a Change Fund, $150.

b. Issued check no. 4 in payment of voucher no. 7.

c. Determined cash sales for the day according to the cash register tapes to be $740.19, while cash on hand was $891.17. A bank deposit was prepared for $741.17.

L.O. 2,5 **Exercise 21-5** Using the net-amount method, record the following transactions in general journal form. Assume the use of a voucher register, check register, and general journal. Identify the book of original entry in which each transaction would be recorded.

Aug. 2 Received from Howell and Son an invoice for merchandise, dated August 1; terms 2/10, n/30; FOB shipping point; $6,869; freight prepaid and added to the invoice, $371 (total $7,240). Issued voucher no. 8114 authorizing payment, and filed voucher for payment on August 8.

16 Discovered that voucher no. 8114 had been filed in error for payment on this date. Refiled it for payment on last day of credit period, September 1.

Sept. 1 Issued check no. 9846 in payment of voucher no. 8114.

L.O. 2,3,4 **Exercise 21-6** Using the gross-amount method, record the following related transactions in general journal form. Assume the use of a voucher register, check register, and general journal. Identify the book of original entry in which each transaction would be recorded.

May 8 Bought merchandise on account from G. R. Brown Company; terms 1/10, n/30; FOB destination; $4,240. Issued voucher no. 6211.

9 Gave a 60-day, 8 percent note to G. R. Brown Company, dated May 9; canceled voucher no. 6211.

July 8 Issued voucher no. 8238, $4,296.53, in favor of G. R. Brown Company for our note: principal $4,240, interest $56.53.

8 Prepared check no. 2773 in payment of voucher no. 8238.

L.O. 2,3,4 **Exercise 21-7** Record in general journal form the following transactions. Assume the use of a voucher register, check register, and general journal. Identify the book of original entry in which each transaction would be recorded.

Feb.   2 Bought shelving on account from Hagen's Cabinet Shop; terms 30 days; $924. Issued voucher no. 716.

Mar.   3 Hagen's Cabinet Shop agreed to accept payment on an install-ment basis as follows: One-third immediately, one-third by March 31, and one-third by April 30. Canceled voucher no. 716 and issued vouchers no. 907 for $308, no. 908 for $308, and no. 909 for $308.

      3 Issued check no. 1168 in payment of voucher no. 907.

    31 Issued check no. 1279 in payment of voucher no. 908.

Apr.   30 Issued check no. 1414 in payment of voucher no. 909.

L.O. 5   **Exercise 21-8**   At the suggestion of the accountant, R. L. Forbes bor-rowed $30,000 from the bank for 30 days at 11 percent. Forbes then used the proceeds to take advantage of discount terms of 2/10, n/30 offered by his supplier of merchandise. Forbes had not previously been taking advantage of the available cash discounts because the cash needed was not always available. Also, he was not convinced that it was worthwhile to borrow money for this purpose. (Hint: The net amount of the purchase is $30,000.)

Instructions

1. State briefly the specific advantage of the loan.
2. What kind of accounting controls should Forbes put into use to make sure that discounts are not overlooked?

Problem Set A

L.O. 2,3   **Problem 21-1A**   The Frobich Company uses a voucher system in which it records invoices at the gross amount. Following are vouchers issued dur-ing June and unpaid on July 1:

Voucher Number	Company	For	Date of Voucher	Amount
835	Sichel and Company	Merchandise, FOB destination	June 27	$1,942.00
838	J. C. Foster	Merchandise, FOB destination	June 30	$3,570.00

The following transactions were completed during July:

July   1 Issued voucher no. 840 in favor of L. C. Meier for July rent, $1,540.

      2 Issued check no. 1018 in payment of voucher no. 840, $1,540.

      6 Bought merchandise on account from Scott Manufacturing Com-pany, $7,024; terms 2/10, n/30; FOB shipping point; freight pre-paid and added to the invoice, $416 (total $7,440). Issued voucher no. 841.

July   9 Issued voucher no. 842 in favor of Piedmont Gas Company for heating bill, $184.

         9 Issued check no. 1019 in payment of voucher no. 842.

         9 Issued check no. 1020 in payment of the full amount of voucher no. 835.

        10 Issued check no. 1021 in payment of voucher no. 838, $3,498.60 ($3,570 less 2 percent discount).

        12 Issued check no. 1022 in payment of voucher no. 841, less the cash discount.

        17 Bought merchandise on account from Irvin, Inc., $5,925; terms 2/10, EOM; FOB destination. Issued voucher no. 843.

        25 Issued voucher no. 844 for a note payable, previously recorded in the general journal: principal $6,750, plus interest of $78. The note is payable to the First State Bank.

        25 Paid voucher no. 844 by issuing check no. 1023.

        31 Issued voucher no. 845 for Wages Payable, $4,552, in favor of the payroll bank account. (Assume that the payroll entry was previously recorded in the general journal.)

        31 Paid voucher no. 845 by issuing check no. 1024.

Instructions

1. Using the voucher issue date, enter the unpaid invoices in the voucher register, beginning with voucher no. 835. Then draw double lines across all columns to separate the vouchers of June from those of July.
2. Enter the transactions for July in the voucher register at the gross amount. Also record the appropriate transactions in the check register.
3. Total and rule the voucher register and the check register.
4. On scratch paper, prove the equality of the debits and credits in the voucher register and check register.

L.O. 2,3,4 **Problem 21-2A** The D. N. Hickman Company, which uses a voucher system, has the following unpaid vouchers on September 30:

Voucher Number	Company	For	Date of Invoice	Amount
7219	La Rose and Robbins	Merchandise, FOB destination	Sept. 22	$11,680.00
7222	Lynch Mercantile	Store Equipment	Sept. 24	$ 4,545.00
7223	Mack and Company	Merchandise, FOB destination	Sept. 27	$ 6,400.00

The D. N. Hickman Company made the following transactions during October:

Oct.   1 Issued voucher no. 7231 in favor of Noble Insurance Company for the premium on a one-year fire insurance policy, $432.

Oct.   1 Paid voucher no. 7219 by issuing check no. 626, $11,446.40 ($11,680 less 2 percent cash discount).

     3 Issued check no. 627 in payment of voucher no. 7231.

     5 Issued voucher no. 7232 in favor of S and F Motor Express for transportation charges on merchandise purchases, $84.

     5 Paid voucher no. 7232 by issuing check no. 628.

     6 Issued check no. 629 in payment of voucher no. 7223, $6,272 ($6,400 less 2 percent cash discount).

   10 Established a Petty Cash Fund of $250. Issued voucher no. 7233.

   10 Paid voucher no. 7233 by issuing check no. 630.

   12 Issued voucher no. 7234 in favor of Higgins and Company for the purchase of merchandise, $9,979; terms 2/10, n/30; FOB shipping point; freight prepaid and added to the invoice, $261 (total $10,240).

   14 Bought office equipment from City Office Supplies, $948; terms n/30. Issued voucher no. 7235.

   16 Received a credit memorandum for $1,040 from Higgins and Company for merchandise returned to them, credit memorandum no. 411.

   17 Issued voucher no. 7236 in favor of Mercer County for six months' property taxes (Prepaid Property Taxes), $1,800.

   17 Paid voucher no. 7236 by issuing check no. 631.

   21 Issued check no. 632 in payment of voucher no. 7234, $9,021.22 ($9,979 less $1,040 return, less cash discount plus freight).

   24 Paid voucher no. 7222 by issuing check no. 633.

   24 Bought merchandise on account from B. N. Hollenbeck, $9,632; terms 2/10, n/30; FOB destination. Issued voucher no. 7237.

   27 Received credit memorandum for $421 from B. N. Hollenbeck for damaged merchandise, credit memorandum no. 1339.

   31 Issued voucher no. 7238 to reimburse Petty Cash Fund. The charges were as follows:

Supplies	$158.92
D. N. Hickman, Drawing	40.00
Miscellaneous Expense	24.30

   31 Issued check no. 634 in payment of voucher no. 7238.

   31 Issued voucher no. 7239 for Wages Payable, $9,447, in favor of payroll bank account. (Assume that the payroll entry was previously recorded in the general journal.)

   31 Paid voucher no. 7239 by issuing check no. 635, payable to payroll bank account.

Instructions

1. Using the voucher issue date, enter the unpaid invoices in the voucher register, beginning with voucher no. 7219. Then draw double lines across all columns to separate the vouchers of September from those of October.

2. Enter the transactions for October in the voucher register at the gross amount. Also record the appropriate transactions in the check register and general journal.

3. Total and rule the voucher register and check register for the transactions recorded for October.
4. On scratch paper prove the equality of the debits and credits in the voucher register and check register.

L.O. 2,3,4   **Problem 21-3A**   The Marler Company uses a voucher system to record invoices at the gross amount. During May of this year it completed the following transactions affecting Vouchers Payable.

May   1 Issued voucher no. 1119 in favor of Larkin Company for the purchase of merchandise having an invoice price of $3,725; terms 30 days; FOB shipping point; freight prepaid and added to the invoice, $175 (total $3,900).

5 Prepared vouchers no. 1120 for $975, no. 1121 for $975, and no. 1122 for $975. The Marler Company incurred this debt because it bought a personal computer from Hammond Company, with terms of $975 cash on delivery, $975 in 30 days, and $975 in 60 days. (Use three lines.)

6 Issued check no. 1426 in payment of voucher no. 1120.

7 Issued voucher no. 1123 in favor of N. D. Drake Company for supplies, $98; terms net 30 days.

10 Prepared voucher no. 1124 in favor of Sever Company for the purchase of merchandise having an invoice price of $8,000 with a 25 percent trade discount (record voucher for $6,000); terms 2/10, n/30; FOB shipping point (freight to be billed separately by the carrier).

11 Prepared voucher no. 1125 in favor of City Real Estate for rent for the month, $1,550.

11 Issued check no. 1427 in payment of voucher no. 1125.

12 Issued voucher no. 1126 in favor of Becker Freight Line for transportation charges on merchandise purchased, $96.

14 Prepared check no. 1428 in payment of voucher no. 1126.

15 Canceled voucher no. 1119 because the invoice is to be paid in two installments, as follows: voucher no. 1127 for $1,950, payable June 1; voucher no. 1128, payable June 15, $1,950. Issued vouchers no. 1127 and no. 1128.

17 Received a credit memo from Sever Company for merchandise returned, $192, credit memo no. 213.

17 Issued check no. 1429 in payment of voucher no. 1124, $5,691.84 ($6,000, less $192 return, less cash discount).

22 Issued voucher no. 1129 in favor of United Telephone Company for telephone bill, $133.62.

22 Prepared check no. 1430 in payment of voucher no. 1129.

31 Prepared voucher no. 1130 for Wages Payable, $3,344, in favor of a payroll bank account. (Assume that the payroll entry was recorded previously in the general journal.)

31 Issued check no. 1431 in payment of voucher no. 1130.

31 Issued voucher no. 1131 in favor of D. N. Marler, the owner, for a personal withdrawal, $1,560.

31 Prepared check no. 1432 in payment of voucher no. 1131.

Instructions

1. Record the transactions for May in the voucher register, the check register, and the general journal.
2. Total and rule the voucher register and the check register.
3. Prove the equality of the debits and credits in the voucher register and the check register.
4. Post the amounts from the registers and the general journal to the Vouchers Payable account.
5. Prepare a schedule of vouchers payable. Compare this total with the balance of the Vouchers Payable account.

L.O. 2,3,4,5   **Problem 21-4A**   The Berger Company, which uses a voucher system, has the following unpaid vouchers on May 31. The firm follows the practice of recording invoices at the net amount.

Voucher Number	Company	For	Date of Invoice	Amount
5033	Calvin and Ball	Store Equipment	May 27	$6,750.00
5038	Harold and Company	Office Equipment	May 28	$7,905.00

The company made the following transactions during June:

June   1 Issued voucher no. 5043 in favor of Region Electric Corp. for electric bill, $192.

2 Paid voucher no. 5043 by issuing check no. 6855.

4 Canceled voucher no. 5033 because the invoice is to be paid in three installments, as follows: voucher no. 5044, payable June 15, $2,250; voucher no. 5045, payable July 1, $2,250; voucher no. 5046, payable July 14, $2,250. Accordingly, issued vouchers no. 5044, no. 5045, and no. 5046.

5 Bought merchandise on account from Edwards Company for $8,100; terms 2/10, n/30; FOB destination. Issued voucher no. 5047 (record invoice at $7,938, using the net amount).

8 N. D. Berger, the owner, withdrew $1,050 for personal use. Issued voucher no. 5048.

8 Prepared check no. 6856 in payment of voucher no. 5048.

10 Harold and Company agrees to accept a sixty-day, 8 percent note, dated June 9. Accordingly, canceled voucher no. 5038.

14 Issued check no. 6857 in payment of voucher no. 5047.

15 Prepared check no. 6858 in payment of voucher no. 5044.

16 Prepared voucher no. 5049 for $932 for sales commissions payable to C. P. Bekins.

16 Issued check no. 6859 in payment of voucher no. 5049.

21 Bought merchandise on account from D. C. Turner Company, $9,600; terms 1/10 EOM; FOB shipping point. Issued voucher no. 5050 (record the invoice as $9,504).

June   23 Issued voucher no. 5051 in favor of Central Express for freight
           bill on purchase from D. C. Turner Company, $92.
        25 Discovered an error in the computations on the invoice from
           D. C. Turner Company, reducing the invoice amount by $360.
           Canceled voucher no. 5050. Issued voucher no. 5052 for
           $9,147.60.
        26 Prepared voucher no. 5053, $571, in favor of Security Savings
           Bank for mortgage payment: principal, $280; interest, $291.
        28 Issued check no. 6860 in payment of voucher no. 5053.
        30 Prepared voucher no. 5054 for Wages Payable, $4,120, in favor of
           a payroll bank account. (Assume that the payroll entry was
           recorded previously in the general journal.)
        30 Paid voucher no. 5054 by issuing check no. 6861.

Instructions

1. Using the voucher issue date, enter the unpaid invoices in the voucher
   register, beginning with voucher no. 5033. Then draw double lines to
   separate the vouchers of May from those of June. Record the total of the
   two vouchers as a balance in the Vouchers Payable account.
2. Record the transactions for June in the voucher register, the check register, and the general journal.
3. Total and rule the voucher register and the check register.
4. Prove the equality of debits and credits in the voucher register and the
   check register.
5. Post the amounts from the registers and the general journal to the Vouchers Payable account, after recording the beginning balance.
6. Prepare a schedule of vouchers payable. Compare this total with the balance of the vouchers payable account.

Problem Set B

L.O. 2,3   **Problem 21-1B**   The Wallich Company uses a voucher system in which
            it records invoices at the gross amount. The following vouchers were issued
            during September and were unpaid on October 1:

Voucher Number	Company	For	Date of Voucher	Amount
618	Stansfield Company	Merchandise, FOB destination	Sept. 26	$2,325.00
621	L. C. Pitcher	Merchandise, FOB destination	Sept. 30	$3,600.00

The following transactions were completed during October:

Oct.   3 Issued voucher no. 623 in favor of Braddock Company for Octo-
          ber rent, $1,110.

Oct.   3 Issued check no. 828 in payment of voucher no. 623, $1,110.

5 Bought merchandise on account from Harlan, Inc., $2,789; terms 2/10, n/30; FOB shipping point; freight prepaid and added to the invoice, $61 (total $2,850). Issued voucher no. 624.

5 Issued check no. 829 in payment of voucher no. 618, $2,301.75 ($2,325 less 1 percent cash discount).

9 Issued voucher no. 625 in favor of Union Electric for electric bill, $108.

9 Issued check no. 830 in payment of voucher no. 625.

9 Issued check no. 831 in payment of voucher 621, $3,528 ($3,600 less 2 percent cash discount).

13 Issued check no. 832 in payment of voucher no. 624, less the cash discount.

16 Bought merchandise on account from Highland Manufacturing Company, $5,130; terms 2/10; FOB destination. Issued voucher no. 626.

25 Issued voucher no. 627 for note payable previously recorded in the general journal: principal, $3,000, plus $36 interest. The note is payable to the Hendricks State Bank.

25 Paid voucher no. 627 by issuing check no. 833.

25 Issued check no. 834 in payment of voucher no. 626, less the cash discount.

31 Issued voucher no. 628 for Wages Payable, $3,874, in favor of the payroll bank account. (Assume that the payroll entry was previously recorded in the general journal.)

31 Paid voucher no. 628 by issuing check no. 835.

Instructions

1. Using the voucher issue date, enter the unpaid invoices in the voucher register, beginning with voucher no. 618. Then draw double lines across all columns to separate the vouchers of September from those of October.
2. Record the transaction for October in the voucher register at the gross amount. Also record the appropriate transactions in the check register.
3. Total and rule the voucher register and the check register.
4. On scratch paper, prove the equality of the debits and credits in the voucher register and the check register.

L.O. 2,3,4   **Problem 21-2B**   The Norris Company, which uses a voucher system, has the following unpaid vouchers on February 28:

Voucher Number	Company	For	Date of Invoice	Amount
3678	Rodriguez and Son	Store Equipment	Feb. 15	$3,885.00
3684	Krueger and Company	Merchandise, FOB destination	Feb. 28	$7,460.00
3686	L. C. Kenney Company	Merchandise, FOB destination	Feb. 28	$9,600.00

The company made the following transactions during March:

Mar.   1 Issued voucher no. 3689 in favor of States Insurance Company for a premium on a three-year fire insurance policy, $780.

2 Paid voucher no. 3678 by issuing check no. 7118, $3,885.

2 Issued check no. 7119 in payment of voucher no. 3689.

4 Issued voucher no. 3690 in favor of Zale Fast Freight for transportation charges on merchandise purchases, $112.

5 Paid voucher no. 3690 by issuing check no. 7120.

7 Issued check no. 7121 in payment of voucher no. 3684, $7,385.40 ($7,460 less 1 percent cash discount).

8 Issued check no. 7122 in payment of voucher no. 3686, $9,504 ($9,600 less 1 percent cash discount).

11 Established a Petty Cash Fund of $250. Issued voucher no. 3691.

11 Paid voucher no. 3691 by issuing check no. 7123.

13 Issued voucher no. 3692 in favor of C. D. Howe Company for merchandise, $13,607; terms 2/10, n/30; FOB shipping point; freight prepaid and added to the invoice, $273 (total $13,880).

15 Received bill for advertising in the *Daily Chronicle*. Issued voucher no. 3693 in the amount of $300.

17 Received a credit memo for $652 from C. D. Howe Company for merchandise returned to them, credit memo no. 439 (pertaining to voucher no. 3692).

20 Issued voucher no. 3694 in favor Macon County for six month's property tax (Prepaid Property Taxes), $2,160.

20 Paid voucher no. 3694 by issuing check no. 7124.

21 Issued check no. 7125 in payment of voucher no. 3692, $12,968.90 ($13,607 less $652 return, less cash discount, plus freight).

23 Bought merchandise on account from Moore and Company, $5,928; terms 1/10, n/30; FOB destination. Issued voucher no. 3695.

27 Received a credit memo for $1,032 for Moore and Company for damaged merchandise, credit memo no. 326 (pertaining to voucher no. 3695).

31 Issued voucher no. 3696 to reimburse Petty Cash Fund. The charges were:

Supplies	$109.32
L. Norris, Drawing	50.00
Miscellaneous Expense	28.56

31 Issued check no. 7126 in payment of voucher no. 3696.

31 Issued voucher no. 3697 for Wages Payable, $7,337, in favor of payroll bank account. (Assume that the payroll entry was recorded previously in the general journal.)

31 Paid voucher no. 3697 by issuing check no. 7127, payable to payroll bank account.

Instructions

1. Using the voucher issue date, enter the unpaid invoices in the voucher register, beginning with voucher no. 3678. Then draw double lines across all columns to separate the vouchers of February from those of March.

2. Enter the transactions for March in the voucher register at the gross amount. Also record the appropriate transactions in the check register and general journal.
3. Total and rule the voucher register and check register for the transactions recorded during March.
4. On scratch paper, prove the equality of debits and credits in the voucher register and check register.

L.O. 2,3,4   **Problem 21-3B**   Brewster Mercantile uses a voucher system in which it records invoices at the gross amount. During October it completed the following transactions:

Oct.   2   Prepared voucher no. 1521 in favor of Larsen and Fitch for the purchase of merchandise having an invoice price of $4,720; terms 30 days; FOB shipping point; freight prepaid and added to the invoice, $80 (total $4,800).

3   Prepared vouchers no. 1522 for $1,080, no. 1523 for $1,080, and no. 1524 for $1,080. The debt arose because Brewster Mercantile bought a personal computer from Norton, Inc. The terms are $1,080 cash on delivery, $1,080 in 30 days, and $1,080 in 60 days. (Use three lines.)

5   Issued check no. 1614 in payment of voucher no. 1522.

9   Issued voucher no. 1525 in favor of Pershing Company for the purchase of supplies, $259.50; terms 30 days.

12   Prepared voucher no. 1526 in favor of Town Realty for rent for the month, $1,540.

12   Issued check no. 1615 in payment of voucher no. 1526.

16   Prepared voucher no. 1527 in favor of Roberts Express for freight charges on merchandise purchases, $74.

16   Prepared voucher no. 1528 in favor of Sanders Company for the purchase of merchandise having an invoice price of $5,400 with a 25 percent trade discount (record voucher for $4,050); terms 2/10, n/30; FOB shipping point.

16   Issued check no. 1616 in payment of voucher no. 1527.

16   Canceled voucher no. 1521 because the invoice will be paid in two installments as follows: voucher no. 1529, payable November 1, $2,400; voucher no. 1530, payable November 15, $2,400. Prepared vouchers no. 1529 and 1530.

17   Received a credit memo from Sanders Company for merchandise returned, $240, credit memo no. 691.

22   Prepared voucher no. 1531 in favor of Union Telephone Company for telephone bill, $132.45.

22   Issued check no. 1617 in payment of voucher no. 1531.

23   Issued check no. 1618 in payment of voucher no. 1528, $3,733.80 ($4,050 less $240 return, less cash discount).

31   Prepared voucher no. 1532 for Wages Payable, $3,449, in favor of payroll bank account. (Assume that the payroll entry was recorded previously in the general journal.)

31   Issued check no. 1619 in payment of voucher no. 1532.

Oct.   31 Prepared voucher no. 1533 in favor of T. N. Morales, the owner, for personal withdrawal, $1,700.

        31 Issued check no. 1620 for payment of voucher no. 1533.

Instructions

1. Record the transactions for October in the voucher register, the check register, and the general journal.
2. Total and rule the voucher register and the check register.
3. Prove the equality of the debits and credits in the voucher register and the check register.
4. Post the amounts from the registers and the general journal to the Vouchers Payable account.
5. Prepare a schedule of vouchers payable. Compare the total with the balance of the Vouchers Payable account.

L.O. 2,3,4,5   **Problem 21-4B**   The Collier Company uses a voucher system by which it records invoices at the net amount. It has the following unpaid vouchers on August 31:

Voucher Number	Company	For	Date of Invoice	Amount
4704	Henreid Company	Store Equipment	Aug. 25	$9,600.00
4710	Tedder, Inc.	Merchandise, FOB destination	Aug. 27	$10,700.00

The company made the following transactions during September:

Sept.   2 Prepared voucher no. 4716 in favor of Seacoast Electric for electric bill, $319.

       2 Paid voucher no. 4716 by issuing check no. 6902.

       2 Bought merchandise on account from Sinco Manufacturing Company, $11,700; terms 2/10, n/30; FOB destination. Prepared voucher no. 4717 (record invoice for $11,466, using the net amount).

       4 Canceled voucher no. 4704 because the invoice is to be paid in three installments, as follows: voucher no. 4718, due September 15, $3,200; voucher no. 4719, due September 30, $3,200; voucher no. 4720, due October 15, $3,200. Accordingly, issued vouchers no. 4718, no. 4719, and no. 4720.

       7 N. R. Sato, the owner, withdrew $1,420 for personal use. Issued voucher no. 4721.

       7 Issued check no. 6903 in payment of voucher no. 4721.

       9 Tedder, Inc., agreed to accept a thirty-day, 9 percent note, dated September 9. Accordingly, canceled voucher no. 4710.

      10 Issued check no. 6904 in payment of voucher no. 4717.

      14 Issued check no. 6905 in payment of voucher no. 4718.

Sept. 17 Prepared voucher no. 4722 for $1,762 for sales commissions expense, in favor of C. P. Payton. The expense was not previously recorded.

17 Issued check no. 6906 in payment of voucher no. 4722, payable to C. P. Payton.

22 Bought merchandise on account from C. C. Manley Company, $13,440; terms 1/10, EOM; FOB shipping point. Issued voucher no. 4723 (record the invoice for $13,305.60).

24 Prepared voucher no. 4724 in favor of C and I Motor Freight for freight bill on the purchase from C. C. Manley Company, $121.

25 Issued check no. 6907 in payment of voucher no. 4724.

25 Discovered an error in the computations on the invoice from C. C. Manley Company, reducing the invoice amount by $440. Canceled voucher no. 4723 and issued voucher no. 4725, $12,870.

29 Prepared voucher no. 4726, $789, in favor of True Savings Bank, for mortgage payment: principal, $412; interest, $377.

29 Issued check no. 6908 in payment of voucher no. 4726.

30 Prepared voucher no. 4727 for Wages Payable, $5,417, in favor of payroll bank account. (Assume that the payroll entry was recorded previously in the general journal.)

30 Paid voucher no. 4727 by issuing check no. 6909.

Instructions

1. Using the voucher issue date, enter the unpaid invoices in the voucher register, beginning with voucher no. 4704. Then draw double lines to separate the vouchers of August from those of September. Record the total of the two vouchers as a balance in the Vouchers Payable account.
2. Record the transactions for September in the voucher register, the check register, and the general journal.
3. Total and rule the voucher register and the check register.
4. Prove the equality of debits and credits in the voucher register and the check register.
5. Post the amounts from the registers and the general journal to the Vouchers Payable account, after recording the beginning balance.
6. Prepare a schedule of vouchers payable. Compare the total with the balance of the Vouchers Payable account.

22 Accounting for Partnerships

Up to this time, we have been dealing entirely with sole proprietorships. In this chapter and the ones that follow, we shall deal with two other forms of business organizations: partnerships and corporations. In the professions and in firms that stress personal service, partnerships are widely used. Each professional practitioner can maintain her or his own clientele yet share with colleagues the expenses of operating an office or clinic. Partnerships are also popular in manufacturing and trade because they afford a means of combining the capital and abilities of two or more persons.

CHARACTERISTICS OF A PARTNERSHIP

A **partnership**, as defined by the Uniform Partnership Act, is an association of two or more persons to carry on, as co-owners, a business for profit. It is a voluntary association, entered into by the parties without compulsion. Certain features of a partnership affect just the partners; other features affect the partners as well as others who are not members of the partnership. Let us examine some of these features.

Co-ownership of Partnership Property

All partners are co-owners of the assets of the partnership. For example, Towne and Dillon formed a 50-50 partnership to run a fuel oil business. The partnership owns two tank trucks of equal value. According to the **co-ownership** concept, each partner owns half of each truck, as well as half of the other assets of the firm.

Limited Life

A partnership may be ended by the death or withdrawal of any partner. Other factors that may bring about the end of a partnership include the bankruptcy or incapacity of a partner, the expiration of the period of time specified in the partnership agreement, or the completion of the project for which the partnership was formed.

Unlimited Liability

Each partner is personally liable to creditors for all the debts the partnership incurs during his or her membership in the firm. When a new partner joins an existing firm, he or she may or may not assume liability for debts incurred by the firm prior to admission. When a partner withdraws from a firm, he or she must give adequate public notice of withdrawal, or he or she may be held liable for debts the partnership incurs after his or her withdrawal.

Mutual Agency

Each partner can enter into binding contracts in the name of the firm for the purchase or sale of goods or services within the normal scope of the firm's business. When the partners agree among themselves to limit the right of any partner to enter into certain contracts in the name of the firm, this agreement is not binding on outsiders who are unaware of its existence.

ADVANTAGES OF A PARTNERSHIP

Here are four advantages of a partnership:

1. Partnerships offer the opportunity to pool the abilities and capital of two or more persons.

2. It is easy to form a partnership, the only requirement being an agreement or mutual understanding by the partners.
3. Legal restrictions are minimal. Although a partnership must have a legal purpose, there are no other limitations on types of business activities.
4. Federal income taxes are not levied against a partnership as an entity, although a partnership must file an information return (Form 1065) containing an income statement, balance sheet, and report of the distributive shares of income (the shares of the year's net income allocated to each partner). A partner has to pay taxes on his or her share of the net income, whether or not this share is actually taken out of the business.

DISADVANTAGES OF A PARTNERSHIP

Here are some disadvantages of a partnership:

1. **General partners** (those who actively and publicly participate in transactions of the firm) have unlimited liability.
2. A partnership has limited life.
3. The actions of one partner are binding on the other partners; this relationship is known as **mutual agency.**
4. The raising of investment capital depends entirely on the partners themselves.
5. It is hard to transfer a partial or entire partnership interest to another person, as the transfer must be agreed to by all partners.
6. There may be some strain in personal relationships (getting along together) among partners as they carry out their daily responsibilities.

PARTNERSHIP AGREEMENTS

Although generally a partnership may be formed on the basis of an oral understanding, it is much better to have the partnership agreement based on a written contract. Although there is no standard form of partnership agreement, the following provisions are usually included:

• Effective date of the agreement
• Names and addresses of the partners
• Name, location, and nature of the business
• Duration of the agreement
• Investment of each partner
• Withdrawals to be allowed each partner
• Procedure for sharing profits and losses
• Provision for division of assets upon dissolution

Let us now look at a typical partnership agreement (Figure 22-1).

FIGURE 22-1

PARTNERSHIP AGREEMENT

L. C. Kibby of San Diego, California, and O. J. Sanford of the same city and state agree as follows:

Recitals of Fact: The parties have this day formed a partnership for the purpose of engaging in and conducting a retail women's wear business in the city of San Diego under the following stipulations, which are a part of this contract:

First: The partnership is to continue for a term of 20 years from January 1 of this year.

Second: The business is to be conducted under the firm name of Hi Fashion Shop, at 1424 West Sixth Street, San Diego, California.

Third: The investments are as follows: L. C. Kibby, cash, $50,000; O. J. Sanford, cash, $50,000. These invested assets are partnership property in which the equity of each partner is the same.

Fourth: Each partner is to devote his or her entire time and attention to the business and to engage in no other business enterprise without the written consent of the other partner.

Fifth: During the operation of this partnership, neither partner is to become surety or bondsman for anyone without the written consent of the other partner.

Sixth: Each partner is to receive a salary of $18,000 a year, payable $750 in cash on the fifteenth and $750 on the last business day of each month. At the end of each annual fiscal period, the net income or the net loss shown by the income statement, after the salaries of the two partners have been allowed, is to be shared as follows: L. C. Kibby, 50 percent; O. J. Sanford, 50 percent.

Seventh: Neither partner is to withdraw assets in excess of his or her salary, any part of the assets invested, or assets in anticipation of net income to be earned, without the written consent of the other partner.

Eighth: In the case of the death or the legal disability of either partner, the other partner is to continue the operations of the business until the close of the annual fiscal period on the following December 31. At that time the continuing partner is to be given an option to buy the interest of the deceased or incapacitated partner at the value of the deceased or incapacitated partner's proprietary interest as determined by the agreement of the continuing partner and the legal representative of the deceased or incapacitated partner. In the event they are unable to agree, then the determination of such value shall be submitted to arbitration in accordance with the rules of the American Arbitration Association. It is agreed that this purchase price is to be paid one half in cash and the balance in four equal installments payable quarterly.

Ninth: At the conclusion of this contract, unless it is mutually agreed to continue the operation of the business under a new contract, the assets of the partnership, after the liabilities are paid, are to be divided in proportion to the net credit of each partner's capital account on that date.

Dated December 28, 19–   *L.C. Kibby*   (Seal)

                                    O. J. Sanford   (Seal)

ACCOUNTING ENTRIES FOR PARTNERSHIPS

The only difference between accounting for a sole proprietorship and accounting for partnerships is in the owners' equity accounts. Otherwise, the accountant uses the same types of assets, liabilities, revenues, and expenses that we discussed before. But because there is more than one owner, it is necessary to have one capital account and one drawing account for each partner. As in the case of sole proprietorships, the capital accounts are involved only when there is a change in investments or when the Income Summary account and the Drawing accounts are closed.

Recording Investments

The accountant makes a separate entry for the investment of each partner. All assets contributed by a given partner are debited to the appropriate asset accounts. If the partnership assumes liabilities, the accountant credits the proper liability accounts, and credits the partner's capital account for the net amount.

Let's take a case of recording initial investments in a partnership: Joan C. Hinds and Nancy A. Morales decide to form a partnership on February 2 for the operation of a jewelry store. Hinds presently owns and operates Hinds's Jewelry Store; she is contributing the assets and liabilities of her store to the new firm. Morales's investment is $20,000 in cash; the following is the entry to record this investment:

	DATE	DESCRIPTION	POST. REF.	DEBIT	CREDIT	
			GENERAL JOURNAL		PAGE 1	
1	19–					1
2	Feb. 2	Cash		20 0 0 0 00		2
3		N. A. Morales, Capital			20 0 0 0 00	3
4		To record the original investment				4
5		of Nancy A. Morales.				5

Both partners have to agree on the monetary amounts at which Hinds's noncash assets are to be recorded. Assume that Hinds's Jewelry Store has the following account balances:

Cash	$ 2,900
Accounts Receivable	18,000
Allowance for Doubtful Accounts	200
Merchandise Inventory	20,400

Equipment				$16,000
Accumulated Depreciation, Equipment				4,500
Notes Payable				1,600
Accounts Payable				8,400

Furthermore, $400 of the Accounts Receivable have been definitely ascertained to be uncollectible; the $400 should not be recorded on the books of the new partnership. Of the remaining $17,600 of Accounts Receivable, there is some doubt as to the collectibility of $500. Assume these amounts have been determined by aging the accounts receivable. Since the values of the merchandise and equipment may be more or less than the amounts recorded on Hinds's books, both parties agree to have an independent appraisal made. Assume the present appraised values of Hinds's merchandise is $21,000 and her equipment is $9,000. Therefore, the accountant records Hinds's investment on page 1 of the general journal as follows:

	DATE		DESCRIPTION	POST. REF.	DEBIT	CREDIT	
7	19–						7
8	Feb.	2	Cash		2 9 0 0 00		8
9			Accounts Receivable		17 6 0 0 00		9
10			Merchandise Inventory		21 0 0 0 00		10
11			Equipment		9 0 0 0 00		11
12			Allowance for Doubtful Accounts			5 0 0 00	12
13			Notes Payable			1 6 0 0 00	13
14			Accounts Payable			8 4 0 0 00	14
15			J. C. Hinds, Capital			40 0 0 0 00	15
16			To record the original investment				16
17			of Joan C. Hinds.				17

The accountant debits Accounts Receivable for the face amount of the accounts taken over by the new partnership and credits Allowance for Doubtful Accounts for the amount estimated to be uncollectible. Any definitely uncollectible customer accounts are excluded from those being taken over by the new business.

The accountant debits the new firm's Merchandise Inventory and Equipment accounts for the amount of their present appraised values. The accumulated depreciation is not recorded, because the appraised value represents the new book value for the partnership.

Additional Investments

Now let's say that eight months have gone by and the new partnership needs more cash. On October 1, the partners each invest an additional $4,000. The entry is shown at the top of the next page.

GENERAL JOURNAL PAGE _28_

	DATE	DESCRIPTION	POST. REF.	DEBIT	CREDIT	
1	19–					1
2	Oct. 1	Cash		8 0 0 0 00		2
3		J. C. Hinds, Capital			4 0 0 0 00	3
4		N. A. Morales, Capital			4 0 0 0 00	4
5		To record additional investments.				5
6						6
7						7
8						8

At the end of the year, before the books are closed, the capital accounts of the partners appear as shown here:

GENERAL LEDGER

ACCOUNT J. C. Hinds, Capital ACCOUNT NO. 301

						BALANCE	
	DATE	ITEM	POST. REF.	DEBIT	CREDIT	DEBIT	CREDIT	
1	19–							1
2	Feb. 2		J1		40 0 0 0 00		40 0 0 0 00	2
3	Oct. 1		J28		4 0 0 0 00		44 0 0 0 00	3
4								4

ACCOUNT N. A. Morales, Capital ACCOUNT NO. 303

						BALANCE	
	DATE	ITEM	POST. REF.	DEBIT	CREDIT	DEBIT	CREDIT	
1	19–							1
2	Feb. 2		J1		20 0 0 0 00		20 0 0 0 00	2
3	Oct. 1		J28		4 0 0 0 00		24 0 0 0 00	3
4								4

Drawing Accounts

Drawing accounts of partners serve the same purpose as the Drawing account of the owner of a sole proprietorship. Debits to the Drawing accounts originate through transactions like those listed below and illustrated in Figure 22-2:

• Withdrawal of cash by a partner, $200.
• Withdrawal of merchandise by a partner, $148.

FIGURE 22-2

	DATE		DESCRIPTION	POST. REF.	DEBIT	CREDIT	
1	*19–*						1
2	*Mar.*	*17*	*J. C. Hinds, Drawing*		*2 0 0 00*		2
3			*Cash*			*2 0 0 00*	3
4			*To record a cash withdrawal.*				4
5							5
6	*May*	*4*	*N. A. Morales, Drawing*		*1 4 8 00*		6
7			*Purchases*			*1 4 8 00*	7
8			*To record a merchandise*				8
9			*withdrawal at cost.*				9
10							10
11							11
12							12
13							13
14							14

DIVISION OF NET INCOME OR NET LOSS

Recall that the closing entries for a sole proprietorship require the following steps:

1. Close the revenue accounts into Income Summary.
2. Close the expense accounts into Income Summary (the expense accounts do not include any payments to partners).
3. Close Income Summary into the Capital account by the amount of the net income or loss.
4. Close the Drawing account into the Capital account.

Objective 1

Prepare a section of an income statement relating to division of net income for a partnership involving division of income on the basis of fractional shares, on the basis of ratio of capital investments, and on the basis of salary and interest allowances.

The only differences between closing entries for a partnership and those for a sole proprietorship pertain to steps 3 and 4. Instead of a single capital account and a single drawing account, in a partnership there are as many accounts of each type as there are partners. Income Summary is closed into the capital accounts by the amount of the net income or loss, and the drawing accounts are closed into the respective capital accounts.

Let's look at step 3, which deals with the division of net income or net loss. The partnership agreement should specify the arrangement for the division of net income or net loss. However, suppose the partnership agreement fails to do this. Then, from a legal standpoint, the partners should share any net income or loss equally. This is true regardless of differences in amounts invested, in special skills provided, or in time devoted to the business. The share of net income (or net loss) allocated to each partner is known as his or her **distributive share.**

Partners may use any one of a number of alternative methods of sharing partnership earnings, or they may use a combination of methods. The variety of methods reflects the different value of the services or investments contributed by individual partners. We shall discuss four methods for sharing partnership earnings:

1. Division of income based on fractional shares
2. Division of income based on the ratio of capital investments
3. Division of income based on salary allowances
4. Division of income based on interest allowances

We shall look at two examples of each method.

In our first example, the partnership of Bates and Cater has a net income of $48,000. In the second, the partnership of Bates and Cater has a net *loss* of $2,000. We shall use the same balances in the capital and drawing accounts for each example, and consider that each method used for dividing net income represents a separate partnership agreement.

The balances of the capital accounts represent the partners' individual investments at the beginning of the year. The balances of the drawing accounts represent the total personal withdrawals during the year. These are shown by T accounts as follows:

L. R. Bates, Capital			P. L. Cater, Capital		
–	+		–	+	
	Balance	50,000		Balance	30,000

L. R. Bates, Drawing			P. L. Cater, Drawing		
+	–		+	–	
Balance	19,000		Balance	10,000	

Division of Income Based on Fractional Shares

Objective 2

Journalize the closing entries for a partnership.

The simplest way to divide net income or loss is to allot each partner a stated fraction of the total. One can establish the size of the fraction by taking into consideration (1) the amount of investment of each partner and (2) the value of services rendered by each partner. Assume that the partnership agreement stipulates that profits and losses are to be divided this way: three-fourths to Bates and one-fourth to Cater.

The accountant may present a report of the division of net income as a separate statement or record it on the income statement, immediately below Net Income.

Net Income of $48,000   If the accountant adopts the latter procedure, the division of net income appears as follows:

Bates and Cater
Income Statement
For Year Ended December 31, 19–

Revenue from Sales:				
Net Income				$48 0 0 0 00
Division of Net Income	L. R. Bates	P. L. Cater	Total	
Fractional Share	$36 0 0 0 00	$12 0 0 0 00	$48 0 0 0 00	

The division of net income is recorded as a closing entry in step 3 of the closing procedure whether or not the partner has withdrawn his or her share. The entry looks like this:

	DATE		DESCRIPTION	POST. REF.	DEBIT	CREDIT	
1	19–		*Closing Entry*				1
2	Dec.	31	Income Summary		48 0 0 0 00		2
3			L. R. Bates, Capital			36 0 0 0 00	3
4			P. L. Cater, Capital			12 0 0 0 00	4
5							5
6							6

The entries for step 4, closing the drawing accounts into the capital accounts, are as follows:

	DATE		DESCRIPTION	POST. REF.	DEBIT	CREDIT	
7	19–		*Closing Entries*				7
8	Dec.	31	L. R. Bates, Capital		19 0 0 0 00		8
9			L. R. Bates, Drawing			19 0 0 0 00	9
10							10
11		31	P. L. Cater, Capital		10 0 0 0 00		11
12			P. L. Cater, Drawing			10 0 0 0 00	12
13							13
14							14

Now let's see what these entries look like by means of T accounts, with steps 3 and 4 labeled:

Income Summary

(3) Closing	48,000	Balance	48,000

L. R. Bates, Capital

–		+	
(4)	19,000	Balance	50,000
		(3)	36,000

P. L. Cater, Capital

–		+	
(4)	10,000	Balance	30,000
		(3)	12,000

L. R. Bates, Drawing

+		–	
Balance	19,000	(4) Closing	19,000

P. L. Cater, Drawing

+		–	
Balance	10,000	(4) Closing	10,000

Note that step 4 is the same for partnerships as for sole proprietorships.

Net Loss of $2,000   The lower portion of the following income statement reflects the net loss. (The parentheses around the totals indicate that the figures are minus numbers.)

	L. R. Bates	P. L. Cater	Total
Revenue from Sales:			
Net Loss			$(2 0 0 00)
Division of Net Loss:	L. R. Bates	P. L. Cater	Total
Fractional Share	$(1 5 0 0 00)	$(5 0 0 00)	$(2 0 0 0 00)

The closing entries and posting to the ledger accounts are shown in Figure 22-3 and the T accounts that follow:

FIGURE 22-3

	DATE	DESCRIPTION	POST. REF.	DEBIT	CREDIT	
1	19–	*Closing Entries*				1
2	Dec. 31	L. R. Bates, Capital		1 5 0 0 00		2
3		P. L. Cater, Capital		5 0 0 00		3
4		Income Summary			2 0 0 0 00	4
5						5
6	31	L. R. Bates, Capital		19 0 0 0 00		6
7		L. R. Bates, Drawing			19 0 0 0 00	7
8						8
9	31	P. L. Cater, Capital		10 0 0 0 00		9
10		P. L. Cater, Drawing			10 0 0 0 00	10
11						11

Income Summary

Balance	2,000	(3) Closing	2,000

L. R. Bates, Capital					P. L. Cater, Capital			
−		+			−		+	
(3)	1,500	Balance	50,000	(3)		500	Balance	30,000
(4)	19,000			(4)		10,000		

L. R. Bates, Drawing					P. L. Cater, Drawing			
+		−			+		−	
Balance	19,000	(4) Closing	19,000	Balance		10,000	(4) Closing	10,000

When partners share net income on a fractional basis, this basis is often expressed as a ratio. We can express Bates's three-fourths and Cater's one-fourth as a 3:1 (3-to-1) ratio.

When you list the division of net income as a ratio and want to turn the ratio into a fraction, do it this way. First add the figures; then use the total as the denominator of the fraction:

3:1   (3 + 1 = 4)   ¾ and ¼

or (in the case of three partners):

5:3:1   (5 + 3 + 1 = 9)   5/9 and 3/9 and 1/9

or (in the case of four partners):

3:2:1:1   (3 + 2 + 1 + 1 = 7)   3/7 and 2/7 and 1/7 and 1/7

Division of Income Based on Ratio of Capital Investments

Allocating earnings to partners on the basis of the amounts of their investment often works well for enterprises whose earnings are closely related to the amount of money invested, such as real estate ventures, cattle feeding operations, and the like. Suppose that Bates and Cater have agreed to share earnings or losses according to the ratio of their investments at the beginning of the year. Let's say that Bates had $50,000 and Cater $30,000 in their capital accounts. One can calculate their respective shares as follows:

Bates	$50,000
Cater	30,000
Total	$80,000

$$\text{Bates's share} = \frac{\$50,000}{\$80,000} = \frac{5}{8} \text{ or } .625 \ (62.5\%)$$

$$\text{Cater's share} = \frac{\$30,000}{\$80,000} = \frac{3}{8} \text{ or } .375 \ (37.5\%)$$

Net Income of $48,000   When the partnership has a net income of $48,000, the accountant determines the distribution like this:

Bates's share of earnings $48,000 × ⅝ (or $48,000 × .625) = $30,000

Cater's share of earnings $48,000 × ⅜ (or $48,000 × .375) = $18,000

The section of the income statement showing the division of net income looks like this:

Revenue from Sales:			
Net Income			$48 0 0 0 00
Division of Net Income:	L. R. Bates	P. L. Cater	Total
Capital Investment Ratio	$30 0 0 0 00	$18 0 0 0 00	$48 0 0 0 00

The accompanying closing entries are as follows:

	DATE	DESCRIPTION	POST. REF.	DEBIT	CREDIT	
1	19–	*Closing Entries*				1
2	Dec. 31	Income Summary		48 0 0 0 00		2
3		L. R. Bates, Capital			30 0 0 0 00	3
4		P. L. Cater, Capital			18 0 0 0 00	4
5						5
6	31	L. R. Bates, Capital		19 0 0 0 00		6
7		L. R. Bates, Drawing			19 0 0 0 00	7
8						8
9	31	P. L. Cater, Capital		10 0 0 0 00		9
10		P. L. Cater, Drawing			10 0 0 0 00	10
11						11
12						12
13						13

Net Loss of $2,000   When the partnership has a net loss of $2,000, the accountant calculates the sharing of the loss as follows:

Bates's share of the loss $2,000 × ⅝ (or $2,000 × .625) = $1,250

Cater's share of the loss $2,000 × ⅜ (or $2,000 × .375) = $750

The section of the income statement showing the division of net loss and the accompanying closing entries looks like this:

	L. R. Bates	P. L. Cater	Total
Revenue from Sales:			
Net Loss			$(2 0 0 0 00)
Division of Net Loss:	L. R. Bates	P. L. Cater	Total
Capital Investment Ratio	$(1 2 5 0 00)	$(7 5 0 00)	$(2 0 0 0 00)

	DATE		DESCRIPTION	POST. REF.	DEBIT	CREDIT	
1	19–		Closing Entries				1
2	Dec.	31	L. R. Bates, Capital		1 2 5 0 00		2
3			P. L. Cater, Capital		7 5 0 00		3
4			Income Summary			2 0 0 0 00	4
5							5
6		31	L. R. Bates, Capital		19 0 0 0 00		6
7			L. R. Bates, Drawing			19 0 0 0 00	7
8							8
9		31	P. L. Cater, Capital		10 0 0 0 00		9
10			P. L. Cater, Drawing			10 0 0 0 00	10
11							11

Note that the entries for step 4—closing the drawing accounts into the capital accounts—are always the same, regardless of whether the firm finishes the year with a net income or a net loss.

Division of Income Based on Salary Allowances

Salary allowances are purely allocations of net income. They are used as a means of recognizing and rewarding differences in ability and in the amount of time devoted to the business. **Salary allowances are different from payments to the partners, which are recorded in the drawing accounts.** They are also different from remuneration to employees, which is recorded as Salaries or Wages Expense. They may be thought of as guaranteed amounts determined without regard to the income of the partnership.

Suppose that Bates's and Cater's partnership agreement provides for yearly salaries of $12,000 and $8,000, respectively, with the remainder of the net income to be divided equally. (It would also be possible to divide the remainder on the basis of the ratio of investments or any other ratio agreed on by the partners.)

Net Income of $48,000   The Division of Net Income section of the income statement when there is a net income of $48,000 is as follows:

Revenue from Sales:			
Net Income			$48 000 00
Division of Net Income:	L. R. Bates	P. L. Cater	Total
Salary Allowances	$12 000 00	$8 000 00	$20 000 00
Remainder Allocated Equally	14 000 00	14 000 00	28 000 00
Net Income	$26 000 00	$22 000 00	$48 000 00

The firm's accountant determines the allocation of the remainder as follows:

Net income	$48,000
Less amount allocated as salaries ($12,000 + $8,000)	20,000
Remainder	$28,000

$$\text{Remainder} \div 2 = \frac{\$28,000}{2} = \$14,000$$

Look at the closing entries:

	DATE	DESCRIPTION	POST. REF.	DEBIT	CREDIT	
1	19–	*Closing Entries*				1
2	Dec. 31	Income Summary		48 000 00		2
3		L. R. Bates, Capital			26 000 00	3
4		P. L. Cater, Capital			22 000 00	4
5						5
6	31	L. R. Bates, Capital		19 000 00		6
7		L. R. Bates, Drawing			19 000 00	7
8						8
9	31	P. L. Cater, Capital		10 000 00		9
10		P. L. Cater, Drawing			10 000 00	10
11						11

Net Loss of $2,000   When salary allowances are stipulated in the partnership agreement, they must be allocated (not necessarily paid) regardless of whether there is enough net income to take care of them.

The accountant determines the remainder as follows:

Net Loss	$(2,000)
Less amount allocated as salaries ($12,000 + $8,000)	20,000
Remainder	$(22,000)

$$\text{Remainder} \div 2 = \frac{\$(22,000)}{2} = \underline{\underline{\$(11,000)}}$$

The income statements and closing entries appear as follows:

Revenue from Sales:						
Net Loss						$(2 0 0 0 00)
Division of Net Loss:	**L. R. Bates**		**P. L. Cater**		**Total**	
Salary Allowances	$12 0 0 0 00		$8 0 0 0 00		$20 0 0 0 00	
Excess of Allowances over Income						
Allocated Equally	(11 0 0 0 00)		(11 0 0 0 00)		(22 0 0 0 00)	
Net Income (Loss)	$1 0 0 0 00		$(3 0 0 0 00)		$(2 0 0 0 00)	

	DATE		DESCRIPTION	POST. REF.	DEBIT	CREDIT	
1	19–		*Closing Entries*				1
2	Dec.	31	P. L. Cater, Capital		3 0 0 0 00		2
3			Income Summary			2 0 0 0 00	3
4			L. R. Bates, Capital			1 0 0 0 00	4
5							5
6		31	L. R. Bates, Capital		19 0 0 0 00		6
7			L. R. Bates, Drawing			19 0 0 0 00	7
8							8
9		31	P. L. Cater, Capital		10 0 0 0 00		9
10			P. L. Cater, Drawing			10 0 0 0 00	10
11							11
12							12
13							13
14							14
15							15

After posting, the owner's equity accounts look like the ones shown at the top of the next page.

Income Summary

Balance	2,000	(3) Closing	2,000

L. R. Bates, Capital

−		+	
(4)	19,000	Balance	50,000
		(3)	1,000

P. L. Cater, Capital

−		+	
(3)	3,000	Balance	30,000
(4)	10,000		

L. R. Bates, Drawing

+		−	
Balance	19,000	(4) Closing	19,000

P. L. Cater, Drawing

+		−	
Balance	10,000	(4) Closing	10,000

As a result of the $2,000 net loss for the year and the activity in the drawing accounts, Bates's capital account decreased by $18,000 (credit $1,000 and debit $19,000); Cater's capital account decreased by $13,000 (debit $3,000 and debit $10,000).

Division of Income Based on Interest Allowances

Sometimes a partnership agreement stipulates an allowance for interest on the capital investment of the partners. This clause acts as an incentive for partners not only to leave their investments in the business but even to increase them. For example, suppose that Bates and Cater, in addition to their salary allowances of $12,000 and $8,000, are allowed 8 percent interest on their capital balances at the beginning of the fiscal year, and the remainder is to be divided equally. Interest allowances, like salary allowances, are just allocations of net income.

Interest allowance for Bates $50,000 × .08 = $4,000

Interest allowance for Cater $30,000 × .08 = $2,400

Net Income of $48,000 The section of the income statement relating to the division of a $48,000 net income appears as follows:

Revenue from Sales:			
Net Income			$48 0 0 0 00
Division of Net Income:	L. R. Bates	P. L. Cater	Total
Salary Allowances	$12 0 0 0 00	$8 0 0 0 00	$20 0 0 0 00
Interest Allowances	4 0 0 0 00	2 4 0 0 00	6 4 0 0 00
Remainder Allocated Equally	10 8 0 0 00	10 8 0 0 00	21 6 0 0 00
Net Income	$26 8 0 0 00	$21 2 0 0 00	$48 0 0 0 00

The accountant figures out the remainder in the following way:

Net Income		$48,000
Less:		
Amount allocated as salaries		
($12,000 + $8,000)	$20,000	
Amount allocated as interest		
($4,000 + $2,400)	6,400	26,400
Remainder		$21,600

$$\text{Remainder} \div 2 = \frac{\$21,600}{2} = \underline{\underline{\$10,800}}$$

And the closing entries look like this:

	DATE		DESCRIPTION	POST. REF.	DEBIT	CREDIT	
1	19–		*Closing Entries*				1
2	Dec.	31	*Income Summary*		48 0 0 0 00		2
3			*L. R. Bates, Capital*			26 8 0 0 00	3
4			*P. L. Cater, Capital*			21 2 0 0 00	4
5							5
6		31	*L. R. Bates, Capital*		19 0 0 0 00		6
7			*L. R. Bates, Drawing*			19 0 0 0 00	7
8							8
9		31	*P. L. Cater, Capital*		10 0 0 0 00		9
10			*P. L. Cater, Drawing*			10 0 0 0 00	10
11							11

Net Loss of $2,000   The accountant handles interest allowances the same way she or he handles salary allowances: Both must be allocated, whether or not there is enough net income to take care of them. The section of the income statement relating to the division of a $2,000 net loss appears as follows:

	L. R. Bates	P. L. Cater	Total	
Revenue from Sales:				
Net Loss			$(2 0 0 0 00)	
Division of Net Loss:	L. R. Bates	P. L. Cater	Total	
Salary Allowances	$12 0 0 0 00	$8 0 0 0 00	$20 0 0 0 00	
Interest Allowances	4 0 0 0 00	2 4 0 0 00	6 4 0 0 00	
Excess of Allowances over Income				
Allocated Equally	(14 2 0 0 00)	(14 2 0 0 00)	(28 4 0 0 00)	
Net Income (Loss)	$1 8 0 0 00	$(3 8 0 0 00)	$(2 0 0 0 00)	

The accountant computes the remainder as follows:

Net Loss		$(2,000)
Less:		
Amount allocated as salaries		
($12,000 + $8,000)	$20,000	
Amount allocated as interest		
($4,000 + $2,400)	6,400	26,400
Remainder		$(28,400)

$$\text{Remainder} \div 2 = \frac{\$(28,400)}{2} = \$(14,200)$$

And the closing entries look like this:

	DATE	DESCRIPTION	POST. REF.	DEBIT	CREDIT	
1	19–	*Closing Entries*				1
2	Dec. 31	*P. L. Cater, Capital*		3 8 0 0 00		2
3		*Income Summary*			2 0 0 0 00	3
4		*L. R. Bates, Capital*			1 8 0 0 00	4
5						5
6	31	*L. R. Bates, Capital*		19 0 0 0 00		6
7		*L. R. Bates, Drawing*			19 0 0 0 00	7
8						8
9	31	*P. L. Cater, Capital*		10 0 0 0 00		9
10		*P. L. Cater, Drawing*			10 0 0 0 00	10
11						11
12						12

After posting, the owner's equity accounts look like this:

Income Summary

Balance	2,000	(3) Closing	2,000

L. R. Bates, Capital

−		+	
(4)	19,000	Balance	50,000
		(3)	1,800

P. L. Cater, Capital

−		+	
(3)	3,800	Balance	30,000
(4)	10,000		

L. R. Bates, Drawing

+		−	
Balance	19,000	(4) Closing	19,000

P. L. Cater, Drawing

+		−	
Balance	10,000	(4) Closing	10,000

FINANCIAL STATEMENTS FOR A PARTNERSHIP

Objective 3

Prepare a statement of partners' equity for a partnership.

We have already talked about how an income statement for a partnership looks with the section on Division of Net Income inserted immediately below Net Income.

Changes in the balances of the partners' capital accounts are recorded in the statement of partners' equity, which is just like a statement of owner's equity for a sole proprietorship, except that there is a separate column for each partner.

Bates and Cater
Statement of Partners' Equity
For Year Ended December 31, 19–

	L. R. Bates	P. L. Cater	Total
Capital, January 1, 19–	$50 0 0 0 00	$30 0 0 0 00	$ 80 0 0 0 00
Net Income for the Year	26 8 0 0 00	21 2 0 0 00	48 0 0 0 00
Total	$76 8 0 0 00	$51 2 0 0 00	$ 128 0 0 0 00
Less Withdrawals During the Year	19 0 0 0 00	10 0 0 0 00	29 0 0 0 00
Capital, December 31, 19–	$57 8 0 0 00	$41 2 0 0 00	$ 99 0 0 0 00

When a partner makes any additional permanent investment after the beginning of the fiscal period, the accountant records this amount right below the beginning balances of the capital accounts.

Partners have to pay federal income taxes on the basis of each partner's distributive share (her or his share of net income) in the business. For example, L. R. Bates's taxable income is $26,800, even though he withdrew only $19,000. He lists $26,800 on his personal income tax return. The Internal Revenue Code decrees that details of the distributive shares of each partner must be recorded on a U.S. Partnership Return of Income (Form 1065).

DISSOLUTION OF A PARTNERSHIP

As we said earlier in this chapter, one disadvantage of a partnership is its limited life. Any change in the personnel of the membership formally ends the partnership. Whenever a partnership dissolves, the main visible result is a change in the names listed in the partnership agreement and a change in the division of net income. However, the routine transactions of the business go on as usual. For example, suppose that a partnership originally consists of A, B, and C. Then C withdraws his or her investment from the firm, and a new partnership emerges: A and B. During the transition, business is carried on as usual. In other words, in a **dissolution,** the original partnership is dissolved by either the sale of one partner's interest in the firm to a new partner or the withdrawal of a partner, but the firm continues to operate as before.

Sale of a Partnership Interest

Objective 4

Journalize entries involving the sale of a partnership interest or withdrawal of a partner.

When a partner retires, the partner may sell her or his interest to a person outside the firm who is acceptable to the remaining partners. Let's say that at the end of a given year P. L. Cater has a capital balance of $31,760 and decides to sell his interest to N. E. Doane for $40,000. The accountant makes the following entry to account for the transfer of ownership:

	DATE		DESCRIPTION	POST. REF.	DEBIT	CREDIT	
1	*19–*						1
2	*Dec.*	*31*	*P. L. Cater, Capital*		31 7 6 0 00		2
3			*N. E. Doane, Capital*			31 7 6 0 00	3
4			*To transfer Cater's equity in*				4
5			*the partnership to Doane.*				5

The difference between $40,000 and $31,760 represents a personal profit to *Cater,* not to the firm. *There has been no change in the partnership's assets or liabilities, and consequently there is no change in the total owner's equity.* However, if the firm is to continue, Bates (the other original partner) must be willing to accept Doane as a new partner.

Withdrawal of a Partner

The partnership agreement should outline a set procedure to be followed when one of the partners withdraws. Such a procedure usually entails an audit of the books and a revaluation of the partnership's assets to reflect current market values.

Partner Withdraws Book Value of His or Her Equity After Revaluation

Suppose that C. M. King is retiring from the partnership of Jones, King, and Luce. The partnership agreement stipulates that net income and net loss shall be shared on an equal basis; it also provides for an audit and revaluation of assets in the event that a partner retires. Figure 22-4 shows the firm's balance sheet, immediately prior to the audit and revaluation.

At this point, an accountant (usually someone from an outside firm) audits the books and makes a fresh appraisal of the firm's assets. This audit and appraisal indicate that Merchandise Inventory is undervalued by

Jones, King, and Luce
Balance Sheet
September 30, 19–

Assets				
Current Assets				
Cash		$28 0 0 0 00		
Accounts Receivable	$8 0 0 0 00			
Less Allowance for Doubtful Accounts	5 0 0 00	7 5 0 0 00		
Merchandise Inventory		47 5 0 0 00		
Total Current Assets			$83 0 0 0 00	
Plant and Equipment:				
Equipment		$27 0 0 0 00		
Less Accumulated Depreciation		11 0 0 0 00	16 0 0 0 00	
Total Assets			$99 0 0 0 00	
Liabilities				
Accounts Payable			$ 7 0 0 0 00	
Partners' Equity				
R. D. Jones, Capital		$46 0 0 0 00		
C. M. King, Capital		24 0 0 0 00		
F. O. Luce, Capital		22 0 0 0 00		
Total Partners' Equity			92 0 0 0 00	
Total Liabilities and Partners' Equity			$99 0 0 0 00	

FIGURE 22-4

$9,800, that Allowances for Doubtful Accounts should be increased by $200, and that Equipment is overvalued by $2,400. The accountant allocates the net difference between debits and credits to the partners' capital accounts, according to their basis for sharing profits and losses, as shown:

	DATE		DESCRIPTION	POST. REF.	DEBIT	CREDIT	
1	19–						1
2	Sept.	30	Merchandise Inventory		9 8 0 0 00		2
3			Allowance for Doubtful Accounts			2 0 0 00	3
4			Equipment			2 4 0 0 00	4
5			R. D. Jones, Capital			2 4 0 0 00	5
6			C. M. King, Capital			2 4 0 0 00	6
7			F. O. Luce, Capital			2 4 0 0 00	7
8			To record the revaluation of				8
9			the assets; net increase in				9
10			owners' equity is $7,200.				10

After the entry has been posted, the partners' equity accounts look like this:

R. D. Jones, Capital			C. M. King, Capital			F. O. Luce, Capital	
−	+		−	+		−	+
	Balance 46,000			Balance 24,000			Balance 22,000
	Sept. 30 2,400			Sept. 30 2,400			Sept. 30 2,400

After the accountant has recorded the revaluation of the firm's assets, C. M. King withdraws cash from the partnership equal to her equity, which leads to the following entry:

	DATE	DESCRIPTION	POST. REF.	DEBIT	CREDIT	
12	19–					12
13	Sept. 30	C. M. King		26 4 0 0 00		13
14		Cash			26 4 0 0 00	14
15		To record the withdrawal of				15
16		C. M. King.				16

Partner Withdraws More Than Book Value of His or Her Equity

Sometimes it happens that a partner withdraws more cash than the amount of his or her capital account. There are two possible reasons for this.

1. The business is prosperous and shows excellent potential for growth.
2. The remaining partners are so anxious for the partner to retire that they are willing to buy out the partner.

When King announced she was going to retire, for example, Jones and Luce agreed to pay her $27,000 for her interest in the partnership. Because the balance of her capital account after the revaluation is $26,400, the excess of $600 must be deducted from the capital accounts of the remaining partners, in accordance with their basis for sharing profits and losses. The general journal entry appears as follows:

	DATE	DESCRIPTION	POST. REF.	DEBIT	CREDIT	
1	19–					1
2	Sept. 30	C. M. King, Capital		26 4 0 0 00		2
3		R. D. Jones, Capital		3 0 0 00		3
4		F. O. Luce, Capital		3 0 0 00		4
5		Cash			27 0 0 0 00	5
6		To record the withdrawal of				6
7		C. M. King.				7

Partner Withdraws Less Than Book Value of His or Her Equity

Sometimes a partner may be so anxious to retire that he or she is willing to take less than the current value of his or her equity just to get out of the partnership, or out of the business. In the firm of Jones, King, and Luce, let's say that King is willing to withdraw if she gets just $21,000 cash out of it. Because the balance of her capital account after the revaluation is $26,400, the difference ($5,400) represents a profit to the remaining partners. The entry to record this situation is as follows:

	DATE	DESCRIPTION	POST. REF.	DEBIT	CREDIT	
5	19–					5
6	Sept. 30	C. M. King, Capital		26 4 0 0 00		6
7		R. D. Jones, Capital			2 7 0 0 00	7
8		F. O. Luce, Capital			2 7 0 0 00	8
9		Cash			21 0 0 0 00	9
10		To record the withdrawal of				10
11		C. M. King.				11

Death of a Partner

The death of a partner automatically ends the partnership, and the partner's estate is entitled to receive the amount of his or her equity. Such a death makes it necessary to close the books immediately so that the accountant can determine the firm's net income for the current fiscal period. Partnership agreements usually provide for an audit and revaluation of the assets at this time. After the accountant has determined the current value of the deceased partner's capital account, the remaining partners and the executor of the deceased partner's estate must agree on the method of payment. The journal entries are similar to those the accountant makes for the withdrawal of a partner. To be certain of having enough cash to meet such a demand, partnerships often carry life insurance policies.

Liquidation of a Partnership

Objective 5

Journalize entries pertaining to the liquidation of a partnership involving the immediate sale of the assets for cash.

A **liquidation** means an end of the partnership as well as of the business itself. This final winding-up process involves selling assets, paying off liabilities, and distributing the remaining cash to the partners. The closing entries are journalized and posted prior to the liquidation.

The accountant makes the necessary journal entries in four steps, as follows:

1. Sale of the assets, using the Loss or Gain from Realization account. The accountant debits this account for losses and credits it for gains. In this respect the account is comparable to the Cash Short and Over account. The word **realization** refers to the sale of the assets for cash.
2. Allocation of loss or gain. The accountant closes the Loss or Gain from Realization account into the partners' capital accounts according to the profit and loss ratio. It must be closed as a separate account because it came into being after the regular closing entries had been recorded.
3. Payment of liabilities. The firm makes a final settlement with all creditors.
4. Distribution of remaining cash to the partners, in accordance with the balances of their capital accounts.

Occasionally it takes a long time to convert merchandise inventory and other assets into cash; on the other hand, things can move quickly. It is impossible to predict how long liquidation operations may take. In the process, several things may happen. We shall discuss only two possibilities here, although you can find more complex situations set forth in more advanced books.

Our first example concerns the partnership of Noyd, Olson, and Poe. The partners share profits and losses as follows: Noyd, one-half; Olson, one-fourth; Poe, one-fourth.

Let's look at an abbreviated balance sheet for this firm (Figure 22-5).

FIGURE 22-5

Noyd, Olson, and Poe
Balance Sheet
June 30, 19–

Assets		
Cash	$10 000 00	
Merchandise Inventory	20 000 00	
Other Assets	40 000 00	
Total Assets		$70 000 00
Liabilities		
Accounts Payable		$ 7 000 00
Partners' Equity		
J. A. Noyd, Capital		
B. N. Olson, Capital	$27 000 00	
G. K. Poe, Capital	24 000 00	
Total Liabilities and Partners' Equity	12 000 00	63 000 00
		$70 000 00

Assets Are Sold at a Profit

Assume that the firm sells its merchandise inventory for $26,000, and the other assets for $48,000. Figure 22-6 shows the journal entries to cover this transaction. (Amounts in parentheses are purely explanatory.)

FIGURE 22-6

	DATE	DESCRIPTION	POST. REF.	DEBIT	CREDIT	
1	19–					1
(1) 2	June 30	Cash ($26,000 + $48,000)		74 0 0 0 00		2
3		Merchandise Inventory			20 0 0 0 00	3
4		Other Assets			40 0 0 0 00	4
5		Loss or Gain from Realization			14 0 0 0 00	5
6		Sold the assets at a gain.				6
7						7
(2) 8	30	Loss or Gain from Realization		14 0 0 0 00		8
9		J. A. Noyd, Capital (½)			7 0 0 0 00	9
10		B. N. Olson, Capital (¼)			3 5 0 0 00	10
11		G. K. Poe, Capital (¼)			3 5 0 0 00	11
12		To allocate the net gain to the				12
13		partners' capital accounts				13
14		according to the profit and loss				14
15		ratio.				15
16						16
(3) 17	30	Accounts Payable		7 0 0 0 00		17
18		Cash			7 0 0 0 00	18
19		To pay the claims of creditors.				19
20						20
(4) 21	30	J. A. Noyd, Capital		34 0 0 0 00		21
22		B. N. Olson, Capital		27 5 0 0 00		22
23		G. K. Poe, Capital		15 5 0 0 00		23
24		Cash			77 0 0 0 00	24
25		To distribute the remaining				25
26		cash to the partners according				26
27		to their account balances.				27

Remember

The balance of Cash before the final distribution to the partners should equal the total of the balances of their capital accounts.

The T accounts for the Cash and capital accounts look like this:

Cash			
+		−	
Balance	10,000	(3)	7,000
(1)	74,000	(4)	77,000

J. A. Noyd, Capital			
−		+	
(4)	34,000	Balance	27,000
		(2)	7,000

B. N. Olson, Capital			
−		+	
(4)	27,500	Balance	24,000
		(2)	3,500

G. K. Poe, Capital			
−		+	
(4)	15,500	Balance	12,000
		(2)	3,500

Assets Are Sold at a Loss: Partners' Capital Accounts Sufficient to Absorb Loss

Now suppose that Noyd, Olson, and Poe sells its merchandise inventory for only $16,000 and its other assets for $32,000. The journal entries would look like those in Figure 22-7.

FIGURE 22-7

	DATE	DESCRIPTION	POST. REF.	DEBIT	CREDIT	
1	19–					1
(1) 2	June 30	Cash ($16,000 + $32,000)		48 0 0 0 00		2
3		Loss or Gain from Realization		12 0 0 0 00		3
4		Merchandise Inventory			20 0 0 0 00	4
5		Other Assets			40 0 0 0 00	5
6		Sold the assets at a loss.				6
7						7
(2) 8	30	J. A. Noyd, Capital (½)		6 0 0 0 00		8
9		B. N. Olson, Capital (¼)		3 0 0 0 00		9
10		G. K. Poe, Capital (¼)		3 0 0 0 00		10
11		Loss or Gain from Realization			12 0 0 0 00	11
12		To allocate the net loss to the				12
13		partners' capital accounts				13
14		according to the profit and loss				14
15		ratio.				15
16						16
(3) 17	30	Accounts Payable		7 0 0 0 00		17
18		Cash			7 0 0 0 00	18
19		To pay the claims of creditors.				19
20						20
(4) 21	30	J. A. Noyd, Capital		21 0 0 0 00		21
22		B. N. Olson, Capital		21 0 0 0 00		22
23		G. K. Poe, Capital		9 0 0 0 00		23
24		Cash			51 0 0 0 00	24
25		To distribute the remaining				25
26		cash to the partners according				26
27		to their account balances.				27
28						28
29						29
30						30

The T accounts for the Cash and capital accounts look like this:

Cash				J. A. Noyd, Capital			
+		–		–		+	
Balance	10,000	(3)	7,000	(2)	6,000	Balance	27,000
(1)	48,000	(4)	51,000	(4)	21,000		

B. N. Olson, Capital				G. K. Poe, Capital			
−		+		−		+	
(2)	3,000	Balance	24,000	(2)	3,000	Balance	12,000
(4)	21,000			(4)	9,000		

SUMMARY

A partnership is an association of two or more persons to carry on, as co-owners, a business for profit. Partnerships are used for professional and service enterprises as well as for small merchandising and manufacturing firms. The main advantage of a partnership is that it makes possible the combining of people's abilities and investments to carry on a business. The main disadvantage is the unlimited liability each partner assumes.

L.O. 1,2,3   The accounting procedure for partnerships differs from that for sole proprietorships only in the owner's equity classification of accounts. Otherwise, partnerships have the same types of assets, liabilities, revenues, and expenses. On the income statement, after the net income is determined, the Division of Net Income section is added. The figures—representing the final allocations of net income to each partner—are used in the entry closing the Income Summary account into the capital accounts. The last step in the closing entries consists of closing each partner's drawing account into his or her capital account.

One can divide the net income for a partnership by any of the following methods (or a combination thereof): fractional-share basis, ratio of capital investments, salary allowances, and interest allowances.

L.O. 4   A partnership ends whenever there is any change in the composition of its membership. This ending is called a dissolution. The effect on the business may simply be a change in the members listed in the partnership agreement and in the capital accounts; or, at the other extreme, it may entail a breakup of the business. In the event of the death of one of the partners, the partnership agreement should provide for an immediate closing of the books and revaluation of the firm's assets.

L.O. 5   Liquidation means going out of business, selling everything for cash, paying off liabilities in cash, and final withdrawals of partners' cash. The steps in the liquidation of a partnership are:

1. Sale of the assets for cash, using the Loss or Gain from Realization account.
2. Allocation of the Loss or Gain from Realization account to the partners' capital accounts.
3. Payment of liabilities.
4. Distribution of remaining cash to the partners.

GLOSSARY

Co-ownership A situation in which each party owns a fractional share of all the assets.

Dissolution The ending of a partnership because of a change in the personnel of the membership and the forming of a new partnership. The transition results primarily in changes in the capital accounts, with routine business being carried on as usual.

Distributive share The share of the net income (or net loss) allocated to each partner.

General partners Partners who actively and publicly participate in the transactions of the firm and have unlimited liability.

Liquidation The ending of a partnership, involving the sale of the assets, payment of the liabilities, and distribution of the remaining cash to the partners.

Mutual agency Each partner may act as an agent of the firm, thereby committing the entire firm to a binding contract.

Partnership An association of two or more persons to carry on, as co-owners, a business for profit.

Realization Conversion into cash, as happens in the case of the sale of assets.

QUESTIONS, EXERCISES, AND PROBLEMS

Discussion Questions

1. Is it possible for one partner to lose a greater amount than the amount of his or her investment in the partnership? Why?
2. What do accountants mean when they discuss the concept of co-ownership of partnership property?
3. To handle the provision for salary allowances used in allocating net income or loss, the accountant debited the Salary Expense account. Is the accountant correct? Why or why not?
4. Moore and Peel are considering forming a partnership. What do you consider the four most important factors to include in their partnership agreement?
5. When assets other than cash are invested in a partnership by one of the partners, at what value are these assets recorded in the books of the partnership?
6. What do you consider the greatest advantage and the greatest disadvantage of the partnership form of business organization?
7. Ash, Best, and Drake are partners. Drake dies, and her daughter claims the right to take her mother's place in the partnership. Explain why Drake's daughter either does or does not have the right to do this.
8. Describe how a dissolution of a partnership differs from a liquidation.

Exercises

L.O. 5   **Exercise 22-1**   Bayer is the senior member of the partnership of Bayer, Caldwell, and Dillon. When Bayer dies, the firm's accountant revalues the assets. The following assets are to be increased in value by these amounts: Merchandise Inventory, $24,000; Building, $64,000. The value of the asset Equipment is to be decreased by $8,000. Assuming that the partnership profit and loss ratio is 2 : 2 : 1 respectively, write the journal entry to show the revaluation of the assets on May 6 prior to dissolution of the firm.

L.O. 4   **Exercise 22-2**   Solomon, a partner in the firm of Rivera, Solomon, and Thorne, sells her share in the partnership (capital balance of $36,000) to Galvan for $28,000. Assuming that Rivera and Thorne are willing to admit Galvan to the firm, give the entry in the firm's books on November 3 to record the change in ownership. Does the withdrawal of Solomon dissolve the firm?

L.O. 1   **Exercise 22-3**   D. L. Holmes, as his original investment in the firm of Holmes and Little, contributes equipment that had been recorded in the books of his own business as costing $80,000, with accumulated depreciation of $52,000. The partners agree on a valuation of $38,000. They also agree to accept Holmes's Accounts Receivable of $40,000, collectible to the extent of 80 percent. Give the journal entry to record Holmes's investment in the partnership of Holmes and Little on June 15.

L.O. 1,2   **Exercise 22-4**   Ardis and Rusk share profits and losses on a fractional-share basis with three-fifths for Ardis and two-fifths for Rusk. This year the firm has a net income of $60,000. The beginning capital balances for the year were $126,000 for Ardis and $84,000 for Rusk. The balances of the drawing accounts are $32,000 for Ardis and $26,000 for Rusk. Journalize the entries to close Income Summary and the partners' drawing accounts on December 31.

L.O. 1   **Exercise 22-5**   The partnership agreement of Beard and Froman provides for salary allowances of $28,000 per year for Beard and $24,000 per year for Froman. They share the remaining balance of net income on the basis of three-fifths for Beard and two-fifths for Froman. The net income amounts to $58,000; calculate the total share for each partner.

L.O. 4   **Exercise 22-6**   Newman is retiring from the partnership of Korn, Morris, and Newman. The profit and loss ratio is 2 : 2 : 1 respectively. After the accountant has posted the revaluation and closing entries, the credit balances in the capital accounts are: Korn, $54,000; Morris, $44,000; and Newman, $22,000. Journalize the entries to record the retirement of Newman under each of the following unrelated assumptions:

a. Newman retires, taking $22,000 of partnership cash for her equity.
b. Newman retires, taking $26,000 of partnership cash for her equity.

L.O. 5   **Exercise 22-7**   Rutledge and Williams are partners who share profits and losses equally. The credit balances of their capital accounts before liquidation are $60,000 and $80,000, respectively. When they liquidate their partnership, they sell the noncash assets and pay all the partnership's liabilities, leaving a balance of $120,000 in cash. What is the amount of the gain or loss on realization? How much cash should be distributed to each partner?

L.O. 5 **Exercise 22-8** The partners Markley, Piper, and Sawyer have a profit and loss ratio of 2:2:1 respectively. They decide to liquidate the firm and to sell off all its assets. After distribution of the firm's loss from realization, the credit balances of the capital accounts are as follows: Markley, $84,000; Piper, $62,000; Sawyer, $74,000. The balance of Cash is $220,000. Write the entry the accountant would make on the books on April 3 to record the distribution of cash.

Problem Set A

L.O. 1,2 **Problem 22-1A** The partnership of A. L. Banini, S. M. Canter, and R. D. Delaney has a net income of $92,850 for the current year. The balances in the capital accounts of the partners at the beginning of the year were $34,500, $39,000, and $48,000, respectively. At the end of the year, the balances of the drawing accounts are $16,500, $19,800, and $18,000, respectively. The partnership agreement stipulates salary allowances as follows: Banini, $16,500; Canter, $21,000; Delaney, $18,000. The partnership agreement also allows interest of 10 percent on the balances of the capital accounts at the beginning of the year. The remainder (after salary and interest allowances) is divided equally among the three partners.

Instructions

1. Prepare the section of the income statement for the current year that deals with division of net income.
2. Prepare the entries to record the closing of the firm's Income Summary and drawing accounts on December 31.
3. Assuming a net income of $40,650, prepare the section of the income statement that deals with division of net income.

L.O. 1 **Problem 22-2A** W. A. Kim and M. C. Love are forming a partnership for a beauty salon and plan to work full time in the firm. Kim will make an initial investment of $30,000 and Love $45,000. They are considering the following plans for the division of net income:

a. Division in the same ratio as the balances of their capital accounts.
b. Interest of 12 percent on the balances of their capital accounts at the beginning of the year, and the remainder of the net income to be divided equally.
c. Salary allowances of $15,000 to Kim and $13,500 to Love based on the value of their services, interest of 9 percent on the balances of their capital accounts at the beginning of the year, and the remainder of the net income to be divided equally.

Instructions

1. Using the form provided in the Working Papers, record the distributive shares of net income for each of the partners, assuming (a) a net income of $45,000, and (b) a net income of $26,000.
2. Which plan is the fairest? Give reasons for your opinion.

L.O. 1,3   **Problem 22-3A**   The following are the adjusted account balances of Allen and Wells as of December 31, the end of the current fiscal year:

Accounts Payable	$ 67,432
Accounts Receivable	53,438
Accumulated Depreciation, Equipment	45,380
R. M. Allen, Capital	60,000
R. M. Allen, Drawing	32,000
Allowance for Doubtful Accounts	1,842
Cash	3,658
Equipment	73,838
Freight In	22,047
General Expenses (control)	14,646
Interest Expense	3,432
Merchandise Inventory	129,452
Notes Payable	20,000
Prepaid Insurance	720
Purchases	529,133
Purchases Returns and Allowances	25,452
Purchases Discount	4,220
Sales	700,490
Sales Returns and Allowances	36,838
Selling Expenses (control)	37,832
C. C. Wells, Capital	48,000
C. C. Wells, Drawing	24,000

There were no changes in the partners' capital accounts during the year. The merchandise inventory at the beginning of the year was $141,234. The partnership agreement provides for salary allowances of $32,000 for Allen and $28,000 for Wells. It also stipulates an interest allowance of 10 percent on invested capital at the beginning of the year, with the remainder of the net income to be divided equally.

Instructions

1. Prepare an income statement for the year.
2. Prepare a statement of partners' equity for the year.
3. Prepare a classified balance sheet for the partnership at the end of the year.

L.O. 5   **Problem 22-4A**   The partnership of Hall, Lewis, and Madison is to be liquidated as of June 30 of this year. The partners share profits and losses in the ratio of 2:2:1 respectively. The firm's post-closing trial balance looks like this:

Hall, Lewis, and Madison
Post-Closing Trial Balance
June 30, 19–

ACCOUNT NAME	DEBIT	CREDIT
Cash	40 3 0 5 00	
Merchandise Inventory	58 8 7 5 00	
Other Assets	45 4 5 0 00	
Accounts Payable		12 6 3 0 00
J. P. Hall, Capital		54 0 0 0 00
C. Y. Lewis, Capital		42 0 0 0 00
T. N. Madison, Capital		36 0 0 0 00
	144 6 3 0 00	144 6 3 0 00

The firm's realization and liquidation transactions are as follows:

July 2 The merchandise inventory sold for $54,000; the other assets sold for $52,000.

2 The accountant allocated the loss or gain from realization to the partners' capital accounts according to the profit and loss ratio.

2 The firm paid its creditors in full.

2 The firm distributed the remaining cash to the partners in accordance with the balances in their capital accounts.

Instructions

1. Record the balances in the selected ledger accounts.
2. Record the liquidating transactions in general journal form.
3. Post the entries to the ledger accounts.

Problem Set B

L.O. 1,2 **Problem 22-1B** The firm of B. N. Davis, F. M. Feldman, and G. W. Huber has a net income of $108,000 for this year. The balances in the capital accounts of the partners at the beginning of the year were $42,000, $46,500, and $54,000, respectively. At the end of the year, the balances of the drawing accounts are $21,000, $25,200, and $20,250, respectively. The partnership agreement stipulates salary allowances as follows: Davis, $21,000; Feldman, $25,500; Huber, $20,250. It also allows 10 percent interest on the balances of the partners' capital accounts at the beginning of the year. The remainder of the net income, after salary and interest allowances, is divided equally.

Instructions

1. Prepare the section of the income statement on the division of net income for the current year.

2. Prepare entries to close the firm's Income Summary and drawing accounts on December 31.
3. Assuming that the net income of the firm is $45,000, prepare the section of the income statement that deals with division of net income.

L.O. 1   **Problem 22-2B**   E. R. Halprin and H. O. Jayson, consulting engineers, are forming a partnership. Both plan to work in the firm on a full-time basis. Halprin's initial investment is $27,000, Jayson's investment $45,000. They are considering the following plans for the division of net income:

a. Division in the same ratio as the balances of their capital accounts.
b. Interest of 9 percent on the balances of their capital accounts at the beginning of the year, and the remainder of the net income to be divided equally.
c. Salary allowances of $24,000 to Halprin and $20,000 to Jayson based on the value of their services, interest of 9 percent on the balances of their capital accounts at the beginning of the year, and the remainder of the net income to be divided equally.

Instructions

1. Using the form provided in the Working Papers, record the distribution of net income for each of the partners, assuming (a) a net income of $56,000, and (b) a net income of $32,000.
2. Which plan is the fairest? Give reasons for your opinion.

L.O. 1,3   **Problem 22-3B**   The following are the adjusted account balances of Abel and Rist as of December 31, the end of this fiscal year:

Accounts Payable	$ 69,416
Accounts Receivable	58,964
Accumulated Depreciation, Equipment	46,820
M. B. Abel, Capital	64,000
M. B. Abel, Drawing	29,600
Allowance for Doubtful Accounts	2,148
Cash	3,742
Equipment	79,128
Freight In	26,834
General Expenses (control)	14,212
Interest Expense	2,942
Merchandise Inventory	126,236
Notes Payable	16,000
Prepaid Insurance	690
Purchases	509,846
Purchases Returns and Allowances	25,690
Purchases Discount	4,428
Sales	684,836
Sales Returns and Allowances	35,872
Selling Expenses (control)	35,562
R. C. Rist, Capital	52,000
R. C. Rist, Drawing	28,800

The merchandise inventory at the beginning of the year was $139,146, and there were no changes in the partners' capital accounts during the year. The partnership agreement provides for salary allowances of $31,200 for Abel and $28,800 for Rist. The agreement also stipulates interest of 12 percent on invested capital at the beginning of the year. The remainder of the net income is to be divided equally.

Instructions

1. Prepare an income statement for the year.
2. Prepare a statement of partners' equity for the year.
3. Prepare a classified balance sheet at the end of the year.

L.O. 5 **Problem 22-4B** The partnership of Hall, Lewis, and Madison is to be liquidated as of November 30 of this year. The partners share profits and losses in the ratio of 2:2:1 respectively. The firm's post-closing trial balance looks like this:

Hall, Lewis, and Madison
Post-Closing Trial Balance
November 30, 19–

ACCOUNT NAME	DEBIT	CREDIT
Cash	37 4 0 0 00	
Merchandise Inventory	67 2 4 0 00	
Other Assets	48 1 6 0 00	
Accounts Payable		15 7 2 0 00
J. P. Hall, Capital		53 8 0 0 00
C. Y. Lewis, Capital		43 6 8 0 00
T. N. Madison, Capital		39 6 0 0 00
	152 8 0 0 00	152 8 0 0 00

The firm's realization and liquidation transactions are as follows:

Dec. 2 The merchandise inventory sold for $76,000; the other assets sold for $36,000.
2 The accountant allocated the loss or gain from realization to the partners' capital accounts according to the profit and loss ratio.
2 The firm paid its creditors in full.
2 The firm distributed the remaining cash to the partners in accordance with the balances in their capital accounts.

Instructions

1. Record the balances in the selected ledger accounts.
2. Record the liquidating transactions in general journal form.
3. Post the entries to the ledger accounts.

23 Corporations: Organization and Capital Stock

LEARNING OBJECTIVES

After you have completed this chapter, you will be able to do the following:

1. Define a corporation.
2. Name at least two advantages and two disadvantages of a corporation.
3. Journalize entries for the issuance of par-value stock.
4. Journalize entries for the issuance of no-par stock.
5. Journalize entries for the sale of stock on the subscription basis.
6. Prepare a classified balance sheet for a corporation, including Subscriptions Receivable, Organization Costs, Paid-in Capital, and Retained Earnings accounts.

Business organizations are usually classified as sole proprietorships, partnerships, or corporations. Corporations are fewest in number, but they account for more business transactions than the other two types of organizations combined. Frequently a firm that begins as a sole proprietorship or a partnership needs more investment capital as it grows and prospers. To raise additional investment capital, the firm incorporates. In other cases, businesses are organized as corporations at the outset. Because of the predominance of corporations, everyone entering the business world should be familiar with the corporate form of organization and its financial structure. We shall be dealing with corporations that issue stock and carry out business activities for the purpose of making profits and distributing the profits to their owners. Nonprofit corporations are those that do not issue stock or distribute profits but carry out activities for charitable, educational, or other philanthropic purposes.

DEFINITION OF A CORPORATION

Objective 1

Define a corporation.

In 1818, Chief Justice John Marshall defined a **corporation** as "an artificial being, invisible, intangible, and existing only in contemplation of the law." A corporation does indeed act as an artificial legal being, deriving its existence from its charter. In every respect it is a separate legal entity, having a continuous existence apart from that of its owners, the stockholders. As an entity, a corporation may own property, enter into contracts, sue in the courts, be sued, and so forth.

ADVANTAGES OF THE CORPORATION

Objective 2

Name at least two advantages and two disadvantages of a corporation.

The corporation offers a number of advantages over the sole proprietorship and the partnership.

1. **Limited liability** As a separate legal entity, a corporation is responsible for its own debts. All that a stockholder can lose is the amount of his or her investment. Since the stockholders are the owners, this is the most important advantage. In contrast, the owners of sole proprietorships and partnerships are personally liable for the entire debt of the business.
2. **Ease of raising capital** A corporation can accumulate more investment capital than a sole proprietorship or partnership because a corporation can sell stock. Some corporations have more than 1 million stockholders. Sole proprietorships and partnerships are limited to the wealth of the few individual owners.
3. **Ease of transferring ownership rights** Ownership rights in a corporation are represented by shares of stock, which can readily be transferred from one person to another without the permission of other stockholders. (Compare this with a partnership, in which the other partners have to give permission for changes in ownership in order for the business to continue.)
4. **Continuous existence** The length of life of a corporation is stipulated in its charter; when the charter expires, it may be renewed. The death, incapacity, or withdrawal of an owner does not affect the life of a corporation, but such a circumstance would cause a partnership to be dissolved or liquidated.
5. **No mutual agency** Stockholders do not have the power to bind the corporation to contracts, unless a given stockholder is an officer. Since owners need not participate in management, the corporation is free to employ the managerial talent it believes can best accomplish its objectives.

DISADVANTAGES OF THE CORPORATE FORM

The corporation also has a number of disadvantages.

1. **Additional taxation** In addition to the usual property and payroll taxes, corporations must pay income taxes and charter fees. Since corporations are separate legal entities, they pay federal and state income

taxes in their own names. Part of the corporation's net income goes to the stockholders in the form of dividends; this money is personal income to the stockholders, and consequently the stockholders have to pay personal income taxes on it. This state of affairs is known as the **double taxation** of corporations. It represents their greatest disadvantage. Charter fees (which are fees paid for the corporation's right to exist) may be considered additional taxes, because they are paid to a state in return for the issuance of a charter.

2. **Government regulation**   Since states create corporations by granting charters, states can exercise closer control and supervision over corporations than over sole proprietorships and partnerships. States often regulate even the amount of net income that a corporation may retain, the extent to which it may buy back its own stock, and the amount of real estate it may own. By contrast, sole proprietorships need only have legal purposes; states impose no further regulations.

FORMING A CORPORATION

To organize a corporation, a person or persons must submit an application for a **charter** to the appropriate official (corporation commissioner or secretary of state) of the state in which the company is to be incorporated. The application is called the **articles of incorporation**. Application requirements vary depending on the state in which the company is incorporated. They generally include at least the following points of information:

- Name and address of the corporation
- Nature of the business to be conducted
- Amount and description of the capital stock to be issued
- Names or name of the promoters or sole incorporator who will serve until the first meeting is held to elect a board of directors

The articles of incorporation must be accompanied by a charter fee, which is based on the dollar amount of maximum stock investment, or **authorized capital**.

When the state officials approve the articles of incorporation, these articles become the charter or governing instrument of the corporation. Shortly after receiving the charter, the promoters or the sole promoter holds an initial meeting to elect an acting board of directors and formulate bylaws. The charter plus the bylaws provide the basic rules for conducting the corporation's affairs. Next, the directors meet to appoint officers to serve as active managers of the business. Then the corporation issues **capital stock** to the subscribers who have paid in full. The shares of stock are in the form of certificates. Since stockholders have come into existence at this point, they now elect a permanent board of directors.

The size of the corporation may vary as to number of stockholders and amount of investment. It may be a small corporation with only a few owners and a minimum investment of $1,000; or it may be a giant corporation, consisting of more than a million owners, with an investment amounting to more than $1 billion. In the small corporation, the stockholders may also be the directors and officers. A corporation whose ownership is confined to a small group of stockholders is called a **closely held corporation**. A corporation whose ownership is widely distributed through a stock exchange or through over-the-counter markets to a large number of stockholders is called an **open** or **public corporation**.

Organization Costs

Let us suppose that a new corporation is forming, starting from scratch, and the organizers call in an accountant to set up the books. The accountant debits the costs of organizing the corporation—such as fees paid to the state, attorneys' fees, promotional costs, travel outlays, costs of printing stock certificates, and so on—to an account titled **Organization Costs**. This account is classified as an **intangible asset**. The Intangible Assets section of the balance sheet appears as a separate category, below Plant and Equipment. The account Organization Costs is like a prepaid expense account, such as Prepaid Insurance, in that eventually it will be written off by means of adjusting entries over a period of years. Organization costs are paid only once, although they benefit the corporation during its entire life, so it seems unfair to list them entirely as expenses of the first year. Income tax laws allow a company to write off its organization costs over a period of five years or more. The adjusting entry is a debit to Organization Cost Expense or Miscellaneous General Expense and a credit to Organization Costs.

Stock Certificate Book

One necessary element of organization costs is the printing of **stock certificates**. In a small corporation, the certificates often have stubs attached. The certificates and stubs are bound in a stock certificate book, rather like a checkbook. The corporation issues the stock certificates only when the stockholder has paid for them in full. Each blank certificate must have written on it the name of the owner, the number of shares issued, and the date of issuance. The stub must show the name and address of the stockholder, the number of shares listed on the stock certificate, and the date of issuance. Both certificates and stubs are numbered consecutively. Figure 23-1 is an example of a stock certificate.

When a transfer of ownership takes place, the stockholder surrenders the stock certificate to the corporation, and the corporation cancels it; the corporation also cancels the matching stub and issues one or more new certificates in the place of these documents. This procedure enables the corporation to maintain an up-to-date record of the name of each stockholder and the number of shares owned by each. A corporation needs

FIGURE 23-1

this information when it pays out dividends and when it sends out notices of annual meetings or other information.

The law requires large corporations whose stocks are listed on major stock exchanges to have independent registrars and transfer agents maintain their records of stock ownership. Banks and trust companies perform this service.

STRUCTURE OF A CORPORATION

The stockholders own the corporation; they delegate authority to the board of directors, which manages the corporation's affairs. (Generally the directors are also stockholders, although this is not always so.) The board of directors, in turn, delegates authority to the officers, who do the actual work of running the business. The officers themselves may also be members of the board of directors. Figure 23-2 on page 774 shows a typical organization chart for a corporation.

Dividends are the share of the corporation's earnings distributed to stockholders. The sources of dividends are the current year's net income after income taxes and the retained earnings of prior years.

FIGURE 23-2

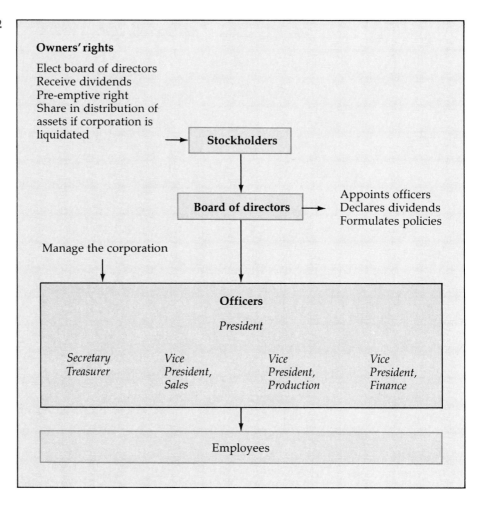

Suppose the corporation issues some new stock. Each original stock-holder then has the right to subscribe to additional shares in proportion to her or his present holding. This feature is known as **preemptive right**. For example, assume that the corporation's new issue consists of 1,000 shares. The present amount of stock outstanding is 10,000 shares, of which Mary Noyes owns 2,000. Her proportion of stock held to stock outstanding is one-fifth (2,000/10,000). Therefore she has the right to subscribe to 200 shares (one-fifth of 1,000 shares) of the new issue.

Stockholders' Equity

The owners' equity in a corporation is called **stockholders' equity**, or **capital**. Just as in sole proprietorships and partnerships, the equity of the owners represents the excess of assets over liabilities. Of the five major classifications of accounts, the main difference with corporations occurs in the Stockholders' Equity classification, in which capital stock accounts replace owners' capital accounts. The **Retained Earnings** account is used to record earnings plowed back into the business.

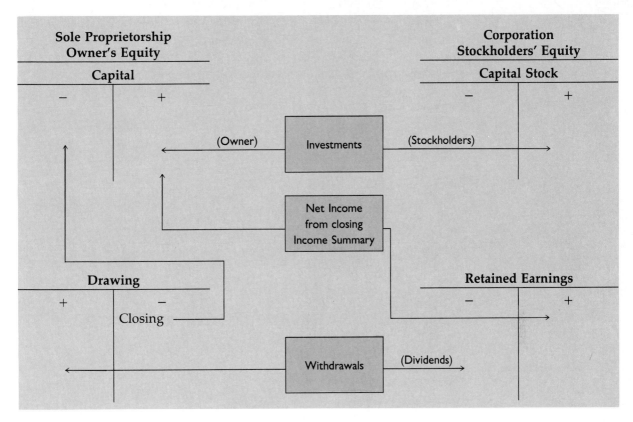

FIGURE 23-3

The T accounts in Figure 23-3 compare accounts for a sole proprietorship with those for a corporation:

CAPITAL STOCK

Capital stock refers to shares of ownership in a corporation. *Authorized capital stock* is the maximum number of shares designated in the charter. **Issued stock** refers to the shares apportioned out to the stockholders. Stock that is actually in the hands of stockholders is called **outstanding stock.** Occasionally, a corporation may reacquire some of the stock it has issued by buying back its own stock or by receiving it as a donation. This reacquired stock is known as **treasury stock;** consequently, the number of shares that have been issued may differ from the number outstanding.

Classes of Capital Stock

To appeal to as many investors as possible, a corporation may issue more than one kind of stock, just as a manufacturer of refrigerators, say, makes different models to please different groups of potential buyers. The two main types of stock are *common* and *preferred.* Each type may have a variety of characteristics. Some may be **par-value stock,** and some may be **no-par stock.** We will be referring to these types of stock frequently. Following is a brief comparison of the characteristics of par-value and no-par stock:

Par-value Stock	No-par Stock
Has a par value (in dollars) printed on the face of the stock certificates.	Has no dollar value printed on the face of the stock certificates.
Has the par value listed in the corporation's charter.	Has no dollar value per share of stock listed in the corporation's charter.
The par value is used to record the shares of stock issued.	The stated value is used to record the shares of stock issued.
Par value can be changed only by amending the corporation's charter.	Stated value is an arbitrary amount and can be changed during a meeting of the board of directors.
Stock issued at an amount above par value is sold at a **premium.**	Stock issued at an amount above stated value is sold **in excess of stated value.**
Stock issued at an amount below par value is sold at a **discount.**	Stocks will not be sold at an amount below stated value since the stated value can be changed readily.
Total par value becomes the **legal capital,** which cannot be withdrawn by stockholders except in liquidation. (*Purpose*: to protect the corporation's assets for the creditors.)	Total stated value becomes the **legal capital,** which cannot be withdrawn by stockholders except in liquidation.
Contingent liability—in case of a liquidation, stockholders who bought stock below par value are liable for the corporation's debts to the extent of the discount.	No contingent liability.

Common Stock

When a corporation issues only one type of stock, it is called **common stock and may be either par-value or no-par stock.** Holders of common stock have all the rights listed above, with voting privilege of one vote for each share of stock.

Preferred Stock

Preferred stock, which is generally par-value stock, is preferred in two ways: (1) the corporation pays dividends on preferred stock before it pays them on common stock, and (2) it pays dividends at a uniform rate. A company is allowed to omit dividend payments altogether. However, if it does pay dividends, it must meet the requirements on preferred stock before paying anything on common stock. The dividend on preferred stock consists of a percentage of the par value of the stock. In the event that the corporation is liquidated, holders of preferred stock are paid off before holders of common stock. In most circumstances, however, holders of preferred stock do not have voting privileges. There are several specific types of preferred stock, so let's discuss each of them briefly.

Cumulative and Noncumulative Preferred Stock   Suppose that a corporation has a bad year and finds that it is not able to pay the dividend on its preferred stock. In this case the dividend is said to be *passed*. Stockholders who own **cumulative preferred stock** get to accumulate the dividends passed in former years (that is, the dividends in arrears). The corporation has to pay these dividends in full before it can pay any dividends to common stockholders. If stockholders own **noncumulative preferred stock,** their dividends in arrears do not accumulate. In other words, if the corporation passes dividends, they are gone forever. Since preferred stockholders naturally want a regular dividend, most preferred stock is cumulative.

Participating and Nonparticipating Preferred Stock   Recall that the dividend on preferred stock consists of an established percentage of the par value of that stock. Some preferred stock, however, provides for the possibility of dividends in excess of this established amount; this kind of preferred stock is called **participating preferred stock.** Holders of participating preferred stock first get the regular dividend that is due them. Then the corporation allocates a stipulated amount to holders of its common stock. And *then* the stockholders who own participating preferred stock are allowed to participate or share in the extra earnings, which are distributed as cash dividends. The dividends of **nonparticipating preferred stock,** on the other hand, are limited to the regular rate. Most preferred stock is nonparticipating.

ISSUING STOCK

Stock is issued when the buyer has paid for it in full or when the corporation has received noncash assets in exchange for its stock. Let us first discuss the issuance of par-value stock and then the issuance of no-par stock. (*Note:* A corporation may issue par-value stock at a figure equal to, above, or below its par value.)

Objective 3

Journalize entries for
the issuance of
par-value stock.

Issuing Stock at Par for Cash

There is a separate ledger account for each class of stock. The accountant
records investments of cash as debits to Cash and credits to the stock accounts for the total amount of the par value. Later we shall deal with
sales of stock in which the cash received is greater than or less than the
par value of the shares issued. Remember that par value is the face value
printed on each stock certificate. This designation of par value is a convenient means of dividing the corporation's capital into units, with the
ownership of each unit known.

For example, the Davidson Corporation is organized on July 16 with
an authorized capital of 4,000 shares of $100-par preferred 8 percent
stock and 20,000 shares of $50-par common stock. On August 1, David-
son issues 1,000 shares of preferred 8 percent stock at par and 10,000
shares of common stock at par. In general journal form, the entry looks
like this:

	DATE		DESCRIPTION	POST. REF.	DEBIT	CREDIT	
1	*19–*						1
2	*Aug.*	*1*	*Cash*		600 0 0 0 00		2
3			*Preferred 8 Percent Stock*			100 0 0 0 00	3
4			*Common Stock*			500 0 0 0 00	4
5			*Issued 1,000 shares of preferred*				5
6			*8 percent stock at par and 10,000*				6
7			*shares of common stock at par.*				7

GENERAL JOURNAL PAGE __1__

According to T accounts, the situation looks like this:

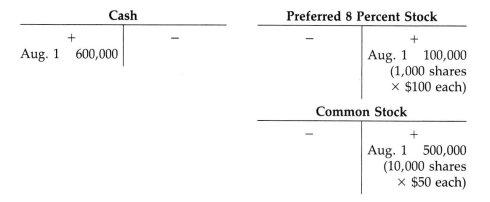

The capital stock accounts (Preferred 8 Percent Stock and Common
Stock) are controlling accounts. The subsidiary ledger is known as the
stockholders' ledger. The stockholders' ledger may consist of the stock
certificate book, or it may be a supplementary record showing the name
and address of each stockholder and the number of shares owned.

Issuing Stock at Par for Noncash Assets

Corporations often accept assets other than cash in exchange for their stock. The Davidson Corporation received equipment, a building, and land in exchange for common stock, as we see in the following journal entry:

	DATE		DESCRIPTION	POST. REF.	DEBIT	CREDIT	
1	*19–*						1
2	*Aug.*	*1*	*Equipment*		*6 0 0 0 00*		2
3			*Building*		*50 0 0 0 00*		3
4			*Land*		*10 0 0 0 00*		4
5			*Common Stock*			*66 0 0 0 00*	5
6			*Exchanged 1,320 shares of*				6
7			*common stock for equipment,*				7
8			*building, and land.*				8

When a corporation accepts an asset other than cash, the accountant records the asset at its fair market value, to present an accurate balance sheet and have a realistic base on which to calculate future depreciation.

Now let's take the case of a corporation that gives shares of its stock to its organizers in exchange for their services in organizing the corporation. In this instance, the corporation receives an intangible asset, Organization Costs. Suppose that the Davidson Corporation issues 100 shares of common stock to its organizers. The accountant handles it this way:

	DATE		DESCRIPTION	POST. REF.	DEBIT	CREDIT	
1	*19–*						1
2	*Aug.*	*1*	*Organization Costs*		*5 0 0 0 00*		2
3			*Common Stock*			*5 0 0 0 00*	3
4			*Issued 100 shares to the pro-*				4
5			*moters in exchange for their*				5
6			*services in organizing the*				6
7			*corporation.*				7

If the fair market value of the asset or service, as in the case of organization costs, is not determinable, then the current market price of the stock on the date the asset or service is acquired is used.

Issuing Stock at a Premium or Discount

A newly organized corporation, such as the Davidson Corporation, generally issues its stock at par. However, after the business has been operating for some time, the directors may realize that they need additional investment capital. Perhaps the business has been so successful that they want to expand it. Or perhaps they need to cover losses suffered during the early years of the business. So the directors decide to issue some new stock. The present market price of the original stock affects the price they can secure for the new shares. The market price of the stock of a corporation is usually influenced by the following factors:

1. The earnings record, financial condition, and dividend record of the corporation
2. The potential for growth in earnings of the corporation
3. The supply of and demand for money for investment purposes in the money market as a whole
4. General business conditions and prospects for the future

When a corporation issues stock at a price above par value, the stock is said to be issued at a **premium**; the premium is the amount by which the selling price of the new stock exceeds the par value. The premium price may be due to the fact that the corporation has performed successfully in the past and has good prospects for growth in earnings in the future. Conversely, when a corporation sells its stock at a price below par value, the stock is said to be issued at a **discount**; the discount is the amount by which the selling price of the new stock falls below the par value. This discount may be due to the fact that the corporation incurred losses during its early period, or perhaps its prospects for the future are not too promising.

Premium on Stock

When a corporation issues stock at a price *above* its par value, the accountant debits Cash or other noncash assets for the amount received, credits the stock account for the par value, and credits a premium account for the difference between the amount received and the par value.

Let's take an example. The Faulkner Corporation issues 500 shares of $100-par preferred 9 percent stock at $103 on July 1. In general journal form, the entry looks like this:

	DATE		DESCRIPTION	POST. REF.	DEBIT	CREDIT	
1	*19–*						1
2	*July*	*1*	*Cash*		51 5 0 0 00		2
3			*Preferred 9 Percent Stock*			50 0 0 0 00	3
4			*Premium on Preferred 9 Percent*				4
5			*Stock*			1 5 0 0 00	5
6			*Issued 500 shares at $103 per*				6
7			*share.*				7
8							8
9							9

According to T accounts, the entry looks like this:

Cash		Preferred 9 Percent Stock	
+	−	−	+
51,500			50,000
(500 shares			(500 shares
× $103 each)			× $100 each)

		Premium on Preferred 9 Percent Stock	
		−	+
			1,500
			(500 shares
			× $3 each)

In the case of par-value stock, the stock account contains only the total par value of the stock. The premium on stock account is treated as an addition to stockholders' equity. Why would buyers be willing to pay a premium for Faulkner's 9 percent preferred stock? The 9 percent rate may be higher than the current market rate for the same type of stock. For example, other companies in comparable financial condition may be paying only 8 percent dividends on their stock.

Discount on Stock

When a corporation issues stock at a price *below* its par value, the accountant debits Cash or other assets for the amount received, credits the stock account for the par value, and debits a discount account for the difference between the amount received and the par value.

It should be mentioned that some states do not permit stock to be issued at a discount. In other states, it may be done only under certain conditions. However, since some states do indeed allow stock to be sold at a discount, we will proceed with an illustration.

Suppose that on July 1 the Faulkner Corporation issues 4,000 shares of $20-par common stock at $19. In general journal form, the entry is as follows:

	DATE		DESCRIPTION	POST. REF.	DEBIT	CREDIT	
1	*19–*						1
2	*July*	*1*	*Cash*		76 0 0 0 00		2
3			*Discount on Common Stock*		4 0 0 0 00		3
4			*Common Stock*			80 0 0 0 00	4
5			*Issued 4,000 shares at $19 per*				5
6			*share.*				6
7							7

In T accounts, the entry looks like this:

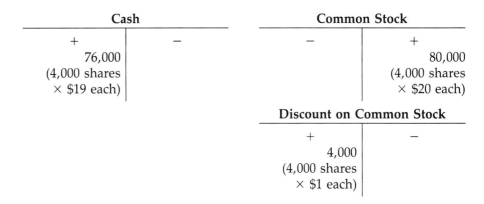

As in the case of par-value stock, the accountant records in the stock account the total *par* value of the stock issued and treats the discount on the stock as a deduction from stockholders' equity. It is a contra account.

Let's review the placement of the major accounts presented thus far in the fundamental accounting equation:

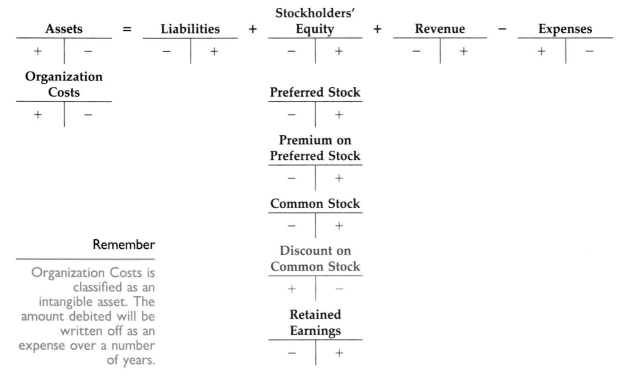

The Stockholders' Equity section of the balance sheet of the Faulkner Corporation—showing the stock, premium, and discount accounts—looks like this:

Stockholders' Equity					
Paid-in Capital:					
Preferred 9 Percent Stock, cumulative, $100 par					
(1,000 shares authorized, 500 shares issued)	$50 0 0 0 00				
Premium on Preferred 9 Percent Stock	1 5 0 0 00	$ 51 5 0 0 00			
Common Stock, $20 par (10,000 shares authorized,					
4,000 shares issued)	$80 0 0 0 00				
Less Discount on Common Stock	4 0 0 0 00	76 0 0 0 00			
Total Paid-in Capital		$127 5 0 0 00			
Retained Earnings		45 0 0 0 00			
Total Stockholders' Equity			172 5 0 0 00		

Notice that the listing of the stock states the par value, the number of shares authorized, and the number of shares issued. The record also describes preferred stock as cumulative and participating; if the stock is noncumulative or nonparticipating, the record does not mention it. Preferred stock is assumed to be noncumulative and nonparticipating unless otherwise stated. **Paid-in Capital** is a main caption under Stockholders' Equity. Preferred stock, and related premium or discount accounts, are always listed before common stock. (A corporation can also issue preferred stock at a discount or common stock at a premium.)

Concerning the Retained Earnings account, note that the amount is not necessarily in the form of cash. Rather than having idle cash, the corporation can get a better return by putting the surplus to work through reinvesting in either merchandise or plant and equipment.

No-Par Stock

Preferred stock generally has a par value. However, common stock may or may not have a par value. If it does not have a par value, it is referred to as *no-par stock*. It used to be the law that all stock had to have par value. Today, corporations in all the fifty states can issue no-par stock. The main advantages claimed for no-par stock are as follows:

1. No-par stock, since it does not have a par value, may be issued without a discount contingent liability.
2. No-par stock prevents misconception on the part of naive stockholders as to the value of the stock. In the case of par stock, investors might believe that the stock is worth the amount printed on the face of the stock certificate. Actually, the market value of the stock may differ markedly from the par value, due to ups and downs of the corporation's past earnings and future prospects.

Stated Value and No-Par Stock

We have said that when all of a company's stock is of the par-value type, the par value of the shares represents the company's legal capital, which stockholders cannot withdraw. This law protects creditors. When various state legislatures passed laws permitting corporations to issue no-par stock, they tried to continue to protect creditors by stipulating that all or part of the amount the corporation receives for its no-par shares be exempt from withdrawal by stockholders. This amount is known as the stock's **stated value**. The minimum stated value per share of no-par stock varies from state to state. In addition, in some states the board of directors of the corporation, if it wishes, may choose a stated value for the company's no-par stock that is higher than the minimum required by state law.

Established Amount of Stated Value

Objective 4

Journalize entries for the issuance of no-par stock.

Keyser Burger Master is located in a state that allows the board of directors of a corporation to designate a stated value for its stock. Accordingly, the board of directors of Keyser Burger Master chooses a stated value of $25 per share for its common stock. On June 20, Keyser issues 1,000 shares at $28 per share, receiving cash. The accountant uses the account titled Paid-in Capital in Excess of Stated Value to record the amount received over and above the stated value.

The accountant's entry, in general journal form, is as follows:

	DATE		DESCRIPTION	POST. REF.	DEBIT	CREDIT	
1	19–						1
2	June	20	Cash		28 0 0 0 00		2
3			Common Stock			25 0 0 0 00	3
4			Paid-in Capital in Excess of				4
5			Stated Value			3 0 0 0 00	5
6			Issued 1,000 shares at $28 per				6
7			share.				7
8							8
9							9
10							10
11							11
12							12
13							13

Next, on September 10, Keyser Burger Master issues an additional 1,000 shares at $30 per share, receiving cash. The entry in general journal form is:

	DATE		DESCRIPTION	POST. REF.	DEBIT	CREDIT	
1	*19–*						1
2	*Sept.*	*10*	*Cash*		*30 0 0 0 00*		2
3			*Common Stock*			*25 0 0 0 00*	3
4			*Paid-in Capital in Excess of*				4
5			*Stated Value*			*5 0 0 0 00*	5
6			*Issued 1,000 shares at $30 per*				6
7			*share.*				7
8							8
9							9
10							10

According to T accounts, the entries look like this:

Cash			
+		**−**	
June 20	28,000		
Sept. 10	30,000		

Common Stock			
−		**+**	
		June 20	25,000
			(stated value)
		Sept. 10	25,000
			(stated value)

Paid-in Capital in Excess of Stated Value			
−		**+**	
		June 20	3,000 (excess)
		Sept. 10	5,000 (excess)

Subscriptions and Stock Issuance

We have been talking about corporations that issue stock for which investors pay in full, either by giving cash or by giving noncash assets or organizational services. However, a corporation often sells its stock directly to investors on a subscription contract (installment) basis. This means that the investor enters into a contract with the corporation, promising to pay at a later date for a specified number of shares at an agreed price. The corporation agrees to issue the shares when the investor has paid for them in full.

Objective 5

Journalize entries for the sale of stock on the subscription basis.

The accountant records the amount of the subscription, which is an asset, in the Subscriptions Receivable account, and credits the par or stated value of the stock to Stock Subscribed, a stockholders' equity account. The accountant then records the difference between the subscription price and the par value under either premium or discount. In the case of no-par stock, the difference between the subscription price and the stated value is recorded under Paid-in Capital in Excess of Stated Value.

As the investor sends in payments, the accountant records them as debits to Cash and credits to Subscriptions Receivable. When the investor finishes paying for all the shares, the accountant records the issuance of the stock as a debit to Stock Subscribed and a credit to Common Stock or Preferred Stock. When investors want subscriptions to both common and preferred stock, the accountant uses separate accounts for each. We can best describe the procedure with some examples.

Subscription Transactions: No-Par Stock   De La Rosa Fine Foods, Inc., a newly organized company, sets up its books with the following transactions involving its own stock:

May   1 Received subscriptions to 10,000 shares of common stock (stated value $10 per share) from various subscribers at $16 per share, with a downpayment of 50 percent of the subscription price.

June   1 Received an additional 30 percent of the subscription price from all subscribers.

July   1 Received an additional 20 percent of the subscription price from all subscribers; then issued the stock.

The general journal entries are shown in Figure 23-4. The items in parentheses are just explanations; they would not actually appear in the journal.

After the accountant has posted these transactions, the T accounts appear as follows:

Cash

+		−
May 1	80,000	
June 1	48,000	
July 1	32,000	

Subscriptions Receivable, Common Stock

+		−	
May 1	160,000	May 1	80,000
		June 1	48,000
		July 1	32,000

Common Stock

−		+	
		July 1	100,000
			(10,000 shares)

Common Stock Subscribed

−		+	
July 1	100,000	May 1	100,000
			(10,000 shares)

Paid-in Capital in Excess of Stated Value

−		+	
		May 1	60,000

Remember

For the sale of common stock on a subscription basis, use Common Stock Subscribed. Do not issue the stock until it is paid for in full.

Common Stock Subscribed represents the total par value or stated value of the shares subscribed. It is considered to be a temporary account to handle subscribed shares that have not yet been paid for in full. When the investors finish paying for all the shares, the accountant records the issuance of stock by debiting the Common Stock Subscribed account and crediting the Common Stock account.

FIGURE 23-4

GENERAL JOURNAL

PAGE _____

	DATE		DESCRIPTION	POST. REF.	DEBIT	CREDIT	
1	19–						1
2	May	1	Subscriptions Receivable, Common				2
3			Stock (10,000 shares at $16 per				3
4			share)		160 0 0 0 00		4
5			Common Stock Subscribed (10,000				5
6			shares at $10 per share)			100 0 0 0 00	6
7			Paid-in Capital in Excess of				7
8			Stated Value ($160,000 − $100,000)			60 0 0 0 00	8
9			Received subscriptions to				9
10			10,000 shares at $16 per share.				10
11							11
12		1	Cash (10,000 shares × $16 per				12
13			share × .5)		80 0 0 0 00		13
14			Subscriptions Receivable,				14
15			Common Stock			80 0 0 0 00	15
16			Received 50 percent of the				16
17			subscription of May 1 on				17
18			10,000 shares.				18
19							19
20	June	1	Cash (10,000 shares × $16 per				20
21			share × .3)		48 0 0 0 00		21
22			Subscriptions Receivable,				22
23			Common Stock			48 0 0 0 00	23
24			Received 30 percent of the				24
25			subscription of May 1 on				25
26			10,000 shares.				26
27							27
28	July	1	Cash (10,000 shares × $16 per				28
29			share × .2)		32 0 0 0 00		29
30			Subscriptions Receivable,				30
31			Common Stock			32 0 0 0 00	31
32			Received 20 percent of the				32
33			subscription of May 1 on				33
34			10,000 shares.				34
35							35
36		1	Common Stock Subscribed		100 0 0 0 00		36
37			Common Stock (10,000 shares ×				37
38			$10 per share)			100 0 0 0 00	38
39			Issued 10,000 shares.				39
40							40
41							41
42							42
43							43
44							44
45							45
46							46

In the ledger accounts for stock issued and subscribed, always list the number of shares in the Item columns. Here is an example for Common Stock and Common Stock Subscribed:

ACCOUNT   *Common Stock*   ACCOUNT NO. *314*

DATE	ITEM	POST. REF.	DEBIT	CREDIT	BALANCE DEBIT	BALANCE CREDIT
19–						
July 1	10,000					
	shares	J1		100 0 0 0 00		100 0 0 0 00

ACCOUNT   *Common Stock Subscribed*   ACCOUNT NO. *316*

DATE	ITEM	POST. REF.	DEBIT	CREDIT	BALANCE DEBIT	BALANCE CREDIT
19–						
May 1	10,000					
	shares	J1		100 0 0 0 00		100 0 0 0 00
July 1		J1	100 0 0 0 00		—	—

Subscription Transactions: Par-Value Stock

Galaxy Motor Inns, Inc., a newly organized company, has the following transactions involving its own stock:

June   15   Received subscriptions to 2,000 shares of preferred 9 percent stock ($100 par value) from various subscribers at $103 per share, with a downpayment of 40 percent of the subscription price.

July   1   Received 30 percent of the subscription price from all subscribers (2,000 shares).

July   15   Received 30 percent of the subscription price from subscribers to 500 shares, and issued 500 shares.

The general journal is shown in Figure 23-5. The items in parentheses are explanations; they would not actually appear in the journal.

All this goes to show that Preferred 9 Percent Stock Subscribed represents the total par value of the shares subscribed. It also points up the fact that a firm does not issue stock until the investor has paid for it in full. Since only 500 shares were paid for in full, the firm issued only 500 shares.

Remember

The amount credited to the stock account is the par or stated value of the stock issued.

FIGURE 23-5

	DATE		DESCRIPTION	POST. REF.	DEBIT	CREDIT	
1	19–						1
2	June	15	Subscriptions Receivable, Preferred				2
3			9 Percent Stock (2,000 shares ×				3
4			$103 per share)		206 0 0 0 00		4
5			Preferred 9 Percent Stock				5
6			Subscribed (2,000 shares × $100				6
7			per share)			200 0 0 0 00	7
8			Premium on Preferred 9 Percent				8
9			Stock (2,000 shares × $3				9
10			per share)			6 0 0 0 00	10
11			Received subscription to 2,000				11
12			shares at $103 per share.				12
13							13
14		15	Cash (2,000 shares × $103 per				14
15			share × .4)		82 4 0 0 00		15
16			Subscriptions Receivable,				16
17			Preferred 9 Percent Stock			82 4 0 0 00	17
18			Received 40 percent of the sub-				18
19			scription of June 15 on 2,000				19
20			shares.				20
21							21
22	July	1	Cash (2,000 shares × $103 per				22
23			share × .3)		61 8 0 0 00		23
24			Subscriptions Receivable,				24
25			Preferred 9 Percent Stock			61 8 0 0 00	25
26			Received 30 percent of the sub-				26
27			scription of June 15 on 2,000				27
28			shares.				28
29							29
30		15	Cash (500 shares × $103 per				30
31			share × .3)		15 4 5 0 00		31
32			Subscriptions Receivable,				32
33			Preferred 9 Percent Stock			15 4 5 0 00	33
34			Received 30 percent, the final				34
35			installment of the subscription				35
36			of June 15, on 500 shares.				36
37							37
38		15	Preferred 9 Percent Stock Subscribed		50 0 0 0 00		38
39			Preferred 9 Percent Stock (500				39
40			shares × $100 per share)			50 0 0 0 00	40
41			Issued 500 shares.				41
42							42
43							43
44							44
45							45
46							46
47							47

Controlling Accounts and Subsidiary Ledgers

Investors may finish paying for subscriptions at different times, whereas the firm issues stock only when the individual subscriber has paid in full. Therefore, the firm's accountant has to maintain an account for each individual subscriber. As a result, the books exhibit the following relationships between controlling accounts and subsidiary ledgers:

Controlling Account	Subsidiary Ledger
Subscriptions Receivable, Preferred 9 Percent Stock	Preferred 9 Percent Stock Subscribers' ledger
Subscriptions Receivable, Common Stock	Common Stock Subscribers' ledger

These records are similar to the Accounts Receivable controlling account and the accounts receivable ledger.

The firm's accountant also has to keep an accurate record of the number of shares owned by each stockholder. Consequently, each stock account is a controlling account:

Controlling Account	Subsidiary Ledger
Preferred 9 Percent Stock	Preferred 9 Percent Stockholders' ledger
Common Stock	Common Stockholders' ledger

As we have said, a small corporation may use its stock certificate book as a subsidiary ledger. Naturally, the accountant must see to it that the information is complete so that the company can declare and pay dividends correctly. Cash dividends are paid on outstanding stock only.

Objective 6

Prepare a classified balance sheet for a corporation, including Subscriptions Receivable, Organization Costs, Paid-in Capital, and Retained Earnings accounts.

ILLUSTRATION OF A CORPORATE BALANCE SHEET

To reinforce your understanding of the accounts introduced in this chapter, examine the balance sheet shown in Figure 23-6 to see where each account is placed. Because this balance sheet covers so many of the concepts just discussed, you will probably want to refer back to it in the future.

In Figure 23-6, notice that Retained Earnings is added separately to Total Paid-in Capital. In this case it is assumed that the Retained Earnings

FIGURE 23-6

Roe Electronics
Balance Sheet
June 30, 19–

Assets			
Current Assets:			
Cash		$ 27 000 00	
Notes Receivable		50 000 00	
Accounts Receivable	$ 419 000 00		
Less Allowance for Doubtful Accounts	12 000 00	407 000 00	
Subscriptions Receivable, Preferred			
9 Percent Stock		14 000 00	
Subscriptions Receivable, Common Stock		30 000 00	
Merchandise Inventory		279 000 00	
Supplies		3 000 00	
Prepaid Insurance		5 00 00	
Total Current Assets			$ 810 500 00
Investments:			
Friedman Equipment Company			
8 Percent Bonds			16 000 00
Plant and Equipment:			
Store Equipment	$ 82 000 00		
Less Accumulated Depreciation	19 000 00	$ 63 000 00	
Delivery Equipment	$ 60 000 00		
Less Accumulated Depreciation	40 000 00	20 000 00	
Total Plant and Equipment			83 000 00
Intangible Assets:			
Organization Costs			8 000 00
Total Assets			$ 917 500 00
Liabilities			
Current Liabilities:			
Notes Payable		$ 20 000 00	
Accounts Payable		281 500 00	
Salaries Payable		3 000 00	
Interest Payable		1 000 00	
Total Liabilities			$ 305 500 00
Stockholders' Equity			
Paid-in Capital:			
Preferred 7 Percent Stock, $50 par (2,000			
shares authorized and issued)	$ 100 000 00		
Less Discount on Preferred 7 Percent Stock	1 000 00	$ 99 000 00	
Preferred 9 Percent Stock, $50 par			
(4,000 shares authorized, 1,500 shares issued)	$ 75 000 00		
Preferred 9 Percent Stock Subscribed			
(500 shares)	25 000 00		
Premium on Preferred 9 Percent Stock	3 000 00	103 000 00	
Common Stock, no-par, stated value			
$10 per share (20,000 shares authorized,			
14,000 shares issued)	$ 140 000 00		
Common Stock Subscribed (2,000 shares)	20 000 00		
Paid-in Capital in Excess of Stated Value	80 000 00	240 000 00	
Total Paid-in Capital		$ 442 000 00	
Retained Earnings		170 000 00	
Total Stockholder's Equity			612 000 00
Total Liabilities and Stockholders' Equity			$ 917 500 00

Remember

Paid-in Capital is a separate heading under Stockholders' Equity, and Preferred Stock accounts are listed first.

account has a $170,000 credit balance. This credit balance represents a surplus, and it is the normal balance. However, if a company had big losses, its Retained Earnings account could have a debit balance, which is called a deficit. On a balance sheet, a Retained Earnings account with a debit balance would be subtracted from Total Paid-in Capital.

NEW ACCOUNTS AND THE FUNDAMENTAL ACCOUNTING EQUATION

The placement and use of the accounts we have introduced in this chapter with respect to the fundamental accounting equation are shown in Figure 23-7 on the opposite page.

SUMMARY

L.O. 1

L.O. 2

A corporation is defined as "an artificial being, invisible, intangible, and existing only in the contemplation of the law." As a form of business organization, the corporation has the following advantages over a sole proprietorship or a partnership: limited liability, ease of raising capital, ease of transferring ownership rights, continuous existence, and no mutual agency. Its disadvantages are additional taxation and government regulation. The structure of the corporation is as follows: The stockholders elect the board of directors, and the board of directors appoints the officers to manage the corporation.

Capital stock may consist of two classes. (1) *Common stock* may be par value or no-par value. Holders of common stock get paid dividends after holders of preferred stock, and common stockholders usually have voting privileges. (2) *Preferred stock* has par value. Stockholders who have preferred stock get paid a definite rate of dividend and are paid before the holders of common stock, although they have no voting privileges. Preferred stock may be cumulative or noncumulative, participating or nonparticipating.

L.O. 3

The entry for the issuance of par-value stock is a debit to Cash and credits to the stock accounts. When stock is exchanged for assets other than cash, those asset accounts are debited. When stock is issued for more than its par value, the accountant must credit a premium account. For stock issued at a discount, a discount account is debited.

L.O. 4

When no-par stock is issued, all the proceeds are credited to the stock account. For no-par stocks with a stated value, the entry credits a paid-in capital in excess of stated value account for amounts higher than the stated value.

L.O. 5

The entry for the sale of stock on a subscription (installment) basis is a debit to a subscriptions receivable account (a current asset) and a credit to a stock subscribed account (a paid-in capital account). When the subscription

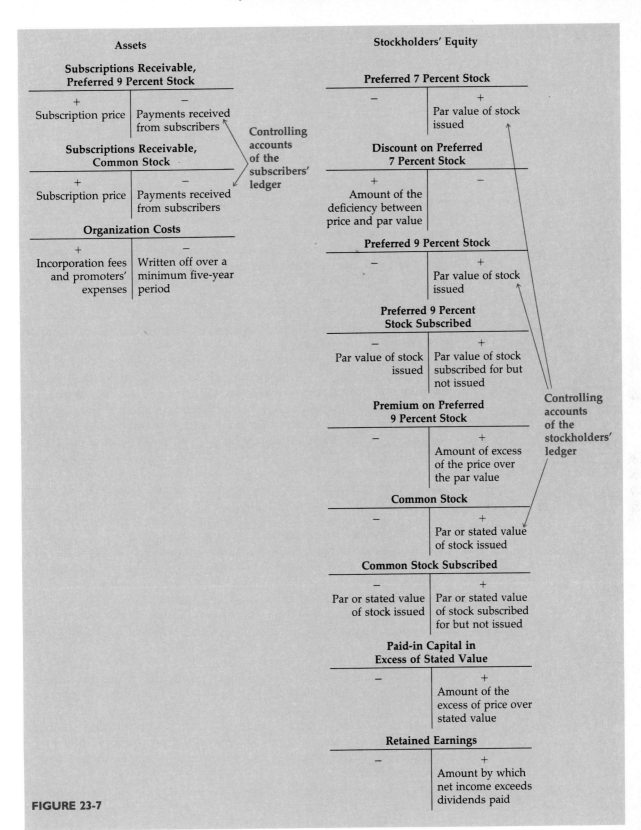

FIGURE 23-7

is paid in full, the entry is a debit to a stock subscribed account and a credit to a stock account.

L.O. 6   The accounts shown in Figure 23-7 are used to prepare a classified balance sheet.

GLOSSARY

Articles of incorporation   Application for a charter.

Authorized capital   The maximum number of shares that may be issued for each class of stock (common and preferred).

Capital stock   General term referring to shares of ownership in a corporation; subdivided into common stock and preferred stock.

Charter   Written right, issued by a state government, for a corporation to exist; approved articles of incorporation.

Closely held corporation   A corporation having a relatively small group of owners.

Common stock   Stock whose owners are paid dividends only after owners of preferred stock have been paid (residual share); holders of common stock have voting privileges.

Corporation   "An artificial being, invisible, intangible, and existing only in contemplation of the law." As such, it is a separate legal entity.

Cumulative preferred stock   When a firm fails to pay dividends during certain years, these dividends may be said to accumulate. When the firm finally pays the accumulated dividends, holders of cumulative preferred stock must be paid these dividends before any dividends can be paid to holders of common stock.

Deficit   Debit or negative balance in the Retained Earnings account.

Discount   The amount by which the issuing price of a stock falls below the par value.

Dividends   Distributions of earnings of a corporation, in the form of either cash or additional shares of stock.

Double taxation   The net income of the corporation is taxed first since the corporation is a separate entity. When the net income is distributed as dividends to stockholders, it becomes part of the personal income of the individual stockholder and is taxed a second time.

Intangible asset   An asset with no physical attributes; this classification includes such accounts as Organization Costs, Franchises, Patents, and Goodwill.

Issued stock   Stock issued by a corporation.

Legal capital   Minimum capital stock investment that a corporation must maintain; capital that is not subject to withdrawal by stockholders; usually equal to par or stated value.

Noncumulative preferred stock   Preferred stock in which dividends in arrears do not accumulate; once they are passed, they are gone forever.

Nonparticipating preferred stock   Stock in which the dividends are limited to the regular rate.

No-par stock   Stock that has no value printed on the stock certificates.

Open or public corporation   A corporation having a large group of owners ordinarily with shares traded on a stock exchange or in over-the-counter markets.

Organization Costs   An intangible asset account; used to record the cost of organizing a corporation, such as fees paid to the state, attorneys' fees, promotional costs, travel expenses, costs of printing stock certificates, and so on.

Outstanding stock   Stock actually in the possession of stockholders (issued stock less the number of shares reacquired by the company).

Paid-in Capital   A caption in the balance sheet listed immediately under Stockholders' Equity. The Paid-in Capital section includes the stock accounts and their related premium or discount accounts.

Participating preferred stock   Holders of preferred stock share in any extra dividends distributed by the corporation after the regular dividend has been paid to holders of preferred stock and a stipulated dividend to holders of common stock.

Par-value stock   Stock in which a uniform face value, indicating the amount per share to be entered in the capital stock account, is printed on the stock certificates.

Preemptive right   To maintain the same proportionate ownership in a corporation in the future as she or he does originally, a stockholder with a preemptive right has the privilege of subscribing to a new issue of stock in the same proportion as her or his present ownership.

Preferred stock   Stock whose holders are paid dividends at a regular rate before any dividends are paid to a holder of common stock. The holder of preferred stock also has preference in the distribution of assets in the event of a liquidation.

Premium   The amount by which the issuing price of a stock exceeds the par value.

Retained Earnings   A stockholders' equity account representing capital generated by the corporation's earnings that remains in the firm; the amount by which net income exceeds dividends paid over the life of the corporation.

Stated value   The amount per share of no-par stock that is recorded in the corporation's stock accounts; an amount designated by the law as being not subject to withdrawal by stockholders.

Stock certificates   Documents giving evidence of ownership of shares of stock; issued only when the stockholder has paid for the shares in full.

Stockholders' equity   The owners' equity in a corporation. Also referred to as _capital_.

Stockholders' ledger   A record showing the name and address of each stockholder and the number of shares owned.

Surplus   Credit or positive balance in the Retained Earnings account.

Treasury stock   A corporation's own stock, which it has issued and which was at one time outstanding, that the firm reacquires; the firm does not intend to cancel the stock.

QUESTIONS, EXERCISES, AND PROBLEMS
Discussion Questions

1. List the names of the subsidiary ledgers for Common Stock and Subscriptions Receivable, Common Stock.
2. In what respect is a corporation a separate legal entity?
3. Name three types of organization costs. How is the account Organization Costs classified on a balance sheet? What eventually happens to Organization Costs?
4. Identify four advantages and two disadvantages of the corporate form of business organization as compared to sole proprietorship and partnership forms. In your opinion, which is the greatest advantage and which is the greatest disadvantage?
5. In regard to common stock, what is the difference between par value and stated value?
6. If a corporation sells its stock at a premium, does the amount of the premium represent revenue to the firm?
7. What is a stock subscription?
8. What is the purpose of Common Stock Subscribed, and what happens to the account?

Exercises

L.O. 3 **Exercise 23-1** Describe the transactions recorded in the following accounts of the Christie Company:

Cash				Common Stock		
(1)	315,000	(2)	1,000		(1)	300,000
					(2)	2,000

Organization Costs			Premium on Common Stock		
(2)	3,000			(1)	15,000

L.O. 3,4 **Exercise 23-2** On June 2, the Macon Corporation issued for cash 9,000 shares of no-par common stock (with a stated value of $12 per share) at $16. On June 17, it issued for cash 600 shares of $100 par preferred 10 percent stock at $108.

a. Give the entries in general journal form for June 2 and June 17.
b. What is the total amount invested by all stockholders as of June 17?

L.O. 3 **Exercise 23-3** The Henderson Corporation is authorized to issue 30,000 shares of $75 par-value common stock. Record the following transactions in general journal form:

Jan.   10 Sold 6,000 shares of common stock at $76 per share; received cash.

Jan.   27 Issued 2,200 shares of common stock in exchange for land and building with a fair market value of $70,000 and $110,000, respectively.

Feb.   3 Sold 1,500 shares of common stock at $77 per share; received cash.

L.O. 4   **Exercise 23-4**   Fedders Explorations, Inc., is authorized to issue 200,000 shares of no-par common stock, $10 stated value. Record the following transactions in general journal form:

Apr.   22 Sold 3,000 shares of common stock at $13 per share for cash.

May   16 Sold 9,000 shares of common stock at $15 per share for cash.

L.O. 3   **Exercise 23-5**   The McMann Corporation was organized on March 7 of this year. The corporation was authorized to issue 800 shares of cumulative preferred 9 percent stock, $100 par value, and 8,000 shares of common stock, $25 par value. Record in general journal form the following transactions, completed during the firm's first year of operations:

Mar.   7 Sold 3,000 shares of common stock at par for cash.

         7 Issued 70 shares of common stock to an attorney in return for legal services pertaining to incorporation. The stock is selling at par.

June   6 Sold 300 shares of preferred stock at $102; received cash.

Sept.   11 Issued 2,600 shares of common stock in exchange for land with a fair market value of $65,000.

L.O. 5   **Exercise 23-6**   Peninsula Machine Shop has authorized capital consisting of 20,000 shares of cumulative preferred 9 percent stock, $100 par value, and 20,000 shares of common stock, $25 par value. Record the following transactions in general journal form:

a. Received subscriptions to 10,000 shares of preferred 9 percent stock at $104 per share, with a downpayment of 50 percent of the subscription price.
b. Received 30 percent of the subscription price from all subscribers.
c. Received 20 percent of the subscription price from all subscribers, and issued the stock certificates.

L.O. 6   **Exercise 23-7**   Demetri's Restaurants, Inc., has a charter authorizing it to issue 2,000 shares of $50 par-value preferred 7 percent stock and 10,000 shares of no-par common stock (stated value $30). The following account balances are from the Balance Sheet columns of the work sheet:

Retained Earnings (debit balance)	$ 56,000
Common Stock Subscribed (2,500 shares)	75,000
Discount on Preferred 7 Percent Stock	3,200
Common Stock	210,000
Preferred 7 Percent Stock	70,000
Paid-in Capital in Excess of Stated Value	42,000

Instructions

Prepare the Stockholders' Equity section of the balance sheet.

L.O. 5 **Exercise 23-8**   Describe the transactions recorded in the following ledger accounts of Kondo Electronics Corporation:

Cash				Common Stock		
(a)	24,000				(a)	20,000
(c)	33,600				(e)	40,000
(d)	22,400					

Subscriptions Receivable, Common Stock

(b)	56,000	(c)	33,600
		(d)	22,400

Common Stock Subscribed

(e)	40,000	(b)	40,000

Paid-in Capital in Excess of Stated Value

		(a)	4,000
		(b)	16,000

Problem Set A

L.O. 3,5 **Problem 23-1A**   The Grand-Way Food Service, Inc., was organized on April 4 of this year and has a charter that stipulates the following authorized capital:

a. 3,000 shares of preferred 7 percent stock, $100 par value
b. 40,000 shares of common stock, $25 par value

Grand-Way Food Service, Inc., completed the following transactions during its first year of operations:

Apr.   8 Received subscriptions to 12,000 shares of common stock at $25 per share; collected 60 percent of the subscription price.
       14 Sold 1,000 shares of preferred 7 percent stock for $97 per share, receiving cash.
May   7 Subscribers to 12,000 shares of common stock paid an additional 20 percent of the subscription price.
June   6 Subscribers to 12,000 shares of common stock paid an additional 20 percent of the subscription price. Grand-Way Food Service, Inc., issued the 12,000 shares of stock.
July   5 Sold 600 shares of preferred 7 percent stock for $94 per share, receiving cash.
Aug.   14 Received subscriptions to 3,000 shares of common stock at $27 per share; collected 50 percent of the subscription price.
Sept. 21 Received subscriptions to 300 shares of preferred 7 percent stock for $97 per share; collected 20 percent of the subscription price.

Instructions

Record the above transactions in general journal form.

L.O. 3,6   **Problem 23-2A**   Three people—Kelly, Haglund, and Howard—organized Newburn Athletic Supply, Inc. The charter of this corporation authorizes capital consisting of the following:

a. 1,600 shares of preferred 9 percent stock, $50 par value
b. 20,000 shares of common stock, $10 par value

During its first year of operations, Newburn Athletic Supply completed the following transactions that affected stockholders' equity:

May
   1 Issued to Kelly 3,000 shares of common stock, at par, for cash.
   2 Bought equipment from Haglund for $32,000. Haglund accepted 3,200 shares of common stock in exchange for the equipment.
   2 Bought land and building from Howard. The fair market value of the land was $18,000 and of the building, $62,000. There is an outstanding mortgage on the property of $32,000, held by Regional Savings Bank. The corporation assumed responsibility for paying the mortgage. Howard accepted common stock at par for her equity.
   5 Paid an attorney $4,200 for reimbursement of state fees and for performing services needed for incorporating the firm.
   7 Issued 100 shares of common stock at par to Kelly for organizational services. The stock is selling at par.

June
   7 Issued 600 shares of preferred 9 percent stock at $52 per share to investors for cash.

July
   3 Issued 400 shares of preferred 9 percent stock at $51 per share to investors for cash.

Instructions

1. Record the above transactions in general journal form.
2. Post the entries to the following accounts: Preferred 9 Percent Stock, Premium on Preferred 9 Percent Stock, and Common Stock.
3. Prepare the Stockholders' Equity section of the balance sheet as of December 31, the end of the first year of operations. Net income after taxes for the year was $42,000, and no dividends were declared during the year. As a result, Retained Earnings has a credit balance of $42,000.

L.O. 6   **Problem 23-3A**   Delite Dairy, Inc., has an authorized capital of 3,000 shares of preferred 10 percent stock, $100 par value, and 25,000 shares of no-par common stock, stated value, $20. The following account balances for the fiscal year ending June 30 of this year are taken from the Balance Sheet columns of the work sheet for the year. The accounts are listed in alphabetical order.

Accounts Payable	$375,280
Accounts Receivable	443,680
Accumulated Depreciation, Building	41,200
Accumulated Depreciation, Equipment	83,300
Allowance for Doubtful Accounts	13,840
Building	256,000
Cash	55,200

Common Stock	$240,000
Common Stock Subscribed	40,000
Equipment	184,000
Land	60,000
Merchandise Inventory	289,000
Mortgage Payable (long-term liability)	84,000
Notes Payable	32,800
Organization Costs	12,840
Paid-in Capital in Excess of Stated Value	70,000
Preferred 10 Percent Stock	160,000
Preferred 10 Percent Stock Subscribed	20,000
Premium on Preferred 10 Percent Stock	3,600
Retained Earnings (credit balance)	168,000
Subscriptions Receivable, Common Stock	17,400
Subscriptions Receivable, Preferred 10 Percent Stock	10,200
Supplies	3,700

Instructions

1. Determine the number of shares of preferred 10 percent stock subscribed and issued.
2. Determine the number of shares of common stock subscribed and issued.
3. Prepare a classified balance sheet.

L.O. 3,4,5,6   **Problem 23-4A**   Gallatin Specialty Advertising was organized on September 1 of this year, with a charter providing for authorized capital as follows:

a. 2,000 shares of preferred 7 percent stock, $50 par value
b. 40,000 shares of no-par common stock, $10 stated value

During the first year of operations, Gallatin Specialty Advertising completed the following transactions:

Sept.   1 Received subscriptions to 8,000 shares of common stock at $12 per share, collecting 30 percent of the subscription price.

3 Bought equipment from Gallatin, one of the promoters, for $32,000. Gallatin accepted 3,000 shares of common stock in return for the equipment. (Credit Paid-in Capital in Excess of Stated Value, $2,000.)

12 Subscribers to 8,000 shares of common stock paid an additional 30 percent of the subscription price.

14 Issued 100 shares of common stock to Gallatin at $12 per share in return for promotional services valued at $1,200.

18 Received subscriptions to 800 shares of preferred 7 percent stock at $47 per share, collecting 40 percent of the subscription price.

25 Paid an attorney $4,140 for paying state fees and for performing services needed for incorporating the firm.

29 Subscribers to 8,000 shares of common stock paid the remaining 40 percent of the subscription price, and Gallatin Specialty Advertising then issued the 8,000 shares.

Oct.   4 Received subscriptions to 3,000 shares of common stock at $14 per share, collecting 50 percent of the subscription price.

9 Subscribers to 800 shares of preferred 7 percent stock paid an additional 30 percent of the subscription price.

30 Subscribers to 3,000 shares of common stock paid the remaining 50 percent of the subscription price, and Gallatin Specialty Advertising issued the 3,000 shares.

Instructions

Record these transactions in general journal form. What is the total paid-in capital?

Problem Set B

L.O. 3,5   **Problem 23-1B**   Bannister Pharmacy, organized on June 4 of this year, has a charter that stipulates the following authorized capital:

a. 6,000 shares of preferred 8 percent stock, $50 par value
b. 30,000 shares of common stock, $20 par value

During the first year of its operations, Bannister completed the following transactions:

June   14 Received subscriptions to 9,000 shares of common stock at $20 per share; collected 50 percent of the subscription price.

July   20 Sold 1,500 shares of preferred 8 percent stock for $48 per share, receiving cash.

Aug.   14 Subscribers to 9,000 shares of common stock paid an additional 30 percent of the subscription price.

Sept.   16 Subscribers to 9,000 shares of common stock paid an additional 20 percent of the subscription price. Next, Bannister Pharmacy issued the 9,000 shares of stock.

Oct.   3 Sold 1,800 shares of preferred 8 percent stock for $47 per share, receiving cash.

Nov.   22 Received subscriptions to 1,600 shares of common stock at $22 per share; collected 25 percent of the subscription price.

Dec.   19 Received subscriptions to 1,200 shares of preferred 8 percent stock for $49 per share, collecting 10 percent of the subscription price.

Instructions

Record the above transactions in general journal form.

L.O. 3,6   **Problem 23-2B**   Three people—Callas, Duncan, and Reeder—organized Freeze-it Cold Storage, Inc., with a charter providing for the following authorized capital:

a. 1,500 shares of preferred 9 percent stock, $50 par value
b. 15,000 shares of common stock, $10 par value

During its first year of operations, Freeze-it Cold Storage completed the following transactions that affected stockholders' equity:

June   5 Issued 3,600 shares of common stock to Callas, at par, for cash.

        6 Paid an attorney $4,050 for performing services related to incorporation as well as for reimbursement of state fees.

        6 Bought equipment from Reeder for $32,140. Reeder accepted 3,214 shares of common stock in exchange for the equipment.

        6 Bought land and building from Duncan. It was determined that the fair market value of the land was $15,900 and of the building, $48,750. There is an outstanding mortgage on the property of $28,500 held by Trent Savings Bank. The corporation assumed responsibility for paying the mortgage. Duncan accepted common stock at par for his equity.

        8 Issued 60 shares of common stock to Callas for organizational services. The stock is selling at par.

July   5 Issued 450 shares of preferred 9 percent stock at $53 per share to investors for cash.

       31 Issued 300 shares of preferred 9 percent stock at $52 per share to investors for cash.

Instructions

1. Record the above transactions in general journal form.
2. Post the entries to the following accounts: Preferred 9 Percent Stock, Premium on Preferred 9 Percent Stock, and Common Stock.
3. Prepare the Stockholders' Equity section of the balance sheet as of December 31, the end of the first year of operations. Net income after taxes for the year was $43,140, and no dividends were declared during the year. As a result, Retained Earnings has a credit balance of $43,140.

L.O. 6   **Problem 23-3B**   Lang Freight-Forwarding Company, Inc., has an authorized capital of 3,000 shares of preferred 9 percent stock, $100 par value, and 30,000 shares of no-par common stock, stated value $20. The following account balances are from the Balance Sheet columns of the work sheet for the fiscal year ended December 31 of this year. The accounts are listed in alphabetical order.

Accounts Payable	$578,160
Accounts Receivable	704,340
Accumulated Depreciation, Building	80,700
Accumulated Depreciation, Equipment	131,190
Allowance for Doubtful Accounts	22,260
Building	396,000
Cash	89,880
Common Stock	360,000
Common Stock Subscribed	90,000
Equipment	289,350
Land	102,000
Merchandise Inventory	475,920
Mortgage Payable (long-term liability)	138,000
Notes Payable	54,600

Organization Costs	$ 21,360
Paid-in Capital in Excess of Stated Value	112,500
Preferred 9 Percent Stock	249,000
Preferred 9 Percent Stock Subscribed	51,000
Premium on Preferred 9 Percent Stock	6,000
Retained Earnings (credit balance)	279,000
Subscriptions Receivable, Common Stock	48,600
Subscriptions Receivable, Preferred 9 Percent Stock	19,200
Supplies	5,760

Instructions

1. Determine the number of shares of preferred 9 percent stock issued and subscribed.
2. Determine the number of shares of common stock issued and subscribed.
3. Prepare a classified balance sheet.

L.O. 3,4,5,6 **Problem 23-4B**   The Stanski Corporation was organized on March 1 of this year, with a charter providing for the following authorized capital:

a. 3,000 shares of preferred 10 percent stock, $50 par value
b. 20,000 shares of no-par common stock, $25 stated value

During the first year of operations, the Stanski Corporation completed the following transactions:

Mar. 2 Bought land from Stanski for $39,000. Stanski accepted 1,200 shares of common stock for the land (credit Paid-in Capital in Excess of Stated Value, $9,000).

4 Received subscriptions to 4,500 shares of common stock at $26 per share, collecting 40 percent of the subscription price.

6 Issued 100 shares of common stock to Stanski, at $26 per share, in return for organizational services.

10 Subscribers to 4,500 shares of common stock paid an additional 30 percent of the subscription price.

13 Paid an attorney $3,940 for performing services and for reimbursement of state fees needed for incorporating the firm.

14 Received subscriptions to 750 shares of preferred 10 percent stock at $52 per share, collecting 20 percent of the subscription price.

21 Subscribers to 4,500 shares of common stock paid the remaining 30 percent of the subscription price; Stanski Corporation then issued the stock.

Apr. 9 Received subscriptions to 3,000 shares of common stock at $27 per share, collecting 50 percent of the subscription price.

17 Subscribers to 750 shares of preferred 10 percent stock paid an additional 40 percent of the subscription price.

23 Sold 300 shares of preferred 10 percent stock at $51 per share for cash.

Instructions

Record these transactions in general journal form. What is the total paid-in capital?

24

Corporations: Work Sheet, Taxes, and Dividends

LEARNING OBJECTIVES

After you have completed this chapter, you will be able to do the following:

1. Journalize entries for corporate income taxes.
2. Journalize closing entries for a corporation.
3. Complete a work sheet for a corporation.
4. Journalize entries for the appropriation of Retained Earnings.
5. Journalize entries for the declaration and issuance of cash dividends.
6. Journalize entries for the declaration and issuance of stock dividends.
7. Complete a corporate statement of retained earnings and a balance sheet, including the following types of accounts: Appropriated Retained Earnings, Stock Dividend Distributable, Dividends Payable, and Income Tax Payable.

Chapter 23 described the entries the accountant makes during the initial organization of a corporation. Now let's assume that the corporation is established and turn our attention to the year-to-year entries for taxes, dividends, and retained earnings.

PROCEDURE FOR RECORDING AND PAYING INCOME TAXES

Determining the net income of a corporation is simply a matter of

Revenue − Expenses = Net income

One could compare most aspects of the revenue and expense accounts of a corporation to the revenue and expense accounts of sole proprietorships and partnerships. The net income of a sole proprietorship and the distributive shares of net income of a partnership are taxable as part of the owners' personal incomes. Since the corporation is a separate legal entity, however, it must pay income taxes in its own name. Corporations are subject to federal income taxes, and many states and cities also impose an income tax on them. We will only talk about the income tax levied by the federal government, but the same basic principles apply to state and city income taxes as well.

To place corporations on a pay-as-you-go basis, the law requires most of them to estimate in advance the amount of their federal income taxes for the forthcoming fiscal year. The corporations then pay the estimated amounts in four quarterly installments during the year. The firm's accountant records each entry as a debit to Income Tax Expense and a credit to Cash. The Income Tax Expense account is handled like any other expense account, except that the accountant usually makes a separate entry closing Income Tax Expense into Income Summary.

At the end of the fiscal year, after the corporation determines the exact amount of its income, it calculates how much income tax it owes. If the amount of income tax the corporation has paid in advance exceeds its tax liability for the year, the accountant debits the amount of the overpayment to Income Tax Paid in Advance, a current-asset account, and credits it to Income Tax Expense. Usually, however, the amount of income tax paid in advance is less than the amount of the tax liability. In this case, the accountant debits the amount of the underpayment to Income Tax Expense and credits it to Income Tax Payable, a current-liability account. The corporation is required to make full payment of its final tax with its income tax return. (The tax return is filed two-and-a-half months after the close of the fiscal year.) The entry is a debit to Income Tax Payable and a credit to Cash.

Corporation Income Tax Rates

Throughout this text, we shall assume corporate income will be subject to federal tax under a three-bracket, graduated-rate structure (the higher the income, the higher the tax rate), as follows:

Taxable Income	Tax Rate, %
First $50,000	15
Next $25,000 ($50,001–$75,000)	25
Over $75,000	34

Also, a 5 percent surtax (extra tax) is imposed on income between $100,000 and $335,000. In effect, the addition of the surtax causes corporations having taxable income above $335,000 to pay a flat 34 percent rate on all taxable income. Following are three examples:

Taxable income of $77,000

Tax on the first $50,000 ($50,000 × .15)	$ 7,500
Tax on the next $25,000 ($25,000 × .25)	6,250
Tax on the next $2,000 ($2,000 × .34)	680
Total tax	$14,430

Remember

Corporations are required to pay income taxes on the amount of their net income; sole proprietorships and partnerships are not taxed directly.

Taxable income of $200,000

Tax on the first $50,000 ($50,000 × .15)	$ 7,500
Tax on the next $25,000 ($25,000 × .25)	6,250
Tax on the next $125,000 ($125,000 × .34)	42,500
Surtax on amount between $100,000 and $200,000	
($100,000 × .05)	5,000
Total tax	$61,250

Taxable income of $460,000

Tax on the first $50,000 ($50,000 × .15)	$ 7,500
Tax on the next $25,000 ($25,000 × .25)	6,250
Tax on the next $385,000 ($385,000 × .34)	130,900
Surtax on amount between $100,000 and $335,000	
($235,000 × .05)	11,750
Total tax	$156,400

Or: Since the taxable income is above $335,000, use the flat tax rate of 34 percent: $460,000 × .34 = $156,400

Income Tax Entries for a Corporation: First Year

Objective 1

Journalize entries for corporate income taxes.

Hoyt Oxygen Supply, Inc., began operations on January 5. The corporation's fiscal year extends from January 1 through December 31. Its authorized capital consists of 200,000 shares of $20 par-value common stock. For the fiscal year, the corporation estimates that its taxable income will be $116,000 and that its income tax will be $28,490:

Tax on the first $50,000 ($50,000 × .15)	$ 7,500
Tax on the next $25,000 (25,000 × .25)	6,250
Tax on the next $41,000 ($41,000 × .34)	13,940
Surcharge on amount between $100,000 and $116,000	
($16,000 × .05)	800
Total tax	$28,490

Here is the way the accountant for Hoyt Oxygen Supply records the payment of this tax:

	DATE		DESCRIPTION	POST. REF.	DEBIT	CREDIT	
1	Year 1						1
2	Apr.	15	Income Tax Expense		7 1 2 2 50		2
3			Cash			7 1 2 2 50	3
4			Paid first quarterly installment				4
5			of estimated federal income tax				5
6			for the year (one-fourth of				6
7			$28,490).				7

	DATE	DESCRIPTION	POST. REF.	DEBIT	CREDIT	
1	Year 1					1
2	June 15	Income Tax Expense		7 1 2 2 50		2
3		Cash			7 1 2 2 50	3
4		Paid second quarterly install-				4
5		ment of estimated federal				5
6		income tax for the year.				6

	DATE	DESCRIPTION	POST. REF.	DEBIT	CREDIT	
1	Year 1					1
2	Sept. 15	Income Tax Expense		7 1 2 2 50		2
3		Cash			7 1 2 2 50	3
4		Paid third quarterly installment				4
5		of estimated federal income tax				5
6		for the year.				6

	DATE	DESCRIPTION	POST. REF.	DEBIT	CREDIT	
1	Year 1					1
2	Dec. 15	Income Tax Expense		7 1 2 2 50		2
3		Cash			7 1 2 2 50	3
4		Paid fourth quarterly install-				4
5		ment of estimated federal				5
6		income tax for the year.				6

At the end of the year, the accountant prepares a work sheet and determines that the taxable income of the corporation for the year is $128,000 ($996,000 in revenues minus $868,000 in costs and expenses). Since the estimated taxable income was $116,000, the additional amount of taxable income is $12,000 ($128,000 − $116,000). The additional tax owed is $4,680, and this amount will first appear as an adjusting entry on the work sheet.

Tax on the first $50,000 ($50,000 × .15)	$ 7,500
Tax on the next $25,000 ($25,000 × .25)	6,250
Tax on the next $53,000 ($53,000 × .34)	18,020
Surcharge on amount between $100,000 and $128,000	
($28,000 × .05)	1,400
Total tax	$33,170
Less estimated tax paid previously	28,490
Additional tax owed	$ 4,680

The adjusting entry is shown below.

	DATE	DESCRIPTION	POST. REF.	DEBIT	CREDIT	
1	Year 1	*Adjusting Entry*				1
2	Dec. 31	Income Tax Expense		4 6 8 0 00		2
3		Income Tax Payable			4 6 8 0 00	3
4						4
5						5

Objective 2

Journalize closing entries for a corporation.

The accountant now records the closing entries. In this example, to save time, we used "Revenues" to represent all temporary-equity accounts having a credit balance and "Expenses" to represent all accounts having a debit balance.

	DATE	DESCRIPTION	POST. REF.	DEBIT	CREDIT	
1	Year 1	*Closing Entries*				1
2	Dec. 31	Revenues		996 0 0 0 00		2
3		Income Summary			996 0 0 0 00	3
4						4
5	31	Income Summary		868 0 0 0 00		5
6		Expenses			868 0 0 0 00	6
7						7
8	31	Income Summary		33 1 7 0 00		8
9		Income Tax Expense			33 1 7 0 00	9
10						10
11	31	Income Summary		94 8 3 0 00		11
12		Retained Earnings			94 8 3 0 00	12
13						13
14						14

Now let's summarize the steps for journalizing the closing entries of a corporation:

1. Close revenue accounts into Income Summary.
2. Close expense accounts into Income Summary.
3. Close Income Tax Expense into Income Summary, by the amount of the actual income tax for the year.
4. Close Income Summary into Retained Earnings, by the amount of the net income after income tax.

As we have said, the Retained Earnings account is classified as a stockholders' equity account. It is a permanent or real account, as opposed to a temporary-equity or nominal account. After the accountant has finished posting to the Retained Earnings account, the account represents accumulated earnings if it has a credit balance. If the Retained Earnings account has a debit balance, it represents a deficit. The accountant posts the entries for the year to the T accounts, as follows:

Cash

+		−	
		Apr. 15	7,122.50
		June 15	7,122.50
		Sept. 15	7,122.50
		Dec. 15	7,122.50

Income Tax Expense

+		−	
Apr. 15	7,122.50	Dec. 31 Clos.	33,170.00
June 15	7,122.50		
Sept. 15	7,122.50		
Dec. 15	7,122.50		
Dec. 31 Adj.	4,680.00		

Revenues

−		+	
Dec. 31 Clos.	996,000	Balance	996,000

Expenses

+		−	
Balance	868,000	Dec. 31 Clos.	868,000

Income Tax Payable

−		+	
		Dec. 31 Adj.	4,680

Income Summary

Dec. 31 (Exp.)	868,000	Dec. 31 (Rev.)	996,000
Dec. 31 (Inc. Tax)	33,170		
Dec. 31 Clos.	94,830		

Retained Earnings

−		+	
		Balance	—
		Dec. 31	94,830

Income taxes are considered to be a necessary expense of conducting a business, and—as stated earlier—the accountant handles the Income Tax Expense account much like any other expense account. However, as stated earlier, it is common practice to make a separate entry closing Income Tax Expense into Income Summary and not to include the amount for income tax with the total amounts for all the other expenses. This procedure makes the amount of taxable income more evident from a quick analysis of Income Summary. Notice in the Income Summary T account illustrated above that the balance of the account prior to transferring the Income Tax Expense balance is $128,000 ($996,000 − $868,000), the taxable income. If the amount of income tax is closed into Income Summary with all the other expenses, the amount of taxable income is not as obvious.

Income Tax Entries for a Corporation: Second Year

The next year begins with a carry-over of the income tax liability for the previous year. Hoyt Oxygen Supply estimates that its net income will be $132,000 and that the related income tax will be $34,730 (verify this figure). Here are the journal entries for Year 2:

	DATE		DESCRIPTION	POST. REF.	DEBIT	CREDIT	
1	Year 2						1
2	Mar.	15	Income Tax Payable		4 6 8 0 00		2
3			Cash			4 6 8 0 00	3
4			Paid tax liability for last				4
5			year, due two and one-half				5
6			months after the close of the				6
7			fiscal year.				7

	DATE		DESCRIPTION	POST. REF.	DEBIT	CREDIT	
1	Year 2						1
2	Apr.	15	Income Tax Expense		8 6 8 2 50		2
3			Cash			8 6 8 2 50	3
4			Paid first quarterly install-				4
5			ment of estimated federal				5
6			income tax for the year				6
7			(one-fourth of $34,730).				7
8							8

	DATE		DESCRIPTION	POST. REF.	DEBIT	CREDIT	
1	Year 2						1
2	June	15	Income Tax Expense		8 6 8 2 50		2
3			Cash			8 6 8 2 50	3
4			Paid second quarterly install-				4
5			ment of estimated federal				5
6			income tax for the year.				6
7							7

	DATE		DESCRIPTION	POST. REF.	DEBIT	CREDIT	
1	Year 2						1
2	Sept.	15	Income Tax Expense		8 6 8 2 50		2
3			Cash			8 6 8 2 50	3
4			Paid third quarterly install-				4
5			ment of estimated federal				5
6			income tax for the year.				6
7							7

	DATE	DESCRIPTION	POST. REF.	DEBIT	CREDIT	
1	Year 2					1
2	Dec. 15	Income Tax Expense		8 6 8 2 50		2
3		Cash			8 6 8 2 50	3
4		Paid fourth quarterly install-				4
5		ment of estimated federal				5
6		income tax for the year.				6
7						7

WORK SHEET FOR A CORPORATION

Objective 3

Complete a work sheet for a corporation.

The second-year work sheet for Hoyt Oxygen Supply, Inc., is shown in Figure 24-1 on pages 814 and 815.

When the accountant is completing the work sheet, he or she must give special treatment to the adjusting entry for the additional income tax. Before recording the adjustment for income tax, the accountant must do the following:

1. Record and total the Trial Balance columns.
2. Record all adjustments except the adjustment for income tax.
3. Extend account balances into the Income Statement columns and tentatively determine the net income before taxes, as shown below. (The accountant's objective, naturally, is to determine the taxable income in advance as a basis for calculating the actual amount of income tax owed. Thus, the trial balance amount for Income Tax Expense must not be extended at this time.)

Remember

At the end of the fiscal period, the adjustment for additional income taxes owed is recorded on the work sheet as a debit to Income Tax Expense and as a credit to Income Tax Payable.

	ACCOUNT NAME	INCOME STATEMENT		
		DEBIT	CREDIT	
1	Sales		1,062 0 0 0 00	1
2	Purchases	729 2 3 4 00		2
3	Purchases Discount		4 8 0 0 00	3
4	Freight In	32 7 6 6 00		4
5	Selling Expenses (control)	130 7 5 0 00		5
6	General Expenses (control)	37 7 1 0 00		6
7	Interest Expense	3 7 2 0 00		7
8	Income Summary	180 5 0 0 00	189 8 8 0 00	8
9		1,114 6 8 0 00	1,256 6 8 0 00	9
10	Income Before Income Tax	142 0 0 0 00		10
11		1,256 6 8 0 00	1,256 6 8 0 00	11
12				12
13				13

4. Calculate the amount of the income tax. The accountant figures the additional income tax this way. (We present two methods; take your choice.) Since both estimated ($132,000) and actual ($142,000) taxable incomes fall in the bracket between $100,000 and $335,000, the 5 percent surtax is involved.

Method 1 Compare the calculations for the taxes based on the estimated and actual taxable incomes.

Estimated Taxable Income $132,000

First $50,000 (15 percent) $50,000 × .15 = $ 7,500
Next $25,000 (25 percent) $25,000 × .25 =   6,250
Next $57,000 (34 percent) $57,000 × .34 = 19,380
Surtax on amount over
  $100,000 (5 percent) $32,000 × .05 =   1,600
Total estimated tax $34,730

Actual Taxable Income $142,000

First $50,000 (15 percent) $50,000 × .15 = $7,500
Next $25,000 (25 percent) $25,000 × .25 =   6,250
Next $67,000 (34 percent) $67,000 × .34 = 22,780
Surtax on amount over
  $100,000 (5 percent) $42,000 × .05 =   2,100
Total actual tax $38,630

The difference is $3,900 ($38,630 − $34,730)

Method 2 Calculate the additional income tax on the difference between estimated and actual taxable incomes ($10,000).

Regular rate, 34 percent of $10,000 = $10,000 × .34 = $3,400
Surtax rate, 5 percent of $10,000   = $10,000 × .05 =   500
Total additional income tax is $3,900

5. Record the adjusting entry of $3,900 in the Adjustments columns of the work sheet and add the column totals.
6. Record the amount of the entire income tax in the Income Statement Debit column and complete the Income Statement columns by determining the income after taxes: $103,370.
7. Extend all remaining figures, including Income Tax Payable and Net Income after Taxes, into the Balance Sheet columns, and complete the Balance Sheet columns.

Financial Statements

Here is an abbreviated income statement for the second year:

Hoyt Oxygen Supply, Inc.
Income Statement
For Year Ended December 31, Year 2

Revenue from Sales:				
Sales				$1 062 0 0 0 00
Income Before Income Tax				142 0 0 0 00
Income Tax Expense				38 6 3 0 00
Net Income After Income Tax				$ 103 3 7 0 00

Hoyt Oxygen Supply, Inc.
Work Sheet
For Year Ended December 31, Year 2

	ACCOUNT NAME	TRIAL BALANCE DEBIT	TRIAL BALANCE CREDIT
1	Cash	13 3 6 0 00	
2	Accounts Receivable	118 1 1 0 00	
3	Allowance for Doubtful Accounts		1 8 2 0 00
4	Subscriptions Receivable, Common Stock	24 5 0 0 00	
5	Merchandise Inventory	180 5 0 0 00	
6	Prepaid Insurance	1 2 2 0 00	
7	Store Equipment	104 7 2 0 00	
8	Accumulated Depreciation, Store Equipment		27 2 5 0 00
9	Office Equipment	28 9 2 0 00	
10	Accumulated Depreciation, Office Equipment		8 4 1 0 00
11	Organization Costs	5 0 0 0 00	
12	Notes Payable		16 0 0 0 00
13	Accounts Payable		62 7 5 0 00
14	Common Stock		200 0 0 0 00
15	Common Stock Subscribed		20 0 0 0 00
16	Premium on Common Stock		2 4 0 0 00
17	Retained Earnings		30 4 3 0 00
18	Sales		1,062 0 0 0 00
19	Purchases	729 2 3 4 00	
20	Purchases Discount		4 8 0 0 00
21	Freight In	32 7 6 6 00	
22	Selling Expenses (control)	126 4 5 0 00	
23	General Expenses (control)	32 7 5 0 00	
24			
25			
26	Interest Expense	3 6 0 0 00	
27	Income Tax Expense	34 7 3 0 00	
28		1,435 8 6 0 00	1,435 8 6 0 00
29	Income Summary		
30	Interest Payable		
31	Income Tax Payable		
32			
33	Net Income After Income Tax		
34			
35			
36			
37			
38			
39			
40			
41			

Step 1

FIGURE 24-1

ADJUSTMENTS DEBIT	ADJUSTMENTS CREDIT	INCOME STATEMENT DEBIT	INCOME STATEMENT CREDIT	BALANCE SHEET DEBIT	BALANCE SHEET CREDIT	
				13 3 6 0 00		1
				118 1 1 0 00		2
	(e) 1 6 8 0 00				3 5 0 0 00	3
				24 5 0 0 00		4
(b) 189 8 8 0 00	(a)180 5 0 0 00			189 8 8 0 00		5
	(f) 5 2 0 00			7 0 0 00		6
				104 7 2 0 00		7
	(c) 4 3 0 0 00				31 5 5 0 00	8
				28 9 2 0 00		9
	(d) 2 7 6 0 00				11 1 7 0 00	10
				5 0 0 0 00		11
					16 0 0 0 00	12
					62 7 5 0 00	13
					200 0 0 0 00	14
					20 0 0 0 00	15
					2 4 0 0 00	16
					30 4 3 0 00	17
			1,062 0 0 0 00			18
		729 2 3 4 00				19
			4 8 0 0 00			20
		32 7 6 6 00				21
(c) 4 3 0 0 00		130 7 5 0 00				22
(d) 2 7 6 0 00						23
(e) 1 6 8 0 00						24
(f) 5 2 0 00		37 7 1 0 00				25
(g) 1 2 0 00		3 7 2 0 00				26
(h) 3 9 0 0 00		38 6 3 0 00				27
						28
(a) 180 5 0 0 00	(b)189 8 8 0 00	180 5 0 0 00	189 8 8 0 00			29
	(g) 1 2 0 00				1 2 0 00	30
	(h) 3 9 0 0 00				3 9 0 0 00	31
383 6 6 0 00	383 6 6 0 00	1,153 3 1 0 00	1,256 6 8 0 00	485 1 9 0 00	381 8 2 0 00	32
		103 3 7 0 00			103 3 7 0 00	33
		1,256 6 8 0 00	1,256 6 8 0 00	485 1 9 0 00	485 1 9 0 00	34
						35
(Step 2)		(Step 3)		(Step 7)		36
						37
(Step 5)		(Step 4)				38
						39
		(Step 6)				40
						41

Step 1: Record and total Trial Balance columns.

Step 2: Record all adjustments except income tax.

Step 3: Extend account balances into Income Statement columns.

Step 4: Determine taxable income and calculate tax.

Step 5: Record adjustment for income tax and complete Adjustments column totals.

Step 6: Record actual income tax in the Income Statement columns and complete the section.

Step 7: Extend account balances into Balance Sheet columns and total the columns.

The order of presentation of financial statements is similar to that of a sole proprietorship:

1. Income statement
2. Statement of retained earnings (counterpart in most respects to the statement of owner's equity)—listing the net income after income tax
3. Balance sheet—listing the ending balance of Retained Earnings

We will look at a complete statement of retained earnings and balance sheet later in this chapter. The balance sheet includes Income Tax Payable as a current liability.

Adjusting and Closing Entries

The next step in the accounting cycle is to take the adjusting entries and closing entries directly from the Adjustments columns of the work sheet and record them in the general journal (Figure 24-2).

Income Statement Net Income Versus Taxable Income

In our example, we've been assuming that the accountant for Hoyt Oxygen Supply determined the income tax for the year as a matter of course by multiplying the corporation's income before taxes for the year (as shown on the income statement) by the tax rate. The accountant maintained that the corporation's income before taxes was its taxable income. Well, in real life, things aren't quite that simple. The net income shown on the income statement may differ considerably from the income reported for tax purposes. Here are some of the reasons why:

1. The depreciation method used for income statement purposes may differ from the method used for tax statement purposes. For example, the firm might use the straight-line method of depreciation for its income statement but rates stipulated in the Tax Reform Act for its tax statement.
2. Some items listed in the income statement, such as interest on state and municipal bonds, are not taxable.
3. A corporation may list certain types of expenditures as assets and consequently not put them on the income statement. These same expenditures may be listed on the tax statement as expenses. For example, a company might not list prepaid advertising on its income statement, whereas it would list it as an expense on its tax statement. Research and development may be another example.

FIGURE 24-2

	DATE		DESCRIPTION	POST. REF.	DEBIT	CREDIT	
1	Year 2		*Adjusting Entries*				1
2	Dec.	31	Income Summary		180 5 0 0 00		2
3			Merchandise Inventory			180 5 0 0 00	3
4							4
5		31	Merchandise Inventory		189 8 8 0 00		5
6			Income Summary			189 8 8 0 00	6
7							7
8		31	Selling Expenses (control)		4 3 0 0 00		8
9			Accumulated Depreciation, Store Equipment			4 3 0 0 00	9
10							10
11		31	General Expenses (control)		2 7 6 0 00		11
12			Accumulated Depreciation, Office Equipment			2 7 6 0 00	12
13							13
14		31	General Expenses (control)		1 6 8 0 00		14
15			Allowance for Doubtful Accounts			1 6 8 0 00	15
16							16
17		31	General Expenses (control)		5 2 0 00		17
18			Prepaid Insurance			5 2 0 00	18
19							19
20		31	Interest Expense		1 2 0 00		20
21			Interest Payable			1 2 0 00	21
22							22
23		31	Income Tax Expense		3 9 0 0 00		23
24			Income Tax Payable			3 9 0 0 00	24
25							25
26			*Closing Entries*				26
27							27
28		31	Sales		1,062 0 0 0 00		28
29			Purchases Discount		4 8 0 0 00		29
30			Income Summary			1,066 8 0 0 00	30
31							31
32		31	Income Summary		934 1 8 0 00		32
33			Purchases			729 2 3 4 00	33
34			Freight In			32 7 6 6 00	34
35			Selling Expenses (control)			130 7 5 0 00	35
36			General Expenses (control)			37 7 1 0 00	36
37			Interest Expense			3 7 2 0 00	37
38							38
39		31	Income Summary		38 6 3 0 00		39
40			Income Tax Expense			38 6 3 0 00	40
41							41
42		31	Income Summary		103 3 7 0 00		42
43			Retained Earnings			103 3 7 0 00	43
44							44
45							45

REASONS FOR APPROPRIATING RETAINED EARNINGS

Since a corporation declares dividends out of its Retained Earnings, the *amount* of dividends is necessarily limited by the amount of Retained Earnings. However, rather than using the entire balance of Retained Earnings for cash or stock dividends (we will discuss cash and stock dividends later), the board of directors may wish to earmark part of Retained Earnings for some specific purpose.

Objective 4

Journalize entries for the appropriation of Retained Earnings.

Such a restriction constitutes an **appropriation of retained earnings.** Let us say that the directors decide they want to provide for future expansion. The board passes a resolution, which is recorded in the minutes of a meeting, restricting or appropriating a certain amount of Retained Earnings for future expansion. The minutes of the meeting represent the source document for the accounting entry. For example, Hoyt Oxygen Supply, Inc., plans to erect its own building. To finance the project, it decides to restrict Retained Earnings for a total amount of $500,000, at the rate of $50,000 per year, for ten years. The accountant makes the following type of entry at the end of each year, after the closing entries:

	DATE		DESCRIPTION	POST. REF.	DEBIT	CREDIT	
1	Year 2						1
2	Feb.	5	*Retained Earnings*		50 0 0 0 00		2
3			*Retained Earnings Appropriated*				3
4			*for Building*			50 0 0 0 00	4
5			*To appropriate Retained*				5
6			*Earnings, as ordered by the*				6
7			*board of directors in meeting*				7
8			*of February 5, Year 2.*				8

This appropriation of Retained Earnings does *not* represent a separate kitty or cash fund of $50,000. Let's look at cash dividends for a moment: If we consider the Retained Earnings account as a well or reservoir from which cash dividends are declared, then this reservoir has dried up by $50,000. **If the corporation does not declare and pay out these dividends, then the firm is preserving its net assets, particularly cash.** Of course, the $50,000 would not necessarily be in the form of cash. Perhaps the company can yield a bigger return by putting the money into merchandise inventory or paying off its debts. By the term *net assets* we mean assets minus liabilities.

At the end of the ten-year period, although there is *not* an actual $500,000 fund of cash, there is an additional $500,000 accumulated in net assets. The corporation can now formulate plans to convert the $500,000 increase in net assets into cash in order to put a downpayment on the building.

When the objective—buying or erecting the building—has been accomplished, the corporation no longer needs to restrict Retained Earnings. The accountant may then make the following entry, reversing the ten previous entries:

	DATE	DESCRIPTION	POST. REF.	DEBIT	CREDIT	
1	*Year 12*					1
2	*Mar. 18*	*Retained Earnings Appropriated for*				2
3		*Building*		*500 0 0 0 00*		3
4		*Retained Earnings*			*500 0 0 0 00*	4
5		*To return to Retained Earnings*				5
6		*the balance in the Retained*				6
7		*Earnings Appropriated for*				7
8		*Building account, as ordered by*				8
9		*the board of directors in the*				9
10		*meeting of March 18, Year 12.*				10

Other examples of appropriated Retained Earnings accounts include:

- Retained Earnings Appropriated for Plant Expansion (no specific objective stated)
- Retained Earnings Appropriated for Bonded Indebtedness (an obligation imposed by contract)
- Retained Earnings Appropriated for Self-Insurance (planning for possible casualty losses)
- Retained Earnings Appropriated for Inventory Losses (in the event of getting caught in a price drop)
- Retained Earnings Appropriated for Contingencies (in the event of a "rainy day")

Remember

An appropriation of Retained Earnings does not result in a decrease in stockholders' equity.

Each appropriated Retained Earnings is labeled "Retained Earnings Appropriated for _____ ." Therefore the account Retained Earnings represents **unappropriated retained earnings**. These accounts appear in a statement of retained earnings, an example of which is illustrated in Figure 24-3 on page 826.

DECLARATION AND PAYMENT OF DIVIDENDS

A dividend is a distribution—of cash, shares of stock, or other assets—that a corporation makes to its stockholders. Dividends are allocated to persons who own stock according to the number of shares they own and according to whether the stock is preferred or common. We shall discuss three types of dividends: cash dividends, stock dividends, and liquidating dividends. Cash dividends and stock dividends reduce Retained Earnings; liquidating dividends reduce Paid-in Capital.

Cash Dividends

A dividend payable in cash—or **cash dividend**—is the most usual form of dividend. It ordinarily represents a share of the current earnings paid to the stockholders as a reward for their investment. The board of directors declares dividends, generally paying cash dividends up to a certain percentage of the firm's net income after income tax. The cash dividend is expressed as a specific amount per share—for example, $1.12 per share. A stockholder who owns 100 shares is thus entitled to $112.

Before a corporation can pay a cash dividend, three things are needed:

1. **Retained Earnings** The company must have a sufficient balance in the unappropriated Retained Earnings account.
2. **An adequate amount of cash** A corporation may have earned large profits, but not all profits are in cash. For example, the revenue may be in the form of charge accounts, such as Accounts Receivable. Cash comes in only when the company receives payments from charge customers.
3. **Formal declaration by the board of directors** The payment of dividends, although it may be a matter of policy, is not automatic. The board of directors must pass the declaration in the form of a motion and record it in the minute book. This minute book is the source document for the accounting entry.

Dividend Dates

Three significant dates are involved in the declaration and payment of a dividend:

1. **Date of declaration** Date on which the board of directors votes to declare dividends. The entry recorded as of this date debits Retained Earnings and credits Dividends Payable.
2. **Date of record** Date as of which the ownership of shares is set. This date determines a person's eligibility for dividends and ordinarily is about three weeks after the date of declaration.
3. **Date of payment** The date payment is made; on this date, the accountant debits the amount to Dividends Payable and credits it to Cash.

Objective 5

Journalize entries for the declaration and issuance of cash dividends.

For example, on January 20, the board of directors of Hoyt Oxygen Supply declares a quarterly cash dividend of $.72 per share (5,000 shares × $.72 = $3,600) to stockholders of record as of February 11, payable on February 20. (Dividends Payable is classified as a current liability.) The entries, in general journal form, are as follows:

DATE	DESCRIPTION	POST. REF.	DEBIT	CREDIT
Year 2				
Jan. 20	Retained Earnings		3 6 0 0 00	
	Dividends Payable			3 6 0 0 00
	To record declaration of			
	quarterly cash dividend on			
	common stock at the rate of			
	$.72 per share to stockholders			
	of record as of February 11,			
	payable February 20, as ordered			
	by board of directors in meeting			
	of January 20.			

DATE	DESCRIPTION	POST. REF.	DEBIT	CREDIT
Year 2				
Feb. 20	Dividends Payable		3 6 0 0 00	
	Cash			3 6 0 0 00
	Payment of quarterly dividend			
	declared on January 20 to			
	stockholders of record as of			
	February 11.			

The Retained Earnings account before closing entries in Year 2 appears as shown below. During the year, an appropriation was made for building, and regular cash dividends were declared and paid. To make the account more understandable, we have included explanations in the Item column:

ACCOUNT Retained Earnings   ACCOUNT NO. 316

DATE	ITEM	POST. REF.	DEBIT	CREDIT	BALANCE DEBIT	BALANCE CREDIT
Year 1						
Dec. 31	Net income			94 8 3 0 00		94 8 3 0 00
Year 2						
Jan. 20	Cash dividend		3 6 0 0 00			91 2 3 0 00
Feb. 5	Appropriation		50 0 0 0 00			41 2 3 0 00
Apr. 20	Cash dividend		3 6 0 0 00			37 6 3 0 00
July 20	Cash dividend		3 6 0 0 00			34 0 3 0 00
Oct. 20	Cash dividend		3 6 0 0 00			30 4 3 0 00

The balance of $30,430 would appear in the Trial Balance column of the work sheet for the year ended December 31, Year 2.

Stock Dividends

Objective 6

Journalize entries for the declaration and issuance of stock dividends.

A **stock dividend** is a distribution, on a pro rata (proportional) basis, of additional shares of a company's stock to the stockholders. In other words, the dividend consists of shares of stock rather than cash. One could describe it as a dividend payable in stock. Generally, stock dividends consist of common stock distributed to holders of common stock. Stock dividends are usually issued by corporations that plow back (retain) earnings in order to finance future expansion.

Suppose that the board of directors of Hoyt Oxygen Supply, Inc., declared a 20 percent stock dividend on October 11 of Year 3 to stockholders of record as of November 1, payable on November 16. The ledger sheet for the Common Stock account on October 11 looks like this in T account form:

Common Stock	
	Balance 200,000
	$40 per share
	(5,000 shares)

Number of shares in the stock dividend:

20 percent of 5,000 shares = <u>1,000</u> shares

The current market value of the shares is $46 per share. The entries, in general journal form, are as follows. (We have put in the calculations just by way of explanation.)

	DATE		DESCRIPTION	POST. REF.	DEBIT	CREDIT	
1	Year 3						1
2	Oct.	11	Retained Earnings (1,000 shares				2
3			× $46 each)		46 0 0 0 00		3
4			Stock Dividend Distributable				4
5			(1,000 shares × $40 each)			40 0 0 0 00	5
6			Premium on Common Stock			6 0 0 0 00	6
7			To record the declaration of				7
8			a 20 percent stock dividend to				8
9			stockholders of record as of				9
10			November 1; payable November				10
11			16, as ordered by board of direc-				11
12			tors in meeting of October 11.				12

	DATE		DESCRIPTION	POST. REF.	DEBIT	CREDIT	
1	Year 3						1
2	Nov.	16	Stock Dividend Distributable		40 0 0 0 00		2
3			Common Stock			40 0 0 0 00	3
4			Issuance of a stock dividend				4
5			(1,000 shares) declared on				5
6			October 11 to stockholders				6
7			of record as of November 1.				7

Stock Dividend Distributable is a stockholders' equity account, representing the total par value of the shares of stock to be issued. If the account is on the books at the time of the preparation of a balance sheet, the accountant lists it in the Paid-in Capital section, just below Common Stock.

The stock dividend—unlike the cash dividend—does *not* result in a reduction of assets. It merely reshuffles the stockholders' equity accounts. The stock dividend increases the Capital Stock accounts and decreases the Retained Earnings account, without making any change in the total stockholders' equity.

The stock dividend has no effect on the porportionate share of ownership held by an individual stockholder. For example, Rosemary Baker owns 500 shares of the corporation's stock, which represents a one-tenth share in the corporation since the total number of shares issued was 5,000. The corporation declares a 20 percent stock dividend. As her part of this dividend, Baker receives 100 shares (20 percent of 500 shares). Her total stock now amounts to 600 shares; the corporation's total issued stock is now at 6,000 shares. Consequently, Rosemary Baker still has a one-tenth share in the ownership (600 shares ÷ 6,000 shares).

Remember

The Stock Dividend Distributable account is used to record the par or stated value of a stock dividend declared, but the stock has not yet been issued to stockholders.

For accounting purposes, corporations make a distinction between a stock dividend of 25 percent or less (small) and a stock dividend of 26 percent or more (large). The above example represented a 20 percent stock dividend, in which the accountant debited Retained Earnings for the fair market value of the shares issued. If the stock dividend had been over 25 percent, the accountant would have debited Retained Earnings for the par or stated value of the shares to be issued.

Reasons for Issuing Stock Dividends

In view of the fact that a stockholder's proportionate share or equity in a company does not change when the company issues a stock dividend, why does a corporation bother with stock dividends? Here are a few reasons:

1. Stock dividends appease stockholders by giving them paper to hold onto. The corporation can conserve its cash, and the stockholders feel

partially satisfied. They didn't get cash, but at least they got something.

2. Stock dividends tend to reduce the market price of the stock. The supply of the stock increases with no immediate offsetting change in the demand for it. Stock with a lower price per share is more easily sold to the public.

3. Stock dividends enable stockholders to avoid income tax liability since the recipients of stock dividends do not have to consider them as income. Therefore, stockholders do not have to pay any income tax on stock dividends.

Remember

A stock dividend does not reduce total stockholders' equity; it is simply an exchange of Retained Earnings for stock.

Liquidating Dividends

A corporation pays **liquidating dividends** when (1) it is going out of existence or (2) it is permanently reducing the size of its operations. It returns to the stockholders all or a part of their investment. For example, in the situation shown below, a corporation has returned all stockholders' investments:

	DATE	DESCRIPTION	POST. REF.	DEBIT	CREDIT	
1		*Common Stock*		240 0 0 0 00		1
2		*Premium on Common Stock*		10 0 0 0 00		2
3		*Cash*			250 0 0 0 00	3
4		*To end the business affairs of*				4
5		*the corporation, the board of*				5
6		*directors during meeting of*				6
7		*August 12 authorized a 100*				7
8		*percent liquidation dividend.*				8
9						9

STOCK SPLIT

When there is a **stock split,** a corporation deliberately splits or subdivides its stock, on the basis of its par or stated value, and issues a proportionate number of additional shares. For example, a corporation with 10,000 shares of $50 par-value stock outstanding may reduce the par value to $25 and increase the number of shares to 20,000. If you own 200 shares before the split, you will own 400 shares after it. The company may call in all the old shares and issue certificates for new ones on a 2-for-1 basis, or it may issue an additional share for each old share. The accountant records a stock split by the entry shown at the top of the next page. (We list the par values by way of explanation.) This 2-for-1 stock split reduces the market price per share by approximately half, thereby increasing the stock's salability. Since each share now costs less, more investors are able to afford the stock.

	DATE	DESCRIPTION	POST. REF.	DEBIT	CREDIT	
1		*Common Stock ($50 par value)*		500 0 0 0 00		1
2		*Common Stock ($25 par value)*			500 0 0 0 00	2
3		*The board of directors have this*				3
4		*day ordered a 2-for-1 stock*				4
5		*split, increasing the outstanding*				5
6		*shares from 10,000 to 20,000,*				6
7		*and reducing the par value from*				7
8		*$50 to $25.*				8
9						9

There is no change in Retained Earnings. The accountant changes the headings of the Capital Stock accounts in the ledger to show the new par or stated value per share and revises the stockholders' ledger to show the new distribution of shares. (As an alternative, some accountants record stock splits with a memorandum entry.)

Minute Book

We have said that the **minute book** is an important source document for any accounting entries involving the declaration of dividends and the appropriation of Retained Earnings. The minute book is just like the minute book of a club: it is a written, narrative record of all actions taken at official meetings of the board of directors. A corporation's minute book may also contain details relating to the purchase of plant and equipment, the obtaining of bank loans, the establishing of officers' salaries, and so on.

STATEMENT OF RETAINED EARNINGS AND A BALANCE SHEET FOR A CORPORATION

Objective 7

Complete a corporate statement of retained earnings and a balance sheet, including the following types of accounts: Appropriated Retained Earnings, Stock Dividend Distributable, Dividends Payable, and Income Tax Payable.

In this chapter, we have discussed a number of possible situations that would affect the status of retained earnings within a given period of time. These changes are reported on a separate financial statement, called a *statement of retained earnings*. Generally, this statement lists only those items that represent significant changes. For example, in the statement of retained earnings of the Kozar Beverage Company, Inc. (Figure 24-3), specific appropriations for plant expansion and possible price declines are listed. The statement of retained earnings for a corporation may be compared, in some respects, to a statement of owner's equity for a sole proprietorship or partnership, with the ending balances appearing in the stockholders' or owner's equity section of a balance sheet.

Remember

The ending balances of
Unappropriated
Retained Earnings and
each Appropriation
account will appear in
the Stockholders'
Equity of the
corporation's balance
sheet.

So that you can better visualize the relationship of the statement of retained earnings to the balance sheet, Figure 24-4 presents the balance sheet for Kozar Beverage Company, Inc.

The accountant may use the account Paid-in Capital from Donation to record a situation in which the corporation receives a material gift. For example, the city of Loganville gave the Kozar Beverage Company an acre of land, valued at $11,650, as an incentive to locate a processing plant there. The accountant for Kozar debited Land and credited Paid-in Capital from Donation for $11,650 each at that time.

FIGURE 24-3

Kozar Beverage Company, Inc.
Statement of Retained Earnings
For Year Ended December 31, 19–

Unappropriated Retained Earnings:			
Unappropriated Retained Earnings, Jan. 1, 19–	$ 112 700 00		
Net Income for the Year	73 000 00	$ 185 700 00	
Less: Cash Dividends Declared	$ 20 000 00		
Stock Dividends Declared	39 500 00		
Transfer to Appropriation for Plant Expansion (see below)	4 000 00		
Transfer to Appropriation for Possible Price Declines (see below)	3 000 00	66 500 00	
Unappropriated Retained Earnings, Dec. 31, 19–			$ 119 200 00
Appropriated Retained Earnings:			
Appropriated for Plant Expansion, Jan. 1, 19–	$ 16 000 00		
Add Appropriation for the Year (see above)	4 000 00		
Appropriated for Plant Expansion, Dec. 31, 19–		$ 20 000 00	
Appropriated for Possible Price Declines, Jan. 1, 19–	$ 15 000 00		
Add Appropriation for the Year (see above)	3 000 00		
Appropriated for Possible Price Declines, Dec. 31, 19–		18 000 00	
Retained Earnings Appropriated, Dec. 31, 19–			38 000 00
Total Retained Earnings, Dec. 31, 19–			$ 157 200 00

FIGURE 24-4

Kozar Beverage Company, Inc.
Balance Sheet
December 31, 19–

Assets				
Current Assets:				
Cash			$ 6 4 2 0 00	
Accounts Receivable	$ 163 3 9 0 00			
Less Allowance for Doubtful Accounts	4 2 9 0 00		159 1 0 0 00	
Subscriptions Receivable, Common Stock			3 5 0 0 00	
Merchandise Inventory			320 2 2 0 00	
Supplies			1 2 5 0 00	
Total Current Assets				$ 490 4 9 0 00
Plant and Equipment:				
Land			$ 40 0 0 0 00	
Building	$ 160 0 0 0 00			
Less Accumulated Depreciation	78 0 0 0 00		82 0 0 0 00	
Equipment	$ 80 7 6 0 00			
Less Accumulated Depreciation	26 7 5 0 00		54 0 1 0 00	
Total Plant and Equipment				176 0 1 0 00
Intangible Assets:				
Organization Costs			$ 7 2 0 0 00	
Patents			7 0 0 0 00	
Total Intangible Assets				14 2 0 0 00
Total Assets				$ 680 7 0 0 00
Liabilities				
Current Liabilities:				
Notes Payable	$ 16 0 0 0 00			
Accounts Payable	85 6 9 0 00			
Income Tax Payable	9 2 0 0 00			
Dividends Payable	4 0 0 0 00			
Interest Payable	9 6 0 00		$ 115 8 5 0 00	
Total Current Liabilities				
Long-Term Liabilities:			54 0 0 0 00	
Mortgage Payable (due July 1, 19–)				$ 169 8 5 0 00
Total Liabilities				
Stockholders' Equity				
Paid-in Capital:				
Preferred 7 Percent Stock, $25 par	$ 125 0 0 0 00			
(5,000 shares authorized and issued)				
Less Discount on Preferred 7 Percent Stock	10 0 0 0 00		$ 115 0 0 0 00	
Common Stock, no-par, stated value $10				
per share (20,000 shares authorized,				
16,000 shares issued)	$ 160 0 0 0 00			
Stock Dividend Distributable (3,950 shares)	39 5 0 0 00			
Common Stock Subscribed (500 shares)	5 0 0 0 00			
Paid-in Capital in Excess of Stated Value	22 5 0 0 00		227 0 0 0 00	
Paid-in Capital from Donation			11 6 5 0 00	
Total Paid-in Capital			$ 353 6 5 0 00	
Retained Earnings:				
Unappropriated Retained Earnings	119 2 0 0 00			
Appropriated:				
For Plant Expansion	$ 20,000.00			
For Possible Price Declines	18,000.00	38 0 0 0 00		
Total Retained Earnings			157 2 0 0 00	
Total Stockholders' Equity				510 8 5 0 00
Total Liabilities and Stockholders' Equity				$ 680 7 0 0 00

FUNDAMENTAL GUIDELINES FOR ACCOUNTING REPORTS

We have called accounting the "language of business." This language is expressed in accounting reports or statements. Accountants want to make sure that their reports are clear and consistent. To make their reports consistent, accountants follow certain guidelines. Three of these fundamental guidelines are full disclosure, materiality, and conservatism.

Full Disclosure

To disclose means "to uncover or make known." The guideline of **full disclosure** requires that anyone preparing a financial statement include enough information so the statement is complete. Relevant information left out of a report or half truths are not acceptable. Information included in the report must not lead the reader to wrong conclusions.

Example: At the end of its report, a business includes a footnote about a lawsuit in which it is involved. The report also states that the case has not been settled and that no financial claim has yet been made against the company. This note prepares the readers to expect a possible financial claim the company may have to pay. The report would not meet the requirement of full disclosure if it failed to mention the lawsuit and the possible claim.

Materiality

If something is "material," it is important and carries weight. The guideline of **materiality** states that relatively important data is included in financial reports. Important data is material; unimportant data is immaterial. Accounting workers deal with many different kinds of financial transactions involving small dollar amounts. These transactions may have very little effect on the results shown in financial statements and would not be likely to influence decisions made by users of the financial statements.

Example: In an annual report of a business reporting a profit of $14 million a year, the understatement of profit by $6,000 may be immaterial. The same understatement of profit for a business reporting an annual profit of $22,000 would be material.

Conservatism

To be conservative means to take the safe route. When faced with a decision about which accounting procedures to apply, accountants generally follow the "safer" principle. They use the alternative that is the least likely to result in an overstatement of income or property value.

Example: An accountant is estimating an amount of money to be received in the future. The accountant must choose between $12,000 and $14,000. **Conservatism** requires the accountant to choose the smaller amount.

SUMMARY

L.O. 1   A corporation, since it is a separate legal entity, must pay a federal corporate income tax. Many state and local governments also levy income taxes on corporations. A corporation has to estimate the federal income tax it will have to pay for the forthcoming year and pay it in four quarterly installments. At the end of the year, when the corporation knows the exact amount of its taxable income, the company accountant makes an adjusting entry either for the amount of the additional tax owed or for the amount of the tax overpaid. Assume that additional tax is owed; in general journal form, the entries look like this:

DATE	DESCRIPTION	POST. REF.	DEBIT	CREDIT
	Income Tax Expense		10 0 0 0 00	
	Cash			10 0 0 0 00
	Installments paid quarterly.			
	Adjusting Entry			
	Income Tax Expense		9 2 0 0 00	
	Income Tax Payable			9 2 0 0 00

If the corporation owes additional taxes, it must pay the balance within two and one-half months following the close of the fiscal year when it files its income tax return. Here is what the entry for one payment would look like:

DATE	DESCRIPTION	POST. REF.	DEBIT	CREDIT
	Income Tax Payable		9 2 0 0 00	
	Cash			9 2 0 0 00
	Payment of additional tax			
	liability.			

L.O. 2   The steps in the closing process for a corporation are as follows:

1. Close revenue accounts into Income Summary.
2. Close expense accounts into Income Summary.
3. Close Income Tax into Income Summary.
4. Close Income Summary into Retained Earnings.

L.O. 3   In completing the work sheet for a corporation, the accountant first determines the amount of taxable income in the Income Statement columns. Next, the accountant backtracks to record the adjusting entry for income tax. Finally, the accountant extends all the remaining current figures into the appropriate columns and completes the work sheet.

L.O. 4   An appropriation of retained earnings is a restriction—or earmarking for a specific purpose—of the Retained Earnings account, making the amount unavailable for dividends. The entry in each case is a debit to Retained Earnings and a credit to Retained Earnings Appropriated for _____ (some specific purpose). The Retained Earnings account, by itself, is unappropriated.

L.O. 5   The entries involving cash dividends are as follows:

Retained Earnings		3 6 0 0 00	
Dividends Payable			3 6 0 0 00
Declaration of cash dividends.			

Dividends Payable		3 6 0 0 00	
Cash			3 6 0 0 00
Payments of cash dividends.			

L.O. 6   The entries involving stock dividends look like this:

Retained Earnings (number of shares × market value per share)		23 0 0 0 00	
Stock Dividend Distributable (number of shares × par value or stated value per share)			20 0 0 0 00
Premium on Common Stock (or Paid-in Capital in Excess of Stated Value)			3 0 0 0 00
Declaration of a stock dividend.			

Stock Dividend Distributable		20 0 0 0 00	
Common Stock			20 0 0 0 00
Issuance of a stock dividend.			

GLOSSARY

Appropriation of retained earnings   A portion of Retained Earnings designated for a specific purpose; the amount appropriated may not be used for cash or stock dividends.

Cash dividend   Distribution of a corporation's earnings to stockholders in the form of cash.

Conservatism   An accounting rule that means that when accountants are faced with major uncertainties as to which alternative accounting procedure to apply, they should choose the procedure that is least likely to overstate a firm's financial position.

Full disclosure   An accounting rule requiring that financial statements and their accompanying footnotes contain all information influencing a user's understanding of a firm's financial position.

Liquidating dividends   Distribution of assets to stockholders when a corporation is going out of existence or is permanently reducing the size of its operations.

Materiality   An accounting rule that refers to the importance of items that significantly affect a firm's financial position.

Minute book   A written narrative of all actions taken at official meetings of the board of directors.

Stock dividend   Distribution of a corporation's retained earnings to stockholders in the form of shares of the corporation's own stock.

Stock split   A deliberate reduction of the par value or stated value of a corporation's stock and the issuing of a proportionate number of additional shares.

Unappropriated retained earnings   The portion of Retained Earnings available for distribution as dividends to the stockholders.

QUESTIONS, EXERCISES, AND PROBLEMS
Discussion Questions

1. List the titles of the two main subdivisions of the Stockholders' Equity section of a balance sheet.
2. Classify each of the following accounts as asset, liability, stockholders' equity, revenue, or expense, and indicate the normal balance of each account:
   a. Common Stock
   b. Subscriptions Receivable, Common Stock
   c. Common Stock Subscribed
   d. Retained Earnings
   e. Paid-in Capital from Donation
   f. Organization Costs
   g. Discount on Preferred 8 Percent Stock
   h. Stock Dividend Distributable
   i. Preferred 8 Percent Stock
   j. Premium on Common Stock
3. Describe the difference between a stock dividend and a stock split.
4. What is included in the Organization Costs account? What happens to the account?
5. How does one write journal entries to eliminate the following accounts: Income Tax Payable, Income Tax Expense?

6. Why aren't stock dividends considered taxable income for the receivers of the dividends when they are received?
7. List the possible titles of five accounts within the Paid-in Capital section of a balance sheet.
8. Explain why an appropriation of retained earnings is not the same thing as setting aside cash. How does a corporation dispose of a retained earnings appropriated account, such as Retained Earnings Appropriated for Building?

Exercises

L.O. 5 **Exercise 24-1**   The dates connected with a cash dividend of $126,000 on a corporation's common stock are March 12, March 29, and April 8. Present the entries in general journal form pertaining to the declaration and payment of the dividend.

L.O. 2 **Exercise 24-2**   The stockholders of Whitman Corporation donated 3,000 shares of no-par common stock to the corporation. Later the corporation sold the stock for $10 per share. Give the journal entries for the receipt and sale of the stock.

L.O. 1,2 **Exercise 24-3**   Describe the entries recorded by letters in the T accounts below:

Income Tax Expense		Cash		Revenues		Retained Earnings	
(a)	(e)		(a)	(c)			(f)
(b)							

Income Summary		Income Tax Payable		Expenses	
(d)	(c)		(b)		(d)
(e)					
(f)					

L.O. 7 **Exercise 24-4**   A corporation's balance sheet includes the following:

Preferred 9 Percent Stock	$135,000
Preferred 9 Percent Stock Subscribed	45,000
Subscriptions Receivable, Preferred 9 Percent Stock	22,290
Discount on Preferred 9 Percent Stock	1,800
Common Stock	225,000
Paid-in Capital in Excess of Stated Value	60,000
Retained Earnings (credit balance)	82,500

a. How much of the paid-in capital is the result of the preferred 9 percent stock?
b. How much of the paid-in capital is the result of the common stock?
c. What is the total stockholders' equity?

L.O. 7   **Exercise 24-5**   Indicate the effect, if any, of each of the following transactions on total retained earnings of Sayers Company, Inc.:

a. Paid Accounts Payable.
b. Wrote off Accounts Receivable against Allowance for Doubtful Accounts.
c. Bought equipment on account, $56,000.
d. The board of directors declared a 20 percent stock dividend to be issued thirty days from the present date.
e. The board of directors voted to appropriate $97,000 for future expansion.
f. Issued 3,000 shares of $20 par-value common stock, receiving $29 per share.
g. Issued the stock dividend declared in transaction **d**.

L.O. 6   **Exercise 24-6**   On December 31, the stockholders' equity of Harris Radiator Repair Company, Inc., is as follows:

Paid-in Capital:			
Common Stock, no par, stated value $30 per			
share (20,000 shares authorized, 17,000			
shares issued)	$ 510 0 0 0 00		
Paid-in Capital in Excess of Stated Value	76 5 0 0 00		
Total Paid-in Capital		$ 586 5 0 0 00	
Retained Earnings:			
Appropriated for Contingencies	$ 90 0 0 0 00		
Unappropriated	201 0 0 0 00		
Total Retained Earnings		291 0 0 0 00	
Total Stockholders' Equity			877 5 0 0 00

On January 6 of the following year, when the stock was selling at $48 per share, the board of directors voted a 20 percent stock dividend, distributable on February 27 to stockholders of record on January 21. Give the entries to record the declaration and distribution of the dividend.

L.O. 7   **Exercise 24-7**   On January 3, the board of directors of King Oyster Company, Inc., votes to appropriate $80,000 of the corporation's unappropriated retained earnings to Retained Earnings Appropriated for Plant Expansion. This is the fourth such appropriation; it gives a balance of $320,000 in Retained Earnings Appropriated for Plant Expansion. On October 11, the corporation buys a warehouse for $344,000 (building, $316,000; land, $28,000), paying $144,000 down and financing the remainder on a mortgage note. Write the entries to record the following:

a. The appropriation of retained earnings on January 3
b. The purchase of the building and land on October 11
c. The release of $320,000 of the Retained Earnings Appropriated for Plant Expansion on October 12

L.O. 7   **Exercise 24-8**   Prepare the Stockholders' Equity section of the balance sheet from the following account balances:

Retained Earnings	$140,000
Subscriptions Receivable, Preferred 10 Percent Stock	40,000
Common Stock, $50 par (20,000 shares authorized)	600,000
Preferred 10 Percent Stock, $100 par (1,000 shares authorized)	40,000
Premium on Common Stock	48,000
Preferred 10 Percent Stock Subscribed	40,000

Problem Set A

L.O. 1,4,5,6   **Problem 24-1A**   Some of the transactions of Alamo Air Service, Inc., during this year are as follows:

Mar. 15 Paid balance due on previous year's federal income tax, $22,500.

Apr. 15 Paid $38,520 for the first quarterly installment of estimated federal income tax for this year.

June 15 Paid $38,520 for the second quarterly installment of estimated federal income tax for this year.

July 12 Declared a cash dividend of $50,400 ($5.04 per share on 10,000 shares, $60 par value) to stockholders of record as of July 22, payable on August 7.

Aug. 7 Paid the cash dividend.

Sept. 15 Paid $38,520 for the third quarterly installment of estimated federal income tax for this year.

18 Declared 10 percent stock dividend on the common stock outstanding to stockholders of record as of September 28, payable on October 6. Current market value of stock: $74 per share.

Oct. 6 Issued stock comprising the stock dividend.

Nov. 14 Declared a cash dividend of $55,440 ($5.04 per share on 11,000 shares) to stockholders of record as of November 30, payable on December 8.

Dec. 8 Paid the cash dividend.

15 Paid $38,520 for the fourth quarterly installment of estimated federal income tax for this year.

31 The board of directors authorized the appropriation of retained earnings for contingencies, $14,400.

31 Recorded $43,920 additional federal income tax allocable to taxable income for the year.

Instructions

Record these transactions in general journal form.

L.O. 3,7   **Problem 24-2A**   The trial balance of Brandon Beauty Supply, Inc., dated December 31 of this year, is shown on the next page.

     To reduce the number of accounts in the trial balance, Selling Expenses (control) is used in place of all selling expenses. Likewise, General Expenses (control) is used in place of all general expenses.

Brandon Beauty Supply, Inc.
Trial Balance
December 31, 19–

ACCOUNT NAME	DEBIT	CREDIT
Cash	14 0 4 0 00	
Notes Receivable	28 9 2 0 00	
Accounts Receivable	315 0 4 8 00	
Allowance for Doubtful Accounts		5 3 8 2 00
Subscriptions Receivable, Preferred 9 Percent Stock	25 8 0 0 00	
Merchandise Inventory	560 2 2 0 00	
Prepaid Insurance	2 5 9 2 00	
Equipment	170 2 2 0 00	
Accumulated Depreciation, Equipment		32 1 9 0 00
Organization Costs	19 2 0 0 00	
Accounts Payable		146 2 9 8 00
Preferred 9 Percent Stock ($100 par)		150 0 0 0 00
Preferred 9 Percent Stock Subscribed		30 0 0 0 00
Premium on Preferred 9 Percent Stock		6 6 0 0 00
Common Stock ($20 stated value)		300 0 0 0 00
Paid-in Capital in Excess of Stated Value		36 0 0 0 00
Retained Earnings		156 0 0 0 00
Sales		3 535 2 0 0 00
Purchases	2 578 5 8 0 00	
Purchases Discount		15 6 0 0 00
Freight In	107 4 4 0 00	
Selling Expenses (control)	397 8 9 0 00	
General Expenses (control)	112 2 0 0 00	
Income Tax Expense	84 5 4 0 00	
Interest Income		3 4 2 0 00
	4 416 6 9 0 00	4 416 6 9 0 00

The corporation's charter stated authorized preferred 9 percent stock amounts to 2,000 shares and authorized common stock amounts to 20,000 shares.

Data for the adjustments are as follows:

a.–b. Merchandise Inventory, December 31 (ending inventory), $576,570.
  c. Additional depreciation of equipment for the year amounts to $12,870; record depreciation under Selling Expenses (control).
  d. Insurance expired during the year, $1,542; record insurance expired under General Expenses (control).
  e. Analysis of Accounts Receivable indicates $10,560 is uncollectible; record estimated bad debt losses under General Expenses (control).
  f. Accrued interest on Notes Receivable, $360.
  g. Additional income tax due for this year, $25,680.
  h. No dividends were declared during the year.

Instructions

1. Record the trial balance on the work sheet (leave two lines for General Expenses control) and complete the work sheet for the year.
2. Prepare an income statement.
3. Prepare a statement of retained earnings.
4. Prepare a classified balance sheet.

L.O. 2,4,5,6,7 **Problem 24-3A**   The Stockholders' Equity section of the balance sheet of Lido Auto Wholesale, Inc., as of January 1 is as follows:

Stockholders' Equity			
Paid-in Capital:			
Preferred 9 Percent Stock $109 par (4,000			
shares authorized, 2,250 shares issued)	$ 225 0 0 0 00		
Premium on Preferred 9 Percent Stock	9 0 0 0 00	$ 234 0 0 0 00	
Common Stock, no par, stated value			
$20 per share (23,000 shares authorized,			
18,000 shares issued)	$ 360 0 0 0 00		
Paid-in Capital in Excess of Stated Value	180 0 0 0 00	540 0 0 0 00	
Total Paid-in Capital		$ 774 0 0 0 00	
Retained Earnings:			
Unappropriated Retained Earnings	$ 191 2 5 0 00		
Appropriated for Expansion	40 5 0 0 00		
Total Retained Earnings		231 7 5 0 00	
Total Stockholders' Equity			1 005 7 5 0 00

Some of the transactions that took place during the year are:

Feb.   24 Declared the regular semiannual $4.50 per share dividend on the preferred stock and a $1.00 per share dividend on the common stock to stockholders of record on March 15, payable on March 23.

Mar.   23 Paid cash dividend declared on February 24.
        27 Received subscriptions to 1,000 shares of common stock at $31 per share, collecting 60 percent of the subscription price.

Apr.   19 Subscribers to 1,000 shares of common stock paid the remaining 40 percent of the subscription price; Lido Auto Wholesale, Inc., then issued the 1,000 shares.

Aug.   24 Declared the regular semiannual $4.50 per share dividend on the preferred stock and $1.20 per share dividend on the common stock to stockholders of record on September 15, payable September 23.

Sept.   23 Paid cash dividends declared on August 24.
Dec.   20 Declared a 10 percent stock dividend on common stock outstanding to stockholders of record on January 15, payable January 23. Fair market value of the stock is $33 per share.

Dec. 31 Increased the appropriation for expansion by $20,000.

31 After the accountant has closed all revenue, expense, and Income Tax Expense accounts, the Income Summary account has a credit balance of $162,000. Closed the Income Summary account.

Instructions

1. Enter in the ledger accounts the balances appearing in the Stockholders' Equity section of the balance sheet as of January 1. In the Item column of the stock accounts, record the word *Balance* on the first line and the number of shares on the second line.
2. Journalize entries in general journal form to record the transactions that occurred during the year and post to the stockholders' equity accounts.
3. Prepare Stockholders' Equity section of balance sheet as of December 31.

L.O. 7 **Problem 24-4A** The account balances taken from the general ledger and statement of retained earnings for Rizzo Door Sales, Inc., are as follows:

a. Preferred 9 percent stock: 3,000 shares authorized, 2,400 shares issued
b. Common stock: 30,000 shares authorized, 20,400 shares issued

Accounts Payable	$294,780
Accounts Receivable	379,080
Accumulated Depreciation, Building	68,400
Accumulated Depreciation, Equipment	74,610
Allowance for Doubtful Accounts	13,860
Building	270,000
Cash	17,460
Common Stock, $15 stated value	306,000
Dividends Payable	14,400
Equipment	139,800
Income Tax Payable	43,800
Land	36,000
Merchandise Inventory	713,610
Mortgage Payable (due April 4, 1995)	126,000
Notes Receivable	36,000
Organization Costs	18,000
Paid-in Capital from Donation	36,000
Paid-in Capital in Excess of Stated Value	66,780
Preferred 9 Percent Stock, $100 par value	240,000
Preferred 9 Percent Stock Subscribed	60,000
Premium on Preferred 9 Percent Stock	3,000
Prepaid Insurance	2,580
Retained Earnings	230,700
Retained Earnings Appropriated for Inventory Losses	12,000
Retained Earnings Appropriated for Plant Expansion	24,600
Stock Dividend Distributable (1,860 shares)	27,900
Subscriptions Receivable, Preferred 9 Percent Stock	30,300

Instructions

Prepare a classified balance sheet dated December 31.

Problem Set B

L.O. 1,4,5,6   **Problem 24-1B**   Some of the transactions of the Baldwin Video Corporation during this fiscal year are as follows:

Mar.   15 Paid balance due on previous year's federal income tax, $44,940.

Apr.   15 Paid $62,100 for the first quarterly installment of estimated federal income tax for current year.

June   15 Paid $62,100 for the second quarterly installment of estimated federal income tax for current year.

July   16 Declared a cash dividend of $68,400 ($6.84 per share on 10,000 shares, $75 par value) to stockholders of record as of July 31, payable August 10.

Aug.   10 Paid cash dividend.

Sept.   15 Declared a 10 percent stock dividend on common stock outstanding to stockholders of record as of September 30, payable on October 9. Current market value of stock: $108 per share (10,000 shares outstanding before stock dividend).

      15 Paid $62,100 for the third quarterly installment of estimated federal income tax for this year.

Oct.   9 Issued stock comprising stock dividend.

Nov.   17 Declared a cash dividend of $79,200 ($7.20 per share on 11,000 shares) to stockholders of record as of November 30, payable on December 9.

Dec.   9 Paid cash dividend.

      15 Paid $62,100 for fourth quarterly installment of estimated federal income tax for this year.

      31 The board of directors authorized the appropriation of retained earnings for plant expansion, $29,400.

      31 Recorded $43,920 additional federal income tax allocable to taxable income for the year.

Instructions

Record the above transactions in general journal form.

L.O. 3,7   **Problem 24-2B**   The trial balance for Bell Luggage, Inc., dated April 30 of this year, is shown on the next page.

    To reduce the number of accounts in the trial balance, Selling Expenses (control) is used in place of all selling expenses. Likewise, General Expenses (control) is used in place of all general expenses.

    The corporation's charter stated authorized preferred 8 percent stock amounts to 1,400 shares and authorized common stock amounts to 20,000 shares.

    Data for the adjustments are as follows:

a.–b. Merchandise Inventory, May 31 (ending inventory), $582,660.

Bell Luggage, Inc.
Trial Balance
May 31, 19–

ACCOUNT NAME	DEBIT	CREDIT
Cash	11 748 00	
Accounts Receivable	346 230 00	
Allowance for Doubtfuı Accounts		5 598 00
Subscriptions Receivable, Common Stock	78 000 00	
Merchandise Inventory	569 010 00	
Store Supplies	1 890 00	
Store Equipment	218 040 00	
Accumulated Depreciation, Store Equipment		34 860 00
Organization Costs	16 260 00	
Notes Payable		30 000 00
Accounts Payable		153 120 00
Preferred 8 Percent Stock ($100 par)		120 000 00
Premium on Preferred 8 Percent Stock		6 000 00
Common Stock ($20 par value)		330 000 00
Common Stock Subscribed		90 000 00
Premium on Common Stock		42 000 00
Retained Earnings		154 800 00
Sales		3 048 900 00
Purchases	2 104 183 00	
Purchases Discount		15 960 00
Freight In	83 117 00	
Selling Expenses (control)	402 912 00	
General Expenses (control)	114 798 00	
Interest Expense	4 620 00	
Income Tax Expense	80 430 00	
	4 031 238 00	4 031 238 00

c. Additional depreciation of store equipment for the year amounts to $12,390; record depreciation expense under Selling Expenses (control).

d. Inventory of store supplies at May 31, $1,302. Use Selling Expenses (control).

e. Analysis of Accounts Receivable indicates $10,470 is uncollectible; record estimated bad debt losses under General Expenses (control).

f. Accrued interest on Notes Payable, $420.

g. Additional income tax due for the current year, $28,260.

h. No dividends were declared during the year.

Instructions

1. Record the trial balance on the work sheet (leave two lines for Selling Expenses control) and complete the work sheet for the year.
2. Prepare an income statement.
3. Prepare a statement of retained earnings.
4. Prepare a classified balance sheet.

L.O. 2,4,5,6,7   **Problem 24-3B**   The Stockholders' Equity section of the balance sheet of Peters Western Wear, Inc., as of January 1 is as follows:

Stockholders' Equity				
Paid-in Capital:				
Preferred 9 Percent Stock, $100 par (8,000 shares	$ 675 0 0 0 00			
authorized, 6,750 shares issued)	27 0 0 0 00	$ 702 0 0 0 00		
Premium on Preferred 9 Percent Stock				
Common Stock, no par, stated value $20 per				
share (90,000 shares authorized, 54,000 shares				
issued)	$ 1 080 0 0 0 00			
Paid-in Capital in Excess of Stated Value	324 0 0 0 00	1 404 0 0 0 00		
Total Paid-in Capital		$2 106 0 0 0 00		
Retained Earnings:				
Unappropriated Retained Earnings	$ 630 0 0 0 00			
Appropriated for Expansion	126 0 0 0 00			
Total Retained Earnings		756 0 0 0 00		
Total Stockholders' Equity			2 862 0 0 0 00	

Some of the transactions that took place during the year are:

May   10   Declared the regular semiannual $4.50 per share dividend on the preferred stock and a $1.30 per share dividend on the common stock to stockholders of record on June 1, payable on June 10.

June   2   Received subscriptions to 9,000 shares of common stock at $27 per share, collecting 70 percent of the subscription price.

           10   Paid cash dividends declared on May 10.

           26   Subscribers to 9,000 shares of common stock paid the remaining 30 percent of the subscription price; Peters Western Wear then issued the 9,000 shares.

Nov.   10   Declared the regular semiannual $4.50 per share dividend on the preferred stock and a $1.50 per share dividend on the common stock to stockholders of record on December 1, payable on December 10.

Dec.   10   Paid cash dividends declared on November 10.

           27   Declared a 5 percent stock dividend on common stock outstanding to stockholders of record on January 14, payable on January 30. Current market value of the stock is $28 per share.

           31   Increased the appropriation for expansion by $50,000.

           31   After the accountant has closed all revenue, expense, and Income Tax Expense accounts, the Income Summary account has a credit balance of $333,000. Closed the Income Summary account.

Instructions

1. Enter in the ledger accounts the balances appearing in the Stockholders' Equity section of the balance sheet as of January 1. In the Item column of the stock accounts, record the word *Balance* on the first line and the number of shares on the second line.
2. Journalize entries in general journal form to record the transactions that occurred during the year and post to the stockholders' equity accounts.
3. Prepare Stockholders' Equity section of balance sheet as of December 31.

L.O. 7   **Problem 24-4B**   Here are the account balances taken from the general ledger and statement of retained earnings for Bristolware, Inc.:

a. Preferred 9 percent stock: 3,000 shares authorized, 2,280 shares issued
b. Common stock: 40,000 shares authorized, 36,000 shares issued

Accounts Payable	$ 338,280
Accounts Receivable	487,290
Accumulated Depreciation, Building	187,200
Accumulated Depreciation, Equipment	102,600
Allowance for Doubtful Accounts	16,920
Building	360,000
Cash	26,130
Common Stock, $15 stated value	540,000
Dividends Payable	24,600
Equipment	218,700
Income Tax Payable	61,800
Land	75,000
Merchandise Inventory	1,027,530
Mortgage Payable (due June 30, 1994)	145,800
Notes Receivable	37,800
Organization Costs	24,000
Paid-in Capital from Donation	21,600
Paid-in Capital in Excess of Stated Value	108,000
Preferred 9 Percent Stock, $100 par value	228,000
Preferred 9 Percent Stock Subscribed	72,000
Premium on Preferred 9 Percent Stock	6,000
Prepaid Insurance	2,880
Retained Earnings	320,100
Retained Earnings Appropriated for Inventory Losses	25,200
Retained Earnings Appropriated for Plant Expansion	48,000
Stock Dividend Distributable	49,950
Subscriptions Receivable, Preferred 9 Percent Stock	36,720

Instructions

Prepare a classified balance sheet dated December 31.

25 Corporations: Long-Term Obligations

LEARNING OBJECTIVES

After you have completed this chapter, you will be able to do the following:

1. Journalize transactions involving the issuance of bonds at a premium or discount.

2. Journalize adjusting entries for amortization of bond premiums and discounts and accrued interest payable.

3. Journalize entries pertaining to the establishment of a bond sinking fund, the receipt of income from sinking fund investments, and the eventual payment of the principal of the bonds.

4. Journalize transactions involving the redemption of bonds.

In our discussions of corporations, we have assumed that the company got the money it needed for building and expansion by selling stock and retaining earnings. There is another possibility: A corporation can borrow money for a long period (five to forty years) by issuing bonds. For all practical purposes, one may consider a bond to be a long-term promissory note. A **bond issue** refers to the total number of bonds that the corporation issues at the same time. Bonds are issued in denominations of $1,000 or $5,000 each, with $1,000 being the most common. You can get a better picture of bonds by comparing them with capital stock.

Bonds	Capital Stock
Bondholders are creditors; they receive interest and are eventually repaid the principal.	Stockholders are owners; they receive dividends.
Bonds Payable is classified as a long-term liability account.	Capital stock is subdivided into Common Stock and Preferred Stock accounts, which are stockholders' equity accounts. (continued)

Bonds	Capital Stock
Interest paid on bonds is a valid expense, which must be paid year after year. Otherwise, bondholders may initiate bankruptcy proceedings against the debtor corporation.	Dividends are distributions of net income, rather than expenses.
Interest expense is deducted to arrive at net income.	Dividends are not deducted to arrive at net income.

CLASSIFICATION OF BONDS

To appeal to investors, corporations have created a wide variety of bonds, each with slightly different combinations of characteristics, just as automobile manufacturers offer different models with various combinations of accessories.

Bonds Classified as to Time of Payment

- **Term bonds** All term bonds have the same term or time period. Thus the entire issue of bonds comes due at the same time. For example, $1,000,000 worth of 10-year bonds issued January 1, 1987, all mature January 1, 1997.
- **Serial bonds** Serial bonds have a series of maturity dates. For example, $1,000,000 worth of bonds issued March 1, 1988, may mature as follows:

$100,000 on March 1, 1993	$100,000 on March 1, 1998
$100,000 on March 1, 1994	$100,000 on March 1, 1999
$100,000 on March 1, 1995	$100,000 on March 1, 2000
$100,000 on March 1, 1996	$100,000 on March 1, 2001
$100,000 on March 1, 1997	$100,000 on March 1, 2002

Bonds Classified as to Ownership

- **Registered bonds** When bonds are registered, the names of the owners are recorded with the issuing corporation. Title to such bonds is transferred when the bonds are sold, just as title to stock is transferred. The corporation pays interest by mailing checks to the registered owners.
- **Coupon bonds** These bonds derive their name from the interest coupons attached to each bond. The interest coupons are payable to bearer, in much the same manner as paper money is. The owners'

names may or may not be listed for the amount of the principal. Figure 25-1 shows the format of a coupon bond.

FIGURE 25-1

Atlas Corporation Bond
$1,000, 20 years, 8 percent
Payable semiannually, April 1 and October 1

$40 Apr. 1, 2006	$40 Oct. 1, 2005	$40 Apr. 1, 2005	$40 Oct. 1, 2004
$40 Apr. 1, 2004	$40 Oct. 1, 2003	$40 Apr. 1, 2003	$40 Oct. 1, 2002
$40 Apr. 1, 1992	$40 Oct. 1, 1991	$40 Apr. 1, 1991	$40 Oct. 1, 1990
$40 Apr. 1, 1990	$40 Oct. 1, 1989	$40 Apr. 1, 1989	$40 Oct. 1, 1988
$40 Apr. 1, 1988	$40 Oct. 1, 1987	$40 Apr. 1, 1987	$40 Oct. 1, 1986

The corporation pays the interest every six months, and each coupon is worth $40. The owner of the bond clips the coupons as they become due and deposits them with a regular commercial bank for collection.

Bonds Classified as to Security

- **Secured bonds** When a bond is secured, it is covered or backed up by mortgages on real estate or by titles to personal property. It may be called a mortgage bond or an equipment trust bond. In case the corporation defaults in its payment of principal or interest, the bondholders, acting through a trustee, may take over the pledged assets.
- **Unsecured bonds** An unsecured bond, also called a **debenture,** is one that is issued just on the corporation's credit standing. Such bonds usually succeed only when issued by financially strong firms.

A bond can have characteristics of all three classifications. For example, if a corporation issues twenty-year mortgage bonds with coupons providing for the payment of interest, the bonds are term bonds, coupon bonds, and secured bonds.

WHY A CORPORATION ISSUES BONDS

A corporation that needs money on a long-term basis has the choice of raising the necessary funds by issuing (1) common stock, (2) preferred stock, or (3) bonds. Each choice has advantages and disadvantages. Since the holders of common stock control the corporation through their voting power, the choice of means of financing is up to them. Stockholders think about the pros and cons of bonds as follows.

Advantages of Issuing Bonds

Bonds offer these advantages:

1. The bond-issuing corporation has the prospect of earning a greater return on the money it raises than it has to pay out in interest. This is known as **leverage.** For example, if a firm can borrow money at an interest rate of 8 percent and use this cash in the business to earn a net income of 15 percent after taxes, then the additional earnings of 7 percent (15 percent − 8 percent) are available to pay dividends to the holders of common stock. Thus, debt is used as a *lever* to raise the owner's rate of return.
2. Interest payments are tax-deductible expenses.
3. Bondholders cannot vote, so common stockholders can retain control of the company's affairs.

Disadvantages of Issuing Bonds

On the other hand, these disadvantages have to be considered:

1. Bondholders are creditors of the corporation, so interest payments must be made to bondholders each year. In contrast, a corporation pays dividends to stockholders only when it has enough money to do so and when the board of directors declares a dividend.
2. The corporation must eventually pay back the principal of the bonds it issues, but it does not have to repay the money it receives from issuing stock.

When a corporation is trying to decide whether to issue additional stock or to issue bonds, an important factor is estimated future earnings and the probable stability of these earnings. The advantages and disadvantages of issuing bonds become apparent in the following example.

Boyer Sand and Gravel, which has 40,000 shares of $50 par-value common stock outstanding ($2,000,000), wishes to raise an additional $1,000,000 for expansion. Boyer is considering three possible ways of raising the money:

- **Plan 1** Issue an additional $1,000,000 of common stock, thereby increasing the total stock outstanding from 40,000 to 60,000 shares.
- **Plan 2** Issue $1,000,000 of 8 percent cumulative preferred stock.
- **Plan 3** Issue $1,000,000 of 7 percent bonds.

Figure 25-2 shows how Boyer Sand and Gravel comes out (1) if it has a yearly income from operations of $420,000 and (2) if it has a yearly income from operations of $60,000. (We assume that the combined federal and state income taxes amount to 40 percent.)

	Income from Operations: $420,000			Income from Operations: $60,000		
	Plan 1	Plan 2	Plan 3	Plan 1	Plan 2	Plan 3
Common Stock now outstanding (40,000 shares)	$2,000,000	$2,000,000	$2,000,000	$2,000,000	$2,000,000	$2,000,000
Additional Common Stock, $50 par (20,000 shares)	1,000,000			1,000,000		
Preferred Stock, 8%, cumulative		1,000,000			1,000,000	
Bonds, 7%			1,000,000			1,000,000
Total Capitalization	$3,000,000	$3,000,000	$3,000,000	$3,000,000	$3,000,000	$3,000,000
Income from Operations (Before Income Tax)	$ 420,000	$ 420,000	$ 420,000	$ 60,000	$ 60,000	$ 60,000
Deduct Bond Interest Expense	0	0	70,000	0	0	70,000
Income (Loss) Before Taxes	$ 420,000	$ 420,000	$ 350,000	$ 60,000	$ 60,000	$ (10,000)
Deduct Federal and State Income Taxes (40%)	168,000	168,000	140,000	24,000	24,000	0
Net Income	$ 252,000	$ 252,000	$ 210,000	$ 36,000	$ 36,000	$ (10,000)
Deduct Preferred Dividends		80,000			80,000	
Earnings Available to Common Shareholders	$ 252,000	$ 172,000	$ 210,000	$ 36,000	$ (44,000)	$ (10,000)
Earnings Available to Common Shareholders	$ 252,000	$ 172,000	$ 210,000	$ 36,000	$ (44,000)	$ (10,000)
Common Stock Shares Outstanding	60,000	40,000	40,000	60,000	40,000	40,000
Earnings per Share of Common Stock	$4.20	$4.30	$5.25	$.60	$(1.10)	$(.25)

FIGURE 25-2

You can see that plan 3 offers the greatest advantage to the original holders of common stock, provided that the company's earnings are large enough to pay the bondholders and still leave a sizable share for the holders of common stock. When the company has a *low* level of earnings, plan 1 is most advantageous to the holders of common stock because there are no prior claims of bondholders or preferred stockholders. The firm can use a combination of the three, but this entails bigger underwriting or financing costs.

ACCOUNTING FOR THE ISSUANCE OF BONDS

Objective 1

Journalize transactions involving the issuance of bonds at a premium or discount.

When a corporation issues bonds at face value, it records the transaction as a debit to Cash and a credit to Bonds Payable. Bonds Payable is a long-term liability account. If there is more than one bond issue, the company keeps a separate account for each. The listing in the balance sheet should identify the issue by stipulating its interest rate and due date.

Remember

Bonds Payable is a long-term liability. It has a normal credit balance.

Bonds Sold at a Premium

The corporation may receive a price for its bonds that is above or below their face value, depending on the rate of interest offered and the general credit standing of the company. If a corporation offers a rate of interest that is higher than the market rate for similar securities, investors may be willing to pay a **premium** for the bonds.

For example, on January 1, Eppler Construction Corporation issues $500,000 of 10 percent, 10-year bonds at 104, with interest payable semiannually, on June 30 and December 31. The term "104" refers to the price of the bonds; it is a percentage of the face value of the bonds, with the percent symbol omitted. This is how people record bond prices. In this example, $500,000 of bonds at 104 means 104 percent of $500,000 ($500,000 × 1.04 = $520,000). [If $1,000,000 worth of bonds, say, had been sold at 106, the price received would have been $1,060,000 ($1,000,000 × 1.06 = $1,060,000).] Eppler's entry to record the sale of the bonds, in general journal form, is as follows:

	DATE		DESCRIPTION	POST. REF.	DEBIT	CREDIT	
1	19–						1
2	Jan.	1	Cash		520 0 0 0 00		2
3			Bonds Payable			500 0 0 0 00	3
4			Premium on Bonds Payable			20 0 0 0 00	4
5			Sold 10-year, 10 percent				5
6			bonds, dated January 1,				6
7			19–, at 104.				7

Premium on Bonds Payable represents the amount received over and above the face value of the bonds. The accountant lists Premium on Bonds Payable right below the bond account in the Long-Term Liabilities section of the balance sheet. To illustrate the placement of Bonds Payable and Premium on Bonds Payable, a partial balance sheet is shown below:

Long-Term Liabilities:		
10 Percent Bonds Payable, due January		
1, 19–	$500 0 0 0 00	
Add Premium on Bonds Payable	20 0 0 0 00	$520 0 0 0 00

The corporation will write off or amortize Premium on Bonds Payable over the remaining life of the bond issue. The entries to pay the interest on the bonds, in general journal form, are shown here:

	DATE		DESCRIPTION	POST. REF.	DEBIT	CREDIT	
1	*19–*						1
2	*June*	*30*	*Interest Expense*		25 0 0 0 00		2
3			*Cash*			25 0 0 0 00	3
4			*Semiannual interest payment*				4
5			*on bonds, face value of*				5
6			*$500,000, 10 percent.*				6
7							7
8							8
9							9
10							10

	DATE		DESCRIPTION	POST. REF.	DEBIT	CREDIT	
1	*19–*						1
2	*Dec.*	*31*	*Interest Expense*		25 0 0 0 00		2
3			*Cash*			25 0 0 0 00	3
4			*Semiannual interest payment*				4
5			*on bonds, face value of*				5
6			*$500,000, 10 percent.*				6
7							7
8							8
9							9
10							10

Adjusting Entry for Bonds Sold at a Premium

Objective 2

Journalize adjusting entries for amortization of bond premiums and discounts and accrued interest payable.

Just what is **amortization?** A company writes off, or *amortizes*, the Premium on Bonds Payable account over the remaining life of the bonds by debiting the account and using Interest Expense as the offsetting credit. The entry appears as an adjusting entry at the end of the fiscal period. It is first recorded in the Adjustments columns of the work sheet, like any other adjusting entry. (The calculation is recorded here purely as a means of explanation.)

	DATE		DESCRIPTION	POST. REF.	DEBIT	CREDIT	
1	*19–*		*Adjusting Entry*				1
2	*Dec.*	*31*	*Premium on Bonds Payable*		2 0 0 0 00		2
3			*Interest Expense ($20,000 ÷*				3
4			*10 years)*			2 0 0 0 00	4
5							5

By T accounts, the entries look like this:

	Cash		
	+	−	
Jan. 1	520,000	June 30	25,000
		Dec. 31	25,000

	Bonds Payable	
−		+
	Jan. 1	500,000

	Interest Expense		
	+	−	
June 30	25,000	Dec. 31 Adj.	2,000
Dec. 31	25,000		

	Premium on Bonds Payable		
−		+	
Dec. 31 Adj.	2,000	Jan. 1	20,000

The adjusting entry reduces the balance of the Interest Expense account from $50,000 to $48,000. The accountant then closes Interest Expense into Income Summary in the amount of $48,000.

In this illustration, we showed the amortization of the bond premium calculated by the straight-line method on an annual basis, which will also be used in the problems. As you can probably see, this is like calculating depreciation by the straight-line method. One can also record the amortization of the bond premium, just as one can record depreciation, on a monthly basis. It should be mentioned, however, that many corporations amortize premiums and discounts on bonds using the effective interest rate method. This method is covered in more advanced accounting courses.

Getting back to our illustration, after the accountant records the adjusting entry, the balance of Interest Expense is $48,000. This amount represents the annual interest expense on the books. Here is another way of looking at it:

Cash to be paid

Face value of the bonds	$500,000	
Interest (20 payments of $25,000 each)	500,000	$1,000,000

Less cash received

Face value of the bonds	$500,000	
Premium on the bonds	20,000	520,000

Remember

Excess of cash to be paid over cash received

(Interest expense for 10 years) $ 480,000

A premium reduces a corporation's total interest expense over the life of the bond.

$$\text{Interest expense per year} = \frac{\$480,000}{10 \text{ years}} = \underline{\$48,000}$$

Bonds Sold at a Discount

When a corporation issues bonds that will pay a rate of interest that is less than the prevailing market rate of interest for comparable bonds, it sells its bonds at less than face value—or at a **discount**.

To demonstrate this, assume that on January 1, Lakeside Motor Inn issues 6 percent, 20-year bonds with a face value of $100,000, at 96, with interest to be paid semiannually on June 30 and December 31.

	DATE		DESCRIPTION	POST. REF.	DEBIT	CREDIT	
1	19–						1
2	Jan.	1	Cash		96 0 0 0 00		2
3			Discount on Bonds Payable		4 0 0 0 00		3
4			Bonds Payable			100 0 0 0 00	4
5			Sold 20-year bonds, 6 percent,				5
6			dated January 1, 19–, at 96.				6

Discount on Bonds Payable is a **contra-liability account**; it is listed on a classified balance sheet as a deduction from Bonds Payable. On a balance sheet, Discount on Bonds Payable is shown like this:

Long-Term Liabilities:		
6 Percent Bonds Payable, due January		
1, 19–	$100 0 0 0 00	
Less Discount on Bonds Payable	4 0 0 0 00	$96 0 0 0 00

The entries, in general journal form, for the payment of interest are as follows:

	DATE		DESCRIPTION	POST. REF.	DEBIT	CREDIT	
1	June	30	Interest Expense		3 0 0 0 00		1
2			Cash			3 0 0 0 00	2
3			Semiannual interest on				3
4			bonds, face value of				4
5			$100,000, 6 percent.				5
6							6
7							7
8							8
9							9

	DATE		DESCRIPTION	POST. REF.	DEBIT	CREDIT	
1	Dec.	31	Interest Expense		3 0 0 0 00		1
2			Cash			3 0 0 0 00	2
3			Semiannual interest on				3
4			bonds, face value of				4
5			$100,000, 6 percent.				5
6							6
7							7
8							8
9							9

Adjusting Entry for Bonds Sold at a Discount

The corporation writes off or amortizes the Discount on Bonds Payable account, as it does the Premium on Bonds Payable account, over the remaining life of the bond issue. The write-off consists of an adjusting entry at the end of the fiscal period. Again, the accountant uses Interest Expense as the offsetting account in the adjusting entry. The adjusting entry, taken from the Adjustments columns of the work sheet, is shown here.

	DATE		DESCRIPTION	POST. REF.	DEBIT	CREDIT	
1			*Adjusting Entry*				1
2	Dec.	31	Interest Expense ($4,000 ÷ 20 years)		2 0 0 00		2
3			Discount on Bonds Payable			2 0 0 00	3
4							4
5							5
6							6
7							7

By T accounts, the entries look like this:

Cash			
+		−	
Jan. 1	96,000	June 30	3,000
		Dec. 31	3,000

Bonds Payable			
−		+	
		Jan. 1	100,000

Interest Expense		
+		−
June 30	3,000	
Dec. 31	3,000	
Dec. 31 Adj.	200	

Discount on Bonds Payable			
+		−	
Jan. 1	4,000	Dec. 31 Adj.	200

The adjusting entry increases the balance of Interest Expense from $6,000 to $6,200. The accountant then closes Interest Expense into Income Summary in the amount of $6,200.

The adjustment for Discount on Bonds Payable results in an increase in the Interest Expense account. Here is how it works:

Remember

A discount increases a corporation's total interest expense over the life of the bonds.

Cash to be paid		
Face value of the bonds	$100,000	
Interest (40 payments of $3,000 each)	120,000	$220,000
Less cash received		
Face value of the bonds	$100,000	
Less discount on the bonds	4,000	96,000
Excess of cash to be paid over cash received		
(Interest expense for 20 years)		$124,000

$$\text{Interest expense per year} = \frac{\$124,000}{20 \text{ years}} = \underline{\underline{\$6,200}}$$

Example: Bonds sold at a premium, whose interest payment dates do not coincide with the end of fiscal year On March 1, Day Fast Freight issues $1,000,000 worth of 20-year, 9 percent bonds, at 103, dated March 1, with interest payable semiannually on September 1 and March 1. The corporation's fiscal year ends on December 31. A diagram of the dates looks like this:

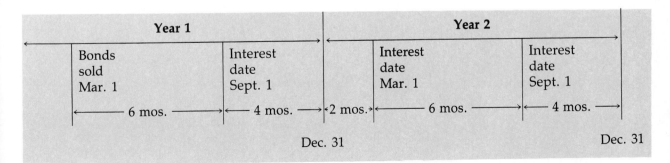

Year 1		Year 2	
Bonds sold Mar. 1	Interest date Sept. 1	Interest date Mar. 1	Interest date Sept. 1
←—— 6 mos. ——→	←— 4 mos. —→ ‹2 mos.›	←—— 6 mos. ——→	←— 4 mos. —→
	Dec. 31		Dec. 31

Since the date on which the interest has to be paid does not coincide with the end of the fiscal year, Day Fast Freight has to make an adjusting entry for the accrued interest for the period from September 1 to December 31. The entries for the first year, in general journal form, are as follows:

	DATE		DESCRIPTION	POST. REF.	DEBIT	CREDIT	
1	Year 1						1
2	Mar.	1	Cash		1,030 0 0 0 00		2
3			Bonds Payable			1,000 0 0 0 00	3
4			Premium on Bonds Payable			30 0 0 0 00	4
5			Sold 20-year bonds,				5
6			9 percent, dated				6
7			March 1, at 103.				7
8							8
9							9

	DATE		DESCRIPTION	POST. REF.	DEBIT	CREDIT	
1	Year 1						1
2	Sept.	1	Interest Expense		45 0 0 0 00		2
3			Cash			45 0 0 0 00	3
4			Semiannual interest on				4
5			bonds ($1,000,000, 9 percent,				5
6			6 months).				6

	DATE		DESCRIPTION	POST. REF.	DEBIT	CREDIT	
1	Year 1		*Adjusting Entries*				1
2	Dec.	31	Premium on Bonds Payable		1 2 5 0 00		2
3			Interest Expense ($30,000 ×				3
4			$\frac{10\ months}{240\ months}$)			1 2 5 0 00	4
5							5
6		31	Interest Expense		30 0 0 0 00		6
7			Interest Payable			30 0 0 0 00	7
8			($1,000,000, 9 percent,				8
9			4 months.)				9
10							10
11			*Closing Entry*				11
12		31	Income Summary		73 7 5 0 00		12
13			Interest Expense			73 7 5 0 00	13
14							14
15							15
16							16

The amortization of the premium on December 31 is for only a part of a year. The next year, however, amortization will be for a full year. The adjusting entry for accrued interest on a bond is like the one for accrued interest on an interest-bearing note payable. In T account form the first-year entries look like this:

Cash

+		−	
Year 1		Year 1	
Mar. 1	1,030,000	Sept. 1	45,000

Interest Expense

+		−	
Year 1		Year 1	
Sept. 1	45,000	Dec. 31 Adj.	1,250
Dec. 31 Adj.	30,000	Dec. 31 Clos.	73,750

Income Summary

Year 1			
(Int. Exp.)	73,750	Closed	

Bonds Payable

−		+	
		Year 1	
		Mar. 1	1,000,000

Premium on Bonds Payable

−		+	
Year 1		Year 1	
Dec. 31 Adj.	1,250	Mar. 1	30,000

Interest Payable

−		+	
		Year 1	
		Dec. 31 Adj.	30,000

Because the adjusting entry for accrued interest opened a new balance sheet account, Interest Payable, Day's accountant has to make a reversing entry as of the first day of the next fiscal year. The reversing entry enables the accountant to follow the regular routine for the payment of six month's interest on March 1 without having to split up the interest over the period between September 1 of one year and March 1 of the following year.

DATE	DESCRIPTION	POST. REF.	DEBIT	CREDIT	
Year 2	Reversing Entry				1
Jan. 1	Interest Payable		30 0 0 0 00		2
	Interest Expense			30 0 0 0 00	3
					4

DATE	DESCRIPTION	POST. REF.	DEBIT	CREDIT	
Year 2					1
Mar. 1	Interest Expense		45 0 0 0 00		2
	Cash			45 0 0 0 00	3
	Semiannual interest on bonds				4
	($1,000,000, 9 percent 6				5
	months).				6

	DATE	DESCRIPTION	POST. REF.	DEBIT	CREDIT	
1	Year 2					1
2	Sept. 1	Interest Expense		45 0 0 0 00		2
3		Cash			45 0 0 0 00	3
4		Semiannual interest on bonds				4
5		($1,000,000, 9 percent 6				5
6		months).				6

Remember

If the interest payment date does not happen to be the same date as the end of a corporation's fiscal period, an adjusting entry must be made at the end of the fiscal period to record the accrued bond interest expense. (It is handled the same way as accrued interest on notes payable.)

	DATE	DESCRIPTION	POST. REF.	DEBIT	CREDIT	
1	Year 2	*Adjusting Entries*				1
2	Dec. 31	Premium on Bonds Payable		1 5 0 0 00		2
3		Interest Expense ($30,000 ×				3
4		$\frac{12\ months}{240\ months}$)			1 5 0 0 00	4
5						5
6	31	Interest Expense		30 0 0 0 00		6
7		Interest Payable ($1,000,000,				7
8		9 percent, 4 months)			30 0 0 0 00	8
9						9
10		*Closing Entry*				10
11	31	Income Summary		88 5 0 0 00		11
12		Interest Expense			88 5 0 0 00	12
13						13

Here are the relevant T accounts from the previous year posted up to date:

Bonds Payable

−		+	
		Year 1 Mar. 1	1,000,000

Premium on Bonds Payable

−		+	
Year 1 Dec. 31 Adj.	1,250	Year 1 Mar. 1	30,000
Year 2 Dec. 31 Adj.	1,500		

Interest Payable

−		+	
		Year 1 Dec. 31 Adj.	30,000
Year 2 Jan. 1 Rev.	30,000	Year 2 Dec. 31 Adj.	30,000

Interest Expense

+		−	
Year 1 Sept. 1	45,000	Year 1 Dec. 31 Adj.	1,250
Dec. 31 Adj.	30,000	Dec. 31 Clos.	73,750
Year 2 Mar. 1	45,000	Year 2 Jan. 1 Rev.	30,000
Sept. 1	45,000	Dec. 31 Adj.	1,500
Dec. 31 Adj.	30,000	Dec. 31 Clos.	88,500

Income Summary

Year 1 (Int. Exp.)	73,750	Year 1 Closed	
Year 2 (Int. Exp.)	88,500	Year 2 Closed	

BOND SINKING FUND

To provide greater security for bondholders, the bond agreement may specify that the issuing corporation make annual deposits of cash into a special fund—called a **sinking fund**—to be used to pay off the bond issue when it comes due. The company keeps the sinking fund separate from its other assets and puts the cash deposited in the sinking fund to work by investing it in income-producing securities. When the bonds mature, the total of the annual deposits, plus the earnings on the investments, should add up to approximately the face value of the bonds. The sinking fund may be controlled by either the corporation or a trustee— usually a bank.

Objective 3

Journalize entries pertaining to the establishment of a bond sinking fund, the receipt of income from sinking fund investments, and the eventual payment of the principal of the bonds.

When the corporation deposits cash in its sinking fund, it records the transaction as a debit to Sinking Fund Cash and as a credit to Cash. When the corporation or the trustee invests the sinking fund cash, the transaction is recorded as a debit to Sinking Fund Investments and a credit to Sinking Fund Cash. **Both Sinking Fund Cash and Sinking Fund Investments are classified as investment accounts.** When the corporation receives interest or dividend income on the investments, it debits Sinking Fund Cash and credits Sinking Fund Income. Sinking Fund Income is classified as an Other Income account on the income statement.

For example, Davison Security Systems issues $100,000 worth of 10-year bonds dated January 1, with the provision that at the end of each of the ten years, it make equal annual deposits in a sinking fund. Davison, which manages its own sinking fund, intends to invest this money in securities that will yield approximately 6 percent per year. Let us assume that, according to compound interest tables, an annual deposit of $7,040 will accumulate to $100,000 in ten years, given the 6 percent annual interest rate.

The following are a few of the many routine transactions that affect the sinking fund during the ten-year period.

• **Annual deposits of cash in bond sinking fund**

	DATE	DESCRIPTION	POST. REF.	DEBIT	CREDIT	
1		*Sinking Fund Cash*		7 0 4 0 00		1
2		*Cash*			7 0 4 0 00	2
3		*Annual deposit in bond sinking*				3
4		*fund, according to bond*				4
5		*agreement.*				5
6						6
7						7
8						8
9						9
10						10
11						11

- **Purchase of investments** (Time of purchase and amount invested may vary.)

	DATE	DESCRIPTION	POST. REF.	DEBIT	CREDIT	
1		Sinking Fund Investments		6 9 8 0 00		1
2		Sinking Fund Cash			6 9 8 0 00	2
3		Bought $7,000 of Consolidated				3
4		Steel 7 percent bonds at 99½,				4
5		plus brokerage commission ($15).				5

- **Receipt of income from investments** (Interest and dividends are received at different times during the year.)

	DATE	DESCRIPTION	POST. REF.	DEBIT	CREDIT	
1		Sinking Fund Cash		4 9 0 00		1
2		Sinking Fund Income			4 9 0 00	2
3		Received interest and dividends				3
4		on sinking fund investments.				4

- **Sale of investments** (Investments may be sold and proceeds reinvested.)

	DATE	DESCRIPTION	POST. REF.	DEBIT	CREDIT	
1		Sinking Fund Cash		18 6 2 0 00		1
2		Sinking Fund Investments			18 4 0 0 00	2
3		Gain on Sale of Sinking Fund				3
4		Investments			2 2 0 00	4
5		Sold sinking fund investments,				5
6		yielding a profit of $220.				6

- **Payment of bonds** (Cash available consists of sinking fund after sale of investments, with addition of last annual deposit, to bring sinking fund up to $100,000.)

	DATE	DESCRIPTION	POST. REF.	DEBIT	CREDIT	
1		Bonds Payable		100 0 0 0 00		1
2		Sinking Fund Cash			100 0 0 0 00	2
3		Paid bond obligation with				3
4		sinking fund cash.				4

REDEMPTION OF BONDS

To protect itself against a decline in market interest rates, a corporation may issue **callable bonds**. Callable bonds give the corporation the right—as stipulated in the bond **indenture**, or agreement—to **redeem** or buy back the bonds at a specified figure, known as the *call price*, which is ordinarily higher than the face value.

The Dean Videocable Corporation issues $2,000,000 worth of 10 percent, 20-year, callable bonds, with a call price of 104. Later, interest rates in general go down. Under the new market conditions, Dean Videocable could sell $2,000,000 worth of bonds at par, with an interest rate of 7 percent. It would pay Dean Videocable to buy back the bonds, even though it would have to pay $2,080,000 for them ($2,000,000 × 1.04) and then turn around and issue new bonds at 7 percent. The annual savings in interest would amount to $60,000 (3 percent of $2,000,000). Even if a corporation's bonds are not callable, it may still buy its own bonds on the open market, if it can find any for sale.

Objective 4

Journalize transactions involving the redemption of bonds.

When a corporation redeems its bonds at a price less than their book value, it realizes a gain. Conversely, if it redeems its bonds at a price that is more than their book value, it incurs a loss. The book value is the sum of the Bonds Payable account and the Premium on Bonds Payable (or Discount on Bonds Payable) account.

For example, Southwest Grocery Company has $500,000 worth of callable bonds outstanding, with a call price of 105; there is an unamortized discount of $2,000. Southwest pays the interest up to date on December 31 and exercises its option of calling in or redeeming the bonds on the same date, December 31. The entry is shown in general journal form. The loss represents the difference between the book value and the price paid (also determined by the difference between debits and credits).

	DATE		DESCRIPTION	POST. REF.	DEBIT	CREDIT	
1	Dec.	31	Bonds Payable		500 0 0 0 00		1
2			Loss on Redemption of Bonds		27 0 0 0 00		2
3			Cash			525 0 0 0 00	3
4			Discount on Bonds Payable			2 0 0 0 00	4
5			To record redemption of bonds				5
6			at 105.				6
7							7

Recall that even if a corporation's bonds are not callable, the firm can buy back the bonds—all of them, or as many as it can find on the open market. For example, Dole Metal Fabricators has $1,000,000 worth of 7 percent coupon bonds outstanding, on which there is an unamortized premium of $30,000. On July 15, Dole buys $100,000 (one-tenth of the original issue) of bonds in the open market at 97, plus fifteen days' accrued interest. The entry, in general journal form, is as follows:

	DATE		DESCRIPTION	POST. REF.	DEBIT	CREDIT	
1	July	15	Bonds Payable		100 0 0 0 00		1
2			Premium on Bonds Payable		3 0 0 0 00		2
3			Interest Expense ($100,000,				3
4			7 percent, 15 days)		2 9 1 67		4
5			Cash			97 2 9 1 67	5
6			Gain on Redemption of Bonds			6 0 0 0 00	6
7			To record redemption of bonds				7
8			at 97 plus accrued interest.				8
9							9

Redemption, in effect, cancels all or a portion of the Bonds Payable account, as well as the accompanying premium or discount. **We shall list Gain (or Loss) on Redemption of Bonds in the income statement under the heading Other Income or Other Expense.** If the gains or losses are significant, they are listed (net of any related income tax effect) under the heading of **Extraordinary Items,** a classification of accounts appearing at the bottom of an income statement. Extraordinary items are unusual in nature and do not occur with any regularity.

BALANCE SHEET

The balance sheet of the D. C. Wall Company, Inc., shown in Figure 25-3, is designed to show you how to place the accounts we introduced in this chapter.

SUMMARY

A bond may be considered a corporation's long-term promissory note. A bond issue is usually subdivided into denominations of $1,000 and $5,000 each. Bondholders are creditors of the corporation; as such, they are entitled to interest payments, as well as repayment of the principal at maturity.

L.O. 1,2   A bond is sold at a premium when the stated rate of interest is *higher* than the existing market rate of interest. A bond is sold at a discount when the stated rate of interest is *lower* than the existing market rate of interest. A corporation amortizes (writes off) premiums or discounts on bonds payable over the remaining life of a bond, beginning at the time the bond is sold. The amortization is recorded as an adjusting entry.

L.O. 3,4   A bond sinking fund increases the security of the bondholders. A corporation redeems its bonds when it wishes to eliminate the debt or to refinance the debt at a lower rate of interest.

FIGURE 25-3

D. C. Wall Company, Inc.
Balance Sheet
December 31, 19–

Assets				
Current Assets:				
Cash			$ 12 0 0 0 00	
Notes Receivable			30 0 0 0 00	
Accounts Receivable	$ 220 0 0 0 00			
Less Allowance for Doubtful Accounts	4 0 0 0 00		216 0 0 0 00	
Merchandise Inventory			647 0 0 0 00	
Supplies			2 0 0 0 00	
Total Current Assets				$ 907 0 0 0 00
Investments:				
Sinking Fund Cash			$ 5 0 0 0 00	
Sinking Fund Investments			84 0 0 0 00	
Total Investments				89 0 0 0 00
Plant and Equipment:				
Land			$ 70 0 0 0 00	
Building	$ 180 0 0 0 00			
Less Accumulated Depreciation	45 0 0 0 00		135 0 0 0 00	
Equipment	$ 222 0 0 0 00			
Less Accumulated Depreciation	32 0 0 0 00		190 0 0 0 00	
Total Plant and Equipment				395 0 0 0 00
Intangible Assets:				
Goodwill			$ 20 0 0 0 00	
Organization Costs			8 0 0 0 00	
Total Intangible Assets				28 0 0 0 00
Total Assets				$1 419 0 0 0 00
Liabilities				
Current Liabilities:				
Accounts Payable			$ 70 0 0 0 00	
Income Tax Payable			8 0 0 0 00	
Dividends Payable			12 0 0 0 00	
Total Current Liabilities				$ 90 0 0 0 00
Long-Term Liabilities:				
6 percent Bonds Payable, due				
December 31, 19–	$ 100 0 0 0 00			
Less Discount on Bonds				
Payable	3 0 0 0 00		$ 97 0 0 0 00	
8 percent Bonds Payable,				
due March 31, 19–	$ 200 0 0 0 00			
Add Premium on Bonds Payable	2 0 0 0 00		202 0 0 0 00	
Total Long-Term Liabilities				299 0 0 0 00
Total Liabilities				$ 389 0 0 0 00
Stockholders' Equity				
Paid-in Capital:				
Common Stock, $10 par (100,000 shares authorized,				
40,000 shares issued)	$ 400 0 0 0 00			
Premium on Common Stock	220 0 0 0 00			
Total Paid-in Capital			$ 620 0 0 0 00	
Retained Earnings:				
Unappropriated Retained Earnings	$ 310 0 0 0 00			
Appropriated For Plant Expansion	100 0 0 0 00			
Total Retained Earnings			410 0 0 0 00	
Total Stockholders' Equity				1 030 0 0 0 00
Total Liabilities and Stockholders' Equity				$1 419 0 0 0 00

GLOSSARY

Amortization   The systematic writing off of a bond premium or discount over the remaining life of the bond.

Bond issue   The total number of bonds that a corporation issues at one time; issued in denominations of $1,000 or $5,000 each.

Callable bonds   Bonds that give the corporation the right to redeem or buy back the bonds at a specified figure, known as the *call price*.

Contra-liability account   A deduction from a liability, such as Discount on Bonds Payable, which is a deduction from the balance of Bonds Payable.

Coupon bonds   Bonds that have interest coupons attached to each bond. These coupons are payable to bearer and may be cashed on interest payment dates.

Debenture   Unsecured bond.

Discount   A bond is sold at less than its face value. The bond will pay a rate of interest less than the prevailing market rate of interest for comparable bonds.

Extraordinary Items   Significant transactions that appear at the bottom of an income statement (net of any related income tax effect) because they are unusual in nature and do not recur with any regularity. They may include gains or losses on redemption of bonds, fire losses, expropriation of property by a foreign government, or major revaluation of a foreign currency.

Indenture   A bond agreement, or contract, between the corporation and its bondholders.

Leverage   Debt used as a lever to raise the owner's rate of return, earning income on borrowed money (as, for example, borrowing money at 8 percent and using it to earn a 15 percent rate of return).

Premium   Excess between the price received and the face value of a bond.

Redeem   Buy back or repurchase bonds from bondholders.

Registered bonds   Bonds whose owners' names are registered with the corporation that issued the bonds.

Secured bonds   Bonds that are covered or backed up by mortgages on real estate or by titles to personal property that may be claimed by the bondholders in the event that the issuing corporation defaults in its payment of principal or interest.

Serial bonds   Bonds of a particular issue that have a series of maturity dates.

Sinking fund   A special fund of cash accumulated over the life of a bond issue to enable the issuing corporation to pay off the bonds when they mature (come due). The fund is kept separate from other assets, and the cash is invested in income-producing securities.

Term bonds   Bonds of a particular issue, all having the same maturity date.

Unsecured bonds   Bonds backed only by the credit standing (good name) of the issuing corporation.

QUESTIONS, EXERCISES, AND PROBLEMS
Discussion Questions

1. How is the bond premium reported on the balance sheet?
2. What is the difference between term bonds and serial bonds?
3. What is the difference between a debenture and an indenture?
4. What do accountants mean by the redemption of callable bonds? What is involved in the journal entry?
5. What are two definite obligations a corporation incurs when it issues bonds?
6. What is a bond sinking fund, and what is its purpose?
7. If the market rate of interest is higher than the rate of interest stated in the bond agreement, will the bonds be sold at a premium or a discount? Why?
8. How is a bond sinking fund classified on a balance sheet?

Exercises

L.O. 1   **Exercise 25-1**   Calculate the total selling price of bonds for the following:

a. Nine $1,000 face value bonds selling at 96 ½
b. Twenty $1,000 face value bonds selling at 103 ¼
c. Fifty $5,000 face value bonds selling at 98 ½
d. Fifteen $5,000 face value bonds selling at 106 ¾

L.O. 1   **Exercise 25-2**   The Marshall Corporation sold $100,000 of face value bonds, receiving $106,000. The Weidler Corporation sold $140,000 of face value bonds, receiving $133,000. How does the Marshall Corporation account for the $6,000 difference between the amount received and the face value? How does the Weidler Corporation account for the $7,000 difference between the amount received and the face value?

L.O. 2   **Exercise 25-3**   On the first day of its fiscal period, a corporation sells $1,000,000 of 10 percent, 10-year bonds at 103. What is the amount of annual amortization of the premium?

L.O. 2   **Exercise 25-4**   On the first day of its fiscal year, Merrill Corporation issues $900,000 of 9 percent, 20-year bonds at 102. What is the net amount of interest expense for this year?

L.O. 3,4   **Exercise 25-5**   Wickham, Inc., has outstanding $600,000 of 10-year sinking fund bonds. At the end of the ninth year after it had issued the bonds, the balance of Wickham's Sinking Fund Investments account is $556,800. List the entries to record the following:

a. The sale of the investments for $564,000
b. The final deposit in the sinking fund, bringing the balance of the account up to $600,000
c. The payment of the bonds

L.O. 1,2   **Exercise 25-6**   Describe the entries in the following T accounts:

Cash	
(1) 2,120,000	(2) 90,000

Bonds Payable	
	(1) 2,000,000

Interest Expense	
(2) 90,000	(4) 4,000
(3) 30,000	(5) 116,000
	(6) 30,000

Premium on Bonds Payable	
(4) 4,000	(1) 120,000

Interest Payable	
(6) 30,000	(3) 30,000

Income Summary	
(5) 116,000	

L.O. 1   **Exercise 25-7**   Two companies are financed as follows:

	L. A. Bourne, Inc.	S. K. Noble, Inc.
Bonds Payable, 9% (issued at face value)	$ 600,000	$ 450,000
Preferred 10% Stock, $100 par	150,000	600,000
Common Stock, $100 par	1,500,000	1,200,000
	$2,250,000	$2,250,000

Each company had an income before taxes and bond interest of $440,000. Assuming a federal corporation income tax of 34 percent, determine for each company the earnings per share on common stock.

L.O. 4   **Exercise 25-8**   The Janders Corporation has the following account balances: Bonds Payable, $1,200,000; Premium on Bonds Payable, $36,000. As a step in redeeming the bond issue, Janders buys $120,000 worth of its bonds on the open market at 96. Give the entry to record the redemption.

Problem Set A

L.O. 1,2   **Problem 25-1A**   During two consecutive years, the Hargraves Corporation completed the following transactions:

Year 1

Jan.   2 Issued $2,000,000 face value 20-year, 9 percent bonds, dated January 1 of this year, at 102. Interest is payable semiannually on June 30 and December 31.

June 30 Paid semiannual interest on bonds.

Dec.   31 Paid semiannual interest on bonds.

        31 Recorded adjusting entry for amortization of premium on bonds.

        31 Closed the Interest Expense account.

Year 2

June 30 Paid semiannual interest on bonds.

Dec.   31 Paid semiannual interest on bonds.

        31 Recorded adjusting entry for amortization of premium on bonds.

        31 Closed the Interest Expense account.

Instructions

Record the transactions in general journal form.

L.O. 1,2   **Problem 25-2A**   United Grocers, Inc., completed the following selected transactions:

Year 1

Mar.	1	Issued $800,000 of 20-year, 9 percent bonds, dated March 1 of this year, at 104. Interest is payable semiannually on September 1 and March 1.
Sept.	1	Paid semiannual interest on bonds.
Dec.	31	Recorded adjusting entry for accrued interest payable.
	31	Recorded adjusting entry for amortization of premium on bonds.
	31	Closed Interest Expense account.

Year 2

Jan.	1	Reversed adjusting entry for accrued interest payable.
Mar.	1	Paid semiannual interest on bonds.
Sept.	1	Paid semiannual interest on bonds.
Dec.	31	Made adjusting entry to record accrued interest payable.
	31	Made adjusting entry to record amortization of premium on bonds.
	31	Closed Interest Expense account.

Instructions

1. Record the transactions in general journal form.
2. Post entries to the Interest Expense account. Label the adjusting, closing, and reversing entries.

L.O. 1,2,3   **Problem 25-3A**   During two consecutive years, the Tracy Medical Clinic completed the following transactions relating to its $9,000,000 issue of 30-year, 8 percent bonds, dated April 1. Interest is payable April 1 and October 1. The corporation's fiscal year extends from January 1 through December 31.

Year 1

Apr.	1	Sold the bond issue at 97.
Oct.	1	Paid semiannual interest on bonds.
Dec.	31	Deposited $79,500 in a bond sinking fund.
	31	Made adjusting entry to record accrued interest payable.
	31	Made adjusting entry to record amortization of bond discount.
	31	Closed Interest Expense account.

Year 2

Jan.	1	Reversed adjusting entry to accrued interest payable.
	4	Bought various securities with sinking fund cash; cost, $73,940.
Apr.	1	Paid semiannual interest on bonds.
Oct.	1	Paid semiannual interest on bonds.

Dec.   31 Recorded receipt of $6,172 of income derived from sinking fund investments, depositing the cash in the sinking fund.
        31 Deposited $110,600 in bond sinking fund.
        31 Made adjusting entry to record accrued interest payable.
        31 Made adjusting entry to record amortization of bond discount.
        31 Closed Interest Expense account.

Instructions

1. Record the transactions in general journal form.
2. Post entries to the Interest Expense account and the Discount on Bonds Payable account. Label the adjusting, closing, and reversing entries.

L.O. 1,2,3 **Problem 25-4A**   On June 1, Ryan Wood Products, Inc., whose fiscal year is the calendar year, issued $12,000,000 of 20-year, 9 percent bonds, dated June 1, with interest payable on June 1 and December 1. The following transactions pertain to the bond issue for the first two years:

Year 1

June   1 Sold the bond issue at 101.
Dec.   1 Paid semiannual interest on bonds.
       31 Deposited $237,000 in a bond sinking fund.
       31 Recorded adjusting entry for accrued interest payable.
       31 Recorded adjusting entry for amortization of bond premium.
       31 Closed the Interest Expense account.

Year 2

Jan.   1 Reversed adjusting entry for accrued interest payable.
       9 Bought various securities with sinking fund cash; cost, $229,600.
June   1 Paid semiannual interest on bonds.
July   1 Recorded receipt of $8,114 of income derived from sinking fund investments, depositing the cash in the sinking fund.
       8 Bought various securities with sinking fund cash, $9,464.
Dec.   1 Paid semiannual interest on bonds.
       31 Recorded receipt of $15,992 of income derived from sinking fund investments, depositing the cash in the sinking fund.
       31 Deposited $335,000 in the bond sinking fund.
       31 Recorded adjusting entry for accrued interest payable.
       31 Recorded adjusting entry for amortization of bond premium.
       31 Closed the Sinking Fund Income account.
       31 Closed the Interest Expense account.

Instructions

1. Record the transactions in general journal form.
2. Post entries to the Interest Expense account and the Premium on Bonds Payable account. Label the appropriate entries in the ledger accounts as adjusting, closing, or reversing.

Problem Set B

L.O. 1,2 **Problem 25-1B** During two consecutive years, the Yates Printing Company, Inc., completed the following transactions:

Year 1

Jan.   1 Issued $1,000,000 face value 20-year, 7 percent bonds, dated January 1 of this year, at 96. Interest is payable semiannually on June 30 and December 31.

June   30 Paid semiannual interest on bonds.

Dec.   31 Paid semiannual interest on bonds.

         31 Recorded adjusting entry for amortization of discount on bonds.

         31 Closed Interest Expense account.

Year 2

June   30 Paid semiannual interest on bonds.

Dec.   31 Paid semiannual interest on bonds.

         31 Recorded adjusting entry for amortization of discount on bonds.

         31 Closed the Interest Expense account.

Instructions

Record the transactions in general journal form.

L.O. 1,2 **Problem 25-2B** Seaside Hotel, Inc., completed the following selected transactions:

Year 1

Apr.   1 Issued $1,200,000 worth of 20-year, 10 percent bonds, dated April 1 of this year, at 105. Interest is payable semiannually on October 1 and April 1.

Oct.   1 Paid semiannual interest on bonds.

Dec.   31 Recorded adjusting entry for accrued interest payable.

         31 Recorded adjusting entry for amortization of premium on bonds.

         31 Closed Interest Expense account.

Year 2

Jan.   1 Reversed adjusting entry for accrued interest payable.

Apr.   1 Paid semiannual interest on bonds.

Oct.   1 Paid semiannual interest on bonds.

Dec.   31 Made adjusting entry to record accrued interest payable.

         31 Made adjusting entry to record amortization of premium on bonds.

         31 Closed Interest Expense account.

Instructions

1. Record the transactions in general journal form.
2. Post the entries to the Interest Expense account. Label the adjusting, closing, and reversing entries.

L.O. 1,2,3   **Problem 25-3B**   During two consecutive years, the Associated Freight Line Corporation completed the following transactions related to its $12,000,000 issue of 25-year, 8 percent bonds, dated May 1 of the first year. Interest is payable on May 1 and November 1. The corporation's fiscal year extends from January 1 through December 31.

Year 1

May   1 Sold bond issue at 98 ½.
Nov. 1 Paid semiannual interest on bonds.
Dec. 31 Deposited $173,250 in a bond sinking fund.
      31 Made adjusting entry to record accrued interest payable.
      31 Made adjusting entry to record amortization of bond discount.
      31 Closed Interest Expense account.

Year 2

Jan.   1 Reversed adjustment for interest payable.
       9 Bought various securities with sinking fund cash; cost, $168,600.
May   1 Paid semiannual interest on bonds.
Nov.   1 Paid semiannual interest on bonds.
Dec. 31 Recorded receipt of $12,994 of income derived from sinking fund investments, depositing cash in sinking fund.
      31 Deposited $258,000 in bond sinking fund.
      31 Made adjusting entry to record accrued interest payable.
      31 Made adjusting entry to record amortization of bond discount.
      31 Closed Interest Expense account.

Instructions

1. Record the transactions in general journal form.
2. Post entries to the Interest Expense account and the Discount on Bonds Payable account. Label the adjusting, closing, and reversing entries.

L.O. 1,2,3   **Problem 25-4B**   On May 1, the Mountain Exploration Corporation issued $9,000,000 worth of 25-year bonds, 9 percent, dated May 1, with interest payable May 1 and November 1. The corporation's fiscal year is the calendar year. The following transactions pertain to the bond issue for the first two years:

Year 1

May   1 Sold bond issue at 103.
Nov. 1 Paid semiannual interest on bonds.
Dec. 31 Deposited $160,500 in a bond sinking fund.
      31 Recorded adjusting entry for accrued interest payable.
      31 Recorded adjusting entry for amortization of bond premium.
      31 Closed the Interest Expense account.

Year 2

Jan.   1 Reversed adjusting entry for accrued interest payable.
      12 Bought various securities with sinking fund cash, $157,400.

May	1	Paid semiannual interest on bonds.
July	1	Recorded receipt of $5,624 of income derived from sinking fund investments, depositing cash in sinking fund.
	2	Bought various securities with sinking fund cash, $7,290.
Nov.	1	Paid semiannual interest on bonds.
Dec.	31	Recorded receipt of $6,331 of income derived from sinking fund investments, depositing cash in sinking fund.
	31	Deposited $201,200 in bond sinking fund.
	31	Recorded adjusting entry for accrued interest payable.
	31	Recorded adjusting entry for amortization of bond premium.
	31	Closed the Sinking Fund Income account.
	31	Closed the Interest Expense account.

Instructions

1. Record the transactions in general journal form.
2. Post entries to the Interest Expense account and the Premium on Bonds Payable account. Label the appropriate entries in the ledger accounts as adjusting, closing, or reversing.

REVIEW OF T ACCOUNT PLACEMENT AND REPRESENTATIVE TRANSACTIONS: CHAPTERS 21 THROUGH 25

Review of T Account Placement

The following display sums up the placement of T accounts covered in Chapters 21 through 25 in relation to the fundamental accounting equation. Color indicates contra accounts.

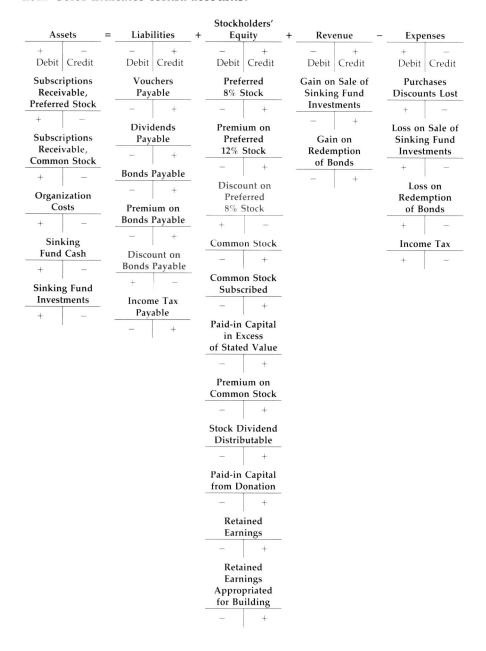

Review of Representative Transactions

The following table summarizes the recording of transactions covered in Chapters 21 through 25, along with classification of the accounts.

Transaction	Accounts Involved	Class.	Increase or Decrease	Therefore Debit or Credit	Financial Statement
Issued voucher for the purchase of merchandise (gross amount)	Purchases (gross) Freight In Vouchers Payable	CMS CMS CL	I I I	Debit Debit Credit	Income State. Income State. Balance Sheet
Paid voucher for purchase of merchandise within discount period (gross amount)	Vouchers Payable Cash Purchases Discount	CL CA CMS	D D I	Debit Credit Credit	Balance Sheet Balance Sheet Income State.

Returned merchandise after original voucher was recorded	Vouchers Payable
	   Purchases Returns
	   and Allowances
		CL
		
		CMS
			D
			
			I
				Debit
				
				Credit
					Balance Sheet
					
					Income State.

Issued voucher for the purchase of merchandise (net amount)	Purchases (net) Freight In Vouchers Payable	CMS CMS CL	I I I	Debit Debit Credit	Income State. Income State. Balance Sheet
Paid voucher for merchandise purchased within discount period (net amount)	Vouchers Payable Cash	CL CA	D D	Debit Credit	Balance Sheet Balance Sheet
Paid voucher for purchase of merchandise after discount period (net amount)	Vouchers Payable Purchases Discount Lost Cash	CL OE CA	D I D	Debit Debit Credit	Balance Sheet Income State. Balance Sheet

Transaction	Accounts Involved	Class.	Increase or Decrease	Therefore Debit or Credit	Financial Statement
Issued a note payable after original voucher was recorded	Vouchers Payable Notes Payable	CL CL	D I	Debit Credit	Balance Sheet Balance Sheet
Paid an interest-bearing note under voucher system	Notes Payable Interest Expense Vouchers Payable	CL OE CL	D I I	Debit Debit Credit	Balance Sheet Income State. Balance Sheet
	Vouchers Payable Cash	CL CA	D D	Debit Credit	Balance Sheet Balance Sheet
Recorded cash investment in a partnership	Cash J. Doe, Capital	CA OE	I I	Debit Credit	Balance Sheet Balance Sheet
Transferred one partner's equity to a new partner	D. Smith, Capital L. Jones, Capital	OE OE	D I	Debit Credit	Balance Sheet Balance Sheet
Partnership assets are sold at a profit	Cash Assets Loss or Gain from Realization	CA Assets OI	I D I	Debit Credit Credit	Balance Sheet Balance Sheet Income State.
Allocated net gain to the partners' capital accounts	Loss or Gain from Realization A. Bell, Capital C. Dale, Capital	OI OE OE	D I I	Debit Credit Credit	Income State. Balance Sheet Balance Sheet
Partnership assets are sold at a loss	Cash Loss or Gain from Realization Assets	CA OE Assets	I I D	Debit Debit Credit	Balance Sheet Income State. Balance Sheet
Sold common stock at par for cash	Cash Common Stock	CA PIC	I I	Debit Credit	Balance Sheet Balance Sheet

Transaction	Accounts Involved	Class.	Increase or Decrease	Therefore Debit or Credit	Financial Statement
Sold preferred 12 percent stock for an amount above par	Cash	CA	I	Debit	Balance Sheet
	Preferred 12 Percent Stock	PIC	I	Credit	Balance Sheet
	Premium on Preferred 12 Percent Stock	PIC	I	Credit	Balance Sheet
Paid corporation state charter fees	Organization Costs	IA	I	Debit	Balance Sheet
	Cash	CA	D	Credit	Balance Sheet
Sold common stock at less than par value	Cash	CA	I	Debit	Balance Sheet
	Discount on Common Stock	PIC	I	Debit	Balance Sheet
	Common Stock	PIC	I	Credit	Balance Sheet
Received subscription for no-par common stock at an amount over stated value	Subscriptions Receivable, Common Stock	CA	I	Debit	Balance Sheet
	Common Stock Subscribed	PIC	I	Credit	Balance Sheet
	Paid-in-Capital in Excess of Stated Value	PIC	I	Credit	Balance Sheet
Received installment on subscription to common stock	Cash	CA	I	Debit	Balance Sheet
	Subscriptions Receivable, Common Stock	CA	D	Credit	Balance Sheet
Issued common stock after receiving last installment on subscription	Common Stock Subscribed	PIC	D	Debit	Balance Sheet
	Common Stock	PIC	I	Credit	Balance Sheet
Paid installment on corporation income tax	Income Tax Expense	Exp.	I	Debit	Income State.
	Cash	CA	D	Credit	Balance Sheet

Transaction	Accounts Involved	Class.	Increase or Decrease	Therefore Debit or Credit	Financial Statement
Adjusting entry for additional corporation income tax	Income Tax Expense Income Tax Payable	Exp. CL	I I	Debit Credit	Income State. Balance Sheet
Closed the Income Tax Expense account	Income Summary Income Tax Expense	— Exp.	— D	Debit Credit	— Income State.
Closed the Income Summary account assuming a net income	Income Summary Retained Earnings	— RE	— I	Debit Credit	— Retained Earnings
Made an appropriation to retained earnings for contingencies	Retained Earnings Retained Earnings Appropriated for Contingencies	RE RE	D I	Debit Credit	Retained Earnings Retained Earnings
Paid interest on corporation bonds	Interest Expense Cash	OE CA	I D	Debit Credit	Income State. Balance Sheet
Sold bonds at an amount over the face value	Cash Premium on Bonds Payable Bonds Payable	CA LTL LTL	I I I	Debit Credit Credit	Balance Sheet Balance Sheet Balance Sheet
Recorded adjusting entry for amortization of bond premium	Premium on Bonds Payable Interest Expense	LTL OE	D D	Debit Credit	Balance Sheet Income State.
Made deposit in bond sinking fund	Sinking Fund Cash Cash	I CA	I D	Debit Credit	Balance Sheet Balance Sheet

Transaction	Accounts Involved	Class.	Increase or Decrease	Therefore Debit or Credit	Financial Statement
Sold bonds at an amount less than face value	Cash	CA	I	Debit	Balance Sheet
	Discount on Bonds Payable	LTL	I	Debit	Balance Sheet
	Bonds Payable	LTL	I	Credit	Balance Sheet
Invested bond sinking fund	Sinking Fund Investments	I	I	Debit	Balance Sheet
	Sinking Fund Cash	I	D	Credit	Balance Sheet
Sold sinking fund investments at a gain	Sinking Fund Cash	I	I	Debit	Balance Sheet
	Sinking Fund Investments	I	D	Credit	Balance Sheet
	Gain on Sale of Sinking Fund Investments	OI	I	Credit	Income State.
Redeemed bonds before maturity at less than book value	Bonds Payable	LTL	D	Debit	Balance Sheet
	Premium on Bonds Payable	LTL	D	Debit	Balance Sheet
	Cash	CA	D	Credit	Balance Sheet
	Gain on Redemption of Bonds	OI	I	Credit	Income State.
Redeemed bonds before maturity at more than book value	Bonds Payable	LTL	D	Debit	Balance Sheet
	Premium on Bonds Payable	LTL	D	Debit	Balance Sheet
	Loss on Redemption of Bonds Payable	OE	I	Debit	Income State.
	Cash	CA	D	Credit	Balance Sheet
Paid bonds at maturity	Bonds Payable	LTL	D	Debit	Balance Sheet
	Cash	CA	D	Credit	Balance Sheet

26 Departmental Accounting

LEARNING OBJECTIVES

After you have completed this chapter, you will be able to do the following:

1. Compile a departmental income statement extended through gross profit.
2. Compile a departmental work sheet.
3. Compile a departmental income statement extended through income from operations.
4. Apportion operating expenses among various operating departments.
5. Compile a departmental income statement extended through departmental margin.

When a company carries on a number of different business activities, the firm should be divided into a number of subdivisions or departments. This enables the company's management to delegate authority to departmental managers, who are held responsible for their respective departments, and to measure the profitability of each department. It is the element of profitability that we are going to discuss in this chapter.

Large companies have greater opportunities to use departmental accounting than small ones. However, even a small business—if it carries on more than one type of business activity—may benefit from departmental accounting. For example, the Chamberlin Company deals in insurance and property management and accounts separately for insurance commissions and management fees. At the end of the fiscal year, Leona and Robert Chamberlin can compare the profitability of each activity with the amount of time and attention they had to devote to the respective activity. On the basis of this comparison, they may decide to spend more time on one activity and less on the other.

For large business firms—those that engage in service, merchandising, or manufacturing—departmental accounting is a must. The accounting reports consist of several levels of income statements recorded on a departmental basis and extended from sales through gross profit or income from operations or departmental margin.

GROSS PROFIT BY DEPARTMENTS

A department's gross profit depends on its sales volume and its markup on the goods sold:

Net sales − Cost of merchandise sold = Gross profit

Gross profit, in the same context, consists of the items listed in the income statement shown in Figure 26-1.

To determine the gross profit of a given department, one needs a separate departmental set of figures for each element entering into the gross profit. There are two methods of obtaining these figures:

1. Keep separate general ledger accounts for each item involved in gross profit, such as a Sales account for each department, a Sales Returns and Allowances account for each department, and so on. Then record the balances of these accounts on the income statement.
2. Keep only one general ledger account for each item involved in gross profit and apportion the balance to the various departments. For example, maintain one Sales account and one Sales Returns and Allowances account for the company, and in addition keep a breakdown of sales and sales returns for each department. Then record the figures for each department on the income statement.

FIGURE 26-1

INCOME STATEMENT

Revenue from Sales:				
Sales				$ 120 0 0 0 00
Less: Sales Returns and				
Allowances			$ 6 0 0 0 00	
Sales Discount			3 0 0 0 00	9 0 0 0 00
Net Sales				$ 111 0 0 0 00
Cost of Merchandise Sold:				
Merchandise Inventory				
(beginning)			$ 48 0 0 0 00	
Purchases		$76 4 0 0 00		
Less: Purchases Returns and				
Allowances	$4 0 0 0 00			
Purchases Discount	2 0 0 0 00	6 0 0 0 00		
		$70 4 0 0 00		
Add Freight In		4 6 0 0 00		
Net Purchases			75 0 0 0 00	
Merchandise Available for Sale			$ 123 0 0 0 00	
Less Merchandise Inventory				
(ending)			52 0 0 0 00	
Cost of Merchandise Sold				71 0 0 0 00
Gross Profit				$ 40 0 0 0 00

Separate Accounts by Departments

Keeping separate accounts by departments yields the most accurate accounting data. One needs separate accounts for each department for Sales, Sales Returns and Allowances, Sales Discount, Purchases, Purchases Returns and Allowances, Purchases Discount, and Merchandise Inventory. For example, Action Enterprises has five departments and uses five Sales accounts, five Sales Returns and Allowances accounts, five Sales Discount accounts, five Merchandise Inventory accounts, and so forth. The special journals contain columns for each departmental account, as in the sales journal in Figure 26-2.

FIGURE 26-2

	DATE	INV. NO.	CUSTOMER'S NAME	POST. REF.	ACCOUNTS RECEIVABLE DEBIT	SALES CREDIT DEPT. A	DEPT. B	DEPT. C	DEPT. D	DEPT. E	
1	19–										1
2	Sept. 1	1698	Carole Barnhart	✓	165 00	165 00					2
3	3	1702	Ralph Muncy	✓	376 00			376 00			3
4	3	1704	Donald Caspar	✓	716 00		716 00				4
15											15
16	30				14 933 00	2 681 00	864 00	4 794 00	3 716 00	2 878 00	16
17					(114)	(411)	(412)	(413)	(414)	(415)	17

SALES JOURNAL　　　PAGE _____

The accountant posts each total to a separate account, as indicated by the ledger account numbers. A company that has many departments and keeps a separate journal column for each may find that the journal becomes quite cumbersome in size. In a situation like this, it is better to post from the sales invoices directly to the departmental sales accounts. (This method is like the process of posting from sales invoices described in Chapter 11.) Another alternative is to establish a controlling account in the general ledger and to record each department in a subsidiary ledger.

Maintaining One General Ledger Account

When a company keeps only one general ledger account for each item involved in gross profit, the accountant has to distribute the total amount among the various departments at the end of the accounting period. To do so, the accountant has to accumulate departmental information on supplementary records. Morgan's Grocery, for example, has a produce, a grocery, and a meat department. Morgan's records sales by department, by having the checkout clerk punch them separately on the cash register. At the end of each day, the sales are recorded in a journal, with the totals being taken from the cash register tapes. Sales are also recorded on a departmental analysis sheet.

Businesses also use separate analysis sheets for sales returns, purchases, purchase returns and allowances, purchase discounts, and so forth. At the end of the accounting period, these analysis sheets give departmental breakdowns for each item.

Gross Profit by Departments

Objective 1

Compile a departmental income statement extended through gross profit.

Based on separate departmental accounts or supplementary analysis sheets

Mattson Company, Inc., has two departments, A and B, and keeps separate accounts for each. The income statement for the fiscal year ending December 31, showing departmental reporting only up to Gross Profit, appears in Figure 26-3 on pages 882 and 883. A skeleton outline of this process is as follows:

From Sales through Gross Profit
Revenue from Sales
Less Cost of Merchandise Sold

Gross Profit
Less Operating Expenses

Income from Operations
Add Other Income
Less Other Expenses

Income Before Income Tax
Less Income Tax Expense

Net Income After Income Tax

INCOME FROM OPERATIONS BY DEPARTMENTS

A company may extend departmental reporting of income to Income from Operations. Mattson Company, Inc., keeps separate accounts for each item that enters into gross profit and apportions the operating expenses between Gross Profit and Income from Operations to department A or department B on a logical basis. (We shall discuss this procedure in detail later.) For emphasis, let us look at the skeleton outline of the income statement:

From Sales Through Income from Operations

Separate departmental accounts or supplementary analysis sheets }

Account balances are apportioned }

Departmentalized
Revenue from Sales
Less Cost of Merchandise Sold

Gross Profit
Less Selling Expenses
Less General Expenses

Income from Operations

Nondepartmentalized
Add Other Income
Less Other Expense

Income Before Income Tax
Less Income Tax Expense

Net Income After Income Tax

Work Sheet for Departmental Accounting

Objective 2

Compile a departmental work sheet.

Each department assumes its share of overhead expenses. Recall once again the sequential steps of the accounting cycle: The accountant records the trial balance in the first columns of the work sheet, formulates and records the adjustments, completes the work sheet, and then uses the work sheet to prepare the income statement. The Income Statement columns of the work sheet for a company that keeps track of income by departments contain debit and credit columns for each department, as well as debit and credit columns titled Nondepartmental. These last two columns include Other Income and Other Expense accounts that are not directly assigned to a department. By the time the accountant gets to the income statement, she or he has already performed calculations apportioning the expenses, which are accordingly subdivided on the work sheet. A sample portion of the work sheet for the Mattson Company is shown in Figure 26-4. (This figure begins on page 884 and continues to page 887.) Various asset, liability, and owners' equity accounts are not shown, but they are included in the totals.

Income Statement for Departmental Accounting

Objective 3

Compile a departmental income statement extended through income from operations.

The income statement contains a set of columns for each department as well as a set of columns for the combined total of all departments. The income statement in Figure 26-5 (pages 888 and 889), which is extended through Income from Operations, is a more representative example than the one shown in Figure 26-4. A discussion of the apportionment of operating expenses between the two departments follows.

FIGURE 26-3

Mattson Company, Inc.
Income Statement
For Year Ended December 31, 19–

		DEPARTMENT A		
1	Revenue from Sales:			
2	Sales		$ 560 0 0 0 00	
3	Less Sales Returns and Allowances		14 2 0 0 00	
4	Net Sales			$ 545 8 0 0 00
5	Cost of Merchandise Sold:			
6	Merchandise Inventory, Jan. 1, 19–		$ 96 4 0 0 00	
7	Purchases	$ 312 1 1 5 00		
8	Less: Purchases Returns and Allowances	(9 5 8 0 00)		
9	Purchases Discount	(5 7 4 0 00)		
10		$ 296 7 9 5 00		
11	Add Freight In	13 0 0 5 00		
12	Net Purchases		309 8 0 0 00	
13	Merchandise Available for Sale		$ 406 2 0 0 00	
14	Less Merchandise Inventory, Dec. 31, 19–		110 0 0 0 00	
15	Cost of Merchandise Sold			296 2 0 0 00
16	Gross Profit			$ 249 6 0 0 00
17				
18	Operating Expenses:			
19	Selling Expenses:			
20	Sales Salary Expense			
21	Advertising Expense			
22	Depreciation Expense, Store Equipment			
23	Miscellaneous Selling Expense			
24	Total Selling Expenses			
25	General Expenses:			
26	Office Salary Expense			
27	Rent Expense			
28	Utilities Expense			
29	Insurance Expense			
30	Bad Debts Expense			
31	Miscellaneous General Expense			
32	Total General Expenses			
33	Total Operating Expenses			
34	Income from Operations			
35				
36	Other Income:			
37	Interest Income			
38	Other Expenses:			
39	Interest Expense			
40	Income Before Income Tax			
41	Income Tax Expense			
42	Net Income After Income Tax			
43				

	DEPARTMENT B			TOTAL			Line
							1
		$ 240 000 00			$ 800 000 00		2
		5 800 00			20 000 00		3
			$ 234 200 00			$ 780 000 00	4
							5
		$ 82 740 00			$ 179 140 00		6
$ 161 175 00				$ 473 290 00			7
(4 756 00)				(14 336 00)			8
(3 274 00)				(9 014 00)			9
$ 153 145 00				$ 449 940 00			10
6 715 00				19 720 00			11
		159 860 00			469 660 00		12
		$ 242 600 00			$ 648 800 00		13
		90 000 00			200 000 00		14
			152 600 00			448 800 00	15
			$ 81 600 00			$ 331 200 00	16
							17
							18
							19
				$ 140 825 00			20
				17 600 00			21
				3 300 00			22
				4 270 00			23
					$ 165 995 00		24
							25
				$ 32 100 00			26
				16 400 00			27
				4 840 00			28
				4 400 00			29
				2 570 00			30
				9 20 00			31
					61 230 00		32
						227 225 00	33
						$ 103 975 00	34
							35
							36
				$ 3 624 00			37
							38
					2 400 00	1 224 00	39
						$ 105 199 00	40
						24 278 00	41
						$ 80 921 00	42
							43

Mattson Company, Inc.
Work Sheet
For Year Ended December 31, 19–

	ACCOUNT NAME	TRIAL BALANCE DEBIT	TRIAL BALANCE CREDIT	ADJUSTMENTS DEBIT	ADJUSTMENTS CREDIT	DEPARTMENT A INCOME STATEMENT DEBIT	DEPARTMENT A INCOME STATEMENT CREDIT
1							
2	Accounts Receivable	82 0 4 0 00					
3	Allowance for						
4	Doubtful Accounts		8 6 2 00		(f) 2 5 7 0 00		
5							
6	Merchandise						
7	Inventory						
8	Department A	96 4 0 0 00		(b) 110 0 0 0 00	(a) 96 4 0 0 00		
9	Department B	82 7 4 0 00		(d) 90 0 0 0 00	(c) 82 7 4 0 00		
10	Prepaid Insurance	5 5 4 0 00			(e) 4 4 0 0 00		
11	Store Equipment	32 4 0 0 00					
12	Accumulated Depre-						
13	ciation, Store						
14	Equipment		21 6 0 0 00		(g) 3 3 0 0 00		
15							
16	Sales						
17	Department A		560 0 0 0 00				560 0 0 0 00
18	Department B		240 0 0 0 00				
19	Sales Returns and						
20	Allowances						
21	Department A	14 2 0 0 00				14 2 0 0 00	
22	Department B	5 8 0 0 00					
23	Purchases						
24	Department A	312 1 1 5 00				312 1 1 5 00	
25	Department B	161 1 7 5 00					
26	Purchases Returns						
27	and Allowances						
28	Department A		9 5 8 0 00				9 5 8 0 00
29	Department B		4 7 5 6 00				
30	Purchases Discount						
31	Department A		5 7 4 0 00				5 7 4 0 00
32	Department B		3 2 7 4 00				
33	Freight In						
34	Department A	13 0 0 5 00				13 0 0 5 00	
35	Department B	6 7 1 5 00					
36	Sales Salary						
37	Expense	140 8 2 5 00				88 6 2 5 00	
38	Advertising Expense	17 6 0 0 00				10 3 3 6 00	
39	Misc. Selling						
40	Expense	4 2 7 0 00				2 9 8 9 00	
41	Office Salary						
42	Expense	32 1 0 0 00				22 4 7 0 00	
43	Rent Expense	16 4 0 0 00				10 2 5 0 00	
44	Utilities Expense	4 8 4 0 00				3 0 2 5 00	
45	Totals carried forward	1,468 5 4 4 00	1,490 4 9 0 00	282 7 4 0 00	279 4 1 0 00	1,037 4 1 4 00	575 3 2 0 00

FIGURE 26-4

DEPARTMENT B INCOME STATEMENT		NONDEPARTMENTAL INCOME STATEMENT		BALANCE SHEET		
DEBIT	CREDIT	DEBIT	CREDIT	DEBIT	CREDIT	
						1
				82 0 4 0 00		2
						3
					3 4 3 2 00	4
						5
						6
						7
				110 0 0 0 00		8
				90 0 0 0 00		9
				1 1 4 0 00		10
				32 4 0 0 00		11
						12
						13
					24 9 0 0 00	14
						15
						16
						17
	240 0 0 0 00					18
						19
						20
						21
5 8 0 0 00						22
						23
						24
161 1 7 5 00						25
						26
						27
						28
	4 7 5 6 00					29
						30
						31
	3 2 7 4 00					32
						33
						34
6 7 1 5 00						35
						36
52 2 0 0 00						37
7 2 6 4 00						38
						39
1 2 8 1 00						40
						41
9 6 3 0 00						42
6 1 5 0 00						43
1 8 1 5 00						44
252 0 3 0 00	248 0 3 0 00	0	0	1,118 7 6 1 00	1,035 8 1 2 00	45

(continued on next page)

| | TRIAL BALANCE | | ADJUSTMENTS | | DEPARTMENT A INCOME STATEMENT | |
ACCOUNT NAME	DEBIT	CREDIT	DEBIT	CREDIT	DEBIT	CREDIT
1 Totals brought forward	1,468 5 4 4 00	1,490 4 9 0 00	282 7 4 0 00	279 4 1 0 00	1,037 4 1 4 00	575 3 2 0 00
2 Misc. General						
3 Expense	9 2 0 00				6 4 4 00	
4 Income Tax Expense	22 2 5 0 00		(h) 2 0 2 8 00			
5 Interest Income		3 6 2 4 00				
6 Interest Expense	2 4 0 0 00					
7	1,494 1 1 4 00	1,494 1 1 4 00				
8 Inc. Summary, A			(a) 96 4 0 0 00	(b) 110 0 0 0 00	96 4 0 0 00	110 0 0 0 00
9 Inc. Summary, B			(c) 82 7 4 0 00	(d) 90 0 0 0 00		
10 Insurance Expense			(e) 4 4 0 0 00		2 5 4 0 00	
11 Bad Debts Expense			(f) 2 5 7 0 00		1 7 9 9 00	
12 Depreciation						
13 Expense, Store						
14 Equipment			(g) 3 3 0 0 00		1 8 4 0 00	
15 Income Tax Payable				(h) 2 0 2 8 00		
16			391 4 3 8 00	391 4 3 8 00	580 2 3 8 00	685 3 2 0 00
17 Net Income (Loss)						
18 by Department					105 0 8 2 00	
19					685 3 2 0 00	685 3 2 0 00
20 Net Income						
21						
22						
23						
24						

Apportionment of Operating Expenses

Objective 4

Apportion operating expenses among various operating departments.

Apportionment of expenses is a crucial element of departmental accounting. It consists of allocating, or dividing, operating expenses among operating departments. One can readily identify some operating expenses as belonging to a given department. For example, suppose that a salesperson makes sales in one department only; the accountant assigns that salesperson's salary or commission directly to that department. However, other operating expenses, such as Miscellaneous Selling Expense or Utilities Expense, cannot be restricted to one department and must be divided between the departments on some equitable basis. Let's look at the operating expenses of the Mattson Company and see how they are apportioned.

FIGURE 26-4
(continued)

DEPARTMENT B INCOME STATEMENT		NONDEPARTMENTAL INCOME STATEMENT		BALANCE SHEET		
DEBIT	CREDIT	DEBIT	CREDIT	DEBIT	CREDIT	
252 0 3 0 00	248 0 3 0 00	0	0	1,118 7 6 1 00	1,035 8 1 2 00	1
						2
2 7 6 00						3
		24 2 7 8 00				4
			3 6 2 4 00			5
		2 4 0 0 00				6
						7
						8
82 7 4 0 00	90 0 0 0 00					9
1 8 6 0 00						10
7 7 1 00						11
						12
						13
1 4 6 0 00						14
					2 0 2 8 00	15
339 1 3 7 00	338 0 3 0 00					16
						17
	1 1 0 7 00		103 9 7 5 00			18
339 1 3 7 00	339 1 3 7 00	26 6 7 8 00	107 5 9 9 00	1,118 7 6 1 00	1,037 8 4 0 00	19
		80 9 2 1 00			80 9 2 1 00	20
		107 5 9 9 00	107 5 9 9 00	1,118 7 6 1 00	1,118 7 6 1 00	21
						22
						23
						24

- **Sales Salary Expense** Mattson allocates the salespersons' salaries to department A or department B according to the names on the payroll register, which lists each employee by department. Department A's share is $88,625; department B's is $52,200.
- **Advertising Expense** Mattson advertises itself in three media: billboards, newspapers, and radio. The cost breakdown is like this:

Billboard advertising	$ 1,600
Newspaper advertising	9,600
Radio advertising	6,400
Total	$17,600

The billboard ads display the name of the company and tell where it is, but they don't advertise the products of department A or department B. Since no specific department is featured, Mattson's accountant

Mattson Company, Inc.
Income Statement
For Year Ended December 31, 19–

#		DEPARTMENT A		
1	Revenue from Sales:			
2	Sales		$ 560 0 0 0 00	
3	Less Sales Returns and Allowances		14 2 0 0 00	
4	Net Sales			$ 545 8 0 0 00
5	Cost of Merchandise Sold:			
6	Merchandise Inventory, Jan. 1, 19–		$ 96 4 0 0 00	
7	Purchases	$ 312 1 1 5 00		
8	Less: Purchases Returns and Allowances	(9 5 8 0 00)		
9	Purchases Discount	$ (5 7 4 0 00)		
10		$ 296 7 9 5 00		
11	Add Freight In	$ 13 0 0 5 00		
12	Net Purchases		309 8 0 0 00	
13	Merchandise Available for Sale		$ 406 2 0 0 00	
14	Less Merchandise Inventory, Dec. 31, 19–		110 0 0 0 00	
15	Cost of Merchandise Sold			296 2 0 0 00
16	Gross Profit			$ 249 6 0 0 00
17				
18	Operating Expenses:			
19	Selling Expenses:			
20	Sales Salary Expense	$ 88 6 2 5 00		
21	Advertising Expense	10 3 3 6 00		
22	Depreciation Expense, Store Equipment	1 8 4 0 00		
23	Miscellaneous Selling Expense	2 9 8 9 00		
24	Total Selling Expenses		$ 103 7 9 0 00	
25	General Expenses:			
26	Office Salary Expense	$ 22 4 7 0 00		
27	Rent Expense	10 2 5 0 00		
28	Utilities Expense	3 0 2 5 00		
29	Insurance Expense	2 5 4 0 00		
30	Bad Debts Expense	1 7 9 9 00		
31	Miscellaneous General Expense	6 4 4 00		
32	Total General Expenses		40 7 2 8 00	
33	Total Operating Expenses			144 5 1 8 00
34	Income (Loss) from Operations			$ 105 0 8 2 00
35				
36	Other Income:			
37	Interest Income			
38	Other Expense:			
39	Interest Expense			
40	Income Before Income Tax			
41	Income Tax Expense			
42	Net Income After Income Tax			

	DEPARTMENT B			TOTAL			
1							
2		$ 240 000 00			$ 800 000 00		
3		5 800 00			20 000 00		
4			$ 234 200 00			$ 780 000 00	
5							
6		$ 82 740 00			$ 179 140 00		
7	$ 161 175 00			$ 473 290 00			
8	(4 756 00)			(14 336 00)			
9	(3 274 00)			(9 014 00)			
10	$ 153 145 00			$ 449 940 00			
11	6 715 00			19 720 00			
12		159 860 00			469 660 00		
13		$ 242 600 00			$ 648 800 00		
14		90 000 00			200 000 00		
15			152 600 00			448 800 00	
16			$ 81 600 00			$ 331 200 00	
17							
18							
19							
20	$ 52 200 00			$ 140 825 00			
21	7 264 00			17 600 00			
22	1 460 00			3 300 00			
23	1 281 00			4 270 00			
24		$ 62 205 00			$ 165 995 00		
25							
26	$ 9 630 00			$ 32 100 00			
27	6 150 00			16 400 00			
28	1 815 00			4 840 00			
29	1 860 00			4 400 00			
30	771 00			2 570 00			
31	276 00			920 00			
32		20 502 00			61 230 00		
33			82 707 00			227 225 00	
34			$ (1 107 00)			$ 103 975 00	
35							
36							
37					$ 3 624 00		
38							
39					2 400 00	1 224 00	
40						$ 105 199 00	
41						24 278 00	
42						$ 80 921 00	

has to apportion the cost of these billboard ads according to gross sales, as follows:

Sales for Department A	$560,000
Sales for Department B	240,000
Total Sales	$800,000

Dept. A's sales as percentage of total: $\dfrac{\$560,000}{\$800,000} = \underline{\underline{70\%}}$

Dept. B's sales as percentage of total: $\dfrac{\$240,000}{\$800,000} = \underline{\underline{30\%}}$

Dept. A's share of cost of billboard advertising:

$$70\% \text{ of } \$1,600 = \$1,600 \times .7 = \underline{\underline{\$1,120}}$$

Dept. B's share of cost of billboard advertising:

$$30\% \text{ of } \$1,600 = \$1,600 \times .3 = \underline{\underline{\$480}}$$

Mattson allocates the cost of its newspaper advertising according to the number of column inches each department uses. In a year, Mattson buys 3,200 inches of newspaper advertising, divided according to departments in the following manner:

Ads for dept. A: 1,920 column inches or $\dfrac{1,920}{3,200} = \underline{\underline{60\%}}$

Ads for dept. B: 1,280 column inches or $\dfrac{1,280}{3,200} = \underline{\underline{40\%}}$

Dept. A's share of cost of newspaper advertising:

$$60\% \text{ of } \$9,600 = \$9,600 \times .6 = \underline{\underline{\$5,760}}$$

Dept. B's share of cost of newspaper advertising:

$$40\% \text{ of } \$9,600 = \$9,600 \times .4 = \underline{\underline{\$3,840}}$$

As for radio advertising, Mattson again allocates cost to the two departments according to the amount of air time each department uses. In a year, Mattson buys 1,250 minutes of radio time, divided according to departments, as shown here:

Ads for dept. A: 675 minutes or $\dfrac{675}{1,250} = \underline{\underline{54\%}}$

Ads for dept. B: 575 minutes or $\dfrac{575}{1,250} = \underline{\underline{46\%}}$

Dept. A's share of cost of radio advertising:

$$54\% \text{ of } \$6,400 = \$6,400 \times .54 = \underline{\underline{\$3,456}}$$

Dept. B's share of cost of radio advertising:

$$46\% \text{ of } \$6,400 = \$6,400 \times .46 = \underline{\underline{\$2,944}}$$

Here is a summary of the Mattson Company's allocation of advertising expense:

Expense	Department A	Department B	Total
Billboard advertising	$ 1,120	$ 480	$ 1,600
Newspaper advertising	5,760	3,840	9,600
Radio advertising	3,456	2,944	6,400
	$10,336	$7,264	$17,600

- **Depreciation Expense, Store Equipment** Mattson keeps a plant and equipment ledger that notes the department in which each piece of equipment is located. The total year's depreciation of the equipment used in department A is $1,840; the total year's depreciation of the equipment used in department B is $1,460.
- **Office Salary Expense** People who work in the office of the Mattson Company get paid a total of $32,100 per year. Mattson apportions the amount of money that is paid in salaries to office workers on the basis of the amount of time the office personnel has to spend on each department. Management estimates that 70 percent of the office force's time is devoted to department A and 30 percent to department B:

Dept. A's share: 70% of $32,100 = $32,100 × .7 = $22,470

Dept. B's share: 30% of $32,100 = $32,100 × .3 = $9,630

- **Rent Expense and Utilities Expense** The Mattson Company rents 40,000 square feet of floor space and allocates the expenses of rent and utilities on the basis of floor space occupied by each department, as follows. (Yearly expense for rent is $16,400; yearly expense for utilities is $4,840.)

Dept. A occupies 25,000 square feet or $\dfrac{25,000}{40,000}$ = 62.5%

Dept. B occupies 15,000 square feet or $\dfrac{15,000}{40,000}$ = 37.5%

Dept. A's share of rent: 62.5% of $16,400 = $10,250

Dept. B's share of rent: 37.5% of $16,400 = $6,150

Dept. A's share of utilities: 62.5% of $4,840 = $3,025

Dept. B's share of utilities: 37.5% of $4,840 = $1,815

In this case, for simplicity, we are assuming that all floor space is of equal value. However, when one is apportioning the rent expense in a multistory building, one has to take into account differences in the value of the various floors and locations.

- **Insurance Expense** The Mattson Company carries insurance policies to cover losses that might result from (1) damage to merchandise or equipment (annual cost, $3,600) and (2) injury incurred by customers while on the premises (annual cost, $800). The cost of the insurance on merchandise and equipment is based on the average cost of the assets held by each department. The average is equal to the cost of assets on hand at the beginning of the year plus the cost of assets on hand at the end of the year, divided by 2. Following are the computations presented in tabular form:

	Computations for Insurance Expense				
Item	**Department A**		**Department B**		**Total**
Merchandise Inventory					
Balance, Jan. 1	$ 96,400		$ 82,740		
Balance, Dec. 31	110,000		90,000		
Total	2)$206,400		2)$172,740		
Average (Total ÷ 2)	$103,200	$103,200	$ 86,370	$86,370	
Store Equipment					
Balance, Jan. 1	$ 19,440		$ 12,960		
Balance, Dec. 31	19,440		12,960		
Total	2)$ 38,880		2)$ 25,920		
Average (Total ÷ 2)	$ 19,440	19,440	$ 12,960	12,960	
Total		$122,640		$99,330	$221,970

$$\text{Dept. A's percentage: } \frac{\$122,640}{\$221,970} = \underline{\underline{55\%}}$$

$$\text{Dept. B's percentage: } \frac{\$99,330}{\$221,970} = \underline{\underline{45\%}}$$

Dept. A's share of property insurance: 55% of $3,600 = $1,980

Dept. B's share of property insurance: 45% of $3,600 = $1,620

The cost of liability insurance (in case of personal injury to customers) is based on sales. Using the same percentages as for billboard advertising, Mattson apportions the cost of liability insurance as follows:

Dept. A's share of liability insurance: 70% of $800 = $560

Dept. B's share of liability insurance: 30% of $800 = $240

Here is a summary of the way Mattson allocates its insurance expense:

Type of Insurance	Department A	Department B	Total
Property insurance	$1,980	$1,620	$3,600
Liability insurance	560	240	800
	$2,540	$1,860	$4,400

- **Bad Debts Expense, Miscellaneous Selling Expense, and Miscellaneous General Expense**   Bad Debts Expense and the miscellaneous expense accounts vary according to the volume of sales. Accordingly, Mattson apportions them on this basis, since volume of sales is a reasonable measure of the benefit each department derives from these accounts.

Item	Department A	Department B	Total
Bad Debts Expense	$1,799	$ 771	$2,570
Miscellaneous Selling Expense	2,989	1,281	4,270
Miscellaneous General Expense	644	276	920
	$5,432	$2,328	$7,760

Division of these expense accounts by department is as follows:

Dept. A's share of bad debts: 70% of $2,570 = $1,799

Dept. B's share of bad debts: 30% of $2,570 = $771

Dept. A's share of miscellaneous selling expense: 70% of $4,270 = $2,989

Dept. B's share of miscellaneous selling expense: 30% of $4,270 = $1,281

Dept. A's share of miscellaneous general expense: 70% of $920 = $644

Dept. B's share of miscellaneous general expense: 30% of $920 = $276

DEPARTMENTAL MARGIN

When a company breaks down its expense figures on a departmental-margin basis, its income statement indicates the contribution each department makes toward the overhead expenses incurred on behalf of the business as a whole. One can divide operating expenses into two classes: (1) **direct expenses,** which are incurred for the sole benefit of a given department and thus are under the control of the department head; (2) **indirect expenses,** which are incurred as overhead expenses of the entire business and thus are not under the control of one department head. For example, Sales Salary Expense is a direct expense since it is incurred purely for the benefit of one department. Property tax on real estate, on the other hand, is an overhead expense incurred for the business as a whole; it is not directly chargeable to one department.

Some operating expenses may be partially direct and partially indirect. For example, Mattson Company's Advertising Expense consisted partially of billboard advertising, which stresses the name and location of the company, and partially of newspaper advertising, which directly benefits separate departments of the company. So the part of the advertising budget that went to billboard advertising is an indirect expense, and the part that went to newspaper advertising is a direct expense. Costs of insurance on merchandise inventories and store equipment are a direct expense; costs of liability insurance are indirect or overhead expenses. When you are classifying an expense as being direct or indirect, use this rule of thumb to identify direct expenses: **If the department were not in existence, then the expense would not be in existence.** The expense must be directly related to the department.

Here is a skeleton outline of an income statement that emphasizes departmental margin:

Objective 5

Compile a departmental income statement extended through departmental margin.

From Sales Through Departmental Margin

Revenue from Sales
Less Cost of Merchandise Sold

Gross Profit
Less Direct Departmental Expenses

Departmental Margin
Less Indirect Expenses

Income from Operations
Add Other Income
Less Other Expense

Income Before Income Tax
Less Income Tax Expense

Net Income After Income Tax

Remember

In any departmental accounting system, it is necessary to keep separate accounts or supplementary records by department for each account involved in determining gross profit on sales.

The income statement shown in Figure 26-6 (pages 896 and 897) presents the same figures that we saw in Figure 26-5 for the Mattson Company. This time, however, they are in the departmental-margin format. You will find it interesting to compare the two.

The Meaning of Departmental Margin

Departmental margin is a measurement of the contribution that a given department makes to the income of the firm, and it is the most realistic portrayal of the profitability of a department. If the company does away with the department, the company's Income Before Taxes will decrease or increase by the amount of the departmental margin. For example, in the case of the Mattson Company, department B had a departmental margin of $18,765; if Mattson eliminated the department, its Income Before Taxes would be reduced by $18,765 (assuming that Mattson didn't create a new department to take the place of department B or expand department A to occupy the void).

In the company's work sheet (Figure 26-4), in which operating expenses were apportioned to departments, department B showed a net loss from operations of $1,107. Department B sustained this loss because it was assigned a number of indirect expenses. If Mattson eliminates department B, these indirect expenses, or overhead, will still exist and will therefore be assigned entirely to department A, thereby accounting in part for the reduction in Income Before Taxes by $18,765 (the amount of the departmental margin).

The Usefulness of Departmental Margin

Income statements that show departmental margin are extremely useful when it comes to controlling a company's direct expenses because the company can hold the head of a given department accountable for expenses directly chargeable to the department. If a department head reduces direct expenses, this action will have a favorable effect on the departmental margin.

A company that manufactures a number of different products can also use the concept of departmental margin to determine the profitability of a particular product. This, clearly, is one of the most important uses of the departmental margin.

Management can use an income statement portraying departmental margin as a tool for making future plans and analyzing future operations. Sometimes such an income statement may even lead to the elimination of a department. For example, The Gonzales Company, Inc., has five departments; its Income from Operations for last year was $120,000, which is about the same as it has been for the past four years. Gonzales's partial income statement, in which all operating expenses are apportioned to the various departments, shows that department E has a Loss from Operations of $9,000. In an abbreviated departmental-margin format, the results of the fiscal year are shown in the table on page 898.

Now suppose that Gonzales eliminates department E. Because department E's departmental margin amounts to $16,000, the Income from Operations of the entire firm will decrease by $16,000 ($120,000 − $104,000 = $16,000). Another factor Gonzales has to consider is possible "spill-over sales" of department E; that is, customers of department E may also buy things in other departments. Also, any change in income

Remember

Direct expenses are those incurred for the sole benefit of a department. If the department did not exist, the expense would not have been incurred.

Mattson Company, Inc.
Income Statement
For Year Ended December 31, 19–

			DEPARTMENT A		
1	Revenue from Sales:				
2	Sales		$ 560 000 00		
3	Less Sales Returns and Allowances		14 200 00		
4	Net Sales			$ 545 800 00	
5	Cost of Merchandise Sold:				
6	Merchandise Inventory, Jan. 1, 19–		$ 96 400 00		
7	Purchases	$ 312 115 00			
8	Less: Purchases Returns and Allowances	(9 580 00)			
9	Purchases Discount	(5 740 00)			
10		$ 296 795 00			
11	Add Freight In	13 005 00			
12	Net Purchases		309 800 00		
13	Merchandise Available for Sale		$ 406 200 00		
14	Less Merchandise Inventory, Dec. 31, 19–		110 000 00		
15	Cost of Merchandise Sold			296 200 00	
16	Gross Profit			$ 249 600 00	
17					
18	Direct Departmental Expenses:				
19	Sales Salary Expense		$ 88 625 00		
20	Advertising Expense		9 216 00		
21	Insurance Expense		1 980 00		
22	Depreciation Expense, Store Equipment		1 840 00		
23	Bad Debts Expense		1 799 00		
24	Total Direct Departmental Expenses			103 460 00	
25	Departmental Margin			$ 146 140 00	
26					
27	Indirect Expenses:				
28	Office Salary Expense				
29	Rent Expense				
30	Utilities Expense				
31	Advertising Expense (billboard)				
32	Insurance Expense (liability)				
33	Miscellaneous Selling Expense				
34	Miscellaneous General Expense				
35	Total Indirect Expenses				
36	Income from Operations				
37					
38	Other Income:				
39	Interest Income				
40	Other Expense:				
41	Interest Expense				
42	Income Before Income Tax				
43	Income Tax Expense				
44	Net Income After Income Tax				

	DEPARTMENT B			TOTAL			
							1
	$ 240 0 0 0 00			$ 800 0 0 0 00			2
	5 8 0 0 00			20 0 0 0 00			3
		$ 234 2 0 0 00			$ 780 0 0 0 00		4
							5
	$ 82 7 4 0 00			$ 179 1 4 0 00			6
$ 161 1 7 5 00			$ 473 2 9 0 00				7
(4 7 5 6 00)			(14 3 3 6 00)				8
(3 2 7 4 00)			(9 0 1 4 00)				9
$ 153 1 4 5 00			$ 449 9 4 0 00				10
6 7 1 5 00			19 7 2 0 00				11
	159 8 6 0 00			469 6 6 0 00			12
	$ 242 6 0 0 00			$ 648 8 0 0 00			13
	90 0 0 0 00			200 0 0 0 00			14
		152 6 0 0 00				448 8 0 0 00	15
		$ 81 6 0 0 00				$ 331 2 0 0 00	16
							17
							18
	$ 52 2 0 0 00			$ 140 8 2 5 00			19
	6 7 8 4 00			16 0 0 0 00			20
	1 6 2 0 00			3 6 0 0 00			21
	1 4 6 0 00			3 3 0 0 00			22
	7 7 1 00			2 5 7 0 00			23
		62 8 3 5 00				166 2 9 5 00	24
		$ 18 7 6 5 00				$ 164 9 0 5 00	25
							26
							27
				$ 32 1 0 0 00			28
				16 4 0 0 00			29
				4 8 4 0 00			30
				1 6 0 0 00			31
				8 0 0 00			32
				4 2 7 0 00			33
				9 2 0 00			34
						60 9 3 0 00	35
						$ 103 9 7 5 00	36
							37
							38
				$ 3 6 2 4 00			39
							40
				2 4 0 0 00		1 2 2 4 00	41
						$ 105 1 9 9 00	42
						24 2 7 8 00	43
						80 9 2 1 00	44

will cause a change in the amount of income tax paid by Gonzales. However, to simplify our analysis, we have omitted income tax from our discussion.

Item	Department E (only)	Departments A to D (only)	Total, Departments A to E	Total, Departments A to D (with E eliminated)
Sales	$120,000	$1,480,000	$1,600,000	$1,480,000
Cost of Merchandise Sold	72,000	880,000	952,000	880,000
Gross Profit	$ 48,000	$ 600,000	$ 648,000	$ 600,000
Direct Departmental Expense	32,000	336,000	368,000	336,000
Departmental Margin	$ 16,000	$ 264,000	$ 280,000	$ 264,000
Indirect Expenses	25,000	135,000	160,000	160,000
Income (Loss) from Operations	($ 9,000)	$ 129,000	$ 120,000	$ 104,000

BRANCH ACCOUNTING

As a means of increasing sales and income, a firm may open branch operations in different locations. This option applies to both merchandising and service enterprises. You can undoubtedly think of numerous examples of chain store outlets in retail fields, such as grocery stores, drug stores, and variety stores. Examples of branch operations in service fields are restaurants, dry cleaners, motels, and service stations.

With the increasing use of data processing equipment, the accounting for branch operations is generally performed (centralized) at the home office. The accounting system is similar to that for departmental accounting, with each branch treated as a department.

SUMMARY

L.O. 1   Income statements, which are extended on a departmental basis from Sales through Gross Profit, are statements in which a company keeps either separate ledger accounts for each department as well as for each element in the Revenue from Sales section and the Cost of Merchandise Sold section or supplementary records of the departmental totals for each element.

COMPUTERS AT WORK

Management Information Systems

While accountants praise computers for eliminating much of the tedious, repetitive work from their profession, managers of a computerized business may value computers most for the speed with which they process and distribute information. A management information system (MIS) can give a manager instant access to every facet of a company's business. Such systems are often extremely expensive to install, but once up and running they provide companies with a clear edge over competitors who still rely on paper and files.

MIS can supply managers with information that goes well beyond what the company bought and sold on a particular day. By keeping customer accounts in a data base, a company can target potential buyers and greatly increase the effectiveness of its advertising. An art gallery, for instance, can keep in a data bank the names of past customers and the artists whose works they have bought. Then when it's trying to promote new works by a particular artist, the gallery can call up the names of people who have bought that artist's works and send them special mailings. Similarly, a department store can keep track of purchases by its best customers in particular departments and send specialized mailings to people likely to be interested in a jewelry or oriental rug sale.

The most radical development in management information systems, and the one likely to have the most effect on the accounting profession, is the expert system. Traditional computers may appear to be "smart," but in fact all they do is follow a set of very precise, rigid instructions. Expert systems, by contrast, are beginning to mimic the human brain in their ability to perform analyses based on experience. Such systems are usually developed in a joint effort of software engineers and experts in the field. These experts program into the expert system's knowledge base both information and the general rules of thumb that the human experts use to draw conclusions and make decisions.

Because new information can be added to an expert system with relative ease, such systems are likely to become popular with accountants. The system can keep track of changes in accounting standards and tax requirements and can help auditors make decisions about such tricky matters as whether a company has made sufficient allowance for bad debts. Perhaps most importantly, an expert system can capture and preserve the years of experience from an old pro who might otherwise retire or die with the secrets of the company's accounts.

Sources: Jon A. Booker and Russell C. Kick, Jr., "Expert Systems in Accounting: The Next Generation of Computer Technology," *Journal of Accountancy*, March 1986, 101–104. "Expert Systems for Accountants: Has Their Time Come?" *Journal of Accountancy*, December 1987, 117–125; John Pallatto, "Neiman-Marcus," *PC Week*, September 2, 1986, 41, 44, 45; Mark Stevens, "Six Small-Business Problems Computers Can Solve," *Working Woman*, September 1987, 33–42.

From Sales through Gross Profit

Based on separate departmental accounts or supplementary analysis sheets

    Revenue from Sales
  − Cost of Merchandise Sold
  = Gross Profit
  − Operating Expenses
  = Income from Operations
  + Other Income
  − Other Expenses
  = Income Before Income Tax
  − Income Tax Expense
  = Net Income After Income Tax

L.O. 2   Accountants use work sheets with separate income statement columns for each department to facilitate the correct apportionment of revenues and expenses.

L.O. 3   A company may extend its income statements on a departmental basis from Sales through Gross Profit or Income from Operations or Departmental Margin.

From Sales through Income from Operations

Based on separate departmental accounts or supplementary analysis sheets

    Revenue from Sales
  − Cost of Merchandise Sold
  = Gross Profit
  − Operating Expenses   { One ledger account for each expense apportioned to various departments
  = Income from Operations
  + Other Income
  − Other Expenses
  = Income Before Income Tax
  − Income Tax Expense
  = Net Income After Income Tax

L.O. 4   In the above format, each department assumes a share of the overhead expenses. The accountant must determine an equitable basis for allocating these expenses among departments.

From Sales through Departmental Margin

Based on separate departmental accounts or supplementary analysis sheets

    Revenue from Sales
  − Cost of Merchandise Sold
  = Gross Profit
  − Direct Departmental Expenses   { Expenses that are directly related to the department
  = Departmental Margin
  − Indirect Expenses
  = Income from Operations
  + Other Income
  − Other Expenses
  = Income Before Income Tax
  − Income Tax Expense
  = Net Income After Income Tax

L.O. 5   In the last format, each department is responsible for only its own share of expenses, consisting of *direct* expenses. Departmental margin represents one department's contribution to the net income of the company as a whole and gives the most realistic portrayal of the department's profitability (or lack of it). A company finds the concept of departmental margin useful in evaluating the present worth of a department, in planning for future operations, and in determining the profitability of a given product. Some operating expenses may be partially direct or partially indirect.

GLOSSARY

Apportionment of expenses Allocating or dividing operating expenses among operating departments.

Departmental margin Gross profit of a department minus the department's direct expenses.

Direct expenses Expenses that benefit only one department and are controlled by the head of the department.

Indirect expenses Overhead expenses that benefit the business as a whole and are not under the control of any one department.

QUESTIONS, EXERCISES, AND PROBLEMS
Discussion Questions

1. Assuming that operating expenses are to be allocated to various departments, on what basis would you allocate the following expenses?
   a. Heating and lighting
   b. Uncollectible accounts
   c. Depreciation of store equipment
   d. Office salaries
   e. Insurance—property and liability
2. In what ways may departmental accounting information be useful?
3. What term is used to refer to the dollar amount representing the excess of departmental gross profit over direct departmental expenses?
4. Describe the difference between a direct and an indirect operating expense.
5. You have been employed as the new manager of a drug store. Previously, the income statement listed total revenue and operating expenses only. The firm can be divided into two departments: pharmacy and variety. You want to know the gross profit for each department. Describe the changes in the accounting system that will be required.
6. Referring to question 5, what benefits do you expect to gain from the departmental information?
7. Department C has a positive departmental margin amounting to $42,000. What does this departmental margin mean as far as the firm is concerned?
8. Why does departmental margin provide a more realistic portrayal of the profitability of a department than gross profit?

Exercises

L.O. 4 **Exercise 26-1** The C and L Grocery occupies an area of 30,000 square feet. The departments and the floor space each department occupies are as follows:

Department	Floor Space
Bakery	1,200 square feet
Grocery	20,100 square feet
Meat	3,600 square feet
Produce	2,400 square feet
Receiving and Storage	2,700 square feet
Total	30,000 square feet

C and L Grocery leases the building for $54,000 per year. Apportion the rent expense to the five departments.

L.O. 1 **Exercise 26-2** The meat department of C and L Grocery buys all its products FOB destination and has the following account balances:

Sales	$516,000
Purchases	276,000
Purchases Discount	6,000
Sales Returns and Allowances	12,000
Merchandise Inventory (beginning)	87,000
Purchases Returns and Allowances	9,000
Merchandise Inventory (ending)	78,000

Determine the amount of the gross profit.

L.O. 4 **Exercise 26-3** Sedgewick Clothiers has annual expenses for salaries of office staff of $17,280, which it allocates to the various departments on the basis of gross sales for each department. Sales by department are as follows:

Department	Gross Sales
Women's clothes	$244,000
Men's clothes	212,000
Accessories	24,000
Total	$480,000

Determine what share of the office salaries expense each of the three operating departments should bear.

L.O. 4 **Exercise 26-4** The premium for public liability insurance for the clothing store in Exercise 26-3 is $570, and the premium for fire and theft insurance on the inventory is $720. The balances of the inventories at the end of the fiscal period are as follows:

Department	Ending Inventory
Women's clothes	$80,000
Men's clothes	60,000
Accessories	20,000
Total	$160,000

How much of the insurance costs should be allocated to each department, given that public liability insurance is apportioned on the basis of gross sales and that property insurance is allocated on the basis of the values of the ending inventories?

L.O. 5 **Exercise 26-5** The following figures apply to Manley and Frank's furniture department:

Sales	$738,000
Direct Departmental Expenses	156,000
Purchases	516,060
Purchases Returns and Allowances	9,000
Freight In	32,940
Interest Expense	6,000
Sales Returns and Allowances	12,000
Merchandise Inventory (ending)	228,000
Indirect Expenses	93,000
Merchandise Inventory (beginning)	198,000

Determine the amount of the departmental margin.

L.O. 4 **Exercise 26-6** Perotti Company apportions depreciation on equipment on the basis of the average cost of equipment. Insurance expense is apportioned on the basis of the combined total of average cost of the equipment and average cost of the merchandise inventory. Depreciation expense on equipment amounted to $9,000. Insurance expense amounted to $3,600. Determine the apportionment of the depreciation expense and the insurance expense based on the following information:

	Average Cost	
Department	Equipment	Inventory
A	$ 45,000	$150,000
B	90,000	180,000
C	45,000	90,000
Total	$180,000	$420,000

L.O. 5 **Exercise 26-7** Lubin, Inc., is considering eliminating its camera department. Management does not believe that the indirect expenses and the level of operations in the other departments will be affected if the camera department closes. Information from Lubin's income statement for the fiscal year ended December 31, which is considered a typical year, is on the next page.

	Camera Department	All Other Departments	Total of All Departments (including Camera)
Sales	$148,000	$1,124,000	$1,272,000
Cost of Merchandise Sold	96,000	792,000	888,000
Gross Profit	$ 52,000	$ 332,000	$ 384,000
Operating Expenses	60,000	222,000	282,000
Income (Loss) from Operations	$ (8,000)	$ 110,000	$ 102,000

Lubin considers that $36,000 of the operating expenses of the camera department are direct expenses. What is the departmental margin of the camera department?

L.O. 3   **Exercise 26-8**   For Lubin, Inc., in Exercise 26-7, prepare an income statement for the forthcoming year, assuming that Lubin discontinues the camera department.

Problem Set A

L.O. 1   **Problem 26-1A**   Bella's Garden Shop has two sales departments: plants and tools. After recording and posting all departments, including the adjustments for merchandise inventory, the accountant presented the adjusted trial balance shown on the next page at the end of the fiscal year.

Instructions

Prepare an income statement to show gross profit for each department and income from operations, as well as net income, for the entire business. Beginning balances of merchandise inventory are as follows: plants, $57,040; tools, $32,106.

L.O. 3   **Problem 26-2A**   Hiram Foster, Inc., has two departments: luggage and accessories. Foster's accountant prepares an adjusted trial balance (shown on page 906) at the end of the fiscal year, after all adjustments, including the adjustments for merchandise inventory, have been recorded and posted. Merchandise inventories at the beginning of the year were as follows: luggage department, $165,520; accessory department, $81,440. The bases for apportioning expenses and the sources of the figures are as follows:

- Sales Salary Expense (payroll register): luggage department, $149,600; accessory department, $96,840
- Advertising Expense (newspaper column inches): luggage department, 1,200 inches; accessory department, 800 inches
- Depreciation Expense, Store Equipment (plant and equipment ledger): luggage department, $19,232; accessory department, $7,640
- Store Supplies Expense (requisitions): luggage department, $836; accessory department, $648

Bella's Garden Shop
Adjusted Trial Balance
September 30, 19–

ACCOUNT NAME	DEBIT	CREDIT
Cash	4 656 00	
Accounts Receivable	46 844 00	
Allowance for Doubtful Accounts		2 282 00
Merchandise Inventory, Plants	50 302 00	
Merchandise Inventory, Tools	35 539 00	
Store Supplies	962 00	
Store Equipment	23 102 00	
Accumulated Depreciation, Store Equipment		15 082 00
Accounts Payable		30 959 00
B. R. Ogdahl, Capital		85 542 00
B. R. Ogdahl, Drawing	22 922 00	
Income Summary	57 040 00	50 302 00
	32 106 00	35 539 00
Sales, Plants		370 136 00
Sales, Tools		257 462 00
Sales Returns and Allowances, Plants	7 142 00	
Sales Returns and Allowances, Tools	6 118 00	
Purchases, Plants	302 685 00	
Purchases, Tools	208 663 00	
Purchases Returns and Allowances, Plants		7 042 00
Purchases Returns and Allowances, Tools		5 136 00
Purchases Discount, Plants		5 150 00
Purchases Discount, Tools		4 310 00
Freight In, Plants	9 361 00	
Freight In, Tools	6 456 00	
Sales Salary Expense	27 162 00	
Depreciation Expense, Store Equipment	4 306 00	
Miscellaneous Selling Expense	548 00	
Office Salary Expense	12 322 00	
Rent Expense	5 922 00	
Utilities Expense	2 414 00	
Bad Debts Expense	638 00	
Miscellaneous General Expense	506 00	
Interest Expense	1 226 00	
	868 942 00	868 942 00

- Rent Expense and Utilities Expense (floor space): luggage department, 5,000 square feet; accessory department, 3,000 square feet
- Insurance Expense (average cost of merchandise inventory, rounded off in dollars): luggage department, $1,208; accessory department, $592 (verify this figure)

Hiram Foster, Inc.
Adjusted Trial Balance
January 31, 19–

ACCOUNT NAME	DEBIT	CREDIT
Cash	9 6 5 2 00	
Accounts Receivable	137 7 8 0 00	
Allowance for Doubtful Accounts		5 2 4 0 00
Merchandise Inventory, Luggage Department	168 2 8 4 00	
Merchandise Inventory, Accessory Department	82 2 7 6 00	
Prepaid Insurance	1 6 8 0 00	
Store Supplies	1 5 2 4 00	
Store Equipment	107 3 6 4 00	
Accumulated Depreciation, Store Equipment		83 6 2 0 00
Accounts Payable		77 3 6 0 00
Sales Tax Payable		2 5 6 8 00
Income Tax Payable		3 4 6 5 00
Common Stock		138 8 8 8 00
Retained Earnings		83 7 5 0 00
Income Summary	165 5 2 0 00	168 2 8 4 00
	81 4 4 0 00	82 2 7 6 00
Sales, Luggage Department		819 6 0 0 00
Sales, Accessory Department		546 4 0 0 00
Sales Returns and Allowances, Luggage Department	23 3 7 0 00	
Sales Returns and Allowances, Accessory Department	3 4 3 2 00	
Purchases, Luggage Department	503 6 9 4 00	
Purchases, Accessory Department	330 4 8 4 00	
Purchases Returns and Allowances, Luggage Department		9 2 3 6 00
Purchases Returns and Allowances, Accessory Department		3 5 8 4 00
Purchases Discount, Luggage Department		10 9 9 2 00
Purchases Discount, Accessory Department		5 9 2 8 00
Freight In, Luggage Department	26 5 1 0 00	
Freight In, Accessory Department	13 7 7 0 00	
Sales Salary Expense	246 4 4 0 00	
Advertising Expense	28 0 0 0 00	
Depreciation Expense, Store Equipment	26 8 7 2 00	
Store Supplies Expense	1 4 8 4 00	
Miscellaneous Selling Expense	1 3 6 0 00	
Rent Expense	16 0 0 0 00	
Utilities Expense	6 4 0 0 00	
Insurance Expense	1 8 0 0 00	
Bad Debts Expense	3 6 0 0 00	
Miscellaneous General Expense	1 6 4 0 00	
Income Tax	45 2 1 5 00	
Interest Expense	5 6 0 0 00	
	2,041 1 9 1 00	2,041 1 9 1 00

- Miscellaneous Selling Expense (volume of gross sales): luggage department, $816; accessory department, $544 (verify these figures)
- Bad Debts Expense (volume of gross sales): luggage department, $2,160; accessory department, $1,440 (verify these figures)
- Miscellaneous General Expense (volume of gross sales): luggage department, $984; accessory department, $656 (verify these figures)

Instructions

Prepare an income statement by department to show income from operations, as well as a nondepartmentalized income statement (using the Total columns) to show net income for the entire company.

L.O. 2   **Problem 26-3A**   The Athletic Station has two departments: bicycle and clothing. The trial balance, as of April 30, the end of the fiscal year, is as follows:

The Athletic Station
Trial Balance
April 30, 19–

ACCOUNT NAME	DEBIT	CREDIT
Cash	10 2 1 0 00	
Accounts Receivable	60 1 8 0 00	
Allowance for Doubtful Accounts		1 5 6 4 00
Merchandise Inventory, Bicycle Department	66 1 0 0 00	
Merchandise Inventory, Clothing Department	47 3 0 0 00	
Prepaid Insurance	8 7 0 00	
Store Equipment	26 9 4 0 00	
Accumulated Depreciation, Store Equipment		12 1 6 5 00
Accounts Payable		58 1 1 0 00
S. E. Olson, Capital		99 1 2 0 00
S. E. Olson, Drawing	23 2 5 0 00	
Sales, Bicycle Department		192 0 0 0 00
Sales, Clothing Department		128 0 0 0 00
Purchases, Bicycle Department	85 8 2 4 00	
Purchases, Clothing Department	65 9 5 2 00	
Freight In, Bicycle Department	3 5 7 6 00	
Freight In, Clothing Department	2 7 4 8 00	
Wages and Commissions Expense	73 1 5 0 00	
Advertising Expense	9 9 0 0 00	
Rent Expense	10 8 0 0 00	
Utilities Expense	2 1 3 0 00	
Miscellaneous Expense	1 3 3 5 00	
Interest Expense	6 9 4 00	
	490 9 5 9 00	490 9 5 9 00

The data for the adjustments are as follows:

a.–d. Merchandise inventories, April 30, the end of the fiscal period: bicycle department, $61,420; clothing department, $43,226

  e. Insurance expired, $615

  f. Estimated uncollectible customer charge accounts (based on an analysis of accounts), $3,662

  g. Depreciation of store equipment for the year, $7,290

  h. Accrued wages and commissions, $512

  i. Accrued interest payable, $206

The bases for apportioning expenses to the two departments are as follows:

- Advertising Expense (column inches of space): bicycle department, $7,920; clothing department, $1,980
- Depreciation Expense (equipment ledger): bicycle department, $5,024; clothing department, $2,266
- Wages and Commissions Expense (time sheets): bicycle department, $47,681; clothing department, $25,981
- Rent Expense, Utilities Expense, Miscellaneous Expense, Bad Debts Expense, Insurance Expense (sales): bicycle department, 60 percent; clothing department, 40 percent.

Instructions

Complete the work sheet.

L.O. 3   **Problem 26-4A**   On December 31, the end of the fiscal year, Ingalls Interiors, a sole proprietorship, has the revenue and expense account and merchandise inventory balances, after adjustments have been recorded, shown in the work sheet on the next page. The store has two departments: carpets and draperies. The values of merchandise inventory on January 1 (beginning) are: carpets, $143,460; and draperies, $71,838.

Essential data for direct expenses (and sources of the figures) are as follows:

a. Sales Salary Expense (sales personnel work in one department only) is allocated as follows: carpets, $95,580; draperies, $40,920.

b. Advertising Expense: Newspaper advertising is allocated as follows: carpets, $9,840; draperies, $2,490.

c. Depreciation: Depreciation of store equipment is apportioned on the basis of the average cost of equipment in each department. The average cost of store equipment is carpets, $22,500; draperies, $7,500.

d. Bad Debts Expense: Department managers are responsible for granting credit on sales made by their respective departments. Bad Debts Expense is allocated as follows: carpets, $3,888; draperies, $1,572.

Instructions

Prepare an income statement to show each department's departmental margin.

Ingalls Interiors
Work Sheet
For Year Ended December 31, 19–

ACCOUNT NAME	ADJUSTED TRIAL BALANCE	
	DEBIT	CREDIT
Merchandise Inventory, Carpets	153 0 9 0 00	
Merchandise Inventory, Draperies	65 3 4 6 00	
Sales, Carpets		562 2 4 8 00
Sales, Draperies		221 7 8 4 00
Sales Returns and Allowances, Carpets	14 3 4 6 00	
Sales Returns and Allowances, Draperies	6 0 1 8 00	
Purchases, Carpets	315 7 6 7 00	
Purchases, Draperies	125 0 0 3 00	
Purchases Returns and Allowances, Carpets		7 9 2 0 00
Purchases Returns and Allowances, Draperies		2 0 5 2 00
Purchases Discount, Carpets		5 9 4 0 00
Purchases Discount, Draperies		2 1 6 0 00
Freight In, Carpets	20 1 5 5 00	
Freight In, Draperies	4 9 3 9 00	
Sales Salary Expense	136 5 0 0 00	
Advertising Expense	12 3 3 0 00	
Depreciation Expense, Store Equipment	9 6 0 0 00	
Bad Debts Expense	5 4 6 0 00	
Office Salary Expense	25 8 0 0 00	
Rent Expense	25 2 0 0 00	
Utilities Expense	3 7 2 0 00	
Insurance Expense	1 1 7 0 00	
Miscellaneous Selling Expense	1 1 2 2 00	
Miscellaneous General Expense	1 0 6 8 00	
Interest Expense	2 2 4 4 00	

Problem Set B

L.O. 1,3 **Problem 26-1B** Hendricks Lumber has two sales departments: lumber and hardware. Hendricks's accountant prepared the adjusted trial balance shown on page 910 at the end of the fiscal year, after all adjustments, including adjustments for merchandise inventory, had been recorded and posted.

Instructions

Prepare an income statement to show gross profit for each department and income from operations, as well as net income for the entire business. Beginning balances of merchandise inventory are as follows: lumber, $235,848; hardware, $217,446.

Hendricks Lumber
Adjusted Trial Balance
December 31, 19–

ACCOUNT NAME	DEBIT	CREDIT
Cash	9 6 2 4 00	
Accounts Receivable	135 5 6 7 00	
Allowance for Doubtful Accounts		4 8 6 0 00
Merchandise Inventory, Lumber Department	258 3 5 7 00	
Merchandise Inventory, Hardware Department	204 5 8 5 00	
Store Supplies	1 5 4 2 00	
Store Equipment	59 0 1 0 00	
Accumulated Depreciation, Store Equipment		38 3 0 4 00
Accounts Payable		143 9 5 5 00
L. T. Hendricks, Capital		361 8 6 0 00
L. T. Hendricks, Drawing	61 2 0 0 00	
Income Summary	235 8 4 8 00	258 3 5 7 00
	217 4 4 6 00	204 5 8 5 00
Sales, Lumber Department		1,120 6 7 7 00
Sales, Hardware Department		945 7 2 0 00
Sales Returns and Allowances, Lumber Department	21 4 2 3 00	
Sales Returns and Allowances, Hardware Department	19 4 2 8 00	
Purchases, Lumber Department	1,011 7 6 0 00	
Purchases, Hardware Department	697 4 0 4 00	
Purchases Returns and Allowances, Lumber Department		15 8 5 2 00
Purchases Returns and Allowances, Hardware Department		13 1 5 2 00
Purchases Discount, Lumber Department		20 5 2 3 00
Purchases Discount, Hardware Department		14 8 8 0 00
Freight In, Lumber Department	31 2 9 2 00	
Freight In, Hardware Department	33 6 2 7 00	
Sales Salary Expense	86 3 7 0 00	
Depreciation Expense, Store Equipment	13 1 4 6 00	
Miscellaneous Selling Expense	5 2 8 00	
Office Salary Expense	17 6 4 0 00	
Rent Expense	14 4 0 0 00	
Utilities Expense	8 6 5 8 00	
Bad Debts Expense	7 2 6 00	
Miscellaneous General Expense	3 6 0 00	
Interest Expense	2 7 8 4 00	
	3,142 7 2 5 00	3,142 7 2 5 00

L.O. 3 **Problem 26-2B** Bryan Book and Software has two sales departments: book and software. After recording and posting all adjustments, including the adjustments for merchandise inventory, the accountant prepared the following adjusted trial balance at the end of the fiscal year:

Bryan Book and Software
Adjusted Trial Balance
December 31, 19–

ACCOUNT NAME	DEBIT	CREDIT
Cash	11 2 8 0 00	
Accounts Receivable	104 6 4 0 00	
Allowance for Doubtful Accounts		5 6 8 0 00
Merchandise Inventory, Book Department	160 6 7 2 00	
Merchandise Inventory, Software Department	74 9 6 2 00	
Prepaid Insurance	1 9 6 8 00	
Store Supplies	1 5 9 6 00	
Store Equipment	128 4 4 0 00	
Accumulated Depreciation, Store Equipment		97 8 5 6 00
Accounts Payable		96 8 4 0 00
Sales Tax Payable		2 6 8 4 00
Income Tax Payable		3 4 9 7 00
Common Stock		223 8 9 0 00
Retained Earnings	27 4 5 0 00	
Income Summary	157 8 5 6 00	160 6 7 2 00
	72 4 4 8 00	74 9 6 2 00
Sales, Book Department		952 0 0 0 00
Sales, Software Department		408 0 0 0 00
Sales Returns and Allowances, Book Department	24 4 8 2 00	
Sales Returns and Allowances, Software Department	1 6 5 2 00	
Purchases, Book Department	599 6 8 6 00	
Purchases, Software Department	288 8 1 8 00	
Purchases Returns and Allowances, Book Department		8 4 5 2 00
Purchases Returns and Allowances, Software Department		2 5 9 2 00
Purchases Discount, Book Department		11 7 6 8 00
Purchases Discount, Software Department		8 5 6 0 00
Freight In, Book Department	21 7 5 0 00	
Freight In, Software Department	8 6 2 6 00	
Sales Salary Expense	243 5 6 4 00	
Advertising Expense	32 0 0 0 00	
Depreciation Expense, Store Equipment	31 6 0 0 00	
Store Supplies Expense	1 2 1 2 00	
Miscellaneous Selling Expense	1 0 4 0 00	
Rent Expense	19 2 0 0 00	
Utilities Expense	7 2 0 0 00	
Insurance Expense	1 6 8 0 00	
Bad Debts Expense	4 4 0 0 00	
Miscellaneous General Expense	1 5 6 0 00	
Interest Expense	3 6 2 4 00	
Income Tax Expense	24 0 4 7 00	
	2,057 4 5 3 00	2,057 4 5 3 00

Merchandise inventories at the beginning of the year were as follows: book department, $157,856; software department, $72,448. The bases (and sources of figures) for apportioning expenses to the two departments are as follows:

- Sales Salary Expense (payroll register): book department, $136,676; software department, $106,888
- Advertising Expense (newspaper column inches): book department, 1,200 inches; software department, 800 inches
- Depreciation Expense, Store Equipment (plant and equipment ledger): book department, $23,284; software department, $8,316
- Store Supplies Expense (requisitions): book department, $640; software department, $572
- Rent Expense and Utilities Expense (floor space): book department, 5,000 square feet; software department, 3,000 square feet
- Insurance Expense (average cost of merchandise inventory, rounded off in dollars): book department, $1,148; software department, $532 (verify these figures)
- Miscellaneous Selling Expense (volume of gross sales): book department, $728; software department, $312 (verify these figures)
- Bad Debts Expense (volume of gross sales): book department, $3,080; software department, $1,320 (verify these figures)
- Miscellaneous General Expense (volume of gross sales): book department, $1,092; software department, $468 (verify these figures)

Instructions

Prepare an income statement by department to show income from operations, as well as a nondepartmentalized income statement (using the Total columns) to show net income for the entire company.

L.O. 2   **Problem 26-3B**   Capra's Cycle has two departments: bicycle and clothing. The trial balance, as of October 31, the end of the fiscal year, is shown on the next page.

The data for the adjustments are as follows:

a.–d. Merchandise inventories, October 31, the end of the fiscal period: bicycle department, $60,000; clothing department, $36,000
   e. Depreciation of store equipment for the year, $7,230
   f. Estimated uncollectible customer charge accounts (based on an analysis of accounts), $2,190
   g. Insurance expired, $585
   h. Accrued wages, $555
   i. Accrued interest payable, $216

The bases for apportioning expenses to the two departments are as follows:

- Wages and Commissions Expense (time sheets): bicycle department, $45,540; clothing department, $19,515
- Advertising Expense (space): bicycle department, $7,680; clothing department, $1,920
- Depreciation Expense (equipment ledger): bicycle department, $5,061; clothing department, $2,169

Capra's Cycle
Trial Balance
October 31, 19–

ACCOUNT NAME	DEBIT	CREDIT
Cash	9 3 0 0 00	
Accounts Receivable	59 4 0 0 00	
Allowance for Doubtful Accounts		1 5 6 0 00
Merchandise Inventory, Bicycle Department	63 0 0 0 00	
Merchandise Inventory, Clothing Department	42 0 0 0 00	
Prepaid Insurance	9 0 0 00	
Store Equipment	27 3 0 0 00	
Accumulated Depreciation, Store Equipment		12 2 1 0 00
Accounts Payable		58 0 8 0 00
C. D. Capra, Capital		99 4 2 0 00
C. D. Capra, Drawing	21 0 0 0 00	
Sales, Bicycle Department		180 0 0 0 00
Sales, Clothing Department		120 0 0 0 00
Purchases, Bicycle Department	86 4 0 0 00	
Purchases, Clothing Department	66 2 4 0 00	
Freight In, Bicycle Department	3 6 0 0 00	
Freight In, Clothing Department	2 7 6 0 00	
Wages and Commissions Expense	64 5 0 0 00	
Advertising Expense	9 6 0 0 00	
Rent Expense	10 8 0 0 00	
Utilities Expense	2 1 7 5 00	
Miscellaneous Expense	1 6 3 5 00	
Interest Expense	6 6 0 00	
	471 2 7 0 00	471 2 7 0 00

- Rent Expense, Utilities Expense, Miscellaneous Expense, Bad Debts Expense, Insurance Expense (sales): bicycle department, 60 percent; clothing department, 40 percent.

Instructions

Complete the work sheet.

L.O. 5 **Problem 26-4B** Modern Decorators is a sole proprietorship. After the firm has recorded adjustments, it has the balances shown in the work sheet on page 914 for revenue and expense accounts and merchandise inventories for its two departments on December 31, the end of the fiscal year. The values of merchandise inventory on January 1 (beginning) are: carpets, $146,130; draperies, $72,420. Essential data for direct expenses (and sources of figures) are shown on page 914.

Modern Decorators
Work Sheet
For Year Ended December 31, 19–

ACCOUNT NAME	ADJUSTED TRIAL BALANCE	
	DEBIT	CREDIT
Merchandise Inventory, Carpets	157 9 8 0 00	
Merchandise Inventory, Draperies	68 9 4 0 00	
Sales, Carpets		569 5 6 8 00
Sales, Draperies		222 4 3 2 00
Sales Returns and Allowances, Carpets	14 4 4 8 00	
Sales Returns and Allowances, Draperies	6 5 5 2 00	
Purchases, Carpets	316 2 3 5 00	
Purchases, Draperies	124 9 3 5 00	
Purchases Returns and Allowances, Carpets		4 9 4 4 00
Purchases Returns and Allowances, Draperies		2 0 1 0 00
Purchases Discount, Carpets		3 5 4 6 00
Purchases Discount, Draperies		2 2 2 0 00
Freight In, Carpets	20 1 8 5 00	
Freight In, Draperies	4 9 3 5 00	
Sales Salary Expense	138 7 8 0 00	
Advertising Expense	12 6 0 0 00	
Depreciation Expense, Store Equipment	9 6 0 0 00	
Bad Debts Expense	5 7 0 0 00	
Office Salary Expense	25 5 6 0 00	
Rent Expense	25 2 0 0 00	
Utilities Expense	3 7 8 0 00	
Insurance Expense	1 2 6 0 00	
Miscellaneous Selling Expense	1 1 7 0 00	
Miscellaneous General Expense	1 0 2 0 00	
Interest Expense	1 8 6 2 00	

a. Sales Salary Expense (sales personnel work in one department only) is allocated as follows: carpets, $97,140; draperies, $41,640.
b. Advertising: newspaper advertising is allocated as follows: carpets, $10,080; draperies, $2,520.
c. Depreciation: Depreciation of store equipment is apportioned on the basis of the average cost of equipment in each department. The average cost of store equipment is $15,000 for carpets and $5,000 for draperies.
d. Bad Debts Expense: Department managers are responsible for granting credit on sales made by their respective departments. Bad Debts Expense is allocated as follows: carpets, $4,104; draperies, $1,596.

Instructions

Prepare an income statement to show each department's departmental margin.

27 Analyzing and Interpreting Financial Statements

As we said in Chapter 1, accounting is the process of analyzing, recording, summarizing, and *interpreting* business transactions. We are now ready to interpret the results: How does one draw conclusions from financial data that have been summarized in financial statements?

The financial condition of a company and the results of operations of business enterprises are of interest not only to owners, employers, and managers but to creditors and to prospective owners and creditors. Everybody is interested in two aspects of an enterprise:

1. Its **solvency,** or its ability to pay its debts
2. Its **profitability,** or its ability to earn a reasonable profit on the owners' investment

This chapter will explain the techniques used to determine solvency and profitability.

TYPES OF COMPARISON

To interpret a set of facts, one has to have something else with which to compare it. In other words, a given set of facts by itself is not significant. For example, if you are told that a certain corporation earned a net income of $56,000 during the past year, this figure by itself is not meaningful. Does this net income indicate a successful year or a poor year? Does it compare favorably with other years or unfavorably? Does it represent a reasonable return on sales and investment or not? How does it compare with the net income of other firms in the same industry?

A company's financial statements are meaningful only if you analyze them on a comparative basis. There are three useful bases for making such a comparison:

1. Statements of the same company for the current year and one or more prior years
2. Financial data for other companies in the same industry
3. Previously established financial standards or objectives

COMPARATIVE STATEMENTS

One technique for analyzing and interpreting financial data is the preparation of comparative statements. Two types of analysis—horizontal and vertical—are commonly used.

Horizontal Analysis

Objective 1

Prepare a comparative income statement and balance sheet involving horizontal analysis.

Income Statement Horizontal analysis compares the same item in a company's financial statements for two or more periods. Let's look at the comparative income statement (Figure 27-1) of Titan Furniture Company, Inc., for 19x4 and 19x5. Later we will look at the comparative balance sheet for this firm.

Note that for each item in the income statement the accountant first expressed the differences—that is, the increases or decreases of 19x5 over 19x4—in dollars and then in percentages. Take the increase in Sales, on the second line, for example. Subtract Sales in 19x4 from Sales in 19x5.

$980,600	Sales for 19x5
− 860,000	Sales for 19x4
$120,600	Increase of 19x5 over 19x4

To calculate the *percentage* of increase in Sales in 19x5 over 19x4, divide the dollar increase by the amount of Sales during the base year. Then round the answer to three decimal places and multiply by 100 to change the decimal to a percentage.

Titan Furniture Company, Inc.
Comparative Income Statement
For Years Ended December 31, 19x5 and December 31, 19x4

	19x5	19x4	INCREASE OR DECREASE AMOUNT	PERCENT
Revenues from Sales:				
Sales	$ 980 600 00	$ 860 000 00	$ 120 600 00	14.0
Less Sales Returns and Allowances	13 700 00	11 400 00	2 300 00	20.2
Net Sales	$ 966 900 00	$ 848 600 00	$ 118 300 00	13.9
Cost of Merchandise Sold:				
Merchandise Inventory, January 1	206 500 00	$ 138 700 00	$ 67 800 00	48.9
Purchases (net)	804 800 00	636 600 00	168 200 00	26.4
Merchandise Available for Sale	$1 011 300 00	$ 775 300 00	$ 236 000 00	30.4
Less Merchandise Inventory, December 31	353 600 00	206 500 00	147 100 00	71.2
Cost of Merchandise Sold	$ 657 700 00	$ 568 800 00	$ 88 900 00	15.6
Gross Profit	$ 309 200 00	$ 279 800 00	$ 29 400 00	10.5
Operating Expenses:				
Selling Expenses:				
Sales Salary Expense	$ 114 650 00	$ 102 400 00	$ 12 250 00	12.0
Delivery Expense	17 700 00	13 700 00	4 000 00	29.2
Advertising Expense	7 900 00	6 900 00	1 000 00	14.5
Depreciation Expense, Equipment	6 800 00	6 600 00	200 00	3.0
Store Supplies Expense	750 00	600 00	150 00	25.0
Total Selling Expenses	$ 147 800 00	$ 130 200 00	$ 17 600 00	13.5
General Expenses:				
Office Salary Expense	$ 33 440 00	$ 27 680 00	$ 5 760 00	20.8
Depreciation Expense, Building	14 200 00	14 200 00	0 00	0
Bad Debts Expense	6 200 00	5 400 00	800 00	14.8
Taxes Expense	6 100 00	5 200 00	900 00	17.3
Insurance Expense	1 100 00	1 000 00	100 00	10.0
Miscellaneous General Expense	860 00	720 00	140 00	19.4
Total General Expenses	$ 61 900 00	$ 54 200 00	$ 7 700 00	14.2
Total Operating Expenses	$ 209 700 00	$ 184 400 00	$ 25 300 00	13.7
Income from Operations	$ 99 500 00	$ 95 400 00	$. 4 100 00	4.3
Other Expenses:				
Interest Expense	8 520 00	7 860 00	660 00	8.4
Income Before Income Tax	$ 90 980 00	$ 87 540 00	$ 3 440 00	3.9
Income Tax Expense	19 920 00	18 010 00	1 910 00	10.6
Net Income After Income Tax	$ 71 060 00	$ 69 530 00	$ 1 530 00	2.2

FIGURE 27-1

$$\frac{\$120,600}{\$860,000} = 860,000\overline{)120,600}^{.1402} = .140 \times 100 = \underline{\underline{14.0\%}}$$

Note: The expression **base year** means the year you are using as a basis for comparison.

As another example, take the change in Sales Returns and Allowances:

$13,700	Sales Returns and Allowances for 19x5
− 11,400	Sales Returns and Allowances for 19x4
$ 2,300	Increase of 19x5 over 19x4

The percentage rate of increase is

$$\frac{\$2,300}{\$11,400} = 11,400\overline{)2,300}^{.2018} = .202 \times 100 = \underline{\underline{20.2\%}}$$

Remember

The percentage of increase is calculated by dividing the dollar amount of increase by the base year amount, rounding the answer to three decimal places, and multiplying by 100.

People appraising an income statement often use the percentage increase of net sales as a basis for comparison. In other words, they compare all other percentage changes with the percentage change in net sales, to see whether the other percentage changes are out of line. If net sales increased 13.9 percent from 19x4 to 19x5, other percentage changes should amount to approximately 13.9 percent also. If they vary considerably from 13.9 percent, they may be out of line, and one should investigate to find the reasons for the difference.

Let's look at the main items on the income statement.

Item	Percentage Change
Net Sales	13.9
Cost of Merchandise Sold	15.6
Gross Profit	10.5
Total Operating Expenses	13.7
Net Income After Income Tax	2.2

You can see that Gross Profit and Net Income are considerably less than the percentage change in sales. Since Gross Profit is determined by subtracting Cost of Merchandise Sold from Net Sales, one should investigate the entire Cost of Merchandise Sold section of the income statement. This is a starting point in accounting for the comparatively small percentage increase in Net Income. The percentage changes of items in the Cost of Merchandise Sold section are as follows:

Item	Percentage Change
Merchandise Inventory, January 1	48.9
Net Purchases	26.4
Merchandise Inventory, December 31	71.2

The merchandise inventory of January 1 was a carry-over from the previous year, but why the large increase in Net Purchases? And look at the large increase in merchandise inventory at the end of the year; buying all that merchandise took a lot of cash. Also, with such a large increase in merchandise inventory, we would expect a larger increase in sales. Is the increase in sales large enough?

Remember

_____

The base year is the earlier year.

Incidentally, a percentage change can be calculated only when a positive amount is reported in the base year. For example, let's say a company had a net loss of $3,500 in Year 1 (base year) and a net income of $2,000 in Year 2. Because the $3,500 is not a positive amount, it is not possible to state the amount of the change as a percentage.

Balance Sheet   Now look at the balance sheet in Figure 27-2, which shows the comparison between 19x5 and 19x4. Again you will see why changes are expressed in both dollars and percentages. Items showing either a large dollar change or a large percentage change stick out like a sore thumb. This time some minus totals show up in the difference column.

The following items are based on data from the comparative balance sheet:

Item	Dollar Increase or Decrease	Percentage Increase or Decrease
Merchandise Inventory	$147,100	71.2
Accounts Payable	42,600	146.9
Cash	(19,100)	(49.4)

Recall that the comparative income statement already exposed the jump in the Merchandise Inventory account. We should also consider the effects of changes in the balances of other related accounts. For example, the fact that Cash is down by 49 percent while Accounts Payable is up by 147 percent may indicate a pending financial crisis. To meet its bills, the firm may be forced to liquidate that big stock of merchandise by

FIGURE 27-2

Titan Furniture Company, Inc.
Comparative Balance Sheet
December 31, 19x5 and December 31, 19x4

	19x5	19x4	INCREASE OR DECREASE AMOUNT	PERCENT
Assets				
Current Assets:				
Cash	$ 19 6 0 0 00	$ 38 7 0 0 00	$ (19 1 0 0 00)	(49.4)
Accounts Receivable	76 7 0 0 00	81 4 0 0 00	(4 7 0 0 00)	(5.8)
Less Allowance for Doubtful Accounts	(3 3 0 0 00)	(2 6 0 0 00)	(7 0 0 00)	(26.9)
Merchandise Inventory	353 6 0 0 00	206 5 0 0 00	147 1 0 0 00	71.2
Prepaid Insurance	2 0 0 0 00	2 1 0 0 00	(1 0 0 00)	(4.8)
Total Current Assets	$ 448 6 0 0 00	$ 326 1 0 0 00	$ 122 5 0 0 00	37.6
Investments:				
Sinking Fund Cash	$ 4 1 0 0 00	$ 5 8 0 0 00	$ (1 7 0 0 00)	(29.3)
Sinking Fund Investments	61 7 0 0 00	59 4 0 0 00	2 3 0 0 00	3.9
Total Investments	$ 65 8 0 0 00	$ 65 2 0 0 00	$ 6 0 0 00	.9
Plant and Equipment:				
Land	$ 40 0 0 0 00	40 0 0 0 00	$ 0 00	0
Building	160 0 0 0 00	160 0 0 0 00	0 00	0
Less Accumulated Depreciation	(56 8 0 0 00)	(42 6 0 0 00)	(14 2 0 0 00)	(33.3)
Equipment	88 6 0 0 00	86 0 0 0 00	2 6 0 0 00	3.0
Less Accumulated Depreciation	(41 0 0 0 00)	(34 2 0 0 00)	(6 8 0 0 00)	(19.9)
Total Plant and Equipment	$ 190 8 0 0 00	$ 209 2 0 0 00	$ (18 4 0 0 00)	(8.8)
Intangible Assets:				
Organization Costs	3 0 0 0 00	4 0 0 0 00	(1 0 0 0 00)	(25.0)
Total Assets	$ 708 2 0 0 00	$ 604 5 0 0 00	$ 103 7 0 0 00	17.2
Liabilities				
Current Liabilities:				
Accounts Payable	$ 71 6 0 0 00	$ 29 0 0 0 00	$ 42 6 0 0 00	146.9
Income Tax Payable	12 8 0 0 00	5 6 0 0 00	7 2 0 0 00	128.6
Dividends Payable	12 0 0 0 00	4 0 0 0 00	8 0 0 0 00	200.0
Salaries Payable	4 2 0 0 00	4 0 0 0 00	2 0 0 00	5.0
Total Current Liabilities	$ 100 6 0 0 00	$ 42 6 0 0 00	$ 58 0 0 0 00	136.2
Long-Term Liabilities:				
Bonds Payable, 6%, due Dec. 31, 19x9	$ 100 0 0 0 00	$ 100 0 0 0 00	0 00	0
Less Discount on Bonds Payable	(2 2 0 0 00)	(2 4 0 0 00)	(2 0 0 00)	(8.3)
Total Long-Term Liabilities	$ 97 8 0 0 00	$ 97 6 0 0 00	$ 2 0 0 00	.2
Total Liabilities	$ 198 4 0 0 00	$ 140 2 0 0 00	$ 58 2 0 0 00	41.5
Stockholders' Equity				
Paid-in Capital:				
Comm Stock, $100 par (4,000 shares authorized, 3,000 shares issued)	$ 300 0 0 0 00	$ 300 0 0 0 00	$ 0 00	0
Premium on Common Stock	86 0 0 0 00	86 0 0 0 00	0 00	0
Total Paid-in Capital	$ 386 0 0 0 00	$ 386 0 0 0 00	$ 0 00	0
Retained Earnings:				
Unappropriated	$ 103 8 0 0 00	$ 66 3 0 0 00	$ 37 5 0 0 00	56.6
Appropriated for Plant Expansion	20 0 0 0 00	12 0 0 0 00	8 0 0 0 00	66.7
Total Retained Earnings	$ 123 8 0 0 00	$ 78 3 0 0 00	$ 45 5 0 0 00	58.1
Total Stockholders' Equity	$ 509 8 0 0 00	$ 464 3 0 0 00	$ 45 5 0 0 00	9.8
Total Liabilities and Stockholders' Equity	$ 708 2 0 0 00	$ 604 5 0 0 00	$ 103 7 0 0 00	17.2

selling it off at cost, or even less. That 200 percent increase in Dividends Payable doesn't look good either. One point in their favor, though, is the decrease in Accounts Receivable. The increase in Allowance for Doubtful Accounts, although relatively small in amount, appears to be unreasonable when expressed as a percentage.

Vertical Analysis

Objective 2

Prepare a comparative income statement and balance sheet involving vertical analysis.

Income Statement Another tool accountants can use to analyze financial statements is **vertical analysis** To use this method, one needs to see, in a single statement, the relationship of components to the whole. In the case of an income statement, *the whole is net sales.* Although each percentage applies to a single item only, one can quickly see the relative importance of each item in the statement. Let's look first at the comparative income statement (Figure 27-3) and then at the comparative balance sheet for Titan Furniture Company, Inc., this time arranged for vertical analysis.

When you arrange an income statement for vertical analysis, you express each item as a *percentage of net sales.* In other words, you divide the total for each item by the total of net sales. Here is how that works.

Gross Profit % = Gross Profit ÷ Net Sales

$$\textbf{Gross Profit \% (19x5)} = \frac{\$309{,}200}{\$966{,}900} = .3198 = \underline{\underline{32.0\%}}$$

$$\textbf{Gross Profit \% (19x4)} = \frac{\$279{,}800}{\$848{,}600} = .3297 = \underline{\underline{33.0\%}}$$

Income from Operations % = Income from Operations ÷ Net Sales

$$\textbf{Income from Operations \% (19x5)} = \frac{\$99{,}500}{\$966{,}900} = .1029 = \underline{\underline{10.3\%}}$$

$$\textbf{Income from Operations \% (19x4)} = \frac{\$95{,}400}{\$848{,}600} = .1124 = \underline{\underline{11.2\%}}$$

Net Income After Income Tax % = Net Income After Income Tax ÷ Net Sales

$$\textbf{Net Income \% (19x5)} = \frac{\$71{,}060}{\$966{,}900} = .0734 = \underline{\underline{7.3\%}}$$

$$\textbf{Net Income \% (19x4)} = \frac{\$69{,}530}{\$848{,}600} = .0819 = \underline{\underline{8.2\%}}$$

One could also interpret the percentages as shown here.

19x5
- For every $100 in net sales, gross profit amounted to $32.00.
- For every $100 in net sales, income from operations amounted to $10.30.
- For every $100 in net sales, net income amounted to $7.30.

Titan Furniture Company, Inc.
Comparative Income Statement
December 31, 19x5 and December 31, 19x4

	19x5		19x4	
	AMOUNT	PERCENT	AMOUNT	PERCENT
Revenue from Sales:				
Sales	$ 980 6 0 0 00	101.4	$ 860 0 0 0 00	101.3
Less Sales Returns and Allowances	13 7 0 0 00	1.4	11 4 0 0 00	1.3
Net Sales	$ 966 9 0 0 00	100.0	$ 848 6 0 0 00	100.0
Cost of Merchandise Sold:				
Merchandise Inventory, Jan. 1	$ 206 5 0 0 00	21.4	$ 138 7 0 0 00	16.3
Purchases (net)	804 8 0 0 00	83.2	636 6 0 0 00	75.0
Merchandise Available for Sale	$1 011 3 0 0 00	104.6	$ 775 3 0 0 00	91.3
Less Merchandise Inventory, Dec. 31	353 6 0 0 00	36.6	206 5 0 0 00	24.3
Cost of Merchandise Sold	$ 657 7 0 0 00	68.0	$ 568 8 0 0 00	67.0
Gross Profit	$ 309 2 0 0 00	32.0	$ 279 8 0 0 00	33.0
Operating Expenses:				
Selling Expenses:				
Sales Salary Expense	$ 114 6 5 0 00	11.9	$ 102 4 0 0 00	12.1
Delivery Expense	17 7 0 0 00	1.8	13 7 0 0 00	1.6
Advertising Expense	7 9 0 0 00	.8	6 9 0 0 00	.8
Depreciation Expense, Equipment	6 8 0 0 00	.7	6 6 0 0 00	.8
Store Supplies Expense	7 5 0 00	.1	6 0 0 00	.1
Total Selling Expenses	$ 147 8 0 0 00	15.3	$ 130 2 0 0 00	15.3
General Expenses:				
Office Salary Expense	$ 33 4 4 0 00	3.5	$ 27 6 8 0 00	3.3
Depreciation Expense, Building	14 2 0 0 00	1.5	14 2 0 0 00	1.7
Bad Debts Expense	6 2 0 0 00	.6	5 4 0 0 00	.6
Taxes Expense	6 1 0 0 00	.6	5 2 0 0 00	.6
Insurance Expense	1 1 0 0 00	.1	1 0 0 0 00	.1
Miscellaneous General Expense	8 6 0 00	.1	7 2 0 00	.1
Total General Expenses	$ 61 9 0 0 00	6.4	$ 54 2 0 0 00	6.4
Total Operating Expenses	$ 209 7 0 0 00	21.7	$ 184 4 0 0 00	21.7
Income from Operations	$ 99 5 0 0 00	10.3	$ 95 4 0 0 00	11.2
Other Expenses:				
Interest Expense	8 5 2 0 00	.9	7 8 6 0 00	.9
Income Before Income Tax	$ 90 9 8 0 00	9.4	$ 87 5 4 0 00	10.3
Income Tax Expense	19 9 2 0 00	2.1	18 0 1 0 00	2.1
Net Income After Income Tax	$ 71 0 6 0 00	7.3	$ 69 5 3 0 00	8.2

FIGURE 27-3

19x4

- For every $100 in net sales, gross profit amounted to $33.00.
- For every $100 in net sales, income from operations amounted to $11.20.
- For every $100 in net sales, net income amounted to $8.20.

Again we see the relative importance in 19x5 assumed by Net Purchases (83.2 percent of Net Sales) and ending Merchandise Inventory (36.6 percent of Net Sales). In the area of Selling Expenses the percentage score of Sales Salary Expense declined slightly over that of 19x4. Advertising Expense as a percentage of Net Sales remained the same. (Is that necessarily a good sign?)

Balance Sheet   When you perform a vertical analysis of a comparative balance sheet, you express each item's figure as *a percentage of total assets*, or as a percentage of total liabilities and owners' equity, which is the same figure. (See Figure 27-4.) For example, suppose you want to find the percentage of total assets represented by Cash, Accounts Receivable, and Merchandise Inventory. In referring to Accounts Receivable, we mean net Accounts Receivable (Accounts Receivable less Allowance for Doubtful Accounts).

Cash % = Cash ÷ Total Assets

$$\text{Cash \% (19x5)} = \frac{\$19,600}{\$708,200} = .0277 = \underline{\underline{2.8\%}}$$

$$\text{Cash \% (19x4)} = \frac{\$38,700}{\$604,500} = .0640 = \underline{\underline{6.4\%}}$$

Accounts Receivable % = Net Accounts Receivable ÷ Total Assets

$$\text{Accounts Receivable \% (19x5)} = \frac{\$73,400}{\$708,200} = .1036 = \underline{\underline{10.4\%}}$$

$$\text{Accounts Receivable \% (19x4)} = \frac{\$78,800}{\$604,500} = .1304 = \underline{\underline{13.0\%}}$$

Merchandise Inventory % = Merchandise Inventory ÷ Total Assets

$$\text{Merchandise Inventory \% (19x5)} = \frac{\$353,600}{\$708,200} = .4993 = \underline{\underline{49.9\%}}$$

$$\text{Merchandise Inventory \% (19x4)} = \frac{\$206,500}{\$604,500} = .3416 = \underline{\underline{34.2\%}}$$

One could also interpret the above percentages as follows:

19x5

- For every $100 in total assets, $2.80 is in the form of cash.
- For every $100 in total assets, $10.40 is in the form of net accounts receivable.

FIGURE
27-4

Titan Furniture Company, Inc.
Comparative Balance Sheet
For Years Ended December 31, 19x5 and December 31, 19x4

	19x5		19x4	
	AMOUNT	PERCENT	AMOUNT	PERCENT
Assets				
Current Assets:				
Cash	$ 19 600 00	2.8	$ 38 700 00	6.4
Accounts Receivable	76 700 00	10.8	81 400 00	13.5
Less Allowance for Doubtful Accounts	(3 300 00)	.5	(2 600 00)	.5
Merchandise Inventory	353 600 00	49.9	206 500 00	34.2
Prepaid Insurance	2 000 00	.3	2 100 00	.3
Total Current Assets	$ 448 600 00	63.3	$ 326 100 00	53.9
Investments:				
Sinking Fund Cash	$ 4 100 00	.6	$ 5 800 00	1.0
Sinking Fund Investments	61 700 00	8.7	59 400 00	9.8
Total Investments	$ 65 800 00	9.3	$ 65 200 00	10.8
Plant Equipment:				
Land	$ 40 000 00	5.6	40 000 00	6.6
Building	160 000 00	22.6	160 000 00	26.5
Less Accumulated Depreciation	(56 800 00)	(8.0)	(42 600 00)	(7.0)
Equipment	88 600 00	12.5	86 000 00	14.2
Less Accumulated Depreciation	(41 000 00)	(5.8)	(34 200 00)	(5.7)
Total Plant and Equipment	$ 190 800 00	26.9	$ 209 200 00	34.6
Intangible Assets:				
Organization Costs	3 000 00	.4	$ 4 000 00	.7
Total Assets	$ 708 200 00	100.0	$ 604 500 00	100.0
Liabilities				
Current Liabilities:				
Accounts Payable	$ 71 600 00	10.1	$ 29 000 00	4.8
Income Tax Payable	12 800 00	1.8	5 600 00	.9
Dividends Payable	12 000 00	1.7	4 000 00	.7
Salaries Payable	4 200 00	.6	4 000 00	.7
Total Current Liabilities	$ 100 600 00	14.2	$ 42 600 00	7.0
Long-Term Liabilities:				
Bonds Payable, 6%, due Dec. 31, 19x9	$ 100 000 00	14.1	$ 100 000 00	16.5
Less Discount on Bonds Payable	(2 200 00)	(.3)	(2 400 00)	(.4)
Total Long-Term Liabilities	$ 97 800 00	13.8	$ 97 600 00	16.1
Total Liabilities	$ 198 400 00	28.0	$ 140 200 00	23.2
Stockholders' Equity				
Paid-in Capital:				
Common Stock, $100 par (4,000 shares authorized, 3,000 shares issued)	$ 300 000 00	42.4	$ 300 000 00	49.6
Premium on Common Stock	86 000 00	12.1	86 000 00	14.2
Total Paid-in Capital	$ 386 000 00	54.5	$ 386 000 00	63.9
Retained Earnings:				
Unappropriated	$ 103 800 00	14.7	$ 66 300 00	11.0
Appropriated for Plant Expansion	20 000 00	2.8	12 000 00	2.0
Total Retained Earnings	$ 123 800 00	17.5	$ 78 300 00	13.0
Total Stockholders' Equity	$ 509 800 00	72.0	$ 464 300 00	76.8
Total Liabilities and Stockholders' Equity	$ 708 200 00	100.0	$ 604 500 00	100.0

- For every $100 in total assets, $49.90 is in the form of merchandise inventory.

19x4

- For every $100 in total assets, $6.40 was in the form of cash.
- For every $100 in total assets, $13.00 was in the form of net accounts receivable.
- For every $100 in total assets, $34.20 was in the form of merchandise inventory.

These percentages accentuate Titan Furniture's poor status with respect to Cash and Merchandise Inventory, as well as their favorable status with respect to Accounts Receivable. Other items that may strike a warning note are the

- Percentage value of plant and equipment declined during 19x5.
- Percentage value of Accounts Payable more than doubled during 19x4.

Our illustrations show full income statements and balance sheets. But sometimes accountants give financial statements in condensed form and put the details in supporting schedules. In this case, the figures are taken from the supporting schedules, and the percentages are worked out the same way. Since the percentages are rounded, the Percent column may not always add to exactly 100 in vertical analysis. The Percent column is never added in horizontal analysis, since it does not involve a common base.

Remember

On an income statement arranged for vertical analysis, each dollar amount is usually expressed as a percentage of net sales. On a balance sheet arranged for vertical analysis, each dollar amount is expressed as a percentage of total assets or total liabilities and stockholders' equity.

TREND PERCENTAGES

Objective 3

Express income statement data in trend percentages.

One may also use percentages to indicate trends or general directions that become evident only when one makes a comparison covering a period of years. Here is the way to calculate the percentages:

1. Select a representative year as the base year.
2. Label the base year 100 percent.
3. Express all other years as percentages of the base year.

Let us say that you have been able to cull the following figures from the income statements for Titan Furniture for 19x1 through 19x5:

Item	Year				
	19x1	19x2	19x3	19x4	19x5
Net Sales	$714,200	$782,380	$806,400	$848,600	$966,900
Cost of Merchandise					
Sold	466,150	519,180	540,300	568,800	657,700
Gross Profit	248,050	263,200	266,100	279,800	309,200

You establish 19x1 as the base year and calculate the trend percentages for Net Sales by dividing the Net Sales of each year by the Net Sales for 19x1:

For 19x2 $714{,}200\overline{)782{,}380} = \underline{\underline{1.0955}}$

For 19x3 $714{,}200\overline{)806{,}400} = \underline{\underline{1.1290}}$

For 19x4 $714{,}200\overline{)848{,}600} = \underline{\underline{1.1882}}$

For 19x5 $714{,}200\overline{)966{,}900} = \underline{\underline{1.3538}}$

You determine trend percentages for Cost of Merchandise Sold and Gross Profit in the same way. Here are the results, with the percentages rounded off as before.

	Year				
Item	**19x1**	**19x2**	**19x3**	**19x4**	**19x5**
Net Sales	100.0%	109.5%	112.9%	188.8%	135.4%
Cost of Merchandise Sold	100.0%	111.4%	115.9%	122.0%	141.1%
Gross Profit	100.0%	106.1%	107.3%	112.8%	124.7%

Observe that over the five-year period, the trend of Net Sales is upward. However, Cost of Merchandise Sold is going up at a more rapid rate. In other words, over the five years, Cost of Merchandise Sold increased faster than Net Sales, resulting in smaller increases in Gross Profit. This is fine if it's the company's plan to achieve a greater volume of sales accompanied by more moderate profits. But if this shrinking Gross Profit is *not* consistent with company policy, then it may be a sign that the company is not passing along its increased costs to its customers.

INDUSTRY COMPARISONS

Vertical analysis, using percentage figures, is very useful when you wish to compare the figures for one company with the average figures for the given industry. Such comparisons are often referred to as **common-size statements** since one expresses all items as percentages of a common base. Again, for the income statement, the common base is net sales. Net sales is set at 100 percent, and all other items are expressed as a percentage of net sales. Trade and marketing associations often gather information and publish common-size statements.

ANALYSIS BY CREDITORS AND MANAGEMENT

Because management is vitally interested in increasing the company's solvency and profitability, managers are concerned with all types of analytical tools and techniques. Because creditors want assurance of being repaid, they are concerned first with the company's solvency and second with its profitability.

How Do Short-Term Creditors and Management Analyze an Enterprise?

Bankers and other short-term creditors are primarily interested in the *current* position of a given firm: Does the firm have enough money coming in to meet its current operating needs and to pay its current debts promptly? (*Current,* to them, means one year or the operating cycle, whichever is longer. This usage is consistent with the way accountants refer to "current assets" and "current liabilities.") Let us use as an example some calculations derived from the comparative financial statements of Titan Furniture for 19x5 and 19x4.

Working Capital

Objective 4a

Compute working capital.

As we stated previously, **working capital** is the excess of current assets over current liabilities. One determines the working capital for Titan Furniture Company as shown in the following equations:

$$\text{Working capital} = \text{Current assets} - \text{Current liabilities}$$

Working capital (19x5) = \$448,600 − \$100,600 = **\$348,000**

Working capital (19x4) = \$326,100 − \$42,600 = **\$283,500**

Titan Furniture has \$348,000 of capital available to work with during 19x5 versus \$283,500 of capital available to work with during 19x4.

Current Ratio

Objective 4b

Compute current ratio.

The relationship of a company's current assets to its current liabilities is known as its **current ratio.** One arrives at this figure by dividing current assets by current liabilities.

$$\text{Current ratio} = \frac{\text{Current assets}}{\text{Current liabilities}}$$

$$\textbf{Current ratio (19x5)} = \frac{\$448,600}{\$100,600} = \underline{\underline{4.5 : 1}}$$

$$\text{Current ratio (19x4)} = \frac{\$326{,}100}{\$42{,}600} = \underline{\underline{7.7 : 1}}$$

A firm's current ratio reveals its current debt-paying ability. Titan Furniture's current ratio of 4.5 : 1 in 19x5 indicates that there is $4.50 of cash coming in within a year from now for every dollar Titan Furniture has to pay out within a year. But the firm was better off in 19x4 because in that year it had $7.70 coming in within the year for every dollar to be paid out within the year.

From the points of view of bankers and other credit grantors, the adequacy of a company's current ratio depends on what type of business the firm is in. A favorable ratio for a merchandising business is generally 2 : 1—higher if the type of merchandise the firm sells is subject to abrupt changes in style. But a public utility, which has no inventories other than supplies, is considered solvent even if its current ratio is less than 1 : 1. Due to the stability of the product involved in the furniture business, a ratio of 4.5 : 1 for Titan Furniture is satisfactory. (*Note:* If the company has changed inventory-valuation methods from one year to another—for example, if it has switched from FIFO to LIFO—a correction should be made in the costs of merchandise inventories; otherwise there is no common base for making a comparison.)

Quick Ratio

The relationship of a company's current assets that can be quickly converted into cash to its current liabilities is known as its **quick ratio** or **acid-test ratio. Quick assets** are cash, current notes receivable, net accounts receivable (that is, accounts receivable less allowance for doubtful accounts), interest receivable, and marketable securities. You do not count inventories and prepaid expenses because they are further removed from conversion into cash than are other current assets. You determine the quick ratio by dividing quick assets by current liabilities.

Objective 4c

Compute quick ratio

$$\text{Quick ratio} = \frac{\text{Quick assets}}{\text{Current liabilities}}$$

$$\text{Quick ratio (19x5)} = \frac{\$19{,}600 + (\$76{,}700 - \$3{,}300)}{\$100{,}600} = \frac{\$93{,}000}{\$100{,}600} = \underline{\underline{.92 : 1}}$$

$$\text{Quick ratio (19x4)} = \frac{\$38{,}700 + (\$81{,}400 - \$2{,}600)}{\$42{,}600} = \frac{\$117{,}500}{\$42{,}600} = \underline{\underline{2.76 : 1}}$$

Titan Furniture's quick ratio of .92 : 1 in 19x5 indicates that there are 92 cents in cash coming in quickly—without involving the liquidation of inventory—for every dollar it has to pay out within a year. For 19x4, there was $2.76 that the firm could realize quickly for every dollar it had to pay out within a year.

A quick ratio of 1 : 1 is normally considered satisfactory. Therefore the quick ratio for Titan Furniture exposes a precarious short-term financial position. One has to consider this quick ratio in conjunction with the company's working capital and its current ratio. Although working capital and current ratio are two indicators of a firm's ability to meet its current obligations, they don't reveal the *composition of its current assets*—a very important factor.

Relationship of Each Current Asset to Total Current Assets

Suppose that you are asked to find out the proportionate positions of each item in the list of current assets of Titan Furniture. Your first step is to compile a schedule of each current asset as it relates to total current assets, as shown in the following illustration:

	DECEMBER 31, 19x5		DECEMBER 31, 19x4	
	AMOUNT	PERCENT	AMOUNT	PERCENT
Current Assets:				
Cash	$ 19 6 0 0 00	4.4	$ 38 7 0 0 00	11.9
Accounts Receivable (net)	73 4 0 0 00	16.4	78 8 0 0 00	24.2
Merchandise Inventory	353 6 0 0 00	78.8	206 5 0 0 00	63.3
Prepaid Insurance	2 0 0 0 00	.4	2 1 0 0 00	.6
Total Current Assets	$ 448 6 0 0 00	100.0	$ 326 1 0 0 00	100.0

As an example, the percentage of cash to total current assets is calculated like this:

$$\frac{\$19,600}{\$448,600} = .0437 = \underline{\underline{4.4\%}}$$

We have already commented on the large increase in the proportion of merchandise inventory (it was 63 percent of current assets in 19x4 but amounts to 79 percent of current assets in 19x5). This change, coupled with the decline in the cash position (12 percent of current assets for 19x4, only 4 percent of current assets for 19x5), reinforces the message we got from the decline in the quick ratio, indicating that the firm may have a hard time paying its current debts.

Analysis of Accounts Receivable

Since money tied up in accounts receivable does not yield any revenue, any firm tries to collect accounts receivable promptly and to keep them at a minimum. It can use the cash it gets from collection of accounts receivable to reduce bank loans or to take advantage of cash discounts. This action reduces the amount of interest expense it has to pay and the cost of the merchandise it buys. It also reduces the risk of loss from bad debts.

Accounts receivable turnover is the number of times charge accounts are turned over (or paid off) per year. A turnover implies a sale on account followed by payment of the debt in cash. One computes this by *dividing net sales on account by average net accounts receivable.* If possible, use the average of the monthly balances of accounts receivable since this method allows for seasonal fluctuations. If you haven't got figures for monthly balances, use the average of the balances at the beginning and the end of the previous year. Current notes receivable from customers are combined with accounts receivable. Here is how it looks for Titan Furniture Company. (You would have to take the beginning balance of Accounts Receivable for 19x4 ($58,400) from the 19x3 balance sheet. Net sales on account were $773,020 for 19x5 and $678,880 for 19x4.)

Objective 4d

Compute accounts receivable turnover.

$$\text{Accounts receivable turnover} = \frac{\text{Net sales on account}}{\text{Average accounts receivable (net)}}$$

$$\frac{\text{Average}}{\text{accounts receivable}} = \frac{\text{Beginning accounts receivable} + \text{Ending accounts receivable}}{2}$$

$$\text{Accounts receivable turnover (19x5)} = \frac{\$773,020}{\dfrac{\$78,800 + \$73,400}{2}} = \frac{\$773,020}{\$76,100} = \underline{\underline{10.16}} \text{ times/yr}$$

$$\text{Accounts receivable turnover (19x4)} = \frac{\$678,880}{\dfrac{\$58,400 + \$78,800}{2}} = \frac{\$678,880}{\$68,600} = \underline{\underline{9.90}} \text{ times/yr}$$

You can use the accounts receivable turnover to determine the number of days that the receivables were on the books. Calculate this by dividing 365 days by the turnover figure:

$$\text{Year (19x5)} = \frac{365 \text{ days}}{10.16 \text{ times per year}} = 35.93 \text{ or } \underline{\underline{36}} \text{ days}$$

$$\text{Year (19x4)} = \frac{365 \text{ days}}{9.90 \text{ times per year}} = 36.87 \text{ or } \underline{\underline{37}} \text{ days}$$

It took an average of one day less in 19x5 to collect accounts receivable than it did in 19x4. This reduction represents a slight improvement in collections for Titan Furniture. Since the company's credit terms are net 30 days, 36 or 37 days is reasonable.

Objective 4e

Compute merchandise inventory turnover.

Merchandise inventory turnover is the number of times a company's average inventory is sold during a given year. One calculates this by *dividing Cost of Merchandise Sold by average Merchandise Inventory.* Here is the calculation for Titan Furniture Company (beginning merchandise inventory for 19x4 taken from the 19x3 balance sheet is $138,700):

$$\text{Merchandise inventory turnover} = \frac{\text{Cost of merchandise sold}}{\text{Average merchandise inventory}}$$

$$\frac{\text{Average}}{\text{merchandise inventory}} = \frac{\text{Beginning merchandise inventory} + \text{Ending merchandise inventory}}{2}$$

$$\text{Merchandise inventory turnover (19x5)} = \frac{\$657,700}{\dfrac{\$206,500 + \$353,600}{2}} = \frac{\$657,700}{\$280,050} = \underline{\underline{2.35}} \text{ times/yr}$$

$$\text{Merchandise inventory turnover (19x4)} = \frac{\$568,800}{\dfrac{\$138,700 + \$206,500}{2}} = \frac{\$568,800}{\$172,600} = \underline{\underline{3.30}} \text{ times/yr}$$

If possible, one should use the average of the monthly balances of Merchandise Inventory (add them and divide by 12). The figure for merchandise inventory turnover varies depending on the type of product involved. One can compare the figure for merchandise inventory turnover for one company with figures for the rest of the industry to use it as a test of merchandising efficiency. Each turnover yields a gross profit or markup to the company. Note that there has been a serious decline in the rate of merchandise inventory turnover for Titan Furniture. This is something to watch.

One may also use the figure for the merchandise inventory turnover to determine the number of days that the merchandise was kept in stock. One calculates this the same way one calculates accounts receivable turnover: dividing 365 days by the turnover figure.

$$\text{Year (19x5)} = \frac{365 \text{ days}}{2.35 \text{ times per year}} = 155.32 = \underline{\underline{155}} \text{ days}$$

$$\text{Year (19x4)} = \frac{365 \text{ days}}{3.30 \text{ times per year}} = 110.61 = \underline{\underline{111}} \text{ days}$$

Note that Titan Furniture's merchandise remained in stock 44 days longer in 19x5 than it did in 19x4. This fact surely calls for an investigation of the company's sales and purchasing practices.

In addition to yielding a higher gross profit, rapid merchandise inventory turnover has other advantages: The money invested in the inventory is tied up for a shorter period of time; storage costs are lower; there is less risk of spoilage (if the merchandise is perishable); there is less risk of change in demand (if the merchandise is affected by changes in style or in business conditions).

How Do Long-Term Creditors and Management Analyze an Enterprise?

Long-term creditors include mortgage holders and bondholders. Whenever specific property has been pledged or mortgaged, long-term creditors have first claim on the property in the event that the company cannot keep up its payments. Even in the case of debentures (unsecured bonds), the bondholders have a prior claim to the general assets of the company, a claim that takes precedence over that of the stockholders. Management is concerned with the company's taking care of its present obligations, as well as preserving its credit standing, and hence its ability to borrow in the future.

Two ratios are particularly useful from the standpoint of long-term creditors:

Objective 4f

Compute ratio of stockholders' equity to liabilities.

• **Ratio of stockholders' equity to liabilities**   When we speak of the ratio of stockholders' equity to liabilities, we are talking about the ratio of the stockholders' investment to the creditors' claims.

In calculating any ratio, we mean the ratio *of* one thing *to* something else. When we write the ratio as a fraction, we put the *of* part in the numerator and the *to* part in the denominator. Look at this calculation for Titan Furniture Company:

$$\text{Ratio of stockholders' equity to liabilities (19x5)} = \frac{\$509,800}{\$198,400} = \underline{\underline{2.57 : 1}}$$

$$\text{Ratio of stockholders' equity to liabilities (19x4)} = \frac{\$464,300}{\$140,200} = \underline{\underline{3.31 : 1}}$$

In 19x5, for every $2.57 of stockholders' investment, the creditors have loaned $1. Titan Furniture's ratio of stockholders' equity to liabilities shows a decline since 19x4, from 3.31 : 1 to 2.57 : 1. Creditors like to see a high proportion of stockholders' equity because stockholders' equity, or owners' equity, acts as a buffer in case the company has to absorb losses. Also, owners often prefer a high proportion of equity to liabilities.

Objective 4g

Compute ratio of the value of plant and equipment to long-term liabilities.

• **Ratio of plant and equipment to long-term liabilities**   There is another factor that provides a margin of safety to mortgage holders and bondholders—the ratio of the value of a firm's total plant and equipment to its long-term liabilities. This ratio also indicates the potential ability of the enterprise to borrow more money on a long-term basis. Let's look at the calculation for Titan Furniture Company:

$$\text{Ratio of plant and equipment to long-term liabilities} = \frac{\text{Plant and equipment}}{\text{Long-term liabilities}}$$

$$\text{Ratio of plant and equipment to long-term liabilities (19x5)} = \frac{\$190,800}{\$97,800} = \underline{\underline{1.95}}$$

$$\text{Ratio of plant and equipment to long-term liabilities (19x4)} = \frac{\$209,200}{\$97,600} = \underline{\underline{2.14}}$$

In 19x5, there is $1.95 book value of plant and equipment for every dollar of long-term liabilities. But in 19x4, there was $2.14 book value of

Remember

To find the ratio of . . . to . . . , divide the "of . . ." amount by the "to . . ." amount. Put a colon and the number 1 to the right of the answer.

plant and equipment for every dollar of long-term liabilities. So this figure too is less favorable.

As we have seen, a firm's creditors and managers may use eight devices to determine the financial position of a firm:

- Working capital
- Current ratio
- Quick ratio
- Relationship of each current asset to total current assets
- Accounts receivable turnover
- Merchandise inventory turnover
- Ratio of stockholders' equity to liabilities
- Ratio of plant and equipment to long-term liabilities

ANALYSIS BY OWNERS AND MANAGEMENT

In addition to being concerned about the solvency and the profitability of a company, the owners, as well as the managers, are vitally interested in the value and return on investment in the company. In many cases the owners are the managers. However, in other situations, managers are employed by the owners. What diagnostic tools do owners and managers use to determine the financial health of their company?

Equity per Share

Objective 5a

Compute equity per share.

When you examine the annual report of a corporation, you encounter the term *equity per share*—also referred to as *book value per share*. If a corporation has only one class of common stock outstanding, equity per share is determined by dividing the total stockholders' equity by the number of shares of stock issued. Here are the calculations for Titan Furniture Company:

$$\text{Equity per share} = \frac{\text{Total stockholders' equity available to a class of stock}}{\text{Number of shares issued and outstanding}}$$

$$\text{Equity per share (19x5)} = \frac{\$509,800}{3,000 \text{ shares}} = \underline{\$169.93} \text{ per share}$$

$$\text{Equity per share (19x4)} = \frac{\$464,300}{3,000 \text{ shares}} = \underline{\$154.77} \text{ per share}$$

When there are shares of preferred stock outstanding, one must deduct the liquidation value, including any dividends in arrears on cumulative preferred stock, to arrive at the stockholders' equity available to holders of common stock. (Remember that in the event of a firm's liquidation, holders of preferred stock are paid before holders of common stock.)

The term *equity per share* does *not* mean the cash value or market value of a share but the amount that would be distributed per share of stock *if* the corporation were to **liquidate** (wind up its affairs by paying off its creditors and selling its assets for cash) without incurring any expenses, gains, or losses in selling its assets and paying its liabilities. The equity per share increases as a firm retains net income. This concept of equity per share is important in contracts involving the sale of stock. For example, a large stockholder might obtain an option to buy the shares of small stockholders at the value of the equity per share as of a certain future date.

Rate of Return on Common Stockholders' Equity

A corporation exists first and foremost to earn a net income for its stockholders. Therefore the rate of return on the common stockholders' equity is important as a means of measuring how good or bad the investment is. This rate is calculated by dividing the net income available to holders of common stock by the *average value* of their equity. Here's the calculation for Titan Furniture (beginning common stock equity for 19x4 is $422,100):

Objective 5b

Compute rate of return on stockholders' equity.

Rate of return on common stockholders' equity

$$= \frac{\text{Net income available to common stock}}{\dfrac{\text{Beginning common stock equity} + \text{Ending common stock equity}}{2}}$$

Rate of return on common stockholders' equity (19x5)

$$= \frac{\$71,060}{\dfrac{\$464,300 + \$509,800}{2}} = \frac{\$71,060}{\$487,050} = .1458 = \underline{\underline{14.6\%}}$$

Rate of return on common stockholders' equity (19x4)

$$= \frac{\$69,530}{\dfrac{\$422,100 + \$464,300}{2}} = \frac{\$69,530}{\$443,200} = .1568 = \underline{\underline{15.7\%}}$$

The rate of return on common stockholders' equity declined 1.1 percent. Management should look into the matter to uncover the possible causes. Again, one begins by looking hard at merchandise inventory, particularly since it represents 49.9 percent of total assets in 19x5.

Earnings per Share of Common Stock

Objective 5c

Compute earnings per share of common stock.

You often see earnings per share of stock listed in financial columns of newspapers. If a corporation has no preferred stock outstanding, you compute the earnings per share of common stock by dividing net income by the average number of common stock shares outstanding during the year. When there is preferred stock, you must first deduct any dividends on preferred stock to arrive at the amount available to common stock (again, as you recall, because dividends on preferred are paid before those on common). Here is the calculation of earnings per share of common stock for Titan Furniture Company:

$$\text{Earnings per share of common stock} = \frac{\text{Net income available to common stock}}{\text{Average number of shares of common stock outstanding}}$$

$$\text{Earnings per share of common stock (19x5)} = \frac{\$71,060}{3,000 \text{ shares}} = \underline{\$23.69}$$

$$\text{Earnings per share of common stock (19x4)} = \frac{\$69,530}{3,000 \text{ shares}} = \underline{\$23.18}$$

Any big change during the year in the *number* of shares outstanding naturally has a vital effect on the amount of earnings per share. That's why a company must consider the average number of shares outstanding and disclose any information relating to stock dividends and stock splits.

Price-Earnings Ratio

Objective 5d

Compute price-earnings ratio.

The **price-earnings ratio** is a measure commonly used to determine whether the market price of a corporation's stock is reasonable. The way you calculate the price-earnings ratio of a company's stock is to divide the market price per share by the annual earnings per share. Let's say that the market price of a share of common stock of Titan Furniture at the end of 19x5 is $132, and that at the end of 19x4 it was $120. Here is how you figure out the price-earnings ratio:

$$\text{Price-earnings ratio} = \frac{\text{Market price per share}}{\text{Earnings per share}}$$

$$\text{Price-earnings ratio (19x5)} = \frac{\$132.00}{\$23.69} = 5.57 = \underline{5.6 : 1}$$

$$\text{Price-earnings ratio (19x4)} = \frac{\$120.00}{\$23.18} = 5.17 = \underline{5.2 : 1}$$

What constitutes a reasonable price-earnings ratio varies from one industry to another. Stocks quoted in the Dow Jones Average usually have about a 15 : 1 price-earnings ratio. Corporations that have shown a large continued growth in earnings over a period of years may have a ratio of more than 30 : 1.

You may also use the price-earnings ratio in this manner: If the acceptable price-earnings ratio for a given stock is 15 : 1 and the earnings per share equal $2.50, it follows that the maximum reasonable price you ought to pay for the stock is $37.50 (that is, $2.50 × 15). But what if the stock is selling for only $20? You may well consider it to be undervalued.

COMPUTERS AT WORK

Spreadsheets and Models

Before VisiCalc was created in 1979, the only way to do complex data analysis and forecasting was to buy expensive time on a mainframe computer. Then "a magic blackboard for numeric calculations," as one of VisiCalc's authors called it, changed the entire business world.[1] Moving from a calculator to a spreadsheet increases an employee's productivity by up to 700 percent, according to one estimate.

Spreadsheets are the single most important reason that businesses have embraced computers. Twenty-six percent of the executives in one survey said they used their computers most often to perform financial analyses with a spreadsheet, over three times as many as said they used word processing. A financial analyst who spent $100,000 one year in timesharing charges on a mainframe computer did the same work the next year on a $5,000 microcomputer with a spreadsheet. One accounting department cut its clerks from 17 to 2 when it began using spreadsheets to prepare the budget and perform what-if analyses.

This miraculous financial tool looks like simple ruled paper divided into rows and columns on the screen. Each individual "cell"—for instance, row 1 column 1—can contain data or can be defined by a formula. Once a spreadsheet has been set up, a user can plug in different numbers or different scenarios and see how the other numbers change. For instance, an accountant can calculate the effect on the company of a change in interest rates or taxes. Because spreadsheets handle such calculations so quickly, people are more likely to use them to explore a number of options thoroughly and to make better decisions as a result.

Spreadsheets do have their drawbacks. It's sometimes hard for anyone to figure out how a particular spreadsheet was set up or what's behind a faulty calculation. To solve some of these problems, and to expand spreadsheets' capacities, software makers have developed financial models. These models can both retrieve and print data in a variety of ways, and the formulas of whole rows and columns can be changed at once. A budget analyst for a chain store used to prepare 250 different spreadsheets, one for each store, then have assistants feed the spreadsheet information manually into a mainframe. Now with a financial model, he can work on all 250 budgets himself, finishing the task in one month instead of four.

Spreadsheets and financial models will probably dominate financial forecasting and analysis for years to come. They speed up processes, improve productivity, and let everyone gaze into a financial crystal ball.

[1] Antonoff, "Spreadsheets," p. 80.

Sources: Michael Antonoff, "Spreadsheets," *Personal Computing*, October 1986, 66–71; Shawn Bryan, "PC Modeling Programs," *Computerworld*, September 15, 1986, 47–57; Cheryl Spencer, "Financial Modeling," *Personal Computing*, April 1987, 69–77.

SUMMARY

A great many people are vitally interested in the financial condition and results of operations of a business enterprise: owners, managers, creditors, prospective owners and creditors, and employees. The status of an enterprise depends on its solvency and profitability. Comparative financial statements are useful in making a line-by-line comparison of items over a period of years.

L.O. 1,2

These statements are compiled using horizontal or vertical analysis. Trend percentages indicate trends or general directions that may become apparent only when one makes a comparison over a period of years. The base year is set at 100 percent.

L.O. 3

Short-term creditors and management use the following techniques:

L.O. 4

Working capital = Current assets − Current liabilities

$$\text{Current ratio} = \frac{\text{Current assets}}{\text{Current liabilities}}$$

$$\text{Quick ratio} = \frac{\text{Cash + Receivables (net) + Marketable securities}}{\text{Current liabilities}}$$

$$\text{Accounts receivable turnover} = \frac{\text{Net sales on account}}{\text{Average accounts receivable (net)}}$$

$$\text{Merchandise inventory turnover} = \frac{\text{Cost of merchandise sold}}{\text{Average merchandise inventory}}$$

Long-term creditors and management use the following ratios:

$$\text{Ratio of stockholders' equity to liabilities} = \frac{\text{Stockholders' equity}}{\text{Liabilities}}$$

$$\text{Ratio of plant and equipment to long-term liabilities} = \frac{\text{Plant and equipment}}{\text{Long-term liabilities}}$$

Owners and managers use the following measures:

L.O. 5

$$\text{Equity per share} = \frac{\text{Total stockholders' equity available to a class of stock}}{\text{Number of shares issued and outstanding}}$$

$$\text{Rate of return on common stockholders' equity} = \frac{\text{Net income available to common stock}}{\text{Average common stock equity}}$$

$$\text{Earnings per share of common stock} = \frac{\text{Net income available to common stock}}{\text{Average number of shares of common stock outstanding}}$$

$$\text{Price-earnings ratio} = \frac{\text{Market price per share}}{\text{Earnings per share}}$$

GLOSSARY

Accounts receivable turnover The number of times charge accounts are paid off per year; a turnover is a sale on account and subsequent repayment.

Acid-test ratio Same as quick ratio.

Base year The year used as a basis for comparison.

Common-size statements Financial statements using vertical analysis expressed as percentages, showing average industrywide figures for companies of similar size that produce the same product or service.

Current ratio Current assets divided by current liabilities.

Horizontal analysis Comparing the same item in the financial statements of an enterprise for two or more periods.

Liquidate To wind up the affairs of a business by paying off the creditors and selling the assets for cash.

Merchandise inventory turnover The number of times a company's average inventory is sold during a given year.

Price-earnings ratio A common measure for deciding whether a stock's market price is reasonable; calculated by dividing the market price per share by the annual earnings per share.

Profitability An enterprise's ability to earn a reasonable profit on the owners' investment.

Quick assets Assets consisting of cash, current notes receivable, net accounts receivable, interest receivable, and marketable securities.

Quick ratio Quick assets divided by current liabilities.

Solvency An enterprise's ability to pay its debts.

Vertical analysis Portraying items in financial statements as percentages (or proportional parts) of a given item on the same financial statement.

Working capital The excess of current assets over current liabilities.

QUESTIONS, EXERCISES, AND PROBLEMS

Discussion Questions

1. In regard to comparative income statements, describe the difference between horizontal analysis and vertical analysis.
2. How does a firm's current ratio differ from its quick ratio?
3. What is the difference between a firm's solvency and its profitability?
4. A firm has a gross profit percentage of 38 percent. What does this mean?
5. What does a decrease in the accounts receivable turnover indicate as far as a firm is concerned?
6. Why are creditors interested in the ratio of stockholders' equity to liabilities? Is it better to have a high ratio or a low ratio?
7. Why is a high merchandise inventory turnover considered beneficial?
8. Which of the following types of business firms would you expect to have a high merchandise turnover?

    a. Florist   d. Auto parts store

    b. Jewelry store   e. Camera store

    c. Supermarket   f. Art gallery

Exercises

L.O. 2 **Exercise 27-1** Using the following revenue and expense data, prepare a comparative income statement, expressing each item for both 19x6 and 19x5 as a percentage of net sales (vertical analysis). Round off to three decimal places. Comment on the results.

	19x6	19x5
Sales (net)	$800,000	$650,000
Cost of Merchandise Sold	640,000	500,000
Selling Expenses	46,000	42,000
General Expenses	22,000	21,000
Income Tax Expense	18,850	17,150

L.O. 1 **Exercise 27-2** Calculate the percentages of increase and decrease for the following items (horizontal analysis). Round off to three decimal places.

	19x6	19x5
Cash	$ 81,000	$ 76,500
Notes Receivable	42,000	48,000
Equipment (net)	183,000	198,000
Retained Earnings	114,000	96,000

L.O. 2,3 **Exercise 27-3** The data below are taken from the financial statements of the Fargo Company. For 19x6, calculate the gross profit percentage, the accounts receivable turnover, and the merchandise inventory turnover.

	19x6	19x5
Sales (net on account)	$900,000	$800,000
Cost of Merchandise Sold	680,000	640,000
Merchandise Inventory (at end of year)	140,000	132,000
Accounts Receivable (at end of year)	90,900	104,000

L.O. 3 **Exercise 27-4** Calculate trend percentages for the following items and comment on the trends. Use 19x0 as the base year. Round off to three decimal places. Comment on the results.

	19x0	19x1	19x2	19x3
Sales (net)	$600,000	$660,000	$726,000	$774,000
Cost of Merchandise Sold	360,000	423,000	480,000	492,000
Merchandise Inventory	63,000	69,000	78,000	90,000

L.O. 4a,b,c   **Exercise 27-5**   The following items are from the balance sheets of C. C. Woodward Company as of December 31, 19x2 and 19x1:

	19x2	19x1
Current Assets:		
Cash and Receivables (net)	$ 180 0 0 0 00	$ 162 0 0 0 00
Merchandise Inventory	270 0 0 0 00	234 0 0 0 00
Total Current Assets	$ 450 0 0 0 00	$ 396 0 0 0 00
Current Liabilities	$ 225 0 0 0 00	$ 180 0 0 0 00

Calculate the following for each year and comment on the company's comparative financial position:

a. Working capital
b. Current ratio
c. Quick ratio

L.O. 5a,b,c,d   **Exercise 27-6**   The Stockholders' Equity section of the balance sheet of the Fouch Corporation is as follows:

Stockholders' Equity		
Paid-in-Capital:		
Common Stock, $5 par (100,000		
shares authorized, 80,000 shares		
issued and outstanding)	$ 400 0 0 0 00	
Premium on Common Stock	120 0 0 0 00	
Total Paid-in Capital	$ 520 0 0 0 00	
Retained Earnings	280 0 0 0 00	
Total Stockholders' Equity		$ 800 0 0 0 00

Net income for the year is $124,000. Stockholders' equity was $760,000 at the beginning of the year. The present market price of the stock is $42 per share. Determine the following:

a. Equity per share
b. Earnings per share
c. Price-earnings ratio
d. Rate of return on common stockholders' equity

L.O. 4d,e;5a,b **Exercise 27-7** The following items are taken from the financial statements of the Ludlum Company. All sales are made on account. Common stock is the only stock issued by Ludlum.

Sales (net on account)	$1,800,000
Plant and Equipment (net)	2,400,000
Average Stockholders' Equity	3,800,000
Long-Term Liabilities	900,000
Net Income	192,000
Average Accounts Receivable (net)	375,000
Average Merchandise Inventory	255,000
Gross Profit	525,000

Compute the following:

a. Accounts receivable turnover
b. Merchandise inventory turnover
c. Ratio of plant and equipment to long-term liabilities
d. Rate of return on common stockholders' equity

L.O. 4a,b,c **Exercise 27-8** The following items are taken from the balance sheet of the Wagner Company.

Cash	$108,000
Accounts Receivable (net)	400,500
Merchandise Inventory	126,000
Prepaid Expenses	4,500
Accounts Payable	180,000
Notes Payable (current)	16,500
Salaries Payable	1,500

Compute the following:

a. Working capital
b. Current ratio
c. Quick ratio

Problem Set A

L.O. 1 **Problem 27-1A** During 19x1, Whaley's Fashion Shoppe put on a big sales promotion campaign that cost $13,200 more than it usually spent for advertising. The condensed comparative income statement for the fiscal years ended December 31, 19x1 and December 31, 19x0 is at the top of the next page.

Instructions

1. Using horizontal analysis, prepare a comparative income statement for the two-year period. Round off percentages to three decimal places.
2. Comment on the percentages of increase or decrease.

Whaley's Fashion Shoppe
Comparative Income Statement
For Years Ended December 31, 19x1 and December 31, 19x0

	19x1	19x0
Revenue from Sales:		
Sales	$ 427 6 8 0 00	$ 324 0 0 0 00
Less Sales Returns and Allowances	35 0 4 0 00	24 0 0 0 00
Net Sales	$ 392 6 4 0 00	$ 300 0 0 0 00
Cost of Merchandise Sold	223 0 2 0 00	177 0 0 0 00
Gross Profit	$ 169 6 2 0 00	$ 123 0 0 0 00
Operating Expenses:		
Selling Expenses	$ 74 8 9 6 00	$ 60 4 0 0 00
General Expenses	22 0 8 0 00	19 2 0 0 00
Total Expenses	$ 96 9 7 6 00	$ 79 6 0 0 00
Income from Operations	$ 72 6 4 4 00	$ 43 4 0 0 00
Other Expense	7 5 0 00	6 0 0 00
Net Income	$ 71 8 9 4 00	$ 42 8 0 0 00

L.O. 2   **Problem 27-2A**   Use the comparative income statement for Whaley's Fashion Shoppe presented in Problem 27-1A.

Instructions

1. Using vertical analysis, prepare a comparative income statement for the two-year period. Round off percentages to three decimal places.
2. Comment on the percentage figures.

L.O. 3   **Problem 27-3A**   Following is the condensed comparative income statement of the Central Electric Corporation:

Central Electric Corporation
Comparative Income Statement
For Years Ended December 31, 19x1, 19x2, 19x3 (thousands of dollars)

	19x1	19x2	19x3
Sales (net)	$9 3 0 0 00	$10 2 0 0 00	$11 4 0 0 00
Cost of Merchandise Sold	6 6 0 0 00	7 4 4 0 00	8 4 4 5 00
Gross Profit	$2 7 0 0 00	$ 2 7 6 0 00	$ 2 9 5 5 00
Operating Expenses:			
Selling Expenses	$1 3 9 5 00	$ 1 4 1 3 00	$ 1 5 8 1 00
General Expenses	9 1 5 00	9 3 0 00	9 3 0 00
Total Operating Expenses	$2 3 1 0 00	$ 2 3 4 3 00	$ 2 5 1 1 00
Income Before Income Tax	$ 3 9 0 00	$ 4 1 7 00	$ 4 4 4 00
Income Tax Expense	1 4 0 00	1 4 3 00	1 5 6 00
Net Income After Income Tax	$ 2 5 0 00	$ 2 7 4 00	$ 2 8 8 00

Instructions

1. Express the income statement data in trend percentages.
2. Comment on any significant relationships revealed by the percentages. Round off to the nearest whole percent (two decimal places).

L.O. 4a,b,c,e;5b,c,d   **Problem 27-4A**   Here is the income statement of Hudson Corporation. The balance sheet is shown on the next page.

Hudson Corporation
Income Statement
For Year Ended December 31, 19x1

Revenue from Sales:		
Sales		$ 705 0 0 0 00
Cost of Merchandise Sold:		
Merchandise Inventory, Jan. 1, 19x1	$ 114 0 0 0 00	
Purchases	460 2 0 0 00	
Merchandise Available for Sale	$ 574 2 0 0 00	
Less Merchandise Inventory,		
Dec. 31, 19x1	121 8 0 0 00	
Cost of Merchandise Sold		452 4 0 0 00
Gross Profit		$ 252 6 0 0 00
Operating Expenses:		
Selling Expenses (control)	$ 139 0 5 0 00	
General Expenses (control)	69 3 0 0 00	
Total Operating Expenses		208 3 5 0 00
Income from Operations		$ 44 2 5 0 00
Other Expense:		
Interest Expense		7 8 0 0 00
Income Before Income Tax		$ 36 4 5 0 00
Income Tax Expense		8 2 5 0 00
Net Income After Income Tax		$ 28 2 0 0 00

The present market price of common stock is $46 per share. At the beginning of the year, stockholders' equity was $193,800.

Instructions

Determine the following, showing the figures you used in your calculations (round off to two decimal places):

1. Working capital
2. Current ratio
3. Quick ratio
4. Merchandise inventory turnover
5. Number of days merchandise inventory kept in stock
6. Rate of return on common stockholders' equity
7. Earnings per share of common stock
8. Price-earnings ratio

Hudson Corporation
Balance Sheet
December 31, 19x1

Assets			
Current Assets:			
Cash	$ 17 2 5 0 00		
Notes Receivable	6 0 0 0 00		
Accounts Receivable (net)	80 5 5 0 00		
Merchandise Inventory	121 8 0 0 00		
Prepaid Expenses	2 1 0 0 00		
Total Current Assets		$ 227 7 0 0 00	
Plant and Equipment:			
Store Equipment (net)	$ 46 8 0 0 00		
Office Equipment (net)	13 6 5 0 00		
Delivery Equipment (net)	77 1 0 0 00		
Total Plant and Equipment		137 5 5 0 00	
Total Assets		$ 365 2 5 0 00	
Liabilities			
Current Liabilities:			
Notes Payable	$ 3 0 0 0 00		
Accounts Payable	32 2 5 0 00		
Total Current Liabilities		$ 35 2 5 0 00	
Long-Term Liabilities:			
Mortgage Payable (due June 30, 19x6)		120 0 0 0 00	
Total Liabilities		$ 155 2 5 0 00	
Stockholders' Equity			
Common Stock, $15 par (10,000 shares authorized and issued)		$ 150 0 0 0 00	
Retained Earnings		60 0 0 0 00	
Total Stockholders' Equity		210 0 0 0 00	
Total Liabilities and Stockholders' Equity		$ 365 2 5 0 00	

Problem Set B

L.O. 1   **Problem 27-1B**   During 19x1, Martin's Floor Coverings put on a sales promotion campaign that cost $17,090 more than it usually spent on advertising. A condensed comparative income statement for the fiscal years ended December 31, 19x1 and December 31, 19x0 is shown on the next page.

Instructions

1. Using horizontal analysis, prepare a comparative income statement for the two-year period. Round off to three decimal places.
2. Comment on the percentages of increase or decrease.

Martin's Floor Coverings
Comparative Income Statement
For Years Ended December 31, 19x1 and December 31, 19x0

	19x1	19x0
Revenue from Sales:		
Sales	$ 470 5 6 0 00	$ 346 0 0 0 00
Less Sales Returns and Allowances	36 4 0 0 00	26 0 0 0 00
Net Sales	$ 434 1 6 0 00	$ 320 0 0 0 00
Cost of Merchandise Sold	278 1 6 0 00	195 2 0 0 00
Gross Profit	$ 156 0 0 0 00	$ 124 8 0 0 00
Operating Expenses:		
Selling Expenses	$ 89 9 6 0 00	$ 69 2 0 0 00
General Expenses	22 4 4 0 00	20 4 0 0 00
Total Expenses	$ 112 4 0 0 00	$ 89 6 0 0 00
Income from Operations	$ 43 6 0 0 00	$ 35 2 0 0 00
Other Expenses	5 6 0 00	4 0 0 00
Net Income	$ 43 0 4 0 00	$ 34 8 0 0 00

L.O. 2   **Problem 27-2B**   Use the comparative income statement for Martin's Floor Coverings presented in Problem 27-1B.

Instructions

1. Using vertical analysis, prepare a comparative income statement for the two-year period. Round off to three decimal places.
2. Comment on the percentage figures.

L.O. 3   **Problem 27-3B**   Following is the condensed comparative income state-ment of the Seahorn Manufacturing Corporation:

Seahorn Manufacturing Corporation
Comparative Income Statement
For Years Ended December 31, 19x6, 19x7, 19x8 (thousands of dollars)

	19x6	19x7	19x8
Sales (net)	$ 16 0 0 0 00	$ 17 6 0 0 00	$ 20 0 0 0 00
Cost of Merchandise Sold	11 4 0 0 00	12 8 0 0 00	15 0 0 0 00
Gross Profit	$ 4 6 0 0 00	$ 4 8 0 0 00	$ 5 0 0 0 00
Operating Expenses:			
Selling Expenses	2 3 6 8 00	2 5 5 4 00	2 6 8 8 00
General Expenses	1 5 6 0 00	1 5 6 0 00	1 5 7 2 00
Total Operating Expenses	$ 3 9 2 8 00	$ 4 1 1 4 00	$ 4 2 6 0 00
Income Before Income Tax	$ 6 7 2 00	$ 6 8 6 00	$ 7 4 0 00
Income Tax Expense	2 2 8 00	2 3 8 00	2 5 3 00
Net Income After Income Tax	$ 4 4 4 00	$ 4 4 8 00	$ 4 8 7 00

Instructions

1. Express the income statement data in trend percentages.
2. Comment on any significant relationships revealed by the percentages. Round off to the nearest whole percent (two decimal places).

L.O. 4a,b,c,e;5b,c,d   **Problem 27-4B**   Here are the year-end financial statements of Henkel Music Store:

<table>
<tr><td colspan="4" align="center">Henkel Music Store
Income Statement
For Year Ended December 31, 19x2</td></tr>
<tr><td>Revenue from Sales:</td><td></td><td></td><td></td></tr>
<tr><td>Sales</td><td></td><td></td><td>$ 810 0 0 0 00</td></tr>
<tr><td>Cost of Merchandise Sold:</td><td></td><td></td><td></td></tr>
<tr><td>Merchandise Inventory, Jan. 1, 19x2</td><td>$ 120 0 0 0 00</td><td></td><td></td></tr>
<tr><td>Net Purchases</td><td>504 6 0 0 00</td><td></td><td></td></tr>
<tr><td>Merchandise Available for Sale</td><td>$ 624 6 0 0 00</td><td></td><td></td></tr>
<tr><td>Less Merchandise Inventory,
  Dec. 31, 19x2</td><td>132 9 0 0 00</td><td></td><td></td></tr>
<tr><td>Cost of Merchandise Sold</td><td></td><td>491 7 0 0 00</td><td></td></tr>
<tr><td>Gross Profit</td><td></td><td>$ 318 3 0 0 00</td><td></td></tr>
<tr><td>Operating Expenses:</td><td></td><td></td><td></td></tr>
<tr><td>Selling Expenses (control)</td><td>$ 168 7 5 0 00</td><td></td><td></td></tr>
<tr><td>General Expenses (control)</td><td>82 9 5 0 00</td><td></td><td></td></tr>
<tr><td>Total Operating Expenses</td><td></td><td>251 7 0 0 00</td><td></td></tr>
<tr><td>Income from Operations</td><td></td><td>$ 66 6 0 0 00</td><td></td></tr>
<tr><td>Other Expenses:</td><td></td><td></td><td></td></tr>
<tr><td>Interest Expense</td><td></td><td>11 4 0 0 00</td><td></td></tr>
<tr><td>Income Before Income Tax</td><td></td><td>$ 55 2 0 0 00</td><td></td></tr>
<tr><td>Income Tax Expense</td><td></td><td>9 5 0 0 00</td><td></td></tr>
<tr><td>Net Income After Income Tax</td><td></td><td>$ 45 7 0 0 00</td><td></td></tr>
</table>

The present market price is $50 per share. At the beginning of the year, stockholders' equity was $175,000.

Instructions

Determine the following, showing the figures you used in your calculations (round off to two decimal places):

1. Working capital
2. Current ratio
3. Quick ratio
4. Merchandise inventory turnover
5. Number of days merchandise inventory kept in stock
6. Rate of return on common stockholders' equity
7. Earnings per share of common stock
8. Price-earnings ratio

Henkel Music Store
Balance Sheet
December 31, 19x2

Assets

Current Assets:			
Cash	$ 21 3 0 0 00		
Notes Receivable	6 0 0 0 00		
Accounts Receivable (net)	77 7 0 0 00		
Merchandise Inventory	132 9 0 0 00		
Prepaid Expenses	1 8 0 0 00		
Total Current Assets		$ 239 7 0 0 00	
Plant and Equipment:			
Store Equipment (net)	$ 46 3 5 0 00		
Office Equipment (net)	14 1 0 0 00		
Delivery Equipment (net)	74 5 5 0 00		
Total Plant and Equipment		135 0 0 0 00	
Total Assets		$ 374 7 0 0 00	

Liabilities

Current Liabilities:			
Notes Payable	$ 3 6 0 0 00		
Accounts Payable	50 7 0 0 00		
Total Current Liabilities		$ 54 3 0 0 00	
Long-Term Liabilities:			
Mortgage Payable (due June 30, 19x8)		115 2 0 0 00	
Total Liabilities			$ 169 5 0 0 00

Stockholders' Equity

Common Stock, $15 par (10,000			
shares authorized and issued)		$ 150 0 0 0 00	
Retained Earnings		55 2 0 0 00	
Total Stockholders' Equity			205 2 0 0 00
Total Liabilities and Stockholder's Equity			$ 374 7 0 0 00

28 Statement of Cash Flows

Certainly the financial statements presented in earlier chapters are important. Each statement serves a specific purpose. The income statement shows the results of operations. The statement of owners' or stockholders' equity shows additional investments by owners and payments to owners. The balance sheet portrays a company's financial condition. However, there are important questions that these statements do not answer. For example, What new assets did the firm invest in (buy) during the year? If liabilities increased during the year, where were the proceeds spent? Or, if liabilities decreased, how were they reduced? Did a corporation's operations for the year generate enough cash to pay dividends? If a corporation issued common stock during the year, what was done with the proceeds?

One wonders, Why can't these questions be answered by the existing financial statements? The income statement is prepared on the accrual basis, and it does not show the amounts of cash either generated or paid. The amounts of cash involved in changes in the balances of assets and liabilities during the year are not shown on the balance sheet. The statement of owners' or stockholders' equity shows only transactions that

949

affect equity accounts. The statement of cash flows was developed to explain the reasons for the inflows and outflows of cash.

A BROAD LOOK AT THE STATEMENT OF CASH FLOWS

Definition

Objective 1

Describe briefly the statement of cash flows and define cash and cash equivalents.

The **statement of cash flows** is a financial statement that explains in detail how the balance of cash and cash equivalents has changed between the beginning and the end of a fiscal period. Some accountants refer to the statement of cash flows as the "where got, where gone" statement of cash. The Financial Accounting Standards Board, in its Statement of Financial Accounting Standards No. 95, now requires a statement of cash flows to be a major part of a full set of financial statements.

Cash and Cash Equivalents　On the statement of cash flows, cash is defined to include both cash, as we think of it, and cash equivalents. **Cash equivalents** are short-term highly liquid investments including money market accounts, U.S. Treasury bills, and commercial paper. When a company has more cash on hand than is needed immediately, it seems logical to put the excess cash to work earning interest. Money market accounts are interest-bearing accounts available at banks. U.S. Treasury bills may be considered short-term government bonds. Commercial paper represents another corporation's short-term interest-bearing notes. All these sources of temporary investments must be convertible into cash within a maximum of ninety days from the date acquired.

Cash equivalents should not be confused with investments in marketable securities, which are held for a longer term. These investments are not combined with the balance of the Cash account on a statement of cash flows.

Purpose

Objective 2

State the purpose of the statement of cash flows.

The main purpose of the statement of cash flows is to provide a summary of information concerning a company's cash receipts and payments during a fiscal period. A secondary purpose is to provide information about a firm's investing and financing activities during a fiscal period.

Uses of the Statement of Cash Flows

Management's Use of the Statement of Cash Flows

Objective 3

State the uses of the statement of cash flows by management, investors, and creditors.

Management uses the statement of cash flows to assess or determine the liquidity of the business, to determine dividend policy, and to evaluate possible investments and means of financing. Management asks the following questions:

Liquidity—Is enough cash being generated for a company to pay its bills?

Dividend policy—Is enough cash being generated for a corporation to establish a regular cash dividend policy?

Investment and financing—If a firm borrows to buy an asset, is enough cash being generated to make the payments?

Investors' and Creditors' Use of the Statement of Cash Flows

Investors (stockholders) are interested in a corporation's ability to pay dividends. Creditors are concerned with a company's ability to pay its liabilities. Both investors and creditors are interested in the firm's ability to generate future cash flows as well as its need for additional financing.

CLASSIFICATIONS OF CASH FLOWS

Objective 4

Identify cash inflows and outflows as operating, investing, or financing activities.

The statement of cash flows classifies cash receipts and payments into three categories: operating activities, investing activities, and financing activities.

Operating Activities

Operating activities, the first category on the statement of cash flows, identify and classify cash inflows and outflows from a variety of sources. *Cash inflows* include cash receipts from customers for the sale of merchandise and services as well as cash receipts in the form of interest and dividend income. Think of the items listed on an income statement including the Revenue from Sales section and then dip into the Other Income section to pick up Interest Income and Dividend Income.

Cash outflows include cash payments for merchandise purchases and operating expenses, such as Wages Expense and Rent Expense. Cash outflows from operating activities also include cash payments in the form of interest and taxes expense. Think of the items listed on an income statement including the Operating Expenses (Selling and General) section and then dip into the Other Expense section to pick up Interest Expense.

Incidentally, when we think about the income statement, we find the accounts Gain on Disposal of Plant and Equipment listed in the Other Income section and Loss on Disposal of Plant and Equipment listed in the Other Expense section. These items generally arise because of investing activities; consequently, they will be included with the sale or purchase of merchandise in the Investing Activities section.

Investing Activities

Investing activities include (1) buying and selling plant and equipment (long-term assets), (2) acquiring and selling investments other than cash equivalents, and (3) making and collecting loans. *Cash inflows* include the cash received from selling plant and equipment as well as investments and from collecting loans. *Cash outflows* include cash paid to purchase plant and equipment, cash loaned to borrowers, and cash invested in another corporation's stocks or bonds.

Financing Activities

Financing activities include cash transactions that involve borrowing from creditors or repaying creditors as well as additional cash investments from owners or transactions that reduce owners' investments. *Cash inflows* include proceeds received from short- or long-term borrowing (issuing notes or bonds) as well as those from issuing stock for cash. *Cash outflows* include repayments of loans (notes and bonds) and payments to owners, including personal withdrawals and cash dividends.

FIGURE 28-1   Figure 28-1 illustrates the classification of cash inflows and outflows.

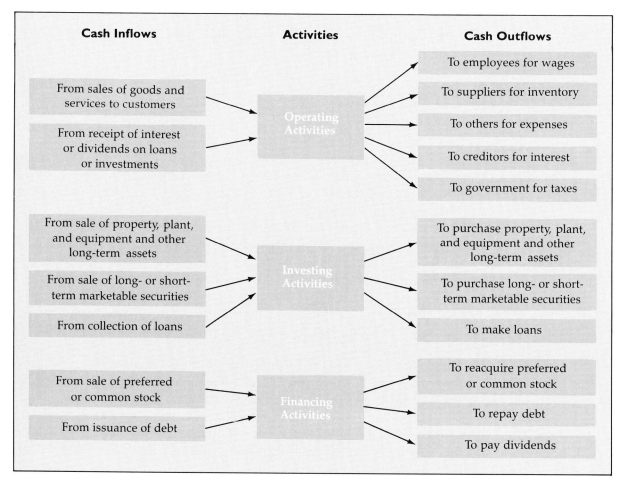

Classifying cash flows into three types of activities helps readers of financial statements to interpret cash flow data. For example, in the following table, companies A, B, and C are similar companies operating in the same industry. Each company has a positive cash flow.

Positive Cash Flow	Company		
	A	B	C
Net cash flows from operating activities: net sales, less cost of merchandise sold, less operating expenses (excluding depreciation), plus interest and dividend income, less interest expense and taxes	$120,000	0	0
Cash flow from investing activities: sale of equipment for cash	0	$140,000	0
Cash flow from financing activities: borrowing from a bank	0	0	$160,000
Net increase in cash	$120,000	$140,000	$160,000

If you were considering investing or loaning money, which company would you choose? Assuming that your decision was based only on this data, you would definitely select Company A. Company A's cash came from operating activities that can be counted on to generate new cash during future years. Company B's cash came from the sale of equipment, which is a "one-shot deal." If the firm is planning to stay in business, this source is not likely to generate cash regularly in the future. Company C's cash came from borrowing, and the principal and interest will have to be paid in the future, possibly resulting in a future drain on cash.

FORM OF THE STATEMENT OF CASH FLOWS

Objective 5

Calculate amounts of cash inflows and outflows involving operating, investing, and financing activities.

The statement of cash flows is divided into the three categories we discussed previously: operating activities, followed by investing activities, followed by financing activities. Within each activity, cash inflows and outflows are shown separately. For example, suppose that a company sells its used equipment for $4,000 in cash. Next, the company turns around and buys new equipment for $30,000, paying cash. Under investing activities, sale of equipment, $4,000, is listed as an inflow of cash. The purchase of equipment, $30,000, is listed as an outflow of cash.

First, we will present an example of a complete statement of cash flows, so that you can see the entire picture. Next, we will follow up by presenting illustrations of four other companies, starting with a one-owner business and working up to a corporation.

Central Corporation
Statement of Cash Flows
For Year Ended December 31, 19–

Cash Flows from (used by) Operating Activities:			
Cash Receipts from:			
Customers		$1 440 0 0 0 00	
Interest and Dividends		6 0 0 0 00	
Total Cash Receipts			$1 446 0 0 0 00
Cash Payments for:			
Merchandise Purchases		$ 520 0 0 0 00	
Operating Expenses:			
Employees	$ 190 0 0 0 00		
Supplies	14 0 0 0 00		
Insurance	3 0 0 0 00		
Total		207 0 0 0 00	
Interest		20 0 0 0 00	
Income Tax		93 0 0 0 00	
Total Cash Payments			840 0 0 0 00
Net Cash Flows from Operating Activities			$ 606 0 0 0 00
Cash Flows from (used by) Investing Activities:			
Purchase of Investments		$ (10 0 0 0 00)	
Sale of Investments		20 0 0 0 00	
Purchase of Plant and Equipment		(30 0 0 0 00)	
Sales of Plant and Equipment		4 0 0 0 00	
Net Cash Flows used by Investing Activities			(16 0 0 0 00)
Cash Flows from (used by) Financing Activities:			
Issuance of Note		$ 10 0 0 0 00	
Issuance of Bonds		210 0 0 0 00	
Repayment of Bonds		(60 0 0 0 00)	
Issuance of Common Stock		140 0 0 0 00	
Payment of Dividends		(50 0 0 0 00)	
Net Cash Flows from Financing Activities			250 0 0 0 00
Net Increase (Decrease) in Cash			$ 840 0 0 0 00

    Actually, the statement of cash flows may be presented using two methods: the direct method and the indirect method. The FASB recommends the direct method, although the indirect method is acceptable. **The direct method primarily involves converting each amount recorded on the income statement from the accrual basis to the cash basis.** The direct method shows the specific sources and uses of cash during a fiscal period. With this method, a separate schedule reconciling net income and net cash flows from operating activities must be provided. This reconciliation is covered in more advanced accounting courses. The indirect method (or reconciliation method) involves a series of adjusting entries made to comparative balance sheet data recorded on a work sheet. Since the direct method is the preferred report format, we will reserve discussion of the indirect method for more advanced accounting texts.

DEVELOPING THE STATEMENT OF CASH FLOWS

Objective 6

Prepare a statement of cash flows using the direct method.

To describe the development of the statement of cash flows, we will use four illustrations. First we need each company's three basic financial statements for the present fiscal period as well as each firm's balance sheet at the end of the previous fiscal period (same as the beginning balance of the present fiscal period). Based on the balance sheets at the beginning and end of the fiscal period, we can compile a comparative balance sheet listing the increases and decreases in all accounts for each of our illustrations.

Illustration I

Our first illustration shows conversions of Supplies Expense, Insurance Expense, Depreciation Expense, and Drawing into cash flows. Bates Spray Service operates on a modified cash basis (page 188), in which revenue is counted only when it is received in cash, and expenses are counted only when they are paid in cash. However, in keeping with Internal Revenue Service regulations, the firm makes adjusting entries for supplies used, insurance expired, and depreciation. The financial statements for Bates Spray Service are presented below and on the next page.

Bates Spray Service
Income Statement
For Year Ended December 31, 19x5

Income from Services		$49 540 00
Expenses:		
Wages Expense	$12 000 00	
Supplies Expense	1 600 00	
Insurance Expense	240 00	
Depreciation Expense	13 200 00	
Total Expenses		27 040 00
Net Income		$22 500 00

Bates Spray Service
Statement of Owner's Equity
For Year Ended December 31, 19x5

C. A. Bates, Capital, January 1, 19x5		$41 200 00
Net Income	$22 500 00	
Less Withdrawals	20 000 00	
Increase in Capital		2 500 00
C. A. Bates, Capital, December 31, 19x5		$43 700 00

Bates Spray Service
Comparative Balance Sheet
December 31, 19x5 and December 31, 19x4

	19x5	19x4	INCREASE OR (DECREASE)
Assets			
Cash	$16 5 2 0 00	$ 7 8 0 00	$15 7 4 0 00
Supplies	9 0 0 00	7 0 0 00	2 0 0 00
Prepaid Insurance	2 8 0 00	5 2 0 00	(2 4 0 00)
Equipment	50 0 0 0 00	50 0 0 0 00	0 00
Less Accumulated Depreciation	(24 0 0 0 00)	(10 8 0 0 00)	(13 2 0 0 00)
Total Assets	$43 7 0 0 00	$41 2 0 0 00	$ 2 5 0 0 00
Owner's Equity			
C. A. Bates, Capital	$43 7 0 0 00	$41 2 0 0 00	$ 2 5 0 0 00
Total Owner's Equity	$43 7 0 0 00	$41 2 0 0 00	$ 2 5 0 0 00

Note the $15,740 increase in Cash in the comparative balance sheet ($16,520 − $780). The purpose of the statement of cash flows is to show how this increase in Cash came about ("where got, where gone"). In essence, the company's income statement must be converted from a modified cash basis (where adjustments were made for supplies used, insurance expired, and depreciation) to a pure cash basis.

Cash Flows from Operating Activities: Convert Revenue and Expenses to Cash Basis

1. **Convert Income from Services to Cash Receipts from Customers.** Since Bates Spray Service records revenue only when it is received in cash, the $49,540 listed as Income from Services on the income statement is the exact amount of cash received.
2. **Convert Wages Expense to Cash Payments to Employees.** Since Bates Spray Service records wages expense only when employees are paid, the $12,000 listed as Wages Expense on the income statment is the exact amount of cash paid.
3. **Convert Supplies Expense to Cash Payments for Supplies.** During 19x5, Supplies increased from $700 to $900. Evidently, Bates Spray Service bought $200 more supplies than it used up during the year. So

$200 more in cash was paid out than the $1,600 listed as Supplies Expense on the income statement. We calculate the cash payments like this:

Supplies Expense	$1,600
+ Ending Supplies	900
= Total	$2,500
− Beginning Supplies	700
= Cash Payments for Supplies	$1,800

4. **Convert Insurance Expense to Cash Payments for Insurance.** During 19x5, Prepaid Insurance decreased from $520 to $280. Evidently, Bates Spray Service did not buy any more insurance. Instead, part of the prepaid insurance simply expired during the year. In other words, the company did not pay any cash out for additional insurance, it simply used up what it had, so the $240 listed as Insurance Expense on the income statement did not cost the firm any cash. We calculate the cash payment like this:

Insurance Expense	$240
+ Ending Prepaid Insurance	280
= Total	$520
− Beginning Prepaid Insurance	520
= Cash Payments for Insurance	$ 0

5. **Convert Depreciation Expense to Cash Payments for Depreciation.** Since the $13,200 listed on the income statement as Depreciation Expense was not paid to anyone, it does not involve cash. Consequently, depreciation is not recorded on a statement of cash flows; it is eliminated.

Cash Flows from Investing Activities   Remember in noting investing activities, we are concerned with changes in plant and equipment. The balance of the Equipment account has not changed during the year. Rather, the balance of Accumulated Depreciation has gone from $10,800 to $24,000. The $13,200 change is accounted for by recording $13,200 as Depreciation Expense on the income statement. Although there is a $13,200 increase in Accumulated Depreciation, this amount is not paid to anyone. Since this is the only change we have, we can say that there have been no cash transactions involving investing activities.

Cash Flows from Financing Activities   As we said earlier, financing activities include additions to or reductions in owner's equity. On the statement of owner's equity, we note a $20,000 withdrawal, which we assume is in the form of cash. The withdrawal will result in a decrease in cash. We can easily check out our assumption that the withdrawals did indeed involve cash by reviewing the transactions affecting the C. A. Bates, Drawing account. Since there were no additional changes reported on the statement of owner's equity, we have gathered all the necessary information we need to prepare our statement of cash flows for Bates Spray Service. Here it is.

Bates Spray Service
Statement of Cash Flows
For Year Ended December 31, 19x5

Cash Flows from (used by) Operating Activities:		
Cash Receipts from Customers		$49 5 4 0 00
Cash Payments for Operating Expenses:		
Employees	$ 12 0 0 0 00	
Supplies ($1,600 + $900 − $700)	1 8 0 0 00	
Total Cash Payments		13 8 0 0 00
Net Cash Flows from Operating Activities		$35 7 4 0 00
Cash Flows from (used by) Financing Activities:		
Payment of Personal Withdrawals	$ (20 0 0 0 00)	
Net Cash Flows used by Financing Activities		(20 0 0 0 00)
Net Increase (Decrease) in Cash		$15 7 4 0 00

Summary of the Conversions in Illustration 1

- **For Prepaid Expenses**   Prepaid expenses include items such as Supplies and Prepaid Insurance.

   Amount of the expense listed on the income statement + the ending balance of the prepaid expense account − the beginning balance of the prepaid expense account = the cash payment for the expense

- Each expense and the amount calculated is listed individually in the operating expenses section under Cash Flows from (used by) Operating Activities.
- **For Depreciation**   The amount of depreciation expense listed on the income statement is canceled out or eliminated.
- **For Personal Cash Withdrawals**   The amount taken from the statement of owner's equity is listed as a negative amount (used by) under Cash Flows from (used by) Financing Activities.

Illustration 2

Our second illustration shows conversions of Income from Services, Wages Expense, Supplies Expense, and purchase of equipment into cash flows. Hogan Company is a one-owner service business operating on the accrual basis. (Revenue is recognized when it is earned, and expenses are recognized when they are incurred.) The financial statements for Hogan Company are presented on the next page.

Hogan Company
Income Statement
For Year Ended December 31, 19x1

Income from Services		$70 0 0 0 00
Expenses:		
Wages Expense	$32 0 0 0 00	
Supplies Expense	4 0 0 0 00	
Depreciation Expense	5 0 0 0 00	
Total Expenses		41 0 0 0 00
Net Income		$29 0 0 0 00

Hogan Company
Statement of Owner's Equity
For Year Ended December 31, 19x1

S. T. Hogan, Capital, January 1, 19x1		$21 0 0 0 00
Net Income	$29 0 0 0 00	
Less Withdrawals	27 0 0 0 00	
Increase in Capital		2 0 0 0 00
S. T. Hogan, Capital, December 31, 19x1		$23 0 0 0 00

Hogan Company
Comparative Balance Sheet
December 31, 19x1 and December 31, 19x0

	19x1	19x0	INCREASE OR (DECREASE)
Assets			
Cash	$ 7 4 0 0 00	$ 3 0 0 0 00	$4 4 0 0 00
Accounts Receivable	10 4 0 0 00	8 4 0 0 00	2 0 0 0 00
Supplies	9 0 0 00	1 0 0 0 00	(1 0 0 00)
Equipment	22 2 0 0 00	21 6 0 0 00	6 0 0 00
Less Accumulated Depreciation	(15 0 0 0 00)	(10 0 0 0 00)	(5 0 0 0 00)
Total Assets	$25 9 0 0 00	$24 0 0 0 00	$1 9 0 0 00
Liabilities			
Accounts Payable	$ 2 7 0 0 00	$ 2 7 0 0 00	$ 0 00
Wages Payable	2 0 0 00	3 0 0 00	(1 0 0 00)
Total Liabilities	$ 2 9 0 0 00	$ 3 0 0 0 00	$(1 0 0 00)
Owner's Equity			
S. T. Hogan, Capital	23 0 0 0 00	21 0 0 0 00	2 0 0 0 00
Total Liabilities and Owner's Equity	$25 9 0 0 00	$24 0 0 0 00	$1 9 0 0 00

Note the $4,400 increase in Cash as shown in the comparative balance sheet ($7,400 − $3,000). To explain this increase, we must first convert the income statement of Hogan Company from the accrual basis to the cash basis. Next, we will look over the statement of owner's equity and the comparative balance sheet to note any possible cash received or paid out that has not shown up in the conversion of the income statement.

Cash Flows from Operating Activities

1. **Convert Income from Services to Cash Receipts from Customers.** Income from Services is in the form of cash and customer charge accounts. During 19x1, Accounts Receivable increased from $8,400 to $10,400. Evidently, $2,000 more was recorded in the charge accounts than was collected in cash. Starting with the $70,000 listed as Income from Services on the income statement, we will say we collected the beginning balance of Accounts Receivable ($8,400) and did not collect the ending balance of Accounts Receivable ($10,400). The amount of cash received from customers is calculated like this:

Income from Services	$70,000
+ Beginning Accounts Receivable	8,400
= Total	$78,400
− Ending Accounts Receivable	10,400
= Cash Receipts from Customers	$68,000

Here's another way of picturing the situation. Assume the company collects its beginning Accounts Receivable first. Next, of the $70,000 listed on the income statement as Income from Services, all but $10,400 (the ending balance of Accounts Receivable) was collected. The calculation looks like this:

Beginning Accounts Receivable	$ 8,400
+ Income from Services	70,000
= Total	$78,400
− Ending Accounts Receivable	10,400
= Cash Receipts from Customers	$68,000

or

Beginning Accounts Receivable	$ 8,400
+ Cash Income from Services ($70,000 − $10,400)	59,600
= Cash Receipts from Customers	$68,000

2. **Convert Wages Expense to Cash Payments to Employees.** We start with the amount shown on the the income statement as Wages Expense, $32,000. During the first part of the year, Hogan Company also paid out to its employees the amount shown as the beginning balance

of Wages Payable, $300, so we add this amount to the $32,000. However, of the $32,000 listed as Wages Expense, $200 was not paid to the employees. The calculation for the amount paid in cash to employees looks like this:

Wages Expense	$32,000
+ Beginning Wages Payable	300
= Total	$32,300
− Ending Wages Payable	200
= Cash Payments to Employees	$32,100

Here's another way of picturing the situation. Assume the company pays its beginning Wages Payable first. Next, of the $32,000 listed on the income statement as Wages Expense, all but $200 (the ending balance of Wages Payable) was paid. The calculation looks like this:

Beginning Wages Payable	$ 300
+ Wages Expense	32,000
= Total	$32,300
− Ending Wages Payable	200
= Cash Payments to Employees	$32,100

or

Beginning Wages Payable	$ 300
+ Cash Wages Expense ($32,000 − $200)	31,800
= Cash Payments to Employees	$32,100

3. **Convert Supplies Expense to Cash Payments for Supplies.** During 19x1, Supplies decreased from $1,000 to $900. Evidently, Hogan Company bought fewer supplies than it used during the year. In other words, Hogan Company had to dip into its inventory of supplies to the extent of $100. So the $4,000 listed as Supplies Expense was $100 more than the amount of cash paid out. The calculation looks like this:

Supplies Expense	$4,000
+ Ending Supplies	900
= Total	$4,900
− Beginning Supplies	1,000
= Cash Payments for Supplies	$3,900

4. **Convert Depreciation Expense to Cash Payments for Depreciation.** As we stated before, no cash is involved in Depreciation Expense, so it is eliminated.

Cash Flows from Investing Activities   We look for clues to identify investment activities by examining changes in plant and equipment accounts. The comparative balance sheet shows that the balance of the Equipment account has increased from $21,600 to $22,200. If we were to review the Equipment ledger account, we would see the posting reference for the one entry recorded this period. When we traced the entry to the journal page, we would find a debit to Equipment for $600 and a credit to Cash for $600. Knowing it was a cash purchase, we would list the purchase of equipment for $600 on the statement of cash flows as an outflow of cash.

Cash Flows from Financing Activities   On the statement of owner's equity, we note a $27,000 personal withdrawal. After reviewing the journal entries affecting the S. T. Hogan, Drawing account, we assume that the $27,000 was paid in cash. On the statement of cash flows, $27,000 is listed as an outflow of cash. Here's the statement of cash flows for Hogan Company:

Hogan Company
Statement of Cash Flows
For Year Ended December 31, 19x1

Cash Flows from (used by) Operating Activities:		
Cash Receipts from Customers		$68 0 0 0 00
Cash Payments for Operating Expenses:		
Employees	$ 32 1 0 0 00	
Supplies	3 9 0 0 00	
Total Cash Payments		36 0 0 0 00
Net Cash Flows from Operating Activities		$32 0 0 0 00
Cash Flows from (used by) Investing Activities:		
Purchase of Equipment	$ (6 0 0 00)	
Net Cash Flows used by Investing Activities		(6 0 0 00)
Cash Flows from (used by) Financing Activities:		
Payment of Personal Withdrawals	$ (27 0 0 0 00)	
Net Cash Flows used by Financing Activities		(27 0 0 0 00)
Net Increase (Decrease) in Cash		$ 4 4 0 0 00

Summary of the Additional Conversion in Illustration 2

• **For Revenue Involving Accounts Receivable—like Income from Services**

Amount of revenue listed on the income statement + the beginning Accounts Receivable − the ending Accounts Receivable.

• **For Accrued Expenses and Their Respective Liabilities—like Wages Expense and Wages Payable**

Amount of expense listed on the income statement + the beginning Wages Payable − the ending Wages Payable.

- **For Purchases of Equipment for Cash** The amount credited to the Cash account in the journal entry for the transaction is listed as a negative amount (used by) under Cash Flows from (used by) Investing Activities.

Illustration 3

Our third example shows conversions of net sales, net purchases, Salary Expense, and Insurance Expense into cash flows. Stengel Company is a one-owner merchandising business operating on the accrual basis. The financial statements for Stengel Company are presented below and on the next page.

Stengel Company
Income Statement
For Year Ended December 31, 19x1

Net Sales			$ 700 0 0 0 00
Cost of Merchandise Sold:			
Merchandise Inventory, January 1, 19x1	$ 126 0 0 0 00		
Net Purchases	514 0 0 0 00		
Merchandise Available for Sale	$ 640 0 0 0 00		
Less Merchandise Inventory, December 31, 19x1	130 0 0 0 00		
Cost of Merchandise Sold		510 0 0 0 00	
Gross Profit		$ 190 0 0 0 00	
Operating Expenses:			
Salary Expense	$ 100 0 0 0 00		
Rent Expense	20 0 0 0 00		
Depreciation Expense, Equipment	22 0 0 0 00		
Supplies Expense	1 6 0 0 00		
Insurance Expense	4 0 0 00		
Total Operating Expenses		144 0 0 0 00	
Net Income		$ 46 0 0 0 00	

Stengel Company
Statement of Owner's Equity
For Year Ended December 31, 19x1

D. N. Stengel, Capital, January 1, 19x1		$ 233 2 0 0 00
Net Income	$46 0 0 0 00	
Less Withdrawals	50 0 0 0 00	
Decrease in Capital		4 0 0 0 00
D. N. Stengel, Capital, December 31, 19x1		$ 229 2 0 0 00

Stengel Company
Comparative Balance Sheet
December 31, 19x1 and December 31, 19x0

	19x1	19x0	INCREASE OR (DECREASE)
Assets			
Cash	$ 32 0 0 0 00	$ 35 0 0 0 00	$(3 0 0 0 00)
Accounts Receivable	45 0 0 0 00	33 0 0 0 00	12 0 0 0 00
Merchandise Inventory	130 0 0 0 00	126 0 0 0 00	4 0 0 0 00
Supplies	6 0 0 00	9 0 0 00	(3 0 0 00)
Prepaid Insurance	1 7 0 0 00	5 0 0 00	1 2 0 0 00
Equipment	136 6 0 0 00	136 6 0 0 00	0 00
Less Accumulated Depreciation	(62 0 0 0 00)	(40 0 0 0 00)	(22 0 0 0 00)
Total Assets	$ 283 9 0 0 00	$ 292 0 0 0 00	$(8 1 0 0 00)
Liabilities			
Accounts Payable	$ 51 5 0 0 00	$ 56 0 0 0 00	$(4 5 0 0 00)
Salaries Payable	3 2 0 0 00	2 8 0 0 00	4 0 0 00
Total Liabilities	$ 54 7 0 0 00	$ 58 8 0 0 00	$(4 1 0 0 00)
Owner's Equity			
D. N. Stengel, Capital	229 2 0 0 00	233 2 0 0 00	(4 0 0 0 00)
Total Liabilities and Owner's Equity	$ 283 9 0 0 00	$ 292 0 0 0 00	$(8 1 0 0 00)

Note the $3,000 decrease in cash. Let's start from the top.

Remember

Cash Flows from Operating Activities

If Accounts Receivable has *increased* between the beginning and the end of the fiscal period, cash receipts from customers will be less than the revenue listed on the income statement. If Accounts Receivable has *decreased* between the beginning and the end of the fiscal period, cash receipts from customers will be more than the revenue listed on the income statement.

1. **Convert Net Sales to Cash Receipts from Customers.** During 19x1, Accounts Receivable increased from $33,000 to $45,000. Evidently, $12,000 more was recorded in the customer charge accounts than was collected in cash. The amount of cash received from customers is calculated like this:

Net Sales	$700,000
+ Beginning Accounts Receivable	33,000
= Total	$733,000
− Ending Accounts Receivable	45,000
= Cash Receipts from Customers	$688,000

2. **Convert Net Purchases to Cash Payments for Merchandise Purchases.** During 19x1, Accounts Payable decreased from $56,000 to $51,500. Evidently, $4,500 more was paid in cash than was recorded as amounts owed to creditors. Starting with the $514,000 listed as Net Purchases on the income statement, we'll say we paid the beginning Accounts

Payable ($56,000) and did not pay the ending Accounts Payable ($51,500). The amount of cash paid to creditors is calculated like this:

Net Purchases	$514,000
+ Beginning Accounts Payable	56,000
= Total	$570,000
− Ending Accounts Payable	51,500
= Cash Payments for Merchandise Purchases	$518,500

Remember

If Accounts Payable has *increased* between the beginning and the end of the fiscal period, cash payments for merchandise purchases will be less than net purchases listed on the income statement. If Accounts Payable has *decreased* between the beginning and the end of the fiscal period, cash payments for merchandise purchases will be more than net purchases listed on the income statement.

Here's another way of picturing the situation. We assume the company pays its beginning balance of Accounts Payable first. Next, of the $514,000, listed on the income statement as Net Purchases, all but $51,500 (the ending balance of Accounts Payable) was paid out. The calculation looks like this:

Beginning Accounts Payable	$ 56,000
+ Net Purchases	514,000
= Total	$570,000
− Ending Accounts Payable	51,500
= Cash Payments for Merchandise Purchases	$518,500

or

Beginning Accounts Payable	$ 56,000
+ Net Purchases Paid in Cash ($514,000 − $51,500)	462,500
= Cash Payments for Merchandise Purchases	$518,500

Operating Expenses   In this section of the statement of cash flows, each expense is listed in the same order as it appears on the income statement.

1. **Convert Salary Expense to Cash Payments to Employees.** On the income statement, the amount listed as Salary Expense is $100,000. On the comparative balance sheet, Salaries Payable increased from $2,800 to $3,200. Evidently, $400 less than the $100,000 listed on the income statement was paid out in cash to employees. The calculation looks like this:

Salary Expense	$100,000
+ Beginning Salaries Payable	2,800
= Total	$102,800
− Ending Salaries Payable	3,200
= Cash Payments to Employees	$ 99,600

2. **Convert Rent Expense to Cash Payments for Rent.** Since there is no amount listed on the balance sheet as Prepaid Rent or Rent Payable, we can conclude that the $20,000 listed on the income statement was indeed paid in cash.

3. **Convert Depreciation Expense to Cash Payments for Depreciation.** Again, since the amount listed as Depreciation Expense is not paid to

anyone, no cash is involved. Depreciation Expense is a noncash expense, so ignore it.

4. **Convert Supplies Expense to Cash Payments for Supplies.** During 19x1, Supplies decreased from $900 to $600. Evidently, Stengel Company used up $300 more in supplies than it bought during the year. $1,600 is listed as Supplies Expense on the income statement, but $300 of that expense resulted from dipping into the company's stock of supplies. The calculation looks like this:

Supplies Expense	$1,600
+ Ending Supplies	600
= Total	$2,200
− Beginning Supplies	900
= Cash Payments for Supplies	$1,300

Remember

If a prepaid expense (like Supplies or Prepaid Insurance) has *increased* between the beginning and the end of the fiscal period, cash payments for the item(s) is more than the amount listed as expense (Supplies Expense or Insurance Expense). If a prepaid expense (like Supplies or Prepaid Insurance) has *decreased* between the beginning and the end of the fiscal period, cash payments for the item(s) is less than the amount listed as expense (Supplies Expense or Insurance Expense).

5. **Convert Insurance Expense to Cash Payments for Insurance.** During 19x1, Prepaid Insurance increased from $500 to $1,700. Evidently, Stengel Company bought more insurance than was used up (expired) during the year. So $1,200 more in cash than the $400 listed as Insurance Expense on the income statement was paid out. The calculation looks like this:

Insurance Expense	$ 400
+ Ending Prepaid Insurance	1,700
= Total	$2,100
− Beginning Prepaid Insurance	500
= Cash Payments for Insurance	$1,600

Cash Flows from Investing Activities No changes in the Equipment account balance occurred between the beginning and end of the fiscal period. However, the Accumulated Depreciation account balance increased by the amount of the year's depreciation expense. Evidently, no equipment was either bought or sold, so no cash is involved. Also, you can note that the balance of the Equipment account has not changed.

Cash Flows from Financing Activities On the Statement of Owner's Equity, we note a withdrawal of $50,000. Let's assume that we trace through the entries involving the Drawing account and note entries debiting D. N. Stengel, Drawing and crediting Cash for a total of $50,000 each. We record $50,000 as an outflow of cash. Putting these cash conversions all together, the statement of cash flows for Stengel Company appears at the top of the next page.

Summary of Additional Conversions in Illustration 3

- **Handling Net Purchases Involving Accounts Payable** This is figured as the amount of net purchases listed on the income statement + the beginning Accounts Payable − the ending Accounts Payable.

Stengel Company
Statement of Cash Flows
For Year Ended December 31, 19x1

Cash Flows from (used by) Operating Activities:					
Cash Receipts from Customers					$ 688 0 0 0 00
Cash Payments for:					
Merchandise Purchases			$ 518 5 0 0 00		
Operating Expenses:					
Employees	$99 6 0 0 00				
Rent	20 0 0 0 00				
Supplies	1 3 0 0 00				
Insurance	1 6 0 0 00				
Total			122 5 0 0 00		
Total Cash Payments				641 0 0 0 00	
Net Cash Flows from Operating Activities				$ 47 0 0 0 00	
Cash Flows from (used by) Financing Activities:					
Payment of Personal Withdrawals			$ (50 0 0 0 00)		
Net Cash Flows used by Financing Activities					(50 0 0 0 00)
Net Increase (Decrease) in Cash					$ (3 0 0 0 00)

Illustration 4

Our final example shows conversions of net sales, net purchases, Wages Expense, Supplies Expense, Property Tax Expense, Insurance Expense, sale of equipment, Interest Expense, bank loan, issuance of stock, and payment of dividends into cash flows. Rex Corporation is a merchandising business operating on an accrual basis. The firm's financial statements are presented on pages 968 and 969.

Note the $7,700 increase in Cash. In spite of having a $13,000 net loss for the year, Rex Corporation winds up with a positive cash flow. Let's proceed to find out why this situation came about.

Cash Flows from Operating Activities

1. **Convert Net Sales to Cash Receipts from Customers.** During 19x8, Accounts Receivable decreased from $69,000 to $58,400. Evidently, $10,600 more was collected in cash than was recorded as net sales. The calculation looks like this:

Net Sales	$614,000
+ Beginning Accounts Receivable	69,000
= Total	$683,000
− Ending Accounts Receivable	58,400
= Cash Receipts from Customers	$624,600

Rex Corporation
Income Statement
For Year Ended December 31, 19x8

Revenue from Sales:		
Sales	$ 620 0 0 0 00	
Less Sales Returns and Allowances	6 0 0 0 00	
Net Sales		$ 614 0 0 0 00
Cost of Merchandise Sold:		
Merchandise Inventory, January 1, 19x8	$ 224 0 0 0 00	
Purchases $473,000.00		
Less Purchases Returns and Allowances 3,000.00		
Net Purchases	470 0 0 0 00	
Merchandise Available for Sale	$ 694 0 0 0 00	
Less Merchandise Inventory, December 31, 19x8	260 0 0 0 00	
Cost of Merchandise Sold		434 0 0 0 00
Gross Profit		$ 180 0 0 0 00
Operating Expenses:		
Wages Expense	$ 123 0 0 0 00	
Rent Expense	20 0 0 0 00	
Depreciation Expense, Equipment	24 0 0 0 00	
Supplies Expense	2 0 0 0 00	
Property Tax Expense	2 0 0 0 00	
Insurance Expense	1 0 0 0 00	
Total Operating Expenses		172 0 0 0 00
Income from Operations		$ 8 0 0 0 00
Other Income:		
Gain on Disposal of Plant and Equipment	$ 5 0 0 0 00	
Other Expenses:		
Interest Expense	26 0 0 0 00	(21 0 0 0 00)
Net Loss		$ (13 0 0 0 00)

Rex Corporation
Statement of Retained Earnings
For Year Ended December 31, 19x8

Retained Earnings, January 1, 19x8		$94 6 0 0 00
Less: Net Loss for the Year	$13 0 0 0 00	
Cash Dividends Declared	16 0 0 0 00	
Decrease in Retained Earnings		29 0 0 0 00
Retained Earnings, December 31, 19x8		$65 6 0 0 00

Rex Corporation
Comparative Balance Sheet
December 31, 19x8 and December 31, 19x7

	19x8	19x7	INCREASE OR (DECREASE)
Assets			
Cash	$ 41 1 0 0 00	$ 33 4 0 0 00	$ 7 7 0 0 00
Accounts Receivable	58 4 0 0 00	69 0 0 0 00	(10 6 0 0 00
Merchandise Inventory	260 0 0 0 00	224 0 0 0 00	36 0 0 0 00
Supplies	3 0 0 00	5 0 0 00	(2 0 0 00)
Prepaid Rent	3 0 0 0 00	3 0 0 0 00	0 00
Prepaid Insurance	9 0 0 00	4 0 0 00	5 0 0 00
Equipment	114 0 0 0 00	143 0 0 0 00	(29 0 0 0 00)
Less Accumulated Depreciation	(47 0 0 0 00)	(35 0 0 0 00)	(12 0 0 0 00)
Total Assets	$ 430 7 0 0 00	$ 438 3 0 0 00	$ (7 6 0 0 00)
Liabilities			
Notes Payable	$ 24 0 0 0 00	$ 0 00	$ 24 0 0 0 00
Accounts Payable	31 6 0 0 00	42 5 0 0 00	(10 9 0 0 00)
Wages Payable	1 0 0 00	4 0 0 00	(3 0 0 00)
Dividends Payable	2 0 0 0 00	3 0 0 0 00	(1 0 0 0 00)
Property Tax Payable	3 0 0 00	1 0 0 00	2 0 0 00
Interest Payable	6 0 0 00	2 0 0 00	4 0 0 00
Total Liabilities	$ 58 6 0 0 00	$ 46 2 0 0 00	$ 12 4 0 0 00
Stockholders' Equity			
Common Stock	$ 306 5 0 0 00	$ 297 5 0 0 00	$ 9 0 0 0 00
Retained Earnings	65 6 0 0 00	94 6 0 0 00	(29 0 0 0 00)
Total Stockholders' Equity	$ 372 1 0 0 00	$ 392 1 0 0 00	$ (20 0 0 0 00)
Total Liabilities and Stockholders' Equity	$ 430 7 0 0 00	$ 438 3 0 0 00	$ (7 6 0 0 00)

2. **Convert Net Purchases to Cash Payments for Merchandise Purchases.**
   During 19x8, Accounts Payable decreased from $42,500 to $31,600. Evidently, $10,900 more in cash was paid for merchandise purchases than the amount listed as net purchases on the income statement. The amount of cash paid to creditors is calculated like this:

Net Purchases	$470,000
+ Beginning Accounts Payable	42,500
= Total	$512,500
− Ending Accounts Payable	31,600
= Cash Payments for Merchandise Purchases	$480,900

Operating Expenses   In preparing this section of the statement of cash flows, list each expense in the order it is presented on the income statement.

1. **Convert Wages Expense to Cash Payments to Employees.**   During 19x8, Wages Payable decreased from $400 to $100. Evidently, $300 more in cash was paid to employees than is recorded as Wages Expense. The calculation looks like this:

Wages Expense	$123,000
+ Beginning Wages Payable	400
= Total	$123,400
− Ending Wages Payable	100
= Cash Payments to Employees	$123,300

2. **Convert Rent Expense to Cash Payments for Rent.**   Since the balance of the Prepaid Rent account has not changed during the year, the $20,000 recorded as Rent Expense on the income statement was paid to the landlord.

3. **Convert Depreciation Expense, Equipment to Cash Payments for Depreciation.**   As we stated previously, depreciation expense does not cost us any cash, so it is eliminated.

4. **Convert Supplies Expense to Cash Payments for Supplies.**   During 19x8, Supplies decreased from $500 to $300. Evidently, Rex Corporation used up $200 more in supplies than it bought. The calculation looks like this:

Supplies Expense	$2,000
+ Ending Supplies	300
= Total	$2,300
− Beginning Supplies	500
= Cash Payments for Supplies	$1,800

5. **Convert Property Tax Expense to Cash Payments for Property Tax.**   During 19x8, Property Tax Payable increased from $100 to $300. Evidently, $200 less was paid out in cash than is recorded as Property Tax Expense. The calculation looks like this:

Property Tax Expense	$2,000
+ Beginning Property Tax Payable	100
= Total	$2,100
− Ending Property Tax Payable	300
= Cash Payments for Property Tax Expense	$1,800

6. **Convert Insurance Expense to Cash Payments for Insurance.**   During 19x8, Prepaid Insurance increased from $400 to $900. Evidently, $500 more was paid in cash than is recorded as Insurance Expense. The calculation looks like this:

Insurance Expense $1,000
+ Ending Prepaid Insurance 900
= Total $1,900
− Beginning Prepaid Insurance 400
= Cash Payments for Insurance $1,500

7. **Convert Interest Expense to Cash Payments for Interest.** During 19x8, Interest Payable increased from $200 to $600. Evidently, $400 less was paid in cash than is recorded as Interest Expense on the income statement. The calculation looks like this:

Interest Expense $26,000
+ Beginning Interest Payable 200
= Total $26,200
− Ending Interest Payable 600
= Cash Payments for Interest $25,600

Note that this situation is similar to the relationship between Wages Expense and Wages Payable.

Before we continue, we should mention that if Rex Corporation had reported income tax expense on its income statement, we would need to convert that amount using the process we've just described. The cash payments for income tax would be listed below the cash payments for interest on the statement of cash flows.

Cash Flows from (used by) Investing Activities

1. **Record Cash Receipts from the Sale of Equipment.** During 19x8, Equipment decreased from $143,000 to $114,000. On the income statement a Gain on Disposal of Plant and Equipment of $5,000 is listed in the Other Income section. In addition Depreciation Expense, Equipment of $24,000 is listed on the income statement. We must examine the general ledger accounts and journals to reconstruct the transactions. The following entry is found in the general journal:

DATE		DESCRIPTION	POST. REF.	DEBIT	CREDIT
19x8					
Jan.	3	Cash		22 000 00	
		Accumulated Depreciation,			
		Equipment		12 000 00	
		Equipment			29 000 00
		Gain on Disposal of Plant and			
		Equipment			5 000 00
		To record the sale of			
		equipment.			

In T account form, the accounts look like this:

Equipment			
1/1/x8 Bal.	143,000	1/3/x8	29,000
12/31/x8 Bal.	114,000		

Accumulated Depreciation, Equipment			
1/3/x8	12,000	1/1/x8 Bal.	35,000
		12/31/x8 Adj.	24,000
		12/31/x8 Bal.	47,000

Cash			
1/3/x8	22,000		

Gain on Disposal of Plant and Equipment		
	1/3/x8	5,000

By reconstructing the entries, we spot the debit to Cash of $22,000. We will list sale of equipment, $22,000, as a positive cash flow.

Cash Flows from Financing Activities

1. **Convert Notes Payable into Cash Receipts from the Issuance of a Note.** During 19x8, Notes Payable increased from $0 to $24,000. We must examine the general ledger account and journals to reconstruct the transaction(s). The following entry is found in the general journal.

GENERAL JOURNAL   PAGE _____

DATE		DESCRIPTION	POST. REF.	DEBIT	CREDIT
19x8					
Oct.	2	Cash		24 0 0 0 00	
		Notes Payable			24 0 0 0 00
		Borrowed from County Bank.			
		Issued 120-day, 10 percent note			
		dated October 2.			

We list the issuance of the note for $24,000 as a positive cash flow under Financing Activities.

2. **Convert Common Stock to Cash Receipts from the Issuance of Common Stock.** During 19x8, Common Stock increased from $297,500 to $306,500. We must examine the general ledger account and journals to reconstruct the transaction(s). The following entry is found in the general journal.

GENERAL JOURNAL   PAGE _____

DATE		DESCRIPTION	POST. REF.	DEBIT	CREDIT
19x8					
June	16	Cash		9 0 0 0 00	
		Common Stock			9 0 0 0 00
		To record the sale of 900 shares			
		of $10 par common stock at par.			

We will list the sale of common stock as a positive cash flow under Financing Activities.

3. **Convert Dividends into Cash Payments of Dividends.** On the statement of retained earnings, we note $16,000 listed as cash dividends. During 19x8, Dividends Payable decreased from $3,000 to $2,000. Evidently, $1,000 more was paid in cash than is recorded as cash dividends. The calculation looks like this:

Cash Dividends Declared	$16,000
+ Beginning Dividends Payable	3,000
= Total	$19,000
− Ending Dividends Payable	2,000
= Cash Payments of Dividends	$17,000

Let's put all these conversions together in the correct format to make up the statement of cash flows for Rex Corporation.

Rex Corporation
Statement of Cash Flows
For Year Ended December 31, 19x8

Cash Flows from (used by) Operating Activities:			
Cash Receipts from Customers			$ 624 600 00
Cash Payments for:			
Merchandise Purchases		$ 480 900 00	
Operating Expenses:			
Employees	$ 123 300 00		
Rent	20 000 00		
Supplies	1 800 00		
Property Tax	1 800 00		
Insurance	1 500 00		
Total		148 400 00	
Interest		25 600 00	
Total Cash Payments			654 900 00
Net Cash Flows from Operating Activities			$ (30 300 00)
Cash Flows from (used by) Investing Activities:			
Sale of Equipment		$ 22 000 00	
Net Cash Flows from Investing Activities			22 000 00
Cash Flows from (used by) Financing Activities:			
Issuance of Note		$ 24 000 00	
Issuance of Common Stock		9 000 00	
Payments of Dividends		(17 000 00)	
Net Cash Flows from Financing Activities			16 000 00
Net Increase (Decrease) in Cash			$ 7 700 00

Summary of Conversions in Illustration 4

- **For Sale of Equipment for Cash**   The amount debited to the Cash account in the journal entry for the transaction is listed as a positive amount under Cash Flows from (used by) Investing Activities.
- **For Accrued Liabilities—like Interest Expense and Interest Payable** This is figured like accrued wages. Here it is the amount of Interest Expense listed on the income statement + the beginning balance of Interest Payable − the ending balance of Interest Payable.
- **For Issuance of a Note**   The amount debited to the Cash account in the journal entry for the transaction is listed as a positive amount under Cash Flows from (used by) Financing Activities.
- **For Issuance of Common Stock**   The amount debited to the Cash account in the journal entry for the transaction is listed as a positive amount under Cash Flows from (used by) Financing Activities.
- **For Cash Dividend Payments**   This is also similar to accrued wages. Here it is the amount taken from the statement of retained earnings listed as cash dividends declared + the beginning balance of Dividends Payable − the ending balance of Dividends Payable.

INTERPRETING THE STATEMENT OF CASH FLOWS

Interpretation of the statement of cash flows begins with the net cash flows from operating activities. Is the net cash flow a positive amount, and how does it compare with net income on the income statement? It is useful to compare the net cash flows from operating activities to see if the company is covering its cash outflows for dividends listed in the Financing Activities section. It is also useful to examine the investing activities section to determine if the company is expanding and how it is being financed. If the expansion is being financed primarily by long-term debt, we can be certain that, unless the expansion produces more cash revenue or a reduction in cash expenses, cash flows from operating activities will decline in the future as interest payments are made.

Anyone who uses financial statements can gather a great deal of information from the statement of cash flows. Having already prepared the statements for the four illustrations, let's take a closer look at Rex Corporation's statement of cash flows to see what we can find out.

Benefits to Users

Managers, investors, and creditors all use the statement of cash flows to judge how a company is doing. Let's see what kinds of conclusions they could draw about Rex Corporation from studying its financial statements, including its statement of cash flows.

Evidently, Rex Corporation is in a precarious financial position. The $7,700 increase in cash is not consistent with the $13,000 net loss. Users of the statement of cash flows are interested in the company's ability to generate enough cash to pay its bills and pay dividends.

Because of limited information, we will simply cite observations and pose questions. The $30,300 negative net cash flows from operating activities is bad news indeed. The $624,600 of cash receipts from customers is offset by the $654,900 of cash payments for operating activities. Evidently, a note payable having a principal of $24,000 was issued. However, the interest rates were quite high, resulting in an excessive amount of interest payments. Is the merchandise inventory saleable? If so, can it be worked down to generate more cash? The $22,000 generated from the sale of equipment is a one-shot transaction. Will the equipment have to be replaced? If so, how will it be financed?

Although the company had a comfortable beginning credit balance of $94,600 in Retained Earnings ($81,600 after closing the net loss into Retained Earnings), the declaration and payment of cash dividends were simply not feasible under the circumstances. Actually, Rex Corporation had to borrow funds to pay its dividends. Although dividends resulted in a cash outflow of $17,000, it is well below the $25,600 cash outflow for interest payments. Despite the fact that interest payments are tax deductible, whereas dividends are not, will Rex Corporation be better off selling stock in the future to finance expansion?

By using other analytical tools, interesting facts are discovered. Rex Corporation's working capital is $305,100 ($363,700 − $58,600); its current ratio is 6.2 : 1 ($363,700 ÷ $58,600); and its quick ratio is 1.7 : 1 ($99,500 ÷ $58,600). However, the firm is still not generating enough cash to pay its bills. Incidentally, the return on stockholders' equity is a dismal negative.

SCHEDULE OF NONCASH INVESTING AND FINANCING TRANSACTIONS

A company occasionally engages in significant transactions that do not affect cash directly. As examples, a corporation may issue a long-term mortgage for the purchase of land and building. Or the company may issue common stock for the land and building. These transactions represent important investing and financing activities, but they would not show up on a statement of cash flows because they do not involve either cash receipts or cash payments. However, since these transactions will affect future cash flows, the Financial Accounting Standards Board has determined that they should be presented in a separate schedule on the statement of cash flows. An example of such a schedule is shown on the next page.

Schedule of Noncash Investing and Financing Transactions						
Issue of Mortgage Payable for Building	$	100	0	0	0	00

In this way, readers of the statement of cash flows will have a complete picture of a company's investing and financing activities.

SUMMARY

L.O. 1   The statement of cash flows explains the changes in cash and cash equivalents between the beginning and the end of a fiscal period. Cash equivalents are short-term (ninety days or less from the date acquired) investments in money market accounts, U.S. Treasury bills, and commercial paper. Commercial paper consists of promissory notes issued by corporations.

L.O. 2   The statement of cash flows provides a summary of information concerning a company's cash receipts and payments during a fiscal period. A secondary purpose is to provide information about a firm's investing and financing activities during a fiscal period.

L.O. 3   The statement of cash flows is useful to management as well as to investors and creditors in assessing or evaluating the liquidity of a business, including the ability of the business to generate future cash flows and to pay its debts and dividends. The statement of cash flows involves converting a company's financial statements from an accrual basis to a cash basis.

L.O. 4   Cash flows are classified as operating activities, investing activities, or financing activities. Operating activities include the cash effects of transactions that enter into the determination of net income after income tax. Investing activities include cash flows involving the making and collecting of loans, the buying and selling of investments, and the buying and selling of plant and equipment. Financing activities include cash flows involving the selling or retiring of bonds, the issuing or paying of notes, the issuing of stock, and payments of personal withdrawals or dividends.

L.O. 5   To calculate cash flows from operating activities:

- Cash Receipts from Customers

  Net Sales + beginning Accounts Receivable
  − ending Accounts Receivable

- Cash Receipts from Interest and Dividends

  Interest Income + beginning Interest Receivable
  − ending Interest Receivable

  Dividend Income + beginning Dividends Receivable
  − ending Dividends Receivable

- Cash Payments for Merchandise Purchases

  Net Purchases + beginning Accounts Payable (trade)
  − ending Accounts Payable (trade)

To determine cash payments for operating expenses:

• Cash Payments to Employees

Wages Expense + beginning Wages Payable − ending Wages Payable

• Cash Payments for Prepaid Expenses (e.g., Supplies, Prepaid Insurance)

Supplies Expense + ending Supplies − beginning Supplies

• Cash Payments for Interest

Interest Expense + beginning Interest Payable − ending Interest Payable

• Cash Payments for Income Tax

Income Tax Expense + beginning Income Tax Payable
− ending Income Tax Payable

To calculate cash flows from investing activities or financing activities:
Changes in the balances of plant and equipment, investments, long-term liabilities, and owner's or stockholders' equity may indicate possible cash inflows or outflows. The amounts of cash involved are determined by exposing the related journal entries.

• Cash Payments of Dividends

Cash Dividends Declared + beginning Dividends Payable
− ending Dividends Payable

L.O. 6   Starting with a company's balance sheet at the beginning and end of the accounting period as well as the income statement and statement of owner's equity for the end of the period, we compile a comparative balance sheet listing the increases and decreases in all accounts. Then we convert changes in account balances to cash flows using the calculations presented in the chapter.

GLOSSARY

Cash equivalents   Items included in the broad definition of cash as used in the statement of cash flows. Included are money market accounts, U.S. Treasury bills, and commercial paper having maturities with a maximum of ninety days from the date acquired.

Financing activities   A category on the statement of cash flows (involving inflows and outflows) that includes borrowing money or repaying loans, and additional cash investments or reductions of owners' investments through cash dividends or personal withdrawals.

Investing activities   A category on the statement of cash flows (involving inflows and outflows) that includes the buying and selling of plant and equipment, the acquiring and selling of investments other than cash equivalents, and the making and collecting of loans.

Operating activities   A category on the statement of cash flows (involving inflows and outflows) that includes cash receipts from customers for the sale of merchandise and services, cash receipts from interest and dividends, cash payments for merchandise purchases, cash payments for operating expenses, cash payments for interest, and cash payments for income taxes.

Statement of cash flows   A financial statement that explains in detail how the balance of cash and cash equivalents has changed between the beginning and the end of a fiscal period. A schedule on the statement presents important noncash investing and financing activities that occurred during the same period.

QUESTIONS, EXERCISES, AND PROBLEMS

Discussion Questions

1. What are the purposes of the statement of cash flows?
2. What is included in the term *cash* as it is used in a statement of cash flows?
3. What are the three categories listed on the statement of cash flows? Give two examples of each category.
4. Sea Lure Corporation has a net loss of $192,000 for the fiscal year but has a positive cash flow of $16,000. What are some conditions that may have caused this to happen?
5. To put part of its cash to work earning a return, Gonzales Company transferred $52,000 from its checking account to a money market account, purchased a $20,000, three-month U.S. Treasury bill, and bought $24,000 of another company's common stock. How will each of these transactions affect the statement of cash flows?
6. What are the effects of the following items on cash flows from operating activities:
   a. Depreciation Expense, $96,000
   b. An increase in Wages Payable, $1,400
   c. A decrease in Accounts Receivable, $12,000
7. Bright Company sold equipment at a loss of $3,000. The equipment cost $94,000 and had accumulated depreciation of $46,000. Describe how this event is handled in the statement of cash flows.
8. In which of the three categories listed on a statement of cash flows would each of the following appear? Also, state for each item whether it represents a cash inflow or a cash outflow.
   a. Cash personal withdrawal
   b. Cash receipts from customers
   c. Cash proceeds from issuing stock
   d. Cash purchase of equipment
   e. Cash payment of interest
   f. Cash sale of investments

Exercises

L.O. 4   **Exercise 28-1**   Primo Bakery, Inc., had the following transactions. Identify each transaction as (1) an Operating Activity, (2) an Investing Activity, (3) a Financing Activity, (4) a noncash transaction, or (5) none of the above.

a. Paid wages to employees
b. Paid interest
c. Sold equipment at a loss
d. Issued common stock for cash

e. Purchased an investment
f. Repaid the principal of a note payable
g. Declared a stock dividend
h. Repaid the principal of a bond payable

L.O. 5   **Exercise 28-2**   The income statement of Dr. McNeill for 19x2 includes Insurance Expense of $5,740. The beginning balance of Prepaid Insurance amounted to $2,760, and the ending balance of Prepaid Insurance amounted to $3,190. Determine the cash payments for insurance by Dr McNeill for the year 19x2.

L.O. 5   **Exercise 28-3**   During 19x2, Herndon Company had net sales of $182,000. During the same year, the beginning balance of Accounts Receivable was $39,000, and the ending balance of Accounts Receivable was $37,500. Determine the amount of cash receipts from customers during the year 19x2.

L.O. 5   **Exercise 28-4**   Income Tax Expense for Romero Corporation was $27,400 for the year 19x2. Between the beginning and end of the year, Income Tax Payable increased by $2,000. Determine the amount of cash payments for income tax during 19x2.

L.O. 4,5   **Exercise 28-5**   All transactions involving Notes Payable and Interest Payable for Shadoff Company during the year 19x2 are presented in the general journal:

GENERAL JOURNAL   PAGE _____

DATE		DESCRIPTION	POST. REF.	DEBIT	CREDIT
19x2		*Reversing Entry*			
Jan.	1	Interest Payable		2 4 0 00	
		Interest Expense			2 4 0 00
Feb.	3	Notes Payable		10 2 0 0 00	
		Interest Expense		8 2 0 00	
		Cash			11 0 2 0 00
		Repayment of note at maturity.			
Dec.	1	Cash		7 0 0 0 00	
		Notes Payable			7 0 0 0 00
		Bank loan, receiving the full			
		principal.			
		Adjusting Entry			
	31	Interest Expense		1 5 0 00	
		Interest Payable			1 5 0 00

Determine the amounts and describe how these transactions are to be recorded on the statement of cash flows.

L.O. 5   **Exercise 28-6**   During 19x1, Palmer Optical had net purchases of $146,000. The beginning balance of Accounts Payable (trade) amounted to $42,000, and the ending balance of Accounts Payable (trade) amounted to $45,000. Determine the cash payments for merchandise purchases for 19x1.

L.O. 5   **Exercise 28-7**   During 19x2, Hernandez and Company had operating expenses of $94,000, including depreciation of $22,000. Also, during 19x2, the beginning balance of Supplies was $2,400, and the ending balance of Supplies was $2,800. The beginning balance of Wages Payable was $1,200, and the ending balance of Wages Payable was $1,000. Assume that operating expenses consisted only of Depreciation Expense, Supplies Expense, and Wages Expense. Determine the total cash payments for operating expenses during the year 19x2.

L.O. 5   **Exercise 28-8**   Following are the T accounts for Equipment and Accumulated Depreciation, Equipment for Weiner Company at the end of 19x1:

Equipment				Accumulated Depreciation, Equipment			
Beg. Balance	84,000	Disposal	18,000	Disposal	9,000	Beg. Balance	62,000
Purchases	27,000					Adjusting	14,000
End. Balance	93,000					End. Balance	67,000

Loss on Disposal of Plant and Equipment	
Disposal	6,000

New equipment was bought for cash, and the used equipment was sold for cash. Compute the amounts to be included in the statement of cash flows, and indicate where these amounts should be shown.

Problem Set A

L.O. 6   **Problem 28-1A**   The financial statements of Hern and Company are presented on page 981.

Instructions

Prepare a statement of cash flows for 19x2.

L.O. 6   **Problem 28-2A**   Marjean Hair Salon uses a modified cash basis. The financial statements for Marjean Hair Salon are presented on page 982.

Instructions

Prepare a statement of cash flows for the year 19x2.

Hern and Company
Income Statement
For Year Ended December 31, 19x2

Revenue:				
Income from Services			$63 6 2 1 00	
Expenses:				
Wages Expense	$29 4 1 0 00			
Rent Expense	6 0 0 00			
Advertising Expense	4 2 0 00			
Utilities Expense	7 6 4 00			
Depreciation Expense, Equipment	8 2 1 0 00			
Supplies Expense	4 7 0 00			
Insurance Expense	2 4 0 00			
Miscellaneous Expense	3 2 2 00			
Total Expenses			40 4 3 6 00	
Net Income			$23 1 8 5 00	

Hern and Company
Statement of Owner's Equity
For Year Ended December 31, 19x2

R. D. Hern, Capital, January 1, 19x2		$65 0 1 8 00	
Net Income	$23 1 8 5 00		
Less Withdrawals	36 0 0 0 00		
Decrease in Capital		12 8 1 5 00	
R. D. Hern, Capital, December 31, 19x2		$52 2 0 3 00	

Hern and Company
Comparative Balance Sheet
December 31, 19x2 and December 31, 19x1

	19x2	19x1	INCREASE OR (DECREASE)
Assets			
Cash	$ 6 7 9 7 00	$11 5 1 7 00	$ (4 7 2 0 00)
Supplies	5 1 6 00	3 2 1 00	1 9 5 00
Prepaid Insurance	1 2 0 00	2 0 0 00	(8 0 00)
Equipment	69 4 0 0 00	69 4 0 0 00	0 00
Less Accumulated Depreciation	(24 6 3 0 00)	(16 4 2 0 00)	(8 2 1 0 00)
Total Assets	$52 2 0 3 00	$65 0 1 8 00	$ (12 8 1 5 00)
Owner's Equity			
R. D. Hern, Capital	$52 2 0 3 00	$65 0 1 8 00	$ (12 8 1 5 00)
Total Liabilities and Owner's Equity	$52 2 0 3 00	$65 0 1 8 00	$ (12 8 1 5 00)

Marjean Hair Salon
Income Statement
For Year Ended December 31, 19x2

Revenue:			
Service Income			$ 117 1 3 0 00
Expenses:			
Salary Expense	$65 4 2 0 00		
Rent Expense	12 0 0 0 00		
Supplies Expense	2 1 9 0 00		
Insurance Expense	4 6 0 00		
Utilities Expense	1 6 8 0 00		
Depreciation Expense, Equipment	1 9 2 0 00		
Depreciation Expense, Furniture	8 3 0 00		
Interest Expense	3 7 0 00		
Miscellaneous Expense	1 1 0 00		
Total Expenses			84 9 8 0 00
Net Income			$ 32 1 5 0 00

Marjean Hair Salon
Statement of Owner's Equity
For Year Ended December 31, 19x2

M. C. Stein, Capital, January 1, 19x2		$21 1 2 0 00
Net Income	$32 1 5 0 00	
Less Withdrawals	37 2 0 0 00	
Decrease in Capital		5 0 5 0 00
M. C. Stein, Capital, December 31, 19x2		$16 0 7 0 00

Marjean Hair Salon
Comparative Balance Statement
December 31, 19x2 and December 31, 19x1

	19x2	19x1	INCREASE OR (DECREASE)
Assets			
Cash	$ 9 6 8 0 00	$13 7 7 0 00	$ (4 0 9 0 00)
Supplies	7 4 0 00	8 1 0 00	(7 0 00)
Prepaid Insurance	7 6 0 00	3 0 0 00	4 6 0 00
Equipment	9 6 0 0 00	9 6 0 0 00	0 00
Less Accumulated Depreciation	(5 7 6 0 00)	(3 8 4 0 00)	(1 9 2 0 00)
Furniture	5 8 4 0 00	5 8 4 0 00	0 00
Less Accumulated Depreciation	(2 4 9 0 00)	(1 6 6 0 00)	(8 3 0 00)
Total Assets	$18 3 7 0 00	$24 8 2 0 00	$ (6 4 5 0 00)
Liabilities			
Notes Payable	$ 2 3 0 0 00	$ 3 7 0 0 00	$ (1 4 0 0 00)
Owner's Equity			
M. C. Stein, Capital	16 0 7 0 00	21 1 2 0 00	(5 0 5 0 00)
Total Liabilities and Owner's Equity	$18 3 7 0 00	$24 8 2 0 00	$ (6 4 5 0 00)

L.O. 6   **Problem 28-3A**   Financial statements for Mangold Fine Clothes are presented below and on page 984.

Instructions

Prepare a statement of cash flows for the year 19x2.

Mangold Fine Clothes
Income Statement
For Year Ended December 31, 19x2

Revenue from Sales:		
Net Sales		$ 854 6 0 0 00
Cost of Merchandise Sold:		
Merchandise Inventory, January 1, 19x2	$ 162 5 7 0 00	
Net Purchases	614 1 2 0 00	
Merchandise Available for Sale	$ 776 6 9 0 00	
Less Merchandise Inventory,		
December 31, 19x2	122 6 5 0 00	
Cost of Merchandise Sold		654 0 4 0 00
Gross Profit		$ 200 5 6 0 00
Operating Expenses:		
Salary Expense	$ 137 9 5 0 00	
Rent Expense	27 0 0 0 00	
Depreciation Expense, Equipment	31 1 4 0 00	
Supplies Expense	3 2 1 0 00	
Insurance Expense	1 5 0 0 00	
Miscellaneous Expense	7 2 0 00	
Total Operating Expenses		201 5 2 0 00
Net Loss		$ (9 6 0 00)

Mangold Fine Clothes
Statement of Owner's Equity
For Year Ended December 31, 19x2

F. R. Mangold, Capital, January 1, 19x2		$ 292 1 4 0 00
Less: Net Loss	$ 9 6 0 00	
Withdrawals for the Year	15 0 0 0 00	
Decrease in Capital		15 9 6 0 00
F. R. Mangold, Capital, December 31, 19x2		$ 276 1 8 0 00

Mangold Fine Clothes
Comparative Balance Sheet
December 31, 19x2 and December 31, 19x1

	19x2	19x1	INCREASE OR (DECREASE)
Assets			
Cash	$ 43 7 7 0 00	$ 31 5 6 0 00	$ 12 2 1 0 00
Accounts Receivable	62 8 4 0 00	47 7 9 0 00	15 0 5 0 00
Merchandise Inventory	122 6 5 0 00	162 5 7 0 00	(39 9 2 0 00)
Supplies	7 1 0 00	6 9 0 00	2 0 00
Prepaid Insurance	2 4 0 0 00	8 0 0 00	1 6 0 0 00
Equipment	182 2 6 0 00	182 2 6 0 00	0 00
Less Accumulated Depreciation	(93 4 2 0 00)	(62 2 8 0 00)	(31 1 4 0 00)
Total Assets	$ 321 2 1 0 00	$ 363 3 9 0 00	$ (42 1 8 0 00)
Liabilities			
Accounts Payable	$ 42 0 8 0 00	$ 67 8 9 0 00	$ (25 8 1 0 00)
Salaries Payable	2 9 5 0 00	3 3 6 0 00	(4 1 0 00)
Total Liabilities	$ 45 0 3 0 00	$ 71 2 5 0 00	$ (26 2 2 0 00)
Owner's Equity			
F. R. Mangold, Capital	276 1 8 0 00	292 1 4 0 00	(15 9 6 0 00)
Total Liabilities and Owner's Equity	$ 321 2 1 0 00	$ 363 3 9 0 00	$ (42 1 8 0 00)

L.O. 6 **Problem 28-4A** Jordan Corporation's financial statements are presented on pages 985 and 986.

Additional information in the records revealed that equipment having a cost of $50,000, and accumulated depreciation of $44,000, was sold for $12,230 cash. Also, 5,000 shares of common stock having a par value of $10 per share were sold for $60,000 cash.

Instructions

Prepare a statement of cash flows for the year 19x1.

Jordan Corporation
Income Statement
For Year Ended December 31, 19x1

Revenue from Sales:			
Sales	$ 994 2 6 0 00		
Less Sales Returns and Allowances	12 1 2 0 00		
Net Sales			$ 982 1 4 0 00
Cost of Merchandise Sold:			
Merchandise Inventory, January 1, 19x1	$ 396 7 0 0 00		
Net Purchases	703 1 0 0 00		
Merchandise Available for Sale	$1 099 8 0 0 00		
Less Merchandise Inventory, December 31, 19x1	421 4 5 0 00		
Cost of Merchandise Sold		678 3 5 0 00	
Gross Profit		$ 303 7 9 0 00	
Operating Expenses:			
Wages Expense	$ 126 4 0 0 00		
Rent Expense	20 0 0 0 00		
Depreciation Expense, Equipment	26 0 0 0 00		
Supplies Expense	2 9 5 0 00		
Insurance Expense	1 2 0 0 00		
Total Operating Expenses		176 5 5 0 00	
Income from Operations		$ 127 2 4 0 00	
Other Income:			
Gain on Disposal of Plant and Equipment	$ 6 2 3 0 00		
Other Expense:			
Interest Expense	7 9 0 00	5 4 4 0 00	
Income Before Income Tax		$ 132 6 8 0 00	
Income Tax Expense		45 1 1 0 00	
Net Income After Income Tax		$ 87 5 7 0 00	

Jordan Corporation
Statement of Retained Earnings
For Year Ended December 31, 19x1

Retained Earnings, January 1, 19x1			$ 116 2 9 0 00
Net Income for the Year	$87 5 7 0 00		
Less Cash Dividends Declared	60 0 0 0 00		
Increase in Retained Earnings		27 5 7 0 00	
Retained Earnings, December 31, 19x1		$ 143 8 6 0 00	

Jordan Corporation
Comparative Balance Sheet
December 31, 19x1 and December 31, 19x0

	19x1	19x0	INCREASE OR (DECREASE)
Assets			
Cash	$ 36 9 2 0 00	$ 10 9 5 0 00	$ 25 9 7 0 00
Accounts Receivable	99 6 4 0 00	73 7 1 0 00	25 9 3 0 00
Merchandise Inventory	421 4 5 0 00	396 7 0 0 00	24 7 5 0 00
Supplies	5 2 0 00	7 9 0 00	(2 7 0 00)
Prepaid Rent	6 0 0 0 00	6 0 0 0 00	0 00
Prepaid Insurance	8 0 0 00	5 0 0 00	3 0 0 00
Equipment	250 9 8 0 00	300 9 8 0 00	(50 0 0 0 00)
Less Accumulated Depreciation	(88 7 0 0 00)	(106 7 0 0 00)	18 0 0 0 00
Total Assets	$ 727 6 1 0 00	$ 682 9 3 0 00	$ 44 6 8 0 00
Liabilities			
Notes Payable	$ 10 4 0 0 00	$ 24 2 0 0 00	$ (13 8 0 0 00)
Accounts Payable	31 7 2 0 00	59 6 4 0 00	(27 9 2 0 00)
Wages Payable	1 0 4 0 00	1 9 9 0 00	(9 5 0 00)
Income Tax Payable	11 2 8 0 00	10 4 6 0 00	8 2 0 00
Dividends Payable	12 0 0 0 00	12 0 0 0 00	0 00
Interest Payable	1 2 0 00	1 1 6 0 00	(1 0 4 0 00)
Total Liabilities	$ 66 5 6 0 00	$ 109 4 5 0 00	$ (42 8 9 0 00)
Stockholders' Equity			
Common Stock	$ 507 1 9 0 00	$ 457 1 9 0 00	$ 50 0 0 0 00
Premium on Common Stock	10 0 0 0 00	0 00	10 0 0 0 00
Retained Earnings	143 8 6 0 00	116 2 9 0 00	27 5 7 0 00
Total Stockholders' Equity	$ 661 0 5 0 00	$ 573 4 8 0 00	$ 87 5 7 0 00
Total Liabilities and Stockholders' Equity	$ 727 6 1 0 00	$ 682 9 3 0 00	$ 44 6 8 0 00

Problem Set B

L.O. 6 **Problem 28-1B** The financial statements of Hoffman Realty are presented on page 987.

Instructions

Prepare a statement of cash flows for 19x2.

Hoffman Realty
Income Statement
For Year Ended December 31, 19x2

Revenue:		
Service Revenue		$71 1 9 0 00
Expenses:		
Commissions Expense	$20 6 4 0 00	
Advertising Expense	5 6 0 0 00	
Automobile Expense	1 2 5 0 00	
Rent Expense	3 6 0 0 00	
Telephone Expense	9 2 0 00	
Depreciation Expense, Automobile	2 2 8 0 00	
Depreciation Expense, Office Equipment	1 2 2 0 00	
Supplies Expense	4 1 0 00	
Utilities Expense	1 6 3 0 00	
Total Expenses		37 5 5 0 00
Net Income		$33 6 4 0 00

Hoffman Realty
Statement of Owner's Equity
For Year Ended December 31, 19x2

L. A. Hoffman, Capital, January 1, 19x2		$22 9 0 0 00
Net Income	$33 6 4 0 00	
Less Withdrawals	30 0 0 0 00	
Increase in Capital		3 6 4 0 00
L. A. Hoffman, Capital, December 31, 19x2		$26 5 4 0 00

Hoffman Realty
Comparative Balance Sheet
December 31, 19x2 and December 31, 19x1

	19x2	19x1	INCREASE OR (DECREASE)
Assets			
Cash	$16 9 6 0 00	$10 2 9 0 00	$ 6 6 7 0 00
Prepaid Rent	9 0 0 00	3 0 0 00	6 0 0 00
Supplies	6 2 0 00	7 5 0 00	(1 3 0 00)
Automobile	11 4 0 0 00	11 4 0 0 00	0 00
Less Accumulated Depreciation	(4 5 6 0 00)	(2 2 8 0 00)	(2 2 8 0 00)
Office Equipment	6 1 0 0 00	6 1 0 0 00	0 00
Less Accumulated Depreciation	(4 8 8 0 00)	(3 6 6 0 00)	(1 2 2 0 00)
Total Assets	$26 5 4 0 00	$22 9 0 0 00	$ 3 6 4 0 00
Owner's Equity			
L. A. Hoffman, Capital	$26 5 4 0 00	$22 9 0 0 00	$ 3 6 4 0 00
Total Liabilities and Owner's Equity	$26 5 4 0 00	$22 9 0 0 00	$ 3 6 4 0 00

L.O. 6   **Problem 28-2B**   Benson Van and Storage's financial statements for the current year are presented below and on the next page.

Instructions

Prepare a statement of cash flows for the year 19x2.

Benson Van and Storage
Income Statement
For Year Ended December 31, 19x2

Revenue:		
Income from Moving Services	$ 124 8 0 0 00	
Income from Storage Rentals	72 7 2 0 00	
Total Income		$ 197 5 2 0 00
Expenses:		
Wages Expense	$ 117 1 0 0 00	
Truck Repair Expense	4 6 4 0 00	
Gas and Oil Expense	3 6 3 0 00	
Insurance Expense	2 8 5 0 00	
Supplies Expense	1 2 4 0 00	
Depreciation Expense, Building	9 6 2 0 00	
Depreciation Expense, Trucks	18 8 0 0 00	
Interest Expense	10 1 0 0 00	
Total Expenses		167 9 8 0 00
Net Income		$ 29 5 4 0 00

Benson Van and Storage
Statement of Owner's Equity
For Year Ended December 31, 19x2

P. R. Benson, Capital, January 1, 19x2		$ 228 0 4 0 00
Net Income	$29 5 4 0 00	
Less Withdrawals	27 0 0 0 00	
Increase in Capital		2 5 4 0 00
P. R. Benson, Capital, December 31, 19x2		$ 230 5 8 0 00

Benson Van and Storage
Comparative Balance Sheet
December 31, 19x2 and December 31, 19x1

	19x2	19x1	INCREASE OR (DECREASE)
Assets			
Cash	$ 368 0 0 00	$ 106 1 0 00	$ 261 9 0 00
Prepaid Insurance	2 6 6 0 00	9 2 0 00	1 7 4 0 00
Supplies	1 1 2 0 00	2 9 0 00	8 3 0 00
Land	32 2 0 0 00	32 2 0 0 00	0 00
Building	314 0 0 0 00	314 0 0 0 00	0 00
Less Accumulated Depreciation	(108 8 0 0 00)	(99 1 8 0 00)	(9 6 2 0 00)
Trucks	94 0 0 0 00	94 0 0 0 00	0 00
Less Accumulated Depreciation	(37 6 0 0 00)	(18 8 0 0 00)	(18 8 0 0 00)
Total Assets	$ 334 3 8 0 00	$ 334 0 4 0 00	$ 3 4 0 00
Liabilities			
Mortgage Payable	$ 103 8 0 0 00	$ 106 0 0 0 00	$ (2 2 0 0 00)
Owner's Equity			
P. R. Benson, Capital	230 5 8 0 00	228 0 4 0 00	2 5 4 0 00
Total Liabilities and Owner's Equity	$ 334 3 8 0 00	$ 334 0 4 0 00	$ 3 4 0 00

L.O. 6   **Problem 28-3B**   Financial statements for The Style Touch are presented below and on the next page.

Instructions

Prepare a statement of cash flows for the year 19x1.

The Style Touch
Statement of Owner's Equity
For Year Ended December 31, 19x1

C. D. Maki, Capital, January 1, 19x1		$ 247 1 7 0 00
Net Income	$33 9 7 0 00	
Less Withdrawals for the Year	40 0 0 0 00	
Decrease in Capital		6 0 3 0 00
C. D. Maki, December 31, 19x1		$ 241 1 4 0 00

The Style Touch
Income Statement
For Year Ended December 31, 19x1

Revenue from Sales:			
Net Sales			$ 742 6 0 0 00
Cost of Merchandise Sold:			
Merchandise Inventory, January 1, 19x1	$ 133 6 7 0 00		
Net Purchases	545 2 8 0 00		
Merchandise Available for Sale	$ 678 9 5 0 00		
Less Merchandise Inventory,			
December 31, 19x1	137 7 5 0 00		
Cost of Merchandise Sold		541 2 0 0 00	
Gross Profit		$ 201 4 0 0 00	
Operating Expenses:			
Salary Expense	$ 109 8 8 0 00		
Rent Expense	24 0 0 0 00		
Depreciation Expense, Equipment	29 6 0 0 00		
Supplies Expense	2 7 5 0 00		
Insurance Expense	1 2 0 0 00		
Total Operating Expenses		167 4 3 0 00	
Net Income		$ 33 9 7 0 00	

The Style Touch
Comparative Balance Sheet
December 31, 19x1 and December 31, 19x0

	19x1	19x0	INCREASE OR (DECREASE)
Assets			
Cash	$ 37 6 4 0 00	$ 38 4 1 0 00	$ (7 7 0 00)
Accounts Receivable	51 1 3 0 00	42 1 6 0 00	8 9 7 0 00
Merchandise Inventory	137 7 5 0 00	133 6 7 0 00	4 0 8 0 00
Supplies	3 7 0 00	9 2 0 00	(5 5 0 00)
Prepaid Insurance	1 8 0 0 00	6 0 0 00	1 2 0 0 00
Equipment	154 9 0 0 00	154 9 0 0 00	0 00
Less Accumulated Depreciation	(118 4 0 0 00)	(88 8 0 0 00)	(29 6 0 0 00)
Total Assets	$ 265 1 9 0 00	$ 281 8 6 0 00	$ (16 6 7 0 00)
Liabilities			
Accounts Payable	$ 20 5 6 0 00	$ 31 9 5 0 00	$ (11 3 9 0 00)
Salaries Payable	3 4 9 0 00	2 7 4 0 00	7 5 0 00
Total Liabilities	$ 24 0 5 0 00	$ 34 6 9 0 00	$ (10 6 4 0 00)
Owner's Equity			
C. D. Maki, Capital	241 1 4 0 00	247 1 7 0 00	(6 0 3 0 00)
Total Liabilities and Owner's Equity	$ 265 1 9 0 00	$ 281 8 6 0 00	$ (16 6 7 0 00)

L.O. 6 **Problem 28-4B** Financial statements for Farley Corporation are presented below and on the next page.

Additional information contained in the records revealed that equipment, having a cost of $47,000 and accumulated depreciation of $35,600, was sold for $18,000 cash. Also, 4,700 shares of common stock having a par value of $10 per share were sold for $54,000 cash.

Instructions

Prepare a statement of cash flows for the year 19x2.

Farley Corporation
Income Statement
For Year Ended December 31, 19x2

Revenue from Sales:			
Sales		$ 886 8 9 0 00	
Less Sales Returns and Allowances		10 7 8 0 00	
Net Sales			$ 876 1 1 0 00
Cost of Merchandise Sold:			
Merchandise Inventory, January 1, 19x2		$ 352 6 2 0 00	
Net Purchases		625 7 6 0 00	
Merchandise Available for Sale		$ 978 3 8 0 00	
Less Merchandise Inventory, December 31, 19x2		375 0 9 0 00	
Cost of Merchandise Sold			603 2 9 0 00
Gross Profit			$ 272 8 2 0 00
Operating Expenses:			
Salary Expense		$ 102 4 9 0 00	
Rent Expense		18 0 0 0 00	
Advertising Expense		6 4 0 0 00	
Depreciation Expense, Equipment		22 1 6 0 00	
Supplies Expense		2 7 1 0 00	
Miscellaneous Expense		9 2 0 00	
Total Operating Expenses			152 6 8 0 00
Income from Operations			$ 120 1 4 0 00
Other Income:			
Interest Income	$ 4 7 0 00		
Gain on Disposal of Plant and Equipment	6 6 0 0 00		
Total Other Income		$ 7 0 7 0 00	
Other Expense:			
Interest Expense		3 2 0 00	6 7 5 0 00
Income Before Income Tax			$ 126 8 9 0 00
Income Tax Expense			38 6 7 0 00
Net Income After Income Tax			$ 88 2 2 0 00

Farley Corporation
Statement of Retained Earnings
For Year Ended December 31, 19x2

Retained Earnings, January 1, 19x2		$ 103 4 9 0 00
Net Income for the Year	$88 2 2 0 00	
Less Cash Dividends Declared	53 0 0 0 00	
Increase in Retained Earnings		35 2 2 0 00
Retained Earnings, December 31, 19x2		$ 138 7 1 0 00

Farley Corporation
Comparative Balance Sheet
December 31, 19x2 and December 31, 19x1

	19x2	19x1	INCREASE OR (DECREASE)
Assets			
Cash	$ 24 8 0 0 00	$ 6 7 4 0 00	$ 18 0 6 0 00
Notes Receivable	0 00	2 8 7 0 00	(2 8 7 0 00)
Accounts Receivable	88 6 7 0 00	63 6 1 0 00	25 0 6 0 00
Merchandise Inventory	375 0 9 0 00	352 6 2 0 00	22 4 7 0 00
Prepaid Advertising	1 2 4 0 00	9 6 0 00	2 8 0 00
Supplies	4 3 0 00	2 1 0 00	2 2 0 00
Equipment	$ 220 3 7 0 00	$ 267 3 7 0 00	(47 0 0 0 00)
Less Accumulated Depreciation	(77 5 3 0 00)	(90 9 7 0 00)	13 4 4 0 00
Total Assets	$ 633 0 7 0 00	$ 603 4 1 0 00	$ 29 6 6 0 00
Liabilities			
Notes Payable	$ 2 6 0 0 00	$ 9 2 0 0 00	$ (6 6 0 0 00)
Accounts Payable	28 2 3 0 00	79 3 2 0 00	(51 0 9 0 00)
Salaries Payable	2 2 0 0 00	2 9 0 0 00	(7 0 0 00)
Income Tax Payable	4 8 3 0 00	5 2 6 0 00	(4 3 0 00)
Dividends Payable	3 9 5 0 00	4 4 7 0 00	(5 2 0 00)
Interest Payable	4 0 00	2 6 0 00	(2 2 0 00)
Total Liabilities	$ 41 8 5 0 00	$ 101 4 1 0 00	$ (59 5 6 0 00)
Stockholders' Equity			
Common Stock	$ 429 5 1 0 00	$ 382 5 1 0 00	$ 47 0 0 0 00
Premium on Common Stock	23 0 0 0 00	16 0 0 0 00	7 0 0 0 00
Retained Earnings	138 7 1 0 00	103 4 9 0 00	35 2 2 0 00
Total Stockholders' Equity	$ 591 2 2 0 00	$ 502 0 0 0 00	$ 89 2 2 0 00
Total Liabilities and Stockholders' Equity	$ 633 0 7 0 00	$ 603 4 1 0 00	$ 29 6 6 0 00

29 Manufacturing Accounting

LEARNING OBJECTIVES

After you have completed this chapter, you will be able to do the following:

1. Prepare financial statements for a manufacturing enterprise.
2. Complete a work sheet for a manufacturing enterprise.
3. Journalize adjusting entries for a manufacturing enterprise.
4. Journalize closing entries for a manufacturing enterprise.

In earlier chapters we dealt with accounting procedures mainly as they apply to service and merchandising enterprises. Now let us turn to another type of business operation: manufacturing.

The accounting principles we have already discussed pertain to manufacturing concerns, but in addition, manufacturers have special procedures to account for manufacturing costs. In this chapter we shall describe how manufacturers determine the total cost of goods manufactured during each accounting period. To acquaint you with the end results, we shall present financial statements of a manufacturer early in the chapter. These statements will enable you to understand the function of the work sheet and its relationship to the financial statements. You may consider this chapter an introduction to accounting for manufacturing operations; a discussion of cost accounting systems is beyond the scope of this text.

COMPARISON OF INCOME STATEMENTS FOR MERCHANDISING AND MANUFACTURING ENTERPRISES

Objective 1

Prepare financial statements for a manufacturing enterprise.

Manufacturing and merchandising companies have the same type of revenue accounts. However, a merchant buys goods in a finished condition and later sells them at a higher price in the same condition. A manufac-

993

turer, on the other hand, buys raw materials, transforms them into finished goods, and later sells the finished goods.

To see how the two types of companies compare, study the following portions of income statements for a merchandising firm and for a manufacturing firm:

A Merchandising Company
Income Statement
For Year Ended December 31, 19–

Sales (net)		$2 000 0 0 0 00
Cost of Merchandise Sold:		
Merchandise Inventory, January 1	$ 400 0 0 0 00	
Net Purchases	1 200 0 0 0 00	
Merchandise Available for Sale	$1 600 0 0 0 00	
Less Merchandise Inventory,		
December 31	250 0 0 0 00	
Cost of Merchandise Sold		1 350 0 0 0 00
Gross Profit		$ 650 0 0 0 00

Penta Manufacturing Company, Inc.
Income Statement
For Year Ended December 31, 19–

Sales (net)		$2 000 0 0 0 00
Cost of Goods Sold:		
Finished Goods Inventory, January 1	$ 400 0 0 0 00	
Cost of Goods Manufactured	1 200 0 0 0 00	
Goods Available for Sale	$1 600 0 0 0 00	
Less Finished Goods Inventory,		
December 31	250 0 0 0 00	
Cost of Goods Sold		1 350 0 0 0 00
Gross Profit		$ 650 0 0 0 00

The main difference in accounting for a merchandising firm and for a manufacturing firm lies in determining the cost of goods (or merchandise) sold.

Merchandising Firm	**Manufacturing Firm**
Beginning Merchandise Inventory	Beginning Finished Goods Inventory
Plus Net Purchases	Plus Cost of Goods Manufactured
Merchandise Available for Sale	Goods Available for Sale
Less Ending Merchandise Inventory	Less Ending Finished Goods Inventory
Cost of Merchandise Sold	Cost of Goods Sold

A manufacturing concern refers to its products as *goods;* a merchandising concern refers to its inventory as *merchandise.* Cost of Goods Manufactured for a manufacturer is the equivalent of Net Purchases for a merchandiser.

STATEMENT OF COST OF GOODS MANUFACTURED

The statement of cost of goods manufactured supports the income statement. Figure 29-1 illustrates such a statement for Penta Manufacturing Company, Inc. **Because Cost of Goods Manufactured is included in the income statement, the accountant naturally prepares the statement of cost of goods manufactured first.**

FIGURE 29-1

Penta Manufacturing Company, Inc.
Statement of Cost of Goods Manufactured
For Year Ended December 31, 19–

Work-in-Process Inventory, January 1			$ 130 0 0 0 00
Raw Materials:			
Raw Materials Inventory, January 1	$ 90 0 0 0 00		
Raw Materials Purchases (net)	230 0 0 0 00		
Cost of Raw Materials Available for Use	$ 320 0 0 0 00		
Less Raw Materials Inventory, December 31	100 0 0 0 00		
Cost of Raw Materials Used		$ 220 0 0 0 00	
Direct Labor		565 0 0 0 00	
Factory Overhead:			
Indirect Labor	$ 120 0 0 0 00		
Supervisory Salaries	110 0 0 0 00		
Heat, Light, and Power	42 0 0 0 00		
Depreciation Expense, Factory Equipment	32 0 0 0 00		
Depreciation Expense, Factory Building	25 0 0 0 00		
Repairs and Maintenance	24 0 0 0 00		
Factory Insurance Expired	22 0 0 0 00		
Factory Supplies Used	14 0 0 0 00		
Miscellaneous Factory Costs	16 0 0 0 00		
Total Factory Overhead		405 0 0 0 00	
Total Manufacturing Costs			1 190 0 0 0 00
Total Cost of Work-in-Process During Period			$1 320 0 0 0 00
Less Work-in-Process Inventory, December 31			120 0 0 0 00
Cost of Goods Manufactured			$1 200 0 0 0 00

ELEMENTS OF MANUFACTURING COSTS

No matter what type of product a manufacturer makes, the three elements that make up the cost of the goods manufactured are *raw materials used*, *direct labor*, and *factory overhead.*

Raw Materials Used

Raw materials are the materials that enter directly into—and become a part of—the finished product. The delivered cost of these materials is the figure one enters as "Raw Materials Used." For example, if you are manufacturing pencils, the raw materials you need are wood, lead, paint, an eraser, and a metal band. Raw materials are also called **direct materials.**

Direct Labor

Direct labor consists of the wages paid to factory employees who work—with machines or hand tools—directly on the materials, to convert them into finished products. The manufacturer debits the Direct Labor account for the gross wages of those who work directly on the raw materials. The cost of direct labor varies directly with the level of production.

Factory Overhead

Factory overhead consists of manufacturing costs (other than raw materials used and direct labor) that cannot be traced directly to products being manufactured. A manufacturer uses Factory Overhead as a controlling account. The specific titles of accounts in the factory overhead subsidiary ledger vary from company to company, with the exact accounts depending on the nature of the company and the information desired. In Figure 29-1 the accounts in the factory overhead ledger are: Indirect Labor; Supervisory Salaries; Heat, Light, and Power; Depreciation Expense, Factory Equipment; Depreciation Expense, Factory Building; Repairs and Maintenance; Factory Insurance Expired; Factory Supplies Used; and Miscellaneous Factory Costs.

Indirect labor is the cost of labor of those people who keep the plant in operation, rather than directly working on production. *Examples:* millwrights, maintenance workers, and timekeepers.

The balance of *Factory Supplies Used* reveals the cost of materials used to keep the plant in operation (oil, grease, and so on). These items are also called **indirect materials.**

Other items that may be included in Factory Overhead are: workers' compensation insurance, payroll taxes on wages of factory employees, taxes on factory building and equipment, taxes on raw materials and work-in-process inventories, patents written off, and small tools written off.

Remember

The cost of manufacturing any product consists of direct (raw) materials, direct labor, and factory overhead.

BALANCE SHEET FOR A MANUFACTURING FIRM

The ending balances of a manufacturing firm's inventory accounts appear in the Current Assets section of the balance sheet, as shown in Figure 29-2 on page 998.

WORK SHEET FOR A MANUFACTURING FIRM

Objective 2

Complete a work sheet for a manufacturing enterprise.

You have seen three financial statements for a manufacturing firm: (1) a statement of cost of goods manufactured, (2) an income statement, and (3) a balance sheet. Since the purpose of a work sheet is to enable the accountant to prepare the necessary financial statements, it follows that the work sheet must have a set of columns for each financial statement. A manufacturer's work sheet must include extra columns for the statement of cost of goods manufactured.

Let us examine the work sheet for Penta Manufacturing Company, Inc., shown in Figure 29-3 (pages 1000 to 1003). First notice that all accounts representing manufacturing costs in the Trial Balance columns have debit balances, just as expense accounts have debit balances. Next, look at the adjusting entries for inventories. (We are assuming that Penta uses a periodic inventory system.) A manufacturer, like a merchandiser, takes two steps to adjust inventory: (1) the accountant takes off (or closes off) the beginning inventory, and (2) the accountant adds on the ending inventory. However, in manufacturing accounting, three inventories are involved: Raw Materials, Work-in-Process, and Finished Goods.

Since Raw Materials and Work-in-Process Inventory appear in the statement of cost of goods manufactured, the accountant adjusts them using the **Manufacturing Summary** account. Since Finished Goods Inventory appears in the income statement, the accountant adjusts it using the Income Summary account. Finished Goods Inventory for a manufacturing firm is equivalent to Merchandise Inventory for a merchandising firm. By T accounts, the adjusting entries are as follows:

Raw Materials Inventory				Work-in-Process Inventory				Manufacturing Summary			
+		−		+		−		**(a)**	90,000	**(b)**	100,000
Bal.	90,000	**(a)**	90,000	Bal.	130,000	**(c)**	130,000	**(c)**	130,000	**(d)**	120,000
(b)	100,000			**(d)**	120,000						

Finished Goods Inventory				Income Summary			
+		−		**(e)**	400,000	**(f)**	250,000
Bal.	400,000	**(e)**	400,000				
(f)	250,000						

Penta Manufacturing Company, Inc.
Balance Sheet
December 31, 19–

Assets				
Current Assets:				
Cash			$ 14 0 0 0 00	
Notes Receivable			50 0 0 0 00	
Accounts Receivable	$ 180 0 0 0 00			
Less Allowance for Doubtful Accounts	6 0 0 0 00		174 0 0 0 00	
Raw Materials Inventory			100 0 0 0 00	
Work-in-Process Inventory			120 0 0 0 00	
Finished Goods Inventory			250 0 0 0 00	
Prepaid Insurance			3 0 0 0 00	
Factory Supplies			2 0 0 0 00	
Total Current Assets				$ 713 0 0 0 00
Plant and Equipment:				
Land			$ 100 0 0 0 00	
Factory Building	$ 500 0 0 0 00			
Less Accumulated Depreciation	275 0 0 0 00		225 0 0 0 00	
Factory Equipment	$ 360 0 0 0 00			
Less Accumulated Depreciation	250 0 0 0 00		110 0 0 0 00	
Office Equipment	$ 62 0 0 0 00			
Less Accumulated Depreciation	45 0 0 0 00		17 0 0 0 00	
Total Plant and Equipment				452 0 0 0 00
Total Assets				$1 165 0 0 0 00
Liabilities				
Current Liabilities:				
Notes Payable	$ 40 0 0 0 00			
Accounts Payable	55 5 5 0 00			
Income Tax Payable	16 0 0 0 00			
Dividends Payable	12 0 0 0 00			
Total Current Liabilities			$ 123 5 5 0 00	
Long-Term Liabilities:				
Bonds Payable (due December 31, 1995)			300 0 0 0 00	
Total Liabilities				$ 423 5 5 0 00
Stockholders' Equity				
Paid-in Capital:				
Common Stock, $10 par (50,000				
shares authorized, 30,000 shares issued)	$ 300 0 0 0 00			
Premium on Common Stock	100 0 0 0 00			
Total Paid-in Capital			$ 400 0 0 0 00	
Retained Earnings			341 4 5 0 00	
Total Stockholders' Equity				741 4 5 0 00
Total Liabilities and Stockholders' Equity				$1 165 0 0 0 00

The other adjustments are like the ones we have already seen. Notice how the figures in the Adjustments columns are transferred to the remaining columns of the work sheet. Just as the accountant transfers the figures on the Income Summary line into the Income Statement columns as separate figures, he or she also transfers the four figures on the Manufacturing Summary lines into the Statement of Cost of Goods Manufactured columns as separate figures, like this:

| ACCOUNT NAME | ADJUSTMENTS | | STATEMENT OF COST OF GOODS MANUFACTURED | | INCOME STATEMENT | |
	DEBIT	CREDIT	DEBIT	CREDIT	DEBIT	CREDIT
Manufacturing Summary	(a) 90 0 0 0 00	(b) 100 0 0 0 00	90 0 0 0 00	100 0 0 0 00		
	(c) 130 0 0 0 00	(d) 120 0 0 0 00	130 0 0 0 00	120 0 0 0 00		
Income Summary	(e) 400 0 0 0 00	(f) 250 0 0 0 00			400 0 0 0 00	250 0 0 0 00

On the work sheet, the accountant transfers the cost of goods manufactured ($1,200,000, the difference between the debit and credit totals in the Statement of Cost of Goods Manufactured columns) to the Income Statement Debit column as shown in the following section of Penta Manufacturing's work sheet. (Cost of goods manufactured can be considered to be the equivalent of Net Purchases for a merchandising firm.)

| ACCOUNT NAME | STATEMENT OF COST OF GOODS MANUFACTURED | | INCOME STATEMENT | |
	DEBIT	CREDIT	DEBIT	CREDIT
	1,420 0 0 0 00	220 0 0 0 00		
Cost of Goods Manufactured		1,200 0 0 0 00	1,200 0 0 0 00	
	1,420 0 0 0 00	1,420 0 0 0 00		

ACCOUNTING CYCLE FOR A MANUFACTURING FIRM

In this discussion of accounting for a manufacturing firm, we presented the financial statements first, to show you the desired end results. Because you were familiar with the statement of cost of goods manufactured, you recognized that the accountant listed each item appearing on the statement in the work sheet in the Statement of Cost of Goods Manufactured columns. Similarly, the accountant listed each item that

Penta Manufacturing Company, Inc.
Work Sheet
For Year Ended December 31, 19–

	ACCOUNT NAME	TRIAL BALANCE DEBIT	TRIAL BALANCE CREDIT	ADJUSTMENTS DEBIT	ADJUSTMENTS CREDIT
1	Cash	14 0 0 0 00			
2	Notes Receivable	50 0 0 0 00			
3	Accounts Receivable	180 0 0 0 00			
4	Allowance for Doubtful Accounts		2 5 0 0 00		(l) 3 5 0 0 00
5	Raw Materials Inventory	90 0 0 0 00		(b)100 0 0 0 00	(a) 90 0 0 0 00
6	Work-in-Process Inventory	130 0 0 0 00		(d)120 0 0 0 00	(c)130 0 0 0 00
7	Finished Goods Inventory	400 0 0 0 00		(f)250 0 0 0 00	(e)400 0 0 0 00
8	Prepaid Insurance	25 0 0 0 00			(i) 22 0 0 0 00
9	Factory Supplies	16 0 0 0 00			(j) 14 0 0 0 00
10	Land	100 0 0 0 00			
11	Factory Building	500 0 0 0 00			
12	Accumulated Deprec., Factory Building		250 0 0 0 00		(h) 25 0 0 0 00
13	Factory Equipment	360 0 0 0 00			
14	Accumulated Deprec., Factory Equipment		218 0 0 0 00		(g) 32 0 0 0 00
15	Office Equipment	62 0 0 0 00			
16	Accumulated Deprec., Office Equipment		40 0 0 0 00		(k) 5 0 0 0 00
17	Notes Payable		40 0 0 0 00		
18	Accounts Payable		55 5 5 0 00		
19	Dividends Payable		12 0 0 0 00		
20	Bonds Payable		300 0 0 0 00		
21	Common Stock		300 0 0 0 00		
22	Premium on Common Stock		100 0 0 0 00		
23	Retained Earnings		214 9 0 0 00		
24	Sales (net)		2,000 0 0 0 00		
25	Raw Materials Purchases	230 0 0 0 00			
26	Direct Labor	565 0 0 0 00			
27	Indirect Labor	120 0 0 0 00			
28	Supervisory Salaries	110 0 0 0 00			
29	Heat, Light, and Power	42 0 0 0 00			
30	Repairs and Maintenance	24 0 0 0 00			
31	Miscellaneous Factory Costs	16 0 0 0 00			
32	Selling Expenses (control)	300 0 0 0 00			
33	General Expenses (control)	143 5 0 0 00		(k) 5 0 0 0 00	
34				(l) 3 5 0 0 00	
35	Interest Expense	18 0 0 0 00			
36	Income Tax Expense	37 4 5 0 00		(m) 16 0 0 0 00	
37		3,532 9 5 0 00	3,532 9 5 0 00		
38	Total carried forward			494 5 0 0 00	721 5 0 0 00
39					
40					
41					

FIGURE 29-3

STATEMENT OF COST OF GOODS MANUFACTURED		INCOME STATEMENT		BALANCE SHEET		
DEBIT	CREDIT	DEBIT	CREDIT	DEBIT	CREDIT	
				14 0 0 0 00		1
				50 0 0 0 00		2
				180 0 0 0 00		3
					6 0 0 0 00	4
				100 0 0 0 00		5
				120 0 0 0 00		6
				250 0 0 0 00		7
				3 0 0 0 00		8
				2 0 0 0 00		9
				100 0 0 0 00		10
				500 0 0 0 00		11
					275 0 0 0 00	12
				360 0 0 0 00		13
					250 0 0 0 00	14
				62 0 0 0 00		15
					45 0 0 0 00	16
					40 0 0 0 00	17
					55 5 5 0 00	18
					12 0 0 0 00	19
					300 0 0 0 00	20
					300 0 0 0 00	21
					100 0 0 0 00	22
					214 9 0 0 00	23
			2,000 0 0 0 00			24
230 0 0 0 00						25
565 0 0 0 00						26
120 0 0 0 00						27
110 0 0 0 00						28
42 0 0 0 00						29
24 0 0 0 00						30
16 0 0 0 00						31
		300 0 0 0 00				32
						33
		152 0 0 0 00				34
		18 0 0 0 00				35
		53 4 5 0 00				36
						37
1,107 0 0 0 00	0 00	523 4 5 0 00	2,000 0 0 0 00	1,741 0 0 0 00	1,598 4 5 0 00	38
						39
						40
						41

(continued on following pages)

| ACCOUNT NAME | TRIAL BALANCE | | ADJUSTMENTS | |
	DEBIT	CREDIT	DEBIT	CREDIT
1 Totals brought forward			494 5 0 0 00	721 5 0 0 00
2 Manufacturing Summary			(a) 90 0 0 0 00	(b)100 0 0 0 00
3			(c)130 0 0 0 00	(d)120 0 0 0 00
4 Income Summary			(e)400 0 0 0 00	(f)250 0 0 0 00
5 Depreciation Expense, Factory Equipment			(g) 32 0 0 0 00	
6 Depreciation Expense, Factory Building			(h) 25 0 0 0 00	
7 Factory Insurance Expired			(i) 22 0 0 0 00	
8 Factory Supplies Used			(j) 14 0 0 0 00	
9 Income Tax Payable				(m) 16 0 0 0 00
10			1,207 5 0 0 00	1,207 5 0 0 00
11 Cost of Goods Manufactured				
12				
13 Net Income After Income Tax				
14				
15				

appeared on the income statement in the Income Statement columns of the work sheet.

To fix the steps in your mind in the proper sequence, let's enumerate the steps in the manufacturer's accounting cycle:

1. Journalize the transactions.
2. Post to the ledger accounts.
3. Prepare a trial balance.
4. Determine the adjustments.
5. Complete the work sheet.
6. Prepare the financial statements.
7. Journalize and post adjusting entries.
8. Journalize and post closing entries.
9. Prepare a post-closing trial balance.

Adjusting Entries

Objective 3

Journalize adjusting entries for a manufacturing enterprise.

After the manufacturer's accountant has assembled the information, she or he records the adjustments in the Adjustments columns of the work sheet, just as the accountant for a merchandising firm does. Here is the information (identified by letter) for the adjustments shown on the work sheet for the Penta Manufacturing Company, Inc.:

a.–b. Cost of the ending raw materials inventory, $100,000
c.–d. Cost of the ending work-in-process inventory, $120,000
e.–f. Cost of the ending finished goods inventory, $250,000

FIGURE 29-3
(continued)

STATEMENT OF COST OF GOODS MANUFACTURED		INCOME STATEMENT		BALANCE SHEET		
DEBIT	CREDIT	DEBIT	CREDIT	DEBIT	CREDIT	
1,107 0 0 0 00	0 00	523 4 5 0 00	2,000 0 0 0 00	1,741 0 0 0 00	1,598 4 5 0 00	1
90 0 0 0 00	100 0 0 0 00					2
130 0 0 0 00	120 0 0 0 00					3
		400 0 0 0 00	250 0 0 0 00			4
32 0 0 0 00						5
25 0 0 0 00						6
22 0 0 0 00						7
14 0 0 0 00						8
					16 0 0 0 00	9
1,420 0 0 0 00	220 0 0 0 00					10
	1,200 0 0 0 00	1,200 0 0 0 00				11
1,420 0 0 0 00	1,420 0 0 0 00	2,123 4 5 0 00	2,250 0 0 0 00	1,741 0 0 0 00	1,614 4 5 0 00	12
		126 5 5 0 00			126 5 5 0 00	13
		2,250 0 0 0 00	2,250 0 0 0 00	1,741 0 0 0 00	1,741 0 0 0 00	14
						15

g. Depreciation of factory equipment, $32,000
h. Depreciation of factory building, $25,000
i. Expired factory insurance, $22,000 (assuming the unexpired portion had already been calculated)
j. Cost of the factory supplies inventory, $2,000
k. Depreciation of office equipment, $5,000
l. Estimated uncollectible accounts, $6,000 (determined by an aging analysis)
m. Income tax, $53,450 (based on a taxable income before income tax of $180,000; the accountant determined this by completing the Income Statement columns of the work sheet without including income tax).

Remember

The raw materials inventory and the work-in-process inventory are adjusted using the Manufacturing Summary account.

The accountant journalizes the adjusting entries as illustrated in Figure 29-4 on page 1004.

Closing Entries

Objective 4

Journalize closing entries for a manufacturing enterprise.

Now we come to the steps one must take in making the closing entries for a manufacturer:

1. Close the costs that appear in the statement of cost of goods manufactured into the Manufacturing Summary account.
2. Close the Manufacturing Summary account into the Income Summary account (by the amount of the cost of goods manufactured).
3. Close the revenue accounts into the Income Summary account.

FIGURE 29-4

GENERAL JOURNAL   PAGE _____

	DATE	DESCRIPTION	POST. REF.	DEBIT	CREDIT	
1	19–	*Adjusting Entries*				1
2	Dec. 31	Manufacturing Summary		90 0 0 0 00		2
3		Raw Materials Inventory			90 0 0 0 00	3
4						4
5	31	Raw Materials Inventory		100 0 0 0 00		5
6		Manufacturing Summary			100 0 0 0 00	6
7						7
8	31	Manufacturing Summary		130 0 0 0 00		8
9		Work-in-Process Inventory			130 0 0 0 00	9
10						10
11	31	Work-in-Process Inventory		120 0 0 0 00		11
12		Manufacturing Summary			120 0 0 0 00	12
13						13
14	31	Income Summary		400 0 0 0 00		14
15		Finished Goods Inventory			400 0 0 0 00	15
16						16
17	31	Finished Goods Inventory		250 0 0 0 00		17
18		Income Summary			250 0 0 0 00	18
19						19
20	31	Depreciation Expense, Factory				20
21		Equipment		32 0 0 0 00		21
22		Accumulated Depreciation,				22
23		Factory Equipment			32 0 0 0 00	23
24						24
25	31	Depreciation Expense, Factory				25
26		Building		25 0 0 0 00		26
27		Accumulated Depreciation,				27
28		Factory Building			25 0 0 0 00	28
29						29
30	31	Factory Insurance Expired		22 0 0 0 00		30
31		Prepaid Insurance			22 0 0 0 00	31
32						32
33	31	Factory Supplies Used		14 0 0 0 00		33
34		Factory Supplies			14 0 0 0 00	34
35						35
36	31	General Expenses (control)		5 0 0 0 00		36
37		Accumulated Depreciation,				37
38		Office Equipment			5 0 0 0 00	38
39						39
40	31	General Expenses (control)		3 5 0 0 00		40
41		Allowance for Doubtful Accounts			3 5 0 0 00	41
42						42
43	31	Income Tax Expense		16 0 0 0 00		43
44		Income Tax Payable			16 0 0 0 00	44
45						45
46						46

FIGURE 29-5

GENERAL JOURNAL   PAGE _____

	DATE		DESCRIPTION	POST. REF.	DEBIT	CREDIT	
1	19–		*Closing Entries*				1
2	Dec.	31	*Manufacturing Summary*		1,200 0 0 0 00		2
3			*Raw Materials Purchases*			230 0 0 0 00	3
4			*Direct Labor*			565 0 0 0 00	4
5			*Indirect Labor*			120 0 0 0 00	5
6			*Supervisory Salaries*			110 0 0 0 00	6
7			*Heat, Light, and Power*			42 0 0 0 00	7
8			*Repairs and Maintenance*			24 0 0 0 00	8
9			*Miscellaneous Factory Costs*			16 0 0 0 00	9
10			*Depreciation Expense, Factory*				10
11			*Equipment*			32 0 0 0 00	11
12			*Depreciation Expense, Factory*				12
13			*Building*			25 0 0 0 00	13
14			*Factory Insurance Expired*			22 0 0 0 00	14
15			*Factory Supplies Used*			14 0 0 0 00	15
16							16
17		31	*Income Summary*		1,200 0 0 0 00		17
18			*Manufacturing Summary*			1,200 0 0 0 00	18
19							19
20		31	*Sales (net)*		2,000 0 0 0 00		20
21			*Income Summary*			2,000 0 0 0 00	21
22							22
23		31	*Income Summary*		470 0 0 0 00		23
24			*Selling Expenses (control)*			300 0 0 0 00	24
25			*General Expenses (control)*			152 0 0 0 00	25
26			*Interest Expense*			18 0 0 0 00	26
27							27
28		31	*Income Summary*		53 4 5 0 00		28
29			*Income Tax Expense*			53 4 5 0 00	29
30							30
31		31	*Income Summary*		126 5 5 0 00		31
32			*Retained Earnings*			126 5 5 0 00	32
33							33
34							34
35							35

4. Close the expense accounts into the Income Summary account.
5. Close the Income Tax Expense account into the Income Summary account.
6. Close the Income Summary account into the Retained Earnings account (by the amount of the net income after income tax).

Following are T accounts for Manufacturing Summary and Income Summary, labeled so that you can readily identify the accounts recorded. These steps are shown in Figure 29-5.

Remember

Manufacturing Summary is closed into Income Summary by the amount of the cost of goods manufactured.

Manufacturing Summary

Raw Materials Inventory, Jan. 1	90,000	Raw Materials Inventory, Dec. 31	100,000
Work-in-Process Inventory, Jan. 1	130,000	Work-in-Process Inventory, Dec. 31	120,000
Raw Materials Purchases	230,000	Closing	1,200,000
Direct Labor	565,000	(To Income Summary)	
Indirect Labor	120,000		
Supervisory Salaries	110,000		
Heat, Light, and Power	42,000		
Repairs and Maintenance	24,000		
Miscellaneous Factory Costs	16,000		
Deprec. Expense, Factory Equipment	32,000		
Deprec. Expense, Factory Building	25,000		
Factory Insurance Expired	22,000		
Factory Supplies Used	14,000		
	1,420,000		1,420,000

Income Summary

Finished Goods Inventory, Jan. 1	400,000	Finished Goods Inventory, Dec. 31	250,000
(From Manufacturing Summary)	1,200,000		

DETERMINING THE VALUE OF ENDING INVENTORIES

We've been talking about the fact that a manufacturer has to record the costs of the ending inventories for (1) raw materials, (2) work in process, and (3) finished goods. The manufacturer first lists these costs in the Adjustments columns of the work sheet and then carries the figures forward into the financial statements. Let us now consider each inventory separately, because each poses a slightly different set of problems.

Raw Materials Inventory

The items that go to make up the raw materials inventory are in the same form they were in when the manufacturer bought them; nothing has been done to them yet. So the accountant first ascertains the quantities on hand and the unit costs and then determines the values of the inventories. The value of the ending inventories may be calculated by either FIFO, LIFO, or weighted-average method. One may also use the lower-of-cost-or-market rule. These alternatives involve periodic inventory systems.

A manufacturer may choose to keep *perpetual inventories*, which provide a continuous or running balance of the firm's inventory. When a firm that uses perpetual inventories buys raw materials, it immediately debits Raw Materials Inventory for the cost of these materials. When the materials are put into production, the manufacturer credits Raw Materials Inventory for the cost of the materials used and debits Work-in-Process. The same debiting and crediting process goes on in the Work-in-Process Inventory and the Finished Goods Inventory accounts, as these materials go through the manufacturing process. If a company keeps perpetual inventories, it verifies the balance of the account periodically by physically counting the goods on hand. Any discrepancy that exists can be handled by an adjusting entry. If there is no discrepancy, then the company does not need to make an adjusting entry involving the inventory.

Work-in-Process Inventory

How does one calculate the cost of the work-in-process inventory? We have seen that the cost of manufacturing any product consists of (1) *raw materials used*, (2) *direct labor expended*, and (3) *factory overhead*. Therefore the manufacturer keeps a record of the amount and cost of raw materials placed in production. The manufacturer also records the cost of direct labor expended on the ending work-in-process inventory.

The third item, factory overhead, consists of a group of accounts such as Heat, Light, and Power; Repairs and Maintenance; and Miscellaneous Factory Costs; to name a few. So the manufacturer cannot calculate the *exact* cost of factory overhead involved in the ending work-in-process inventory and must therefore estimate this cost. The firm does this by using a percentage of the direct labor cost involved in the ending inventory.

Remember

Exact factory overhead cost can't be traced directly to specific products being manufactured, so the cost must be allocated by a predetermined factory overhead rate.

The reasoning here is that since factory overhead is closely related to the level of production, and since the level of production varies directly with the amount of direct labor, the cost of factory overhead should be regarded as a percentage of direct labor. For example, Heat, Light, and Power is part of factory overhead and varies directly with the level of production.

One may determine the percentage figure for factory overhead from the most recent statement of cost of goods manufactured. The factory overhead rate for the Penta Manufacturing Company, Inc., is as follows:

$$\text{Factory overhead rate} = \frac{\text{Factory overhead}}{\text{Direct labor}} = \frac{\$405,000}{\$565,000} = .72 = \underline{\underline{72\%}}$$

Since the process of factory overhead cost allocation is beyond the scope of this course, we will leave further discussion of this topic for more advanced accounting texts.

SUMMARY

The same accounting principles that govern the accounts of service and merchandising enterprises also govern those of manufacturing companies. The additional element that enters into the accounting for manufacturing firms is the determination of the cost of goods manufactured.

L.O. 1   We presented the financial statements first to show you how the accounts
L.O. 2   introduced here for a manufacturer are recorded on the work sheet. Each
figure appearing in the statement of cost of goods manufactured also appears in the work sheet columns labeled Statement of Cost of Goods Manufactured; likewise, each figure appearing in the income statement also appears in the columns labeled Income Statement.

L.O. 3   In making the adjusting entries, the accountant adjusts the inventories
appearing in the statement of cost of goods manufactured (raw materials
and work-in-process) into the Manufacturing Summary account and adjusts
the inventories appearing in the income statement (finished goods) into the
Income Summary account.

L.O. 4   In making the closing entries, the accountant first closes all manufactur-
ing-cost accounts into the Manufacturing Summary account. Next the accountant closes Manufacturing Summary (now representing the cost of
goods manufactured) into the Income Summary account. All other adjusting
and closing entries are handled in the usual manner.

The manufacturer determines the costs of the work-in-process and
finished-goods inventories by adding the cost of the raw materials used, the
cost of the direct labor, and the estimated cost of factory overhead, which is
figured as a percentage of the cost of direct labor. For an example, refer to
the table below: In our illustration of the Penta Manufacturing Company, we
established the rate for factory overhead as being 72 percent of direct labor.

Item	Work in Process		Finished Goods	
Raw materials used	$ 51,200	00	$107,240	00
+ Direct labor	40,000	00	83,000	00
+ Factory overhead (72% of direct labor)	28,800	00	59,760	00
	$120,000	00	$250,000	00

GLOSSARY

Direct labor   Wages paid to factory employees who work with machines
or hand tools directly on raw materials to convert them into finished
products.

Direct materials   Delivered cost of raw materials used in manufacturing
products.

Factory overhead   All manufacturing costs except raw materials used and
direct labor that cannot be traced directly to products being manufactured. Examples: heat, light, and power; repairs and maintenance; indirect labor; indirect materials.

Indirect labor   That portion of the cost of work performed by workers who
keep the plant in operation—such as factory maintenance workers and
timekeepers—rather than workers who are directly occupied with production; considered to be part of factory overhead.

C MPUTERS AT WORK

The Factory of the Future

The factory of the future is almost here. Relying heavily on advanced computerized accounting procedures, it will require a fundamental rethinking of many accounting assumptions and practices.

At the heart of the new factory are robots and automatic machine tools, computer-integrated-manufacturing (CIM), and just-in-time techniques. The idea of "economy of scale" has been replaced by "economy of scope or variety." Versatility and quality are now key terms.

Robots now have such delicate "hands" and "eyes" that they can perform all the operations of assembling a computer or making a rug, whether choosing the right parts out of trays and soldering them in the computer housing or monitoring yarn's weight, moisture, and quality. Robots on the production line may be supplied with materials by other robots that make trips to the storeroom. And the storeroom itself is getting smaller and smaller, as vendors deliver, "just in time," smaller quantities of supplies more frequently than they used to. Space is saved and nothing sits around for months waiting to get used.

CIM systems keep all this automation—and even the human workers involved—integrated and running smoothly. The computers monitor every facet of the factory's operations, from raw materials to new orders. Because computers and robots are so versatile and easily programmed for new tasks, engineers can design a new product on a computer in a CIM factory, give it to other computers that check the design, and then program robots and machine tools to manufacture the product.

The theory behind such factories is that CIM allows a manufacturer to respond to customer desires so quickly, making a variety of top-quality products, that it will still profit, despite a loss in economies of scale. But accounting systems have a difficult time figuring quality and flexibility into a company's balance sheets. For years, accountants have helped manufacturers focus on variable costs; the fixed costs of the plant itself were stable, based on mature technology. Because of the focus on cutting variable costs, the factory of the future is often presented as a way to save on labor, a major variable. However, while robots and CIM often eliminate assembly-line jobs, they may require more trained, highly paid workers. It's hard to justify investing in new factory technology in order to eliminate a few hundred low-paying jobs.

Instead, accountants must now reckon with the fact that fixed costs account for as much as 70 percent of the total costs of a flexible manufacturer. Accountants need to look at the new factory's costs in different ways, factoring in the value of expanding market share and of maximizing the output of an existing work force.

Sources: "Factory of the Future," *The Economist*, May 30, 1987, 50; Kasra Ferdows and Wickham Skinner, "The Sweeping Revolution in Manufacturing," *The Journal of Business Strategy*, Fall 1987, 64–69; Michael Sheehan, "Broadloom Automation," *Manufacturing Systems*, May 1987, 58–59.

Indirect materials   Factory supplies, such as oil, grease, and cleaning fluids, used to keep the plant in operation; considered part of factory overhead.

Manufacturing Summary   An account used to make adjustments to Raw Materials and Work-in-Process accounts; similar to Income Summary.

Raw materials   Delivered cost of materials (also called *direct materials*) to be used in producing the finished goods; the materials that enter directly into and become a part of the finished product.

QUESTIONS, EXERCISES, AND PROBLEMS
Discussion Questions

1. Name the three major elements involved in manufacturing costs.
2. What inventory accounts appear in a manufacturing company's chart of accounts?
3. Which inventories appear in the statement of costs of goods manufactured?
4. What is the purpose of the Manufacturing Summary account?
5. Which inventory of a manufacturing firm is handled in the same way as the merchandise inventory of a merchandising firm?
6. Name five accounts that you would consider to be factory overhead costs.
7. Why is cost of goods manufactured entered in the Statement of Cost of Goods Manufactured Credit and the Income Statement Debit columns on a work sheet?
8. Does the Manufacturing Summary account have a balance during the fiscal period? Explain your answer.

Exercises

L.O. I   **Exercise 29-1**   From the following balances, calculate the cost of the ending work-in-process inventory, which contains the following three elements:

Raw materials used	$108,000
Direct labor	120,000
Factory overhead (75% of direct labor cost)	

L.O. I   **Exercise 29-2**   From the following balances, determine the cost of goods manufactured:

Cost of Goods Sold	$1,275,000
Finished Goods Inventory, March 1	300,000
Finished Goods Inventory, March 31	225,000

L.O. I   **Exercise 29-3**   From the following balances, determine the cost of the raw materials used:

Raw Materials Purchases	$900,000
Raw Materials Inventory, August 31	160,000
Raw Materials Inventory, August 1	120,000

L.O. 1 **Exercise 29-4** Prepare a statement of cost of goods manufactured, using any of the following balances you need:

Raw Materials Purchases	$420,000
Raw Materials Inventory, June 30	50,000
Raw Materials Inventory, June 1	30,000
Work-in-Process Inventory, June 1	150,000
Work-in-Process Inventory, June 30	200,000
Finished Goods Inventory, June 30	80,000
Direct Labor	600,000
Factory Overhead	450,000
Finished Goods Inventory, June 1	90,000

L.O. 1 **Exercise 29-5** From the data in Exercise 29-4, determine the percentage of factory overhead to direct labor. Assume that the cost of the work in process on June 30 is $200,000, comprising raw materials of $60,000 and direct labor of $80,000. How much is the factory overhead? Verify the figure by means of the percentage of factory overhead to direct labor.

L.O. 2 **Exercise 29-6** The Statement of Cost of Goods Manufactured columns and the Income Statement columns of the work sheet for the Finch Manufacturing Company for the year ended December 31 are as follows. Finch's beginning inventory of raw materials is $10,000; its beginning inventory of work in process is $48,000. Prepare a statement of cost of goods manufactured.

ACCOUNT NAME	STATEMENT OF COST OF GOODS MANUFACTURED DEBIT	CREDIT	INCOME STATEMENT DEBIT	CREDIT
Sales				450 0 0 0 00
Raw Materials Purchases	80 0 0 0 00			
Direct Labor	200 0 0 0 00			
Indirect Labor	4 0 0 0 00			
Heat, Light, and Power	2 0 0 0 00			
Miscellaneous Factory Costs	1 0 0 0 00			
Selling Expenses (control)			42 5 0 0 00	
General Expenses (control)			17 5 0 0 00	
Income Tax Expense			28 1 0 0 00	
Manufacturing Summary	10 0 0 0 00	15 0 0 0 00		
	48 0 0 0 00	50 0 0 0 00		
Income Summary			40 0 0 0 00	45 0 0 0 00
	345 0 0 0 00	65 0 0 0 00		
Cost of Goods Manufactured		280 0 0 0 00	280 0 0 0 00	
	345 0 0 0 00	345 0 0 0 00	408 1 0 0 00	495 0 0 0 00
Net Income After Income Tax			86 9 0 0 00	
			495 0 0 0 00	495 0 0 0 00

L.O. 1   **Exercise 29-7**   From the information in Exercise 29-6, prepare an income statement for the Finch Manufacturing Company. Beginning inventory of finished goods is $40,000.

L.O. 4   **Exercise 29-8**   From the information in Exercise 29-6, journalize the closing entries for the Finch Manufacturing Company.

Problem Set A

L.O. 3,4   **Problem 29-1A**   Here is the statement of cost of goods manufactured for the Sarbo Manufacturing Company:

Sarbo Manufacturing Company
Statement of Cost of Goods Manufactured
For Year Ended December 31, 19–

Work-in-Process Inventory, January 1			$ 240 0 0 0 00
Raw Materials:			
Raw Materials Inventory, January 1	$ 500 0 0 0 00		
Raw Materials Purchases (net)	780 0 0 0 00		
Cost of Raw Materials Available for Use	$1 280 0 0 0 00		
Less Raw Materials Inventory, December 31	530 0 0 0 00		
Cost of Raw Materials Used		$ 750 0 0 0 00	
Direct Labor		1 200 0 0 0 00	
Factory Overhead:			
Indirect Labor	$ 220 0 0 0 00		
Supervisory Salaries	190 0 0 0 00		
Depreciation Expense, Factory Equipment	130 0 0 0 00		
Heat, Light, and Power	38 0 0 0 00		
Depreciation Expense, Factory Building	37 6 0 0 00		
Repairs and Maintenance	28 4 0 0 00		
Factory Supplies Used	24 0 0 0 00		
Factory Insurance Expired	17 6 0 0 00		
Property Tax on Factory Building	14 4 0 0 00		
Miscellaneous Factory Costs	12 8 0 0 00		
Total Factory Overhead		712 8 0 0 00	
Total Manufacturing Costs			2 662 8 0 0 00
Total Cost of Work-in-Process During Period			$2 902 8 0 0 00
Less Work-in-Process Inventory, December 31			520 0 0 0 00
Costs of Goods Manufactured			$2 382 8 0 0 00

Instructions

1. Journalize the adjusting entries for the Raw Materials Inventory and the Work-in-Process Inventory.
2. Journalize the closing entries for manufacturing costs.
3. Post the entries to the Manufacturing Summary account.
4. Journalize and post the entry to close the Manufacturing Summary account.

L.O. 1,2 **Problem 29-2A** The trial balance of the McBain Products Company, Inc., as of December 31 of this year, is shown below:

McBain Products Company, Inc.
Trial Balance
December 31, 19–

ACCOUNT NAME	DEBIT	CREDIT
Cash	4 2 0 0 00	
Accounts Receivable	35 8 0 0 00	
Allowance for Doubtful Accounts		1 4 5 0 00
Raw Materials Inventory	45 0 0 0 00	
Work-in-Process Inventory	71 3 0 0 00	
Finished Goods Inventory	68 2 0 0 00	
Prepaid Factory Insurance	1 8 0 0 00	
Factory Supplies	3 0 0 0 00	
Machinery	84 0 0 0 00	
Accumulated Depreciation, Machinery		42 0 0 0 00
Accounts Payable		29 3 0 0 00
Common Stock		100 0 0 0 00
Paid-in Capital in Excess of Stated Value		20 0 0 0 00
Retained Earnings		70 0 0 0 00
Sales		638 7 5 0 00
Raw Materials Purchases	70 0 0 0 00	
Direct Labor	209 7 0 0 00	
Indirect Labor	79 9 0 0 00	
Heat, Light, and Power	16 0 0 0 00	
Machinery Repairs	9 0 0 0 00	
Selling Expenses (control)	139 9 5 0 00	
General Expenses (control)	60 0 5 0 00	
Income Tax Expense	3 6 0 0 00	
	901 5 0 0 00	901 5 0 0 00

You are given the following information for the adjustments:

a.–f. Year-end inventories: raw materials, $43,000; work-in-process, $63,400; finished goods, $69,250.

g. Allowance for Doubtful Accounts to be increased by $800 (debit General Expenses (control)).

h. Cost of the factory supplies inventory, $1,000.

i. Estimated depreciation of factory machinery, $8,750.

j. A study of the company's insurance policies shows that $1,200 of factory insurance expired during the year.

k. Accrued direct labor, $300; accrued indirect labor, $100; accrued sales commissions, $100 (credit Wages and Commissions Payable).

l. Additional income tax, $1,208.

Instructions

1. Prepare a work sheet.
2. Prepare a statement of cost of goods manufactured.
3. Prepare an income statement.

L.O. 1,3,4   **Problem 29-3A**   The columns reflecting the statement of cost of goods manufactured and the income statement from the work sheet of Nesta Sporting Goods Company, Inc., as of December 31, the end of the fiscal year, are shown below. Beginning inventory of raw materials is $138,240; beginning inventory of work in process is $248,800.

Instructions

1. Prepare a statement of cost of goods manufactured.
2. Prepare an income statement.
3. Journalize the adjusting entries for the inventories.
4. Journalize the closing entries.

ACCOUNT NAME	STATEMENT OF COST OF GOODS MANUFACTURED DEBIT	CREDIT	INCOME STATEMENT DEBIT	CREDIT
Sales				2,999 9 2 0 00
Sales Returns and Allowances			24 8 0 0 00	
Sales Discounts			23 6 0 0 00	
Selling Expenses (control)			358 9 8 0 00	
General Expenses (control)			145 7 2 0 00	
Raw Materials Purchases	769 0 0 0 00			
Direct Labor	965 8 0 0 00			
Indirect Labor	221 2 4 0 00			
Heat, Light, and Power	53 9 6 0 00			
Factory Supervision	53 9 0 0 00			
Rent, Factory	32 0 0 0 00			
Machinery Repairs	31 8 0 0 00			
Depreciation Expense, Machinery	31 6 8 0 00			
Factory Supplies Used	12 4 0 0 00			
Factory Insurance Expired	7 6 0 0 00			
Small Tools Expense	2 5 2 0 00			
Miscellaneous Factory Costs	1 3 6 0 00			
Loss on Disposal of Equipment			17 2 0 0 00	
Interest Expense			13 6 0 0 00	
Income Tax Expense			86 0 0 0 00	
Manufacturing Summary	138 2 4 0 00	143 2 0 0 00		
	248 8 0 0 00	252 9 8 0 00		
Income Summary			362 8 0 0 00	373 4 4 0 00
	2,570 3 0 0 00	396 1 8 0 00		
Cost of Goods Manufactured		2,174 1 2 0 00	2,174 1 2 0 00	
	2,570 3 0 0 00	2,570 3 0 0 00	3,206 8 2 0 00	3,373 3 6 0 00
Net Income After Income Tax			166 5 4 0 00	
			3,373 3 6 0 00	3,373 3 6 0 00

L.O. 1   **Problem 29-4A**   Here are adjusting and closing entries on the books of
Maynard Paint Company at the end of the fiscal year, May 31:

	DATE		DESCRIPTION	POST. REF.	DEBIT	CREDIT	
1	19–		*Adjusting Entries*				1
2	May	31	Manufacturing Summary		86 7 0 0 00		2
3			Raw Materials Inventory			86 7 0 0 00	3
4							4
5		31	Raw Materials Inventory		78 4 9 0 00		5
6			Manufacturing Summary			78 4 9 0 00	6
7							7
8		31	Manufacturing Summary		110 7 4 0 00		8
9			Work-in-Process Inventory			110 7 4 0 00	9
10							10
11		31	Work-in-Process Inventory		106 4 2 0 00		11
12			Manufacturing Summary			106 4 2 0 00	12
13							13
14			*Closing Entries*				14
15		31	Purchases Discount		3 8 4 0 00		15
16			Manufacturing Summary			3 8 4 0 00	16
17							17
18		31	Manufacturing Summary		954 5 3 0 00		18
19			Raw Materials Purchases			236 7 0 0 00	19
20			Direct Labor			488 9 4 0 00	20
21			Indirect Labor			48 7 4 0 00	21
22			Supervision			69 4 8 0 00	22
23			Depreciation of Machinery			50 0 0 0 00	23
24			Depreciation of Factory Building			20 0 0 0 00	24
25			Heat, Light, and Power			14 2 0 0 00	25
26			Repairs and Maintenance			12 7 9 0 00	26
27			Property Tax, Machinery			1 8 5 0 00	27
28			Property Tax, Factory Building			2 2 0 0 00	28
29			Factory Supplies Used			6 8 7 0 00	29
30			Factory Insurance Expired			1 8 0 0 00	30
31			Miscellaneous Factory Costs			9 6 0 00	31
32							32
33		31	Income Summary		963 2 2 0 00		33
34			Manufacturing Summary			963 2 2 0 00	34
35							35
36							36
37							37
38							38
39							39

Instructions

Prepare a statement of cost of goods manufactured for the year.

Problem Set B

L.O. 3,4   **Problem 29-1B**   Here is the statement of cost of goods manufactured for the Epler Manufacturing Company:

Epler Manufacturing Company
Statement of Cost of Goods Manufactured
For Year Ended June 30, 19–

Work-in-Process Inventory, July 1			$ 80 0 0 0 00
Raw Materials:			
Raw Materials Inventory, July 1	$ 136 0 0 0 00		
Raw Materials Purchases (net)	197 5 0 0 00		
Cost of Raw Materials Available for Use	$ 333 5 0 0 00		
Less Raw Materials Inventory, June 30	130 0 0 0 00		
Cost of Raw Materials Used		$ 203 5 0 0 00	
Direct Labor		291 0 0 0 00	
Factory Overhead:			
Indirect Labor	$54 2 0 0 00		
Supervisory Salaries	38 0 5 0 00		
Depreciation Expense, Factory Equipment	36 0 0 0 00		
Depreciation Expense, Factory Building	10 9 0 0 00		
Heat, Light, and Power	9 3 0 0 00		
Repairs and Maintenance	7 2 0 0 00		
Factory Supplies Used	6 9 5 0 00		
Factory Insurance Expired	3 8 0 0 00		
Property Tax on Factory Building	3 7 5 0 00		
Miscellaneous Factory Costs	3 5 5 0 00		
Total Factory Overhead		173 7 0 0 00	
Total Manufacturing Costs			668 2 0 0 00
Total Cost of Work-in-Process for Period			$ 748 2 0 0 00
Less Work-in-Process Inventory, June 30			87 5 0 0 00
Cost of Goods Manufactured			$ 660 7 0 0 00

Instructions

1. Journalize the adjusting entries for the Raw Materials Inventory and the Work-in-Process Inventory.
2. Journalize the closing entries for manufacturing costs.
3. Post the entries to the Manufacturing Summary account.
4. Journalize and post the entry to close the Manufacturing Summary account.

L.O. 1,2   **Problem 29-2B**   The trial balance of the Bonnard Manufacturing Corporation as of December 31 of this year is shown below:

Bonnard Manufacturing Corporation
Trial Balance
December 31, 19–

ACCOUNT NAME	DEBIT	CREDIT
Cash	4 3 5 0 00	
Accounts Receivable	34 7 0 0 00	
Allowance for Doubtful Accounts		1 3 5 0 00
Raw Materials Inventory	45 8 0 0 00	
Work-in-Process Inventory	71 0 5 0 00	
Finished Goods Inventory	69 2 0 0 00	
Prepaid Factory Insurance	2 1 0 0 00	
Factory Supplies	3 0 0 0 00	
Machinery	85 5 0 0 00	
Accumulated Depreciation, Machinery		43 2 0 0 00
Accounts Payable		27 4 5 0 00
Common Stock		100 0 0 0 00
Paid-in Capital in Excess of Stated Value		25 0 0 0 00
Retained Earnings		65 4 0 5 00
Sales		645 7 0 0 00
Raw Materials Purchases	69 9 5 0 00	
Direct Labor	210 6 4 0 00	
Indirect Labor	80 7 3 0 00	
Heat, Light, and Power	16 2 0 0 00	
Machinery Repairs	9 8 0 0 00	
Selling Expenses (control)	141 7 1 0 00	
General Expenses (control)	59 3 7 5 00	
Income Tax Expense	4 0 0 0 00	
	908 1 0 5 00	908 1 0 5 00

You are given the following information for the adjustments:

a.–f. Year-end inventories: raw materials, $42,700; work-in-process, $64,200; finished goods, $70,350.

g. Estimated depreciation of factory machinery, $9,250.

h. A study of the company's insurance policies shows that $1,550 of factory insurance expired during the year.

i. Allowance for Doubtful Accounts to be increased by $775 (debit General Expenses (control)).

j. Accrued direct labor, $360; accrued indirect labor, $120; accrued sales commissions, $140 (credit Wages and Commissions Payable).

k. Ending factory supplies inventory, $1,100.

l. Additional income tax, $1,160.

Instructions

1. Prepare a work sheet.
2. Prepare a statement of cost of goods manufactured.
3. Prepare an income statement.

L.O. 1,3,4 **Problem 29-3B** Here are the columns reflecting the statement of cost of goods manufactured and the income statement in the work sheet of the Sero Pump Corporation as of December 31, the end of the fiscal year. Their beginning inventory of raw materials is $142,920; their beginning inventory of work-in-process is $253,400.

ACCOUNT NAME	STATEMENT OF COST OF GOODS MANUFACTURED DEBIT	STATEMENT OF COST OF GOODS MANUFACTURED CREDIT	INCOME STATEMENT DEBIT	INCOME STATEMENT CREDIT
Sales				3,016 4 8 0 00
Sales Returns and Allowances			25 2 0 0 00	
Sales Discounts			24 0 0 0 00	
Selling Expenses (control)			373 9 0 0 00	
General Expenses (control)			147 2 2 0 00	
Raw Materials Purchases	764 0 0 0 00			
Direct Labor	973 8 0 0 00			
Indirect Labor	221 6 8 0 00			
Heat, Light, and Power	55 2 4 0 00			
Factory Supervision	53 8 6 0 00			
Rent, Factory	36 0 0 0 00			
Machinery Repairs	35 8 4 0 00			
Depreciation Expense, Machinery	34 7 6 0 00			
Factory Supplies Used	9 8 0 0 00			
Factory Insurance Expired	7 2 0 0 00			
Small Tools Expense	2 4 8 0 00			
Miscellaneous Factory Costs	1 3 0 0 00			
Loss on Disposal of Equipment			16 0 0 0 00	
Interest Expense			15 2 0 0 00	
Income Tax Expense			83 0 0 0 00	
Manufacturing Summary	142 9 2 0 00	147 6 4 0 00		
	253 4 0 0 00	265 6 8 0 00		
Income Summary			369 2 0 0 00	385 6 0 0 00
	2,592 2 8 0 00	413 3 2 0 00		
Cost of Goods Manufactured		2,178 9 6 0 00	2,178 9 6 0 00	
	2,592 2 8 0 00	2,592 2 8 0 00	3,232 6 8 0 00	3,402 0 8 0 00
Net Income After Income Tax			169 4 0 0 00	
			3,402 0 8 0 00	3,402 0 8 0 00

Instructions

1. Prepare a statement of cost of goods manufactured.
2. Prepare an income statement.
3. Journalize the adjusting entries for the inventories.
4. Journalize the closing entries.

L.O. 1   **Problem 29-4B**   Here are adjusting and closing entries that appear on the books of the Bailor Cedar Shingle Company at the end of the fiscal year, December 31.

	DATE		DESCRIPTION	POST. REF.	DEBIT	CREDIT	
1	19–		*Adjusting Entries*				1
2	Dec.	31	*Manufacturing Summary*		88 7 7 0 00		2
3			*Raw Materials Inventory*			88 7 7 0 00	3
4							4
5		31	*Raw Materials Inventory*		90 6 1 8 00		5
6			*Manufacturing Summary*			90 6 1 8 00	6
7							7
8		31	*Manufacturing Summary*		112 8 2 0 00		8
9			*Work-in-Process Inventory*			112 8 2 0 00	9
10							10
11		31	*Work-in-Process Inventory*		116 8 4 0 00		11
12			*Manufacturing Summary*			116 8 4 0 00	12
13							13
14			*Closing Entries*				14
15		31	*Purchases Discount*		4 2 1 0 00		15
16			*Manufacturing Summary*			4 2 1 0 00	16
17							17
18		31	*Manufacturing Summary*		794 8 7 0 00		18
19			*Raw Materials Purchases*			254 9 6 0 00	19
20			*Direct Labor*			339 4 6 0 00	20
21			*Indirect Labor*			38 4 8 0 00	21
22			*Supervision*			58 6 4 0 00	22
23			*Depreciation of Machinery*			42 0 0 0 00	23
24			*Depreciation of Factory Building*			24 0 0 0 00	24
25			*Heat, Light, and Power*			12 8 2 0 00	25
26			*Repairs and Maintenance*			9 6 8 0 00	26
27			*Property Tax, Machinery*			1 2 7 0 00	27
28			*Property Tax, Factory Building*			1 8 4 0 00	28
29			*Factory Supplies Used*			9 4 7 0 00	29
30			*Factory Insurance Expired*			1 2 0 0 00	30
31			*Miscellaneous Factory Costs*			1 0 5 0 00	31
32							32
33		31	*Income Summary*		784 7 9 2 00		33
34			*Manufacturing Summary*			784 7 9 2 00	34
35							35

Instructions

Prepare a statement of cost of goods manufactured for the year.

Glossary of Terms
Chapters 1 Through 15

ABA number   The number assigned by the American Bankers Association to a given bank. The first part of the numerator denotes the city or state in which the bank is located; the second part denotes the bank on which the check is drawn. The denominator indicates the Federal Reserve District and the routing number used by the Federal Reserve Bank.

Account form   The form of the balance sheet in which assets, liabilities, and owner's equity are placed side by side, with assets on the left side and liabilities and owner's equity on the right side.

Accounting   The process of analyzing, classifying, recording, summarizing, and interpreting business transactions in financial or monetary terms.

Accounting cycle   The steps in the accounting process that are completed during the fiscal period.

Account numbers   The numbers assigned to accounts according to the chart of accounts.

Accounts   The categories under the main headings of Assets, Liabilities, and Owner's Equity.

Accounts Receivable   Accounts used to record the amounts owed by charge customers. These accounts represent credit, usually extended for thirty-day periods.

Accounts receivable ledger   A subsidiary ledger that lists the individual accounts of charge customers in alphabetical order.

Accrual basis   An accounting method by which revenue is recorded when it is earned, regardless of when it is received, and expenses are recorded when they are incurred, regardless of when they are paid.

Accrued wages   The amount of unpaid wages owed to employees for the time between the last payday and the end of the fiscal period.

Adjusting entry   An entry to help bring the books up to date at the end of the fiscal period.

Adjustments   Internal transactions that bring ledger accounts up to date, as a planned part of the accounting procedure. They are first recorded in the Adjustments columns of the work sheet.

Assets   Cash, properties, and other things of value owned by an economic unit or business entity.

Balance sheet   A financial statement showing the financial position of a firm or other economic unit on a given date, such as June 30 or December 31. The balance sheet lists the balances of the assets, liabilities, and owner's equity accounts.

Bank charge card   A bank credit card, like the credit cards used by millions of private citizens. The card holder pays what she or he owes directly to the issuing bank. The business firm deposits the credit card receipts; the amount of the deposit equals the total of the receipts, less a discount deducted by the bank.

Bank reconciliation A process by which an accountant determines whether there is a difference between the balance shown on the bank statement and the balance of the Cash account in the firm's general ledger. The object is to determine the adjusted (or true) balance of the Cash account.

Bank statement Periodic statement that a bank sends to the holder of a checking account listing deposits received and checks paid by the bank, as well as debit and credit memorandums.

Blank endorsement An endorsement in which the holder (payee) of a check simply signs her or his name on the back of the check. There are no restrictions attached.

Book balance of cash The balance of the Cash account in the general ledger before it is reconciled with the bank statement.

Book value The cost of an asset minus the accumulated depreciation.

Business entity A business enterprise, separate and distinct from the persons who supply the assets it uses. Property acquired by a business is an asset of the business. The owner is separate from the business and occupies the status of a claimant of the business.

Canceled checks Checks issued by the depositor that have been paid (cleared) by the bank and listed on the bank statement. They are called canceled checks because they are canceled by a stamp or perforation, indicating that they have been paid.

Capital The owner's investment, or equity, in an enterprise.

Cash discount The amount a customer can deduct for paying a bill within a specified period of time; used to encourage prompt payment. Not all sellers offer cash discounts.

Cash funds Sums of money set aside for specific purposes.

Cash payments journal A special journal used to record all transactions in which cash goes out, or decreases.

Cash-receipts-and-disbursements basis An accounting method by which revenue is recorded only when it is received in cash, and all expenses are recorded only when they are paid in cash.

Cash receipts journal A special journal used to record all transactions in which cash comes in, or increases.

Certified Public Accountant (CPA) An independent licensed professional who provides services to clients for a fee.

Change Fund A cash fund used by a firm to make change for customers who pay cash for goods or services.

Chart of accounts The official list of the ledger accounts in which transactions of a business are to be recorded.

Check writer A machine used to imprint the amount in figures and words on the check itself.

Closing entries Entries made at the end of a fiscal period to close off the revenue and expense accounts; that is, to make the balances of the temporary equity account equal to zero. This is also referred to as *clearing the accounts*.

Combined journal A journal format widely used by professional and service-type enterprises in place of a general journal; designed to make the recording and posting of transactions more efficient.

Compound entry   A transaction that requires more than one debit or more than one credit to be recorded.

Contra account   An account that is contrary to, or a deduction from, another account; for example, Accumulated Depreciation entered as a deduction from Equipment.

Controlling account   An account in the general ledger that summarizes the balances of a subsidiary ledger.

Cost of Merchandise Sold   Merchandise Inventory at beginning of fiscal period, plus net purchases, minus Merchandise Inventory at end of fiscal period. Terms often used to describe the same things are *cost of goods sold* and *cost of sales:*

Merchandise Inventory (beginning)
Plus Net Purchases
Merchandise Available for Sale
Less Merchandise Inventory (ending)
Cost of Merchandise Sold

Cost principle   A purchased asset should be recorded at its actual cost (the agreed amount of a transaction).

Credit   The right side of a T account; to credit is to record an amount on the right side of a T account. Credits represent increases in liability, capital, and revenue accounts and decreases in asset, drawing, and expense accounts.

Credit memorandum   A business form provided by the seller to a buyer who has either returned a purchase (or part of a purchase) for credit or been granted an allowance for damaged goods. The seller records the amount of the credit memorandum under the Sales Returns and Allowances account.

Creditor   One to whom money is owed.

Credit period   The time the seller allows the buyer before full payment on a charge sale has to be made.

Crossfooting   The process of totaling columns in a journal or work sheet to make sure that the sum of the debit totals equals the sum of the credit totals.

Cross-reference   The ledger account number in the Posting Reference column of the journal or the journal page number in the Posting Reference column of the ledger account.

Current assets   Cash and any other assets or resources that are expected to be realized in cash or sold or consumed during the normal operating cycle of the business (or one year if the normal operating cycle is less than twelve months).

Current liabilities   Debts that are due within the normal operating cycle of a business, usually within one year, and that are normally paid from current assets.

Current ratio   A firm's current assets divided by its current liabilities. Portrays a firm's short-term-debt-paying ability.

Current Tax Payment Act   Requires employers to withhold employees' federal income tax as well as to pay and report the tax.

Debit The left side of a T account; to debit is to record an amount on the left side of a T account. Debits represent increases in asset, drawing, and expense accounts and decreases in liability, capital, and revenue accounts.

Denominations Varieties of coins and currency, such as quarters, dimes, and nickels and $1 and $5 bills.

Deposit in transit A deposit not recorded on the bank statement because the deposit was made between the time of the bank's closing date for compiling items for its statement and the time the statement is received by the depositor, also known as a *late deposit*.

Deposit slips Printed forms provided by a bank so that customers can list all items being deposited; also known as *deposit tickets*.

Depreciation An expense, based on the expectation that an asset will gradually decline in usefulness due to time, wear and tear, or obsolescence; the cost of the asset is therefore spread out over its estimated useful life. A part of depreciation expense is apportioned to each fiscal period.

Double-entry accounting The system by which each business transaction is recorded in at least two accounts and the accounting equation is kept in balance.

Economic unit Includes business enterprises and also nonprofit entities, such as government bodies, churches, clubs, and fraternal organizations.

Eighth-of-a-month periods Periods used to determine the due date of tax deposits, designated by the Internal Revenue Service as follows: from the 1st to the 3rd of the month, from the 4th to the 7th of the month, from the 8th to the 11th of the month, from the 12th to the 15th of the month, from the 16th to the 19th of the month, from the 20th to the 22nd of the month, from the 23rd to the 25th of the month, and from the 26th to the last day of the month. (All dates are inclusive.)

Employee One who works for compensation under the direction and control of the employer.

Employee's individual earnings record A supplementary record for each employee showing personal payroll data and yearly cumulative earnings and deductions.

Employee's Withholding Allowance Certificate (Form W-4) This form specifies the number of exemptions claimed by each employee and gives the employer the authority to withhold money for an employee's income taxes and FICA taxes.

Employer identification number The number assigned each employer by the Internal Revenue Service for use in the submission of reports and payments for FICA taxes and federal income tax withheld.

Endorsement The process by which the payee transfers ownership of the check to a bank or another party. A check must be endorsed when deposited in a bank because the bank must have legal title to it in order to collect payment from the drawer of the check (the person or firm who wrote the check). In case the check cannot be collected, the endorser guarantees all subsequent holders (*Exception:* an endorsement "without recourse").

Equity The value of a right to or financial interest in an asset or group of assets.

Exemption An amount of an employee's annual earnings not subject to income tax. The term is also called a *withholding allowance*.

Expenses The costs that relate to the earning of revenue (the cost of doing business); examples are wages, rent expense, interest expense, advertising expense; may be paid in cash or at a later time (Accounts Payable).

Fair Labor Standards Act (Wages and Hours Law) An act requiring employers whose products are involved in interstate commerce to pay their employees time-and-a-half for all hours worked in excess of 40 per week.

Fair market value The present worth of an asset, or the amount that would be received if the asset were sold to an outsider on the open market.

Federal unemployment tax A tax levied on the employer only, amounting to .8 percent of the first $7,000 of total earnings paid to each employee during the calendar year. This tax is used to supplement state unemployment benefits.

FICA taxes Social Security taxes paid by both employers and employees under the provisions of the Federal Insurance Contributions Act. The proceeds are used to pay old-age and disability pensions.

Financial position The resources or assets owned by an economic unit at a point in time, offset by the claims against those resources; shown by a balance sheet.

Fiscal period or year Any period of time covering a complete accounting cycle, generally consisting of twelve consecutive months.

FOB destination The seller pays the freight charges and includes them in the selling price.

FOB shipping point The buyer pays the freight charges between the point of shipment and the destination. Payment may be made directly to the carrier upon receiving the goods or to the supplier, if the supplier prepaid the freight charges on behalf of the buyer.

Footings The totals of each side of a T account, recorded in small pencil-written figures.

Form 940 An annual report filed by employers showing total wages paid to employees, total wages subject to federal unemployment tax, total federal unemployment tax, and other information. Also called the *Employers Annual Federal Unemployment Tax Return*.

Form 941 A report showing the tax liability for withholdings of employees' federal income tax and FICA tax as well as the employer's share of FICA tax. Total tax deposits made in the quarter are also listed on this Employer's Quarterly Federal Tax Return.

Form W-2 A form containing information about employee earnings and tax deductions for the year. Also called *Wage and Tax Statement*.

Form W-3 An annual report sent to the Social Security Administration listing the total wages and tips, total federal income tax withheld, total FICA taxable wages, total FICA tax withheld, and other information for all employees of a firm. Also called the *Transmittal of Income and Tax Statements*.

Freight In The account used to record transportation charges on incoming merchandise intended for resale.

Fundamental accounting equation An equation expressing the relationship of assets, liabilities, and owner's equity.

FUTA taxes   Taxes paid only by employers under the provisions of the Federal Unemployment Tax Act. The proceeds are used to provide financial support for the maintenance of government-run employment offices throughout the country.

General expenses   Expenses incurred in the administration of a business, including office expenses and any expenses that are not wholly classified as Selling Expenses or Other Expenses.

Generally accepted accounting principles (GAAP)   The rules or guidelines used for carrying out the accounting process.

Gross pay   The total amount of an employee's pay before any deductions.

Gross profit   Net Sales minus Cost of Merchandise Sold, or profit before deducting expenses:

Net Sales
Less Cost of Merchandise Sold
Gross Profit

Income statement   A financial statement showing the results of business transactions involving revenue and expense accounts over a period of time: total revenue minus total expenses.

Income Summary   An account brought into existence in order to have a debit and credit with each closing entry.

Independent contractor   Someone who is engaged for a definite job or service who may choose her or his own means of doing the work. This person is not an employee of the firm for which the service is provided. (*Examples:* appliance repair, plumber, freelance artist, CPA firm.)

Interim statements   Financial statements prepared during the fiscal year, covering a period of time less than the entire twelve months.

Internal control   Plans and procedures built into the accounting system with the following objectives: (1) to protect assets against fraud and waste, (2) to yield accurate accounting data, (3) to promote an efficient operation, and (4) to encourage adherence to management policies.

Invoice   A business form prepared by the seller that lists the items shipped, their cost, terms of the sale, and the mode of shipment. It may also state the freight charges. The buyer considers it a purchase invoice; the seller considers it a sales invoice.

Journal   The book in which a person makes the original record of a business transaction; commonly referred to as a *book of original entry*.

Journalizing   The process of recording a business transaction in a journal.

Ledger   A book, a loose-leaf binder, or a whole filing system containing all the accounts of an enterprise.

Ledger account   A complete record of the transactions recorded in each individual account.

Liabilities   Debts, or amounts, owed to creditors.

Liquidity   The ability of an asset to be quickly turned into cash, either by selling it or by putting it up as security for a loan.

Long-term liabilities   Debts payable over a comparatively long period, usually more than one year.

Matching principle   The revenue for one time period is matched up or compared with the expenses for the same time period.

Merchandise inventory   A stock of goods that a firm buys and intends to resell, in the same physical condition, at a profit.

MICR   Magnetic ink character recognition; the characters the bank uses to print the number of the depositor's account and the bank's number at the bottom of checks and deposit slips. The bank also prints the amount of the check in MICR when the check is deposited. A number written in this characters can be read by electronic equipment used by banks in clearing checks.

Mixed accounts   Certain accounts that appear in the trial balance that are partly income statement amounts and partly balance sheet amounts—for example, Prepaid Insurance and Supplies.

Modified cash basis   An accounting method by which revenue is recorded only when it is received in cash. Expenditures classified as expenses are recorded only when they are paid in cash. Exceptions are made for expenditures on items having a useful life of more than one year and for certain prepaid items. For example, expenditures for supplies and insurance premiums can be _prorated_, or spread out over the fiscal periods covered. Expenditures for long-lived items are recorded as assets and later depreciated or written off as an expense during their useful lives.

Net income   The result when total revenue exceeds total expenses over a period of time. The final figure on an income statement after all expenses have been deducted from revenues. Also called _net profit_.

Net loss   The result when total expenses exceed total revenue over a period of time.

Net pay   Gross pay minus deductions. Also called take-home pay.

Net purchases   Total purchases less the sum of Purchases Returns and Allowances and Purchases Discount plus Freight In:

Purchases
Less Purchases Returns and Allowances
Less Purchases Discount
Plus Freight In
Net Purchases

Net sales   Sales, minus Sales Returns and Allowances and minus Sales Discount:

Sales
Less Sales Returns and Allowances
Less Sales Discount
Net Sales

Nominal or temporary-equity accounts   Accounts that apply to only one fiscal period and that are to be closed at the end of that fiscal period, such as revenue, expense, Income Summary, and Drawing accounts. This category may also be described as all accounts except assets, liabilities, and the Capital account.

Normal balance   The plus side of a T account.

Notes receivable (current) Written promises to pay received from customers and due in a period of less than one year.

NSF (Not Sufficient Funds) check A check drawn against an account in which there are *Not Sufficient Funds:* this check is returned by the depositor's bank to the drawer's bank because of nonpayment; also known as a *dishonored check.*

Outstanding checks Checks that have been written by the depositor and deducted on his or her records but have not reached the bank for payment and have not been deducted from the bank balance by the time the bank issued its statement.

Payee The person to whom a check is payable.

Payroll Tax Expense A general expense account used for recording the employer's matching portion of the FICA tax, the federal unemployment tax, and the state unemployment tax.

Petty Cash Fund A cash fund used to make small immediate cash payments.

Petty cash payments record A record indicating the amount of each petty cash voucher and the accounts to which they should be charged.

Petty cash voucher A form stating who got what from the Petty Cash Fund, signed by (1) the person in charge of the fund, and (2) the person who received the cash.

Physical inventory An actual count of the stock of goods on hand; also referred to as a *periodic inventory.*

Plant and equipment Long-lived assets that are held for use in the production or sale of other assets or services; also called *fixed assets.*

Post-closing trial balance The listing of the final balances of the real accounts at the end of the fiscal period.

Posting The process of transferring figures from the journal to the ledger accounts.

Promissory note A written promise to pay a definite sum at a definite future time.

Purchase order A written order from the buyer of goods to the supplier, listing items wanted as well as terms of the transaction.

Purchase requisition A form used to request the Purchasing Department to buy something. This form is intended for internal use within a company.

Purchases An account for recording the cost of merchandise acquired for resale.

Purchases Discount An account that records cash discounts granted by suppliers in return for prompt payment; it is treated as a deduction from Purchases.

Purchases journal A special journal used to record the buying of goods on account. It may be used to record the purchase of merchandise only. Or, it may be a multicolumn journal, or invoice register, used to record the buying of anything on account.

Purchases Returns and Allowances The account used by the buyer to record a reduction granted by the supplier either for the return of merchandise or as compensation for damage to the merchandise. The entry in the buyer's account is based on a credit memorandum received from the supplier.

Qualified endorsement An endorsement in which the holder (payee) of a check avoids future liability in case the drawer of the check does not have sufficient funds to cover the check by adding the words "without recourse" to the endorsement on the back of the check.

Quarter A three-month interval of the year, also referred to as a *calendar quarter*, as follows: first quarter, January, February, and March; second quarter, April, May, and June; third quarter, July, August, and September; fourth quarter, October, November, and December.

Real or permanent accounts The accounts that remain open (assets, liabilities, and the Capital account in owner's equity) and that have balances that will be carried over to the next fiscal period.

Report form The form of the balance sheet in which assets are placed at the top and the liabilities and owner's equity are placed below.

Restrictive endorsement An endorsement, such as "Pay to the order of (name of bank), for deposit only," that restricts or limits any further negotiation of a check. If forces the check's deposit since the endorsement is not valid for any other purpose.

Revenues The amounts a business earns; examples are fees earned for performing services, sales, rent income, and interest income; may be in the form of cash, credit card receipts, or accounts receivable (charge accounts).

Reversing entries The reverse of certain adjusting entries, recorded as of the first day of the following fiscal year.

Sales A revenue account for recording the sale of merchandise.

Sales Discount An account that records a deduction from the original price, granted by the seller to the buyer for the prompt payment of an invoice. The cash discount from the seller's point of view; in the buyer's books this is a *purchases discount*.

Sales journal A special journal for recording the sale of merchandise on account only.

Sales Returns and Allowances The account a seller uses to record the physical return of merchandise by customers or a reduction in the bill because merchandise was damaged. Sales Returns and Allowances is treated as a deduction from Sales. This account is usually evidenced by a credit memorandum issued by the seller.

Sales tax A tax levied by a state or city government on the retail sale of goods and services. The tax is paid by the consumer but collected by the retailer.

Selling expenses Expenses directly related to the sale of merchandise, such as salaries of sales staff, advertising expenses, and delivery expenses.

Separate entity concept A business is treated as being a separate economic or accounting entity. The business is independent or stands by itself; it is separate from its owners, creditors, and customers.

Service charge The fee the bank charges for handling checks, collections, and other items. It is in the form of a debit memorandum.

Signature card The form a depositor signs to give the bank a sample of the official signatures of any persons authorized to sign checks. The bank uses it to verify the depositor's signature on checks, on cash items that the depositor(s) may endorse for deposit, and on other business papers that the depositor(s) may present to the bank.

Slide An error in placing the decimal point of a number.

Sole proprietorship One of the three primary forms of business ownership; a one-owner business.

Source documents Business papers such as checks, invoices, receipts, letters, and memos that furnish proof that a transaction has taken place.

Special journals Books of original entry in which one records specialized types of repetitive transactions.

Statement of owner's equity A financial statement showing how—and why—the owner's equity, or capital, account has changed over the financial period.

State unemployment tax A tax levied on the employer only. Rates differ among the various states; however, they are generally 5.4 percent or higher of the first $7,000 of total earnings paid to each employee during the calendar year. The proceeds are used to pay subsistence benefits to unemployed workers.

Straight-line method A means of calculating depreciation in which the cost of an asset, less any trade-in value, is allocated on an average basis over the useful life of the asset.

Subsidiary ledger A group of accounts representing individual subdivisions of a controlling account.

Summarizing entry An entry made to post the column totals of the special journals to the appropriate accounts in the general ledger. It is also used when individual sales invoices are posted directly to the accounts receivable ledger. The summarizing entry represents the one entry made in the general journal to record the total sales on account for a period of time and posted to the general ledger.

T account form A form of account shaped like the letter T; one side is for entries on the debit, or left, side, and one side is for entries on the credit, or right, side.

Temporary-equity accounts Accounts whose balances apply to one fiscal period only, such as revenues, expenses, and the Drawing account. Temporary-equity accounts are also called *nominal accounts.*

Trade discounts Substantial reductions from the list or catalog prices of goods, granted by the seller.

Transaction An event affecting an economic entity that can be expressed in terms of money and that must be recorded in the accounting records.

Transposition An error that involves interchanging, or switching around, the digits during the recording of a number.

Trial balance A list of all ledger account balances to prove that the total of all the debit balances equals the total of all the credit balances.

Two-column general journal A general journal in which there are two money columns used for debit and credit amounts.

Unearned revenue   Revenue received in advance for goods or services to be delivered later; considered to be a liability until the revenue is earned.

Withdrawal   The taking of cash or goods out of a business by the owner for his or her own personal use. (This is also referred to as a *drawing*.) A withdrawal is treated as a temporary decrease in the owner's equity since it is anticipated that it will be offset by net income.

Workers' compensation insurance   This insurance, usually paid for by the employer, provides benefits for employees injured or killed on the job. The rates vary according to the degree of risk inherent in the job. The plans may be sponsored by states or by private firms. The employer pays the premium in advance at the beginning of the year, based on the estimated payroll. The rates are adjusted after the exact payroll is known.

Workers' compensation laws   State laws guaranteeing benefits for employees who are injured or killed on the job.

Working capital   A firm's current assets less its current liabilities. The amount of capital a firm has available to use or to work with during a normal operating cycle.

Work sheet   A working paper used by accountants to record necessary adjustments and provide up-to-date account balances needed to prepare the financial statements.

Index

Note: Boldface indicates a key term and the page where it is defined.

Accelerated Cost Recovery System
  (ACRS), 670
Accelerated depreciation, 649,
  650–654, **672**
Account(s)
  contra, 648
  contra-liability, 520, 851, **862**
  controlling, 619–620
  in departmental accounting, 879
  doubtful, 574
  note given to secure extension of
    time on, 513–515, 541, 542–543
  T form, *see* T accounts
  uncollectible, *see* Bad debt(s)
  See also specific account titles
Accounting
  accrual basis of, 573
  allowance method of, 573–576, **594**
  for bad debts, 571–594
  for bond issuance, 848–856
  branch, 898
  computers and, 620–621, 623
  consistency in, 616, **622,** 655, **672**
  departmental, 877–901
  expert systems and, 899
  for inventory valuation, 605–624
  for manufacturing enterprise,
    993–1008
  for merchandising enterprise,
    993–995
  for notes payable, 509–533
  for notes receivable, 541–563
  for partnerships, 733–761
  for plant and equipment valuation,
    645–672
  software for, 623
  for valuation of receivables, 571–594
  voucher system of, 697–718
Accounting cycle, for manufacturing
  enterprise, 999, 1005–1006
Accounts Payable account
  changing to Notes Payable account,
    513–515
  See also Vouchers Payable account
Accounts Receivable account
  aging of, 577–579, **594**
  analysis of, 929–931
  book value of, 574, 576, **594**

changing to Notes Receivable
  account, 541
computerized collections and, 595
dishonored notes receivable and, 547
estimating bad debts on basis of,
  576–581
valuation of, 571
Accounts receivable turnover, 930, **938**
Accrual basis, of accounting, 573
**Accrued interest income on notes
  receivable,** 555–558, **562**
Accrued interest on notes payable,
  524–526, **533**
Accumulated Depreciation account,
  648
Acid-test ratio, 928–929, **938**
Adjusting entries
  for bad debts, 574–575, 578, 580–581,
    585
  for bonds, 850
  for corporation, 809
  for manufacturing enterprise,
    997–999, 1004
  for organization costs, 772
  for perpetual inventories, 619
  for premiums, 853–856
Adjustments
  for notes payable, 524–529
  for notes receivable, 555–558
Age (Accounts Receivable), 577–579,
  594
Allowance(s), salary, division of
  income based on, 746–747
Allowance for Doubtful Accounts
  account
  adjusting entries and, 585
  in balance sheet, 575, 576
  classification of, 574
**Allowance method of accounting for
  bad debt losses,** 573–576, **594**
Amortization, 862
  of bond discount, 852
  of bond premium, 850
Apportionment of expenses, 886–893,
  901
Appropriation of retained earnings,
  818–819, **831**
Articles of incorporation, 771, **794**

Asset(s)
  current, 607, 928–929
  depreciation of, *see* Depreciation
    discarding or retiring, 658–660
  exchange of, 664–667
  fixed, 645
  intangible, 772, **794**
  issuing stock at par for, 779
  merchandise inventory, 607
  noncash, 779
  note given in exchange for, 516–517
  note received in exchange for,
    544–545
  partnership and, 734, 737
  purchase of, 697
  quick, 928, **938**
  relationship to total current assets, 929
  sale of, 660–663, 693
  useful life of, 648
Authorized capital, 771, **794**
Automobiles, depreciation of, 688, 691

Bad debt(s)
  accounting for, 571–594
  adjusting entries for, 574–575, 578,
    580–581, 585
  allowance method of accounting for,
    573–576, **594**
  collection of accounts previously
    written off and, 588–590
  computerized collections and, 595
  income taxes and, 572
  matching with sales, 573, 582–584
  specific charge-off method of
    accounting for, 590–592, **594**
  write-off method for, 584–588
Bad Debts Expense account
  closing of, 584–585
  estimating, 576–584
  on income statement, 575, 578–579
Bad Debts Recovered account, 592
Balance sheet
  Allowance for Doubtful Accounts
    account in, 575, 576
  bonds and, 861 (illus.)
  comparative, 919–921, 923–925
  of corporation, 790–792, 826, 827
    (illus.)

Balance Sheet (cont.)
  horizontal analysis of, 919–921
  intangible assets in, 772
  for manufacturing enterprise, 997,
    998
  Merchandise Inventory account in,
    607
  for partnership dissolution, 753–754,
    757
  Plant and Equipment account in, 667
  Stockholders' Equity in, 782–783
  vertical analysis of, 923–925
Balance sheet equation, *see*
    Fundamental accounting equation
Bank
  analysis of financial statements by,
    927
  note collection by, 515
Bankruptcy, 588, 590, **594**
  partnerships and, 734
Base year, 918, **938**
Beginning inventory, 609
Board of directors, 771
  dividends and, 820
  minute book of, 825, **831**
Bond(s)
  accounting for issuance of, 848–856
  adjusting entries for, 850, 852–853
  balance sheet and, 861 (illus.)
  callable, 859, **862**
  classification of, 844–845
  coupon, 844–845, **862**
  discount on, 851–853, **862**
  premium on, 848–851, 853–856, **862**
  reasons for issuing, 845–848
  redemption of, 859–860
  registered, 844, **862**
  secured, 845, **862**
  serial, 844, **862**
  sinking fund, 857–858, **862**
  stock comparison, 843–844
  term, 844, **862**
  unsecured, 845, **862**
Bondholders, analysis by, 931
Bond issue, 843, **862**
Bonds Payable account, 848
Book of original entry
  check register as, 702
  voucher register as, 702
Book value
  per share, 933–934
  trade-in value and, 664–667
  withdrawal of partnership equity
    and, 753–756
Book value of Accounts Receivable,
    574, 576, **594**
Branch accounting, 898
Buildings
  determining costs of, 646, 647
  See also Plant and equipment

Callable bonds, 859, **862**
Call price, of bonds, 859
Capital
  authorized, 771
  corporations and, 770, 774
  legal, 776, **794**
  paid-in, 783, **795**
  working, 927, **938**
  See also Owner's equity;
    Stockholders' equity
Capital expenditures, 656, **672**
Capital stock, 771, **794**
  classes of, 775–777
  See also Stock
Cash
  internal control of, 697
  issuing stock at par for, 778
  sources and uses of, *see* Statement of
    cash flows
Cash account
  inflows and outflows of, 951–953
  See also Statement of cash flows
Cash discount
  net-amount system and, 714–716,
    718
  voucher system and, 714
Cash dividends, 820, **831**
  cash flows and, 951
Cash equivalents, 950, **977**
Charge accounts
  changing to note, 513–515, 541,
    542–543
  entries to write off, 585–588
  See also Accounts receivable
Charter, for corporation, 771, **794**
Check register, 703–704, 705 (illus.)
Clearing the accounts, *see* Closing
    entries
Closely held corporation, 772, **794**
Closing entries
  Bad Debts Expense account and,
    584–585
  for corporation, 809, 817
  Interest Expense account and,
    527–528
  for manufacturing enterprise,
    1005–1006
  for partnership, 740
Collection
  by bank, 515
  of dishonored note, 547–548
Common-size statements, 926, **938**
Common stock, 776, **794**
  assets in exchange for, 779
  earnings per share of, 934–935
  with no par value, 783
  rate of return and, 934
  See also Stock
Comparative statements
  horizontal analysis and, 916–921, **938**

  industry, 926
  trend percentages and, 925–926
  vertical analysis and, 921–925
Compound entry, to write off
    uncollectible accounts, 587
Computer(s)
  bad debt collections and, 595
  depreciation and, 669
  embezzlement using, 717
  expert systems and, 899
  inventory and, 623
  management information systems
    and, 899
  manufacturing enterprise and, 1009
  perpetual inventories and, 620–621
  software for, 623
  spreadsheets and, 936
Computer-integrated-manufacturing
    (CIM), 1009
Conservatism, 828, **831**
Consistency principle, 616, **622,** 655,
    672
Contingent liability, 550, **562**
Continuous existence, of corporation,
    770
Contra account, 648
Contracts, partnership, 734, 735
Contra-liability account, 520, 851, **862**
Contribution margin, by department,
    893–898
Controlling account
  Merchandise Inventory account as,
    619–620
  stock and, 778, 790
  Store Equipment account as, 667
Co-ownership, 734, **761**
Corporation(s), 769, **794**
  advantages and disadvantages of,
    770–771
  appropriation of retained earnings
    by, 818–819, **831**
  balance sheet for, 790–792, 826, 827
    (illus.)
  bonds and, *see* Bond(s)
  closely held, 772, **794**
  closing entries for, 809, 817
  declaration and payment of
    dividends by, 819–824
  financial statements for, 813, 816
  formation of, 771–773
  fundamental accounting equation
    and, 793
  income statement for, 813
  income taxes of, 770–771, 805–812
  liability of, 770
  liquidation of, 933–934
  minute book of, 825, **831**
  nonprofit, 769
  open or public, 772, **795**
  ownership of, 770, 772, 774–775

regulation of, 771
statement of retained earnings for,
    825, 826 (illus.)
stock of, 771–790. *See also* Stock
structure of, 773–775
work sheet for, 812–817
Cost(s)
    fixed, 1009
    variable, 1009
Cost of Goods Sold account, 994
Cost of Merchandise Sold account,
    619, 994
Coupon bonds, 844, 845 (illus.), **862**
Credit
    department, 572
    ratings, 572
    See also Promissory notes
Creditors, financial statement analysis
    by, 927–933
Cumulative preferred stock, 777, **794**
Current assets
    Merchandise Inventory account and,
        607
    quick ratio and, 928
    relationship to total current assets,
        929
Current liabilities, 513
Current operations, as source of
    working capital, 927
Current ratio, 927–928, **938**

Data base management systems
    (DBMS), 623
Date of declaration, 820
Date of payment, 820
Debenture, 845, **862**
Deficit, 792, **794**
Departmental accounting, 877–901
    apportionment of operating
        expenses in, 886–893
    contribution margin in, 893–898
    gross profits and, 878–880
    income from operations and,
        880–893
    income statement for, 878, 880–881,
        882–883 (illus.), 893–895,
        896–897 (illus.)
    work sheet for, 881, 884–887 (illus.)
Departmental margin, 893–898, **901**
Depreciation
    accelerated, 649, 650–654, **672**
    Accelerated Cost Recovery System of,
        670
    calculating, 649–655
    comparison of methods for, 654–655
    computers and, 669
    double-declining-balance method
        for, 650–652
    functional, 647
    income taxes and, 668, 670

of land, 646
Modified Accelerated Cost Recovery
    System of, 670, 686–694
nature and recording of, 647–648
net income and, 667
for periods of less than a year,
    655–656
physical, 647
of plant and equipment, 647–656
sale of asset and, 693
straight-line method of, 649–650
sum-of-the-years'-digits method of,
    652–654
units-of-production method of, 650
useful life and, 648
Depreciation base, 648, **672**
Depreciation Expense account, 648
Direct expenses, 893–894, 895, **901**
Direct labor, 996, 1007, **1008**
Direct materials, 996, **1008**
Discount(s), 533, 794, 862
    on bonds, 851–853, **862**
    cash, 714–716
    on notes payable, 518–519, 520–521,
        526–529, **533**
    on notes receivable, 548–555, **562**
    on stock, 776, 780, 781–783, **794**
Discounting a note payable, 518–519,
    520–521, 526–529, **533**
Discounting a note receivable,
    548–555, **562**
Discount period, 549, **562**
Discounts Lost account, 715–716, **718**
Dishonored note receivable, 546–548,
    562
Dissolution, of partnership, 752–760,
    761
Distributive share, 740, **761**
Dividends, 773, **794**
    appropriation of retained earnings
        and, 818–819
    cash, 820, **831**
    dates, 820–821
    declaration and payment of, 819–824
    liquidating, 824, **831**
    passing on, 777
    stock, 822–824, **831**
Double-declining-balance method of
    depreciation, 650–652
Double taxation, 771, **794**
Doubtful accounts, *see* Allowance for
    Doubtful Accounts account
Drawing account, partnership and,
    739–740
Due date
    determining, 512–513
    on voucher, 700

Earnings, per share, 934–935. *See also*
    Income

Economic Recovery Act of 1981, 670
Embezzlement, using computers, 717
Employees, loans to, 542
Ending inventory, 608–609
Endorsement, of notes, 515, 548, 550
Equipment, *see* Plant and equipment
Equity
    partnership dissolution and, 753–756
    per share, 933–934
    See also Owner's equity;
        Stockholders' equity
Errors, vouchers and, 712–713
Expenditures
    capital, 656, **672**
    extraordinary-repairs, 656–658, **672**
    revenue, 656, **672**
Expenses
    apportionment of, 886–893, **901**
    cash flows and, 952
    direct, 893–894, 895, **901**
    general, 891–893
    indirect, 893–894, **901**
    operating, 886–894
    voucher system and, 701–702
Expert systems, 899
Extraordinary Items, 860, **862**
Extraordinary-repairs expenditures,
    656–658, **672**

Factory automation, 1009
Factory overhead, 996, 1007, **1008**
Factory Supplies Used account, 996
Fees, protest, 552, **563**
FIFO, *see* First-in, first-out method
Fifteen-year property, 687, 691
Financial Accounting Standards Board
    (FASB), 950
Financial statements
    analyzing and interpreting, 915–938
    comparative, 916–925
    for corporation, 813, 816
    fundamental guidelines for, 828–829
    horizontal analysis of, 916–921, **938**
    industry comparisons and, 926
    for manufacturing enterprise,
        993–999
    for merchandising enterprise,
        607–609, 993–995
    for partnership, 741, 752
    trend percentages and, 925–926
    vertical analysis of, 921–925
    See also specific statements
Financing activities, 952, **977**
Financing transactions, schedule of,
    975–976
First-in, first-out (FIFO) method,
    613–614, **622**
Fiscal period, notes payable and, 519,
    520–521, 524–529
Five-year property, 687, 688–689

Fixed assets, 645
Fixed costs, 1009
FOB destination, inventory and, 610
FOB shipping point, inventory and, 610
Form 1065, 752
Fractional-share basis, division of
    income on, 741–744
Full disclosure, 828, 831
Functional depreciation, 647
Fundamental accounting equation,
    corporate transactions and, 793

Gain
    on exchange of asset, 664
    on sale of asset, 662–663
Gain on Disposal of Plant and
    Equipment, 663, 672
General expenses, 891–893
General journal
    dividends payable and, 821
    Notes Payable account entries in,
        514–523
    Notes Receivable account entries in,
        542–548
General ledger
    departmental accounting and,
        879–880
    posting from voucher register to, 703
    See also Ledger accounts
General partners, 735, 761
Gross profit
    by departments, 878–880
    estimating value of inventories and,
        637–642

Half-year convention, in depreciation,
    687
Horizontal analysis, 916–921, 938

Income
    division, for partnership, 740–751
    taxable versus net, 816
Income statement
    Bad Debts Expense account on, 575,
        578–579
    comparative, 916–919, 921–923, 924
    for corporation, 813
    for departmental accounting, 878,
        880–883
    departmental margin and, 893–897
    Extraordinary Items on, 860, **862**
    gain or loss on redemption of
        bonds, 860
    gross profit in, 638–641
    horizontal analysis of, 916–919
    Merchandise Inventory account on,
        607–609
    for partnership, 741
    Sinking Fund Income on, 857
    vertical analysis of, 921–923, 924

Income taxes
    bad debts and, 572
    corporation and, 805–812
    depreciation and, 668, 670
    double taxation and, 771, **794**
    inventory valuation and, 616
    partnership and, 752
Incorporation, *see* Corporation(s)
Indenture, 859, 862
Indirect expenses, 893–894, 901
Indirect labor, 996, 1008
Indirect materials, 996, 1010
Installment purchase, of stock, 785–788
Intangible asset, 772, 794
Interest, 533
    accrued, on notes payable, 524–526,
        533
    accrued, on notes receivable,
        555–558, **562**
    allowances, division of partnership
        income based on, 749–751
    calculating, 510–512
    deducting in advance, 518–519,
        520–521
    on promissory notes, 510–512
Interest Expense account, 513, 519
Interest Income account, 547, 556–558
Interest Payable account, 525–526
Interest Receivable account, 558
Internal control, objectives of, 697. *See*
    also Voucher system
Internal Revenue Service, *see* Income
    taxes
Inventory(ies)
    beginning, 609
    computers and, 623
    ending, 609–610
    need for, 610–611
    periodic, 607, **622**
    perpetual, 607, 617–621, **624**, 1006
    physical, 610–611
    raw materials, 1006–1007
    work-in-process, 1007
    See also Inventory valuation;
        Merchandise Inventory account
Inventory valuation
    accounting for, 605–624
    estimating, 632–642
    first-in, first-out (FIFO) method,
        613–614, **622**
    importance of, 607–609
    income taxes and, 616
    last-in, first-out (LIFO) method,
        614–615, 616, **622**
    lower-of-cost-or-market rule and, 617
    for manufacturing enterprise,
        1006–1007
    methods of assigning costs and,
        611–616
    net income and, 607–609

specific-identification method, 612,
    624
weighted-average cost, 613, **624**
Investing activities, 952, 977
Investment, of partnership, 737–739,
    744–746. *See also* Equity
Invoice, voucher system and, 698,
    699–700
Issued stock, 775, 794

Journal, *see* General journal; Journal
    entries
Journal entries
    for asset disposal, 659, 660
    bond sinking fund and, 857–858
    for corporate income taxes, 807–808
    for loss or gain on redemption of
        bonds, 859–860
    perpetual inventory and, 618–619
    subscription stock and, 787

Labor
    direct, 996, 1007, **1008**
    indirect, 996, **1008**
Land
    depreciation of, 646
    determining costs of, 646–647
    determining improvement costs,
        647
Land Improvements, 647, 672
Last-in, first-out (LIFO) method,
    614–615, **622**
    tax effect of, 616
Ledger accounts
    departmental, 879–880
    for stock, 778
    See also T accounts; *specific account*
Legal capital, 776, 794
Leverage, 846, 862
Liabilities
    contingent, 550, **562**
    corporations and, 770, 776
    long-term, 513
    partnership and, 734, 737
    plant and equipment and, 932–933
    stockholders' equity ratio and, 932
    voucher system and, 701–702
LIFO, *see* Last-in, first-out method
Limited liability, of corporation, 770
Limited life, of partnership, 734
Liquidate, 934, 938
Liquidating dividends, 824, 831
Liquidation, of partnership, 756–760,
    761
Liquidity, 951
Loans
    employee, 542
    notes given to secure, 517, 543–544
    personal, 543–544
    See also Promissory notes

Long-term liabilities, 513
  plant and equipment ratio and, 932–933
Loss
  on division of partnership, 740–751
  on exchange of asset, 664
  on sale of asset, 660–662
Loss on Disposal of Plant and Equipment, 660, **672**
Loss or Gain from Realization account, 757
Lower-of-cost-or-market rule, 617, **622**

Maker, 510, **533**
Management
  departmental margin and, 895
  financial statement analysis by, 927–935
  statement of cash flows and, 950–951
  voucher system as tool for, 713–714
Management information systems (MIS), 899
Manufacturing enterprise
  accounting cycle for, 999, 1005–1006
  accounting for, 993–1008
  adjusting entries for, 997–999, 1004
  balance sheet for, 997
  closing entries for, 1005–1006
  computers and, 623, 1009
  cost elements, 996
  income statement for, 993–995
  inventory valuation and, 1006–1007
  perpetual inventory system and, 621
  statement of cost of goods manufactured for, 995
  work sheet for, 997–999, 1000–1003
Manufacturing Summary account, 997, 999, 1002–1006, **1010**
Markdowns, retail inventory method and, 635–637
Markups, 878
  normal, 633
  retail inventory method and, 635–637
Matching principle, 573
Materiality, 828, **831**
Materials
  direct, 996, **1008**
  indirect, 996
Maturity date, 511, **533**
  determining, 512–513
Maturity value, 548, **562**
Merchandise, notes received in exchange for, 544–545
Merchandise Inventory account
  controlling, 619–620
  in financial statements, 607
  under perpetual inventory system, 617–620
  See also Inventory valuation

Merchandise inventory turnover, 930, **938**
Merchandising enterprise
  financial statements for, 607–609
  income statement for, 993–995
  perpetual inventory system and, 617–620
Midquarter convention, in depreciation, 692
Minute book, 825, **831**
Modified Accelerated Cost Recovery System (MACRS), 670, 686–694
Mortgage holders, analysis by, 931
Moving average, 620, **622**
Mutual agency, 734, 735, **761**

Net-amount system, 714–716, **718**
Net income
  of corporation, 805, 816
  depreciation and, 667
  inventory valuation and, 607–609
  partnership division of, 740–751
  taxable income versus, 816
Net loss, partnership division of, 740–751
Net profit, *see* Net income
Net sales, in financial statement analysis, 921
Noncash assets, issuing stock at par for, 779
Noncash investing, schedule of, 975–976
Noncumulative preferred stock, 777, **794**
Nonparticipating preferred stock, 777, **794**
Nonprofit corporations, 769
No-par stock, 776, 783–784, **795**
  stated value and, 784
  subscription transactions and, 786–788
Normal markup, 633
Note(s), *see* Promissory notes
Notes payable
  accounting for, 509–533
  accrued interest on, 524–526
  adjustments for, 524–529
  discount on, 518–519, 520–521, 526–529, **533**
  issuing after voucher has been recorded, 709–710
  schedule of, 524
  transactions involving, 513–524
Notes Payable account, 509
Notes payable register, 523–524, **533**
Notes receivable
  accounting for, 541–563
  accrued interest income on, 555–558, **562**
  adjustments for, 555–558

  discounting, 548–555, **562**
  dishonored, 546–548, **562**
  endorsement of, 515
  schedule of, 555
  transactions for, 542–546
Notes Receivable account, 509
Notes receivable register, 555, **563**
Notice of maturity, 515, **533**

Open corporation, 772, **795**
Operating activities, **978**
  cash flows from, 974
  income from, 880–893
  on statement of cash flows, 951
Operating expenses
  apportionment of, 886–893
  classes of, 893–894
Organization chart, 774
Organization Costs account, 772, **795**
Other Expense, 513
Outstanding stock, 775, **795**
Overhead, factory, 996, **1008**
Owners, financial statement analysis by, 933–935
Owner's equity
  corporations and, 774–775
  partnership and, 737

Paid-in Capital, 783, **795**
Paid-in Capital in Excess of Stated Value account, 784–785
Paid vouchers, 706
Participating preferred stock, 777, **795**
Partnership, 733–734, **761**
  advantages and disadvantages of, 734–735
  agreements, 735, 736 (illus.)
  characteristics of, 733–734
  closing entries for, 740
  co-ownership of property in, 734
  death of partner and, 756
  dissolution of, 752–760, **761**
  division of net income or net loss in, 740–751
  Drawing accounts of, 739–740
  financial statements for, 741, 752
  general, 735, **761**
  income taxes and, 752
  investments of, 737–739, 744–746
  liability and, 734
  limited life of, 734
  liquidation of, 756–760, **761**
  mutual agency feature of, 734
  sale of assets of, 756
  sale of interest in, 753
  withdrawal of partner from, 753–756
Par-value stock, 776, **795**
  issuing, 778–783
  subscription transactions and, 788–789

Payee, 510, **533**
Periodic inventory system, 607, **622**
Perpetual inventory, 607, 617–621, **624**
  electronic data processing and,
    620–621
  for manufacturing enterprise, 621
Physical depreciation, 647
Physical inventory, 610–611
  for spot check, 637
Plant and equipment
  capital and revenue expenditures
    for, 656
  in classified balance sheet, 667
  depreciation of, 647–656
  discarding or retiring, 658–660
  exchange of, 664–667
  extraordinary-repairs expenditures
    for, 656–658
  initial costs of, 645–646
  ledger, 667–668
  long-term liabilities ratio to, 932–933
  records for, 667–668
  selling, 660–663
  valuation of, 645–672
Posting
  of retained earnings, 810
  from voucher register, 703
Preemptive right, 774, **795**
Preferred stock, 777, **795**
Premium, 776, 779–781, **795, 862**
  adjusting entry for, 853–856
  on bonds, 848–851, **862**
  on Bonds Payable account, 849–850
Price-earnings ratio, 935, **938**
Price extensions, 698, **718**
Principal, 511, **533**
Proceeds, 518, **533**
Profitability, 915, **938**
Promissory notes, 509–510, 510 (illus.),
  533
  calculating interest on, 510–512
  classification of, 513
  due date determination, 512–513
  end-of-fiscal-period adjustments for,
    524–529, 555–558
  face value of, 519
  maturity date of, 511
  principal, 511
  renewal of, 521–524, 545–546
  transactions involving, 513–524, 542–546
  See also Notes payable; Notes
    receivable
Protest fee, 552, **563**
Public corporation, 772, **795**
Purchases
  internal control of, 697–698
  of long-term assets, 952

Quick assets, 928, **938**
Quick ratio, 928–929, **938**

Rate of return on common
  stockholders' equity, 934
Raw materials, 996, 1007, **1010**
Raw materials inventory, 1006–1007
Realization, 757, **761**
Receivables, *see* Accounts Receivable
  account
Redeem, 859, **862**
Registered bonds, 844, **862**
Retail inventory method, 632–637
  markups and markdowns and,
    635–637
Retained earnings, 774, **795**
Retained Earnings account
  appropriation of, 818–819, **831**
  deficit in, 792
  dividend payments and, 821
  posting to, 810
  surplus in, 792
Revenue(s), matching of, 573
Revenue expenditures, 656, **672**
Reversing entry, for bond interest, 855

Salary allowances, division of
  partnership income based on,
    746–749
Sales
  of assets, 660–663, 693, 756
  comparative financial statements
    and, 918
  departmental accounting and, 878
  expenses, apportionment of, 887,
    890–891
  matching bad-debt losses with, 573,
    582–584
  of partnership assets, 756
  of partnership interest, 753
  of stock, 952
Secured bonds, 845, **862**
Serial bonds, 844, **862**
Seven-year property, 687, 689–690
Sinking fund, 857–858, **862**
Software
  for depreciation, 669
  for inventory, 623
Solvency, 915, **938**
  analysis by creditors and
    management of, 927
**Specific charge-off method of
  accounting for bad debt losses,**
  590–592, **594**
Specific-identification method, 612,
  624
Spot-check, of inventory, 637
Spreadsheets, financial analysis using,
  936
Stated value, 784–785, **795**
Statement of cash flows, 949–977, **978**
  classifications of, 951–953
  definition of, 950

  development of, 955–974
  form of, 953, 954 (illus.)
  interpreting, 974–975
  use of, 950–951
Statement of cost of goods
  manufactured, 995
Statement of financial position, *see*
  Balance sheet
Statement of income and expenses, *see*
  Income statement
Statement of owner's equity, for
  partnership, 752
Statement of retained earnings, 825,
  826 (illus.)
Statute of limitations, 589, **594**
Stock
  authorized, 771, 775
  bond comparison, 843–844
  capital, 771, 775–777, **794**
  certificates, 771, 772–773, **795**
  common, 776, **794**
  discount on, 776, 780, 781–783,
    794
  dividends on, 774, **794**
  dividends paid in, 822–824, **831**
  equity per share, 933–934
  issuance of, 777–790
  issued, 775, **794**
  no-par, 776, 784, 786–788, **795**
  outstanding, 775, **795**
  par-value, 776, 778–783, 788–789,
    795
  preferred, 777, **795**
  premium on, 776, 779–781, **795**
  sale of, 952
  stated value of, 784–785, **795**
  subscription transactions for,
    785–790
  treasury, 775, **795**
  types of, 775–777
  See also Capital stock
Stock certificates, 771, 772–773, **795**
Stock dividends, 822–824, **831**
Stockholders' equity, 774–775, **795**
Stockholders' equity to liabilities ratio,
  932
Stockholders' ledger, 778, **795**
Stock split, 824–825, **831**
Store Equipment account, 667
Straight-line method of depreciation,
  649–650
Subscriptions, stock issuance and,
  785–790
Subsidiary ledger
  for plant and equipment, 667–668
  stockholders', 778, 790, **795**
  Unpaid Voucher file as, 704
Sum-of-the-years'-digits method of
  depreciation, 652–654
Surplus, 792, **795**

T accounts, 681, 870
  for bad debts, 574, 578
  for bonds, 856
  for depreciation, 658, 659
  discount on notes payable and, 520
  for interest income, 557
  for manufacturing enterprise, 1006
  notes payable and, 515
  notes receivable and, 543
  for perpetual inventory, 617
  for stock, 782
Taxation, double, 771, **794.** *See also*
  Income taxes
Tax Reform Act of 1986, 572, 670
  requirements of, 593
Ten-year property, 687, 692
Term bonds, 844, **862**
Thirty-one-and-one-half-year property,
  687, 691
Three-year property, 687
Tickler file, 714, **718**
Trade-in value, book value and,
  664–667
Transactions
  internal, 648
  review of, 681–685, 871–875
Treasury stock, 775, **795**
Trend percentages, 925–926

Twenty-seven-and-one-half-year
  property, 687, 691
Twenty-year property, 687, 691

**Unappropriated Retained Earnings,
  831**
Uncollectible accounts, *see* Bad debts
Uniform Partnership Act, 733
Unit cost, 611
Units-of-production method, of
  depreciation, 650
Unsecured bonds, 845, **862**
Useful life, of asset, 648
U.S. Partnership Return of Income
  (Form 1065), 752

Valuation
  of inventory, *see* Inventory valuation
  of receivables, 571–594
Variable costs, 1009
Vertical analysis, 921–925, **938**
Voucher(s), 698, **718**
  characteristics of, 699
  correcting errors and, 712–713
  filing, 706
  installment payments and, 710–712
  issuing note payable after recording
    of, 709–710

  preparation and approval of,
    699–700
  unpaid, 704, 706
Voucher register, 702–703, 704–705
  (illus.), **718**
  posting from, 703
Vouchers Payable account, 701–702
Voucher system, 718
  adjustments in, 706–713
  check register and, 703–704
  expenses and, 701–702
  invoices and, 698, 699–700
  as management tool, 713–714
  net-amount method and, 714–716
  objectives of, 697–698

Weighted-average cost, 613, **624**
Withdrawal, from partnership,
  753–756
Working capital, 927, **938**
Work-in-process inventory, 1007
Work sheet
  for corporations, 812–817
  for departmental accounting, 881,
    884–887
  for manufacturing enterprise,
    997–999, 1000–1003
Write-off, 572